# Essential Skills for Struggling Learners

# Essential Skills for Struggling Learners
## A Framework for Student Support Teams

by

**Erik von Hahn, M.D.**
Developmental-Behavioral Pediatrician
Center for Children with Special Needs, Floating Hospital for Children
Associate Clinical Professor of Pediatrics
Tufts University School of Medicine
Boston, Massachusetts

with

**Sheldon H. Horowitz, Ed.D.**
Senior Advisor
National Center for Learning Disabilities
Washington, DC

**Caroline Linse, Ed.D.**
Senior Lecturer
School of Social Sciences, Education, and Social Work
Queen's University Belfast
Belfast, Northern Ireland

Baltimore • London • Sydney

**Paul H. Brookes Publishing Co.**
Post Office Box 10624
Baltimore, Maryland 21285-0624
USA

www.brookespublishing.com



Typeset by Progressive Publishing Services, York, Pennsylvania.
Manufactured in the United States of America by Sheridan Books, Inc., Chelsea, Michigan.

The information provided in this book is in no way meant to substitute for a medical or mental health practitioner's advice or expert opinion. Readers should consult a health or mental health professional if they are interested in more information. This book is sold without warranties of any kind, express or implied, and the publisher and authors disclaim any liability, loss, or damage caused by the contents of this book.

The individuals described in this book's case examples are composites or real people whose situations are masked and are based on the authors' experiences. In all instances, names and identifying details have been changed to protect confidentiality.



Figures 1.1, 1.2, and 2.1 were created by Holly R. Fischer, MFA, Ann Arbor, Michigan.

**Library of Congress Cataloging-in-Publication Data**

Names: Hahn, Erik von, author. | Horowitz, Sheldon H., author. | Linse, Caroline T., author.
Title: Essential skills for struggling learners: A framework for student support teams / by Erik von Hahn with Sheldon H. Horowitz and Caroline Linse.
Description: Baltimore: Paul H. Brookes Publishing, Co., [2020] | Includes bibliographical references and index.
Identifiers: LCCN 2019008002 (print) | ISBN 9781681252551 (pbk.)
Subjects: LCSH: Learning disabilities. | Learning disabled children—Education. | Slow learning children—Education. | Remedial teaching.
Classification: LCC LC4704 .H337 2020 (print) | LCC LC4704 (ebook) | DDC 371.9—dc23
LC record available at https://lccn.loc.gov/2019008002
LC ebook record available at https://lccn.loc.gov/2019980460

British Library Cataloguing in Publication data are available from the British Library.

2023 2022 2021 2020 2019

10 9 8 7 6 5 4 3 2 1

# Table of Contents

# A Note on the Chapter Appendices

Each chapter includes appendices that offer two practical forms for use by school professionals. The first, the Skills Framework, functions as a quick reference tool, offering a summary of the key skills, behaviors that indicate learning difficulty as related to that skill, and sample educational objectives and strategies presented in each chapter. The second, the Skills Observation Sheet, provides structure for observing and taking notes on a student's skills and behaviors.

Purchasers of this book may download, print, and/or photocopy the Skills Frameworks and Skills Observation Sheets for professional, educational, or clinical use. These materials are included with the print book and are also available at **www.brookespublishing.com/Hahn/material** for both print and e-book buyers.

# About the Authors

**Erik von Hahn, M.D.**

Dr. Erik von Hahn has worked with children with diverse disabilities for more than 20 years. He has extensive consultative relationships with schools, especially in Massachusetts, and earlier in his career in New Hampshire. He has developed a deep understanding of children with disabilities, as seen through the lens of the school professionals who serve them.

In addition to his consultative practice with schools, Dr. von Hahn maintains a clinical practice in a teaching hospital. He uses his experience working with schools to help families in the clinic communicate successfully with their child's school team. As part of his academic duties, Dr. von Hahn has substantial teaching duties with Tufts University School of Medicine. He provides training and supervision of future Developmental-Behavioral Pediatricians, future general pediatricians, and future allied health care professionals in social work, speech pathology, and psychology. Finally, Dr. von Hahn provides regular continuing education services to both educators and local general pediatricians in their practice. Successful service to children with disabilities occurs when adults can work successfully with one another. All of Dr. von Hahn's clinical and teaching encounters emphasize service to children with disabilities through collaboration among home, school, and clinic.

**Sheldon H. Horowitz, Ed.D.**

Dr. Sheldon H. Horowitz is a Senior Advisor at the National Center for Learning Disabilities. Prior to his arrival at NCLD, he directed hospital-based evaluation and treatment programs in outpatient psychiatry and in developmental and behavioral pediatrics, as well as having taught at the primary, secondary, and college levels, and served as a consultant to school districts throughout the New York City metropolitan region. He has published in the areas of fetal alcohol effects in children, language-based learning disabilities, and disorders of hyperactivity and attention and has contributed content and expertise to several web sites in the area of learning disabilities. Dr. Horowitz is a regular presenter at professional conferences and is frequently cited in the popular press on topics including parenting children with learning disabilities and other special needs, attention-deficit/hyperactivity disorder, assessment and evaluation, evidence-based interventions, parent advocacy and special education policy reform, post-secondary transition, and LD throughout the life span.

**Caroline Linse, Ed.D.**

Dr. Caroline Linse is a Senior Lecturer at Queen's University, Belfast, where she teaches in the School of Social Sciences Education and Social Work. She teaches in the TESOL (Teaching English to Speakers of Other Languages) program and works directly with current and future teachers who must address cultural and linguistic diversity as a core element of the instruction that they deliver. She has worked in a variety of countries with learners and teachers from different cultural and linguistic traditions.

# Acknowledgments


**Erik von Hahn**

In addition to thanking my collaborating authors for sharing their knowledge, wisdom, and insights, I would like to thank personally the following mentors and colleagues for countless reasons that can never be captured fully, but are summarized here:

- Judith Palfrey, M.D.: For bringing me to Boston and introducing me to the world of developmental-behavioral pediatrics
- Kathleen Braden, M.D., and Carol Curtin, LICSW: For believing in me
- Gordon Harper, M.D., and Joshua Sparrow, M.D.: For teaching me about how to speak with children
- The School Partnership Program at Crotched Mountain Rehabilitation Center, in Greenfield, NH: For teaching me about educational practices and therapeutics in schools and for helping me to lay the groundwork for this book
- Public schools in Massachusetts and New Hampshire, and especially Brookline Public Schools, Brookline, MA: For inviting me and integrating me into your teams, and for the countless team meetings we have held together to brainstorm about students and their needs
- For the Center for Children with Special Needs at the Floating Hospital for Children/Tufts Medical Center in Boston, MA: For your constantly engaging, supportive, and cheerful learning environment
- For the children, youth, and families: For your ever-patient teaching to me about what really matters and for making my career worthwhile

**Sheldon H. Horowitz**

From my very first conversation with Erik, I knew that this book would be special in so many ways. I am grateful to have been given the opportunity, and privilege, to coauthor this book with him and with Caroline, and I look forward to the next steps in deepening our collaborative work together.

I must also acknowledge colleagues and friends at the National Center for Learning Disabilities (NCLD), my professional home for the past 23 years. Their unwavering commitment to serving individuals with learning and attention issues across the life span has allowed me to hone my voice, work closely with members of NCLD's Professional Advisory Board (of which Erik is one), and grow personally and professionally in ways that are too numerous to mention.

To the entire team at Brookes, my heartfelt thanks for believing in the impact we all know this book will have for educators and others whose efforts are a lifeline of support for children and their families.

And finally, a huge thank you to Lauren. Doing what I love most, with the encouragement ("Are you almost done with the chapter?") of the person I love most . . . it doesn't get better than that.

**Caroline Linse**

I am very appreciative of the work that Erik has done and the much-needed efforts and strategies to help professionals from different orientations work together to benefit children.

I am also grateful to the team at Brookes who have been instrumental in shaping the manuscript into a book that will help professionals from a variety of disciplines work together for the sake of the learners.

# Introduction

## WHO THIS BOOK IS FOR

Throughout the book, we use the term *school professional* to encompass a range of professionals who work with children in school settings and are responsible for addressing the needs of diverse learners; such professionals include school psychologists, general and special educators, therapists, speech-language pathologists, and other school-based practitioners. We hope that professionals with diverse training and different levels of experience will gain new insights about how children develop and learn. School professionals with less experience may use the book's content to gain deeper insight into the developmental and educational needs of children. Although more experienced practitioners may find some chapters to be a review of their current understanding, all school-based professionals will find the book's frameworks useful for interprofessional communication.

Readers of this book will inevitably be both novice and expert, depending on the chapter and topic at hand. The breadth of topics in this book allows all team members to play both roles. Through teaching and interprofessional training guided by this volume, all team members can enjoy the same or a similar level of expertise in many of the frameworks presented in this book.

## GOAL OF THIS BOOK

This book intends to strengthen partnerships. By mastering the vocabulary and concepts presented in this book, teams will find the frameworks useful for organizing team meetings and in the development of intervention plans. The frameworks provide a structure for effective communication among team members.

This book is also intended to strengthen partnerships with professionals outside of school. It is designed to be used for communication with professionals who may be involved in the student's care outside of school, fostering consistency for the student across settings. Further, the book's frameworks can facilitate communication and collaboration with parents, who may need guidance in understanding the educational and therapeutic approaches needed by their child while at school.

Finally, and most important, a goal of this book is to help strengthen school professionals' partnerships with students. It is not only adults and professionals who need the vocabulary and the knowledge presented in this book. Students also need to understand the concepts and the vocabulary presented in this book at their developmental level. When the adults have a shared terminology to enhance communication with one another, they will also be able to find a way to enhance their communication with the student. When the professionals involved in a student's education have terms to describe the skills that the student needs to build, they can also speak to the student about those skills and how to develop them.

## FEATURES AND OBJECTIVES OF THIS BOOK

This book will be useful to you because:

1. It can expand your knowledge base in your area of expertise.
2. It can serve as a platform for teaching your colleagues about what you know about students and their needs.
3. It will deepen your understanding and appreciation for the work done by your colleagues.
4. It will help you to become a good observer of students. Observable behaviors serve the purpose of identifying both the skills that the student brings to learning and the skills that the student needs to continue to build. Observable behaviors also assist in making a diagnostic determination. See text box entitled "The Limitations of Diagnostic Categories." By developing your observation skills, you will understand your students more deeply and be able to participate in their education more successfully.
5. It helps with team-building and creates cohesion.

### The Limitations of Diagnostic Categories

When professionals identify the student who is struggling, they are often called on to identify the educationally disabling condition. In the educational setting, the disabling condition is determined by the educational codes used in special education law (Individuals with Disabilities Education Act [IDEA]). In the health care setting, disabling conditions are identified and categorized by the International Classification of Diseases (ICD) or the *Diagnostic and Statistical Manual of Mental Health Disorders (DSM).*

From time to time, this book highlights how observable behaviors can be associated with diagnostic or handicapping conditions. As a starting point for any student-related discussion, it can be useful to identify a student's handicapping condition, because it offers a global view of the student's needs and is useful for administrative purposes. However, it is not the primary intention of this book to use observable behaviors for this purpose. Diagnostic labels are usually not sufficient for determining student's needs because they are not specific enough.

Diagnostic conditions are not specific because the same symptoms, behaviors, and skill gaps commonly occur in multiple diagnostic conditions. Students often end up qualifying for more than one diagnosis, each of which may need to be addressed in the student's intervention plan (Gage, Lierheimer, & Goran, 2012; Gillberg, Fernell, & Minnis, 2013; Pettersson, Anckarsater, Gillberg, & Lichtenstein, 2013). For example, very high percentages of children with attention-deficit/hyperactivity disorder (ADHD), autism spectrum disorder (ASD), and disruptive behavior disorders, have co-occurring learning disabilities (Dickerson Mayes & Calhoun, 2006). A very high percentage of children with a psychiatric disorder have a coexistent language impairment (Bishop, 2004; Camarata, Hughes, & Ruhl, 1988; Im-Bolter & Cohen, 2007). Many students with disabilities or emotional or behavioral impairments have motor impairments or developmental coordination disorders (Cairney, Veldhuizen, & Szatmari, 2010; Gustafsson et al., 2014). Any one diagnostic condition is commonly associated with other diagnostic conditions.

Because of their lack of specificity, diagnostic categories do not inform educational practice very clearly. This is especially true in children, whose needs change by age and grade. Two students with ADHD may need very different types of educational supports, depending upon their age and the expression of their diagnosis. Some supports, such as making eye contact, speaking slowly, and ensuring the student's comprehension, are as important for the student with ADHD as they are for the student with autism, intellectual impairment, language impairment, or hearing impairment. Identification of the diagnosis or the disabling condition, on its own, is therefore not sufficient for determining the student's educational program, objectives, or strategies.

## HOW THIS BOOK WORKS

This book presents 11 frameworks. Each framework represents an area of child development. Frameworks presented in this book are dedicated to language skills, motor skills, reading skills, and so forth. Each framework consists of a collection of skill sets and skills (the *essential skills*). For any given framework, the team needs to be able to discuss which of these skills the student has mastered and which ones the student needs to develop further. By identifying these skills, the team can understand more clearly the educational goals and objectives that should be considered for the student's educational program.

The 11 frameworks presented in this book are divided into three sections: Neurological, Developmental, and Educational. The purpose of dividing the frameworks into these three different types is primarily conceptual and is intended to help organize ideas presented in this book. All learning requires the entire brain, not just one part or the other. Although the first three frameworks are categorized as neurological in nature and are manifestations of typical biological growth and development, all of the skills in each framework rely on neurology. Although the final three frameworks are categorized as academic and develop only through educational exposure, the full development of all of the skill sets and skills in each of the frameworks depends upon education, training, and environmental opportunities and demands. The frameworks, organized by category and in order of chapter appearance are the following:

Neurological Frameworks

1. Vision
2. Hearing
3. Motor skills

Developmental Frameworks

1. Formal language skills
2. Pragmatic language skills
3. Social skills
4. Executive skills
5. Affect and self-regulation skills

Educational Frameworks

1. Reading
2. Writing
3. Math

Each of the 11 frameworks consists of skill sets and skills that are essential for learning and for successful participation at school and elsewhere. Each framework is summarized and available for quick reference in an appendix to each chapter. The frameworks are also available on the book's web site for online download (see A Note on the Chapter Appendices). Each chapter is designed around the framework and structured in the following manner:

1. **Introduction and general definitions.** The chapter begins with general and introductory information about the framework to be discussed. This overview orients the reader to the framework presented in that chapter.
2. **How the framework was constructed.** This section shares a selection of the research and resources used in developing the framework. A major function of the book is to provide consistent terms to describe essential skills for learning. In reviewing a diverse range of resources, we often discovered a lack of consensus about which terms best describe the key aspects of child development that underlie learning, and which skill sets and skills are the most essential skills to include. This section briefly explains the logic that was used for including or excluding specific terms for each framework.
3. **How can this framework help me?** This section discusses why the framework is helpful or important to learning, in both special and general education.
4. **The framework: Terms and definitions.** This section is the heart of each chapter. It presents the key terms and definitions of the framework and its associated skill sets and skills. Skills are presented in a sequence of least complex to most complex that mirrors typical child development and shows how each skill supports successful learning.
5. **Performance difficulties.** Missing or underdeveloped skill sets and skills account for a student's learning difficulty. This section helps the reader identify the student who is struggling. It defines what constitutes performance difficulties in a given framework. It shows how learning difficulties are linked to observable behaviors, and how those behaviors are linked to missing or underdeveloped skill sets and skills. This section also helps school professionals identify skills sets and skills that are present. In the IEP Builder later in the chapter, the professional will use missing or underdeveloped skills sets and skills to identify the student's strengths. By identifying what the student *can* do, professionals can help the student *do more.*
6. **How to set up an observation.** This section explores how to make behavioral observations of students when they are not performing successfully. It provides instruction to assist professionals of all levels of experience in gathering classroom observations to share with other members of the team. Sharing observations can help identify targets for intervention or can help the team determine whether a formal evaluation is needed. After a formal evaluation, professionals can reexamine the student's performance and continue to make links among the student's classroom performance, the student's performance during standardized measures, and the underlying skill sets and skills that the student still needs to develop. Each chapter includes a Skills Observation Sheet to provide structure for notetaking while observing a student's skills. These forms are also available on the book's web site for download.
7. **IEP Builder.** This section offers specific educational objectives, teaching strategies, and teaching accommodations to help improve performance in the developmental domain. Once school professionals conduct and analyze observations to identify learning difficulties, school teams can use these objectives, strategies, and accommodations to assist in the development of an intervention plan. This includes building an Individualized Education Program (IEP) when needed. The content in this section is aligned with the skills and skill sets presented earlier in the chapter. This section of the chapter helps professionals apply the chapter's terms and concepts directly to their work with students.

8. **Case Example.** This section provides case examples. Case Examples are based on actual observations made of many students by the lead author. Each case consists of observations made of more than one student to enhance the teaching value of the case and to ensure privacy. The Case Example provides further explanation of how to make behavioral observations, how to make links between the observations and the skill sets and skills of that chapter, and how to organize educational objectives and strategies using the framework as presented in that chapter.

9. **Summary.** Each chapter ends with a summary and final notes to transition the reader to the skills discussed in the subsequent chapter.

The book also includes a number of illustrative figures, explanatory boxes, and boxes on Working With Culturally and Linguistically Diverse Learners. These boxes deepen understanding of the subject material and aid in practical application. Two appendices with further guidelines on implementing the frameworks are also available in the back of the book.

## WHAT THIS BOOK CAN DO FOR YOU

This book provides the terms needed to identify the skill sets and skills that students require to succeed in school. For students who are struggling, the frameworks presented will help the team to identify more quickly the specific skills that need to be developed. Through a shared vocabulary and common knowledge, team members can more easily share what they know, recognize the expertise of each member more clearly, and help each team member support the team as a whole more successfully. The frameworks facilitate shorter and more focused meetings that can lead to effective planning decisions more quickly. Further, the school professional will feel more confident in making key educational decisions and become more skilled in selecting meaningful educational objectives and in monitoring the student's progress. Finally, this book will improve the professional's communication with the student and the student's family. By sharing knowledge successfully with students and their family, the student is more likely to learn from the educational objectives and strategies that the practitioner has prepared to foster their success.

## REFERENCES


Bishop, D. V. M. (2004). Specific language impairment: Diagnostic dilemmas. In L. Verhoeven & H. van Balkom (Eds.), *Classification of developmental language disorders: Theoretical issues and clinical implications* (pp. 309–326). Mahwah, NJ: Lawrence Erlbaum.

Cairney, J., Veldhuizen, S., & Szatmari, P. (2010). Motor coordination and emotional–behavioral problems in children. *Current Opinion in Psychiatry, 23*(4), 324–329.

Camarata, S. M., Hughes, C. A., & Ruhl K. L. (1988). Mild/moderate behaviorally disordered students: a population at risk for language disorders. *Language, Speech, and Hearing Services in Schools, 19*(2), 191–200.

Dickerson Mayes, S., & Calhoun, S. L. (2006). Frequency of reading, math, and writing disabilities in children with clinical disorders. *Learning and Individual Differences, 16*(2), 145–157.

Gage, N. A., Lierheimer, K. S., & Goran, L. G. (2012). Characteristics of students with high-incidence disabilities broadly defined. *Journal of Disability Policy Studies, 23*(3), 168–178.

Gillberg, C., Fernell, E., & Minnis, H. (2013). Early symptomatic syndromes eliciting neurodevelopmental clinical examinations. *Scientific World Journal, 2013*(3), 710570.

Gustafsson, P., Kerekes, N., Anckarsater, H., Lichenstein, P., Gillberg, C., & Rastam, M. (2014). Motor function and perception in children with neuropsychiatric and conduct problems: Results from a population based twin study. *Journal of Neurodevelopmental Disorders, 6*(11), 2–10.

Im-Bolter, N., & Cohen, N. J. (2007). Language impairment and psychiatric comorbidities. *Pediatric Clinics of North America, 54*(3), 525–542.

Pettersson, E., Anckarsater, H., Gillberg, C., & Lichtenstein, P. (2013). Different neurodevelopmental symptoms have a common genetic etiology. *Journal of Child Psychology and Psychiatry, 54*(12), 1356–1365.

# I

# Neurological Frameworks

# Vision Skills

## INTRODUCTION AND GENERAL DEFINITIONS

Section I focuses on neurological functions and associated skills necessary for learning. Although all of the skill sets discussed in this book have a neurological basis, the three discussed in this first section (vision, hearing, and motor skills) are especially dependent on intact biological structures. The term *neurological* is used for this section to highlight the importance of biology. Without intact neurological structures, it is more difficult for students to develop the skills that are discussed in this chapter and the two that follow. This chapter is focused on vision and will introduce key components of vision, all of which are critical to successful functioning at school and elsewhere.

As a first step, it is important to recognize that vision is a complex skill set that includes unique and separate components. Because of the many skills discussed in each chapter, frameworks were organized into skill sets and skills. The term *skill set* refers to a category or group of skills. Skill sets are further divided into component functions and skills. When one considers all of the skills that make up each framework, the importance of categorizing skills this way becomes clear. For example, normal vision does not include only the function or the skill of seeing objects clearly at near and at a distance. Normal vision includes many other functions and skills, such as the capacity to see clearly, even if lighting conditions change. Normal vision includes being able to use of the full field of vision, extending nearly 180 degrees in all directions and involves the ability to see colors. It allows for the capacity to notice subtle differences in reflected light to make out differences in depth or surface texture, a capacity used to notice changes in ground surfaces while walking or in facial expressions while speaking to a friend. Vision not only allows us to understand three-dimensional space that is visible but also allows us to understand three-dimensional space that is imagined. Further, normal vision is dependent on motor skills. The motor skills required to move the eyes allow us to look at and focus on objects that are either stationary or moving, as well as to look at and focus on objects, while we are ourselves moving. In sum, vision consists of many skills. Impairments in any of the different components that contribute to vision can interfere with the functions and skills just listed and can affect participation at school and elsewhere. As will be evident later in this chapter and throughout the book, it is important and challenging to organize so many skills into a logical framework.

The reader will notice that these first chapters (vision, hearing, and motor skills) list anatomical structures in addition to skill sets and skills. This chapter first presents key aspects of visual anatomical structures. The Vision Skills Framework then introduces the visual functions and skills that are so important to learning. The chapter goes on to explain how to set up an observation and how to build an intervention plan or an individualized education program (IEP) with objectives and strategies focused on vision. It wraps up with a Case Example of a child with a vision impairment and provides a brief summary and conclusion.

There are four anatomical and functional aspects to vision:

1. Ocular muscles
2. Ocular structures: Cornea, pupil, iris, lens, and retina
3. Connections between the eye and the brain: Optic nerve, optic chiasm, optic tract, and geniculate body (These connections and the connections to the visual cortex are collectively referred to as the *visual axis*.)
4. Neurological structures that support visual processing by the brain: Connections between the geniculate body and visual cortex; connections between the visual cortex and other parts of the brain

Each of these aspects is discussed in more detail in the framework section that follows.

## TERMINOLOGY USED IN CONSTRUCTING EACH OF THE FRAMEWORKS OF THIS BOOK

Each chapter uses information about typical child development to identify functions, skill sets, and skills. This book differentiates biological structures and functions from skills and abilities that emerge through typical child development and through learning. One way to consider these different terms is from the perspective of nature versus nurture. *Nature* refers to the neurological or biological endowment of the child, with its associated structures and functions. *Nurture* refers to the experiences, education, and training that children receive that help to shape the way the brain develops and allow them to perform successfully in the world. To lay the groundwork for all the frameworks presented in the book, this section will discuss the nature–nurture distinction at greater length, using vision as an example.

In this book, the term *nature* pertains to bodily structures and functions. Bodily structures are anatomical parts of the body such as organs, limbs, and their components. Body functions are the ways that body parts and systems work, including psychological and neurological functions of the brain (World Health Organization, 2007). Examples of bodily functions and structures include breathing by the lungs, digesting by the gastrointestinal tract, and movement by the muscles. In the case of vision, bodily structures include the lens of the eye (and its function of focusing light rays on the retina) and the retina (and its function of transforming light information into electrical impulses that are then delivered to the brain). These structures and their associated functions are all largely present at birth, though some changes occur with growth and development following birth. For example, in the case of the eyes, some visual functions, such as visual acuity, change with growth and development in the first year or two of life. Like most bodily functions, visual functions emerge early in life and do so in a largely spontaneous manner as long as the infant or toddler maintains good health. Vision is therefore primarily about the unfolding of nature rather than the influence of nurture. The three neurological frameworks of this book (i.e., vision, hearing, and motor skills) are all categorized in this way.

Nurture, in contrast, refers to the experiences, education, and training that children and youth receive over time. Nurture also includes the responsiveness of the environment to the child. Nurture allows the child's nature to flourish and expand into a variety of skills and abilities. Skill sets and skills emerge from intact neurological and bodily structures and functions but only when children and youth are provided with the right environmental stimulation, training or practice, and education (nurture).

Skills are learned capacities that develop through nurture. Skills do not involve the use of any assistive devices, technologies, or accommodations. *Skills* and *skill sets* refer to most of the behaviors discussed in this book, such as interpreting visual information and its three-dimensionality, listening to sounds and identifying words, using the motor system to walk or run, manipulating the tongue and lips to produce speech, making a decision to go outdoors instead of watching television, or thinking about someone else's feelings by paying attention to his or her behaviors. *Abilities*, in contrast, refer to behaviors that make use of tools, assistive devices, technologies, and/or accommodations. Abilities are those skills that develop with tool use, use of instruments, or use of accommodations or supports. For example, using tools, a person can feed him- or herself using a spoon. Sometimes, a person needs adaptations of the spoon in order to self-feed, such as a larger handle to account for a clumsy grasp. Using a hearing aid, a person may be better able to listen and engage in conversation. Using a cane, a person may be able to walk. Using computer software, a person may be better able to use expressive language through a speech-generating device. This same logic applies to the ability to play the piano or the ability to draw. Abilities do not necessarily refer to the skills that students with disabilities develop through accommodations; they refer to any skill that emerges through use of a tool, an instrument, or a support of some kind. The distinction between skills and abilities is not always clear. That said, the distinction is useful conceptually, especially when students do not show the development of skills as expected but can perform successfully when accommodations are provided. For the purposes of this book, the distinction between skills and abilities chiefly applies to students who may need accommodations in order to perform as well as their peers.

This book is dedicated to a description of the early emerging skills and abilities seen in typically developing children and youth. This book presents the *essential skills* that children and youth need to thrive. Although these skills and abilities may seem to emerge in a spontaneous manner in typically developing children, most of them are dependent on successful child–environment interactions. They emerge through nurture, not from nature alone. Regardless of the framework, the terms *skill sets*, *skills*, and *skills-building* all refer to those skills that that emerge out of intact structures and functions and through typical child development. Biological and neurological functions undergo physical growth, develop and refine with age, and result in new skills and abilities. It is through healthy interactions with the environment and through education and training that children and youth develop these skills and learn how to perform successfully in the world. The skill sets and skills discussed in this book emerge in a relatively predictable manner in typically developing children. Each of the frameworks presented in this book lists these functions, skill sets, and skills in a hierarchy that proceeds from least to most. The hierarchy often mirrors typical child development but is not intended to provide an accurate description of child development. Rather, the frameworks are useful for organizing educational objectives in a developmentally appropriate manner.

The dividing line between each of these definitions (bodily structures and functions, skill sets, and skills) is not always crystal clear. Nonetheless, the distinctions among the three terms is useful conceptually. It helps to organize the presentation of information throughout the frameworks in this book. See Colenbrander (2010b) and Hyvärinen (2010) for a similar discussion of the same distinctions. See also Box 1.1, which places the discussion of nature and nurture into a larger context and highlights the importance of defining terms accurately.

### BOX 1.1. Nature, Nurture, and the World Health Organization

The World Health Organization (WHO) highlights nature and nurture through its two classification systems: The International Classification of Diseases (ICD) and the International Classification of Functioning (ICF). The ICF has a version for children and youth, the ICF-CY (International Classification of Functioning–Children and Youth) (WHO, 2007).

*(continued)*

**BOX 1.1.** *(continued)*

The ICD focuses on body structures and bodily functions, which is a focus on nature. In contrast, the ICF focuses on a person's functioning in the environment and the environmental factors that can affect a person's activity and participation in life. Its focus is on nurture. Both the ICD (which fits into a medical model) and the ICF (which fits into a social model) are important in describing and cataloging a person's state of well-being and establishing healthy functioning. Both of these models can be considered and should not be seen as competing perspectives. That said, sometimes it is difficult to know which model is the right one to use for a given situation. Does disease or injury need to be eliminated, so that a person can function more successfully? Should the environment provide accommodations and reduce demands on the individual? Or does the individual need to develop skills and abilities? At what point does the student need intervention by a health care practitioner, support from a school professional, or a change of environmental demands? When might it be appropriate to stop focusing on nature and instead direct our attention to nurture? These questions pervade all the frameworks in this book and are important to consider as children and youth, especially those with disabilities, live their lives and receive services in different settings. Educational success and the successful participation of students with disabilities at schools depend on an understanding of the influence of nurture on nature. Just as is true for the two classification systems of the WHO, educators and professionals working in schools need to develop an understanding of where nature ends, where nurture begins, and the often complex and changing relationship between the two throughout the course of development.

Even though the educational model fits more closely with the social model, students' experiences in school are not simply about changing the environment or creating environmental opportunities. Education is the path to developmental growth. Education helps people develop skill sets, skills, and abilities. It changes people. We argue that education changes nature. It enhances the biological endowment of people by helping them build skills and abilities. Sometimes, the impact of education on nature is just as powerful as the impact of any medical intervention. The student who has impaired vision, hearing, or motor structures and functions can still learn to participate successfully in the world. The same holds true for all of the frameworks discussed in this book.

The difference between the three categories of frameworks presented in this book lies primarily in how much any framework is an expression of nature versus nurture. The first three frameworks (the neurological frameworks of vision, hearing, and motor functions and skills) rely more heavily on intact neurology and the successful unfolding of nature. However, this book will illustrate that vision, hearing, and motor functions must be nurtured over time and with experience in order to become more fully developed skill sets and skills. The last three frameworks (the educational frameworks for reading, writing, and math) are almost entirely the result of nurture. They depend on intact neurology, but only develop with explicit instruction and education. The middle section of this book, dedicated to the developmental frameworks, lies in between these two competing perspectives. The distinction between nature and nurture will be highlighted from time to time throughout this book.

At times, especially in the case of children with disabilities, nature does not supply all the structures and functions for the typical unfolding and development of important skills. Students can have a biological or structural limitation in vision, hearing, and motor skills just as they can have a biologically determined limitation in their development of language skills, executive skills, or emotion-management skills. These children and youth need more nurturing.

They need more explicit training or instruction to acquire skills that other children acquire more spontaneously or more easily. In some cases, certain skills cannot emerge successfully, because bodily structures or functions have been disrupted, are absent or underdeveloped, or are slow to develop. For example, a child with a vision impairment or with cerebral palsy may never fully develop some of the skill sets and skills discussed in this book. In such cases, children and youth may need to acquire compensatory skills, so that they can perform successfully. Similarly, a child with a language impairment, an impairment in executive skills, or an impairment in emotion-regulation may also need to acquire compensatory skills. However, many of the skills discussed in this book depend upon education and training and not just on biology. Nurture plays an important role. Compensatory skills are not always as well-developed as the skills that usually emerge when there is no impairment to begin with but can allow for very successful functioning. In some cases, compensatory skills only emerge through the use of accommodations. In this case, the compensatory skills are referred to as *abilities*. They are commonly dependent on technologies or accommodations. Whether because of biological limitations or lack of educational exposure, more nurture can help to build underdeveloped skills.

## HOW THIS FRAMEWORK WAS CONSTRUCTED

The visual functions and visual skills described in this framework are discussed using terminology found in reference texts and review articles on the subject. The text that follows in this section represents a synthesis of information contained in the References section. There is relatively good agreement here about how to label and define the functions and skills related to vision, with only minor variations in terminology among authors. The reader is invited to review this chapter's references to deepen understanding of this important area of development.

## HOW CAN THIS FRAMEWORK HELP ME?

This chapter is designed to serve as an introduction to important visual functions and visual skills. The terms and definitions in this chapter will help professionals to identify performance difficulties in vision, and to discuss with colleagues the vision functions and skills of students. The chapter provides important terms needed to communicate about a student's current function and his or her educational/therapeutic goals and objectives. For the expert, this chapter is designed to serve as a platform for teaching. By using the terms presented in this chapter, the expert can share his or her knowledge of vision with other less experienced colleagues through daily collaboration or through interprofessional training. The chapter also helps all professionals, no matter their experience, communicate with students and their families about key aspects of vision and visual skills.

In addition to sharing and defining important terms related to vision, the Vision Skills Framework can help school teams think strategically about how to optimize visual function and enhance visual skills for the student with a vision impairment. Although strategies to enhance visual functioning are especially important for the student with vision impairment, some of the strategies discussed in this chapter may also be useful to students who do not have a vision impairment. When visual information is presented optimally, a variety of students with and without disabilities may find it easier to focus their attention and complete their work. For example, use of computers to change font size, illumination, colors, or contrast can be helpful for students who become distracted or fatigued by excess visual stimulation. Judicious use of lighting, font size, color, and reduction of visual clutter (among other examples) can reduce visual processing demands for a student with significant cognitive impairments and thereby facilitate the student's focus on the content of the visual material instead. Students with limited cognitive skills can benefit from visually modified materials, such as photographs or fine line drawings, to communicate important concepts, instead of relying upon the interpretation of printed words or symbols. See Box 1.2 for additional examples. This chapter will introduce strategies to help school professionals optimize the presentation of visual information in their classrooms. The strategies do not always require special technologies or teaching methods and are often already available in general education classrooms. As noted above, many of these strategies do not need to be reserved only for students with a vision impairment.

**BOX 1.2. Vision Is Important Everywhere**

Consider how words, paragraphs, and other elements are presented in this chapter. Decisions about the visual organization of information on this page were made with the intention of improving visual attention. By using bold, large font for headings and subheadings, some information on the page is visually highlighted, whereas other information recedes into the background. Boxes signal additional information and help the reader to organize information differently than would be the case if all of the information were incorporated into the body of the text. Figures serve as their own visual focus, again highlighting content in a different way.

Visual strategies and the organization of visual information are used in many different walks of life: In the presentation of material on the Internet, in how print appears on the page, and in how furniture is set up in a home or public setting. A classroom can also be organized visually. For example, a rug sets off a corner of the room into a space designated for group-learning activities. Information on the walls can be visually organized and positioned in ways that prioritize what students should see first or be able to reference at different times during the school day. Be sure to put information at the level of students' sight line if you want them to notice what you have put on the walls! In printed text, visual salience influences what the eye is drawn to first, second, third, and last. Separating ideas through the use of bold font and colors helps to differentiate key ideas from supporting ideas, main teaching points from supplementary teaching points, just as in this book. By making use of visual strategies, educators and therapists can improve a student's ability to focus and learn.

## VISION SKILLS FRAMEWORK: TERMS AND DEFINITIONS

There are several overlapping and interrelated skill sets and skills that pertain to vision. Information about ocular structures and ocular health are presented first. The remainder of the information is dedicated to skill sets: Oculomotor skills, visual functions related to the globe (the eyeball), and visual processing skills. Although all frameworks in this book discuss both functions and skills, the Vision Skills Framework primarily focuses on functions, as visual competencies are more highly dependent on nature rather than nurture.

The framework, which is summarized and available in Appendix 1.1 for quick reference, includes the following:

1. Ocular structures and ocular health: Important structures of the eye globe
    a. Cornea
    b. Lens
    c. Ciliary body

    d. Retina
    e. Optic nerve
    f. Oculomotor muscles
2. Oculomotor functions and skills: The muscles that move the eye and that affect the shape of the lens
    a. Scanning
    b. Localizing
    c. Fixation and focus
    d. Tracking
    e. Tracing
3. Ocular functions related to the eye globe
    a. Acuity and focus
    b. Visual fields
    c. Contrast sensitivity
    d. Light–dark adaptation
    e. Color vision
4. Visual processing functions and skills
    a. Stereopsis and depth perception
    b. Object recognition functions
    c. Spatial awareness and motor planning

Each of the sets and their corresponding skills and functions will be explained in depth in the sections that follow.

## Ocular Structures and Ocular Health

The Vision Skills Framework first introduces information about ocular structures and ocular health. Ocular structures consist of the structures that make up the eye globe. Ocular functions are the functions of the eye globe. The Vision Skills Framework involves the structures of the eyes described in the following sections. Figures 1.1 and 1.2 are diagrams of each of these anatomical and functional areas.

***Cornea*** The cornea is the most exterior portion of the eye globe. It is clear, covers the area over the iris, and functions to protect the eye from damage, such as from sand or dirt.

***Iris*** The iris is a colored muscle. People usually notice the iris when looking at someone's eyes, because it is colored differently from one person to the next. The iris is a circular muscle that opens and closes, controlling the amount of light that falls into the lens. It surrounds the pupil, which is an open space that lies on top of the lens and underneath the cornea.

***Lens*** The lens is a crystal-like structure inside the eye. The purpose of the lens is to focus light rays on the retina. The lens focuses light rays onto the retina by *accommodating*, the act of changing the shape of the lens to focus light rays on the retina. Accommodation is performed by

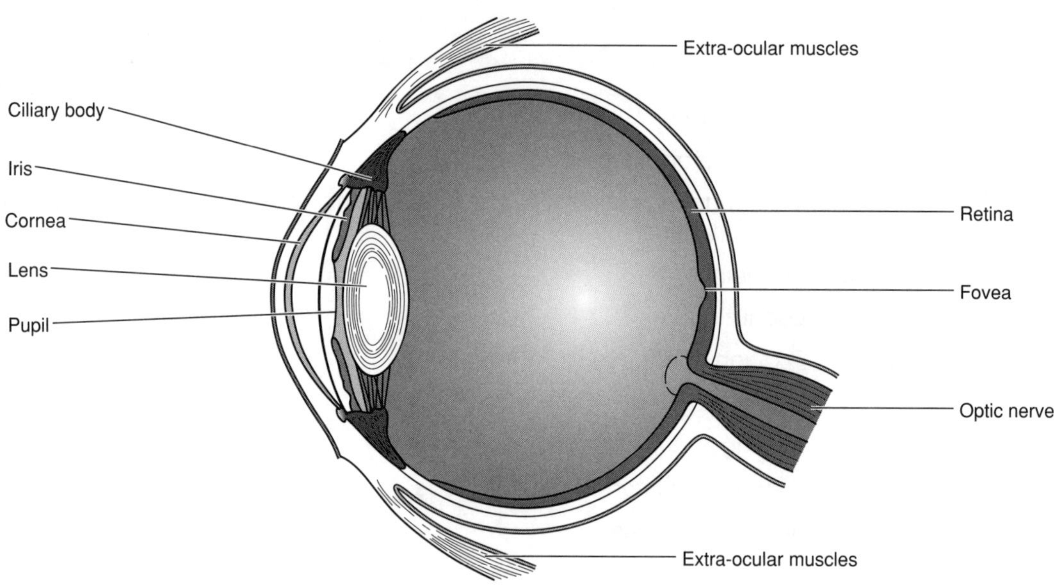


**Figure 1.1.** Key components of ocular anatomy, including the ciliary body, iris, cornea, lens, pupil, retina, and optic nerve.

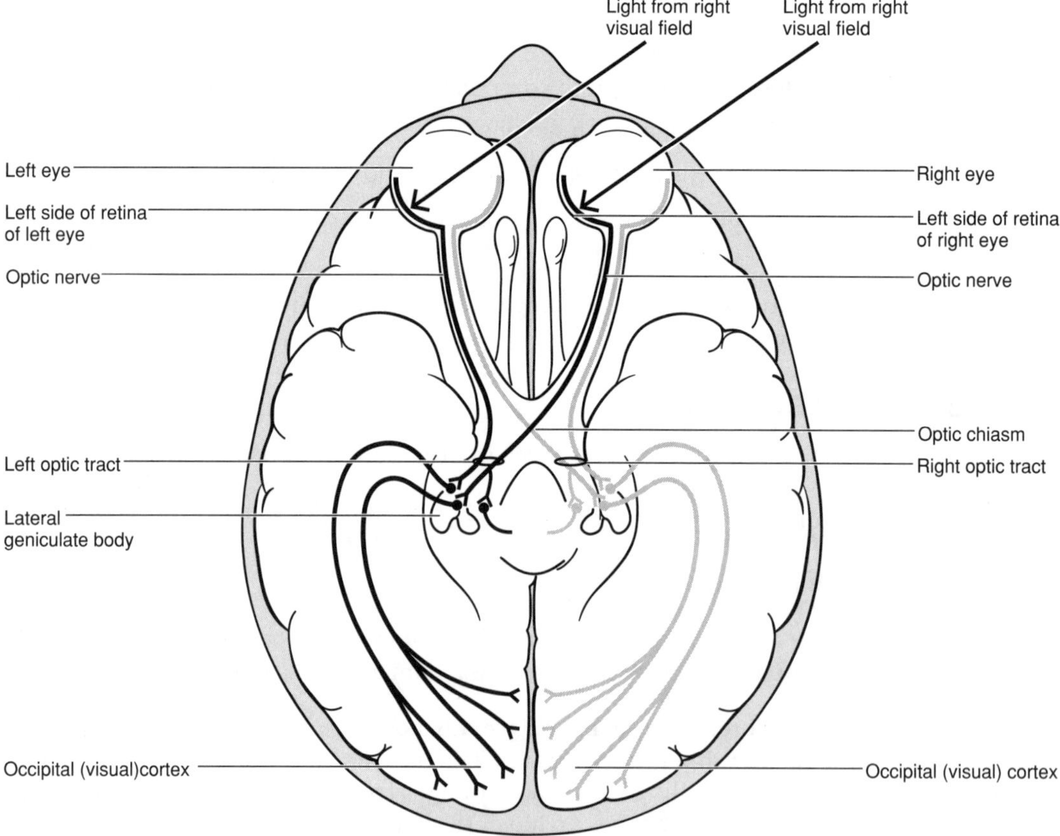


**Figure 1.2.** This diagram illustrates the connections between the eyes and the brain, including the optic nerves, optic chiasm, optic tracts, and geniculate bodies. The black-shaded pathway shows how light from the right side of a person's visual field lands on the left side of each retina. The left side of the retina then transmits this light information to the left side of the brain via both optic nerves, the left optic tract, and the left geniculate body. The converse is also true.

the ciliary body, a muscle located inside the eye. It changes the shape of the lens by contracting or relaxing its tension on the lens. When the ciliary body changes the shape of the lens, it allows light from different distances to become focused successfully on the retina. This process allows for clear vision at different distances. All of the visual skills discussed in this chapter must be applied to visualizing objects located at different distances from the eyes. Distance effects are important to take into consideration when discussing visual functions and visual skills. A student may not have any visual difficulties at one distance but may have performance difficulties at another. See Box 1.3 for more information.

**BOX 1.3. Vision at Different Distances**

Distance is often classified as near, middle, far, and distant spaces, as follows:

- Near space: 3–12 inches
- Middle space: 1–6 feet
- Far space: 6–20 feet
- Distant space: 20 feet and greater

The ranges listed above are a good reference for near point and far point vision. A person with myopia cannot see objects clearly when they are too far away. In contrast, a person with hyperopia cannot see objects clearly when they are too close. In both cases, the lens is unable to accommodate enough to allow clear vision of either distant or near objects. Presbyopia is the term used when adults become middle aged and need to wear glasses to see clearly something held close to the eyes, such as fine print in a book. Presbyopia refers to an age-related difficulty with accommodation, especially for objects at near.

The eyes and the brain have to account for differences in distance. For example, oculomotor muscles are used differently if the object being visualized is at near or distant space. Features of the environment, such as color and lighting, affect vision differently, depending on whether the object is at near or distant space. Throughout the chapter, it is important to take into consideration not only which function, skill set, or skill is under discussion but also how each is affected by the distance of the object(s) from the eyes.

***Retina*** The retina is the most posterior (farthest back) portion of the inside of the eye (see Figure 1.1). The retina consists of two types of cells: Rods and cones. Cones distinguish different wavelengths of light and allow for color vision. Rods distinguish between different intensities of light and are especially important for night vision or when light levels are low. The rods and cones of the retina convert light information into electrical impulses that are recognizable by the brain. The signals from the retina are transmitted to several regions in the brain to perform functions such as opening or closing the pupil to control the amount of light entering into the eye, or to detect motion and assist with stabilizing the individual using the motor system. Light information from the retina also informs the hypothalamus about circadian (recurring naturally in a 24-hour cycle) changes in light and dark. Finally, light information from the retina is transmitted to the lateral geniculate body and then to higher cortical centers to allow for visual processing.

***Optic Nerve*** The optic nerves are the most posterior portion of the eye and carry the electrical impulses from the retina to the brain. As demonstrated by the black-shaded pathway in Figure 1.2, light from the right side of a person's visual field lands on the left side of each retina. The left side of the retina then transmits this light information to the left side of the brain via both optic nerves, the left optic tract, and the left geniculate body. Similarly, light from the left side of a person's visual field lands on the right side of each retina. The right portion of the retina then transmits light information to the right side of the brain via both optic nerves, the right optic tract, and the right lateral geniculate body. The X-shape formed when the optic nerves cross in the brain is called the optic chiasm. Light information from the left side of a person's visual field is processed by a person's right cerebral hemisphere; light information from the right side of a person's visual field is processed by a person's left cerebral hemisphere.

***Oculomotor Muscles*** There are six oculomotor muscles that are attached at the four quadrants of the eyes (top, bottom, left, and right). Two additional oculomotor muscles have an oblique orientation, extending from the top or bottom of the eye globe in a diagonal orientation. They make it possible for the eye globes to rotate. All six oculomotor muscles help to move the eyes in many different directions.

## Oculomotor Functions and Skills: How the Eyes Move

Oculomotor muscles are positioned around the eye globe and move the eyes in all directions. They also act to keep the eye still when needed. Oculomotor skills mature early in life. Whereas oculomotor functions serve the purpose of moving the eyes in different directions, oculomotor skills serve the more specific purpose of understanding visual information, making use of visual information, and helping to navigate the environment. The oculomotor behaviors described in this section are skills because they are related to a person's successful functioning in the environment. They might need to be developed explicitly in some students with a vision impairment. In typically developing children, eye movements, especially scanning, develop in response to the environment within the first year of life. Other skills described later in this section develop long after age 1 year, in conjunction with the development of motor skills of the body as a whole. The following sections provide more specific information about the development of oculomotor skills, which are also the focus of training in students with low vision who must learn to use residual vision effectively. The information here is summarized in Lueck and Heinze (2004) and Lueck (2004a) and in other standard references that describe oculomotor functions and skills.

***Scanning*** *Scanning the environment* refers to large, sweeping movements that people make with the head and eyes to locate (localize) an object of interest and then fixate (defined below) on it. Scanning requires gaze shift, moving the eyes to let go of the first visual stimulus in order to look at a second object or second visual stimulus. This letting go is a specific oculomotor function, but it is also a skill, because it matures and becomes more efficient with age and experience. Scanning is used to locate objects in distant and far space. Scanning is needed to walk through a room and avoid obstacles, or to find one's way in an unfamiliar building or in the community. In near and middle space, scanning is needed for reading controls on a panel or looking at different images on a computer screen or different objects on a desk. In near space, think of tracing (defined below) as equivalent to scanning.

***Localizing*** After scanning, the student needs to localize the object of interest, meaning he or she needs to recognize where the target of interest is located. Localization is both a cerebral (cognitive) and an ocular skill. Localization requires a prior understanding of where to scan in order to find a necessary object or item. For example, localization is necessary for finding the beginning of a page, the correct dial on a machine, the price of a grocery store item that is located on a shelf in a store, or an object in the environment that one wishes to pick up. All of these skills are cognitive skills, acquired through experience. Once an object is localized, the eyes then have to fixate. Localizing is thus a combination of strategic scanning and then fixating successfully. Fixating is described below.

***Fixation and Focus*** Normal vision requires being able to control when to move the eyes and when to keep them still. Oculomotor skills are required for moving the eyes, as well as for keeping the eyes in one position, stabilizing the eyes, and preventing any additional movements. In addition to stabilizing the eyes, the oculomotor muscles of each eye also must be coordinated with one another. Both eyes have to be able to look at the same object at the same time. Convergence (keeping both eyes positioned in the same position) is the ability to keep both eyes fixated on a target, whether the target is stationary or moving. After fixating, focusing is required to see the object or other visual target clearly. Focusing refers to the ability to change the shape of the lens so that light is focused on the retina. The ciliary body, a muscle located inside the eye, changes the shape of the lens. This creates a clear image on the retina.

Fixating and focus are possible in part because the child knows what portion of the eye to use. He or she moves the head, the eyes, or the object being viewed so that its image can be focused on the fovea of the retina. The fovea is the portion of the retina that has the greatest density of photoreceptive cells and allows for the most precise perception of objects, including seeing colors.

***Tracking*** Tracking is the ability to follow a moving object in the environment, such as following the trajectory of a moving car in the street or following the path of a person walking across the room. During tracking, the eyes remain on the target during all movement directions: Horizontal, vertical, circular, and diagonal. When tracking successfully, the eyes move at the same rate as the object being tracked—the eyes do not move more quickly or more slowly than the object. The two eyes track together as conjugate movements, meaning both eyes are held in the same position and move together in tandem.

Tracking is used not only to follow moving targets in the environment. It is also used to determine one's position in space in relation to the moving object(s). For example, tracking is used to cross the street safely while also following the movements of oncoming traffic. The same type of skill is needed in many sports activities. Among other skills, the successful athlete is able to coordinate body position and movements in relation to a moving ball and in relation to moving teammates. The skill of tracking is continually refined and enhanced, depending on the environmental demands.

***Tracing*** Tracing is a type of scanning. It involves visually following a stationary line in the environment. For distance vision, the child uses lines in the environment to move her or his visual attention from one place in the environment to another. For example, a person with vision impairment might use lines in the environment to locate important targets for localization. By tracing the vertical lines of a building, he or she can subsequently locate the lines of the curb and then finally locate a traffic light. Tracing in near vision occurs when using the eyes to follow the movement of a pen across a page or when following the movement of a needle when sewing. Tracing is a relatively simpler skill than tracking, because the object being traced is stationary. In the case of printing or sewing, the pace of the moving object is controlled by the person who is looking at the object. This is a less demanding skill than having to watch a moving object whose pace of movement is under someone else's control.

## Ocular Functions

The cornea, iris, lens, and retina are the primary structures of the eye globe. These structures serve the function of accepting sensory information (light) and transmitting this information to the optic nerve, which then transmits light information to the brain. Ocular functions are discussed in more detail in the sections that follow. The information presented in this section is summarized from Lennie and Van Hemel (2002). It can also be found in other standard references that discuss vision.

***Visual Acuity*** Visual acuity is a measure of the ability to resolve fine detail. It develops to maturity in the first year of life. Visual acuity is the most commonly assessed visual function and is the only function measured during a routine vision screening. Typically, such assessments use an eye chart, such as the type of chart used by the school nurse or in in a doctor's office. Visual acuity charts use optotypes (figures or letters of different sizes) to test the capacity of the eyes to resolve fine detail. Each line of the chart consists of a series of symbols (usually letters or numbers); each of the symbols on each line is the same size and is equally spaced. Each line of the chart uses progressively smaller symbols. As the viewer proceeds down the chart, the lens has to accommodate more and more to resolve the details.

A visual acuity measure does not capture all the other visual functions and skills discussed in this chapter. In other words, passing a visual acuity measure does not guarantee that the person has normal vision. It is a good first measure to use when assessing vision, but impairments in a variety of visual functions and skills may be present even if the visual acuity test results are normal.

***Visual Field and Visual Field Defects*** The visual field is the perceived space on either side of both eyes that is visible when the person is looking straight ahead. The normal visual field measures as an oval-shaped field that is a bit less than 180 degrees in width. Each eye has its own visual field, though there is substantial overlap between the two. A (learned) skill associated with use of the visual field is to recognize when something is located outside the visual field and to move the eyes or the head to orient the eyes toward the object so that it lies within the visual field. This skill develops within the first year of life. With the awareness of what might lie just outside the visual field, the person can make adjustments, such as turning the head, turning the eyes, or shifting the position of an object so that it lies within the visual field.

***Contrast Sensitivity*** Contrast sensitivity refers to the ability to detect differences in brightness between an object and its background. The higher the person's sensitivity to contrast, the lower the degree of contrast that the individual can detect. A common example used to illustrate this concept is to compare the degree of contrast in a pastel painting with an oil painting. The contrast between colors in a pastel drawing is lower than the contrast between colors in an oil painting. For a person with low contrast sensitivity, it is harder to detect differences in colors and to identify lines and borders in the pastel drawing. The reduced contrast makes it more difficult to identify the objects portrayed in the pastel drawing. An oil painting that uses strong differences in color between objects or between foreground and background has higher contrast. In the painting, it is easier to detect differences in color and to identify lines and borders. For a person with low contrast sensitivity, the oil painting will be easier to see, whereas the pastel drawing will be more difficult to see. To understand contrast in paintings and drawings, see Box 1.4.

### BOX 1.4. Value and Saturation

*Value* and *saturation* are terms that are pertinent to the topic of contrast sensitivity. The value of a color is its lightness or darkness. The saturation of a color is its intensity. Pastel colors have lower value (brightness) and lower saturation (intensity), whereas neon paints have high value and high saturation. Objects or colors similar in value or saturation have a low level of contrast between them and are more difficult to distinguish from one another.

Two shades of pastel blue have less contrast between them, as is the case for two shades of neon yellow. Objects or colors with different value and different saturation have a higher level of contrast and are easier to distinguish from one another. A pastel drawing has lower contrast than a drawing made with bright colors.

One skill that students develop in their art classes is that of understanding relationships among colors, value, and saturation. The painter can manipulate colors, their value, and their saturation to create higher or lower contrast between different aspects of the painting. By manipulating these variables, the artist can create the illusion of colors that may not actually be present. Using differences in contrast, the painter can also create the illusion of shadow and light, foreground and distance, without using any lines or even perspective. Color and contrast can be used to enhance or diminish the three-dimensionality of the painting, for example, or can bring attention to one part of the canvas while reducing attention to other parts of the canvas. Vision specialists use knowledge of contrast sensitivity to enhance visual attention or facilitate visual interpretation of objects and pictures for individuals with vision impairment.

The issue of contrast sensitivity has practical implications, beyond the appreciation of art and painting. Contrast sensitivity is used to help locate an object that is partially hidden within a cluttered array of objects or an object that is placed on a patterned background. Contrast sensitivity is also used to understand depth, for example, to notice the difference between foreground and background and to notice differences between near and far objects. The capacity to distinguish between objects or surfaces that are nearer or farther away influences a person's ability to walk down a flight of stairs or to walk through a hallway. Unless distant objects are lit more brightly, nearby objects normally appear as brighter than distant objects. A person with low contrast sensitivity will have difficulty making out the difference between near and distant objects unless the lighting is sufficiently different between the two. Noticing differences in surface texture also depends on noticing differences between what lies in the shadow and what lies closer to the surface. Contrast sensitivity is necessary to detect these differences when walking on an uneven surface but is also needed to detect differences in facial expressions. Changes in facial expression involve only very small changes in the contrast between the lighter foreground and the darker background. These differences are more difficult to detect if contrast sensitivity is low.

The person with higher contrast sensitivity can detect subtle differences in lighting between foreground and background in distant space, between foreground and background for uneven surfaces in middle space, between foreground and background as facial expressions change, and/or between objects that have to be retrieved from a within a cluttered array or that are located on a patterned background (middle and near space). The person with low contrast sensitivity will have difficulty with all of the visual demands just listed. As objects change in size (usually as objects get larger or are magnified), contrast sensitivity can improve (Markowitz, S. N., 2006). This is known as contrast acuity.

***Light–Dark Adaptation and Light Sensitivity*** The eye spontaneously adjusts to changes in lighting. This ability occurs through rapid changes in the opening of the eye, controlled by the iris. When a person exits a dimly lit room and enters into bright sunshine, the iris contracts and reduces the amount of light that reaches the retina. This function is important because it ensures that only a moderate or reasonable level of light ever reaches the retina.

***Color Vision*** Normal color discrimination develops by the end of the first year of life, even if color identification (the capacity to identify colors by name) occurs somewhat later.

The capacity to see different colors not only enhances visual pleasure but also affects the capacity to distinguish between objects.

## Visual Processing Functions and Skills: How the Brain Understands and Uses Visual Information

Visual processing refers to what the brain does with the visual information delivered to it by the eyes (Goodale, 2010). Nearly half of all cortical (cerebral) neurons are devoted to the processing of visual information (Schiefer & Hart, 2007). This underscores the importance of vision in the life of humans. Although visual processing is defined as something that occurs in the brain, successful visual processing requires an intact visual axis: It starts with intact ocular structures that lie outside the brain and includes all of the nerves and structures related to vision that are located inside the brain. See the description of the visual axis in next paragraph.

Effective visual processing starts with the best light information. The best light information is delivered to the retina when there is good light in the environment and when oculomotor functions and the structures and functions of the eye globe are all intact. Light information is then transmitted by the retina to the optic nerves. The optic nerves connect the eyes with the brain. Each optic nerve connects at the optic chiasm and then connects to the geniculate body in each cerebral hemisphere. The geniculate body then connects to the visual cortex, and the visual cortex connects to other regions of the brain. All of the neuro-anatomical components just listed make up the visual axis and have to be intact for successful visual processing to occur.

Visual processing reflects any of the interconnections that occur between light information delivered by the eyes to the visual cortex and the subsequent interconnections that can occur with all the other regions of the brain. Visual processing includes depth perception, object recognition functions, visual-motor functions, and imaginary functions. Visual processing includes the integration of visual information with higher cognitive functions, such as hearing and touch; with motor skills; and with general knowledge such as reading, writing, and math or personal experience and general knowledge. The sections that follow discuss some of these visual processing functions and skills in more detail.

***Visual Processing and Depth Perception (Stereopsis)*** As discussed above, the function of contrast sensitivity helps in understanding depth; for instance, when walking down stairs, differences in contrast between the higher and the lower steps provides information about the location of the steps and the point at which depth changes. Depth perception is also possible because of differences in the visual field between each eye. Each eye takes in slightly different information because each eye does not have exactly the same field of vision. When both eyes are functioning successfully together, the slightly different visual perspectives from each eye are delivered to the brain. The brain integrates this information and creates a three-dimensional representation that includes depth and distance (Markowitz, S. N., 2006). This capacity is known as stereopsis, which is critical in helping the individual navigate the environment successfully. Stereopsis is a basic, or fundamental, type of visual processing. It develops over the first year of life as the infant learns to look at and explore three-dimensional space.

***Visual Processing and Object Recognition*** Information from the visual cortex is distributed to two important brain regions, the temporal and parietal lobes. This section focuses on the temporal connections. The pathway that carries visual information from the primary visual cortex to the temporal lobe is called the ventral stream. This pathway is important for the perception and recognition of colors, objects, and faces (Dutton, Cockburn, McDaid, and Macdonald, 2010; Zihl, Schiefer, & Schiller, 2007). Information carried by this pathway is then integrated with other brain regions. Connections are made with sensory modalities such as hearing and touch, with motor skills, and with general knowledge. The ventral stream skills develop with age. The infant and toddler have to recognize and identify objects. The toddler also learns to interpret or understand photos or drawings and understands that photos and drawings represent objects and are not the same as the actual objects. Visual recognition demands can be placed into a hierarchy, as described in the following sections.

*Objects* Seeing or looking at objects requires the lowest level of visual interpretation. The object is what it is: An object. The visual interpretation required is to know what the object is used for and what it is called. Infants and toddlers recognize objects when they see them, though they often also rely on tactile or other cues to understand the nature of what they see. With increasing knowledge, they combine visual information with information about the use or function of the object. They then learn that different objects can be of the same type (e.g., all cups are cups, even though two cups can look different from each other). They learn to recognize similarities in form and function. The skill of identifying two different objects as being the same is subsequently linked with language skills. The toddler can now identify the cup using a word.

*Photographs* Although a photograph is an object (i.e., it is a piece of paper with colors on it), it is also a representation. It is a picture of an object and it can thus represent (stand in the place of) an object. Infants do not understand photographs as representing an object; they only understand that a photograph is a piece of paper with colors on it. Understanding that a photograph is a representation of an object is a skill that is acquired after the first year of life. A common initial manifestation of this skill occurs when a toddler correctly identifies the photo of a person as being that person and knows that the photo is not the actual person.

*Fine Line Drawings* Fine line drawings are similar to photographs in their demands on visual processing. Toddlers and preschoolers can understand that fine line drawings represent objects in the real world, as long as the level of detail provided is clear and as long as the drawing has the colors and contrasts needed to identify the object(s) or person(s) clearly.

*Schematic Drawings and Pictographs* Schematic drawings and pictographs require a higher level of visual processing than do objects, photographs, or fine line drawings. They contain less visual information, and as a result, they require greater interpretation. To interpret and understand pictographs, more visual recognition functions and skills are needed. The person viewing the schematic drawing or pictograph has to make connections with familiar objects or scenarios by filling in the gaps with prior experiences or using general knowledge. For example, a simple line drawing of a teapot produced with a black pen is more schematic than a fine line drawing of a teapot with colors that highlight its three-dimensional nature. A pictograph or icon, such as the sign for a bathroom in public places, is even more schematic. Interpretation of the icon requires prior knowledge or prior experience to understand its meaning. Pictographs and schematic drawings are interpretable by preschoolers and young school-age children if they are provided with instruction. Comprehension of pictographs and icons is a learned skill.

*Symbols: Letters, Numbers, and Words* Symbols such as the letters of the alphabet, numbers, and the printed word are highly symbolic and require the highest level of visual interpretation. Printed text, which is a form of visual information, has to be connected via recognition functions and recognition skills to the language center as well as with general knowledge housed in other parts of the brain. The interpretation is visual but also linguistic and cognitive. The capacity to interpret symbols such as printed letters or words (i.e., the understanding that the printed material represents objects, actions, or other information) is present by the early school-age years. At this point, visual processing is no longer a function; it is a skill. Nurture has acted on nature and has linked visual information with other types of knowledge and other types of skills, such as language and reading decoding skills and general knowledge.

***Visual Processing and Visual-Spatial Perception and Motor Planning*** The section above showed that information from the occipital (visual) cortex is carried to the temporal lobe and allows for object recognition functions. In contrast, information carried from the visual cortex to the parietal lobe allows for visual-spatial and visual-motor skills. Occipitoparietal connections are referred to as the dorsal stream (Dutton et al., 2010). Dorsal stream functions are associated with visual-spatial perception and orientation (Zihl et al., 2007). Dorsal stream functions and skills include skills such as understanding and interpreting depth and distance, awareness of physical space, understanding maps and routes, and awareness of mathematical space. The dorsal stream allows for hand-eye coordination, following a map to find one's way in space, and maintaining one's orientation in space. It integrates vision information with motor functions and motor skills. Based on the delivery of good light (visual) information, and based on successful recognition of that visual information, children and youth need to be able to act on what they see. For example, young children learn to use visual information to create a three-dimensional understanding of their environment. They learn how to locate items or places that are not yet visible (e.g., a toy that they know is located in another room). They learn to avoid obstacles and how to judge distances. Using this new understanding of distance and space, they can also acquire other skills. They can learn to judge the time needed to traverse certain distances. They can use their understanding of distance, space, and timing to enhance motor control and perform more skillfully in sports activities. When young children learn to draw, they learn how to use visual fine motor skills to produce lines, shapes, and simple stick figures. With age, children learn that lines and shapes can be manipulated to produce the illusion of three dimensions, for example, a three-dimensional house. The artist advances this skill further, using more and more visual strategies to create the illusion of three dimensions in two-dimensional space.

***Advances in Visual Processing*** Advances in visual processing occur through repeated cycles of recognition, mentalizing (imagining and reflecting on what was seen), and (motor) production. For example, an artist can render an image of three dimensions in two dimensions by using pencil, pen, or paint. The artist also applies visual processing when producing a sculpture. Using a mental image of a three-dimensional object, person, or place, the sculptor produces a three-dimensional representation of that object, person, or place. Dorsal stream functions and the appreciation of three-dimensional space include understanding space when there is no light information, as occurs when producing an architectural drawing for a new building or when solving math problems. Persons who are legally blind can still have an understanding of three-dimensional space, a skill they acquire through auditory and tactile cues and from experience.

## GENERAL COMMENTS ABOUT THE TERM *PERFORMANCE DIFFICULTIES* IN THIS BOOK

Performance difficulties, as defined in this book, are caused by a lack of development of the skill sets and skills described in each of the frameworks. Performance difficulties can occur when there is an injury to bodily structures or functions, when there is a lack of nurture, and/or when there is a lack of quality instruction. The goal for school professionals is to identify performance difficulties when they occur and, subsequently, to identify the types of activities (experiences) needed to nurture the student's growth and development.

Performance difficulties often manifest as atypical behaviors, or as behaviors that are unexpected for the student's chronological age. The recognition of performance difficulties is often the first step in the process of assisting a student. As defined in this book, stating that a student has a performance difficulty is the same as stating that the student is missing certain essential skills. Professionals can choose their preferred term for the situation: Performance difficulty, or missing or underdeveloped skill sets or skills. The missing skills can be developed through nurture.

Each of the frameworks provides an organizational structure for understanding the essential skills discussed in this book. The frameworks are useful for identifying performance difficulties. Each time a school professional identifies performance difficulties in a student, the framework can be used to identify which skills are missing. In turn, the professional can also identify which of the earlier-emerging skills in the framework might be present, and which of those skills could be developed further. More nurture, such as intentionally targeted instruction and intervention, may be needed to make up for the missing or underdeveloped skills.

## PERFORMANCE DIFFICULTIES IN VISION

Successful performance in vision is always related to intact biological structures and biological functions. Students who do not have intact structures and functions may show a variety of impairment-related behaviors. They often also have impairments in areas outside of vision, such as motor skills, language skills, and/or general cognition (Rahi & Solebo, 2012). It can be challenging to identify performance difficulties that are related to vision specifically and to separate vision performance difficulties from performance difficulties that might be associated with the other frameworks in this book. The sections that follow provide examples of vision performance difficulties and relate those performance difficulties to their underlying (missing or underdeveloped) visual skills.

### Performance Difficulties Related to Ocular and Overall Health Status

Different from other chapters, this section starts out by asking the reader to consider medical information. Medical risk factors for vision impairment are important to identify, because they are the first clue that a performance difficulty might exist. These medical factors are not challenging to identify if the student's medical history is available and if the school nurse or another medical provider can review the student's medical record. Performance difficulties related to vision often occur in certain medical conditions such as individuals who were born with extreme prematurity, or who have cerebral palsy, or known eye diseases. When medical conditions like these are uncovered as part of a review of the student's medical history, school professionals should think more carefully about the student's vision. If medical risk factors are present, the school nurse should communicate with the student's health care provider to ask whether a vision assessment is required. If the family prefers, the school nurse can provide a list of observations and questions related to vision, which the student's family can then share with the student's medical providers. Boxes 1.5 and 1.6 provide information about whether additional medical evaluations are needed.

**BOX 1.5. Medical Conditions That Can Be Associated With Vision Difficulties**

The following conditions can potentially be associated with visual performance difficulties:

1. Prematurity and associated retinopathy of prematurity
2. Prematurity and associated cerebral palsy, intraventricular hemorrhage, periventricular leukomalacia, and/or hydrocephalus
3. Cerebral palsy due to causes other than prematurity
4. Spastic diplegia

*(continued)*

**BOX 1.5.** *(continued)*

5. Intellectual disability
6. Epilepsy
7. Traumatic brain injury
8. Ocular injuries or diseases associated with eye disease
9. Chromosomal disorders associated with eye conditions

When one of these conditions is noted in the student's medical record, the school nurse's input is important because she or he can help determine whether there is an associated vision impairment. The school nurse should take into consideration the student's visual acuity test results, the student's medical history, and a history of other student performance difficulties. Together with the student support team, the school nurse can then decide whether additional evaluation of the visual system is needed.

Before considering whether a medical condition exists, it is important to confirm that the student has undergone a visual acuity assessment and that refractive errors have been corrected. A failed vision screening (visual acuity test) is an automatic reason for concern about the integrity and health of ocular structures. Probing for medical factors further, the school nurse can ask whether there is anything about the student's visual behaviors or medical history that suggests difficulties with ocular structures or with ocular health. Any child who has experienced eye disease, eye injury, a neurological disease, or a head injury (among others) is at risk for damage to ocular structures, the optic nerve, and/or pathways and regions in the brain dedicated to the processing of vision. Students who were born prematurely, especially those who spent the first weeks of life in an intensive care unit, are at risk for vision impairment due to retinal or cerebral injury. Some students may have an eye disease such as glaucoma, which also causes damage to the retina. Cerebral palsy is an important risk factor for vision impairment.

In cases such as the ones listed here, it is important for the child's eyes and ocular health to be assessed by a vision specialist, such as an ophthalmologist or an optometrist. At the outset, it is important to know whether the student has any active medical difficulties related to vision, whether the student is at risk for vision difficulties because of medical conditions, or whether there are no risk factors related to the student's vision. Medical factors should be addressed before making any attempts at observing or interpreting the student's visual skills. As discussed later in this chapter, the interpretation of the student's visual behaviors will be different based on whether there are untreated medical conditions that affect vision.

### BOX 1.6. Different Causes and Types of Vision Impairment

Vision impairment can occur because of difficulties with one or more of the anatomical structures described in the following and as shown in Figure 1.2:

1. Oculomotor muscles surrounding the eyes
2. Structures of the eye globe
3. The optic nerve that brings light information from the retina to the geniculate body

4. Connections between the lateral geniculate body and the visual cortex
5. The dorsal and ventral streams that emanate from the visual cortex and connect vision information with other brain regions

In developing countries, causes of vision impairment are more likely related to the eye globe than to the brain. In Western countries, the opposite is true. Cerebral vision impairment (impairment in the visual cortex and its connections to the rest of the brain) is the most common form of vision impairment. In Western countries, the next most common cause of vision impairment is retinopathy of prematurity, followed by optic nerve hypoplasia (Steinkuller et al., 1999; Thompson & Kaufman, 2003). Coexisting intellectual disability, cerebral palsy, and/or epilepsy are common (Mervis, Boyle, & Yeargin-Allsopp, 2002; Ozturk, Er, Yaman, & Berk, 2016). In developing countries, vision impairment is more commonly the result of infections and other causes related to the eye globe, for example, corneal disease (Kong, Fry, Al-Sammarraie, Gilbert, & Steinkuller, 2012).

## Performance Difficulties and Oculomotor Skills

Students need to learn to navigate their environment. Students with vision impairment may have difficulty in finding their way in three-dimensional space, whether that space is the classroom, the school building, or the larger community. Students who have difficulty in this area can have one or several performance difficulties related to oculomotor skills, ocular skills, and/or visual processing skills. Oculomotor skills are the focus for discussion here.

The skills of tracking, scanning, and localizing are all needed for navigating three-dimensional space. Students with this type of vision impairment may come to the attention of school professionals because they have already been enrolled for instruction with an orientation and mobility specialist or might already have been identified as needing an instructional assistant or a cane. The student may not have difficulty in navigating familiar environments or in avoiding immediate obstacles. However, the student may have greater difficulty in new environments and/or in navigating larger environments such as walking in the community. Even though oculomotor skills are so critical for orientation and mobility, all visual functions and skills are needed for successful orientation and mobility. In other words, oculomotor dysfunctions and an absence of oculomotor skills may occur in isolation but (more commonly) co-occurs with other types of visual dysfunctions such as those discussed in subsequent sections. When students are not navigating the environment but instead need to navigate a desktop or work on a computer, they are less reliant on oculomotor skills and depend on visual functions related to the eye globe. Scanning and localization skills are still required but within a much smaller field of vision.

## Performance Difficulties and Ocular Functions and Skills

The following sections provide examples of vision impairments related to the eye globe.

***Performance Difficulties and the Visual Fields (Field Defects)*** Field defects can show up as the loss of vision within a portion of the visual field. The student may fail to see objects or parts of objects even when they are placed within full view of the student. If the student moves the eyes (or if the practitioner moves the object), it may then become visible. Whereas a field defect can occur on one side or the other (or can occur in the upper or lower portion of the student's visual field), it can also occur in the form of spots or rings within the field. These are referred to as scotomas. A scotoma can prevent a student from seeing the entirety of an object and might result in their seeing only parts of objects in central or peripheral vision, even when the object is placed quite close. A skill that students can develop when they have a known field defect is the recognition or awareness that objects sometimes lie outside their visual field followed by the response to move the eyes or the head in order to see the object fully. In fact, these students can often be seen turning their head into an awkward position to optimize use of the field. This behavior can occur during activities that demand orientation and mobility in space (distance vision), as well as during desktop activities (near vision). In near space, the student may position objects to one side or another in order to see the object clearly.

***Performance Difficulties and Contrast Sensitivity*** Students with low contrast sensitivity can have difficulty seeing or paying attention to important visual information because their contrast sensitivity is too low. They may not notice differences between foreground and background, affecting depth perception as they walk in their environment. They may not be able to see objects in near space that are placed on a similarly colored background. They may also have difficulty seeing similarly colored objects within a cluttered array of objects or picking out objects lying on a patterned background. Students with low contrast sensitivity can also have difficulty noticing changes in facial expression.

Students with low contrast sensitivity end up focusing their visual attention on high-contrast features of the visual field. When walking through space, these students might notice only those features of the environment that are clearly different from the background, such as a bright exit sign in a hallway or a white object against a dark background. When looking at faces, the student may focus only on high-contrast features such as the eyebrows, the hairline, and/or the lips, while not noticing changes in the expression of the eyes or the mouth. They may recognize only extremes of emotion and not recognize more subtle changes in facial expression.

***Performance Difficulties and Light Sensitivity*** Some students have difficulty seeing excessively bright or dark environments or have difficulty adjusting between the two light conditions. They may be sensitive to excessive light (photophobia) or may be attracted to light sources specifically because they are easier to see. They can exhibit night blindness. For any given individual, the optimal level of light, and the optimal wavelength of light, varies by type of visual impairment (Markowitz, S. N., 2006). Some students with visual impairment may perform poorly with high levels of white light and may perform successfully with lower levels of light. For others, the reverse might be true. Still others may need lighting within a narrow wavelength (e.g., light within the blue color spectrum), which is obtained through the use of filters. Glare is an aspect of light–dark adaptation and refers to the degree of reflected light in the environment. Some students may show their light sensitivity in situations of glare, which occurs when sunlight reflects off sand or snow or other light-colored surfaces.

***Performance Difficulties and Color Vision*** Not all individuals can distinguish between colors effectively, which can interfere with effective visual function. Color blindness is often unrecognized, because a student who has never seen certain types of colors will not know that he or she is missing out on parts of the visual spectrum. Color blindness can interfere with the successful interpretation of visual information if colors are used to demarcate different parts of a visual stimulus. By changing the contrast between colors (changing value and saturation), difficulties related to color blindness can be reduced.

## Performance Difficulties and Visual Processing

Visual processing depends on the successful delivery of light information by the eyes to the brain. Any of the performance difficulties discussed above would be expected to affect visual processing. When a student does not notice differences in contrast or color or shows light sensitivity, he or she is no longer successfully registering all the light information in the environment.

When a student has reduced visual fields or has impairments in oculomotor functions/skills, she or he may not take in all the visual information present in the visual field. As a result, the light information that is delivered to the brain is reduced and the brain has less information to work with in order to understand the environment. The following sections provide more detailed examples of performance difficulties in visual processing.

***Performance Difficulties and Depth Perception (Stereopsis)*** Students with performance difficulties in visual processing can have difficulty with depth perception. Difficulties with depth perception can result in more difficulty navigating the environment, which may manifest as clumsiness or difficulty finding targets. Depth perception difficulties can be due to difficulties with stereopsis or can be due to difficulties with contrast sensitivity.

***Performance Difficulties and Object Recognition Functions and Visual-Motor Skills*** Even though the visual functions of the oculomotor muscles and the eye globe all mature within the first year or two of life, visual processing skills take much longer to develop. The development of visual processing skills depends as much on intact visual and neurological structures (nature) as it does on experience (nurture). Children learn to recognize objects and to recognize symbolic information such as photographs, drawings, symbols, letters, and numbers. Age and experience allow a student to take in visual information and then develop three-dimensional representations from two-dimensional drawings, for example. Children learn to comprehend symbolic information, such as letters, numbers, or symbols. They learn to imagine spaces in the mind's eye, instead of relying on concrete representations of space. A student with very limited cognitive skills would not be expected to have developed the full range of visual processing skills. This affects the ability to understand three-dimensional space and to recognize objects. The student's underdeveloped visual processing then affects how successfully the student moves in space or how that student performs visual-motor tasks. Many of the performance difficulties discussed in the above sections can be due to difficulties with visual processing, regardless of whether the eyes deliver good light information to the brain. Difficulties with oculomotor skills and ocular functions/skills can appear the same as difficulties in the processing of visual information by the brain. See Box 1.7 for an extended list of behaviors that suggest vision performance difficulties.

## BOX 1.7. Behaviors That Suggest Vision Performance Difficulties and That May Require a Medical Evaluation

The atypical behaviors listed here are categorized by the underlying visual skills that are potentially missing or underdeveloped. When thinking about visual performance difficulties, it is useful to be thinking simultaneously about the interventions that might be helpful to the student. Visual performance difficulties are grouped here using the structure of the Vision Skills Framework. However, atypical visual behaviors and visual performance difficulties can sometimes fall into more than one of the skill sets listed in the framework. They can be caused by one or several different types of impairments along the visual axis. The main point in grouping the following typical visual behaviors is to assist with choosing interventions and in building skills. Information here was synthesized from articles by Matsuba and Soul (2010); Dutton, Cockburn, McDaid, and Macdonald (2010); Dutton, Macdonald, Drummond, Said:Kasimova, and Mitchell (2010); and Sargent, Salt, and Dale (2010).

*(continued)*

**BOX 1.7.** *(continued)*

1. Low vision (low visual acuity)
   a. Holds objects too near to the eyes
   b. Sits too close to the television screen: less than 60-cm distance, or closer for a handheld screen
   c. Misses objects that are obvious to the normally sighted person, such as a bright ball on green grass
2. Atypical visual behaviors, visual sensory-seeking behaviors
   a. Light gazing
   b. Finger flicking in front of the eyes
   c. Eye-pressing or eye-poking behaviors
   d. Roving eye movements
3. Color vision
   a. Inability to discriminate objects by color
   b. Inability to name colors
4. Contrast sensitivity
   a. Has difficulty seeing at far distances unless provided with adequate lighting
   b. Cannot discriminate facial expressions
   c. Cannot identify details in a fine line drawing
   d. Does better with an illuminated object in an otherwise dark space
5. Difficulties related to visual fields
   a. Head tilting when viewing objects or when walking in the environment
   b. Has difficulty finding the beginning of a line when reading
   c. Has difficulty finding the next word when reading
   d. Walks out in front of traffic
   e. Bumps into doorframes or partly opened doors; bumps into furniture; bumps into low-lying items, such as low furniture or objects on the floor
   f. Misses pictures or words on one side of the page
   g. Leaves food on one side of the plate untouched
6. Light–dark adaptation
   a. Avoids extremes of bright light
   b. Has difficulty with transitions between dark and light spaces
7. Difficulty with visual processing functions (object recognition functions and skills)
   a. The following developmental age levels are useful when analyzing visual behaviors that require the student to respond using language to name objects. Students

need to have the following language age levels in order to name the following types of objects and symbols:

- Naming objects: from 18 months
- Naming pictures: from 21 months
- Matching symbols: from 30 months
- Naming pictograms: from 33 months
- Naming letters: from 42 months

b. Has difficulty recognizing familiar objects, such as the family car, shapes, animals, after already having developed knowledge of these objects

c. Has difficulty managing a complex visual scene, such as in the examples listed here:

- Able to attend to only one object in a visual scene at a time
- Difficulty finding a toy in a toybox
- Difficulty finding a preferred food item on a grocery store shelf
- Difficulty finding an object on a patterned background
- Difficulty finding an item of clothing in a pile of clothes
- Difficulty finding food on a plate
- Tendency to get lost in crowded situations

d. Has difficulty seeing a distant object

e. Has difficulty reading, particularly crowded text

f. Has difficulty with recognizing persons

- Difficulty finding a close friend or relative who is standing in a group
- Difficulty recognizing close relatives in real life or from photographs
- Mistakenly identifies strangers as being familiar
- Difficulty interpreting facial expressions or seems uninterested in looking at faces
- Relies on nonvisual information such as a person's voice, clothing, or odor to identify that person

8. Difficulty coordinating visual functions with mobility

a. Has difficulty negotiating floor boundaries, for example, looks down when crossing over a boundary, even if the surface is smooth

b. Has difficulty walking over uneven surfaces and uses tactile cues to cross between a tiled and a carpeted floor

c. Has difficulty negotiating stairs and curbs, especially when going down (gets stuck, freezes, refuses to step down, or trips when stepping down), difficulty using escalators and with getting on and off

*(continued)*

**BOX 1.7.** *(continued)*

d. Has difficulty managing obstacles; bumps into furniture, out of keeping with overall motor skills; gets angry when furniture is moved; makes excessively large head or body movements to accommodate for difficulty with oculomotor skills; has difficulty navigating a room with excess visual clutter

e. Has difficulty managing spaces; quiet spaces, crowded spaces, or open spaces generate anxiety and/or disruptive behaviors

9. Difficulty coordinating vision with arm or hand movements
   a. Has inaccurate or atypical visually guided reach, such as reaching for food items, eating utensils, pencils
   b. Knocks over items during visually guided reach
   c. Reaches for objects while simultaneously looking away from the object
10. Difficulty recognizing and responding to objects in motion
    a. Has difficulty seeing things that are moving quickly, such as small animals; does not see or respond to fast-moving objects, such as traffic
    b. Avoids watching fast-moving television and/or chooses to watch slow-moving television
    c. Has difficulty catching a ball
11. Impaired orientation
    a. Gets lost in known locations and new environments
    b. Has difficulty finding one's way in the community
12. Impaired attention
    a. Has difficulty performing more than one visual task at a time; difficulty performing visual tasks while also performing an auditory task
    b. Exhibits marked frustration at being interrupted
    c. Bumps into things when walking and talking at the same time
13. Variability in visual performance
    a. May perform better in the early hours of the day as opposed to later in the day; performance wanes when tired, feeling hungry, or when feeling unwell

## SETTING UP OBSERVATIONS: GENERAL COMMENTS ON THIS BOOK

An important goal of this book is to help school professionals make good observations of their students. A good observation consists of an accurate description of a student's performance. The first step is to be descriptive (include a good level of detail) and to be objective, not interpretative. Each chapter in this book includes a Skills Observation Sheet in the appendix; professionals can use this form to apply the framework to their practice and to structure their observations.

During the observation, professionals should pay close attention to each student behavior and take detailed notes. Although interpretation is critical for understanding the behaviors, professionals should engage in interpretation and analysis only after the observation is completed. Each chapter will provide examples of how to gather information about student behaviors in an objective manner.

After completing the observation and taking time to reflect, professionals can begin the process of interpretation and analysis to identify which skills are developing appropriately, which skills are underdeveloped, and how any skill gaps might best be addressed. The frameworks presented in each chapter help to make connections between the observation and the resulting interpretation. The interpretation occurs in response to a question: "What does this behavior tell me about the framework of interest?" Alternatively, the school professional can ask, "For the framework of interest, what do the student's behaviors tell me about the skills that he or she has already mastered? Which skills are missing?" As a general rule, skills listed at the top of each framework (i.e., at the beginning) are more basic and emerge earlier in typically developing children than those listed toward the bottom. They are also more commonly present in students (regardless of disability) than those skills listed later in the framework. That said, many students with disabilities need to develop *all* the skills in a given framework, not just those at the top. With practice, professionals will become more accurate at identifying the full range of skills that are either present or absent (or underdeveloped) in any given student and for any given framework.

Although it is important to identify performance difficulties, it is equally important to identify performance successes. It is just as important to identify the skills that the student is missing as it is to describe those that are present. Only by identifying both can the professional make good interpretations and decide how best to intervene on behalf of the student.

## SETTING UP AN OBSERVATION FOR VISION

As noted, performance difficulties tend to capture the observer's attention first. In the case of vision skills, for example, the observer might first notice that the student bumps into objects, uses groping motions of the hands to find her or his way around a desktop, holds the head at an angle in order to read, or holds objects too close to the face and uses touch to explore them. Atypical behaviors such as these can be a first sign that the student may be having performance and learning difficulties. Box 1.7 lists commonly observable behaviors a teacher or other school professional might notice in the classroom setting that are related to underdeveloped or missing visual functions and skills.

The observable behaviors chosen for this section are relatively specific to vision. However, any observable behavior in any student is likely to have more than one possible explanation. In fact, some of the atypical behaviors discussed in this chapter could be related to factors that lie entirely outside of vision. For example, a student's inability or uninterest in looking at faces or recognizing people may be related to visual processing difficulties and can also be related to difficulties with social cognition. The Social Skills Framework (Chapter 6) discusses the importance of eye contact and social attention and is another framework for interpreting some of the visual behaviors of students. A student who is clumsy may have difficulties with visual perception and visual-motor skills. The student might also show those behaviors because of difficulties with the motor system or because of inattention. The Motor Skills Framework (Chapter 3) discusses the skill of coordination, whereas the Executive Skills Framework (Chapter 7) discusses the skill of paying attention. Thus, for any observable behavior, it is important for the school professional to consider more than one of the frameworks presented in this book. The observer has to decide which framework(s) are the most relevant or the most informative for understanding the student's skills.

Conducting observations, developing an objective description, and interpreting student behaviors should be done in an iterative manner. For any given student, more observations and more attempts at interpreting those observations helps to improve the accuracy of the interpretation by using the best framework(s). By learning about all the frameworks, the professional will gain a deeper understanding of which behaviors to look for and how to interpret them. As the professional becomes more skilled at identifying relevant behaviors and interpreting them accurately, so too will it become easier to determine the best intervention plan.

Although the task might at first seem daunting, the frameworks facilitate effective observation and analysis. They also allow school professionals to share the workload with colleagues. No one practitioner will master all of the frameworks nor be capable of making all of the observations and interpretations needed to address all of the student's needs. The main goal for the reader at this point is to know that interpretations of student behaviors can be made in a systematic and structured manner using one or several of the frameworks. Each school professional needs to develop an understanding of the frameworks, skill sets, and skills he or she can identify with confidence as being present. The professional needs to know which frameworks, skill sets, and skills he or she can identify with confidence as being absent or underdeveloped. Finally, the professional needs to know what he or she does not know. For those performance difficulties and observable behaviors that the professional is not able to interpret, it is important to ask colleagues to perform the observations and make relevant interpretations.

## HOW TO SET UP AN OBSERVATION FOR VISION

In this book, the How to Set Up an Observation sections are designed to help school professionals make descriptive as well as accurate interpretations. For this chapter, the focus is on making accurate observations of performance difficulties and skills related to vision. To begin, the observer is reminded that good observations and the successful interpretation of those behaviors depends on stable ocular health. Observations will be less useful for making educational decisions if there are any ongoing, unaddressed, or evolving medical conditions. This statement is true for any student, not just the student with a vision impairment. Students need to have generally stable health before behavioral observations will be consistent and can be interpreted successfully. It is important for the school nurse to verify that no ongoing or untreated medical condition(s) may be present that might affect the student's behaviors, visual or otherwise. The boxes in this chapter provide suggestions for the school nurse, so that medical factors related to vision are considered. The references for this chapter provide medical checklists for vision that the school nurse may find useful. When obtaining samples of student behaviors, it is best to choose behaviors that are common and necessary for participation at school. Managing one's belongings, working at a desktop, following classroom rules, reading, writing, and so forth are all examples of the types of behaviors that can and should be used for making observations. Within each of these common school-related activities, professionals can make more detailed observations to understand the student's skills within each of the domains discussed in this book.

### Selection of the Student

School professionals should conduct an observation of any student who they know or suspect to have a vision impairment. It is especially important to conduct observations of vision on those students who have risk factors related to vision.

***Obtain Sample Visual Behaviors*** As discussed above, many or most of the observations for vision should be made within the context of everyday classroom and school activities. School professionals can use Appendix 1.2, the Vision Skills Observation Sheet, to structure their observation for vision. The sections that follow outline how to make everyday classroom activities relevant for observing visual skills.

***Observations of Oculomotor Skills*** A commonly used test of oculomotor skills is to ask the student to move the eyes in all directions (up, down, to the right, and to the left). Sample oculomotor behaviors can be obtained by asking the student to perform basic movements such as these. When making observations, the school professionals should note whether the student's eyes move together, and whether both eyes can move the full arc in all directions. Other examples of how to assess oculomotor skills include organizing the materials or print on a desktop and seeing whether the student can scan the items in a left-to-right, top-to-bottom manner. The student should be able to do so without having to move his or her head. The observer should note whether the student can scan a desktop or computer screen and can locate important symbols, icons, or objects. Alternatively, oculomotor skills can be assessed through activities such as asking the student to copy a drawing and seeing whether the student can make scanning movements between two locations at a desktop. In this scenario, drawing requires two skill sets: Oculomotor skills and visual-motor skills.

In middle and distant space, the observer can verify whether the student can scan the environment to locate/localize important objects or landmarks. For example, the observer can ask the student to describe or show where things are located in the classroom or in a larger space. The capacity to do so requires scanning skills. Scanning skills are also needed to navigate three-dimensional space. To navigate successfully, the student needs either to reach or to avoid obstacles or landmarks in near and far space. For example, professionals can observe whether the student can find important locations in the building such as the cafeteria, bathroom, or main office. The observer may notice that the student bumps into objects or seems to get lost. It is especially important to distinguish performance difficulties due to factors not related to vision. For example, some of the activities just described depend on language and motor skills, not only on vision.

***Observations of Ocular Functions and Skills*** To make observations of behaviors related to ocular functions and skills, the student should be observed at a desktop and asked to identify objects, photographs, fine line drawings, symbols, and letters and numbers. The observer can also ask the student to identify colors and shapes or to label other visual information. For instance, the observer might ask the student to point at a named object and describe the objects as appearing clear or fuzzy. The lighting, font size, contrast between foreground and background, and/or the colors can then be varied to see whether the student's visual behaviors or overall participation improve. Field defects can show up as an oculomotor difficulty. Students with field defects are known to move the head instead of moving the eyes in order to see an object more fully. They may be able to improve their vision by holding the head to one side. The observation can be used to introduce backlighting, for example, shining a light on the desktop from behind the student, instead of from above or from in front of the student. This strategy can help determine whether changes in lighting improves the student's vision and allow for more normal visual behaviors. For students who do not have strong language skills, the observations just suggested may need to be made based on spontaneous reaching or play behaviors to understand what the students can see. Students who hold objects too closely, ignore objects named by the observer, or seem to lack interest in looking at any of the objects may have vision difficulties.

***Observations of Visual Processing Skills*** Visual processing consists of more complex understanding and use of visual information. For example, visual processing includes understanding the meaning of visual information, being able to discuss or talk about that information, or being able to act on that information through the motor system. Visual processing starts with depth perception, the ability to recognize what is closer and what is farther away.

Depth perception is important for finding one's way in space. Visual recognition functions and skills can be observed by providing objects, photographs, fine line drawings, symbols, and/or printed words and asking the student to identify the visual information, discuss it, or make use of it to reach personal or classroom goals. To assess visual-motor functions and skills, the observer should note whether the student pairs visual recognition functions/skills with other types of skills such as motor skills. The observation might also look at whether the student can navigate well through the space or can copy drawings or print letters or words.

## Analyze and Interpret the Observations

The visual behaviors discussed above are evaluated in a more precise manner by a functional vision specialist, who is trained to make the types of observations suggested in this chapter and augments the observations suggested above using specialized testing materials. School professionals should not expect to draw firm conclusions about a student's visual functions and skills without the support or guidance of a vision specialist. For any given atypical or unexpected behavior, there may be more than one explanation for the student's performance. The same observable behavior may be due to an impairment in oculomotor skills, ocular skills, and/or visual processing skills. The same observable behavior could also be due to an impairment in language skills, motor skills, or another developmental domain. Sometimes, an impairment in visual skills may be present without any obvious behavioral manifestations. The purpose of the observations suggested in this chapter is to help school professionals who may not be specialists in this area understand the link between observable behaviors and visual skills. By doing so, the professional's daily interactions and observations of student behavior will become easier to interpret. Better interpretations can then lead to more clearly defined educational goals and objectives, as well as the best therapeutic intervention or strategy to introduce. For any observable behavior or set of behaviors, school professionals should aim to accurately describe the student's behaviors, discuss the observations with the functional vision specialist, and then use this information to interpret the behavior. Use the following sections as a guide for interpretation.

***Analysis and Interpretation of Behaviors for Oculomotor Skills*** Behavioral observations should be made to help determine whether the student can move both eyes in tandem while looking at stationary objects. The student should also be able to keep both eyes in tandem while following a moving target. These skills should be present over the full range of eye movements. Notably, any of the skills discussed in this chapter (i.e., ocular functions, visual processing functions) may influence and interfere with the student's ability to use oculomotor skills. Oculomotor skills may look as though they are impaired, when, in fact, ocular and visual processing functions are affected.

***Analysis and Interpretation of Behaviors for Visual Acuity*** A variety of unexpected or atypical behaviors can occur when visual acuity is affected. The best way to assess acuity is through a visual acuity test, as long as the student has the language skills needed to participate. Other behaviors may suggest that visual acuity is not yet in place. For example, a student who holds objects very close to the face, or who cannot see distant objects, may have difficulties with visual acuity.

***Analysis and Interpretation of Behaviors for Visual Fields*** Field defects manifest behaviorally when the student fails to notice visual stimuli in a predictable manner, for example, he or she always fails to notice things on one or the other side. Field defects can also manifest when the student holds objects at an odd angle or always places objects in a particular position on the desktop. The observational data should be analyzed to consider whether the student is able to see the full visual field. If the student tilts her or his head at an odd angle or seems to ignore objects or stimuli in certain portions of the field, the field may be decreased in size.

***Analysis and Interpretation of Behaviors for Light Sensitivity*** Light sensitivity manifests through light-avoidance behaviors. School professionals should consider whether the student's behaviors suggest that she or he seems a preference for either low or high levels of light, or a slow adaptation during transitions between light and dark spaces.

***Analysis and Interpretation of Behaviors for Color Vision*** This analysis considers whether the student is able to recognize colors. Normally, this skill is measured by asking the student to name colors.

***Analysis and Interpretation of Behaviors for Contrast Sensitivity*** The student should be able to perform successfully when there is a low level of contrast between foreground and background. One way to assess contrast sensitivity is to ask the student to retrieve objects from within a cluttered array. Another way to assess contrast sensitivity is to ask the student to notice subtle changes in facial expressions, especially when the lighting is not optimal. During a functional visual assessment with a specialist, contrast sensitivity is measured using specifically designed visual stimuli.

***Analysis and Interpretation of Behaviors for Stereopsis and Depth Perception*** The student should be able to navigate the environment, such as reaching a destination in the building or walking down stairs without support. When walking through the environment, be sure to observe whether the student makes use of tactile or auditory cues to navigate successfully, as opposed to relying on vision alone. Be sure to provide physical supports if the student is at risk of falling.

***Analysis and Interpretation of Behaviors for Visual Recognition Functions/Skills*** The student should be able to recognize objects, photographs, fine line drawings, or symbols, depending on the student's overall developmental age. Students with developmental delay may not be able to identify or select symbols such as letters, for example, but may be able to identify or select objects or photographs. Visual recognition skills include paying visual attention to others such as when socializing and being able to identify others visually. The student should be able to recognize facial features in order to recognize other people and should not have to rely upon familiar articles of clothing or the sound of someone's voice to identify the person.

***Analysis and Interpretation of Behaviors for Visual-Motor Functions/Skills*** The student should be able to use vision to guide motor behaviors when navigating the environment, when using tools or instruments successfully, and for printing and drawing, among other activities. The student should be able to detect errors using vision alone and then make attempts at correcting those errors. Error detection and correction should occur without having to rely on tactile or auditory cues.

***Analysis and Interpretation of Behaviors for Visual Processing: Mentalizing Visual Information*** At times, a vision impairment may manifest as difficulty visualizing three-dimensional space when offered two-dimensional information (e.g., difficulty understanding geometric forms in math or difficulty producing representational drawings).

***Analysis for Variability in Visual Functions and Visual Skills*** At times, a vision impairment may manifest as variability in visual performance. For example, some students appear to have variations in their visual functions and skills. They may be especially vulnerable to visual difficulty when they are tired or hungry or feel unwell. The type of variation described here is more likely to occur in students with a significant disability such as cerebral palsy with substantial cognitive impairments.

### Conclusions About Making Observations and Analyzing Successfully

Making good observations and accurate interpretations is a complex task that becomes easier with practice. The frameworks and associated skills presented in this chapter are intended to guide the interpretation of behavioral observations. Notably, professionals should always take into consideration more than one framework rather than quickly focusing the analysis on specific skills sets and skills within any one framework.

## GENERAL COMMENTS ABOUT THE INTERVENTION PLAN AND IEP BUILDER FOR EACH OF THE CHAPTERS OF THIS BOOK

The IEP Builder is perhaps the most important section in each chapter of this book. The purpose of the IEP Builder is to provide specific examples of how to help improve student performance. The IEP Builder includes strategies that can be used in both general and special education. It describes sample educational objectives and strategies relevant to that chapter, which can be used by school teams to inform the development of an intervention plan or an IEP. It does not include the development of measurable objectives or make more than general suggestions about service delivery to students.

When performance difficulties are identified, school professionals should make an interpretation of the underlying skill sets or skills that might be missing or underdeveloped. School professionals then need to identify the underlying skill sets and skills that are developing successfully. In fact, it is through the identification of those skills that are developed or are developing more successfully that the professionals can identify appropriate educational goals, objectives, strategies, and/or accommodations. It is the underlying strengths (skills and abilities) of the student that can end up supporting growth for the framework as a whole. As school professionals monitor developmental growth in each student, they also enhance their observational and interpretative skills. Each subsequent observation of the student helps the professionals to better understand the student's skills, to measure progress more accurately, and to select educational objectives, strategies, and accommodations more precisely the next time. Observations, descriptive analyses, interpretations, and measuring progress are all interrelated. This iterative process is true for each of the frameworks presented in this book.

## IEP BUILDER

The IEP Builder for vision provides sample educational objectives and strategies to enhance a student's visual performance. Many of the educational objectives discussed will be dedicated to teaching the student compensatory skills to accommodate for oculomotor dysfunctions, field defects, reduced contrast sensitivity, absent or impaired color vision, difficulties with depth perception, and so forth. The same compensatory skills can be used regardless of whether the structural or functional impairment is at the level of the ocular structures, the optic nerve, neurological connections to the visual cortex, or connections to other brain regions. In other words, many of the vision rehabilitation and visual strategies discussed in this chapter help support the entire visual system, not just specific anatomical sites or specific visual functions. For example, strategies such as optimizing lighting or teaching the use of auditory or tactile cues are potentially as useful to the student with a retinal dysfunction as they are for the student with cerebral visual dysfunctions and visual processing difficulties. Enhancing contrast between foreground and background may be as useful to the student with impairments in color vision as it is for students with other types of visual dysfunctions. The information shared in this section of the chapter is synthesized using several of the references in the References section, especially from Lueck (2004a, 2004b, 2004c, 2004d) and Lueck and Heinze (2004).

The vision rehabilitation specialist should work together with the school professional who may be less specialized in this field and help to identify strategies that improve the student's performance. See Box 1.8 for more information about how to share the workload when strategizing for the student.

**BOX 1.8. Selecting the Right Team Members**

Before building an IEP, a team must be assembled, composed of the professionals best qualified to choose educational objectives and strategies, that will help the student make developmental progress. This chapter is especially useful in highlighting the contribution of diverse specialists, all of whom have somewhat different roles, and all of whom can assist students with vision impairment and visual performance difficulties. Making use of as many members of the team as possible to help teach the student is always a desired goal. Even less experienced members of the team can assist the student with a vision impairment.

Damaged or injured ocular structures are addressed by a medical practitioner, such as an ophthalmologist or optometrist, who can repair or improve ocular structures and functions through the use of medications, surgery, or prescription eyeglasses. When eye structures have undergone maximum repair or treatment, vision can still be improved through vision habilitation and rehabilitation.

The focus in a school setting is habilitation (the building of new skills) or rehabilitation (the building of skills that were present and then lost). When building visual skills, several professionals may be involved, such as a functional vision specialist, vision rehabilitation specialist, or teacher of the visually impaired. Some ophthalmologists and optometrists are certified as low vision rehabilitation specialists. More commonly, vision rehabilitation is carried out by the functional vision specialist, orientation and mobility trainers, teachers of the visually impaired, and occupational therapists (Markowitz, M., 2006; Whitaker & Scheiner, 2012). The purpose of vision rehabilitation is to help maximize residual function by developing visual skills. By developing visual skills, the individual can use her or his vision as successfully as possible (Colenbrander, 2010a).

A functional vision specialist or teacher of the visually impaired can optimize how visual information is presented to the eyes, making desktop and environmental information visually accessible to the student. An occupational therapist can work with students with vision impairment in teaching fine motor and adaptive skills (Whitaker & Scheiner, 2012). It is important for the school team and the student to know what each professional can do and to help coordinate all the different vision interventions that the student may need. It is also important for the specialists to provide instruction or guidance to less experienced professionals, so that all members of the team, not just the experts, can help to support the student with a vision impairment. The concept of team members sharing the workload while also providing interprofessional training and support is a constant theme in this book.

## Medical and Health-Related Interventions for Ocular Structures and Ocular Health

Interventions for ocular structures include interventions such as surgery to clear up or replace a cloudy cornea, prescription glasses to assist with accommodation difficulties of the lens, laser surgery to change the shape of the lens or to prevent deterioration of the retina, or medications to reduce ocular disease and/or improve ocular health. School professionals are not normally involved in the assessment or treatment of ocular structures or ocular functions and do not normally provide medical interventions. The main goal for school professionals who work with students with a vision impairment is to make good observations and ask good questions when ocular health is a concern. This function can be provided by the school nurse or by some of the vision specialists mentioned in this section. Medically related questions should be transmitted to a health care professional such as an ophthalmologist or optometrist who can determine whether any medical interventions are required to repair or improve the health or the function of ocular structures (Lueck, 2004c).

## Educational Objectives and Strategies for Oculomotor Skills

The following sections provide information about the types of educational objectives, strategies, and accommodations that are useful for a variety of students with vision impairment. The reader should review these sections with the goal of understanding the recommendations that are likely to flow from a specialist who has conducted an assessment of the student's functional vision.

***Educational Objectives and Strategies for Scanning and Tracing*** Students all need to be taught to scan or trace from left to right and top to bottom. The student with vision impairment may need to be taught this skill in an explicit manner. As examples, students with oculomotor dysfunctions, field defects, and low visual acuity will likely need instruction in scanning and tracing. They can learn to scan in a systematic manner by scanning sequentially, scanning in overlapping swaths, and scanning the entire visual area. The degree of effort will vary for near, middle, and distance vision and will depend on the student's capacity for near versus distant vision. However, regardless of the type of visual information, whether it is print, objects on a desktop, or navigating the environment, the basic strategy remains the same. At times, use of the motor system as a whole can help compensate for underdeveloped or missing oculomotor skills. By making movements of the entire head, a student can compensate for missing or underdeveloped oculomotor skills.

Students with developmental delay or with severe vision and/or cognitive impairments may need physical supports to be able to move their body, head, or eyes sequentially from left to right. Physical supports might mean seating supports to keep the head upright or use of the hands of an adult to help move the head in more than one direction. For other students, verbal instruction may be enough. Near vision scanning skills can be trained by placing objects in a predictable order on the desktop. Then, the student would be taught to scan from left to right and top to bottom in a systematic manner. The same type of organized approach can be used to teach a student to scan the environment and then localize an object of interest. The student may need to be taught positional and spatial concepts such as left, right, up, down, close, and farther away.

***Educational Objectives and Strategies for Orientation and Mobility Training*** Orientation and mobility skills require students to move their eyes, as described above, to find their way in space. The concepts discussed above are important aspects of orientation and mobility training. Orientation and mobility training also involves teaching the use of tactile and auditory cues. Students who are legally blind may need specific training in the use of a cane (which provides both tactile and auditory cues) and may need explicit instruction in understanding and anticipating the location, position, and distance of objects. At the desktop, objects can be used for their tactile information to indicate points on the schedule, to indicate which activity will be occurring next, and the like.

Students with residual vision and/or those students with visual processing difficulties may benefit from learning to identify the location of specific objects, symbols, or landmarks in the school building as they navigate that environment. Having symbols of a specific color that indicate that they are in a particular hallway or that outline a specific path to certain locations in the school building can enhance the students' independence in navigating the school building. For example, yellow stars can be used to indicate the path to the cafeteria, whereas blue squares indicate the path to the principal's office. If the student has sufficient vision to start using other types of markers, these specialized visual supports can be gradually taken away. They can instead be paired with natural geographic markers such as an exit sign or other markers such as the stairway, the elevator, the purple classroom door, and so forth. Each of these landmarks can be used to help the student find his or her way around the building. For example, the student can learn a script such as "The purple exit door is halfway between the classroom and the cafeteria." Students who have language skills can benefit from this type of instruction but may not think about using strategies such as these unless instructed to do so. Tactile landmarks can also be useful. For example, sandpapered traction tape on the floor can serve the purpose of guiding a student toward certain important locations in the building.

***Educational Objectives and Strategies for Ocular Functions*** Most of the strategies used to improve ocular functioning are accommodations and would not be considered educational objectives. The Educational Accommodations for Vision section later in this chapter discusses the different types of modifications that enhance ocular functioning. That said, an important educational objective should be to teach the students how to advocate for their own visual needs. This can be accomplished by teaching the student the vocabulary associated with successful functional vision. The student should learn to identify the visual strategies that seem to help her or him the most. By learning the terms of the Vision Skills Framework and the strategies listed in the Educational Accommodations for Vision section, students can begin to advocate for their own needs as well.

***Educational Objectives and Strategies for the Visual Field*** With some experimentation, the student can discover what size objects and images and/or what size font works best for her or his visual acuity, field defects, or other factors. Educational objectives in this case could include teaching the student about these different accommodations and having the student use trial and error to choose the accommodations that work best. For example, when training oculomotor skills, the student can be trained to use just the eyes and to avoid using head tilt or head motions to localize a visual stimulus. The idea is to keep the student's head in an upright or neutral position and train the student to move his or her eyes or to change the position of the object in order to see it. This strategy can be difficult when walking and looking for landmarks or objects in the environment, as the student may need to tilt the head for optimal viewing.

Students with visual field defects need to learn how to position objects to maximize use of their vision and they also need to learn the vocabulary needed to direct others to assist with optimal placement of objects or images. To do this, the student will need to learn vocabulary for positional concepts (e.g., *higher, lower, right side, left side, center, right of center*). When viewing objects, the student will need to learn to keep the head mid-line (i.e., avoid tilting the head) and change the position of objects to see them clearly.

***Educational Objectives and Strategies for Enhancing Contrast*** The student can learn about the strategies used to enhance contrast, for example, through judicious use of lighting and choice of dark background and by using contrasts in color, value, and saturation. Ideally, the student would learn the definitions of the technical terms listed here and elsewhere in this chapter. However, many students will need to learn vocabulary that is developmentally more appropriate. Terms such as "more light" or "lighter color" and "darker color" may be sufficient for some students as they advocate for their needs.

***Educational Objectives and Strategies for Light–Dark Adaptation*** Students can learn to adjust lighting, make use of color filters, verbalize difficulties with excess light and glare, or verbalize difficulties with insufficient light.

***Educational Objectives and Strategies for Depth Perception and Distance*** Orientation and mobility training can help the student with visual impairment to use auditory and tactile cues to identify distance, depth, and space. See the Educational Objectives and Strategies for Orientation and Mobility Training section.

## Educational Accommodations for Vision

Many of the strategies used for the student with a visual impairment consist of accommodations. Accommodations do not teach students new skills but can enhance students' functioning and result in the development of new abilities. For example, use of a cane to navigate one's way through a building is an example of an accommodation that helps to develop a new ability (navigating the environment) by making use of auditory and tactile cues. Different types of tactile and auditory inputs can be used to teach orientation and mobility, not just those that result from using a cane. It is important to train the student to make use of accommodations as independently as possible. This means that the student needs to be taught to request or access accommodations when they are needed. The accommodations that follow can help improve functional vision.

***Accommodations for a Variety of Ocular Functions*** Accommodations for a variety of ocular functions include adjusting the size of the objects or print. Changing the size of the object or print can help accommodate for visual dysfunctions such as acuity, field size, and fixation skills, among others. Some students may perform better with smaller font and smaller objects, whereas others may perform better with a larger font or with larger objects or pictures. Objects also can be placed at different distances, as vision may improve when the object is nearer or farther away.

***Accommodations to Enhance Contrast*** Accommodations to enhance visual contrast include the following:

*Reducing Visual Clutter* Reduction in visual clutter accommodates for difficulties with contrast sensitivity and also accommodates for scanning weaknesses. Visual clutter may need to be reduced at the desktop but may also need to be reduced for the classroom as a whole. For many students, a classroom with less rather than more visual stimulation works better. For example, visual processing demands are reduced when all the furniture is only one color, when different sections of the classroom are demarcated from one another as different color zones, and/or when visual information on the walls is organized into columns and rows. At the desktop, visual clutter can be reduced by presenting information in clearly demarcated rows and columns. Organizing visual information carefully simplifies the task of scanning.

*Using a Dark Background* At the desktop, contrast can be enhanced by placing objects on a dark-colored desktop or by changing the background color of a computer screen display.

*Using Lighting Strategically* Shine a light on the desktop while keeping the rest of the classroom slightly darker. This accommodation can make it easier for the student to focus on objects or activities of interest and reduce visual attention to nonsalient objects. Similarly, the student may be more successful in localizing and fixating on an object when it is well lit and when surrounding objects are not as well lit. Some experimentation may be needed to find the right intensity of light.

*Accommodating for Color Blindness* Reducing the number of different colors can help reduce visual clutter and can be helpful to students who are color blind. Color blindness can affect contrast sensitivity, depending on the colors being used. A student who cannot discern the full array of colors may also have more difficulty separating objects and images from one another. More highly contrasting colors, especially those colors that the student is able to differentiate, can help enhance contrast sensitivity.

***Accommodations for the Visual Field*** Accommodations for the visual field include the following:

*Ensuring Correct Placement Within the Visual Field* Students may need materials placed strategically. They may benefit from having visual information placed in the center, higher or lower than the center, or to the left or right side. In some cases, the student should weigh in on what is best.

*Reducing Scanning Demands* Visually salient information should be placed in front of the student. The student can be taught to localize visually important information by teaching positional concepts. For example, a teacher might train the student to follow instructions such as "look up" or "look on the right-hand side," 'lower than that," and so forth.

*Making Use of Objects of Reference* For students with a small visual field and for students with a variety of other vision impairments, objects of reference can help identify persons and objects. Objects of reference might consist of a bracelet of a certain color that is worn by only one specific person. When the bracelet is placed into the student's visual field, the student knows who is there. The bracelet may be offered for the student to see or touch, communicating who is present. Objects of reference are very useful for deafblind students, as long as the student has some residual vision. Objects of reference are also useful for students with impairments in their visual processing. Some experimentation may be needed to see if objects of reference help the student to perform better. Adults working with students can also choose to wear a specific colored shirt or to wear a specific colored smock. A dark smock can at the same time improve contrast sensitivity.

***Accommodations for Light–Dark Adaptation*** A slower transition between light and dark environments can help the student accommodate to transitions between light and dark. Lighting intensity can be reduced or enhanced. Light shining from behind the student (instead of overhead or in front of the student) can also reduce sensitivity to light. Colored filters can be helpful in reducing exposure to those wavelengths that provoke sensitivity, and polarizing filters can reduce glare. These filters can be used when the student is exposed to fluorescent lighting or very bright light situations. The choice of lighting should be determined by a functional vision specialist, though some experimentation may be required to find the solution.

***Accommodations for Depth Perception and Distance*** Colors and contrast can be used to highlight the contrast between distance and depth. In distant and middle space, symbols of different shapes or colors can be used to highlight pathways through the school building. For example, colored lines, symbols, arrows, or icons with a printed word can lead to different locations in the building. Arrows might lead the student to the main office, whereas colored lines might lead to the cafeteria. In middle to near space, stairs can be highlighted at the edges with a lighter or darker colored strip. In near space, contrast can be enhanced on the desktop by using a dark background, by using highly contrasting colors, or by using lighting judiciously.

***Accommodations for Object Recognition Functions and Skills*** Deficits in higher order visual processing and in recognition functions can be addressed by changing the degree of symbolic representation. A hierarchy of complexity is helpful to take into consideration here. The lowest level of visual processing demands exists for objects, especially when these are displayed using judicious lighting and with high contrast against a dark background. From here, the level of visual processing increases as students are asked to recognize and extract meaning from photographs, drawings, symbols, and/or letters. Students with cognitive impairment who cannot interpret symbols (e.g., letters, words, numbers) can use photographs, drawings, and pictographs for learning. Photographs can be especially successful, particularly when photographs are taken of the student's own environment. Photographs taken for the student should be clear and consistent in size and magnification and have appropriate background for optimal contrast.

***Accommodations for Visual-Motor Functions and Skills*** All the strategies listed above can be used to help build visual-motor skills in distant, middle, and near space. The student may need clearly recognizable objects, building features, pictures, or symbols. From here, the student can learn how to scan the environment for those objects, building features, pictures, or symbols. Subsequently, the student can learn to use their motor system to access objects or building features, using motor skills such as reaching, grasping, or walking.

***Accommodations for Variability in Visual Function*** Some students, particularly those with cerebral vision impairment, may show variations in their capacity to see. For these students, it can be difficult to know which of the above strategies is the most effective, since their functions can vary from day to day or even from hour to hour. Variation in function can occur with variations in the level of alertness or fatigue, level of hunger, level of wellness, or level of sensitivity to environmental stimuli in general. It may require several observations to know how to optimize vision for these students. An assessment of the student's responsiveness to interventions and to accommodations is another way to determine which interventions and accommodations are the most useful. See Box 1.9 for a list of vision accommodations that can be trialed with the student and that can help determine the student's vision needs. More observations over time and under different environmental conditions can help identify the strategies that appear to be the most helpful.

### BOX 1.9. Vision Accommodations

**Reduce Demands on Scanning, Tracking, and Tracing**

1. Optimize viewing distance.
2. Optimize the size of objects or font at near distance.
3. Find the right amount of space between items on the desktop or at near distances.
4. Organize items into a logical sequence on the desktop.
5. For middle distance and far vision, reduce obstacles, enhance visibility of landmarks in the environment through use of color and lighting; provide visual cues that help locate objects or items in the classroom or destinations in the building.
6. Make use of auditory and tactile cues to reduce demands on scanning, tracking, and tracing.
7. Allow more time for scanning, tracking, and tracing.

**Reduce Demands on Ocular Functions**

1. *Acuity.* At near, optimize the size of items, either slightly larger or slightly smaller. This applies to the size of objects, pictures, and font size.
2. *Field.* At near, place items in the optimal portion of the visual field.

3. *Contrast.* Optimize contrast by using a dark background and/or primary colors (enhance contrast by increasing difference in the value or saturation of colors), creating clear spaces or clear demarcations between visual stimuli. Desktop should be dark. Personnel presenting visual targets should have solid, dark-colored clothing or a smock.
4. *Lighting.* Optimize lighting, for example, use backlighting, reduce use of overhead lighting. Consider use of polarized lenses or consider use of single-color lighting.
5. *Visual clutter.* Decrease the visual complexity or visual clutter by reducing color, using bold colors, enhancing contrast between foreground and background, organizing visual materials into rows and columns.

**Reduce Demands on Visual Processing**
All of the accommodations listed above also reduce visual processing demands.

1. *Depth perception.* Reduce demands on depth perception by highlighting changes in depth in the environment (e.g., stairs) through use of contrasting colors, lighting, and tactile cues.
2. *Object recognition functions.* Reduce demands on object recognition functions by reducing the level of symbolism, for example, use drawings or photographs instead of symbols or icons, when possible. Use objects instead of photographs if needed. Make use of objects of reference to help a student quickly identify familiar persons, places, or objects that might otherwise be difficult for the student to see because of problems with the visual field or because the visual targets are moving. Objects of reference can be a bracelet, hairband, or article of clothing always worn by the same person and not by anyone else.
3. *Object recognition functions.* Use visual identification tags for familiar objects or places. Objects and locations in the environment can be identified by using a symbol, a color, or an icon to help the student rapidly identify everyday utensils needed by the student, other items that belong to the student, or locations that are important for the student to be able to locate quickly.
4. *Object recognition and motion.* Reduce demands on recognition functions at near when persons or objects are moving. For example, changes in facial expression may need to be exaggerated or repeated. Videotaped material may need to be viewed more than once or may need to be broken down into still images.
    a. Reduce demands on visual-motor functions by either simplifying visual demands (strategies listed above) or by reducing motor demands.
    b. Use auditory and tactile cues to assist with visual-motor demands.
    c. Allow more time for visual processing.
    d. Ensure that the student is not tired, hungry, or feeling unwell.

***Accommodations for Students Who Are Not Visually Impaired*** Use of the accommodations listed above can facilitate learning for students who may not have a vision impairment. Delayed or limited overall cognitive development can account for delays or limited visual processing skills. Demands on oculomotor skills can be reduced by organizing visual information into rows and columns and/or by reducing the number of visual stimuli that the student needs to scan. Demands on ocular functions can be reduced by using lighting judiciously, by enhancing contrast, by reducing visual clutter, and by keeping objects mid-line within the student's visual field. Demands on visual processing can be reduced by using visual information that is more concrete and less symbolic. Students who are inattentive or who have learning difficulty could potentially also benefit from these strategies. By reducing demands on oculomotor skills, ocular sensory functions, and/or visual processing skills, the student can potentially expend more mental energy on other aspects of learning.

## CASE EXAMPLE

Yoshe is a 12-year-old student with vision impairment. She has attended her current school for several years and is well known to the staff and student body. Yoshe has come a long way in working with her current team. When she first entered the school, she often appeared anxious or upset. It took her a while to learn to work successfully with the adults in her classroom. Everyone feels very positive about the many gains she has made in her program. As part of her triennial review, her team was interested in summarizing her visual skills and needs. Yoshe will be transitioned into high school in the coming year. Her team wants to make sure that all relevant visual information is transmitted successfully to the receiving team at her high school.

### Medical Information Pertinent to Yoshe

Yoshe has a vision impairment, a result of complications related to her premature birth. She often fails to pay attention to objects or persons on her left hand side (left-sided neglect). Yoshe has both ocular impairments and central nervous system–related impairments that affect her vision. Her ocular health is now stable but includes retinal detachment. The retinal detachment, on the right side of the retina of both eyes, resulted in a left-sided field defect. However, the retinal detachment in each eye is different in scope, and the field defect in each eye is therefore difficult to characterize. In general, she does not notice objects or movements on her left side. However, she does respond to visual stimuli at mid-line and to the right of mid-line. Her cornea and lens are intact. She has normal color vision and contrast sensitivity.

Yoshe can walk securely in familiar environments and can use her right arm and hand successfully, though not always very smoothly or efficiently. Yoshe also has global learning delays. She currently shows consistent mastery of preschool concepts and is working on an early school-age curriculum. She has started to identify whole words. She understands basic math concepts such as more and less, and she has started to count and identify numerals.

### Observations of Yoshe

The following list of observations and accommodations describe some of Yoshe's visually related behaviors. These observations were gathered by her present team to share with the new team that will work with her in high school.

#### *Oculomotor Skills*

Yoshe's teachers remind her to keep her head at mid-line and to use purposeful scanning motions to make sure that she truly sees all of the objects and images that might be in her visual field. This is true for desktop work and for orientation and mobility demands (i.e., navigating her environment). Yoshe is not always able to see objects in distant or far space and does not always recognize people or objects in distant or far space.

### *Ocular Functions*

Yoshe needs objects placed to her right side or near the center, so that visual information is transmitted to the left (intact) side of both of her retinas. As mentioned, Yoshe's team has noticed that she does not always recognize people from a distance. Yoshe usually has a very neutral facial expression when looking at others. She seems to inspect the faces of others in an unusual manner, especially when she is not familiar with the person. Her team wondered whether she is trying to identify facial features that will help her identify the person again at a subsequent visit. At the same time, she is often prone to speaking to others without looking at their face. She turns her face to her social partner only when prompted to do so.

### *Visual Processing Skills*

During an observation of her performance at desktop activities, Yoshe showed that she can read fine print. When reading, she scans from left to right but can do so only with exaggerated head movements to accommodate for her left field defect. She can identify and discuss pictures in picture books. She can identify all the letters of the alphabet and their sounds. Reading skills are limited to sight word recognition. She is not yet decoding any words. Yoshe appears to be most comfortable using printed material with a 14-point font. She does better when teaching staff present drawings and objects one at a time, and when they ask her to scan carefully from left to right when looking at objects on her desk or when looking at a computer screen. In her classroom, lighting is optimized so that it shines on her desk from behind. Overhead lighting is kept low. These strategies reduce glare and enhance contrast. Her desk has a dark blue background, which helps her to focus her vision on the object or book that is placed on top of the desk.

Yoshe has a visual schedule, that is designed to be read from top to bottom. This format appears to be easier for her because vertical scanning circumvents her left-sided field defect. Yoshe cannot remember a schedule very easily, but she always likes to know what is next. Her team is mindful to keep her daily schedule nearby, as she prefers the visual reminder. When the schedule changes when there's a field trip or a special assembly, she often seems agitated and keeps asking, "What's next?" or "What's going on?" Simply providing her with verbal information about the schedule seems not to be sufficient. Her team accommodates her needs by always providing both visual and verbal information pertaining to her schedule and to time intervals. This helps make her feel more secure about the events of the day. Yoshe's attention span is short, and she usually works for 15-minute periods. This attention span is appropriate for her overall cognitive abilities.

During an observation of her gait, Yoshe walks slowly and does not always scan the environment to make up for her left visual field defect, but when reminded, she can do so. She is hesitant when descending stairs, slowing stretching her foot out to find the edge of each step before stepping downward.

## Case Analysis of Yoshe

Yoshe's visual limitations have already been identified by a teacher of the visually impaired. Many appropriate vision interventions and accommodations are already in place. That said, it is important for the team to continually observe Yoshe's visual behaviors, with and without the accommodations, so they can be more strategic in using visual accommodations and in monitoring their effectiveness and can help Yoshe make maximal use of her vision. Accommodations and interventions sometimes have to be modified, especially as the student makes developmental progress, or when the student transitions to a new classroom or a new school building. The following sections further analyze Yoshe's visual needs.

### *Analysis of Yoshe's Ocular Health*

Yoshe is followed by an ophthalmologist. Yoshe underwent laser correction of her retinal detachment, but residual field defects persist. She has regular (annual) checkups with the ophthalmologist. The team does not have any concerns about the need for additional amelioration or correction of ocular structures, as her ocular health is stable.

### *Analysis of Yoshe's Oculomotor Skills*

Yoshe has full movement of both eyes in all directions. However, she does not always make use of her oculomotor skills when she should. Her orientation and mobility specialist is teaching her to use her vision consistently by scanning and tracing consistently in both near and distant space. It is harder for Yoshe to track moving objects, given her vision impairment. She tends to be clumsy in her scanning, which is sometimes a bit jerky. If she moves about slowly and scans consistently, she does not bump into objects. However, she does not always anticipate moving classmates and can inadvertently bump into them. Safety awareness in the community is a concern. For now, she needs one-to-one attention when moving through any environment.

### *Yoshe's Ocular Functions and Skills*

Yoshe has a left-sided field defect. She sometimes gets agitated or angry when someone enters into her left visual field without warning and she is taken by surprise. The team is careful to say something to her when approaching from the left, to alert her attention to her left side. Materials on her desktop are always presented to the right of mid-line or at mid-line, so they are placed in the best portion of her visual field. In near space, the team uses appropriate font size, judicious use of color and lighting, and reminders to use her vision skills strategically whenever they present materials to her.

### *Analysis of Yoshe's Visual Processing Skills*

Yoshe has difficulty with depth perception, as is evident from her hesitation when going down stairs and her use of tactile cues to assist her. Placing high-contrast material at the edges of the stairs has helped her understand differences in depth, but this accommodation is not available for all stairs in all settings. Yoshe continues to have difficulty with depth perception at distance. She navigates her environment slowly, in part for this reason. She is not always able to find her way in the school building and needs a lot of support in finding her way in unfamiliar settings.

### *Yoshe's Visual Recognition Skills*

Yoshe has difficulty looking at faces in social situations. It is not yet clear if optimizing lighting and enhancing contrast would help her to read faces more successfully. She seems to become overwhelmed by faces and appears not to know how to register all of the visual information in faces. Perhaps for this reason, she tends not to look at them. Her tendency to touch objects to her face also seems to suggest a desire to see the object through touch. Yoshe does have the visual processing and object recognition skills to identify objects and she can also identify objects in photos and in drawings. At times, lighting and contrast need to be optimized so that she can interpret visual information accurately.

### *Yoshe's Visual-Motor Skills*

Visual-motor skills are another area of difficulty for Yoshe. Although she can move her body normally, she does not coordinate her vision with her movements very successfully. Yoshe's occupational therapist is working with her to help improve visual fine motor skills for adaptive tasks.

### *Yoshe's Ability to Mentalize Visual Space*

Yoshe can move about with relative ease when she is in a familiar environment. This suggests that she can imagine space and can function in space when her mental map corresponds to the real world. It is not yet clear how Yoshe will function as she learns math concepts. Currently, she can count and can identify numbers, but she does not show an understanding of one-to-one correspondence and does not show that she is developing her number sense or a number line.

## Educational Objectives and Strategies for Yoshe

The following sections describe some of the educational objectives and strategies that might be useful for Yoshe. She needs to develop all her visual skills and abilities and has to develop some skills both with and without the assistance or benefit of accommodations.

### *Educational Objectives and Strategies for Oculomotor Skills for Yoshe*

Yoshe needs to develop good scanning and tracking skills in both near and distant space. Since she is capable of good scanning when prompted to do so, an objective for her is to rely less often on adult prompts and to use scanning and tracking skills more spontaneously, more consistently, and without adult prompting. She also needs to learn to position her head properly and to position items properly, so that she maximizes use of her visual fields. By not always stepping in to address her visual needs and by use of indirect feedback (e.g., "I wonder if you can see what's in front of you" or "Remember to use your strategies"), adults can expand Yoshe's successful use of her vision and help her to perform more independently. Her team is measuring progress by measuring the degree of support that she needs (physical support, verbal directives, indirect verbal support, or no support). The objective is to reduce the level of adult support. She is learning the vocabulary for concepts related to oculomotor skills, such as *scanning* ("Look on both sides") and *tracking* ("Watch what's moving") and is also learning positional concepts.

### *Educational Objectives and Strategies for Ocular Functions and Skills for Yoshe*

Yoshe's team has discovered the types of visual strategies and accommodations that seem to help her the most. Specifically, materials need to be placed in the right side of her visual field. Backlighting and placement of objects on a dark background are often also needed. Even though she can sometimes see clearly without accommodations, her overall performance improves when the accommodations are used consistently. Yoshe is now ready to identify the accommodations used on her own. By teaching her the vocabulary of her visual accommodations and by teaching her to experiment with visual strategies, her team is making sure she is learning to advocate for her own vision needs. She can learn words related to important concepts such as *fields* and *position* ("Look at everything on the table top" or "Look in all directions"), *contrast* ("Where is your dark desktop?"), and *lighting* ("Do you need more light on your desktop? Do you need less light in the room?") and how to describe what strategies work best for her. Her teachers allow her to experiment with different visual conditions, comparing her level of comfort and her success with and without lighting, contrast, and correct placement of items.

### *Educational Objectives and Strategies for Visual Processing Skills for Yoshe*

Yoshe has mature object recognition skills, meaning that she can distinguish between objects, photographs, fine line drawings, icons, and symbols. She is able to identify different types of objects and their functions. At times, she has greater difficulty with object recognition functions at far and distant space, a result of her difficulties with ocular functions. Her visual-motor processing skills are more difficult to measure because of her motor impairment. Even when she might recognize objects and understand three-dimensional space, she often makes errors in her motor performance because of her field defect and because of her hemiparesis. The team did not include any specific educational objectives for her visual processing skills and decided to use oculomotor functions and ocular functions as targets in identifying their educational objectives.

### Accommodations for Yoshe

Yoshe's vision impairment is successfully accommodated, as explained in the Observations section above. The best accommodations for Yoshe depend on vision demands in near space, as opposed to middle, distant, and far space. Yoshe's vision specialist had to try a number of different approaches to identify exactly how and when certain accommodations would work best for her. For example, it took some experimenting to determine where to place objects into her visual field, what type of lighting and contrast to use, and what size of object or print was most suitable for her. It also took some time to determine how to help her use her oculomotor skills (scanning, tracking, tracing) during orientation and mobility demands; see Box 1.9.

### Working With Culturally and Linguistically Diverse Learners

School professionals should keep the following elements in mind when working with culturally and linguistically diverse learners on vision skills:

#### *Color Vision*

It is very common for educators working with children learning English as a second language (ESL) to use colors as a point of reference (e.g., "Point to the man with the red shirt"). Colors are one of the first vocabulary items taught to ESL learners and this approach should be modified for learners who have color vision difficulties.

Educators may also need to account for cultural considerations related to color. For example, in some Asian cultures it is extremely inappropriate to write people's names in red. The only names written in red are for people who have died.

#### *Vision Acuity Test Example*

For some students from other cultures, visual acuity tests should be modified. For example, avoid vision acuity tests that include the letters *B* and *V*, and *A*, *E*, and *I*. In Spanish, *B* and *V* can sound identical and be easily confused. The letters *A*, *E*, and *I* are difficult because of the way they exist differently in English and Spanish. The letter *A* in English sounds like /ah/ in Spanish; the letter *E* in Spanish sounds like the long *A* in English. The letter *I* in Spanish sounds like the letter *E* in English.

## CONCLUSIONS

This chapter presented the Vision Skills Framework. The next two chapters are dedicated to the remaining two neurological frameworks of this book, hearing skills and motor skills. This chapter and the two that follow highlight how nurture can act on nature, especially when nature did not unfold as intended, when bodily structures are injured, and when bodily functions are affected. Children and youth with injury or impairment to their vision, hearing, and motor system are less common in special education than are children with difficulties in other areas. Nonetheless, students with performance difficulties in vision, hearing, and motor skills are important to understand because they help school professionals understand students with disabilities in general. Many of the educational objectives, strategies, and accommodations that these children and youth need are also useful for students with other types of performance difficulties. The information contained in these first three chapters helps to set the stage for the second and third sections, developmental and educational foundations for learning.

## REFERENCES


Colenbrander, A. (2010a). Assessment of functional vision and its rehabilitation. *Acta Ophthalmologica, 88,* 163–173.

Colenbrander, A. (2010b). Towards the development of a classification of vision-related functioning: A potential framework. In G. N. Dutton & M. Bax (Eds.), *Visual impairment in children due to damage to the brain* (pp. 282–294). New York, NY: Wiley-Blackwell.

Dutton, G. N., Cockburn, D., McDaid, G., & Macdonald, E. (2010). Practical approaches for the management of visual difficulties due to cerebral visual impairment. In G. N. Dutton & M. Bax (Eds.), *Visual impairment in children due to damage to the brain* (pp. 217–226). New York, NY: Wiley-Blackwell.

Dutton, G. N., Macdonald, E., Drummond, S. R., Said:Kasimova, S., & Mitchell, K. (2010). Clinical features of perceptual and cognitive visual impairment in children with brain damage of early onset. In G. N. Dutton & M. Bax (Eds.), *Visual impairment in children due to damage to the brain* (pp. 106–116). New York, NY: Wiley-Blackwell.

Goodale, M. A. (2010). The functional organization of the central visual pathways. In G. N. Dutton & M. Bax (Eds.), *Visual impairment in children due to damage to the brain* (pp. 5–15). New York, NY: Wiley-Blackwell.

Hyvärinen, L. (2010). Classification of visual functioning and disability in children with visual processing disorders. In G. N. Dutton & M. Bax (Eds.), *Visual impairment in children due to damage to the brain* (pp. 265–281). New York, NY: Wiley-Blackwell.

Kong, L., Fry, M., Al-Sammarraie, M., Gilbert, C., & Steinkuller, S. (2012). An update on progress and the changing epidemiology of causes of childhood blindness worldwide. *JAAPOS, 16*(6), 501–507.

Lennie, P., & Van Hemel, S. B. (Eds.). (2002). Assessment of vision in infants and children. In *Visual impairment: Determining eligibility for Social Security benefits.* Washington, DC: National Academies Press. Retrieved from http://www.nap.edu

Lueck, A., & Heinze, T. (2004). Interventions for young children with visual impairments and students with visual and multiple disabilities. In A. H. Lueck (Ed.), *Functional vision: A practitioner's guide to evaluation and intervention* (pp. 277–341). New York, NY: AFB Press.

Lueck, A. H. (2004a). Overview of functional evaluation. In A. H. Lueck (Ed.), *Functional vision: A practitioner's guide to evaluation and intervention* (pp. 89–107). New York, NY: AFB Press.

Lueck, A. H. (2004b). Overview of intervention methods. In A. H. Lueck (Ed.), *Functional vision: A practitioner's guide to evaluation and intervention* (pp. 257–275). New York, NY: AFB Press.

Lueck, A. H. (2004c). Comprehensive low vision care. In A. H. Lueck (Ed.), *Functional vision: A practitioner's guide to evaluation and intervention* (pp. 89–107). New York, NY: AFB Press.

Lueck, A. H. (Ed.). (2004d). *Functional vision: A practitioner's guide to evaluation and intervention.* New York, NY: AFB Press.

Markowitz, M. (2006). Occupational therapy interventions in low vision rehabilitation. *Canadian Journal of Ophthalmology, 41,* 340–347.

Markowitz, S. N. (2006). Principles of modern low vision rehabilitation. *Canadian Journal of Ophthalmology, 41,* 289–312.

Matsuba, C., & Soul, J. (2010). Clinical manifestations of cerebral visual impairment. In G. N. Dutton & M. Bax (Eds.), *Visual impairment in children due to damage to the brain* (pp. 41–49). New York, NY: Wiley-Blackwell.

Mervis, C. A., Boyle, C. A., & Yeargin-Allsopp, M. (2002). Prevalence and selected characteristics of childhood vision impairment. *Developmental Medicine and Child Neurology, 44,* 538–541.

Ozturk, T., Er, D., Yaman, A., & Berk, A. T. (2016). Changing trends over the past decade in the aetiology of childhood blindness: A study from a tertiary referral center. *British Journal of Ophthalmology, 100,* 166–171.

Rahi, J. S., & Solebo, A. L. (2012). Childhood eye disorders and visual impairment. In D. Hollar (Ed.), *Handbook of children with special health care needs* (pp. 131–152). New York, NY: Springer.

Sargent, J., Salt, A., & Dale, N. (2010). Children with severe brain damage: Functional assessment for diagnosis and intervention. In G. N. Dutton & M. Bax (Eds.), *Visual impairment in children due to damage to the brain* (pp. 181–193). New York, NY: Wiley-Blackwell.

Schiefer, U., & Hart, W. (2007). Functional anatomy of the human visual pathway. In U. Schiefer, H. Wilhelm, & W. Hart (Eds.), *Clinical neuro-ophthalmology: A practical guide* (pp. 19–28). Berlin, Germany: Springer.

Schiefer, U., Wilhelm, H., & Hart, W. (Eds.). (2007). *Clinical neuro-ophthalmology: A practical guide.* Berlin, Germany: Springer.

Steinkuller, P. G., Du, L., Gilbet, C., Foster, A., Collins, M. L., & Coats, K. (1999). Childhood blindness. *Journal of the American Academy for Pediatric Ophthalmology and Strabismus, 3*(1), 26–32.

Thompson, L., & Kaufman, L. M. (2003). The visually impaired child. *Pediatric Clinics of North America, 50,* 225–239.

Whitaker, D. B., & Scheiner, E. M. (2012). Evaluating school-aged children with visual disabilities. In D. Hollar (Ed.), *Handbook of children with special health care needs* (pp. 153–158). New York, NY: Springer.

World Health Organization. (2007). *International classification of functioning, disability and health: Children & youth version*. Geneva, Switzerland: WHO.

Zihl, J., Schiefer, U., & Schiller, J. (2007). Central disturbances of vision. In U. Schiefer, H. Wilhelm, & W. Hart (Eds.), *Clinical neuro-ophthalmology: A practical guide* (pp. 185–194). Berlin, Germany: Springer.

APPENDIX 1.1 **Vision Skills Framework**

The Vision Skills Framework is summarized here. School professionals can use this form as a quick reference for the skill sets and skills that need to be taken into consideration when making observations and developing an intervention plan.

| Structures and skill sets | Structures, functions, and skills | Examples of functions and skills in action | Sample medical conditions or performance difficulties | Potential interventions, strategies, accommodations, or educational objectives |
|---|---|---|---|---|
| Ocular structures and ocular health | Cornea | Protects the eye; allows light to shine through the pupil | Cloudy cornea due to metabolic or other illness<br>Astigmatism is an example of corneal dysfunction. It results in an uneven corneal surface, affecting how light rays shine through the pupil and onto the lens. | Conditions that affect the cornea may be treated with prescription glasses, medications and/or surgery. |
| | Lens | Focuses light rays onto the retina | Cloudy lens due to metabolic or other illness (e.g., cataracts)<br>The lens might not change shape sufficiently to focus light successfully on the retina. | Conditions that affect the lens can be treated with prescription eyeglasses, medications and/or surgery.<br>Prescription glasses circumvent problems with the lens by focusing light rays before they reach the lens, can adjust for inability of the lens to accommodate properly. |
| | Ciliary body | Changes the shape of the lens to adjust for near and distance vision | Problems in ciliary muscle function | Prescription glasses help to accommodate when the ciliary body and lens do not successfully focus light rays onto the retina. |
| | Retina | Gathers light information and transmits it as neurological impulses to the optic nerve | Retinopathy of prematurity, retinal diseases, and other conditions can result in retinal dysfunction and cause field defects, defects in color vision, defects in night vision, among other problems. | Medications and surgery can be used to treat retinal conditions.<br>Many of the accommodations and strategies listed in Chapter 1, such as higher contrast, judicious use of lighting to enhance contrast and reduce light sensitivity, use of color, changing the saturation/value of color, help reduce the effects of retinal dysfunction.<br>Positioning and judicious use of object, picture and/or font size can help reduced the impact of field defects. |
| | Optic nerve | Transmits light information from the retina to the brain | Dysfunctions or injury to the optic nerve and to the visual pathways in the brain can result in the same types of dysfunctions listed above. | Optic nerve dysfunction and dysfunctions of the visual pathways in the brain are often addressed by using the accommodations discussed in Chapter 1 and as listed in this table. |

*(continued)*

| Structures and skill sets | Structures, functions, and skills | Examples of functions and skills in action | Sample medical conditions or performance difficulties | Potential interventions, strategies, accommodations, or educational objectives |
|---|---|---|---|---|
| Oculomotor functions and skills | Scanning | Ability to move the eyes so as to scan the room or scan the visual field from left to right and top to bottom. Strategic scanning is needed by any student who has vision impairment. | Oculomotor dysfunctions may diminish the capacity to scan in all directions.<br>Strabismus is one example of oculomotor dysfunction and makes it difficult for both eyes to move together in tandem. Any of the retinal dysfunctions can make systematic scanning more difficult to achieve, thus interfering with localizing and fixating. | Ensure good head position when teaching all of the oculomotor skills listed here; orientation and mobility training addresses many of the skills listed in this section. |
| | Localizing | Ability to identify a sought-for object, person, or item from within the visual field | Inability to move the eyes in all directions can interfere with localization.<br>Inability to guess or know where items are located can interfere with scanning and therefore also with localizing. | Orientation and mobility training addresses many of the skills listed in this section. Use of the accommodations listed previously can make it easier to identify salient visual information and can thereby improve scanning and localizing indirectly. |
| | Fixation and focus | Ability to keep both eyes from moving so that they can both focus on the sought-for object, person, or item and see it clearly | Inability to keep the eyes fixated (i.e., to keep the eyes from moving) so that the ciliary body can adjust the shape of the lens and thereby focus successfully. | Use of the accommodations listed previously can make it easier to identify salient visual information and can thereby improve scanning, localizing, and fixation indirectly. |
| | Tracking | Ability to follow a moving target with the eyes in far and middle distance; the viewer can be stationary or can also be in motion | Impairments in oculomotor skills or in whole-head or whole-body movement can affect tracking skills. | Teach effective use of oculomotor skills and of whole-head and whole-body movement so as to track successfully.<br>Orientation and mobility training addresses many of the skills listed in this section. |
| | Tracing | Ability to follow a moving target in near space; handwriting and sewing are two example activities that require tracing, following a moving object in near space | Inability to keep the eyes from moving while attempting to trace<br>Inability to control whole-head or whole-body movements while attempting to trace | Keep head held steadily. |
| Ocular functions | Acuity and focus | Ability to hold the eyes steadily and use the ciliary body to change the shape of the lens so as to see clearly at near and far distance | Problems with the oculomotor muscles, the ciliary body, or the lens can affect the ability to focus, or the ability to focus on objects at varying distances from the eyes. | Use of prescription glasses<br>Keep head held steadily to allow time for the lens to focus on an object.<br>Use of correct object size, photo or picture size, font size<br>Use of the accommodations listed previously can make it easier to identify salient visual information and can thereby make it easier to focus. |

| Structures and skill sets | Structures, functions, and skills | Examples of functions and skills in action | Sample medical conditions or performance difficulties | Potential interventions, strategies, accommodations, or educational objectives |
|---|---|---|---|---|
| | Visual fields | Ability to see all items located in any position inside the visual field, which normally extends nearly 180 degrees horizontally and vertically | Problems with the retina, optic nerves, or other visual pathways of the central nervous system can disrupt the visual field and diminish or change its size.<br>A scotoma is a circular field defect in the middle of the visual field. | Teach scanning skills.<br>Place objects strategically inside the intact portion of the visual field.<br>Use of correct object size, photo or picture size, and font size<br>Teach the student to anticipate and look into the direction of those portions of the field where objects are normally not visible. |
| | Contrast sensitivity | The capacity to differentiate items within the visual field when they are closely matched in color, value, saturation, and/or lighting | Problems with the retina, optic nerve, or visual pathways in the central nervous system can interfere with contrast sensitivity, which can make it difficult to distinguish similarly colored objects or to differentiate objects within the visual field that are similar in saturation, value, or brightness.<br>Students with low contrast sensitivity may find it difficult to select items from a cluttered array.<br>Low contrast sensitivity can also make it difficult to differentiate foreground from background and can therefore interfere with depth perception. | Make use of strategies that enhance contrast. For example, enhance the contrast between foreground and background in near or distant space by judicious use of lighting, color, saturation, and value. A blue background often helps to highlight lighter-colored items in the foreground. A dark background with a well-lit foreground can also enhance contrast.<br>Make use of backlighting by placing the light source behind the student, not in front or above.<br>Teach students the vocabulary needed to advocate for their own needs. |
| | Light–dark adaptation | The capacity to move between different lighting conditions without experiencing discomfort, blindness, or other vision difficulties | Temporary inability to see as lighting conditions change<br>Oversensitivity to bright lights | Allow for extra time to adjust between different lighting conditions.<br>Make judicious use of lighting to allow the student to adjust more easily to different lighting conditions. |
| | Color vision | The capacity to see all colors in the color spectrum | Retinal dysfunction or absence of some of the cones (specialized cells) of the retina can interfere with the capacity to see the full color spectrum (color blindness). | Make use of those colors that are visible to the student.<br>Reduce use of colors that the student cannot see, especially when contrast sensitivity is an issue. |

*(continued)*

| Structures and skill sets | Structures, functions, and skills | Examples of functions and skills in action | Sample medical conditions or performance difficulties | Potential interventions, strategies, accommodations, or educational objectives |
|---|---|---|---|---|
| Visual processing functions and skills | Stereopsis and depth perception | The capacity to use both eyes for recognizing when an object is at near or far distance | Impaired fixation of one or both eyes or impaired vision in one eye can affect the capacity to perceive depth. | Orientation and mobility training can assist with depth perception, making use of tactile and auditory cues.<br>Enhancing contrast and making judicious use of lighting can facilitate depth perception.<br>Optimize visual aspects of the environment, such as use of colored lines or symbols in the environment, to enhance the student's awareness of different locations in the building. |
| | Object recognition functions | The capacity to recognize objects, similarities between objects, and to guess at the identity of the object even when it is partially hidden, poorly lit, or presented as a drawing or symbol | Difficulty recognizing objects when they are not properly lit, are partially hidden, are presented in the form of a photo instead of an object, or are presented in the form of a drawing or symbol instead of a photo or object.<br>Many of the vision skills listed in this table act together to help individuals interpret objects in the environment.<br>Different kinds of impairment, at all points along the visual axis, can interfere with object recognition functions. | Making use of tactile or auditory cues can help with object recognition functions.<br>Enhancing contrast and making judicious use of lighting can facilitate object recognition.<br>Select the correct level of visual complexity when presenting information visually: Objects, photos, fine-line drawings, symbols, and/or printed words. |
| | Spatial awareness and motor planning | The capacity to use vision to understand three-dimensional space, either of an object or within architectural space (the space in which the student finds him- or herself)<br>The capacity to use the motor system to manipulate objects successfully with or without using vision<br>The capacity to navigate through the environment smoothly and effectively with or without using vision | Difficulty understanding three dimensions of objects and/or of the environment<br>Many of the different visual skills listed in this table allow students to perceive three-dimensional space. Different types of impairments, at all points along the visual pathways in the brain, can interfere with spatial awareness and motor planning.<br>Motor impairments alone can also affect spatial awareness and motor planning. | Making use of tactile or auditory cues can help with object recognition functions.<br>Enhancing contrast and making judicious use of lighting can facilitate object recognition.<br>Orientation and mobility training assists students with spatial awareness and motor planning. |

## APPENDIX 1.2 Vision Skills Observation Sheet

| Structures and skill sets | Functions and skills | Example skills or deficits in this student | Example strategies or interventions that appear to help the student perform more successfully |
|---|---|---|---|
| Ocular structures and ocular health | Cornea<br><br>Lens<br><br>Ciliary body<br><br>Retina<br><br>Optic nerve | | |
| Oculomotor functions and skills | Scanning<br><br>Localizing<br><br>Fixation and focus<br><br>Tracking<br><br>Tracing | | |
| Ocular functions | Acuity and focus<br><br>Visual fields<br><br>Contrast sensitivity<br><br>Light–dark adaptation<br><br>Color vision | | |
| Visual processing functions and skills | Stereopsis and depth perception<br><br>Object recognition functions<br><br>Spatial awareness and motor planning | | |

# Hearing Skills

## INTRODUCTION AND GENERAL DEFINITIONS

Hearing is the second of the three neurological frameworks. Chapter 1 highlighted the complexity of the topic of vision. Vision is not just about visual acuity, and it is not sufficient to know whether a student passed a vision screening test in order to determine whether the student can see. The same applies to hearing. To understand whether someone can hear means more than knowing whether a person passed or failed a hearing screening test. A hearing screening test, like a vision screening test, measures only a limited range of hearing skills. A hearing screening test measures the ability to hear loud and soft sounds at different pitches (high-pitched and low-pitched sounds). Yet, the capacity to hear sounds consists of other skills as well. For example, normal hearing includes the ability to discriminate among different types of sounds. The person who can hear can often identify the location of a sound and can determine whether a sound source is moving. Not all of these skills are assessed during a routine hearing screening. Hearing consists of a collection of functions and skills and is not just a question of acuity.

The capacity to hear sounds has to be integrated into many different central nervous system functions and skills. This integration occurs for hearing just as it does for vision. For example, when listening to someone talking, it is not sufficient to hear speech sounds (the sounds produced by a person who is speaking). Speech sounds need to be connected with an understanding of language, as well as with an understanding of the identity of the speaker. The listener typically knows that the speaker is a man or a woman. The listener can identify whether the speaker is a familiar or an unfamiliar person. In the classroom, hearing has to be integrated with language skills, such as reading, writing, and classroom participation. Students need to be able to hear the voice of their teacher or of their classmates and understand the information (language) being transmitted. Similarly, they need to be able to imagine hearing someone's voice when reading or when writing. An important goal of this chapter is not only to introduce school professionals to the complexity of sound and the complexity of hearing, but also to allow them to make relevant connections between speech, hearing, language, academic learning, and other important brain functions and skills. Hearing is a critical foundation for learning.

## HOW THIS FRAMEWORK WAS CONSTRUCTED



This framework is a synthesis of knowledge and best practices drawn from the references provided at the end of the chapter. The terms and definitions discussed in this chapter conform to those used in standard reference texts on hearing. There is generally good agreement in the field about the terminology, and so the terms presented here should be familiar to audiologists, speech pathologists, teachers of the hearing impaired, and other specialists interested in hearing. By learning about the terms and concepts discussed in this chapter, school professionals will find other resources on sound and hearing more straightforward and easier to access and understand.

As part of this general introduction, it is useful to make a distinction between the subject of sound and the subject of hearing. The term *sound* refers to the study of sound waves. Sound waves are a type of energy. The study of sound belongs in the realm of physics. In contrast, the term *hearing* refers to the biological functions involved in changing physical properties of sound waves into neurological signals. *Hearing* refers to central nervous system functions and skills that interpret sound signals and give them meaning or purpose (Yost, 2013a). Hearing is the subjective experience of sound. See Box 2.1 for additional information.

### BOX 2.1. The Physics of Sound and the Experience of Hearing

It is useful to understand the differences and the relationships between the terms *sound* and *hearing*. Sound is merely a type of energy that has certain physical properties. It does not have any meaning or purpose. When sound energy is transformed into neurological impulses, it is experienced as hearing. Hearing and listening involve an interpretation of sound information, giving it meaning and purpose. Key terms related to sound include the *pressure/amplitude*, *frequency*, and *timing/phase*. Parallel key terms related to hearing include *decibels* and *pitch*, as well as *timing*, *phase*, and *patterns*. A sound that has high pressure or a high amplitude is experienced as loud. It is considered to have a higher decibel level. A sound that has a high frequency is experienced as having a high pitch. Differences between types of sound (e.g., speech, a musical instrument, or random noise) are caused by variations in timing, phase, or patterns. Variations in timing, phase, and patterns of sound help differentiate sounds from one another. So even though leaves rustling in the wind can have a similar pitch and loudness as some speech sounds (e.g., whispering), the two types of sounds are still very easy to distinguish from each other. Speech sounds have much more complex temporal patterns and are therefore easily differentiated from the leaves rustling. Variations in timing or phase also help the listener identify aspects of sound such as its location or position in space. This chapter uses terms that apply to hearing more often than terms that apply to sounds.

## HOW CAN THIS FRAMEWORK HELP ME?

The Hearing Skills Framework is designed to help professionals understand key concepts, terms, and definitions related to sound and to hearing. The purpose of this framework is to introduce school professionals to hearing functions and hearing skills and to discover how intact hearing supports successful performance in the classroom. This framework will be useful to members of most school teams. Whenever possible, the information presented in this chapter should be reviewed with the in-district audiologist, teacher of the hearing impaired, or speech pathologist, all of whom have training and expertise in hearing. Any one of these specialists can use the concepts and terms presented in this chapter to help school teams understand the hearing needs of students. See Box 2.2 to learn more about the role of the audiologist.

**BOX 2.2. The Role of the Audiologist in the Education of Children With Hearing Impairment**

Audiologists should be included as members of the school team and/or should be available through consultation. Their role is to explain the results of auditory screening and evaluation and to assist in educational planning for students with hearing impairment and/or auditory processing disorders (APDs). Comprehensive audiological services are needed to reduce the negative effects of hearing loss and/or APDs, to maximize the student's auditory learning, and to maximize the student's communication skills. Audiological services are provided to improve listening skills, to prevent further hearing loss, and to create environments that are acoustically accessible.

The audiologist should perform the following functions:

1. Identify the student with hearing loss.
2. Determine the nature, degree, and extent or range of hearing loss.
3. Refer to medical professionals for the habilitation of hearing.
4. Provide habilitative services for speech production and language comprehension
5. Provide auditory training (improve listening skills).
6. Provide instruction in speech reading (lip reading).
7. Provide hearing evaluation.
8. Provide counseling to school team and to the family.
9. Ensure that hearing aids are functioning normally.
10. Ensure provision of other assistive devices and services.
11. Ensure the impact of poor hearing on all aspects of the child's life, not just hearing and communication skills but also psychosocial adjustment and performance in other settings.
12. Select and implement appropriate instructional materials and media.
13. Provide suggestions for how to structure the learning environment with acoustic modifications.
14. Provide compensatory skill training to support academic deficits.

---

ASHA (2002). ASHA: Guidelines for audiological service provision in schools. Retrieved from asha.org

The classroom is an aural-oral environment. As such, the concepts and terms discussed in this chapter apply to a substantial portion of the student body, not just those with identified hearing impairment. Although the focus of this chapter is on hearing, it is important to remember that hearing is only the first step in an important chain. Hearing leads to listening, to language comprehension, to speaking, and to reading and writing. Hearing is the physical ability to receive sound, whereas listening is the mental activity of attending to sound. To listen successfully, students need to know what to listen for. The critical example relevant to this book is when students have to listen selectively for speech sounds and not listen to other types of sounds. A majority of language and academic learning occurs through this chain of events: Hearing speech sounds, listening to speech sounds, producing speech (speaking), and understanding the associated language concepts (language comprehension). This is as true for the (silent) skills of reading and writing, as it is for conversations between students, teachers, and peers. So, even though this chapter is focused on hearing, the reader is invited to consider the effect of hearing on listening, speech production, and literacy in those who may have difficulty hearing.

Many students, especially those who are still young, do not have fully developed hearing, listening, or language skills. When children are acquiring their home or heritage language, it is usually done on a one-to-one basis. Parents, older siblings, or other caregivers adjust the volume and rate of their speech, so that the young child can hear and listen successfully. If a child has mild hearing loss, the caregiver may speak slightly louder or more slowly to ensure the child has understood. These caregiver behaviors help improve the chances that the student's hearing will lead to listening, language development, and speaking. However, when a student is in a classroom full of other learners, the teacher cannot always make the same number of adjustments to compensate for the hearing loss of a learner. It is therefore important for teachers to think about the quality of the auditory signal that they deliver to their students. All students depend on a quality auditory signal for good hearing and for subsequent successful listening, language comprehension, and language development. The quality of the auditory signal is as important for the hearing-impaired student as it is for the student body as a whole. This chapter provides suggestions for maximizing the quality of the auditory signal, so that the student's chances of listening and language comprehension can improve.

## HEARING SKILLS FRAMEWORK: TERMS AND DEFINITIONS

The Hearing Skills Framework is similar in structure to the Vision Skills Framework. The framework begins by presenting key aspects of hearing anatomy (hearing structures). It then describes hearing functions as they relate to those structures. Chapter 1 shared that the majority of visual functions develop over a relatively short period of time (i.e., over the first year of life or so). It also highlighted that, through nurture, visual functions become more and more integrated with central nervous system functions and expand to become visual skills. The same holds true for hearing functions. Hearing functions are present before birth. The unborn child can hear sounds, and newborns and infants can distinguish between soft and loud sounds. Newborns can distinguish between the familiar sound of their mother's voice as distinct from sounds produced by other female speakers. Hearing functions and skills rapidly develop during the first year of life to include other important functions, such as the ability to locate the origin of sounds, the identity of different types of sounds, and the identity of different speakers. With nurture, hearing functions evolve into hearing skills (or listening skills) as they get linked with and integrated into the central nervous system. The Hearing Skills Framework is summarized and available in Appendix 2.1 for quick reference.

### Auditory Structures

This section briefly presents basic structures related to hearing. The purpose of this review is to orient the reader to the basic structures and associated functions of hearing. A school team would not normally be expected to provide interventions or treatments related to the anatomical structures of the ear or hearing. Interventions of this type are the purview of audiologists in particular. However, it is useful to understand normal hearing anatomy as a basis for understanding hearing functions and skills presented later in this chapter. Intact hearing structures allow for normal hearing (auditory) functions. In turn, normal auditory functions are a prerequisite for the subsequent development of successful hearing skills. The anatomical structures of hearing are discussed in the sections that follow and are labeled in Figure 2.1.

The framework includes the following terms, which are defined and explained in the sections that follow:

1. Auditory structures
    a. External ear
    b. Middle ear
    c. Inner ear
    d. Auditory nerve
2. Auditory functions
    a. Decibels and intensity
    b. Frequency and pitch
    c. Temporal aspects of sound and hearing: Phase and pattern discrimination
3. Auditory processing skills
    a. Temporal aspects of sound and hearing: Discriminating between different types of sounds by detecting patterns of intensity, pitch, and phase over varying time intervals
    b. Binaural skills and sound localization: Detecting the position of a sound source, its distance from the listener, and its movements
    c. Binaural skills: Fusion and separation of sound signals
        i. Detection of signals in noise
        ii. Diotic and dichotic listening tasks
    d. Auditory closure: Using higher order cognition to understand sounds
    e. Responding to sound and motor planning

***External Ear and Ear Canal*** The external ear consists of the external ear canal and the pinna. The external ear canal leads to the tympanic membrane. The functions of the pinna of the ear and external ear canal are to modify auditory signals (sounds) that reach the exterior portion of the ear canal and deliver those signals to the tympanic membrane. The pinna is designed to dampen some sounds, especially those that are not delivered directly to the external ear canal. In contrast, the ear canal amplifies sounds.

***Middle Ear*** The middle ear is located between the tympanic membrane and the inner ear. Three small bones, called the auricular bones, are located inside the middle ear. The function of the auricular bones is to enhance and transmit the energy of sound waves to the basilar membrane. The basilar membrane separates the middle ear from the inner ear. Sound pressure is transmitted from the basilar membrane to the cochlea primarily by the auricular bones inside the middle ear. Some sound pressure is also transmitted to the basilar membrane through the air in the middle ear.

***Inner Ear and the Cochlea*** The inner ear consists of the cochlea, which contains hair cells. The cochlea accepts sound pressure waves at the basilar membrane and transmits these pressures through the cochlear fluid to the hair cells. Some sound pressure information is also transmitted to the cochlear fluid via the bones of the skull.

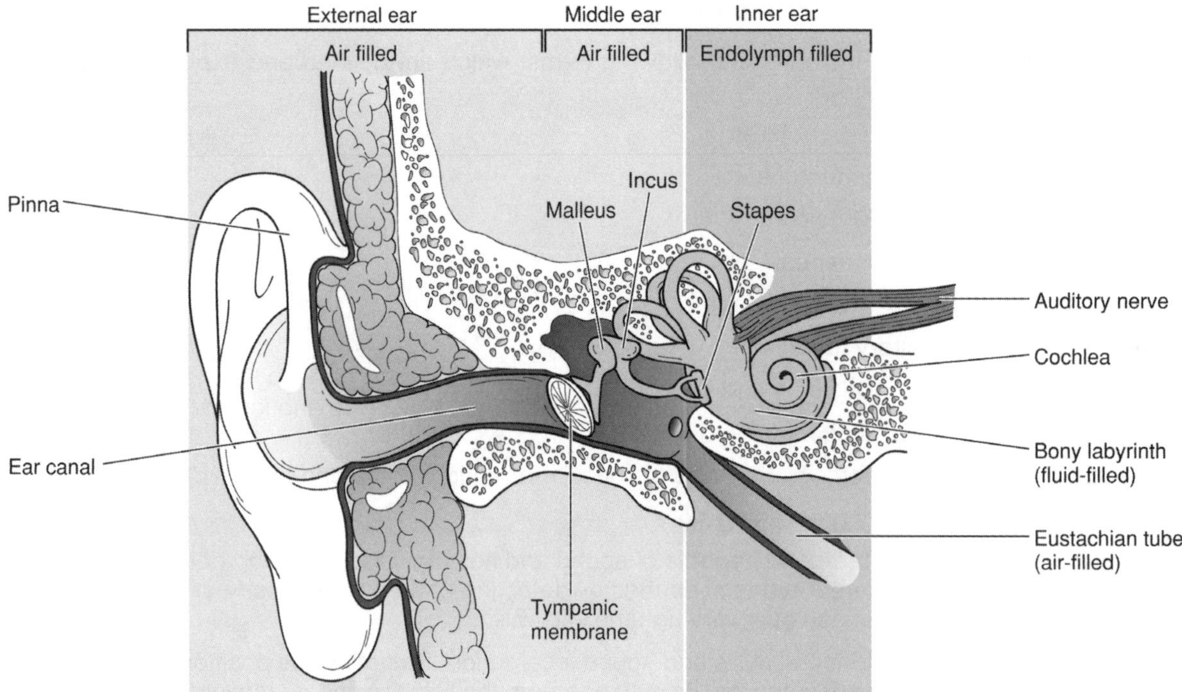


**Figure 2.1.** Key aspects of the ear and hearing anatomy, which include the external, middle, and inner ear and the pinna, ear canal, tympanic membrane, cochlea, and auditory nerve.

***Hair Cells*** The hair cells are located inside the cochlea. The function of the hair cells is to transduce the sound pressure waves into neurological impulses, which are collected by the auditory nerve.

***Auditory Nerve*** Nerves that exit from each of the hair cells gather together as the auditory nerve. The auditory nerve exits from the cochlea and carries the transduced sound information to other parts of the brain.

***Central Nervous System Components of Hearing*** The auditory nerve connects with a variety of central nervous system networks, with auditory information obtained from the other ear, and with both of the auditory cortexes (the region in each temporal lobe of the brain dedicated to the interpretation of auditory information). In turn, the auditory cortex sends auditory information to other parts of the brain, such as the motor cortex, the cerebellum, and other sites. Sharing auditory information with other parts of the brain allows the listener to respond to the auditory information just received.

## Auditory (Hearing) Functions

The following terms pertain to auditory functions. When reading these terms, it is important to know that they pertain to the experience of *hearing*. Review Box 2.1 as a reminder of the difference between sound and hearing.

***Decibels*** The loudness or softness of sounds that humans can hear is referred to as the *intensity of sound*. The intensity of sound is related to the sound's pressure and amplitude. The capacity to identify loud and soft sounds is assessed using a measure called the *decibel*. Decibels are a way to describe the hearing experience of the intensity of sounds through the audible range of human hearing. See Box 2.3 for a more detailed description. Normal hearing, which is present from birth, refers to the capacity to hear sounds through the full range of audible hearing, ranging from nearly zero to 140 decibels.



### BOX 2.3. Understanding Decibels

During a behavioral audiometry examination, the audiologist measures a person's sensitivity to different sound pressures. These sound pressures are measured as sound pressure levels (SPL) or sound sensation levels (SSL) or intensity units. Decibel units (dB) are based on the sound pressures and intensities produced by the types of sound sources commonly heard by humans as the sound arrives at the ears. It is important to remember that the pressure and intensity of any sound at its *source* is not the same as the pressure and intensity of that sound as it arrives at the *ears*. Some pressure and intensity are lost as sound travels from its source and interacts with the environment. In the audiologist's sound booth, sound pressure and intensities are delivered to the ears in a standardized manner and in the absence of environmental interferences. The following descriptive hearing experiences are mapped on to specific sound pressure levels that are produced in an audiologist's sound booth. Each sound pressure/hearing experience is matched to a decibel level:

1. 0 dB SPL: Softest sound a person with normal hearing can hear
2. 10 dB SPL: Normal breathing
3. 20 dB SPL: Whispering
4. 40 dB SPL: Refrigerator hum
5. 50 dB SPL: Rainfall
6. 60 dB SPL: Normal conversation
7. 95 dB SPL: Motorcycle
8. 110 dB SPL: Shouting in an ear
9. 120 dB SPL: Thunder
10. 140 dB SPL: Firecrackers

A sound with high pressure or higher decibel number is experienced as being louder. A sound with a lower pressure or lower decibel number is experienced as being softer. A decibel is a ratio that compares a given sound with the least amount of sound that is still audible to the human ear. Because the dynamic range of hearing is so large, decibel units are related to one another logarithmically. As decibels increase from 0 to 140, they increase in a logarithmic relationship. A sound that is experienced as twice as loud has about 10 times the pressure. The experience of sound also depends on background noise. A sound can be experienced as very loud in a quiet room, whereas the same sound heard outside along with traffic noise might not be experienced as loudly (American Speech-Hearing-Language Association [ASHA], 2018; Centers for Disease Control [CDC], 2018).

***Pitch*** Sound pressure, sound intensity, and decibels form only one important aspect of sound and hearing. The second important aspect of sound and hearing is its frequency. Frequency is measured as hertz (Hz) or kilohertz (kHz). The listener experiences differences in frequency (a property of sound) as differences in pitch (a property of hearing). For instance, a flute produces high-frequency sounds, whereas a tuba produces low-frequency sounds. The female voice typically consists of high-frequency sounds, whereas the male voice consists of low-frequency sounds. In both cases (musical instrument or voice box), the former is experienced as being higher in pitch, whereas the latter is experienced as being lower in pitch. Infants and children preferentially listen to higher pitched sounds, whereas senior citizens, who often lose high-frequency hearing functions, may preferentially hear and listen for sounds at lower frequencies. Further, some languages emphasize certain pitches more than others. For example, Hungarian has a very low pitch, whereas Chinese has a very high one. It is important to be able to hear through the full range of loudness (decibels) and the full range of pitches (hertz). Without this capacity, it is more difficult to develop the full range of speech sounds in spoken language. It is also more difficult to understand the full range of language transmitted by those speech sounds.

When audiologists test hearing functions, they test for both the capacity to hear different loudness levels of sounds (measured as decibels), as well as different pitches of sound (measured as hertz or kilohertz). The auditory functions of hearing loud and soft sounds and high and low pitches are fully mature within the first year of life. Figure 2.2 shows the relationship between decibels (hearing level) and hertz (frequency) in a blank audiogram. Frequency is plotted on the X-axis, spanning low to high pitches. Hearing level is represented on the Y-axis in decibels ranging from quiet at the top of the axis (–10) to loud at the bottom (140). Figure 2.3 provides a graphic representation of a person with normal hearing in both ears. The *X*s represent the hearing of the left ear, whereas the *O*s represent the hearing of the right ear.

Whenever a person can hear sounds between 8 and 40 dB, he or she is considered to have normal hearing. If an infant or child cannot hear sounds that have a loudness of at least 40 dB, he or she is considered moderately hearing impaired. A person who is deaf is unable to hear sounds that are much louder, for example, 100 dB or greater. Hearing loss at 100 dB or greater is considered a severe or profound hearing loss.

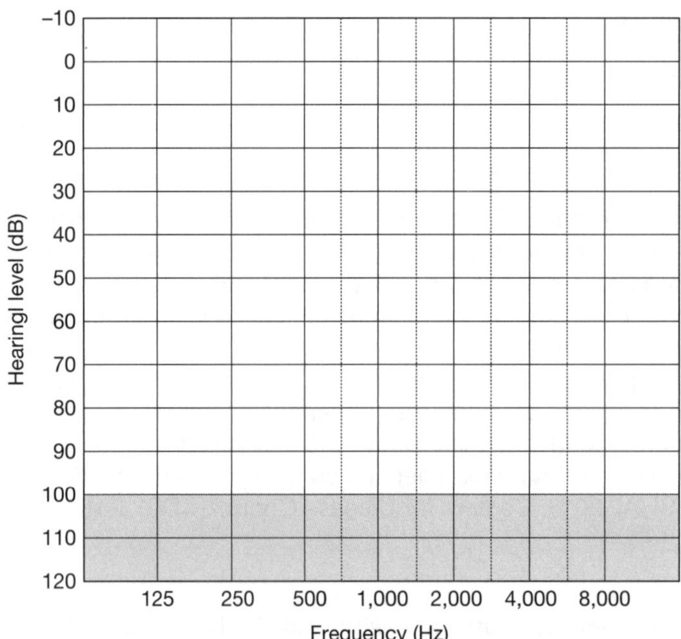


**Figure 2.2.** A blank audiogram. The X-axis represents frequency of the tone, whereas the Y-axis represents the hearing level in decibels. This empty audiogram shows the range of normal hearing in humans.

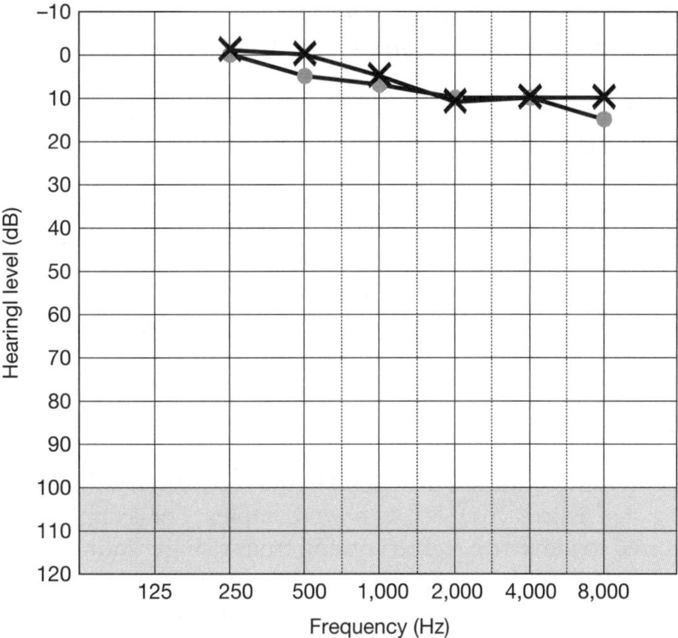


**Figure 2.3.** An audiogram of a person with normal hearing.

The audiogram in Figure 2.2 is known as a behavioral audiogram. A behavioral audiogram requires the person being tested to be capable of following the audiologist's instructions. The person being tested must be able to communicate with the audiologist using spoken language or gestures. Thus, even though the hearing functions shown in the audiogram are present at birth, it would not be possible to test an infant's hearing using a behavioral audiogram. Hearing in infants is tested using measures that do not rely on behavioral responses.

***Temporal Aspects of Sound*** The third important auditory function is related to temporal aspects of sound. Most sound waves consist of a mixture of pressures (loudness) and frequencies (pitch). Sound waves are typically complex, not simple. Each of the pressure peaks and frequencies within a sound phase can have differently timed phases and can occur in different patterns. The human ear discriminates between different types of sound sources using temporal differences in sound wave production such as these.

Temporal patterns between sound waves occur because of patterns embedded in the sound wave. Fine-grained patterns might occur within a single sound wave over the course of a few milliseconds or over tens of milliseconds. Coarser patterns might occur over longer time intervals within a sound wave (e.g., over hundreds of milliseconds, seconds, or even longer intervals). When speaking about sounds, the term *fine structure* refers to the patterns that might occur over milliseconds, whereas the term *temporal envelope* refers to patterns that occur over longer intervals, such as hundreds of milliseconds. The next section reviews parallel terms as related to the experience of hearing. A nearly infinite number of different sounds can be produced by the environment, depending on the pattern produced by changing pressures, changing amplitudes, and the patterns of those changes over very short or longer intervals of time.

The ability to discriminate temporal patterns of sound pressures and sound frequencies, over different time intervals, is present at birth. For example, infants respond preferentially to speech sounds as opposed to other types of sounds and can even respond preferentially to their own parents' speech as opposed to the speech of other adults. This capacity is due to the characteristics of speech sounds: Their intensity, their pitch, and their temporal patterns. The section Temporal Patterns Detection and Sound Discrimination looks at sound wave patterns in greater detail.

## Auditory Processing Skills

The previous section made the point that auditory functions consist primarily of transducing sound information into hearing information. Sound wave information (pressure, frequency, phase, and temporal patterns) are converted or *transduced* into neurological impulses and are experienced as differences in intensity, pitch, phase, and temporal patterns. Notice that the terms *phase* and *temporal patterns* have the same meaning when discussing the physics of sound as well as the experience of hearing. Auditory processing skills are those skills related to the analysis and processing of sound after their initial transduction (Griffiths, 2002). Auditory processing involves perceiving the differences in the aspects of sound just listed and assigning meaning to those differences.

Auditory processing skills are described in the sections that follow. The hierarchy proceeds from processing that is less complex to more complex. For example, the amount of auditory processing required to identify a sound coming from a single sound source is less complex than when the brain has to process multiple sounds coming from multiple sources. A good example of a very simple auditory processing demand is illustrated by the listening demands made during a hearing test in an audiology clinic. The audiologist performs hearing tests in a sound booth. This allows for the delivery of single tones (called pure tones), which are delivered to the ears at different volumes and frequencies. The listener has to identify only the pitch and the volume of the sound. There are no interfering noises. However, in real life it is very rare for sounds to arrive to the ears as pure tones. Usually, sound arrives to the ears as multiple, complex sound waves. Most of the sounds that arrive to the ears come from multiple sources and have also been subject to interference from other sound sources and from reflected sound waves. As a result, auditory processing is required to interpret most sounds. For example, a complex listening task occurs when the listener has to discriminate her or his dining partner's speech in a restaurant with background music, competing voices, and lots of reverberation and echoing. Whether being used for a listening task of low or high complexity, auditory processing skills involve the analysis and interpretation of the different types of sound. It occurs in the central nervous system, after sound information has been transduced into neurological impulses. The neuroanatomy of these different auditory processing functions and skills is not clear. Auditory processing skills do not follow clearly defined neurological boundaries (Dawes & Bishop, 2009). The following sections discuss auditory processing skills in greater detail.

***Temporal Patterns Detection and Sound Discrimination*** Early in life, auditory processing starts as the processing of temporal aspects of sound. An infant is capable of discriminating between different sound sources based on sound wave pressure (intensity), sound wave frequency (pitch), and temporal aspects of sound. However, the infant is not yet registering all of the differences in sounds and does not necessarily ascribe meaning to those sounds. The infant may therefore not know how to respond to the sounds.

Pressure, pitch, and timing help us to identify different types of sounds. For example, wind blowing through leaves produces a relatively small range of sound pressures (intensities) and frequencies (pitch). The variations in sound pressures and frequencies is relatively narrow. The sound patterns produced by these variations occurs over a short time interval (e.g., milliseconds to a second or so). In contrast, a musical instrument can produce many more sound pressures and frequencies and produces many more temporal patterns. Patterns of a short duration (e.g., hundreds of milliseconds) can account for difficult-to-describe features of an instrument's sound such as timbre, tone, or resonance. Longer sound patterns that occur over seconds or minutes can produce effects that account for rhythm, theme, and/or melody.

Speech sounds are yet more complex. In speech, temporal patterns at a fine-grained level of analysis might account for the tone or resonance of a person's voice. Sound patterns that occur over hundreds of milliseconds or over an entire second account for differences in phonemes (e.g., vowels versus consonants), gaps between phonemes (e.g., gaps between sounds within a word or between two words), or prosodic stress (within words, one syllable is stressed more than the others). Sound patterns that occur over one to several seconds account for differences in intonation and emotional expressiveness in language. To understand all these different aspects of speech sounds, the listener must be capable of identifying not only changes in intensity and pitch but also changes in the timing of intensity and pitch over varying time intervals.

As infants enter the toddler and preschool years, they become more and more capable of discriminating many different types of sounds and sound sources and can also respond to them with greater discrimination. Only at later ages do humans develop their listening skills to identify and respond to some of the features of sound discussed above, such as appreciating differences between musical instruments or differences in rhythm, theme, or melody. See Boxes 2.4 and 2.5 for additional information about how sound discrimination skills develop with age.



**BOX 2.4. Infants and Speech Recognition**

As discussed in the Auditory Functions section, temporal differences in sound are detectable as early as the newborn period. However, the capacity to discriminate temporal patterns matures and changes over the course of the first year of life. Initially, infants are biologically programmed to identify and discriminate among different speech sounds. For example, infants as young as 1 month old can distinguish between the speech sounds *ba* and *pa*. Both of these speech sounds are present in English as well as in other languages. This discrimination ability is a phonetic capacity, the general capacity to discriminate between speech sounds. Infants can actually identify more than just the phonetic contrast. For example, for the same speech sound, they can discriminate between male and female speakers, and even between two male or two female speakers (Flavell, Miller, & Miller, 2002). During the first year of life, infants can discriminate between all of the phonetic contrasts that exist in all languages. However, by the end of the first year, they have already started to differentiate their listening.

By the end of the first year, infants lose the ability to discriminate phonetic contrasts between all languages. They become attuned to the phonetic contrasts within their heritage language in particular. There is a biologically determined transition from the perception of phonetically relevant contrasts (differences in phonemes between two or more different languages) to phonemically relevant contrasts (differences in phonemes within the heritage language). There is a transition to preferring the phonemically relevant contrasts of the child's heritage language before the age of 1 year. This transition occurs at the same time that infants are learning how to localize sounds (Franco, 1997). As infants become more skilled at identifying all of the different sounds within their heritage language, they become less capable of doing so in other languages.

Further refinement in temporal pattern discrimination occurs with the acquisition of language, at some point before the first birthday. The infant and toddler can now discriminate between different words and phrases and is able to use these discrimination skills in the service of speech-sound identification, speech-sound production, and associated language comprehension and language expression. The temporal patterns detected here are changes or shifts in sound patterns that extend over single phonemes, over single words, and over single sentences.

### BOX 2.5. Speech Sounds: The Complexity of the Human Vocal Apparatus as a Sound Source

Speech sounds consist of complex sound waves that are produced by the vibrating vocal cords. The vocal apparatus can produce a very wide range of sound frequencies and also produces a range of sound pressures. For example, vowel sounds are generally lower in frequency, ranging from 90 to 300 Hz. Consonants typically produce higher frequency sounds, ranging from 600 to 6,000 Hz. Consonants produce sound pressures that are 10–15 dB lower than vowels or diphthongs (two-vowel combinations). In addition, vowel and consonant sounds are discriminated on the basis of the time needed to produce them. For example, vowel sounds take longer to produce than consonants.

The human vocal apparatus is a very complex sound source. First of all, people each have differently sized and differently shaped vocal cords and voice boxes. Second, the voice box can change in size and shape. The nasal and oral cavities increase or decrease in size depending on the position of the tongue and cheeks, or whether the lips are closed or open. Speech sounds are different from one another because of differences in how the vocal cords vibrate as the voice box changes in size and shape. All of the differences in speech sounds can be recognized only by the listener with intact auditory functions and auditory processing skills. The listener detects differences in sound pressure, sound frequency, and temporal aspects of sound to discriminate among all of the different speech sounds within and between speakers.

Table 2.1 further outlines typical development of hearing functions and skills, based on chronological age. The capacity to hear is present prior to birth. Prior to and after birth, the hearing system has to mature so that the full range of sound frequencies can be detected at normal sound levels. Newborns have less sensitive hearing than adults and need generally louder noises in order to hear as well as adults. Adult levels of noise perception are reached within the first year of life. During the first year, infants approach a more optimal level of hearing for higher frequency sounds before they reach this optimal level for lower frequency sounds (Flavell et al., 2002). This finding explains, in part, the infant's preference for speech produced by women as opposed to men.

**Table 2.1.** Typical development of hearing skills and interface with language acquisition

| Age (months) | Typical development |
|---|---|
| 0–4 | Startles to loud sounds, quiets to mother's voice, momentarily ceases activity when sound is presented at a conversational level |
| 5–6 | Correctly localizes to sound presented in a horizontal plane; begins to imitate sounds in own speech repertoire or at least reciprocally vocalize with an adult |
| 7–12 | Correctly localizes to sound presented in any plane; responds to name, even when spoken quietly |
| 13–15 | Points toward an unexpected sound or to familiar objects or persons when asked |
| 16–18 | Follows simple directions without gestural or other visual cues; can be trained to reach toward an interesting toy at mid-line when a sound is presented |
| 19–24 | Points to body parts when asked; by 21–24 months, can be trained to perform play audiometry, where the child learns to respond to a sound by placing a toy in a container |

Adapted from Auditory Development and Early Intervention (2002). In Northern, J. L., & Downs, M. P. *Hearing in Children* (5th Ed.). (Chapter 5, pp.132 and 138). Philadelphia, PA: Lippincott, Williams, and Wilkins.

## Hearing Skills Needed for the Development of Language

In order to develop language, children need adequate exposure to speech sounds specifically, and they need to capitalize on the brain's innate ability to distinguish phonemes. Children also need exposure to language in general, and they need to capitalize on the brain's natural ability to develop word and sentence structures. The exposure to language must be adequate in both quality and quantity, which means that the auditory signal needs to be sufficiently clear and occur sufficiently often. For a child with a hearing impairment, and especially the child who has only partial hearing impairment, it is particularly important to consider the quality of the auditory/acoustic signals. These children need accessible auditory/linguistic input, in meaningful interactions, with skilled speakers of the native language (Matkin & Wilcox, 1999; Mayer, 2007; Yost, 2013b).



***Binaural Skills: Localizing Sounds and Sound Sources*** Localization is another key auditory processing skill. Infants show this skill when they spontaneously turn toward a sound source. The capacity to localize sound emerges prior to 6 months of age for sounds located in the horizontal plane and after 6 months of age for sounds located in the vertical plane. Initially, reflexive hearing functions help infants orient to the location of a sound. Over the course of the first year of life, and especially once the infant becomes a toddler who can crawl or walk, reflexive hearing functions are superseded by more purposeful and conscious hearing skills that help the toddler understand and identify the location of the sound source. After 1 year of age, localization skills include the capacity to judge the distance between the listener and the sound source and the ability to judge whether the sound source is stationary or moving.

Locating sound sources depends on binaural skills. Binaural skills allow the child to compare differences in the sound wave information collected by each ear. Interaural differences in how sound waves arrive at both ears help the listener understand the position of the sound source. Even if both the sound source and listener are stationary, sound may arrive differently at each ear due to differences in the phase (timing of the cycle), intensity (decibels), and reflected sound waves (reverberation) that arrive at each ear. These three interaural differences are discussed briefly in the following sections.

*Interaural Phase Differences* Interaural phase differences are registered when the same sound arrives at each ear at slightly different points in the sound wave's cycle. A sound might arrive at one ear at the peak of its cycle, whereas it arrives at the other ear midway or at the trough of its cycle. This minute temporal difference is detected by the brain when the sound information is delivered at very slightly different time intervals by the two auditory nerves that extend from each inner ear. Differences in phase between the two ears indicate to the listener that the sound is located to one side or the other and is not located at an equal distance from both ears.

*Interaural Differences in Amplitude and Intensity* Interaural differences in amplitude or intensity are also registered when the same sound arrives at each ear at slightly different times. Sound loses amplitude and intensity the farther it travels. As such, sound arrives slightly earlier to the ear that is facing the sound source and slightly later to the ear that is not facing the sound source. Sound that arrives earlier to the ear that is facing the sound source is less degraded and is therefore perceived as louder. The sound that arrives at the farther ear is slightly lower in amplitude and is perceived as somewhat softer. Interaural differences in the amplitude (intensity; loudness) of sound therefore provides a clue about the where the sound is coming from.

*Interaural Differences in Reflected Waves* Finally, interaural differences may also be registered because of differences in direct versus reflected sound waves. The first wave of sound that arrives at the ears plays the largest role in determining the location of the sound. However, the ratio of direct versus reflected sound also provides clues for judging the relative distance from the source. The ear that is closer to the sound source will receive sound more directly, with less impedance by the objects in the environment, with less impedance by the bony structures of the skull and the pinna of the ear, and with a smaller number of reflections or reverberations. The ear that is located farther from the sound source will receive sound after it has passed through objects in the environment, after it has passed through bony structures of the skull, and/or after it has passed over the pinna of the ear. The ear that is located farther away from the sound source may also receive more reflected or reverberated sound waves. Reflected waves can be different in pressure or amplitude because of loss of pressure or frequency. Reflected waves also arrive at different points in the sound's phase. All of these factors amplify interaural differences and can provide clues for interpreting the location of sound. See Box 2.6 for additional information about reverberation and how the environment can affect sound waves.

## BOX 2.6. Acoustics

Acoustics is the study of how sound is affected by the environment. The environment usually consists of multiple (vibrating) sound sources that can all produce sounds. For example, there may be multiple people, objects, or instruments that all produce sounds. They can produce sounds one after the other or all at the same time. Two sound sources can produce sounds that end up interacting with one another. Two sound sources can also interact via reflections off objects or surfaces in the environment. All of these interactions affect the amplitude, frequency, and phases of the sound waves as they arrive at the ear. By the time a sound wave arrives at the listener's ear, the sound wave may have undergone several changes and might be perceived quite differently by the listener.

### Ambient Noise

Ambient noise is undesired noise. In classrooms, any noise not related to the teacher's voice would be considered an ambient noise. In a concert hall, any noise not related to the production of music could be ambient noise. Ambient noise can be both internal and external to the room. Internal ambient noise comes from a sound source in the room (e.g., another person speaking). External ambient noise might come from people speaking in the hallway or from street traffic or other environmental noises outside the building. Ambient noise can interfere with sound through masking (defined below) and other effects. Ambient noise is measured in terms of decibels, or the overall pressure or amplitude that background sound sources produce collectively.

### Reverberation

Reverberation refers to how sound is reflected by objects and surfaces in the environment. Reverberation time is a unit of measurement for how long it takes for reflected sound to reach a smaller portion of its original pressure. For example, reverberation could be a measure of how long it takes for a reflected sound wave to reach one half of its original pressure. A room with highly absorptive surfaces, such as carpets or thick curtains, has a short reverberation time. The sound waves are impeded or absorbed more quickly, and sound pressure/amplitude dissipates more quickly. The original sound is less disrupted by reflected sound waves and can therefore be heard more clearly. A teacher's voice in a room with absorptive surfaces, therefore, can sometimes be heard more easily because ambient noise is absorbed more quickly. There is less competition with ambient sounds for hearing the teacher's voice. In contrast, the teacher's voice may be more difficult to hear in a room that has hard surfaces that do not absorb sound successfully (i.e., the room has a long reverberation time). The sound of the teacher's voice can therefore be affected by reflected (reverberating) ambient sounds, making the original sound more difficult to hear. A reverberation time of 1 second or so is typically considered to be too long for an optimal listening experience, especially regarding speech sounds in a classroom setting.

**Masking**

Masking is the study of how sounds interact or interfere with one another. Two sounds that are similar in frequency tend to mask each other more than two sounds with very different frequencies. This occurs because of the way that hair cells in the inner ear are activated. Even though the hair cells and the auditory nerve are designed to become activated by a particular frequency, more hair cells are activated by the same sound frequency if that sound is louder. Some of the neighboring hair cells can get activated at the same time, creating some confusion about the actual pitch of the sound. Lower frequency sounds tend to mask higher frequency sounds more so than vice versa.



***Binaural Skills: Locating the Distance From Static and Moving Sound Sources*** As infants and toddlers become familiar with certain sounds, they learn to make judgments about their distance from the sound source and become more skilled at identifying specific sound sources and their location. Instead of simply turning toward a sound source, an older infant or toddler can actively seek out the sound source. Older infants and toddlers have object permanence, meaning they can remember the existence of something even if it is not immediately visible. They can also move about (they can creep, crawl, cruise, or walk). Using both object permanence and their ability to explore three-dimensional space, they can look for a sound source that is not visible.

Moving the body through space serves to exaggerate interaural differences in the experience of sound, as discussed above. By moving the body, the listener gains information about the location of a sound source. For example, by tilting the head (or, as adults sometimes do, by cupping the ear), the young listener discovers that she or he can exaggerate interaural sound differences and decide which locations to move toward or away from. By moving his or her body through space, the toddler learns that sound degrades and gets softer with distance and is louder with proximity. With more time and experience, the toddler can identify what a familiar sound should sound like when it is close or what it should sound like when it is farther away, regardless of whether or not the toddler is moving.

Identifying the actual distance away from a sound source takes some interpretation and is dependent on experience and general knowledge about sounds and environments. For example, an audio recording of a door slamming or a person shouting can be played at reduced volume and give the impression of being a sound source that is located far away even though the recording device is playing nearby. Only with experience do humans learn to understand the position in space of a sound source, its location, their distance from the sound source, and whether the sound is moving. The judgments that a person needs to make to identify these spatial features of sound sources depend on the type of sound source, the environment, and general knowledge about how sound behaves in different types of environments.

***Binaural Skills: Fusion and Separation of Sound Signals Coming From Multiple Sound Sources*** The binaural skills of fusion and separation are necessary when the listener has to discriminate two sound sources that produce sound waves simultaneously. The listener has to decide either to suppress one sound source in favor of the other or to separate, attend, and respond to both. Young children are commonly distracted by competing sounds. They do not have good separation and fusion skills. By the age of 10 years, they are better able to ignore irrelevant sounds and to maintain their focus in an environment with competing signals. However, until age 12, they continue to rely on multiple cues to correctly identify speech sounds (especially consonants) and only reach adult-level maturity at the age of 14 years (Bailey, 2010; Crandell & Smaldino, 2000). The reader should take this information into consideration when thinking about the auditory input provided to most children and the type of input they need. Failure to provide a good auditory input diminishes their capacity to hear, discriminate, and respond to important sounds in their environment.

There are several auditory processing skills that enable adults to perform more successfully than children when exposed to competing sound signals. Adults have more advanced auditory discrimination skills because of more advanced temporal pattern detection. They are better able to fuse sound information from the same sound source as it arrives to both ears, even when the quality of the signal is different between the two ears. They can differentiate and separate sounds coming from two or more sound sources. Because of past experiences and general knowledge, they can more successfully prioritize some sounds as more relevant, while suppressing others. This allows them to focus on relevant sounds only.

***Detection of Signals in Noise*** Amplitude (intensity), frequency (pitch), and temporal pattern differences in sound all allow for the differentiation of sounds that simultaneously arrive at both ears from more than one sound source. Amplitude, frequency, and temporal differences between the hum of an air conditioner and speech sounds are easily differentiated. Separating background music from speech sounds is more difficult but is still easier than separating background speech sounds from a signal speech sound (e.g., classroom teacher's voice and background speech from the teacher's aide). The greater the differences in amplitude, frequency, and temporal patterns, the easier it is to discriminate the two sound sources.

The ability to identify the location of the sound source(s) also helps to make the discrimination. Knowing that a sound comes from a specific location helps to either enhance or suppress attention to that sound. Both binaural separation and binaural fusion skills are needed here. Binaural separation helps to separate two sound sources (and allows for suppression of one of the sound sources as needed). Binaural fusion helps to amplify the same sound source, especially when that sound arrives to each ear at different phases, or when the sound arrives to one ear as more degraded because of distance and/or reverberation effects. Regardless of the extent of differences in the sound waves produced by the sound sources, young children are distracted more often by a background noise than would be the case for an older child, adolescent, or adult.

***Separating and Fusing Two Sounds Sources: Dichotic and Diotic Listening Skills*** At times, sounds from two sound sources arrive at both ears and compete for auditory attention. In a dichotic listening task, each sound source delivers sound preferentially to one ear. In a diotic listening task, each sound source delivers sound information to both ears. The auditory processing skill required here is to differentiate the two sound sources and to be able either to suppress one source in favor of the other or to respond to both sound sources.

Differentiation of sounds requires both separation and fusion skills. Separation skills depend on the auditory processing skills discussed in the section above: Differences in pressure, frequency, temporal pattern, and location assist in separating sounds. Auditory fusion skills help to augment the signal, especially when that signal is located to one side or the other and arrives in a more degraded form to one ear as opposed to the other. A more mature child or adolescent is able to perform these several auditory processing skills more successfully than a less mature child. The skill of auditory closure, discussed in the next section, also plays a role.

***Auditory Closure: Higher Order Cognition in the Identification of Sound Sources*** The successful interpretation of the type, location, and distance of a sound source occurs more successfully when the auditory signal is received clearly by both ears and has not undergone degradation. A degraded auditory signal can occur because of poor sound production at the sound source (e.g., mumbled speech, a poor recording) or in unfavorable listening circumstances. Unfavorable listening circumstances include factors such as the location of the sound source (i.e., the sound source is too far away), sound-absorbing effects (the sound gets muffled by sound-absorbing features of the environment), masking effects (the sound is degraded because of other sound waves that interfere with the signal sound), or reverberation effects (the signal sound reverberates or echoes off objects and walls, increasing the complexity of the sound wave and making it more difficult to interpret). Box 2.6 discusses these terms and features of sound in more detail. When an auditory signal is degraded, it is more difficult to differentiate from background noises or competing signals, and more judgment is needed to determine the nature of the sound source. Auditory closure refers to the judgment needed to localize and identify a sound source and to assign meaning to that sound source, especially when sound quality and listening circumstances are unfavorable. Auditory closure involves use of prior knowledge of sound sources (what different sound sources are supposed to sound like), more advanced language skills (what words or sentences are likely being transmitted), and other aspects of cognition (environmental or social features that help to judge the location and meaning of the sound).

Sound is subject to interpretation. Auditory closure involves making a conscious decision or judgment about the sound and then using that judgment to determine the nature or meaning of the sound. Whatever the sound, the listener must make an interpretation about whether the sound is related to undifferentiated noise, an environmental noise such as wind blowing through leaves, music, speech, or another sound. More active interpretation is needed if the sound signal is degraded. Judgments about what likely has caused a sound then help the person to listen more carefully for expected or unexpected patterns that fit or do not fit the interpretation. If the subsequent sound patterns continue to fit the expected pattern, the listener has shown good auditory closure skills. As an example, once a sound is identified as music, the listener can then start to differentiate components of music such as melody, rhythm, beats, different instruments and their relationships to rhythm, melody, or theme. A similar phenomenon occurs once a listener identifies a sound as speech. The listener continues to listen for expected speech sounds, such as expected words, the expected pitch associated with the male or female voice, and so forth. When sound information is missing, such as occurs in degraded speech, the brain can compensate for the missing information. With good auditory closure, the brain can still make accurate interpretations about the identity of the sound source, the location of the sound source, the different components of sound within the sound source, and the different meanings contained in the sound (music appreciation, speech-language information).

Children need sound delivered to them under more optimal conditions than adults would require because they lack the experience and general knowledge of what types of sounds come from what types of sound sources and what different sounds mean. Auditory closure skills are especially limited when the listener is exposed to new situations, new experiences, or new vocabulary words. Young children have less general knowledge about sounds (and language) on which to rely. They are exposed to new situations and new expectations more often. Their auditory closure skills are therefore less mature, and they are less likely to respond successfully to degraded auditory inputs.

***Responding to Sounds and Motor Planning*** As discussed in Chapter 1, auditory information is shared with other parts of the brain, allowing the listener to dedicate attention differently, to perform a motor response, or to learn a new concept. Part of intact auditory processing skills involve responding appropriately to the auditory information, perhaps by turning the head toward the sound, using a hand signal to respond to the sound, responding with a one-word answer, or enhancing attention to the signal without showing any motor behaviors. In a motor response, a child could move to a new location to get closer to or farther away from the sound source.

## PERFORMANCE DIFFICULTIES IN HEARING

Schools are an aural-oral environment. It is difficult to overemphasize the role of good hearing in a student's performance at school. Hearing issues, whether related to a hearing impairment or to poor classroom acoustics, are an underappreciated cause for learning difficulty. Any behavioral, learning, or attention difficulty in the classroom should prompt educators and other school-based professionals to ask whether the student might have a hearing impairment and/or to consider whether there are environmental factors that interfere with hearing.

In high-income regions, the global prevalence of hearing impairment in children and youth is in the range of 0.4% (Stevens et al., 2011). The number of children served under the category of hearing impairment in schools in the United States is 1.2% (ASHA, 2018). These figures give the reader an indication of how often hearing impairment is typically identified. However, when considering hearing difficulties, it is important to remember that most children with hearing impairment can still hear. Most children and youth with identified hearing impairment have residual hearing. Only 0.05%–0.1% of children have profound hearing loss, that is, no hearing functions at all (Cushing & Papsin, 2015). Students with a hearing impairment may escape notice because they are able to hear in some circumstances. Even when a student passes a hearing screening test, a hearing impairment can still exist. For example, a hearing screening test does not take into consideration all of the auditory processing skills discussed in this chapter. Further, the poor acoustics of most classrooms can be a cause for hearing difficulty and are not taken into consideration in a standard hearing screening assessment. This is an especially important consideration for students with milder forms of hearing impairment (ASHA Guidelines, 2018). It is always important to compare the student's performance in acoustically favorable environments (including but not limited to the acoustically controlled environment of the audiologist's sound booth) against the student's performance in everyday settings. Listening conditions in the student's environment are not always favorable; a student may live next to loud neighbors or on a busy street. The student's actual hearing skills and abilities in her or his environment can be different from her or his performance in a more controlled environment. The student's actual hearing skills need to be identified to determine the need for intervention.

This section offers guidance on when to refer a child for a formal audiological evaluation for suspected hearing difficulty. By studying this chapter and this section, the reader is expected to be able to identify suspected hearing impairment and generate a list of specific questions to ask the audiologist. The reader should also be able to use the information presented in this chapter to speak with the student's audiologist to learn about the student's hearing skills and limitations. Following a student's evaluation with an audiologist, teaching staff should be able to understand under what conditions a student with a hearing impairment can hear successfully and under what conditions hearing would be challenging; see Boxes 2.7 and 2.8. The audiologist should be able to describe the student's hearing impairment and make suggestions for accommodations or modifications to improve the student's performance.

The following sections provide examples of different types of hearing impairment. The type of hearing impairment will help professionals understand what their role might be in offering accommodations and supports to ensure a positive learning environment for the student.

**BOX 2.7. Questions to Ask the Hearing Specialist**

1. What is the decibel loss of hearing for this student?
2. Which types of frequencies are the most affected?
3. How much is each ear affected?
4. When listening conditions are favorable, what types of listening tasks would be expected to cause difficulty for this student?
   a. Hearing noises or environmental sounds
   b. Hearing music
   c. Hearing amplified music
   d. Hearing speech
   e. Hearing amplified speech
   f. Hearing loud noises
   g. Identifying the location of a sound
5. When listening conditions are not favorable, what types of listening tasks would be expected to cause difficulty for this student?
   a. Hearing speech when there is background noise
   b. Hearing speech when there is background music
   c. Hearing speech when there are background voices
   d. Hearing two competing signals (e.g., two voices speaking simultaneously)
   e. Hearing successfully when the auditory signal is degraded
   f. Determining the location of a sound
6. Ask the following about the acoustic features of the listening environment:
   a. How favorable or unfavorable are the acoustics for this child's classroom? For other parts of the school building such as the hallway, cafeteria, or gymnasium?
   b. What speaker behaviors would assist this student? Consider the location or position of the speaker, the pitch, and the volume of the speaker's voice.
   c. What type of amplification device or system might be effective for this student?

**BOX 2.8. Observable Behaviors Associated With Hearing Difficulty**

Students who may have a hearing impairment may exhibit the following behaviors:

1. Tendency to ask others to repeat themselves
2. Tendency to misinterpret a spoken message
3. Difficulty hearing audio or video at a volume normally found audible by other listeners

*(continued)*

**BOX 2.8.** *(continued)*

4. Difficulty hearing in the classroom when seated too far from the speaker (teacher or student)
5. Difficulty understanding conversation in a group
6. Annoyance and aversion to suboptimal listening conditions (e.g., sensitivity to background noises or noises outside the classroom)
7. Delays or difficulties in speech development, communication, academic performance, and learning skills
8. Difficulty producing speech sounds. Difficulty producing speech sounds can occur in the presence of normal hearing but is especially common when the speaker is not able to hear and/or discriminate speech sounds.
9. Speech-language difficulties. Any student with any type speech-language difficulty should be considered for formal hearing evaluation. Hearing impairments, even subtle hearing impairments, are associated (and are often causally associated) with speech-language development.
10. Academic difficulties. These are often associated with hearing impairment. The student may show poor reading decoding and reading comprehension skills, poor writing skills, inattention, and difficulty participating in oral discussion.
11. Psychosocial development. Psychosocial difficulties such as isolation, social exclusion, shyness, embarrassment, annoyance, oppositionality, refusal to participate in activities, confusion, and helplessness may be associated with hearing impairment, and is sometimes causally associated with hearing impairment.

## Severity of Hearing Impairments: Decibels and Frequency Loss

Normal hearing refers to normal hearing functions and skills for sounds in the 0–15 dB range. Hearing disability starts when hearing in the better ear is compromised at sound intensity levels higher than 15 dB. Hearing loss may be mild, moderate, severe, or profound. A mild hearing impairment is defined as the inability to hear sounds in the 15–40 dB range. A moderate degree of hearing impairment is present when a person cannot hear sounds at 40–100 dB. A severe or profound level of hearing impairment is present when a person cannot hear sounds as loud as 100 dB or higher.

The severity of a person's hearing impairment is measured as the average hearing threshold for the better ear, in decibels. Like any number that is averaged, the average hearing loss for a given person tells only part of the story. The actual impact of the hearing loss depends on more than just the average loss. For example, the degree of hearing loss can vary between the two ears. The degree of hearing loss can also vary depending on the frequency of the sound and on environmental factors. A hearing test normally assesses hearing across several frequencies, as most students with hearing impairment do not have a uniform loss of hearing at all frequencies and may not have the same severity of loss in both ears (ASHA, 2018, Dale, 1962). It is useful to know whether hearing loss affects certain frequencies more than others (e.g., low- versus high-frequency hearing loss). It is also useful to know which ear has the greater impairment. Figure 2.4 shows an audiogram for a hearing test conducted at multiple frequencies; data on the student's left ear are marked with Xs, whereas data on the student's right ear are marked with Os. This audiogram reveals bilateral hearing loss. It also shows that hearing loss is greater in the right ear than in the left ear for this student.

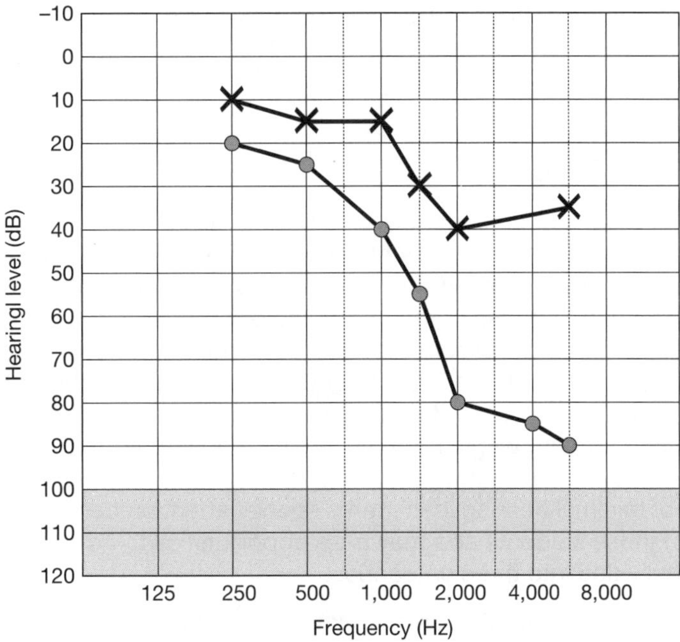


**Figure 2.4.** An audiogram that reveals bilateral hearing loss. Data on the left ear are marked with *X*s, and data from the right ear are marked with *O*s.

## Hearing Performance: Quality of the Sound Signal and Environmental Acoustics

Even when the severity of hearing impairment of a student is understood, school professionals still need to know how the student's hearing impairment manifests with different signal sounds (the sounds of interest or of importance, usually the teacher's voice) and in different acoustic environments. When a hearing impairment does not affect all frequencies and is mild, it is tempting to think that the degree of impairment is mild. However, the degree of impairment will vary, depending on the sound source and on the environment. For example, the student with a mild hearing impairment might have greater difficulty with fusion of sounds, especially when a more degraded signal arrives at the poorer hearing ear. This will increase difficulties in locating sounds and/or in focusing attention on the sound signal. In the classroom, hearing the teacher's or a classmate's voice can be affected, especially if the sound source is not stationary or changes position. See Table 2.2 for a description of different severities of hearing impairment

**Table 2.2.** A description of different ranges of hearing impairment, from mild to severe, and degree of associated handicap

| Average threshold | Description | What can be heard without amplification | Probable needs |
|---|---|---|---|
| 0–15 dB | Normal hearing | All speech sounds | None |
| 16–25 dB | Slight hearing loss | Vowel sounds heard clearly; may miss unvoiced consonant sounds | Consider use of hearing aid, speech reading (lip reading), auditory training, speech therapy, preferential seating |
| 26–30 dB | Mild hearing loss | Hears only some speech sounds, the louder voiced sounds | Hearing aid; lip reading; auditory training; speech therapy |
| 31–50 dB | Moderate hearing loss | Misses most speech sounds at normal conversational level | Consider interventions listed above; consider special classroom |
| 51–70 dB | Severe hearing loss | Hears no speech sounds in normal conversations | Consider all of the above interventions; probably needs special classroom |
| ≥71 dB | Profound hearing loss | Hears no speech or other sounds | All of the above; may also need special classroom |

From Auditory Development and Early Intervention (2002). In Northern, J. L., & Downs, M. P. *Hearing in Children* (5th Ed.). (Chapter 5, pp.132 and 138). Philadelphia, PA: Lippincott, Williams, and Wilkins.

and suggested accommodations in the classroom. See Box 2.9 for a more ample discussion on minimal hearing loss.



### BOX 2.9. Minimal Hearing Loss

There is evidence that students identified as having mild hearing impairment can be at risk for not performing successfully at school. These students may have difficulty hearing sounds between 15 and 40 dB. Their difficulties might not be identified during routine hearing testing because of the controlled environment in which the hearing testing occurs. However, in a classroom setting that is often noisy, mild hearing impairment might have substantial effects on learning and on participation. The student's minimal hearing loss may be associated with social-emotional as well as learning difficulties, just as is the case for a student with a more severe hearing impairment (Bess, Dodd-Murphy, & Parker, 1998).

The issue of minimal hearing loss merits special attention because school teams may not be aware of those students and may miss opportunities to assist them. Minimal hearing loss can be divided into three categories:

1. Unilateral hearing loss (UHL): Air-conduction pure-tone average is greater than 20 dB in the impaired ear
2. Mild bilateral hearing loss (MBHL): Pure-tone average is between 20 and 40 dB HL in both ears
3. High-frequency hearing loss (HFHL): Air-conduction thresholds are greater than 25 dB at two or more frequencies above 2 kHz

Children with minimal hearing loss face more challenges than do their peers with normal hearing and may need additional resources. Difficulties in understanding speech could occur in unfavorable or adverse listening environments. For example, a student may have special difficulty hearing different pitches. The higher pitched female voice may be more difficult to understand than the lower pitched male voice (or vice versa). Both types of speech might be understood successfully when the speaker is nearby but may become more difficult for the student when the speaker is at some distance away. Speech might be more difficult to hear when it is delivered along with other voices, background noise, or outside noises. When the hearing loss affects one ear more than the other, binaural skills can be affected. A student may lose sound localization skills, an important mechanism for identifying the location of a sound source and also for differentiating between sound sources. The student with localization difficulties may be especially sensitive to the position of the speaker's voice when listening. Even though students with minimal hearing loss might hear successfully in adverse listening conditions some of the time, they may not be able to do so over long time intervals. As a result of the extra strain involved in perceiving speech successfully, these students may experience more stress and may show more behavioral disturbances such as noncompliance, impatience, hyperactivity, impulsivity, resistance and oppositionality, and/or anxiety.

---

*Source:* Winiger, Alexander, & Diefendorf (2016).

## Auditory Processing Difficulties

Any student with hearing impairment (in decibels and frequency) will also have difficulty in auditory processing. However, auditory processing difficulties can also occur on their own. Even when sounds arrive successfully at each ear, and even when the ears transduce those sounds into neurological impulses, auditory processing difficulties can interfere with understanding the auditory signal. They can manifest with the same types of behavioral difficulties as described for impairments in hearing functions. As discussed earlier in the chapter, auditory processing includes the capacity to identify and discriminate between different types of temporal patterns over different time intervals. Therefore, sound discrimination skills can be impaired when auditory processing skills are affected. In addition, binaural skills are affected. It is more difficult for the student with auditory processing weaknesses to identify the location of a sound, to fuse sound signals coming to both ears when the signal is weak or degraded because of acoustic factors, to separate sound signals when there is signal competition, and to use higher order cognition (general knowledge, language skills) to comprehend degraded sound signals (auditory closure). The primary deficits encountered in classroom settings are typically related to the issue of separating speech sounds from competing background noises. Children and youth in classrooms may also need to identify and make sense of degraded auditory signals, especially if classroom acoustics are not favorable.

Auditory processing skills are not mature during the early and middle childhood years. Children have developmentally expected difficulty with auditory processing, especially prior to the age of 10 years. For example, young children have difficulty separating sound sources when multiple sound signals arrive to the ears. They may not be able to determine relevant from nonrelevant sounds. They may not be able to integrate sound information to understand the location or the type of the sound source. They are more easily distracted by environmental sounds and may preferentially listen to nonrelevant sounds at times. Younger children have more limited auditory closure skills. For example, children who are still mastering speech-sound identification and language skills do not have the same cognitive resources to fill in the blanks, as it were, when auditory signals are suboptimal (degraded), or when they have to listen to multiple auditory inputs simultaneously. All of these limitations would be expected to affect how well a child perceives signal speech. Even if children can successfully perform some auditory processing skills, children cannot usually sustain their attention as long as adults can. They would therefore not be expected to sustain their attention during complex or demanding listening tasks for long periods of time. As is true for hearing impairment, the classroom teacher will depend on the audiologist to identify an auditory processing disorder in a student. See Box 2.10 for a more in-depth discussion.

### BOX 2.10. Definition and Identification of Central Auditory Processing Disorders

The behavioral profile of children with auditory processing disorders (APDs) is often the same as children with specific language impairment, attention-deficit/hyperactivity disorder (ADHD), and phonological processing disorders. It is also much the same behavioral profile as for children with hearing impairment, especially mild impairment. When making behavioral observations of students, a teacher in a classroom would therefore have difficulty separating behaviors resulting from APDs from those associated with hearing impairment, language impairment, ADHD, or problems with phonological processing. Hearing skills, language skills, attention skills, and phonological processing

*(continued)*

**BOX 2.10.** *(continued)*

skills all require engagement with sound and the connection of sound with language. Not all students are successful in their language development. Therefore, some clinicians argue that APDs may simply be the result of poor engagement with sounds and language rather than impaired hearing or impaired auditory processing (Moore, Ferguson, Edmondson-Jones, Ratib, & Riley, 2010). Even among audiologists there exists disagreement about how to identify APDs and whether the conditions can be separated from any of the other conditions listed here (Kraus & Anderson, 2016).

Although it is difficult to separate APDs from the other conditions listed above, there are some students whose listening difficulty is related to auditory processing alone. They have a specific deficit in understanding distorted speech, competing speech, and/or paying attention to speech in competition with background noise (Keith, 1999). All of the different interventions discussed in this chapter can be useful to the student with APD, even if the identification and diagnosis are uncertain.

## HOW TO SET UP AN OBSERVATION FOR HEARING

By understanding the tie between hearing impairments and performance difficulties in the classroom, school professionals can make informed observations of students who may have hearing impairments. The behaviors most likely to be observable include poor comprehension, poor expressive language skills, a short attention span, off-task behaviors, disruptive behaviors, and poor academic skills. Students may also express a lot of anxiety or frustration. Virtually any performance difficulty in the classroom could potentially be attributed to hearing impairment.

Hearing impairment is variable and depends on the quality of the sound source and the acoustics of the environment. Professionals must use judgment in determining which behaviors are related to hearing impairment and which behaviors may be related to other factors. The examples that follow describe specific hearing impairment–related behaviors.

### Select the Student

To begin an observation, school professionals should select a student who has already been identified as having a hearing impairment or a student whom they suspect to have one. For a student who has a hearing impairment, the observer should review the audiologist's report and also speak with the audiologist, who can provide information about the specific features of the student's hearing impairment. Refer to this chapter to understand the terms used by audiologists and review some of the hearing skills that might be affected. The audiologist can provide clarification as needed.

For students who are suspected of having a hearing impairment that is not yet confirmed, school professionals should make notes about why they suspect a hearing impairment. It is important to keep in mind that hearing impairment might be present only with certain sound sources, with degraded signals, in noisy environments, or when there are two or more competing sound sources. These difficulties can occur even after a student has passed a hearing screening test. Good observations can be shared with the audiologist to enhance the value of the audiological assessment. If hearing impairment is not confirmed, the behavioral observations will still be useful, as they can be interpreted using one or several of the other frameworks in this book (e.g., formal language skills, reading skills, or executive skills).

## Consider Classroom and Environmental Acoustics

Before conducting a hearing observation, school professionals should consider the environment in which the student learns and socializes. The analysis should examine how well *any* student can hear speech and other relevant input in this environment. Professionals should consider the following:

1. Ambient noise inside the classroom
2. Ambient noise from outside the classroom
3. Ambient noise from outside the building
4. Reverberation time: Short or long
5. Masking

Each of these variables affects classroom acoustics and can affect performance of any student. It is important that professionals are aware of these variables within the classroom environment before conducting an observation of a student who may have performance difficulty related to hearing.

## Make Observations

Some student behaviors may be very easy to identify as being the result of hearing loss. An important first step is to ask the students about whether they believe hearing to be difficult in the school environment or elsewhere. The students' responses will depend upon their age and language skills, and they may not even recognize their hearing impairment. However, many students will be able to share some insights.

Before observations begin, students should be informed about the process. School professionals can explain that they are sampling the student's hearing skills in different conditions and they hope to learn together about the best ways to deliver speech sounds or other auditory information. School professionals can use Appendix 2.2, the Hearing Skills Observation Sheet, to structure their observation for hearing. The observation should include circumstances in which the student is exposed to different intensities and pitches. For instance, the observer might call the student by name and make a request from different places in the room and by using different speaking behaviors. In this case, the observer should consider the following: Did the student respond when called by name? Did he or she understand the request? Does it make a difference to speak from different angles or from different distances? Does it make a difference to speak toward one ear or the other? Speaking from nearby is likely to result in a better response than speaking to the student from far away. In this case, the observer should consider the following: Does it make a difference to speak in a lower voice or a higher voice? Does it make a difference to articulate more slowly and clearly? Does it make a difference to exaggerate the prosody or to speak in a more monotone voice? If the student has residual hearing, it is important to conduct these trials while staying outside the student's line of sight. Alternatively, the observer can cover the lips and maintain a neutral facial expression. This reduces visual cues that the student might use to understand what the speaker is saying.

If the student does not respond successfully, the observer should add eye contact and remain within the student's line of sight. The observer may learn that he or she should always speak only after first initiating eye contact and/or after the student's attention is obtained by touching or providing a different type of physical or visual prompt. The student may need to look at others for the purposes of speech reading (lip reading), and/or may rely on changes in facial expressions or gestures in order to respond.

After different speaker conditions and speaker behaviors have been trialed, the observer should ask whether the student has a preference. The student should provide feedback about which speaker conditions or speaker behaviors seem to be the most useful by answering the following:

- Do you prefer it if I speak to you close up and nearby, or can I speak with you from a distance?
- Do you prefer it if I speak from the front of the room, the back of the room, or off to one side?
- Do you prefer it if I speak close to your right ear or close your left ear?
- Do you prefer it if I speak loudly or softly?
- Do you prefer it if I speak with a low voice or a high voice?
- Do you prefer it if I speak to you only after we've made eye contact?
- Do you prefer it if I make a lot of changes in my facial expressions and use gestures, or does it not matter?
- Do you prefer it if I speak more slowly and exaggerate my lip movements, or does it not matter?

The observer may need to trial different speaking conditions in different acoustic environments. For example, it is useful to know how the speaking conditions listed above do or do not affect the student's hearing skills when speaking with the student in a small, quiet room versus a classroom with an average level of background noise. The observer can also try out different speaking conditions and speaking behaviors in noisy environments such as the cafeteria or the hallway. The observation could even occur outside of the school building. Through repeated observations, the observer can learn about what types of speaking conditions or speaking behaviors seem to work best for the student. The observer's voice, ability to use nonverbal communication with facial expressions and gestures, ability to enunciate more clearly, and the specific acoustic environment may all create opportunities or barriers for optimal hearing for the student. Ideally, all of the adults who work with the student will make similar observations and determine what works best with their voice, their environment, and their activities. If the student uses an amplification system, such as a hearing aid, be sure to ask the audiologist what instructions the student was given about the amplification system, when it should or should not be used, or how to adjust the system depending on the environment (if at all). See the Accommodations for Hearing section later in this chapter for more information about amplification systems.

## Analyze and Interpret the Observations

Depending on the student's responses, the observer can gather valuable information about what constitutes optimal speaker behaviors and optimal listening (acoustic) conditions for the student. Be sure to share the observations with the specialist (audiologist, teacher of the hearing impaired) to determine with accuracy which types of speaking conditions appear to be the most effective for the student. The initial observations are useful in determining whether a formal audiological evaluation is needed. They can help identify hearing impairment. They can also help identify any changes that might need to be made for the student over time. For example, the audiologist may discover that the student needs a different type of hearing aid, a new amplification system, or different acoustic modifications. Even if none of the initial observations of concern end up being related to a hearing impairment and are instead the result of a language impairment or an impairment in executive skills, the observer's conversations with the student and the observations are likely to result in the use of strategies that can help improve the student's performance. Many of the speaker behaviors and speaker conditions discussed above can improve the performance of students with other types of learning difficulties. Students with language impairment and students with difficulty regulating their attention might benefit from some of the strategies discussed here.

The primary obligations in building an IEP or an intervention plan for the student with hearing impairment is to ensure that the student can successfully access the curriculum. A variety of educational objectives can and should be developed to help the student manage her or his hearing impairment optimally, with different communication partners, in different environments, and for different activities. The strategies listed in the How to Set Up an Observation section should be discussed with the student. To the extent possible, the student should be involved actively in choosing those speaker-related behaviors or conditions that optimize hearing and listening skills.

## Educational Objectives and Strategies for Hearing

A school team will not be able to modify the severity of the hearing impairment, which is the purview of health care providers. As such, many of the educational objectives relate to self-advocacy and helping the student to make the best use of accommodations and assistive technology. The school team can make the school environment more accessible by teaching the student how to maximize participation.

***Optimal Hearing and Listening Conditions*** The student should learn about his or her optimal hearing and listening conditions that apply in different settings. The student should understand how to identify preferred variables, such as the pitch of the speaker's voice, the location of the speaker, which ear is preferred for listening, the level of ambient noise, and any preferences related to visual communication or lip reading.

***Comprehension Failures*** Students with hearing impairment should be taught to recognize comprehension failures and given strategies to respond to communication breakdowns. Strategies might include asking for clarification or asking the speaker to write down what was said. The student may also need to practice paying attention to nonverbal aspects of communication to facilitate overall comprehension (Keith, 1999).

***Differences in Strategy Use Between Acoustic Environments*** The student should learn about different acoustic environments and discover what types of acoustic strategies seem to optimize hearing. The student should acquire the vocabulary needed to describe hearing and listening preferences in different environments. For example, the student can learn about how close he or she needs to be to hear the speaker properly in different environments. The student can also learn terms and phrases to request repetition or to request different forms of communication from a variety of communication partners, including familiar and unfamiliar adults and peers. For example, the student may need to learn to use scripts such as, "I did not catch what you said, can you repeat that please?" or, the student can say, "This is a noisy place. I sometimes need to use my eyes to understand what people are saying. Can you repeat a bit more slowly please?" Older students can learn how to describe optimal hearing conditions to peers and/or to adults in community settings.

***Use of Trusted Adults*** Not all students who have hearing impairment will necessarily be comfortable discussing their hearing preferences with all their communication partners. They may even prefer that speakers not use any individualized behaviors or strategies. Reluctance to use communication strategies commonly stems from a desire not to be singled out from peers. Some students may not have the language skills needed to acquire the educational objectives as presented here. Adults may have to rely on what they consider to be the best speaker behaviors and speaker conditions and use those behaviors in a manner that feels the most respectful to the student. Over time, the student may gain the confidence needed to advocate for his or her own hearing and listening needs or may acquire the language skills needed to do so. The student may become more willing to advocate for preferred speaker behaviors and conditions, especially if these can lead to more meaningful social connections. If the student is not able to advocate personally, a useful strategy could be for the student to identify trusted adults who can play the role of advocate on their behalf.

***Speech Reading, Gesture, and Instruction in Sign Language*** For some students with hearing impairments, the intervention plan or IEP may need to include specialized instruction and educational objectives for speech reading (lip reading), gesturing, or American Sign Language or other forms of manual language. A student with hearing impairment who has underdeveloped spoken and written language skills may need specialized instruction in phonics, morpho-syntax, and narrative in their heritage language. See Chapter 4 for additional information.

## Accommodations for Hearing

Accommodations for hearing flow logically from the educational objectives and strategies discussed above. Some symptoms of hearing impairment and many symptoms of auditory processing disorders are not separable from language impairment and executive dysfunctions (Dawes, Bishop, Sirimanna, & Bamiou, 2008). As such, many of the teaching strategies that are used for students with language impairment and attention-regulation challenges also apply to the student with hearing impairment and to the student with auditory processing difficulty.

For the student with a hearing impairment and/or APDs, most of the accommodations will be designed to maximize the student's capacity to hear and to discriminate speech sounds (Keith, 1999). Highlighting the most relevant sounds in an environment is also known as increasing the signal-to-noise ratio. Specific recommendations should come from the audiologist or other specialist who can examine the acoustics of the environments in which the student functions, while also evaluating the specific hearing needs of the student. Enhancing the signal-to-noise ratio is an accommodation that should be considered for the entire classroom. All children, especially younger children, require a higher signal-to-noise ratio than do adults. Commonly reported levels of classroom noise and reverberation interfere with speech perception for many typically developing children and youth, not just those who may have a hearing impairment. As their hearing skills do not mature until mid-adolescence, it is especially important to offer acoustically sound learning environments to all children and youth (Crandell & Smaldino, 2000). Accommodations should be designed for both the individual student and the classroom as a whole.

***Optimize Speaker Behaviors and Speaker Conditions*** Accommodations should be provided to optimize speaker behaviors and speaker conditions. Strategies include optimizing the location, position, and distance between the person speaking and the student, adjusting the loudness and pitch of communication, integrating one-to-one instruction, and using repetition and check-ins for comprehension. When feasible, professionals should provide audio recordings of presentations so that learners can review the material on their own.

***Make Use of Visual Communication Systems*** Visual communication systems include pictures, gestures, facial expressions, speech reading, manual communication (e.g., manual spelling, use of hands to communicate concepts), and American Sign Language. Students might also be taught lip reading skills. Visual communication systems should be offered and used if they enhance communication with and by the student.



***Optimize Acoustic Conditions*** The student with a hearing impairment may need instruction to be delivered in an acoustically optimal environment. Optimizing the acoustics of the classroom requires input from an audiologist or other specialist who can take measures of current classroom background noise (ambient noise) and reverberation levels. The accommodations that result from making changes to the classroom would likely be useful for a substantial proportion of students in any given classroom, not just those who may have a hearing impairment. Many students perform less well in noisy classrooms (Dockrell & Shield, 2006). Young students in particular need optimal acoustic and listening conditions in order to learn successfully.

Classroom acoustics can be improved by reducing background noise from outside and inside the classroom. This can occur through use of barriers outside the school building, such as planting trees to reduce traffic noise. Noise-canceling measures, such as using sound-absorbent building materials in hallways and classrooms or heating, cooling, lighting, and bathroom systems that do not produce excess noise, can also be useful. Classroom acoustics can also be improved by reducing the amount of reverberation, even when background noise is not a concern. Noise-dampening and sound-absorbing interventions such as thick curtains and carpeting can reduce the impact of reverberation. Classroom furniture and spacing may also be arranged to produce the most optimal distance between the teacher and the student(s). Good design and attention to detail throughout the construction or renovation process of learning environments can ensure conformance to the standard acoustic requirements for optimal learning (American National Standard, 2002; Marttila, 2004; Picard & Bradley, 2001; Rosenberg, 2010).

Teachers also benefit from acoustically optimized classrooms, as they are less likely to experience voice fatigue (American Academy of Audiology, 2011). It is critical to optimize the acoustic environment for students as much as for teachers.

***Make Use of Amplification Systems*** Individual students with hearing impairment may require an amplification system, which increases the signal-to-noise ratio. They improve the student's capacity to use residual hearing maximally. An amplification system can take the form of a hearing aid or an FM (frequency modulation) system. A hearing aid increases the amplitude of all sounds that reach the student's ear. An FM system amplifies the teacher's voice with a microphone that delivers the sound signal to a speaker located in the student's ear. A sound-field system amplifies the teacher's voice to all students or to groups of students, depending on how many speakers are located in the room. All three of these amplification systems can help the student pay closer attention to the teacher's voice and participate more successfully in classroom activities.

## CASE EXAMPLE

Robin is a 10-year-old student who is in the third grade. She was identified as having a mild hearing impairment when she was a toddler. A hearing assessment was undertaken when she failed to acquire language at age level. She has been followed closely by her audiologist ever since her hearing impairment was identified. Not all teachers in her school are aware of her hearing impairment. She can function very well in many classroom and school settings, and her social nature has endeared her to many at her school.

## Robin's Hearing Functions and Hearing Skills

Robin's hearing impairment was labeled as mild. She had a 20-dB loss in the right ear and a 30-dB loss in the left ear, especially for frequencies in the mid-range. Her parents have always insisted that she can hear normally. They report no concerns in the home setting. In the classroom setting, her hearing also appears to be normal, but only when her teacher speaks with her directly. Robin's hearing is equally good no matter who speaks with her. However, her listening skills do vary by hearing conditions, and they sometimes vary by speaker. Her teachers were able to provide this valuable insight to her parents by sharing the strategies that they use in the classroom to facilitate and improve Robin's listening. Without realizing it, her parents had already discovered what her teachers knew and were doing at school. They turn their attention to her, make eye contact, and sometimes speak more slowly or repeat what they say. They usually do not have to speak with her in noisy settings, and they are very familiar speakers. Because of her familiarity with them and because of the hearing and listening environment of the home, Robin's hearing and listening skills at home appear normal.

At school, adults who are familiar with her can identify her listening readiness by making eye contact. When they know that she is in listening mode, they have no difficulty communicating with her. Her language comprehension is at age and grade level for routine interactions of the school day. That said, when Robin is distracted or when she is in a noisy environment, she is much less likely to listen as carefully as she should. At times, she fails to understand what is said to her. She does not always recognize communication failures. Peers who are close friends have been successful at making physical or eye contact with her when they notice communication breakdowns. However, not all peers repair communication breaks with her when they arise. Robin's language skills are all within an age-appropriate level for conversational speech. However, her writing is less mature than that of her peers. She tends to write in simple sentences and her vocabulary is not as well developed as that of her peers.

## Robin's Auditory Processing Skills

Robin's team did not assess all her auditory processing skills. Her audiologist stated that her auditory processing skills are normal. However, Robin does not always make full use of her auditory processing skills. Her awareness of sound, and her capacity to listen to sounds, varies by environment. She does not always realize that someone is speaking to her and does not always recognize noises coming from different locations. She has difficulty understanding competing speech sources unless she is making eye contact with the person speaking. She is now learning to recognize the difference in her listening skills, depending on the location and hearing environment. She recognizes that she does not hear or listen as well in the cafeteria or on the playground. At this point, she seems to not mind having only a few friends or speaking only to those who are right next to her. By not wearing an amplification system, she does not stand out among her peers.

## Robin's Hearing Accommodations

Robin's audiologist recommended an FM system for her, but Robin does not always wear it, unless she is in her small classroom with familiar peers. She uses the FM system inconsistently when she attends the larger classroom. She does not wear an amplification device on the playground or in other areas. In the small classroom, and with the FM system in place, hearing and listening are not a challenge. Use of her FM system is less critical in the smaller classroom, but she notices that listening is less effortful when she uses it. Robin's use of the FM system in the larger classroom is also inconsistent. In both settings, adults working with her have learned that she typically needs one-to-one attention in order to hear and listen. For now, these strategies appear to be sufficient to keep her engaged and have been sufficient for her to develop and maintain positive peer relations.

## Accommodations for Robin

Accommodations for Robin are described in the history above and consist primarily of her FM system. As discussed, Robin does not use this accommodation consistently. In fact, she should be using the FM system more consistently in the larger classroom. One of her classrooms is especially subject to reverberation, and she clearly performs much better in that classroom when using her FM system.

## Educational Objectives for Robin

Robin's IEP now includes self-advocacy skills. Robin is learning to identify hearing and listening strategies that help to improve her performance. She is also learning to speak with familiar adults and peers about her hearing skills and needs. Her school team is not convinced that she is making full use of these accommodations and strategies. Partly because of her age and partly for social reasons, Robin appears to not always appreciate the extent of her hearing needs. She may not want to make herself stand out among her peers. Her team continues to help her notice listening and comprehension failures and have started to ask her what she can do to help improve her listening and her comprehension. Robin usually responds successfully to adult prompts at self-advocacy, but she is not yet advocating for herself consistently when left to her own devices.

## Working With Culturally and Linguistically Diverse Learners

When teaching culturally and linguistically diverse learners, school professionals should keep the following approaches in mind:

### *Consider Previous Experience With Listening Skills*

Learners may or may not have developed consistent listening skills, depending on the context and curriculum that they have experienced. In some cultures and contexts, learners will have a great deal of experience in hearing and listening as part of the overall curriculum. These students will be more accustomed to an assessment that involves auditory input, such as class discussion or an oral examination. In other countries, students will not have been assessed in any way with auditory input. It is important for assessors to be aware that learners from different countries may or may not be familiar with auditory assessment. Students who are not proficient in English may need to have the directions for auditory assessments repeated or may need them translated into their heritage language.

### *Adjust Volume and Rate of Speech to Meet the Learner's Needs*

The range of sounds and sound frequencies differ in different languages. For example, Hungarian has a very low pitch, and Chinese has a very high one. These factors can be important when a student is first exposed to English. When learners are acquiring the home or mother tongue, it is usually done on a one-to-one basis where the parents, older siblings, or other caregivers can adjust their volume and rate of speech based on how the child or learner reacts. If a child has mild hearing loss, the caregiver may speak slightly louder or slower in order to ensure the child has understood. When individuals are learning a second or additional language in a classroom full of learners, the teacher should make adjustments to compensate for a hearing loss. It is especially important for English-language learners with hearing loss to receive a quality auditory signal and for the teacher's voice to be heard easily and clearly. These learners may also qualify for accommodations when taking a test.

## CONCLUSIONS

This chapter outlined the Hearing Skills Framework. The two neurological frameworks introduced thus far, hearing and vision, are both sensory input systems. Vision and hearing functions and skills are highly dependent on intact structures (nature). We hope that these two chapters have also highlighted the importance of nurture, because vision and hearing functions have to develop and expand into vision and hearing skills. Both vision and hearing help to guide the motor system for successful action and participation in the activities of daily life. The next chapter is focused on motor skills and helps to clarify this important connection.

## REFERENCES


American Academy of Audiology. (2011). Position statement on classroom acoustics. Retrieved from www.audiology.org, guidelines and standards.

American National Standard. (2002). Acoustical performance criteria, design requirements, and guidelines for schools. Acoustical Society of America.

American Speech-Language-Hearing Association (ASHA). (2019). Hearing loss: Beyond early childhood. Retrieved from www.asha.org

American Speech-Language-Hearing Association (ASHA). (2018). Retrieved from www.asha.org/public/hearing/Audiogram/ and www.asha.org/public/hearing/Configuration-of-Hearing-Loss/

American Speech-Language-Hearing Association (ASHA). The prevalence and incidence of hearing loss in children. Retrieved from https://www.asha.org/PRPSpecificTopic.aspx?folderid=8589934680§ion=Incidence_and_Prevalence

American Speech-Language-Hearing Association (ASHA). Guidelines for audiological service provision in schools. Retrieved from https://www.asha.org/policy/gl2002-00005/

American Speech-Language-Hearing Association. Retrieved from https://www.asha.org/public/hearing/loud-noise-dangers/

Bailey, T. (2010). Auditory pathways and processes: Implications for neuropsychological assessment and diagnosis of children and adolescents. *Child Neuropsychology, 16*(6), 521–528.

Bess, F., Dodd-Murphy, J. U., & Parker, R. A. (1998). Children with minimal sensorineural hearing loss: Prevalence, educational performance, and functional status. *Ear and Hearing, 19*(5), 339–354.

Centers for Disease Control (CDC). (2018). Retrieved from https://www.cdc.gov/nceh/hearing_loss/what_noises_cause_hearing_loss.html

Crandell, C. C., & Smaldino, J. J. (2000). Classroom acoustics for children with normal hearing and with hearing impairment. *Language, Speech and Hearing Services in Schools, 31*, 362–370.

Cushing, S. L., & Papsin, B. C. (2015). Taking the history and performing the physical examination in a child with hearing loss. *Otolaryngology Clinics of North America, 48*, 903–912.

Dale, D. M. C. (1962). *Applied audiology for children.* Springfield, IL: Charles C. Thomas Publisher.

Dawes, P., & Bishop, D. (2009). Auditory processing disorder in relation to developmental disorders of language, communication, and attention: A review and critique. *International Journal of Language and Communication Disorders, 44*(4), 440–465.

Dawes, P., Bishop, D. V. M., Sirimanna, T., & Bamiou, D. E. (2008). Profile and aetiology of children diagnosed with auditory processing disorder (APD). *International Journal of Pediatric Otorhinolaryngology, 72*(4), 483–489.

Dockrell, J. E., & Shield, B. M. (2006). Acoustical barriers in classrooms: The impact of noise on performance in the classroom. *British Educational Research Journal, 32*(3), 509–525.

Flavell, J., Miller, P., & Miller, S. (2002). *Cognitive development* (4th ed.). Upper Saddle River, NJ: Pearson.

Franco, F. (1997). The developmental of meaning in infancy. In S. Hala (Ed.), *The development of social cognition* (pp. 95–148). New York, NY: Psychology Press.

Griffiths, T. D. (2002). Central auditory processing disorders. *Current Opinion in Neurology, 15*, 31–33.

Keith, R. W. (1999). Clinical issues in central auditory processing disorders. *Language, Speech, and Hearing Services in Schools, 30*(4), 339–344.

Kraus, N., & Anderson, S. (2016). Auditory processing disorder: Biological basis and treatment efficacy. In C. G. Le Prell, E. Lobarinas, A. N. Popper, & R. R. Fay (Eds.), *Translational research in audiology, neurotology, and the hearing sciences* (pp. 51–80). Switzerland: Springer.

Marttila, J. (2004). Listening technologies for individuals and the classroom. *Topics in Language Disorders, 24*(1), 31–50.

Matkin, N. D., & Wilcox, A. M. (1999). Considerations in the education of children with hearing loss. *Pediatric Clinics of North America, 46*(1), 143–152.

Mayer, C. (2007). What really matters in the early literacy development of deaf children. *Journal of Deaf Studies and Deaf Education, 12*(4), 411–431.

Moore, D. R., Ferguson, M. A., Edmondson-Jones, A. M., Ratib, S., & Riley, A. (2010). Nature of auditory processing disorder in children. *Pediatrics, 126*(2), e382–e390.

Northern, J. L. (2001). Hearing and hearing loss in children. In J. L. Northern & M. P. Downs (eds.), *Hearing in children* (5th ed., p. 21). Baltimore, MD: Lippincott Williams and Wilkins.

Picard, M., & Bradley, J. S. (2001). Revisiting speech interference in classroom. *Audiology, 40*(5), 221–244.

Rosenberg, G. G. (2010). Classroom acoustics. *Seminars in Hearing, 31*(3), 188–202.

Smith, R. J. H., & Gooj, A. (2019) Hearing loss in children: Screening and evaluation. In *Up to Date Online*. Philadelphia, PA: Wolters Kluwer. Retrieved from https://www.uptodate.com/contents/hearing-loss-in-children-screening-and-evaluation

Stevens, G., Flaxman, S., Brunskill, E., Mascarenhas, M., Mathers, C. D., & Finucane, M. (2011). Global and regional hearing impairment prevalence: An analysis of 42 studies in 29 countries. *European Journal of Public Health 23*(1), 146–152.

Theunissen, S. C., Rieffe, C., Kouwenberg, M., De Raeve, L. J., Soede, W., Briaire, J. J., & Frijns, J. H. (2014). Behavioral problems in school-aged hearing-impaired children: the influence of sociodemographic, linguistic, and medical factors. *European Child & Adolescent Psychiatry, 23*(4), 187–196.

Winiger, A. M., Alexander, J. M., & Diefendorf, A. O. (2016). Minimal hearing loss: From a failure-based approach to evidence-based practice. *American Journal of Audiology, 25*, 232–245.

Yost, W. A. (2013a). Auditory perception. In W. A. Yost (Ed.), *Fundamentals of hearing: An introduction*. Leiden, the Netherlands: Brill.

Yost, W. A. (2013b). The world we hear, an introduction. In W. A. Yost (Ed.), *Fundamentals of hearing: An introduction*. Leiden, the Netherlands: Brill.

## APPENDIX 2.1 Hearing Skills Framework

The Hearing Skills Framework is summarized here. School professionals can use this form as a quick reference for the skill sets and skills that need to be taken into consideration when making observations and developing an intervention plan.

| Structures and skill sets | Structures, functions, and skills | Examples of functions and skills in action | Sample medical conditions or performance difficulties | Potential interventions, strategies, accommodations, or educational objectives |
|---|---|---|---|---|
| Auditory structures | External ear | The external ear (pinna) reduces the effect of interfering sound waves while the external ear canal enhances delivery of signal to the ear drum and middle ear. | Malformation in the external ear can impair noise-reducing and signal-amplifying functions of the external ear. | Improve signal-to-noise ratio by modifying classroom acoustics and/or by use of signal-enhancing systems |
| | Middle ear | The middle ear contains the three auditory ossicles, which transmit the physical energy of sound waves to the inner ear. | Middle ear fluid can interfere with the function of the ossicles.<br>Damage to the ossicles can interfere with the transmission of physical sound wave energy to the inner ear. This is referred to as *conductive hearing loss*. | Placement of pressure-equalizing (PE) tubes to ensure normal function of the ossicles.<br>Hearing aid, frequency modulator (FM) system, or other amplification system<br>Optimize classroom acoustics by reducing ambient noise and/or by improving the signal-to-noise ratio. |
| | Inner ear | The inner ear accepts physical energy of sound waves and transduces (transforms) this energy into neurological impulses. | Damage to the inner ear prevents the formation of neurological impulses. This is referred to as sensory-neural hearing loss. The hearing loss can reduce the capacity to hear sounds at different intensities (decibels) and at different frequencies (hertz). | Use of amplification systems, such as a hearing aid, an FM system, among others, can help to amplify those sounds that remain audible. Cochlear implants can partially reverse the inner ear's inability to transduce sound waves into neurological impulses.<br>Use of visual cues or sign language may be needed. |
| | Auditory nerve | The auditory nerve accepts neurological impulses as transduced by the inner ear. It then shares these neurological impulses with the auditory cortex and other parts of the brain. | Damage to the auditory nerve cannot be reversed.<br>Residual hearing is amplified through use of amplification systems. | Use of visual cues or sign language may be needed.<br>Some students may benefit from tactile cues if they are also visually impaired. |
| Auditory functions | Decibels/ intensity | The ability to hear all sounds, soft and loud, through the normal range of hearing | Hearing loss in one or both ears, for soft sounds or for both soft and loud sounds<br>Hearing loss can range from mildly impaired (loud sounds remain audible) to profoundly impaired (even loud sounds are not audible). | Use of hearing aids to amplify sounds across all frequencies<br>Teachers and peers can modify speech so that it is louder or more clearly articulated to ensure improved hearing and listening. Visual cues may be needed.<br>Teachers and peers can modify their position in relation to the student's ears to maximize hearing in the better-hearing ear.<br>Improve classroom acoustics by reducing ambient noise or through the use of amplification systems. |

| Structures and skill sets | Structures, functions, and skills | Examples of functions and skills in action | Sample medical conditions or performance difficulties | Potential interventions, strategies, accommodations, or educational objectives |
|---|---|---|---|---|
| | Frequency/ pitch | The ability to hear all sounds, low frequency to high frequency, through the normal range of human hearing | Hearing loss for certain frequencies, such as low frequency or high frequency hearing loss | Use of hearing aids to amplify those frequencies that are the most affected<br>Teachers and peers can modify speech to be higher or lower in pitch to ensure improved hearing and listening; visual cues may be needed.<br>Teachers and peers can modify their position in relation to the student's ears, to maximize hearing in the better-hearing ear.<br>Improve classroom acoustics by reducing ambient noise or through the use of amplification systems. |
| | Temporal aspects of sound and hearing | The capacity to recognize and differentiate sound patterns<br>Sounds are made up of different patterns of loudness (decibels), and pitch (frequency), and also include sound gaps (no sound). These (temporal) patterns extend over milliseconds, hundreds of milliseconds, and seconds.<br>Differences in these patterns allow for the differentiation of sound sources, such as speech sounds, animal noises, noises made by objects, noises made by musical instruments. | The student may be able to detect sounds but not be able to differentiate between different types of sounds, (e.g., inability to differentiate between speech sounds, animal sounds, or sounds produced by musical instruments). This type of impairment would normally be associated with a severe hearing loss. | Use of visual cues and sign language may be needed.<br>Teachers and peers can modify speech, as indicated previously.<br>Improve classroom acoustics by reducing ambient noise or through the use of amplification systems. |
| Auditory processing skills | Temporal aspects of sound and hearing | Capacity to differentiate between similar sounds. For example, the capacity to differentiate male and female voice, between two male speakers, between sounds made by two woodwind instruments, and/or between the sounds made by two different dogs. | The student may have difficulty in detecting differences in sounds such as those listed previously. For example, loss of hearing at certain frequencies can make it more difficult to differentiate speech sounds produced by two different male speakers. | Train auditory processing skills to enhance auditory processing in unfavorable listening environments. |
| | Binaural skills and sound localization | The capacity to localize a sound source | The student may not be able to identify whether a sound source is on the left or the right side. Students with unilateral hearing loss are at risk for this type of difficulty. | Train auditory skills to be able to localize sounds when the source is not visible and/or when the source is moving. For example, make use of changes in head or body position, make use of visual cues and/or auditory closure skills to help identify sources of sound in different locations and when those sources are moving. |

*(continued)*

| Structures and skill sets | Structures, functions, and skills | Examples of functions and skills in action | Sample medical conditions or performance difficulties | Potential interventions, strategies, accommodations, or educational objectives |
|---|---|---|---|---|
| | | The capacity to localize a sound source and estimate its distance away from the listener | The student may not be able to identify and localize a sound source that is coming from a different room or that is not visible. | |
| | | The capacity to localize a sound source that is moving | The student may have difficulty identifying and localizing a sound source when the sound source is moving, such as a moving car. | |
| | Binaural skills and the fusion and separation of sounds | The capacity to discriminate signal (speech) sounds from background (ambient) noise | The student may have difficulty discriminating signal from ambient noise.<br>The student may have difficulty discriminating signal from ambient noise when the speech signal is degraded or when the acoustics are not favorable.<br>Many young students can have difficulties such as the ones listed here. | Train binaural skills to help discriminate speech sounds from other sounds.<br>Teach the use of visual cues to enhance hearing and listening.<br>Improve signal-to-noise ratio by use of an FM or sound field system.<br>Increase or enhance the signal-to-noise ratio by improving classroom acoustics.<br>Change teacher/peer behaviors so that they speak more slowly, provide more visual cues, and check for comprehension more often. |
| | Auditory closure | The capacity to detect and interpret sound sources even when the sound signal is degraded—for example, the capacity to hear and understand degraded speech from a poor audio recording, during poor telephone reception, or from poorly articulated or highly accented speech | The student may have difficulty identifying and interpreting sound sources, especially when these are unfamiliar. They are less able to guess at or know about the nature of a sound if the signal is not optimal, or to understand suboptimal speech sounds or accented speech. | Teach the use of auditory closure to help students anticipate sounds; make use of visual and tactile cues to interpret sounds.<br>Change teacher/peer behaviors so that they speak more slowly, provide more visual cues, and check for comprehension more often. |

APPENDIX 2.2 **Hearing Skills Observation Sheet**

| Structures and skill sets | Functions and skills | Example skills or deficits in this student | Potential interventions, strategies, accommodations, or educational objectives |
|---|---|---|---|
| Auditory structures | External ear | | |
| | Middle ear | | |
| | Inner ear | | |
| | Auditory nerve | | |
| Auditory functions | Decibels/ intensity | | |
| | Frequency/ pitch | | |
| | Temporal aspects of sound and hearing | | |
| Auditory processing skills | Temporal aspects of sound and hearing | | |
| | Binaural skills and sound localization | | |
| | Binaural skills and the fusion and separation of sounds | | |
| | Auditory closure | | |

# Motor Skills



## INTRODUCTION AND GENERAL DEFINITIONS

Chapters 1 and 2 reviewed the neurological frameworks of vision and hearing. As with vision and hearing, it is difficult to overemphasize the importance of the motor system. The motor system is important for survival. In order for humans to survive in the world, they have to perform motor actions. These actions emerge very early in life and include actions such as eating, walking, and speaking. The motor system is also critical in learning. Complex actions, such as writing or performing adaptive, vocational, and/or recreational tasks, all reflect learning. For the student, motor impairment can affect participation in learning and the ability to show what was learned. Speech and more subtle behaviors such as smiling, frowning, and gesturing also have to be learned or acquired. Without the motor system, pragmatic language skills are affected and communication is less clear. The motor system is key to survival, but it also allows for learning, for communication, and for expressing what was learned.

The motor system does not just respond to information and to cognition. It does not merely reflect or respond to what was learned. The motor system also influences what the brain knows and how the brain thinks. Through movement, the brain discovers new experiences that can result in acquiring new knowledge. Motor activity therefore affects thought and can improve cognition (Sibley & Etnier, 2003). Motor activity may be especially important in improving self-regulation (den Heijer et al., 2017; Pirrie & Lodewiyk, 2012). Although it is difficult to show the causal relations between movement and cognition (Zach, Shoval, & Lidor, 2017), there exists a rich literature that shows how student performance improves when students participate in physical activities (Howie & Russell, 2012). The converse is also true: Motor performance difficulties are highly correlated with academic and cognitive performance difficulties (Houwen, Visser, van der Putten, & Vlaskamp, 2016; Lopes, Santos, Pereira, & Lopes, 2013). It is important to know that students with diverse types of disabilities commonly have motor impairments and motor performance difficulties (Pieters et al., 2012). These performance difficulties can be the result of issues in physical structures and functions, such as low muscle tone (hypotonia), joint laxity (looseness), or spasticity (muscle contraction causing stiffness or tightness). These difficulties may also be related to problems in the coordination of movement or in understanding how to use the motor system (i.e., cognition) (Fournier, Hass, Naik, Lodha, & Cauraugh, 2010; Shetreat-Kline, M., Shinner, S., & Rapin, I., 2014; Vuijk, Harman, Scherder, & Visscher, 2010; Webster, Majnemer, Platt, & Shevell, 2005).

Motor impairments in students with disabilities are sometimes overlooked because other aspects of the student's disability are prioritized. For example, a student's learning disability or diagnosis of autism may become the focus of the IEP, whereas motor performance difficulties are not taken into full consideration. Practitioners should always consider motor performance difficulties in any student with a disability. All students should learn how to use the motor system and should participate in movement to the best of their ability (Fournier et al., 2010; Lopes et al., 2013; Zwicker, Missiuma, & Boyd, 2009). An intact and well-functioning motor system is important to successful performance in the world. Taking into account all the literature on motor skills and cognition, the Centers for Disease Control and Prevention (CDC) recommends daily physical education or activities to help improve academic performance (U.S. Department of Health and Human Services, 2010) and to prevent obesity (Lambourne & Donnelly, 2011). These recommendations apply equally to students with intact motor skills and to students with motor performance difficulties.

## HOW THIS FRAMEWORK WAS CONSTRUCTED

The Motor Skills Framework is based on commonly used terms related to motor structures and functions on the one hand and motor skills and abilities on the other. The Motor Skills Framework provides terms that are useful in describing a student's motor performance. These terms are borrowed from literature in physical and occupational therapy, developmental disabilities, and developmental medicine.

### Motor System Terminology Depends on the Purpose of the Terms

The terminology used to describe aspects of the motor system can vary, depending on the purpose of the definitions. Terms related to the motor system may be used to describe anatomical features of the motor system (e.g., nerves, muscles, ligaments, joints, and bones) or to describe muscle functions (e.g., contraction and relaxation, range of motion, or strength). The motor system can also be described according to the types of movements that it produces. The terms *motor pattern* or *movement pattern* refer to the types of movements produced by the body. These terms are useful because they break movement (a fluid phenomenon) into recognizable components or units.

Movement is sometimes described in terms of its function or purpose instead of the underlying movement patterns. For example, professionals might speak about a student's handwriting skills or dressing skills as an identifiable type of movement. Handwriting and dressing skills are certainly critical, but they are not a motor or movement pattern. They are the result of sequences of movement patterns. Finally, movement is controlled by the brain and depends upon cognition. The cognitive aspects of movement are referred to as *motor control* and include components such as visual spatial awareness, comprehension of the purpose of the task at hand, and prior knowledge and experience. All these aspects of the motor system are considered in the framework and should be considered in working with students.

### The Motor Skills Framework Takes Into Consideration Patterns of Development

The framework takes into consideration the four aspects of the motor system introduced above: Structures and functions, movement patterns, movement sequences (also referred to as functional movement sequences), and motor control. Consistent with the other frameworks in this book, motor skills are described in a hierarchy that is based on observable behaviors that emerge during typical early childhood development. Movement in young children emerges in relatively predictable ways. Sitting, standing, walking, and running are all movement patterns. They emerge during typical childhood development in roughly the order listed. Similarly, reaching, swatting, grabbing, and pincer control are movement patterns that also emerge roughly in the order listed. The reader is invited to consider the typical developmental trajectory of movement patterns as one organizing principle for the Motor Skills Framework. See Box 3.1.

The framework synthesizes key ideas from typical motor development and uses these ideas to help describe movement more accurately.

Key texts and review articles used to construct this framework include those by Barnett (2008); Burton and Miller (1998); Campbell (1994); Carr and Shepherd (2000); Gallahue and Ozmun (2002); Kramer and Hinojosa (2010); Tecklin (1999); and Wilson (2005).



### BOX 3.1. Developmental Patterns in the Acquisition of Movement

**Proximal to Distal**

Core muscles of the spine, abdomen, and pelvis (proximal muscles) must develop before peripheral (distal) muscles can be put to effective use. Humans develop postural control (control of the spine) before they develop control over peripheral movement (movement of the head, arms, and legs).

**Gross Movement Patterns Versus Small or Fine Movement Patterns**

Motor development proceeds from using large and less accurate movement patterns before proceeding to smaller, more refined, and more precise movement patterns. For instance, walking with a broad gait is a larger and less accurate movement pattern than walking on a balance beam or walking as part of a dance performance. Reaching and swatting are larger and less accurate movements than reaching for and picking up a pencil. Crumpling a piece of paper is a larger and less accurate movement pattern than folding a piece of paper to produce an origami swan.

**Complexity and Differentiation of Movement Patterns**

Motor skills proceed from simpler motor and movement patterns to more complex patterns. In the course of development, basic patterns are combined with one another to produce more complex patterns. Depending on environmental demands and opportunities, children will develop motor patterns differently. Access to play items, to people, and to different places all influence how movement becomes differentiated and refined.

**Increasing Control Over Force and Speed in Movement**

As people master new motor skills, they gain increasing control over force and speed. When children first learn how to walk, they do not have control over the speed. With age, they learn to walk and run more quickly. As they age further, they learn to control the speed of walking to suit the circumstances, moving both quickly and slowly as the need arises. When reaching and swatting, people show less control over force and speed than when they reach precisely to pick up a pencil. When holding a pencil, they first show less control over the force and speed of use than occurs with later practice. These early emerging patterns apply equally to learning to play basketball, ski, or how to play the piano.

**Purpose: Stability, Locomotion, and Object Manipulation**

Over the course of typical child development, movement patterns develop to provide stability and support before they develop to provide locomotion and object manipulation. Stability (e.g., stable sitting or stable standing) is needed for locomotion and object manipulation to become possible (e.g., manipulating objects in the hands, catching a ball). In turn, locomotion can improve stability. For example, when a child has peers and a ball to play with, he or she has to learn how to combine object manipulation skills such as throwing and catching with a locomotion skill (running). The child's stability patterns are stressed in play activities such as these. In the process, they also mature. Similarly, when a child is provided with a pencil and asked to write, prolonged sitting is also required. In both examples, new movement patterns help to develop greater stability, and vice versa.

## HOW CAN THIS FRAMEWORK HELP ME?

As shared in the sections above, discussion of a student's motor performance requires an understanding of the different components of the motor system and how those components develop with age and with practice. It is often easy to identify a student's motor performance as normal as opposed to not normal or skilled as opposed to clumsy. However, these descriptive terms are not very precise and do not lead to well-targeted intervention strategies. The goal of this framework is to help school professionals describe differences in motor performance accurately and clearly. The description has to reflect differences in the less mature versus the more mature performance of children and youth.

Describing to colleagues what has been observed requires a shared set of terms and definitions. This chapter provides a framework to describe motor performance and motor performance difficulties using a set of terms that are more precise and help identify the student's motor skills and needs. The framework offers a common understanding for teams to discuss and analyze formal assessment findings among themselves, with the student, and with the student's family. Finally, the Motor Skills Framework can be used to organize educational goals, objectives, and strategies to help the student improve her or his motor performance.

## MOTOR SKILLS FRAMEWORK: TERMS AND DEFINITIONS

As with vision and hearing skills, motor activities require intact motor structures and motor functions. Motor structures include the nerves, muscles, ligaments, joints, and bones of the musculoskeletal system. Motor functions include the capacity of muscles to shorten and lengthen. Movement is possible because of motor structures and functions.

All infants are born with motor structures and motor functions. Some of the developments in movement after birth emerge so spontaneously that they may appear to be neurologically based and an expression of nature only. Examples include developing the social smile, reaching with the arm to touch a caregiver's face, and rolling from supine (face upwards) to prone (face downwards), amongst other early movement skills. Although these types of skills emerge so spontaneously in life, they are considered to reflect stimulation by the environment. They are the result of nurture acting on nature. Authors make the distinction between nature and nurture by referring to this type of movement as functional movement (Campbell, 1994) or as movement skills (Burton & Miller, 1998). This chapter uses the term *movement skills* in order to stress the importance of environmental stimulation (nurture) and the types of interventions normally used in the school setting. Movement skills will be discussed in terms of their patterns, sequences, force, and speed. As is true for all the frameworks of this book, the terms are presented in a hierarchy that progresses from least to most complex. The framework is summarized and available in Appendix 3.1 for quick reference.

The Motor Skills Framework includes the following terms and definitions:

1. Motor structures
2. Motor functions
3. Movement patterns
    a. Rudimentary movement patterns
    b. Fundamental movement patterns
    c. Differentiated movement patterns

4. Functional movement sequences
5. Motor control: Nonmotor aspects of movement
    a. Control of speed and force in movement
    b. Spatial awareness (use of visual, auditory, proprioceptive, and vestibular information)
    c. Executive skills
    d. Motivation
    e. Comprehension



These terms and concepts are explained in the sections that follow.

## Motor Structures

Motor structures are the nerves, muscles, ligaments, joints, and bones that make up the musculoskeletal system. Intact nerves, muscles, ligaments, joints, and bones are needed for normal movement to occur. All muscles are present at birth, but they continue to grow after birth. Increases in muscle length and size occur as joints, ligaments, and bones also grow.

## Motor Functions

Motor functions are the involuntary and voluntary movement of muscle fibers. In order to contract and relax voluntarily, muscles must be connected to nerves that communicate with the central nervous system. Contraction and relaxation result in shorter and longer muscles, respectively. When muscles shorten or lengthen, they create movement over a joint. With increasing age, there is ever greater control over ever smaller portions of the motor system. Ever more refined movement is possible because the central nervous system has more and more differentiated control over smaller and smaller numbers of muscle fibers. This differentiated control comes with neurological development, increasing awareness, and practice and experience.

## Movement Patterns

Movement always occurs in patterns and is therefore more complex than are muscle functions. First, muscles do not contract or relax in isolation. A single muscle always moves in relation to and alongside other muscles. For instance, flexing and extending at the elbow requires both the biceps and the triceps muscle, as well as the actions of other muscles, to move. Movement occurs when clusters of muscle fibers, muscles, or groups of muscles move together. Very often, as one muscle or muscle group contracts, another muscle or muscle group has to relax. This pattern holds for peripheral muscles and for central muscles. When these combinations of contraction and relaxation occur, a physical change occurs in posture, position, and/or location. Movement occurs when a collection of muscles relaxes and contracts together and produces movement over one or several joints.

*Movement patterns* is the term given to the cluster of muscle groups that move at any given point in time. It is a way to describe the components or units of movement. In the example above, the movement pattern is the flexion and extension of the elbow. A movement pattern typically includes a description of the purpose of the movement. Flexion and extension of the elbow occur during the movement patterns of grabbing or throwing, for example. The movement pattern could have another name if the purpose were different. For example, elbow flexion and extension also occur during hammering. Important or common movement patterns that are the subject of observation and analysis during a physical or occupational therapy evaluation include sitting, standing, walking, running, jumping, hopping, skipping, throwing, catching, grasping, and manipulating. All these movement patterns are identified by the purpose that they serve, not by their anatomical features. It is not possible to label all the different purposes that movement can have, as purposes of movement can be nearly limitless. It is also not practical to describe all the different anatomical components that the same movement can have. Movement patterns shift and change depending on the circumstances. See Box 3.2 for a description of different types of movement patterns. One way to organize and label movement patterns is to identify them as stability patterns, locomotion patterns, and object manipulation patterns. Commonly, all three purposes for movement are present in any movement pattern. The simple categorization scheme proposed in Box 3.2 may be useful in labeling movement patterns not specifically discussed in this chapter. All professionals involved in observing movement will find these terms useful.

### BOX 3.2. How to Describe and Identify Movement Patterns

The following terms can be helpful in the description or categorization of movement patterns:

**Stability**

All purposeful movement patterns depend on movement in some joints, with stability in others. Some muscles and joints must be kept stable so that others can move. In elbow extension and flexion, both movements require stability of the shoulder and the upper spine. Walking requires stability of the lower spine and pelvis.

The components of movement that are stable (head, shoulder, and spine) can be referred to as the postural aspect of the movement pattern. The terms *position* and *balance* are also used to describe the stability aspect of movement patterns. However, *stability* does not mean that there is no movement at all. In fact, stability is itself a type of movement. Stability requires small changes in the relaxation and contraction of opposing muscles as the center of gravity changes during movement. The main difference between stability and postural control (during which movement is not always visible) and other movement patterns such as walking or reaching (during which movement is visible) is that the movement that underlies posture and stability is very subtle. It may not be immediately visible, even though it is indeed a movement.

Posture and stability are not just expressed in the vertical plane; they are expressed in all planes. A stable posture is just as important to maintain in the vertical position for sitting and standing as it is in the horizontal position during push-ups or in the lateral plane during a boxing match or while performing a gymnastics routine on a balance beam. Even though stability is usually the work of core muscles, such as the spinal, abdominal, and pelvic muscles, stability can also be provided by distal muscles, joints, and bones. With age, humans develop postural control for an increasing number of body positions and body movements and also make use of the limbs to assist with positional control. During a headstand, for example, the hands and arms maintain stability as much as the core muscles do. During bimanual tasks, one hand confers stability (e.g., to hold a jar or to hold down a piece of paper), while the other hand moves (e.g., to open the jar's lid or to manipulate a pencil).

**Locomotion**
Movement through space is referred to as *locomotion.* Humans move past objects and through space. Typically, we think of locomotion as a function of the legs. Walking and running are the most efficient ways to move through space. However, locomotion can also occur through creeping, crawling, or rolling on the ground. Locomotion can occur using the arms, such as doing a walking handstand, or using the hands and arms on a jungle gym.

**Object Manipulation**
Humans move objects in space. This third aspect of movement is *object manipulation.* Movement of objects can occur with any part of the body. It can occur over large distances or over only a millimeter or two. When using the large muscles of the body, object manipulation can consist of pushing the body against an object, using either the arms or the back. When using the legs, it can involve kicking a ball. When using the hands, it can mean opening jar or producing handwriting or playing an instrument.

**Identifying and Describing Specific Movement Patterns**
Each of the three primary descriptors—stability, locomotion, and object manipulation—apply to a nearly limitless number of movement patterns. The challenge for the observer who wishes to describe movement patterns is in isolating them into individual actions when movement is so fluid. Movement patterns shift and change without clearly defined boundaries between them. Even when a movement pattern is identified, it takes some judgment to decide which muscles and joints are involved and how to break the pattern down into the components of stability, locomotion, and object manipulation. Just as movement patterns are difficult to separate from one another, so too are the functions of stability, locomotion, and object manipulation difficult to separate.

The sections that follow introduce some of the basic movement patterns that emerge in typical early childhood development. These movement patterns are often identified and subject to analysis by physical and occupational therapists and other specialists.

***Random Movements and Reflexes*** Stability and movement can be identified starting at the beginning of life. The newborn has very limited stability and shows much more random than purposeful movement. Some of the seemingly organized movement patterns seen in newborns are actually reflexive in nature and do not serve a conscious purpose or goal. The grasping reflex (infant closes the hands when the palm is stroked) and the Moro reflex (infant spreads the arms rapidly and then brings them together when jolted or jostled) are two examples of reflex behaviors that appear functional but do not have a conscious or purposeful goal. Only several weeks after birth do stability and purposeful movement emerge. Once stability (e.g., postural control of the neck or back) emerges as a movement skill, the infant can start to move the body in more purposeful ways. Purposeful movement in the infant can include opening and closing the hands, reaching for a mobile or for the caregiver's face, rolling, pushing up by the hands and arms, or sitting.

***Basic or Rudimentary Movement Patterns*** The basic or rudimentary movement patterns serve as building blocks for more complex movement patterns that develop later. Those that emerge within the first year of life include the following:

1. Rolling
2. Sitting

3. Crawling (using the arms and shoulders to slide the rest of the body along the floor)
4. Creeping (on hands and knees, using the arms and legs to move across the floor)
5. Standing
6. Cruising (walking while holding on to a support such as the edge of a table or a handrail)
7. Reaching (overhand movement of the arms to bring the hand close to an object)
8. Grabbing (fingers and thumb all close together to hold on to an object)
9. Rake grasp (fingers hold on to an object, separately from the thumb)
10. Use of the thumb against the other fingers in grasping.

A majority of the movement patterns in the first year of life reflect improvements in stability (i.e., improved ability to maintain a posture, a position, or balance). Stability patterns are considered movement patterns even though they involve only limited movement; see Box 3.2. These movement patterns have very limited locomotion or object manipulation functions. Locomotion and object manipulation are not the primary skills achieved during the first year.

***Fundamental Movement Patterns*** Fundamental movement patterns emerge during the toddler and preschool years. They are possible because rudimentary movement patterns are already in place. Fundamental movement patterns require the stability developed during the first year but are more clearly examples of locomotion and object manipulation. Locomotion includes the following:

1. Walking
2. Running
3. Jumping
4. Hopping
5. Skipping

Object manipulation includes the following:

1. The ability to kick, catch, and push objects
2. Pincer grasp (index finger opposed to the thumb)
3. One-hand skills: Crushing, crumpling, squeezing (e.g., one-hand skills useful for holding a spoon or a cup)
4. Bimanual skills: Holding an object securely in one hand while performing an action on the object with the other hand (e.g., holding a container to open the lid of a jar, securing a piece of paper in order to print or write, holding a pencil in a mature grasp while forming legible letters and words)

***Differentiated Movement Patterns*** Movement patterns must become more refined, or more differentiated, in order to be useful in different contexts and under different conditions. Differentiated movement patterns consist of more refined rudimentary and fundamental movement patterns. They also consist of a larger repertoire of movement patterns that help link rudimentary and fundamental movement patterns. The transition from rudimentary to fundamental to differentiated movement patterns does not involve any clear cutoff points. The following sections provide some examples of how movement patterns become more differentiated.

*Different Conditions* Movement patterns are differentiated when used under different conditions. For example, walking first emerges as a skill at approximately 13 months of age. However, walking looks quite different in a 13-month-old than it does in a 6-year-old. The gait is initially wide based and with age, it becomes narrower and more secure. As walking becomes more differentiated, there is less extraneous movement of the upper body because of improved upper body control. More differentiated walking occurs as a child develops a narrower base of support, which is important as a child learns to walk on uneven surfaces or when a child learns to walk on a balance beam. Differentiation of movement patterns is also required when movement has to occur within a moving environment, such as when walking inside a moving bus, when crossing the street and avoiding cars, and when playing sports with a moving ball and navigating among moving team players.

Object manipulation using upper limb and hand movements also serves to illustrate differentiation. For example, grasping becomes more differentiated when children learn to grasp a piece of paper rather than a spoon or cup. Similarly, grasping also becomes more differentiated when grasping a heavy cup with a large handle that is filled with water. The grasp has to be firm and requires use of the whole hand. In contrast, the grasp required for holding an empty, smaller cup with a small handle does not need to be as firm and might not need to make use of the whole hand.

*Combinations of Movement Patterns* Differentiation of movement patterns occurs when movement patterns are combined. By interacting with the environment, the infant and toddler create complex movement patterns from basic movement patterns. Walking is paired with turning the body or the head. Walking is transformed into running, which is then combined with turning the head and body to play tag. Running is combined with throwing and catching while also turning and stopping to play sports. All of these developments involve greater differentiation of rudimentary and fundamental movement patterns: All of them involve greater differentiation of stability, locomotion, and object manipulation. Differentiation of stability movements occurs when stability is needed to maintain posture and balance in the vertical, horizontal, and lateral planes. Differentiation and improvements in locomotion occur as the legs and arms are used to help move the body through space. Differentiation and improvements in object manipulation occur as arms, legs, and hands are all used to move objects through the environment.

*Linking of Movement Patterns Using Transitional Movement Patterns* When embedded into a sequence, motor patterns also become more differentiated. Movement patterns must be adjusted and refined, so that they can be linked with the movement that occurred just before and just after the movement pattern under analysis. Transitional movement patterns help link rudimentary and fundamental movement patterns, allowing for movement in sequence or series. See Box 3.3 to learn more about how movement patterns can become more and more differentiated with age and experience.

**BOX 3.3. An Analysis of Walking: A Fundamental Movement Pattern**

Walking is a fundamental movement pattern. The movement pattern consists of stability at the lower back and the pelvis, accompanied by alternating forward and backward movements of the upper legs at the pelvis. However, the motor pattern looks different with developmental improvements. It also looks different when environmental circumstances change. The following points help in understanding developmental improvements

*(continued)*

**BOX 3.3.** *(continued)*

in walking. Notice the types of adjustments that have to occur so that walking remains secure and purposeful under changing circumstances and for different purposes:

1. Upright posture. Upright posture has to be secure. The toddler should be able to use spinal and pelvic control to stand and not need the arms to maintain a stable posture.
2. Length of steps. Short steps become longer; step size becomes more controlled to suit the circumstances.
3. Base of support. Base of support is initially wide, and then narrows.
4. Initial movements. Initially, movements are jerky and involve whole-body movement. With improvements, movements become smoother and the upper body no longer moves with the lower body.
5. Feet. Initially, feet land flat. With improvements, the heel lands before the toe makes contact with the floor.
6. Arms and upper body. Initially, arms and upper body might show a lot of movement. With improvements, arms are closer to the body and movement of the upper body is more and more limited.
7. Walking under different circumstances. Walking becomes possible on uneven surfaces, in a moving vehicle, on a balance beam, and while carrying heavy objects
8. Speed of walking. Speed of walking is more controlled.
9. Purpose of walking. Walking can be a stroll in the park, a power walk (i.e., rapid walk), or part of a theatrical performance. Walking becomes more and more differentiated as motor control influences how walking is applied in a particular environment or in a specific activity.

## Functional Movement Sequences

Movement typically occurs in sequences. Movement sequences consist of multiple, varied movement patterns that are linked with one another to reach a goal or produce an outcome. The movement sequence serves an adaptive, vocational, or recreational purpose. As examples, a motor sequence could be all of the movement patterns involved in the following: Getting dressed, completing personal hygiene, doing the laundry, performing a dance routine, or playing basketball. Breaking these activities down, consider that dressing involves use of the hands to grab and pull, while standing on one foot, lifting the other foot, and pushing the legs through a pair of pants or moving the arms through a shirt. During household tasks, a person may need to squat, stand up, lift, dump, wipe, or crawl on the knees. Many different movement patterns exist within a given movement sequence. To understand movement sequences, the observer has to carry out an analysis of all of the rudimentary and fundamental movement patterns that make up the sequence. See Box 3.4 for a more detailed discussion.

**BOX 3.4. Task Analysis and Movement Sequences**

Task analysis is the process of analyzing movements in sequence to produce a description of the movement patterns that make up a given activity. Task analysis is commonly applied to self-care activities and is often undertaken by an occupational therapist working with a student with a motor impairment. For example, the activity of drinking requires reaching, grabbing, holding the cup steady, bringing the cup to the mouth, tipping the cup, and making the oral motor movements of drinking. The activity of washing the hands requires turning on and off the faucet, adjusting the temperature of the water by manipulating the faucet, holding on to a bar of soap using the right amount of force (or pumping soap from a dispenser), making rolling motions of the soap between the two hands, placing the hands under the running water, turning off the faucet, and finally drying the hands. The purpose of the analysis is to identify all of the movement patterns needed to reach the goal.

The purpose of doing a task analysis for a student with a motor impairment might be to teach the student how to perform certain movement patterns so that he or she can complete the full sequence. The student may practice portions of the sequence by learning one movement pattern at a time. With practice, the student learns to link movement patterns and complete the entire sequence with greater and greater independence. Alternatively, the occupational therapist may need to find ways to adjust the demands on the student so that certain movement patterns are no longer needed. For example, the occupational therapist might decide to change the size of the handle of the cup, change the handles on the faucet, or make other modifications so that the student can reach the goal without having to perform all of the usual movement patterns.

The concept of task analysis can be applied to the analysis of movement more generally and can serve more than one purpose. The practitioner starts by identifying an adaptive, vocational, or recreational goal or purpose. The practitioner then analyzes the movement patterns needed to reach that goal or serve that purpose. When a student is not performing successfully, the practitioner then has to make some decisions. Should the student master the missing or underdevelopment movement patterns, so that she or he can reach the goal? Should the practitioner modify the movement sequence, so that the student no longer needs to perform all of the usual movement patterns? Is the purpose of therapy to reach the functional goal, such as drinking or dressing? Is the purpose of therapy to improve the student's movement patterns and to help the student master and differentiate new movement patterns? The answers to questions such as these depend on the student and the situation. For educators and other school professionals, the goal should be to identify the movement patterns needed for a specific outcome. In consultation with colleagues, educators and other school professionals can then decide what educational objectives are the right ones for the situation.

As explained in Box 3.4, the analysis of movement sequences can be used to help understand the motor skills and needs of students with a motor impairment. However, the analysis of movement sequences is not something that should apply only to a student with a motor impairment or even necessarily to students with learning difficulty. Analysis of movement sequences is useful for any student who is mastering a new skill. An analysis of basketball, for example, could consist of identifying the essential movement patterns of playing the game, including running (forward and backward), jumping, throwing, catching, dribbling, stopping, twisting, and stepping sideways. The instructor would teach the student about the different movement patterns required in basketball. The student would then practice those movement patterns as separate units, as linked units, and then as units linked into a series. The same logic applies to swimming, dance, gymnastics, and other team sports.

Even a seemingly simple and well-differentiated movement pattern, such as walking, might be the subject of task analysis when walking is integrated into a more complex movement sequence. For instance, an actor on the stage may need to differentiate walking in a more complex way to convey emotion or intention. He or she might stomp when walking to convey anger or tiptoe to convey the need for secrecy. Differences in the posture, in the size of the steps, in the speed of walking, and/or in the movements of other parts of the body (hunched shoulders, clenched fists, a facial grimace or smile) can all convey different emotions and different intentions in the simple act of walking. Several movement patterns, linked with walking, create a much more differentiated type of walking.

In the examples cited, the observer and the student can learn about component movements by analyzing movement sequences and their purpose. Through the analysis, both teacher and student can identify, practice, and master specific movement patterns. They can learn about how movement patterns are differentiated and refined depending on the purpose. They can discover how those movement patterns can be linked into a movement sequence, how to make links smoothly, and how to reach a functional goal. Control of speed and force, discussed in the next section, also influences the shape (appearance), fluency, and the functional outcome of the movement patterns.

## Motor Control

The aspects of movement discussed in the previous sections are dependent on intact nerves, muscle fibers, ligaments, joints, and bones. These aspects of movement also depend on the emergence of rudimentary, fundamental, and differentiated movement patterns. Most of these movement patterns emerge in most children as the environment places demands on the motor system. Children learn to reach, sit, stand, walk, run, and develop a pincer grasp because of environmental demands, opportunities, purposes, and goals that invite them to do so. These basic movement patterns become more differentiated as environmental demands and opportunities increase and as the child gains control over factors such as force and speed.

The skilled motor performance depends not only on a motor system that is responding to the environment, but also on an understanding of the purpose and the goals of the movement and how to best produce the right movement patterns and sequences for the environmental situation. This internalized understanding is referred to as *motor control*. Motor control is the capacity to choose the right movement patterns and sequences to respond successfully to the situation. Motor control includes factors such as control over force and speed, spatial awareness, executive skills, motivation, and overall cognition. Students with good motor control make use of these factors, as well as knowledge from prior experience, to make good decisions about how to use their motor system. Successful motor control also includes choosing the environment, the purposes, and the goals of the movement. Stated differently, movement requires an activation of the entire brain. Important components of motor control are discussed in the sections that follow. Be sure also to read Box 3.5 to learn more about how to assess motor control.

### BOX 3.5. What Does *Well-Coordinated* Mean? What Does *Clumsy* Mean?

An important aspect of motor control is the capacity to perform movement in a coordinated and efficient manner. It may be difficult to describe why one student's performance looks more coordinated or more efficient than the performance of another. One student's performance might appear better because the movements are more precise, refined, or complex. The untrained observer commonly refers to the difference as being more coordinated. The corollary is that the less skilled performance is often referred to as more clumsy. However, terms such as *less well-coordinated* or *more clumsy* are not very precise terms to use when the goal is to improve a student's motor performance. It is important to be able to describe the student's performance more accurately. By making good observations, a practitioner can identify the factors that account for a more coordinated or more clumsy performance.

To make good observations, it is important to know that differences in coordination are not always visible when observing a movement pattern in isolation. Be sure to observe several different movement patterns, not just one or two. Be sure to observe movement patterns during movement sequences, such as a dressing routine or a vocational task. Clumsiness may or may not show up when observing basic movement patterns such as walking and running. It might not even show up during basic movement sequences such as managing daily routines or participating in an exercise routine during a physical education class. Sometimes clumsiness or lack of coordination might show up only during a complex movement pattern (e.g., simultaneous jumping and throwing, simultaneous reaching and grasping with a pincer grasp). Clumsiness may show up only within longer sequences of movement (e.g., sports activities, vocational activities) or during unfavorable conditions such as movement that has to take place within a moving environment or within a confined space.

A well-coordinated performance is a performance that is more highly differentiated. Each movement pattern is more clearly differentiated from the next movement pattern. Movement patterns are linked more smoothly with one another. The mover uses just the right amount of force and speed to carry out the movement efficiently. A clumsy performance, in contrast, involves less clearly differentiated movement patterns. The transition between movement patterns during a movement sequence is slower or less precise. The overall efficiency is lower because of less control over force and speed.

Clumsiness can be due to more than one factor. It may occur because of problems with muscle tone or joint laxity. Clumsiness may also be due to lack of experience with certain movement patterns or movement sequences. Anyone who is learning a new movement pattern or movement sequence is likely to be clumsy. Finally, clumsiness may also be due to one or several motor control processes (spatial awareness, executive skills, motivation). The description just outlined applies to all learners: The preschooler who is learning how to get dressed, the school-age child who is learning about playing team sports at school, the child or adolescent who is learning how to ski for the first time, or the cook and the surgeon learning about the fine motor skills of their professions. Clumsiness and coordination occur for a reason. They can also be identified and described using the terms presented here.

Coordinated movement has the following features:

1. Precision. Movement patterns are clearly differentiated from one another and are also differentiated to suit the purposes of a specific situation.

2. Lack of extraneous movements. While one part of the body is moving, other parts of the body remain still or do not move. If other parts of the body are also moving, they are controlled differently or separately. When jumping, only the lower limbs are moving. When jumping while also throwing, the upper limbs are controlled separately from the lower limbs. Movement in the upper limbs does not affect the movement of the lower limbs.

3. Efficiency in reaching a goal. Only the necessary movement patterns and sequences are used in reaching the goal. There are no extraneous or excess movement patterns or sequences. Extraneous movements are avoided because of more precise control of movement in each part of the body. Extraneous movements are also avoided by analyzing movement sequences and using motor control processes to reduce the movement to its essentials. Movement sequences can be analyzed and reduced to only their most essential movement patterns while still reaching the goal.

Motor control is a broad concept that includes those factors not primarily related to muscles and joints. Motor control consists of the cognitive aspects of movement. Successful movement is dependent on many brain activities and many of the frameworks discussed in this book. In particular, successful movement is dependent on the skills in the following sections:

***Control of Speed and Force in Movement*** Part of the maturation in movement includes developing greater control over speed and force. The degree of differentiation of movement patterns, as well as the control of speed and force, distinguish the advanced performance in skiing, gymnastics, and dance (as examples) from the performance of the beginner. These same features of movement are true for a person completing activities of the daily routine (such as dressing and personal hygiene) or in a vocational task (such as repairing a bicycle). Any activity can be carried out as less or more differentiated. Any activity can be carried out slowly and clumsily or smoothly and precisely. Subtle differences in the force and speed of movement can distinguish the efficient and expert performance from the performance of the beginner.

***Spatial Awareness*** Vision, hearing, and vestibular and proprioceptive inputs all provide information about the position of the body and objects in space. The vestibular apparatus of the inner ear provides information about one's position in space (e.g., vertical, horizontal, or lateral position). Proprioceptive input refers to the awareness of the limbs in relation to one another and in relation to surrounding space. Hearing and vision enhance the information provided through the vestibular apparatus and through proprioceptive inputs. All this information is necessary for choosing the right movement patterns, movement sequences, force, and speed for a given situation. Spatial awareness helps determine how big the movement should be, how long the movement needs to continue, and how fast or forceful the movement should be.

***Executive Skills*** Movement has to be planned into sequences, and those sequences need to be carried out efficiently. As an example, learning how to play strategically in basketball relies on executive skills such as working memory. The player has to remember any strategies discussed with teammates prior to the game, remember the rules of the game, and also remember where players are located during the game in order to play successfully. Executive skills also apply to vocational tasks. In a vocational task, working memory and sequencing and planning are necessary to complete the task accurately and to reach the goal as intended. For example, a pastry chef has to master specialized movement patterns (measuring, mixing, pouring). All steps have to be completed successfully, and none can be left out. The component steps and their associated movement patterns have to be carried out in the correct order. The sequence should be carried out using the smallest number of steps possible. Without the executive skills of working memory, planning, and organizing (see Chapter 7 for definitions), there is a risk that the goal will not be reached. In a work environment, financial outcomes are especially dependent on efficiency.

***Motivation*** A person's state of emotional awareness and her or his motivation for a task can have a significant influence on the outcome of the motor skill or activity. A student's motivation for winning a baseball game (e.g., if he or she prefers reading books) or for making a cake (e.g., if she or he prefers playing soccer) will influence how much time the student takes to master the motor skills involved in playing basketball or baking. Motivation affects motor performance, because it influences how much practice time the student is likely to dedicate to the activity and how well the student will master the movement sequences required in each.

## PERFORMANCE DIFFICULTIES IN MOTOR SKILLS

One might think it is easy to identify the student with motor performance difficulties, but this is not always the case. To provide effective supports or interventions, school professionals need to consider more than what might be gleaned from an initial impression. Information needs to be gathered on which aspect of motor skills might be the most involved and on how the student's motor performance could be improved. To address performance difficulties effectively, the description of a student's motor performance should include a details of the student's motor structures and functions, movement patterns, movement sequences, and motor control. These aspects of movement should be considered and integrated into the development of objectives and strategies that can help to improve the student's motor performance.



### Impairments in Motor Structures and Motor Functions

Impairments in motor structures and functions can occur in the nerves, muscles, ligaments joints, and bones. An impairment can manifest as reduced range of motion, because of structural problems in the joints or ligaments or because of an impairment in muscle or central nervous system function. Sometimes reduced muscle tone and joint laxity result in greater difficulty differentiating movements and reduced motor control. Motor conditions such as cerebral palsy and hypotonia both reflect structural and functional impairments of the motor system. They can affect all of the aspects of movement discussed in this chapter. Developmental coordination disorder, another common medical condition, may also be related to impairments in motor structures and functions. However, some of the primary impairments in developmental coordination disorder may be attributed to other aspects of the motor system, such as executive skills or spatial awareness (i.e., components of motor control) (Barnett, 2008).

The novice practitioner is not expected to accurately identify impairments in the structures or functions of the motor system. A specialist, such as a physical or occupational therapist, can help identify these conditions and can help the student access health care services as needed. That said, all school professionals should be able to identify situations where impairments in motor structures and functions are likely and when specialist consultation is needed. Movement patterns are likely to be slow, jerky, or associated with extraneous movement. There may be an absence of movement in some parts of the body altogether.

### Performance Difficulties Related to Impairments in Movement Patterns

Impairments in motor structures and functions can cause impairments in rudimentary and fundamental movement patterns. These impairments can also occur when a student is mastering a new skill. When skills do not develop securely, it is more challenging for the student to show differentiation of movement, movement in sequences, and motor control. For example, a typically developing child first learns to walk and run before learning to play ball. While playing ball, the child needs to combine a previously secure fundamental skill (running) with grabbing, jumping, and throwing. In the process, the running looks less secure or less precise as the new movement patterns are incorporated into running. Similarly, as reaching and grabbing a cup is applied to cups of different sizes or that are filled with different volumes of water, the fundamental movement (grabbing) may look less secure. By observing the same movement pattern applied to new circumstances, it is possible to identify difficulties in the differentiation of movement. Difficulties in the differentiation of movement are important to identify in all students, those who are mastering a new skills, as well as those who should have mastered a skill a long time ago.

### Performance Difficulties Related to Movement Sequences

As in the execution of movement patterns, students are likely to have difficulty performing movements in sequence if they have not mastered the component movement patterns.

Problems can occur at any place within the sequence and may include several difficulties, not just one. The result is that important functional tasks do not get completed or are completed inefficiently. For example, even though a student may be able to perform parts of a dressing routine, his or her execution of the full sequence of getting dressed may be inefficient or incomplete.



## Performance Difficulties Related to Motor Control

Successful movement is dependent on many brain activities and many of the frameworks discussed in this book. Movement can be negatively affected and can look more clumsy or less well coordinated when vision, hearing, and vestibular inputs are not providing needed information to the motor system. The student cannot perform motor tasks as accurately, smoothly, or efficiently when these critical sensory inputs are not available. In such a student, fundamental movement patterns, such as walking or running, may be proficient. However, visual-motor demands required for dressing or for playing sports may be affected.

***Control of Speed and Control of Force*** Control of speed and force and the planning and organization of movement can be analyzed by looking at movement sequences. As movement patterns become more differentiated, they should also be associated with greater force and speed. Force and speed may apply most clearly to the successful athlete but may also apply to vocational tasks and even to handwriting. Force and speed contribute to both the differentiation and the efficiency of movement. Transitions between movement patterns are faster and more precise. Difficulties due to insufficient force and speed may manifest as a clumsy or inefficient performance. Videotaping can help to capture and analyze the observation. With practice, the student should show improvements in the control over force and speed.

***Spatial Awareness*** Vision, hearing, and vestibular and proprioceptive inputs all provide information about the position of the body and objects in space. The vestibular apparatus of the inner ear provides information about one's position in space (e.g., vertical, horizontal, lateral position). Proprioceptive input refers to the awareness of the limbs in relation to one another and in relation to surrounding space. Hearing and vision enhance the information provided through the vestibular apparatus and through proprioceptive inputs. All this information is useful for choosing the right movement patterns, movement sequences, force, and speed for a given situation. Spatial awareness helps determine how big the movement should be, how long the movement needs to continue, and how fast or forceful the movement should be. A student can have motor difficulties because of limited spatial awareness. In such a student, fundamental movement patterns, such as walking or running, may be proficient. However, visual-motor demands required for dressing or for playing sports may be affected.

***Executive Skills*** Underdeveloped executive skills and executive dysfunctions can affect the success of movement. Some students may not be able to participate in complex motor activities such as a game of basketball or soccer, because inattention and problems with working memory may affect how they use their motor system. They may not perform well in a vocational task because they may forget important steps, because they do not have the attention and focus to review their performance for error detection and error correction procedures, or because of poor planning. Some vocational and adaptive tasks have to be carried out in a specific order, without which the outcome is not successful. Motor performance difficulties may manifest as a result of difficulties in executive skills and not just because of a motor impairment.

***Motivation*** Finally, motivation can influence how well motor patterns and motor tasks are carried out and completed. A student who lacks the motivation to perform well, due to unsuccessful past attempts, may not desire to attempt new movement patterns or new adaptive or vocational tasks. Motivation affects motor performance, because it influences how much practice time the student is likely to dedicate to the activity and how well the student will master the required movement sequences.

## HOW TO SET UP AN OBSERVATION OF MOTOR SKILLS

The practitioner should select naturalistic activities to make observations of the student and to learn about the student's neurodevelopmental foundations, focusing on a student's motor foundations. Motor performance difficulties occur in many students with disabilities and often co-occur with disorders such as autism, intellectual disability, learning disabilities, and attention-deficit disorders.



### Select a Student

To get started, school personnel should identify the student whose motor performance requires closer examination. It can be useful to observe movement patterns in many or most of the students already identified as having a disabling condition. Motor performance difficulties are commonly encountered in children and youth with diverse disabilities. It is also useful to analyze movement patterns in students as they master new skills, regardless of disability status. The purpose of the observation is to generate a good description of the student's current movement patterns and sequences and to use the description for educational planning purposes. If the analysis suggests motor performance difficulties, a formal evaluation with a specialist such as a physical or occupational therapist should be considered.

### A Special Note About Students With Impairments in Motor Structures or Functions

Educators and other school professionals do not need to be able to accurately identify problems with motor structures or functions. However, they should know when to ask if motor structures or motor functions are the underlying cause of the student's motor performance difficulties. Students with substantial motor impairments may have very limited mobility, for example, in the case of malformations or injury to bones, ligaments, or joints. Spasticity and hypotonia are two common motor functions that can be the cause of motor performance difficulties. Joint laxity and excess mobility over a joint are also relatively common. Quivering, random, or sudden jerky motions not under the control of the student are signs of problems in motor structures and functions. When educators encounter motor impairments such as the ones listed here, it is more likely that specialist consultation will be needed.

### Select the Motor Activities to Be Observed

Observation of movement should occur during different activities. For any given function or purpose, the school professional should observe movement at all levels of complexity: Rudimentary movement patterns, fundamental movement patterns, differentiation of the movement patterns, and movement sequences. Practitioners should also consider aspects of motor control, such as speed and force of movement, planning and efficiency of movement, and whether the movement sequences reach their intended purpose or goal. Movement usually happens very quickly. Professionals new to conducting these targeted observations may find it easier to conduct the observation by viewing the student's performance on video. Alternatively, professionals can focus on a handful of motor activities that commonly occur during the school day and develop expertise in describing the movement patterns that underlie those tasks or activities. Examples of important movement patterns to identify and describe are outlined below. Appendix 3.2, the Motor Skills Observation Sheet, summarizes these key patterns and skills and can be used as a tool to structure motor skills observations.

***Rudimentary Movement Patterns*** Rudimentary movement patterns are primarily involved in maintaining stability, posture, position, and balance.

*Sitting* Mature and secure sitting skills involve sitting with an erect posture that allows for free movement at the shoulders. The observer should discern whether the student can sit securely. The seated student should be able to move the shoulders and arms freely. The student should be able to sit without excessive movement and without changing position too often. Depending on the student's age, the student should be able to sit for prolonged periods. Notice whether the student shifts position too often, seems to slide out of her or his seat too often, or gets up to walk about the room too often. Behaviors such as these suggest muscle fatigue, especially for those muscles responsible for stability.

*Standing* Mature standing involves standing with an erect posture that allows for free movement at the shoulders and at the hips. The observer should consider whether the student stands with an erect or a slouched posture. The student should be able to stand still, without excessive movement. Students should also be able to stand while moving at the hips and shoulders without difficulty. Some preschool children may still be mastering these standing skills. Kindergarten and first-grade students may not be able to sit for prolonged periods.

***Fundamental Movement Patterns*** Fundamental movement patterns rely on stability but serve the purpose of locomotion and/or object manipulation.

*Walking* The observer should assess whether the student walks using an alternating gait and a narrow or wide base of support. Each foot should lift before the student places it on the floor again. The feet should not drag or shuffle, and the heel should strike the floor before the rest of the foot lands on the floor. The student should walk in a relatively straight line and be able to avoid obstacles. The student should have control over the upper limbs, without excessive movement. Some preschool-age children may still be mastering these skills.

*Running* The student should be able to run securely in a straight line and on a narrow base of support. There should be no excessive movement of the upper body or the upper limbs.

*In-Hand Skills* The student should be able to grasp, release, and transfer objects and use fingers independently. The student should have a pincer grasp (index finger apposed to the thumb). If the pincer grasp is not present, the observer should notice whether the student is able to produce a grasp using all fingers against the palm of the hand, against the thumb, or using the index finger only. The grasp should be secure, and the student should not drop things easily. By the time the student enters first grade, he or she should have a mature tripod grasp of a pencil or pen.

*Bimanual Skills* Bimanual skills include coordinating two different types of movement between the two hands. The observer should note whether the student is able to bring both hands together at mid-line and hold an object while manipulating it. This movement pattern usually involves using one hand for stability and the other hand for manipulation. Examples include opening a jar or taking off a lid, securing a piece of paper while printing or drawing, and securing a piece of paper while cutting with scissors. If the student can perform this kind of activity, the observer should note whether the student's performance is secure or shaky, precise or imprecise.

***Differentiated Movement Patterns*** Both rudimentary and fundamental movement patterns have to be adjusted, refined, and modified to suit different circumstances and to be embedded into different activities.

*Differentiated Sitting* Sitting for prolonged periods requires greater motor skill than sitting for a short period. Sitting in a firm chair is different from sitting on the floor with the legs crossed (or not), which is different again from sitting in a chair that is too big or too small. When making observations of sitting, the student should be assessed in different situations and at different times and activities. The observer should consider whether the student sits with an erect or slouched posture. The observer should notice the amount of movement of the body and how often the student shifts position or has to get out of the seat altogether.



*Differentiated Standing* Standing in line while waiting to go outside or while waiting to get a food item in the cafeteria or waiting during a sports activity may all look somewhat different. The observer should notice the same behaviors as discussed in the previous section. For example, standing should be secure in different locations and for different purposes. The student should not have to shift position too often or lean on objects or peers.

*Differentiated Walking and Running* Walking and running can look different depending on whether the floor or ground is uneven or whether the student is avoiding obstacles such as other students in the hallway or furniture in the classroom. Walking and running also look different when walking on a balance beam, when going through an obstacle course in physical education classes, or when playing team sports. The observer should notice whether there are changes under different conditions or whether the walking and running appear to be more insecure under certain conditions.

*Differentiated Object Manipulation* Grasp, transfer, release, and pincer grasp may look somewhat different depending on the task. Grasping a jacket and grasping a zipper or a pencil require somewhat different degrees of finger skills. Grasping might also look different when using a pencil for a prolonged period. When observing students grasp different objects under different conditions, notice whether the student is able to separate fingers and what type of grasping pattern is used (e.g., whole hand grasp, all fingers against the thumb, or index finger to the thumb). Handwriting is a special example of differentiated object manipulation. The observer can focus on whether the student shows a mature tripod grasp while writing and can review printing or writing samples as the observation. When there are doubts or concerns, educators should refer to an expert (e.g., occupational therapist) to conduct a more careful observation. It is important to remember that some hand skills are affected because of performance difficulties in rudimentary movement patterns such as sitting and standing. Insecure posture or stability patterns can affect the hands and can result in secondary performance difficulties in handwriting or other hand skills.

*Differentiation of Movement Patterns in a Movement Sequence* Another way to analyze differentiation of a movement pattern is to observe the pattern within a movement sequence. Choose an activity (e.g., dressing or playing basketball) and then choose a portion of the activity that could be called a movement sequence (e.g., putting on pants, putting on a jacket, dribbling a ball). By narrowing the observation, it becomes easier to identify relevant movement patterns and to assess their level of differentiation. When rudimentary and fundamental movement patterns are not well differentiated, the student may show slow or jerky transitions between the patterns contained within a movement sequence.

Young children and students who are acquiring a new skill will not be expected to perform all movement sequences securely or efficiently. The movement sequences listed in a subsequent section are especially useful for school professionals to consider when learning how to observe movement.

***Movement Sequences*** Observers can consider the following movement sequences for assessment of a student's motor status:

*Participating in Classroom Routines* Shifting between sitting, standing, and walking is one simple sequence to consider observing. For instance, a teacher might observe the student when he or she is instructed to finish work, put it away, stand up, get outdoor clothing, and then stand in line. This movement sequence includes movement patterns such as sitting, standing, walking, reaching, and grabbing. For each of these movement patterns, the observer should consider how securely the posture is maintained, the quality of the movement pattern (how differentiated the movement pattern is, so that it fits into this particular movement sequence), how smoothly the transition between movement patterns occurs, and how swiftly the entire sequence is completed.

*Dressing* The observation can include the movement sequence of dressing, when the student puts on a jacket to go outside at recess or changes shoes to play a sport. The movement patterns in this case include hand skills such as reaching, grasping, releasing, and transferring. The observer should notice combinations of movement patterns, such as grasping a jacket with one hand while then making a reaching movement to push the arm through the sleeve or standing while bending to tie shoelaces. The observer should note how smoothly the tasks are carried out within the sequence. There may be excessive pauses or extraneous movements between each step in the sequence. The transition between movement sequences may be smooth or irregular.

*Washing Hands* Hand washing requires grasp, transfer and release (if there is a bar of soap), bimanual manipulation of soap, shaking off excess water, and drying motions. If a bar of soap is used, the task requires having just the right amount of force in order to be effective. If a soap dispenser is used, pumping and collecting soap must occur. The observer should notice how securely the student can position the arms and hands to perform this activity successfully. It can be useful to notice whether the student uses only gross movements of the whole hand or is able to separate the fingers to rub soap between them.

*Handwriting* School professionals may choose to observe the student at a handwriting task (e.g., writing several sentences in print or cursive). This movement sequence requires very small changes in the movements of the hands and fingers. The observer can identify different grasping patterns (tripod grasp of the pencil or pen using the index finger, thumb, and second finger, versus a grasp that includes several fingers, versus a fisted grasp) and note how fluidly the hand is used to form letters. Although letter formation and a writing sample are important to analyze, real-time observations are necessary to help understand which aspects of movement may need remediation. Handwriting is a highly differentiated set of movement patterns. Although educators and other school professionals are not expected to identify which movement patterns will require remediation, it is important to be able to analyze handwriting in real time and to appreciate the success of the student's performance. It is also important to be able to analyze handwriting samples and to decide which students may need a formal assessment with an occupational therapist.

*Playing Sports* The observation can occur as the student engages in sports activities such as basketball or soccer, gymnastics, or dancing. Many fundamental movement patterns are linked in sequences during a sports activity. Two or more movement patterns may need to be linked and produced simultaneously, such as running and catching in baseball or jumping and turning in ballet. Movement patterns must be more highly differentiated to be linked smoothly and carried out at different speeds and with different degrees of force. The observer should also examine the transitions between movements.

***Motor Control*** In some cases, movement performance difficulties are related to motor control. Movement sequences may be quick or slow. Movement may be forceful or gentle. Changes in speed may increase or reduce extraneous movement. The observer should comment upon speed, force, and precision in movement. Some students can perform movements successfully when they are rehearsed or practiced, but they have difficulty mastering new skills because of aspects related to motor control. For example, handwriting, drawing, self-care, and navigating the environment can all be affected by underdeveloped spatial awareness. Difficulties with sequencing, planning, and efficiency can occur in a student who is hyperactive or impulsive. That student might not be able to bring the working memory and planning skills needed to show a good motor performance. To understand spatial awareness, consider reviewing Chapters 1 and 2. To understand executive skills, consider reading Chapter 7. Lack of comprehension as related to motor instructions can affect a student's motor performance, as can lack of motivation. All of these motor control factors are important to consider and address when working with a student to improve her or his motor performance.



## Analyze and Interpret the Observations

It is important to proceed systematically when analyzing and interpreting movement. For any given observation, a successful analysis has to take into consideration motor structures, motor functions, and movement patterns. Movement patterns can be divided into rudimentary, fundamental, and differentiated. From there, the observer also has to take into consideration how smoothly movement patterns are linked with one another, their force and speed, and whether the functional outcome of the movement (the goal) is reached successfully. These latter aspects of movement relate to motor control. For each of the aspects of movement listed here, the observer has to determine whether the movement is successful or not so successful. Depending on the age of the student, some motor performance difficulties may be expected. Motor performance difficulties should also be expected when a student is mastering a new motor skill or motor activity. The purpose of the observation, then, is primarily to identify targets for intervention, regardless of whether the student is performing at the level expected for age. Whenever possible, the novice observer should speak with specialists, such as an occupational or physical therapist or a physical education teacher, to corroborate initial impressions and to learn from their expertise. As discussed earlier in this chapter, educators are not expected to identify impairments in motor structures or motor functions. Some of these may be obvious to the untrained observer. However, analysis of movement is more complex in the case of impairments.

The development of successful movement at all levels of analysis outlined in this chapter is important for all students, not just those who may have motor performance difficulties. For any student, an analysis of motor skills can lead to an intervention plan with clearly defined educational objectives, strategies, and/or accommodations. When building the student's intervention plan or IEP, the educational team must find a successful balance between treating or improving motor structures and functions and developing motor skills, motor abilities, and social participation.

## Educational Objectives and Strategies for Motor Skills

A hierarchy of therapeutic and educational objectives can be developed using the Motor Skills Framework as presented in this chapter. Interventions and objectives may need to be developed to enhance motor functions, movement patterns (i.e., rudimentary, fundamental, and differentiated), functional movement sequences, and/or motor control. At the beginning of the hierarchy (motor structures and functions), students can improve their performance when they participate in traditional physical therapy interventions, such as stretching or strengthening exercises. These and other neuromuscular interventions are more appropriately offered by health care providers but are sometimes appropriate to deliver in a school setting as well.

A more functional approach, often favored by therapists working in both health care and educational settings, is to develop educational objectives by first identifying important tasks or activities for the student. This means identifying functional motor sequences that have an adaptive, vocational, or recreational purpose. The sequences are then broken down into rudimentary, fundamental, and differentiated movement patterns. Educational objectives are designed for each of the levels of analysis just listed. Objectives can also be developed to help the student move more smoothly between movement patterns, to improve force and speed of movement, and/or to improve the final outcome and reach important goals.

For a student with more substantial motor limitations, self-care tasks such as dressing, personal hygiene, and eating may serve as the objectives for teaching and learning. Task-oriented training can help to improve overall movement and participation while also helping the student to master rudimentary or fundamental movement patterns (Männistö, Huovinen, Kooistra, & Larkin, 2006; Martin, Baker, & Harvey, 2010). Task-oriented training is often combined with neurodevelopmental approaches to enhance strength and tone (e.g., in students with cerebral palsy) (Liptak & Murphy, 2011). The motor component of the training could improve movement patterns, differentiation of movement patterns, and transitions between movement patterns.

In addition to the adaptive tasks of the day, the team may choose to help the student develop motor patterns that are related to vocational activities. These could include developing the motor patterns and sequences needed to participate in recycling tasks, cleaning tasks, food preparation or serving tasks, or building maintenance skills. For example, the student can learn about wiping, stirring, cleaning, scrubbing, holding and sorting, and stacking. Within each of these, the student can learn about how to apply just the right amount of force or speed. The student can also learn about efficiency. During a multiple-step sequence, such as cleaning up a workshop area, a kitchen area, or a building area, the student should be encouraged to think about how many steps are involved or how the task could be made more efficient.

For other students, recreational activities may serve as the platform for learning. The student may be ready to master more highly differentiated movement patterns, transitions between movement patterns, and movement sequences in gymnastics, dance, soccer, or other recreational or sports activities. The student may be ready to learn about moving fluidly between movement patterns, moving with more control over force and speed, and learning to move with greater efficiency to win a game or to achieve higher mastery goals.

***Educational Objectives for Rudimentary, Fundamental, and Differentiated Movement Patterns*** Rudimentary movement patterns are often affected due to problems in motor structures and functions (muscles, ligaments, joints, and bones) and are discussed in the Accommodations section. Rudimentary movement patterns undergird all movement. For the student who already has the capacity to sit and stand, it is important to teach about the importance of stability in movement and how posture and positioning are foundations for successful movement. Awareness of the role of neck, back, pelvic, and abdominal muscles can help improve motor performance. For students who are ready to learn about fundamental movement patterns, practice in fundamental movement patterns such as walking, running, hopping, skipping, throwing, catching, grabbing, and so forth can be a focus for instruction. As the student learns about and masters different fundamental movement patterns, he or she can be challenged to differentiate those movement patterns by learning to perform under different circumstances. Students can differentiate movement patterns by practicing those movement patterns on uneven surfaces, at different speeds, with different levels of force, and as a part of new movement sequences.

***Educational Objectives for Movement Sequences*** For students who already have a good repertoire of fundamental movement patterns, it can be helpful to focus instruction to help them transition more smoothly, more quickly, or with changing force or speed between movement patterns. The movement patterns should be part of a movement sequence that fulfills adaptive, vocational, or recreational purposes. The student with a motor impairment may wish to learn how to complete self-care, adaptive tasks, and some vocational tasks more smoothly or more efficiently. The student without motor impairments may wish to apply this type of instruction to vocational and recreational activities. The activities used for this type of instruction might include use of mechanical equipment in a workshop setting, such as motor sequences needed for food preparation or landscaping work, or more skilled movement patterns as required in sports, dance, or gymnastics.



***Educational Objectives for Motor Control*** Students must acquire a variety of adaptive, vocational, and recreational skills as part of their instruction at school. When teaching students about these different purposes of movement, educators will also need to teach motor control skills. To develop motor control skills, students will need to learn about and build spatial awareness, executive skills, motivation, and overall cognition (i.e., understanding the purpose of the motor activity and learning from doing the activity). In some cases, instruction in movement requires prior instruction in some of the aspects of motor control discussed in this chapter. Adaptive, vocational, and recreational activities may require content knowledge such as the purpose of the task or activity or the outcome expected for that task or activity. The student may require reading, writing, and math skills, or may require executive skills, as part of mastering the motor sequence. For example, if the task involves food preparation, motor skills may need to be combined with knowledge of food science, reading, and math (measurement). If the task involves building or repairing an object, motor skills may need to be combined with knowledge about materials and methods. If the activity involves sports, the student may need content knowledge about rules of the game, rules that apply during a competition, and their relationship to the motor skills involved. Content knowledge and many of the skills described in this book may influence the student's ability to participate in the motor sequences that make up the adaptive, vocational, or recreational activity. Context therapy and comprehensive motor programming (Männistö et al., 2006) are examples of how the function or purpose of movement can be used as the platform for learning to use the motor system.

## Accommodations for Motor Performance Difficulties

As is the case for most of the skills discussed in this book, accommodations for the student with motor performance difficulties should typically be offered only when the student is not expected to be capable of mastering certain types of movements. Accommodations can be used to focus on mastery of higher order objectives (e.g., objectives related to motor control processes or related to specific functional or adaptive purposes). For example, it might not be appropriate to teach a student who uses a wheelchair or a standing walker to kick and run in a game of soccer or to perform landscaping tasks. However, the student can and should still be included in soccer games or landscaping if this participation allows the student to master other types of skills, such as motor control skills. Teaching about motor skills can be designed to ensure participation and to enhance general knowledge and should not be designed to enhance only motor skills specifically (Imms, 2008). The environment or the activity may need to be modified, so that the student can participate. School professionals can consider the accommodations in the following sections to help enhance overall participation.

***Accommodations for Motor Structures and Functions*** Students with motor impairments that affect the muscles, ligaments, joints, or bones may need accommodations to perform successfully at school, including to perform motor skills and to participate in other activities that might occur over the course of a school day. Such accommodations may be prescribed by a health care provider and might include the use of braces, orthotic supports, a stander, walker, or cane. School professionals should be aware of the types of supports that a student may need and know when to ask for assistance in using these types of accommodations.

***Accommodations for Rudimentary and Fundamental Movement Patterns*** Students who are not able to sit, stand, or walk may need physical supports such as a stander, seating supports, walker, cane, and/or wheelchair. They may need supports for navigating the school building (e.g., circumventing stairs, reducing the distance needed to travel between classes, or having a means to travel over uneven surfaces, or within a moving environment).



***Accommodations for Movement in Sequences: Adaptive and Vocational Tasks and Recreational Activities*** Even with rudimentary and fundamental movement patterns in place, some students may have difficulty performing motor activities in sequence. This may be due to poor differentiation of movement patterns, fatigue, problems with force and/or speed, or difficulty remembering all the steps involved in a sequence. Sequences may need to be shortened or modified. For example, the full range of self-care and personal hygiene may be beyond the level of a student's motor skills. The goal for the student may be to complete portions of self-care and personal hygiene only, while relying on physical assistance, environmental accommodations such as specially designed tools, or memory aids to ensure a good functional outcome. The student may have the ability to sit for a length of time while doing classroom activities or to walk certain distances to get from one class to the next. However, the student may need assistive devices to perform successfully, may need motor demands curtailed, or may need to use an elevator so as not to fatigue his or her motor system.

As examples, adaptive demands can be reduced by changing the shape, size, or weight of important everyday objects such a pencil, spoon, or cup. Adaptive and vocational demands can be reduced when fasteners on clothing are eliminated or modified. Demands related to motor skills can be reduced during vocational activities when mechanical instruments or items needed for food preparation are placed within easy reach, when their weight or size is altered, and when grips are added for easier grasping. During sports or recreational activities, the weight and size of a ball can be altered to improve participation in sports activities, or the rules can be changed to accommodate for wheelchairs or other means of locomotion. The movement patterns and sequences can be modified for dance or sports routines. The educational goal of the vocational or recreational event can be modified by changing the focus or purpose for the student. A student can help organize a recreational event or can identify specific vocational skills that are personally more accessible or more meaningful.

***Accommodations Related to Motor Control*** Some students may need modifications or accommodations made in relation to motor control aspects of movement. A student may need support to be able to organize materials, instruments, or objects needed to fulfill vocational activities. A student with a vision impairment may need more tactile cues embedded in the motor activity, for example, the addition of different colors or textures to objects so that they are more easily identified. Another student may need a social story related to the adaptive, vocational, or recreational activity to help organize his or her understanding of the activity and its purpose and outcome.

***Environmental Accommodations*** In considering environmental accommodations, the analysis of movement is no longer the primary focus of the observer. Rather, the analysis must be focused on environmental barriers (Verschuren, Lesley, Dominique, & Marjolijn, 2012). Context therapy is an example of how a practitioner can make social participation the primary goal of a motor activity by conducting an almost exclusive analysis of the environment, instead of conducting an analysis of the student's motor skills. It is a useful model for understanding how to facilitate participation primarily as opposed to building motor skills primarily

(Darrah et al., 2011). An analysis of the environment might lead to building wider doorways, making surfaces more even, and offering handrail supports. Many of these accommodations are already mandated by disability rights laws, though they may not always be in place in all parts of a building or in all locations. The analysis might also take into consideration factors such as accessibility and location. When the location of a motor activity is changed, new access opportunities might open up for the student with a motor impairment (e.g., open field versus a gymnasium).

The environment includes adults and peers who may not have any experience with students who have motor performance difficulties. The analysis of the environment might need to consider the (often limiting) attitudes of teaching staff or peers, such as could occur for students with cerebral palsy (Kramer, Olsen, Mermelstein, Balcells, & Liljenquist, 2012). The adults and peers who interact with the student may need to learn about the student's perspectives and wishes. They may also need to learn what it means to be helpful and how students with motor performance difficulties sometimes perceive the efforts of their more able peers as unhelpful. The student's description of personal preferences is likely the best source of information for changing the attitudes of others. The student can be taught advocacy skills so that the environment could change. For example, the student could learn how to articulate her or his preferences and prepare a short narrative to inform others about how to be the most helpful. The student may need to clarify and explain to peers how they should help in pushing the wheelchair, how they can help with the walker, and why no help at all is sometimes the best approach. Advance planning can help the student think about how to navigate different terrains, how to make use of different transportation options, and how to access different environments. The environment can become friendlier for the student with motor performance difficulties when the student can share the experience of having a motor impairment and can help eliminate any misconceptions. By sharing this information, students with motor performance difficulties can enhance motor control factors such as executive skills and motivation and can improve participation and performance. By sharing their perspectives, they can end up feeling empowered to influence the world around them in positive ways (Kramer et al., 2012).

Regardless of the balance chosen for motor skills building and accommodations for motor performance difficulties, the goal of motor skills instruction should always be to improve the student's overall independence and social participation (Martin, Baker, & Harvey, 2010; Msall, 2010; Palisano et al., 2012). Ideally, teaching and learning related to the motor system will help improve all aspects of the motor system: Motor structures, motor functions, motor skills, and motor abilities. The program should address the motor system at the level of motor functions, rudimentary and fundamental movement patterns, movement sequences, and motor control. It should emphasize successful adaptive, prevocational, and recreational outcomes. The program should prevent musculoskeletal complications and provide teaching in areas such as language, spatial awareness, language skills, general understanding, and executive skills (Campbell, 1994). The program should take into consideration both the limitations and the abilities of the student with motor performance difficulties. It should actively engage the student in joint decision making whenever possible (Kramer et al., 2012).

## CASE EXAMPLE

Julian is a 9-year-old boy with mild learning difficulty. His overall academic performance is close to grade level, with special education supports in place for reading, writing, and math. Now that Julian is in the third grade, he is expected to sit and work independently for longer periods of time. His teacher noticed that he is not able to sit still for as long as his peers. He often shifts position in his seat and gets up to request water or to go to the bathroom. His teacher initially thought that he might have an attention-deficit/hyperactivity disorder and allowed him more motor breaks. However, she is uncertain about how difficult it is for him to sustain his attention because he can focus well some of the time. Julian's teacher also noticed that he is more clumsy than his peers. She asked his second-grade teacher about Julian's attention status. His second-grade teacher also provided motor breaks but did not seem as concerned about clumsiness. After closer observation, Julian's teacher wondered whether he might have low muscle tone and associated muscle fatigue. Before consulting with the in-district occupational therapist, she selected the following movement patterns and sequences to observe his motor system more carefully:

## Sitting (Rudimentary Movement Patterns)

When sitting at his desk, Julian often supports his head using his hand with his elbow on his desk. This works well when he is participating in classroom activities. However, when he has to use his hands to complete work, he starts to become more fidgety and seems unable to find a comfortable position. When he is seated on the floor, he usually leans against the bookcase, even though this means that he ends up sitting just outside the circle during group learning activities on the carpet.

## Walking and Running (Fundamental Movement Patterns)

Julian can walk and run successfully but he trips more easily than other children and often knocks things over or runs into things. By observing his walking gait more closely, Julian's teacher noticed that he has a flat-footed gait. He places the whole foot on the floor and makes a bit of a slapping sound as he walks. The amount of noise he makes varies, depending on what kind of shoes he is wearing. His walking patterns seem to be acceptable for most situations, and his upper body control appears normal. He typically masters sports moves more slowly than his peers, and he is not always able to carry them out smoothly. While observing him along with his physical education teacher, Julian's teacher noticed that he looks more awkward when he runs. His gait becomes broader and his upper body moves about more, making him appear clumsy. Julian is becoming self-conscious about his ability to perform in sports activities. He recently complained to his physical education teacher that he is not good at sports, prompting the teacher to spend extra time to help him master movement patterns in sports activities.

Julian's teacher discussed her observations with his parents. She believes that Julian needs to be seen by the occupational therapist, to determine whether there are any seating supports or other accommodations that could be useful. Julian's parents were very familiar with Julian's difficulty with motor skills. He was much slower to learn to perform self-care than his older brother, they explained, though his performance now seems normal to them. Because he does not perform well in team sports, his parents decided to enroll him in swimming classes. Although he is not the greatest swimmer yet, he enjoys swimming classes and he is learning to improve his stroke.

## Analysis and Interpretation of Julian's Motor Skills

Julian presents with motor behaviors that are very common for a student with low muscle tone and/or joint laxity. Julian's teacher would not be expected to identify a problem with structures or functions (muscles, ligaments, joints, bones), but she was able to make accurate observations of his movement patterns and discovered that his motor performance is not as secure as the performance of his peers. Although rudimentary and fundamental movement patterns are in place and are generally secure, she was able to identify that his movement patterns are not as well differentiated as they should be for his age. He shows extraneous (upper body) movements when running. He can perform movements in sequence, for example, adaptive skills such as personal care. However, when stressed by novel tasks, or by demands on speed or force, his movement patterns look less secure and his performance slows down. He acquires new movement patterns more slowly than his peers and completes tasks and activities more slowly than his peers even for familiar movement sequences.



## Educational Objectives, Strategies, and Accommodations for Julian

### *Accommodations for Sitting*

Julian may need accommodations for his low muscle tone. Seating should be designed to fit his body size and to provide extra support. His back should be at 90 degrees in relation to his hips, and his knees also should have a 90-degree bend with feet firmly placed on the floor. In addition, supports on either side (e.g., armrests or, better yet, supports around his pelvis) might help to secure an optimal seating posture. With optimized seating posture, he might be freer to use his arms to complete desktop work. Seating supports may help him with his handwriting skills. Because he will not have to lean on his elbows during writing, his hands will be freed up for handwriting.

### *Accommodations for Handwriting*

Students such as Julian commonly have difficulty with handwriting. Handwriting difficulty can be related to the student's difficulty maintaining postural control during prolonged sitting. It may be useful to reduce handwriting demands for a student such as Julian. Keyboarding, voice dictation software, and/or use of a scribe can be considered. These accommodations reduce handwriting demands and would allow Julian to concentrate on higher order writing demands such as composition. A decision to reduce handwriting demands should be made only after a reassessment of his capacity for handwriting and appropriate seating supports are in place.

### *Teaching Movement Patterns and Sequences*

Julian is capable of mastering new movement sequences. Currently, all self-care and adaptive skills are secure. However, it took him longer than his brother to learn self-care skills at home, and he tends to take a bit longer to complete personal care than other children his age. When he has to acquire new motor sequences, he is clumsy and tends to master new movement sequences slowly. The expectation for a student such as Julian should be that he will participate fully in adaptive and vocational activities. His team suspects that this will be possible whenever the activity does not require precise control over force and speed. He should be able to perform all the adaptive and prevocational demands of a household routine (e.g., personal care, food preparation, cleaning, yardwork). However, because he is slow to master new movement patterns and new movement sequences, more time and attention may be needed to teach him new motor and movement skills.

Sports activities are likely to be challenging. This does not mean that Julian should not participate in sports. However, it is important to consider that team sports may be especially taxing. It is harder for students such as Julian to participate in motor activities when they have to perform in a moving environment, such as playing successfully with moving players and a moving ball. In team sports, motor skills have to be carried out strategically and in cooperation with team players. The demands on spatial awareness, speed, and executive skills are higher. Julian's level of motivation might help overcome some of these barriers. If he is especially keen on playing team sports, he may also practice movement patterns and sequences enough to be able to play with his peers. However, Julian may also be more content to improve his motor skills in individual sports, such as swimming or track and field. Julian's parents had already decided to enroll him in swimming classes. They made this decision based on his difficulty keeping up with peers in team sports. It is important to ensure that students like Julian participate in movement, even if they need a lot of encouragement to do so. Students with low muscle tone are prone to being overweight if they move about less. Julian's parents noticed that when he is not swimming, he often ends up playing video games. They would like to keep him active so that he burns up calories and does not end up gaining excess weight.



## Working With Culturally and Linguistically Diverse Learners

School professionals should keep the following elements in mind when working with culturally and linguistically diverse learners on motor skills:

### *Left Handedness Versus Right Handedness*

Children may exhibit motor difficulty if they are not using their preferred hand for different activities such as eating or coloring. In some cultures, there is pressure for all children to be right handed even if their natural inclination is to use the left hand. Hygiene is one reason that members of cultural groups want individuals to be right handed so that only one hand is used for touching food and the other is used for cleaning one's body.

### *Utensils Used for Eating*

Depending on their cultural background, children may have learned to eat with chopsticks. They may appear awkward or clumsy when using eating utensils such as a knife or fork. In some cultures, people hold both the knife and fork when eating a dish that requires cutting food, while in other cultures the knife should be put down before using the fork for eating. In still other cultures, it is not polite to have a knife at the table at all. It can be useful to check what the norms are for the use of utensils among your students. It is important to explain the school rules and regulations regarding zero tolerance to culturally and linguistically diverse families. They may not be aware that many school districts do not allow children to bring knives of any kind to school.

## CONCLUSIONS

This chapter concludes Section I, dedicated to neurological foundations for learning. Chapters in this section highlighted the difference between structures and functions, on the one hand, and skills and abilities, on the other. Structures and functions pertain to the anatomical and functional aspects of the body. They emerge as an expression of nature. Skills and abilities, on the other hand, are related to nurture. Nurturing nature occurs by providing the right opportunities and the right instruction. Biologically endowed functions, such as being able to move muscle fibers across a joint, can be enhanced and expanded into skills and abilities that enhance survival and participation and foster further development and learning.

The distinction between nature and nurture also applies to the developmental foundations for learning in Section II. When discussing developmental foundations for learning in the upcoming chapters, the distinction among structures, functions, skills, and abilities is less clearly defined anatomically. The skills that we will discuss in Section II are developed in the brain, though the anatomical location for those skills and their connections with the motor system are not always easy to define anatomically. Humans are biologically programmed to acquire many of the skills that we will discuss in Section II, as was the case for the neurological foundations we covered in the first three chapters. Many different parts of the brain can and do support the developmental skills and abilities to be discussed in the upcoming chapters.



## REFERENCES


Barnett, A. L. (2008). Motor assessment in developmental coordination disorder: From identification to intervention. *International Journal of Disability, Development and Education, 55*(2), 113–129.

Bradley, N. S. (2011). Motor control: Developmental aspects of motor control in skill acquisition. In S. K. Campbell (Ed.), *Physical therapy for children* (pp. 87–150). Philadelphia, PA: WB Saunders.

Burton, A. W., & Miller, D. E. (1998). *Movement skill assessment*. Champaign, IL: Human Kinetics.

Campbell, S. K. (1994). The child's development of functional movement. In S. K. Campbell (Ed.), *Physical therapy for children* (pp. 3–37). Philadelphia, PA: Saunders.

Campbell, S. K. (2011). The child's development of functional movement. In S. K. Campbell (Ed.), *Physical therapy for children* (pp. 37–86). Philadelphia, PA: WB Saunders.

Carr, J., & Shepherd, R. (2000). A motor model for rehabilitation. In J. Carr & R. Shepherd (Eds.), *Movement science: Foundations for physical therapy in rehabilitation* (2nd ed., pp. 33–39). New York, NY: Aspen Publishers.

Darrah, J., Law, M. C., Pollock, N., Wilson, B., Russell, D. J., Walter, S. D., . . . Galup, B. (2011). Context therapy: A new intervention approach for children with cerebral palsy. *Developmental Medicine & Child Neurology,* 53(7), 615–620.

den Heijer, A. E., Groen, Y., Tucha, L., Fuermaier, A. B. M., Koerts, J., Lange, K. W., et al. (2017). Sweat it out? The effects of physical exercise on cognition and behavior in children and adults with ADHD: A systematic literature review. *Journal of Neural Transmission, 124*(Suppl. 1), S3–S26.

Fournier, K. A., Hass, C. J., Naik, S. K., Lodha, N., & Cauraugh, J. H. (2010). Motor coordination in autism spectrum disorders: A synthesis and meta-analysis. *Journal of Autism and Developmental Disorders, 40*(10), 1227–1240.

Gallahue, D. L., & Ozmun, J. C. (2002). *Understanding motor development. Infants, children, adolescents, adults* (5th ed.). New York, NY: McGraw Hill.

Houwen, S., Visser, L., van der Putten, A., & Vlaskamp, C. (2016). The interrelationships between motor, cognitive, and language development in children with and without intellectual and developmental disabilities. *Research in Developmental Disabilities, 53–54,* 19–31.

Howie, E., & Russell, R. P. (2012). Physical activity and academic achievement in children: A historical perspective. *Journal of Sport and Health Science, 1,* 160–169.

Imms, C. (2008). Children with cerebral palsy participate: A review of the literature. *Disability and Rehabilitation, 30*(24), 1867–1884.

Kramer, J. M., Olsen, S., Mermelstein, M., Balcells, A., & Liljenquist, K. (2012). Youth with disabilities' perspectives of the environment and participation: A qualitative meta-synthesis. *Child: Care, Health and Development, 38*(6), 763–777.

Kramer, P., & Hinojosa, J. (Eds.). (2010). *Frames of reference for pediatric occupational therapy* (3rd ed.). Philadelphia, PA: Lippincott and Williams and Wilkins.

Lambourne, K., & Donnelly, J. E. (2011). The role of physical activity in pediatric obesity. *Pediatric Clinics of North America, 58*(6), 1481–1491.

Liptak, G. S., & Murphy, N. A. (2011). Providing a primary care medical home for children and youth with cerebral palsy. Council on Children with Disabilities. *Pediatrics, 128*(5), e1321–e1355.

Lopes, L., Santos, R., Pereira, B., & Lopes, V. P. (2013). Associations between gross motor coordination and academic achievement in elementary school children. *Human Movement Science, 32*(1), 9–20.

Männistö, J.-P., Huovinen, T., Kooistra, L., & Larkin, D. (2006). A school-based movement programme for children with motor learning difficulty. *European Physical Education Review, 12*(3), 273–287.

Martin, L., Baker, R., & Harvey, A. (2010). A systematic review of common physiotherapy interventions in school-aged children with cerebral palsy. *Physical and Occupational Therapy in Pediatrics, 30*(4), 294–312.

Msall, M. E. (2010). Developing preschool surveillance tools for adaptive functioning: Lessons for neurooncology. *European Journal of Paediatric Neurology, 14*(5), 368–379.

Palisano, R. J., Begnoche, D. M., Chiarello, L. A., Bartlett, D. J., Westcott-McCoy, S., & Chang, J-J. (2012). Amount and focus of physical therapy and occupational therapy for young children with cerebral palsy. *Physical & Occupational Therapy in Pediatrics, 32*(4), 368–382.

Pieters, S., De Block, K., Scheiris, J., Eyssen, M., Desoete, A., Deboutte, D., et al. (2012). How common are motor problems in children with a developmental disorder: Rule or exception? *Child: Care, Health and Development, 38*(1), 139–145.

Pirrie, A. M., & Lodewiyk, K. R. (2012). Investigating links between moderate-to-vigorous physical activity and cognitive performance in elementary school students. *Mental Health and Physical Activity, 5*, 93–98.

Shetreat-Klein, M., Shinner, S., & Rapin, I. (2014). Abnormalities of joint mobility and gait in children with autism spectrum disorders. *Brain and Development, 36*(2), 91–96.

Sibley, B. A., & Etnier, J. L. (2003). The relationship between physical activity and cognition in children: A meta-analysis. *Pediatric Exercise Science, 15*, 243–256.

Tecklin, J. S. (1999). *Pediatric physical therapy* (3rd ed.). Philadelphia, PA: Lippincott Williams and Wilkins.

U.S. Department of Health and Human Services, Centers for Disease Control and Prevention. (2010). The association between school-based physical activity, including physical education, and academic performance. Retrieved from http://www.cdc.gov/healthyyouth/health_and_academics/pdf/pa-pe_paper.pdf

Verschuren, O., Lesley, W., Dominique, H., & Marjolijn, K. (2012). Identification of facilitators and barriers to physical activity in children and adolescents with cerebral palsy. *Journal of Pediatrics, 161*(3), 488–494.

Vuijk, P. J., Harman, E., Scherder, E., & Visscher, C. (2010). Motor performance of children with mild intellectual disability and borderline intellectual functioning. *Journal of Intellectual Disability Research, 54*(Pt. 11), 955–965.

Webster, R., Majnemer, A., Platt, R. W., & Shevell, M. I. (2005). Motor function at school age in children with a preschool diagnosis of developmental language impairment. *Journal of Pediatrics, 146*(1), 80–85.

Wilson, P. H. (2005). Practitioner review: Approaches to assessment and treatment of children with DCD: An evaluative review. *Journal of Child Psychology and Psychiatry, 46*(8), 806–823.

Zach, S., Shoval, E., & Lidor, R. (2017). Physical education and academic achievement—literature review 1997–2015. *Journal of Curriculum Studies, 49*(5), 703–721.

Zwicker, J. G., Missiuma, C., & Boyd, L. A. (2009). Neural correlates of developmental coordination disorder: A review of hypotheses. *Journal of Child Neurology, 24*(10), 1273–1281.

APPENDIX 3.1 **Motor Skills Framework**

The Motor Skills Framework is summarized here. School professionals can use this form as a quick reference for the skill sets and skills that need to be taken into consideration when making observations and developing an intervention plan.

| Structures and skill sets | Structures, functions, and skills | Examples of functions and skills in action | Sample medical conditions or performance difficulties | Potential interventions, strategies, accommodations, or educational objectives |
|---|---|---|---|---|
| Motor structures | Bones<br>Joints<br>Ligaments<br>Muscles<br>Nerves | All of the structures listed here need to be intact for optimal motor function and optimal movement. | There are many medical conditions that affect the integrity of the motor structures listed here.<br>Examples include cerebral palsy, muscular dystrophy, low muscle tone, rheumatological diseases, musculoskeletal injuries, among others. | A very wide variety of treatments and interventions may be needed by a student whose motor structures have been affected. Surgery, medications, braces, orthotics, and physical therapy interventions are just a few of these. |
| Motor functions | Relaxation and contraction of muscles, movement across a joint | Muscles relax and contract and thereby produce movement across a joint. These functions are present prior to birth. | Muscles have to be able to contract and relax. This creates movement across a joint. Impairments in relaxation/contraction can occur in any of the medical conditions listed previously. The impairment sometimes lies in the muscle fibers and nerves (e.g., spasticity or hypotonia) and sometimes in the ligaments, joint cavity, or bones.<br>Movement problems can manifest at birth or long after birth, depending on the medical condition. | A very wide variety of treatments and interventions may be needed by a student whose motor functions are affected. Surgery, medications, braces, orthotics, and physical therapy interventions are just a few of these. A physical and/or occupational therapist can assist in identifying motor impairments and, along with the family, can help explain the types of medical interventions that may be in use. |
| Movement patterns | *Rudimentary gross motor patterns:* Rolling, sitting, crawling, standing, cruising<br>*Rudimentary fine motor patterns:* Grabbing with full hand, rake grasp, finger-to-thumb grasp | The movement patterns of rolling, sitting, crawling, standing, and cruising are essential first steps toward more advanced movement skills. They are mastered in the first year of life in typically developing children. | Not all students can perform the rudimentary movement patterns listed here. Cerebral palsy, hypotonia, and other structural impairments or motor dysfunctions can interfere with rudimentary movement patterns. | A variety of interventions, such as surgery, medications, braces, orthotics, and physical therapy, can be used to support impairments in motor structures and functions. They are commonly determined by physicians and other health care professionals working in the health care system. An important goal for the school team should be to help the student develop the rudimentary movement patterns listed here. They serve as a platform for fundamental movement patterns and for more independent functioning. |

*(continued)*

| Structures and skill sets | Structures, functions, and skills | Examples of functions and skills in action | Sample medical conditions or performance difficulties | Potential interventions, strategies, accommodations, or educational objectives |
|---|---|---|---|---|
| | | | | At times, the goal may be to provide accommodations when rudimentary movement patterns cannot be taught or learned. For example, a student may instead learn to stand using a stander or may learn to grab using adaptive equipment.<br><br>The physical and/or occupational therapist can help determine if the goal is to help the student develop independent performance in rudimentary movement patterns, to develop performance using devices or supports as accommodations, or to not aim to develop these movement patterns. |
| | *Fundamental gross motor locomotion patterns:* Walking, running, jumping, hopping, skipping<br><br>*Fundamental gross motor object manipulation patterns:* Kicking, catching, pushing objects | The movement patterns of walking, running, jumping, hopping, and skipping are essential components of more advanced movement skills. They are typically acquired in the second and third years of life.<br><br>The object manipulation patterns of kicking, catching, and pushing are essential components of more advanced movement skills. They are acquired in the preschool years. | Not all students can perform the fundamental gross motor locomotion and object manipulation patterns listed here. Cerebral palsy, hypotonia, and other structural impairments or motor dysfunctions can interfere with fundamental movement patterns | A variety of interventions can be used to support impairments in motor structures and functions so that fundamental movement patterns become more successful. These are commonly determined by physicians and other health care professionals working in the health care system. An important goal for the school team should be to help the student develop the fundamental movement patterns listed here. They serve as a platform for more independent functioning.<br><br>At times, the goal may be to provide accommodations when fundamental movement patterns cannot be acquired. For example, a student may instead learn to stand using a stander, may learn to walk using a walker, or may need to be taught how to use a wheelchair. |

| Structures and skill sets | Structures, functions, and skills | Examples of functions and skills in action | Sample medical conditions or performance difficulties | Potential interventions, strategies, accommodations, or educational objectives |
|---|---|---|---|---|
| | *Fundamental fine motor object manipulation skills:* One-hand skills—pincer grasp, crushing, crumpling, squeezing<br>*Fundamental fine motor object manipulation skills:* Bimanual skills—holding onto an object in one hand while performing an action on the object with the other hand (e.g., opening a jar, writing) | The one-hand movement patterns of pincer gasp, crushing, crumpling, and squeezing are essential components of more advanced movement skills. They are typically acquired in the second and third years of life.<br>The bimanual movement patterns listed here are essential next steps toward more advanced movement skills. They are typically acquired in the preschool years. | Not all students can perform one-hand and bimanual movement patterns listed here.<br>Cerebral palsy, hypotonia, and other structural impairments or motor dysfunctions can prevent the successful emergence and execution of fundamental movement patterns. Postural hypotonia is a relatively common and sometimes underidentified cause, in addition to the conditions listed previously. | A variety of interventions can be used to support impairments in motor structures and functions so that fundamental movement patterns in the fine motor domain can become more possible. An important goal for the school team should be to help the student develop the fundamental movement patterns listed here. They serve as a platform for more independent functioning. |
| | *Differentiated movement patterns*<br>All of the movement patterns listed previously can be used under different circumstances and for different purposes. | Differentiation of movement develops in the preschool and school-age years. It continues throughout life, especially whenever a new movement pattern is acquired. | Not all students can differentiate their rudimentary or fundamental movement patterns or combine them.<br>A student may succeed in producing rudimentary and fundamental movement patterns, but then not be able to use those movement patterns under changing circumstances, such as walking on uneven surfaces, object manipulation for objects that vary in size, shape, or weight, or when moving within a moving environment. This difficulty reflects the lack of differentiation of movement patterns.<br>Undifferentiated movement patterns are performed in an overly rigid or predictable manner and are not adapted to the environment. | An important goal for the school team should be to help the student differentiate any of the fundamental movement patterns discussed in the preceding rows. This means teaching the student how to use fundamental movement patterns in different circumstances, under different environmental conditions, using different types of objects, and so on.<br>The goal should be to enhance the student's independence as much as possible. At times, differentiation may not be a goal. Instead, accommodations, such as changing or modifying the environment to assist with locomotion or modifying the size, shape, or weight of an object, can be used as a strategy to help the student develop fundamental movement skills. |

*(continued)*

| Structures and skill sets | Structures, functions, and skills | Examples of functions and skills in action | Sample medical conditions or performance difficulties | Potential interventions, strategies, accommodations, or educational objectives |
|---|---|---|---|---|
| Movement sequences | Adaptive, vocational, and recreational movement sequences | Rudimentary, fundamental, and differentiated movement patterns get linked into a series of movements.<br><br>The movement sequence is then used to reach an adaptive, vocational, or recreational goal. For example, linked movement patterns allow a student to perform all of the movements required to wash and to dress self (personal care, an adaptive skill), to complete a recycling task (a vocational skill), or to play basketball (a recreational skill). | Students who have difficulty in differentiating their movement patterns may also have difficulty in linking movements into a sequence or series. They may not be able to perform adaptive, vocational, or recreational activities successfully. | An important goal for the school team should be to help the link movement patterns to reach adaptive, vocational, and/or recreational goals.<br><br>The goal should be to enhance the student's independence as much as possible. Adaptive goals such as self-care should always be a priority for any student, even if self-care is dependent on accommodations or adaptive equipment. The next goal should be for the student to develop vocational and recreational skills.<br><br>Adaptive equipment can be used to enhance independence in self-care and vocational and recreational sequences and activities. |
| Motor control | Force and speed in movement | Adaptive, vocational, and recreational movement sequences have to be performed with the right force, speed, and precision. Brushing teeth requires just the right force so that all teeth are cleaned successfully but the gums are not damaged in the process. A recycling task has to be done at the right speed in order to meet productivity requirements. Playing basketball requires the right force, speed, and precision so that the ball gets from one end of the court to the other and into the hoop.<br><br>Force, speed, and precision are skills that all students can work toward but are commonly a goal for students who do not have substantial motor impairment. | Not all students learn to apply force, speed, and precision successfully in their movement patterns. Lack of practice is a common reason, especially for novel tasks. Any substantial motor impairment (e.g., lack of movement across a joint or spasticity due to cerebral palsy) will prevent the student from working toward force, speed, and precision. Even mildly low tone can be interfering. | The development of force, speed, and precision in movement commonly depends on intact motor structures and motor functions. Any student who is still developing the movement sequences needed for adaptive, vocational, and recreational interests should be considered for extra practice opportunities so that force, speed, and precision are also possible. At times, the goal may need to be to teach about force, speed, and precision using adaptive equipment. At times, control of force and speed may not be primary goals, but precision can continue to be a primary goal. |

| Structures and skill sets | Structures, functions, and skills | Examples of functions and skills in action | Sample medical conditions or performance difficulties | Potential interventions, strategies, accommodations, or educational objectives |
|---|---|---|---|---|
| | Spatial awareness<br>Executive skills<br>Motivation<br>Comprehension | A variety of cognitive skills, such as the ones listed here, influence a student's motor performance. This can occur whether or not any motor impairment exists. Motor skills are always more precise and more successful when the student has the cognitive skills listed in the column to the left. | Cognitive factors can influence successful movement whether or not there is a motor impairment of any kind. A student can perform poorly in motor tasks when he or she lacks spatial awareness.<br>Developmental coordination disorder can fall into this category. Students can also be inefficient or imprecise in their motor skills when they are too easily distracted, when they forget steps that need to be completed as part of a motor sequence, when they are not motivated by the task, or when they have not understood task demands.<br>Not understanding a task demand can be due to multiple factors, such as language impairment or a learning disability. | Students who have difficulty with spatial awareness can be taught strategies to enhance their spatial awareness through auditory and tactile cues. See Chapter 1. Students who have difficulties in their executive skills, motivation, and/or comprehension may need other strategies to help them perform successfully in motor tasks. See relevant chapters for suggestions.<br>Accommodations could be needed for underdeveloped executive skills, language skills, reading skills, or math skills, for example. Their role depends on the extent to which these skills are important in any given adaptive, vocational, or recreational activity. The student may need to build motivation for learning in general before he or she is able to build motivation for the motor task at hand.<br>Motor skills can serve as an excellent platform for learning and can be used to enhance motivation for learning, especially when the motor system is an area of strength for the student.<br>Many students experience greater success when they have to master language skills, academic skills, executive skills, or other types of skills when the learning activity includes a motor component.<br>Adaptive, vocational, and/or recreational skills are all important to use as a platform for learning. |

*(continued)*

APPENDIX 3.2 **Motor Skills Observation Sheet**

| Structures and skill sets | Functions and skills | Example skills or deficits in this student | Potential interventions, strategies, accommodations, or educational objectives |
|---|---|---|---|
| Motor structures | Bones<br><br>Joints<br><br>Ligaments<br><br>Muscles<br><br>Nerves | | |
| Motor functions | Relaxation and contraction of muscles, movement across a joint | | |
| Movement patterns | *Rudimentary gross motor patterns:* Rolling, sitting, crawling, standing, cruising<br><br>*Rudimentary fine motor patterns:* Grabbing with full hand, rake grasp, finger-to-thumb grasp<br><br>*Fundamental gross motor locomotion patterns:* Walking, running, jumping, hopping, skipping<br><br>*Fundamental gross motor object manipulation patterns:* Kicking, catching, pushing objects<br><br>*Fundamental fine motor object manipulation skills:* One-hand skills—pincer grasp, crushing, crumpling, squeezing<br><br>*Fundamental fine motor object manipulation skills:* Bimanual skills—holding onto an object in one hand while performing an action on the object with the other hand (e.g., opening a jar, writing)<br><br>*Differentiated movement patterns:* All of the movement patterns listed previously can be used under different circumstances and for different purposes | | |
| Movement sequences | Adaptive, vocational, and recreational movement sequences | | |
| Motor control | Force and speed in movement<br><br>Spatial awareness<br><br>Executive skills<br><br>Motivation<br><br>Comprehension | | |

# II

# Developmental Frameworks

# Formal Language Skills



## INTRODUCTION AND GENERAL DEFINITIONS

Language is a critical part of learning at school. It underlies and influences almost all aspects of the school day, including a student's classroom participation and reading and writing skills. Although the topic of language generally includes all types of communication, this chapter is dedicated to the narrower definition of language as it occurs in the aural-oral context. Later chapters of this book revisit language skills in relation to reading and writing and the role of language in print.

Speech pathologists often divide language into the following three aspects: *Form, content,* and *function* or *use* (ASHA, 1993). The *form* of language refers to the components of language, such as sounds, words, and grammatical markers, or the structures of language such as word order in sentences. Components and structures give language its form. The form of language is the subject of this chapter. Here, the term *formal language* does not refer to the type of language used in formal settings, such as when writing an essay for publication or when delivering a presentation to colleagues. The terms *content* and *use* are defined later in this chapter and in the next chapter.

## HOW THIS FRAMEWORK WAS CONSTRUCTED

The Formal Language Skills Framework is based on divisions of language forms that are commonly agreed upon by linguists. Although some of the details differ among linguists (e.g., Crystal, 1997; Strazny, 2005; Thompson, 2003), there is agreement that language can be divided into the following components:

1. Sounds (phonetics and phonology)
2. Grammar (morphology and syntax)
3. Meaning (content)

The focus of this chapter is on the forms of language. Although language content and language use are equally important, they are not addressed in the Formal Language Skills Framework. The *content* of language refers to the meaning of the forms, such as the ideas or concepts that a speaker conveys through language. The *use* and the *function* of language (the terms can be used interchangeably) are not listed here. They both refer to how a speaker chooses the right language forms to convey the intended meaning successfully in a given context. For example, the form and content of language may have to be simplified when speaking with children, when speaking with nonnative speakers of English, or when speaking to an audience having limited familiarity with a given topic. Chapter 5, Pragmatic Language Skills, addresses the issue of language *use*. Successful use of language requires choosing the right language forms and content to meet the needs of the listener.

### Language Functions and Language Skills



The Formal Language Skills Framework uses the term *skills* very explicitly. Recall the distinction between biologically determined *functions* (as consistent with World Health Organization terminology, presented in Chapter 1) and *skills* (the expansion, through nurture, of biologically endowed functions into a broad range of skills). Humans are biologically programmed to listen to language and to speak. As discussed in Chapter 2, the capacity to discriminate among all the different sounds available for language (phonemic awareness) is a biologically endowed skill that is present from birth and develops during infancy. Humans are also biologically programmed to produce sounds and speechlike noises when, as infants, they coo and babble. Both phonemic awareness and the capacity to produce speechlike sounds are biologically endowed language functions. However, they are enhanced and refined through exposure to language and become integrated into a more complex set of language skills. For example, over the first years of life, infants and toddlers expand their awareness of the phonemes of their heritage language and then learn to reproduce those sounds in their speech and use the sounds as words. There is strong evidence that language skills depend on environmental exposure to language and that a proportion of students who do not have strong language skills were not exposed to a rich language environment (Hoff, 2006). For all students and perhaps especially for students with language impairment, it is important to provide a language-rich environment and explicit instruction in language (Golinkoff, Hoff, Rowe, Tamis-Lemonda, & Hirsh-Pasek, 2018).

## HOW CAN THIS FRAMEWORK HELP ME?

This chapter, which opens the section dedicated to developmental frameworks, highlights the importance of language in education. Language is everywhere. Listening, speaking, reading, and writing all require language skills. In fact, most of classroom learning occurs through language (Bloom, 2003). Difficulties in comprehension and production of language can affect students' success in reading, writing, and math (Grizzle & Simms, 2009; Harrison, McLeod, Berthelsen, & Walker, 2009).

This chapter is designed to deepen school professionals' understanding of and appreciation for language and its forms. The framework is designed to help identify successful language performance in the classroom by showing the practitioner what to look for. The terms presented here will help the practitioner describe a student's language performance during naturalistic or qualitative observations. They can also help in discussing observations made during a standardized measure as administered by the speech pathologist and create links to language objectives for the student's educational program. The framework also allows for a deeper understanding of reading and writing skills, as will be discussed in those chapters.

As is true for all the skills discussed in this book, the Formal Language Skills Framework can help practitioners identify the student's strengths (the skills that the student has already developed) to then determine which skills the student needs to develop further. The terms presented in this chapter can help school team members discuss a student's formal language skills with colleagues, with the student, and with the student's family. By making good observations, practitioners can fulfill their legal obligation to provide a written description of the student's classroom performance as part of a formal evaluation under disability rights law (Section 504 of the Rehabilitation Act and the Americans with Disabilities Act [ADA]) and special education law (Individuals with Disabilities Education Act [IDEA]). If the student is found eligible for services, practitioners can use the terms presented in this chapter to discuss with colleagues which educational goals and objectives to include in the student's IEP and how to measure the student's progress. A comprehensive discussion of the student's formal language skills can help everyone on the team understand the student's needs and allows all team members to participate in helping the student to improve language skills. By making repeated observations of a student's language performance over time, all practitioners can measure progress in the student's formal language skills and assess responsiveness to the teaching and intervention plan.



## FORMAL LANGUAGE SKILLS FRAMEWORK: TERMS AND DEFINITIONS

The framework presented in this section provides a detailed breakdown of the language skills, expanding on the terms and concepts introduced earlier in the chapter. The framework is intended to provide a deep understanding of language to help school professionals discuss a student's language skills more knowledgeably with colleagues, the student's family, and the student. Knowledge of these terms and definitions can also help guide proactive thinking about appropriate educational objectives to improve the student's language performance and to measure progress more successfully.

The Formal Language Skills Framework consists of the following skill sets and skills:

1. Sounds
   a. Phonemes and phonological awareness
   b. Articulation
2. Words
   a. Vocabulary
   b. Semantics
3. Sentences
   a. Morphology
   b. Syntax
4. Paragraphs: Narrative and discourse
   a. Heaps
   b. Sequences
   c. Linking devices
   d. Number of elements
   e. Tailoring the narrative to the needs of the audience

Each of the skills sets and corresponding skills listed in the framework above is defined and explained further in the sections that follow. The Formal Language Skills Framework is also summarized and presented in Appendix 4.1 for quick reference.

## Sounds

Language consists of sounds. Early in life, children begin to learn language by discriminating between noises and speech sounds. In the first year of life, infants listen preferentially to speech sounds, and they learn to discriminate between those sounds and to produce the sounds. The sounds of a language are referred to as *phonemes*. The capacity to discriminate between different phonemes is referred to as *phonemic awareness* or *phonological awareness*. In English, there are 45 phonemes. Each of the vowels and consonants used in speaking English is a phoneme. Sound combinations, such as /ch/ or /th/, are also phonemes. Each letter and many letter combinations of the alphabet represent one or more phonemes (Crystal, 1997).

Phonological awareness is the capacity to hear and discriminate among all the phonemes in a language. It is a biologically endowed skill. Children and youth need phonological awareness to produce sounds in speech (speech sounds). Speech-sound production is the process of producing phonemes by the lips, tongue, cheeks, and vocal apparatus. *Articulation* refers to how well or how poorly a student produces speech sounds.

Production of speech sounds begins in infancy and first shows up as babbling. Babbling emerges without any exposure to language and is a neurologically based function. Consisting of consonant–vowel sounds, such as "ba-ba" or "da-da," babbling emerges regardless of whether an infant is exposed to language; it also emerges in hearing-impaired infants who may not be able to hear spoken language. *Jargon* refers to the production of speechlike sounds and emerges in the second half of the first year of life. In contrast to babbling, jargon emerges only when an infant hears language on a consistent basis. It is not as repetitive as babbling, consists of a larger number of consonants and vowels, and includes changes in intonation (a rising and falling of the voice). It does not consist of true words and sounds very much like speech. True speech-sound production is evident once an infant or toddler speaks her or his first words.

Most speech sounds emerge during the toddler years. Articulation of speech sounds is largely mastered by the time a child reaches the age of 4 years. Although some articulation errors can persist after the age of 4 years in typically developing children, their speech is 100% intelligible to an unfamiliar listener. Prior to age 4 years, children's speech is not always as intelligible (Simms, 2016). Mastery of both phonological awareness and speech-sound production are critical pre-reading skills. Both phonological awareness and speech-sound production allow students to hear, discriminate, and produce the sounds of English as they apply to letters and letter combinations. When students have established their phonological awareness and have mastered speech-sound production, they can be understood successfully and can participate with greater confidence at school. They can later learn about how speech sounds are related to letters and letter combinations in print. See Chapter 9.

## Words and Vocabulary

Effective communication requires a *word bank, lexicon*, or *vocabulary* (Gagne, 2005). These terms all refer to the number of words that a person can understand and/or use. Vocabulary can be both receptive and expressive. A person's receptive vocabulary refers to the number of words that the person understands. Expressive vocabulary refers to the number of words that a person can use when communicating. A person's receptive vocabulary is typically larger than their expressive vocabulary. This pattern remains true over the life span. For example, toddlers learn the meaning of words before they learn to speak those words. As children and youth age, they are exposed to more new words, understand the meaning of those words, and subsequently learn how to use the words in their communications. A comprehensive lexicon or word bank is needed for them to understand and communicate ideas successfully when speaking and later, for reading and writing.

Vocabulary development is highly variable. It depends upon exposure and the demands of the environment. However, some patterns do exist. Typically developing children learn about and master common words and common concepts before they master more complex words or concepts. For example, children learn to use nouns and verbs before they learn about adjectives or adverbs. Children also tend to learn about commonly experienced nouns and verbs before less common ones. Early in life, children learn about categories of words, such as animals or clothing. Only later do children learn about words that describe language. Children and youth first master general words about language, such as *word root, opposite* (antonyms), or *simile*. With advancing age, students' vocabulary continues to develop as they master new concepts, such as learning the vocabulary for specific fields of study such as science or math. When students have a solid word bank, they can perform more successfully in school. They can understand more complex ideas, expressed by a peer or by a teacher. They can also express more complex ideas in their conversations with others and in their written work.



## Sentences: Morphemes and Syntax (Morpho-syntax)

*Morphemes* and *syntax* are the two terms that are important to understand when considering the structures of sentence-level language. They are commonly combined as *morpho-syntax* and are sometimes referred to as *grammar*. Depending on the resource, the word *grammar* can sometimes also refer to correct word choice (semantics or content) (Crystal, 1997). The following sections define morphemes and syntax in more detail.

## Morphemes

A morpheme consists of one or more phonemes tied together. For example, the phonemes /a/ and /n/ combine to form the morpheme /an/. The morpheme /an/ can then be used as part of a larger word, such as the word *analogy*. Sometimes, a morpheme is a subunit of a word, as shown in the word *analogy*. However, a morpheme can also be a word on its own, such as the word *an*. Morphemes are considered the smallest unit of meaning. However, many morphemes do not have any meaning on their own. They commonly need to be part of a word or part of a sentence to have meaning. For instance, even though *an* is itself a word, it does not have any meaning without other words connected to it. When *an* is connected to the word *apple*, it changes the meaning of the word. "An apple" means something different from "the apple," which is also different from "this apple," and so forth.

Morphemes influence the meaning of words and sentences. Key morphemes include the small joining words and the beginnings and endings of words, such as *a, an, and*, and *the*; prepositions such as *on* and *in*; and pronouns such as *his* and *mine*. Each of these words is made up of one or more phonemes. They do not mean anything on their own, although they do influence the meaning of the sentence. For example, the phrase "the ball in the box" does not mean the same thing as the phrase "the ball on the box." The morphemes /in/ and /on/ influence what ball is being referred to. Morphemes that serve as beginnings and endings of words also change the meaning of the sentence. For example, the beginning morpheme /dis-/ creates a negation. The endings /-ed/ or /-s/ change the word to the past tense or change the meaning of the word to a plural or possessive.

Brown's classic work (1973) is still used by speech pathologists in their observations of language and in their choice of therapeutic goals and objectives, because it offers a framework for understanding typical language development as it relates to morphemes and syntax (Crystal, 1997, Chap. 16; Feldman & Aronoff, 2005; see Table 4.1 for an adaptation of Brown's hierarchy). Literature on the development of morphemes and grammar focuses on the typical acquisition of morphemes and on the mean length of utterance (MLU), a measure of the number of words that a young child uses per sentence. This measure is useful in understanding sentence-level language development up to an MLU of three or four words. There exists somewhat limited agreement about the order in which these sentence-level (grammatical) aspects of language are acquired, and the developmental trajectory also varies depending on the language. A clear trajectory for the development of grammar thus remains elusive. Partly because of this, the most appropriate order in which to teach mastery of the above morphemes is also uncertain (Balason & Dollaghan, 2002; Hadley, 2014; Lahey, 1994).

**Table 4.1.** Brown's Hierachy of Morphemes in order of typical acquisition

| Grammatical morpheme | Example |
|---|---|
| Present progressive (-ing) | Baby cry**ing**. |
| in | Juice **in** cup. |
| on | Book **on** table. |
| Plural regular (-s) | Daddy have tool**s**. |
| Past irregular | Doggie **ate** bone. |
| Possessive ('s) | Jake**'s** apple. |
| Uncontractible copula (used as main verb) | This **is** mine. |
| Articles (a, the) | **A** red apple.<br>**The** big house. |
| Past regular (-ed) | He jump**ed** high. |
| Third person regular (-s) | Susie drink**s**. |
| Third person irregular | Baby **does** patty-cake.<br>Kitty **has** a toy. |
| Uncontractible auxiliary | **Are** you thirsty?<br>She **was** running.<br>He **is**. (Response to "Who's crying?") |
| Contractible copula | It**'s** cold outside. |
| Contractible auxiliary | Mommy**'s** crying. |

From American Speech-Language-Hearing Association. (n.d.). Grammatical morphemes in order of acquisition. Retrieved from https://www.asha.org/Practice-Portal/Clinical-Topics/Late-Language-Emergence/Grammatical-Morphemes-in-Order-of-Acquisition/

*Note:* All grammatical morphemes are typically acquired by about 4 years of age.

*Source:* Brown's (1973).

***Syntax*** *Syntax* refers to word order. Words in sentences must be in the correct order for the sentence to be meaningful. There is both a form and a content aspect to syntax. It does not make sense to say, "Store to I am going" or "Give the ball Billy to Jim." These sentences do not have the right form (word order) and therefore have unclear meaning (content). To make these sentences meaningful, the word order needs to be changed. It makes sense to say, "I am going to the store" and "Billy gives the ball to Jim." By changing the word order, the sentences become meaningful. The correctly written sentence not only included a change in word order, it also required a change in morphemes. The error in the word *give* was corrected by adding the morpheme /s/.

Morpho-syntax develops with age. The toddler transitions from using simple phrases consisting of two or three words to speaking in longer and more complete sentences. Simple sentences that each express one idea develop to become more complex sentences that can express more than one idea. As part of routine exposure to language, and as part of instruction in English Language Arts, students learn to speak in sentences that have more than one clause. Those sentences can then express complex relationships, such as which event or concept came first or how two events or two ideas are causally related to each other. When students can use English morpho-syntax successfully, they can understand and participate in conversations with peers and adults and can perform successfully in reading comprehension and written expression. Sentences are largely without any errors by the time a child reaches 6–8 years of age (Macroy-Higgins & Kolker, 2017).

## Discourse and Narrative

*Discourse* and *narrative* refer to language involving more than one sentence. The sentences can be part of a multisentence exchange between two people, such as a conversation or an interview.

The sentences can also be part of a lecture, a story, an explanation of how to do something, a description of an event, or something else entirely. When people deliver information in two or more sentences, they are using discourse or speaking in narrative. This section provides a set of terms to help school professionals analyze and describe paragraph-level spoken discourse and narrative. The terms presented here are useful in analyzing discourse such as stories, explanations, or descriptions. All these examples of discourse are referred to as narrative in this chapter. The topic of discourse and narrative is also revisited in Chapter 5. That chapter discusses the pragmatics of discourse and narrative and discusses the use of language in conversations between two or more people.

Just as the forms of language affect meaning at the level of words and sentences, the form of narrative also affects its meaning. A good narrative is structured in predictable ways. Without a solid structure, the content or meaning of the narrative is less clear (Crystal, 1997). The forms of narrative and discourse are described in different ways, depending on the author or the purpose of the analysis.



***Elements, Goal Path, and Evaluation in Narrative*** The description of narrative provided in this section applies to many different types of multiple-sentence language samples. Multiple-sentence language samples might be delivered as a story, as a lecture, or (in written language) as an essay. There are three aspects of narrative: The number of elements in the narrative, the goal path of the narrative, and the narrator's evaluation of the elements and the goal path (summarized by Boudreau, 2008). The elements of a narrative are the persons, places, and events of the narrative. The second aspect of narrative is the goal path. The goal path consists of an initiating event, is followed by one or more additional events, and finishes with a resolution. The goal of the story can be about the goal of the main character(s) or about the goals of the narrator. The third aspect of narration, the evaluation of the narrative, refers to how the narrator "ties it all together." The narrator must explain the interrelationships between the elements of the story and the goal path. These interrelationships are often made clear when the narrator uses linking devices, that is, words and phrases such as *because* or *as a result,* that illuminate the connections between the elements of the story and the goal path. The appearance of linking devices marks a developmental accomplishment in the narrative skills of children.

***A Developmental Hierarchy for Elements, Goal Path, and Evaluation*** This section proposes an outline of how narrative develops with age. The paragraphs that follow provide a hierarchy of narrative skills. This hierarchy is useful for analyzing a student's narrative skills and for selecting educational objectives for enhancing a student's narrative skills.

*Narrative in Heaps* A narrative delivered in heaps (a term borrowed from Appleby, 1978) contains the right information (i.e., about persons, places, and events) and the right elements. However, the elements are not necessarily delivered in the right order, and the interrelationships between the elements are unclear. Many typically developing preschoolers deliver narratives in heaps. Only with adult prompting do the sequence and the interrelationships of persons, places, and events become clear (Hedburg & Stoehl-Gammon, 1986).

*Narrative in Sequence* The next stage in narrative development occurs after the preschool years. For example, by 5–6 years of age, typically developing students are often able to deliver a narrative in a proper sequence, with a beginning, middle, and end. Young students often link each sentence or each event with the words *and then* repeatedly. This linking device is helpful for identifying the temporal sequence of the story, even if it is not sufficient for understanding all of the interrelationships between persons, places, and events.

*Narrative in Temporal Sequence and/or With Causal Links* Midway through the early school years (first through third grade), students start to improve their narratives so that it is easier to follow the logic of the narrative. Linking devices and a clearer delivery of the causal relations in the story now emerge. The elements (people, situations, events) of the narrative are not only delivered in the right order, they are also delivered with some information about why the order occurred (*evaluation*). The student might use words and phrases such as *and then, because, after that,* or *even though* to explain connections between elements of the story.

*Narrative With Subplots, Characters, Attributions, and Intentions* As narrative skills progress, the narrative shows greater complexity. For example, elementary school–age students can add more information to the elements of the story (persons, places, events) and can have more than one goal path (e.g., subplots, narrative within the narrative). The narrative may have a richer description, and the student may reveal more interrelations among all the elements.



*Narrative That Is Tailored to the Needs of the Audience* The amount of information delivered in the narrative must suit the needs of the intended audience. Understanding the needs of the audience is a skill acquired not only through convention but also through awareness of social norms. For example, a student who is sharing a narrative with a familiar or unfamiliar adult, a class or a classmate, or a same-age friend will change how much information he or she delivers to make sure that the listener in each situation understands what was said. Tailoring the narrative to the needs of the audience is an example of language *use* and is discussed further in Chapter 5.

The student who has secure narrative skills can participate more fully at school. As narrative skills develop, students can engage in longer conversations with peers. They listen more attentively. They show stronger reading comprehension skills as they learn to summarize (aloud or to themselves) narrative in text. They show stronger writing skills as they start to produce their own written text. They start to understand and express complex ideas in content areas of the curriculum.

## PERFORMANCE DIFFICULTIES IN FORMAL LANGUAGE SKILLS

Performance difficulties in formal language can affect a variety of classroom participation behaviors and may affect academic outcomes. Consider the following classroom participation behaviors, as selected from report cards reviewed by the lead author in his clinical practice. The skills listed here are commonly assessed as part of a student's overall performance in kindergarten through grade four.

- Listens carefully and follows directions from adults
- Asks and answers questions to seek help, get information, or deepen understanding
- Listens attentively in small groups; listens attentively in large groups
- Follows rules for group discussion; participates in group discussions; participates in discussions by listening actively and contributing knowledge and ideas; stays on topic during discussion
- Produces complete sentences when appropriate to the situation
- Expresses self clearly, utilizing appropriate grammar
- Demonstrates understanding of a text read aloud or information presented orally
- Retells information from a story; describes people, places, things, and events with relevant details

The classroom participation behaviors listed above depend upon formal language skills and are commonly assessed by educators. The same list applies to pragmatic language skills, as will be discussed in the next chapter. Given how commonly these skills are assessed, teachers who work with students will have a sense of what constitutes grade-level performance versus a below-grade-level performance.

Difficulties in the skills listed above are associated with language performance difficulties. The behaviors are dependent on all four skill sets of the Formal Language Skills Framework. Failure to develop these skills may be due to a language impairment. Consider the examples in the following paragraph, adapted from Wolf (2011), for a more detailed list of language performance difficulties that educators and other school professionals could also identify in their students:

## Performance Difficulties in Speech Skills or Articulation

Students may have difficulty producing speech sounds. Articulation may be poor with preserved intelligibility, that is, the teacher and peers can still make out what the student is saying. Articulation may also be associated with reduced intelligibility such that the student is not always understood by others. Articulation errors can occur consistently or inconsistently. For example, some students struggle to articulate only certain phonemes, such as saying /f/ for the phoneme /th/. Other students may misarticulate primarily the beginning sounds or the ending sounds of words. In others, the articulation errors appear to be inconsistent. All the language performance difficulties just listed are associated with speech-sound disorders. They can be due to a hearing impairment, to muscle tone and muscle coordination difficulties, or developmental delay. A speech-language pathologist might identify a student as having an articulation disorder, childhood apraxia of speech, or a developmental delay, based on the student's performance in speech-sound production.



## Performance Difficulties in Phonological Awareness

In receptive language (listening comprehension), students might have difficulty discriminating the sounds of English and differentiating between words that sound similar. They may have difficulty understanding spoken language and would typically also have difficulty in sounding out words. Phonological awareness difficulties can occur in students with poor hearing or auditory processing disorders (APD). They can also occur in students who are learning English as a second language (ESL) or students with a specific language impairment. Difficulty understanding rhymes in spoken language and relating letters to speech sounds are potentially important markers of speech-sound problems and are associated with later difficulties in reading. Difficulty with phonics (decoding and spelling), discussed in Chapters 9 and 10, can be a marker and the result of performance difficulties in phonological awareness.

## Performance Difficulties in Vocabulary

In receptive language, a student who does not have a strong vocabulary may seem confused and struggle to understand instructions. In expressive language, a student with limited vocabulary might show compensatory behaviors. For example, instead of speaking smoothly and using accurate words that match the situation, the student might instead use filler words. The student might overuse phrases such as "the thing" or "the, you know, like . . ." or use imprecise words. The student might even use incorrect words, creating confusion for the listener, such as using the word *magician* for *musician*. For students with language difficulties such as these, a speech pathologist might identify the students as having a specific language impairment or an expressive language impairment.

## Performance Difficulties in Morpho-syntax

In receptive language, a student with difficulty understanding the morpho-syntax of English might take excess time to respond to questions. He or she might appear not to listen attentively and might not follow instructions successfully. In expressive language, the student might produce sentences that are too short. The MLU should be greater than 3.5 words by age 4 years and should be greater than 4.5 words by 5 years (Wolf, 2011). The student might have difficulty using morphemes correctly and might produce grammatically incorrect sentences. For example, the student might say *in* instead of *on* or *she* instead of *her,* thus altering the meaning of the sentence. The student might persist in using regular past tense endings, such as saying *I runned* instead of *I ran.*

### Performance Difficulties in Discourse/Narrative

The student might only be able to produce one or a few sentences in response to discourse demands, instead of speaking at greater length. For example, the student might summarize a story using one or two sentences and miss important elements. The discourse might not be presented in a logical sequence, or the interrelationships between ideas might be unclear. The discourse might contain too much information or, conversely, too little information. The student might forget too many details in delivering the narrative or might include excessive information.



## HOW TO SET UP AN OBSERVATION OF FORMAL LANGUAGE

The type of observation proposed for formal language skills, and throughout this book, is structured, qualitative, and naturalistic. It is intended to mimic everyday language demands and is a critical aspect of any evaluation (Dockrell & Marshall, 2015; Farmer & Mendoza, 2007). The reader may wish to review the list of classroom participation behaviors taken from kindergarten to grade four report cards presented in the prior section. Each of the examples in that list requires sentence-length comprehension and expression. It can be useful to start the process of making observations by keeping these already familiar observations in mind, even for students who are in higher grades.

Naturalistic observations from the classroom are needed to understand how the student uses language in everyday contexts. Naturalistic observations help to identify performance difficulties and help in making referral decisions if a standardized assessment is needed. If a standardized assessment was completed, be sure to ask the speech pathologist to interpret the naturalistic observations and compare them with the student's performance during the assessment. All of these observations help to inform the choice of educational objectives. Note that the qualitative observations as proposed below should be divided into both receptive and expressive aspects of formal language skills. There may be a significant difference between what the student can understand and what the student can produce or express.

### Choose a Way to Measure Skills

To conduct a qualitative observation, it is important to have a method for quantifying behaviors. The quantification of naturally occurring behaviors is a critical aspect of making behavioral observations in children in general. Specific examples of how to do this are offered in Chapters 7 and 8. The main factor here is to ensure that what was witnessed during the observation is a consistent behavior that occurs across settings. All of the adults who know the student can make observations, on different days and in different locations, and can help ensure that the observations are consistent. It is important to know that observations made on one day accurately reflect the student's everyday language behaviors across settings and over time.

### Select the Student

To get started, school professionals should identify the student whose language will be analyzed. The student's report card will often indicate whether there are concerns. Any student with performance difficulties in classroom participation merits a more detailed observation. All the classroom participation behaviors listed at the beginning of the prior section (Performance

Difficulties in Formal Language Skills) are important to review. Classroom participation behaviors that are graded as "not yet at grade level" may signal the need for a more careful observation. Students with difficulties in their reading and writing skills may also warrant a more careful observation of language.

## Select Activities

To set up a qualitative observation, the observer should choose activities that mimic everyday classroom demands for that student. These could be looking at a storybook together, reading a section of a chapter book, engaging in a classroom discussion with peers, or holding spontaneous conversations in the hallway or on the playground. Professionals will have to use their judgment about what type of activity is best for each student. The goal here is to find an activity that offers a naturally occurring language sample that can be used to assess the student's comprehension and use of language. Even if the student already receives speech-language services, the observation outside the therapy sessions will prove to be worthwhile. The observation will provide information about how to speak with the student, and what types of responses to expect from the student, during everyday classroom demands. Professionals can also use the Formal Language Skills Observation Sheet in Appendix 4.2 to provide further structure to their observations.



## Obtain a Language Sample

A simple way to obtain a language sample is to ask the student to generate a narrative by looking at a picture. Alternatively, the observer can ask the student to retell a story after having heard it read out loud. Many pictures or picture books in classrooms for young children can serve as the stimulus for producing a narrative and for obtaining a language sample. When selecting the pictures, the observer should consider the student's narrative skills. For a developmentally younger child, the pictures should be detailed and should provide clues that help the student understand the temporal and causal links between one picture and the next. For a student with more advanced language skills, the language sample can be obtained using a book or set of pictures that are more open ended. These two types of pictures offer a different level of support.

Language samples can also be gathered through conversations with the student. For example, a teacher might ask the student to share information about an interest, describe a fun activity that she or he did with friends or with the family, discuss a field trip or a family trip that the student may have taken recently, or hold a conversation using puppets, dolls, action figures, or toy animals. The observer can make an audiorecording of the student's language sample.

The observer should take notes throughout the interaction. Alternatively, the observer can make audioclips or, preferably, videoclips to use in transcribing the conversation after the interaction has occurred. Even capturing a 1- or 2-minute segment of the conversation will prove valuable for the analysis.

## Analyze and Interpret the Observations

After obtaining the language sample, the observer should analyze and then summarize his or her thoughts about the student's performance for each of the Formal Language Skills discussed in the framework. The observer can review and analyze the language sample for the following types of difficulties:

***Analysis of Phonological Awareness*** The student should be able to discriminate between phonemes and not be confused by similar-sounding words. The student should be able to segment words into their component phonemes. For example, if the observer asks the student to segment the words into their component sounds, he or she can prompt the student this way:

"Say 'cowboy.' Now, say 'cowboy' without saying 'boy'." Another way to assess segmentation is to ask the student to count the number of sounds in words or to produce each sound contained in a word one after the other.

***Analysis of Articulation*** The student should not make articulation errors past the age of 6 or 7 years. Any articulation errors should not interfere with the observer's comprehension. If the student is difficult to understand, it can be useful to make an estimate, by percentage, of the student's intelligibility. For example, is the student 100% intelligible? Is he or she 75% intelligible? Less than 75% intelligible? It can also be useful to describe where the articulation errors tend to occur. For example, the articulation errors might occur only for certain sounds. The articulation errors might occur only at the beginning or at the end of the words. Some students make inconsistent articulation errors. These are harder to capture but are very important to identify if present.



***Analysis of Words/Vocabulary/Lexicon*** For learners who function at an early developmental stage of language, the observer may wish to document how many words the student is able to understand. The student might show comprehension at the single-word level, either by showing comprehension with a nod or shake of the head, by responding correctly to testing demands, or by other actions that convey their comprehension. The student might use single words. For some students whose vocabulary is very limited, such as a student with severe cognitive impairment, it can be useful to document and generate a list of words that the student has mastered. This list indicates not only the extent of the student's expressive language development, but also serves as a platform for expanding the student's vocabulary. For students who already speak in phrases or sentences, the analysis may look somewhat different. The student may seem to speak fluently but may use filler words, such as "um, the thing," or "you know, like, the stuff." The observer may need to determine if the student uses fillers too often, or if the student uses incorrect words altogether. Overly simple sentences and lack of description can be a signal of a low vocabulary count.

***Analysis of Morphemes and Syntax*** The observer should verify that the student understands sentence-length speech. This can be done by using sentences of different lengths, for example, five to six words versus ten to twelve words. The observer can also use some humor and speak in grammatically incorrect sentences. Students still mastering grammar might be confused by small changes in the sentence, such as changes in the pronoun (he/she) or changes in prepositions (in/on/under). If the observer changes the word order to change the meaning of the sentence, or to render the sentence meaningless, verify that the student understands the difference. For example, the observer could say, "Billy the bear was under the bridge when he threw the ball." And then say, "The ball was under the bear when Billy threw it to the bridge." The observer could then ask which sentence does not make sense, or could ask the student to respond to a comprehension question for each. Expressively, verify whether the student makes excessive grammatical errors. The observer can ask the student to produce language samples in response to a storybook or a set of toys. The observer can analyze the language sample for correct use of tenses, correct use of possessives, and correct use of pronouns. The observer should document the length of the sentences produced. The observer should also make a note of the number of words in each sentence, whether the words respect rules of syntax (order), and whether or not the sentences make sense. For some students, difficulties in morpho-syntax are very obvious. The Case Example at the end of the chapter provides one such example. For other students, difficulties in the production of sentence-level speech might be less obvious. For example, some students with a specific language impairment can produce grammatically correct sentences most of the time. Their language difficulty becomes evident only when the observer notices that their sentences are usually short, consisting of only one clause, and often contain only a basic vocabulary.

***Analysis of Narrative/Discourse*** Receptively, notice whether or not the student is listening attentively and appears to understand a story read to her or him. Some students need pictures to help focus their attention and to help them understand the story line. Other students can comprehend the narrative based on a verbal retell alone. Observers can assess comprehension by asking the student to respond to a question by pointing at the right picture or to respond verbally. The observer can also ask the student to retell the story. If the student's narrative appears to be disorganized or is not intelligible, it might be because of a language comprehension problem. The student may produce an unintelligible narrative because he or she did not understand the story that he or she was supposed to retell. Just as likely, the student may have a language production problem, even if comprehension is intact. Regardless of the cause, it can be useful to characterize the student's production of narrative using the terms discussed in this chapter. It is useful to know if the narrative was delivered in heaps or in a sequence and whether or not there were any linking devices. It is useful to know if the narrative improves when the student has pictures to support the verbal output or if pictures do not make any difference at all. Young children will produce a narrative that lacks a coherent order, whereas school-age children can typically produce a narrative that is correctly ordered. More advanced details to look for include remembering enough details, telling about all the events in the story, and using linking devices that help clarify narrative. Notice whether the narrative is too long, with excessive detail and a lack of focus. Notice whether the narrative too short, with too few details.



## Discuss Findings With Colleagues

After analyzing the observation, school professionals should discuss the student's performance with colleagues, including the student support team, the special education team, and the speech pathologist, as appropriate. The observer can share the transcript or the audio/videoclip and describe what language barriers he or she observed for the student. The discussion should consider the following: Which component(s) of language may not be at age or grade level? Have other colleagues noticed the same performance difficulties? Is the difficulty occurring in different settings and is it a consistent finding? Is a formal evaluation needed? The team members should offer their opinion of the observer's analysis and recommend next steps in providing supports or intervention for that student.

After an observation and after discussion with the team, specific educational objectives can be selected for inclusion in the student's educational program. The following paragraphs provide some general suggestions that are often appropriate for the student with language learning difficulty.

## General Comments About Language Learning

For all students with language-learning difficulty, adults should verify that they receive exposure to high-quality language. This includes the hearing-impaired student. Adults who work with students with more limited language skills should deliver language slowly and with repetition. Sentences may need to be shortened. The instructor may need to pause to ensure that the student has understood correctly and then ask the student to share his or her understanding of the task or situation (Garnet & Farmer, 2007). The student with a hearing impairment can improve understanding of spoken English while also learning sign language (Easterbrooks, 1999, 2008). For all students with language impairment, but especially for those students with hearing impairment, it is important to consider the quality of the acoustic signal (the teacher's voice) in relation to background noise.

Improving a student's language abilities involves more than just providing speech-language services during a therapy session. Teachers, peers, and the family should all be engaged in the teaching process (Wolf, 2011). Whereas there are multiple theories about how typically developing children acquire language, many different strategies can be effective. Strategies for any given student should be selected based on what works best for that individual student. Students can improve their language skills using direct instruction that integrates the terms and definitions presented in this chapter. The student can be taught to recognize the language forms that she or he has already mastered, and the teacher can use this base to build on and enhance the current skill sets. For example, the student can be taught about discriminating and producing new sounds, understanding and using new words, recognizing and using new grammatical structures, and/or developing more advanced narrative skills. Exercises can be created to enhance the student's skills in each of these areas, using a direct instructional approach.

Students can also improve their language skills using a contextual approach. As the student acquires new knowledge or participates in new experiences, the student is taught about the sounds, words, grammatical structures, and narrative structures needed to understand and describe the newly acquired knowledge or experiences. These latter skills can be acquired through student-teacher interactions, as well as through student-peer interactions. Language learning occurs best when different approaches are used simultaneously. This means not only providing direct instruction about the forms of language but also providing language instruction during naturally occurring communication with the student. Language instruction should also occur within the context of other learning demands such as reading, writing, and in content areas. (Chapman, 2000; Clark, 2004; Hoff, 2006). The integration of language instruction with reading and writing instruction is discussed further in Chapters 9 and 10. The student and teacher(s) should set goals mutually (Wolf, 2011). Whatever the learning context, the teacher should be sure to teach about both form (phonemes, vocabulary, and morpho-syntax) and content (current or prior experiences and knowledge). Chapter 5 is important to review for additional terms related to language and its use in social contexts.

## Educational Objectives and Strategies for Teaching Formal Language Skills

The Formal Language Skills Framework provides a structure that can be used for both teaching and learning. The objectives for formal language learning will depend on the individual needs of the student. Most students will benefit from language instruction in all the skills presented in the Formal Language Skills Framework: Sounds, words, sentences, and paragraphs. The specific goals and objectives chosen for teaching formal language skills will depend on what language skills the student needs to develop the most. The team should always make use of a speech pathologist's expertise, whenever available. One of the objectives for students already showing sentence-level speech should be to teach the definition of the terms listed in the Formal Language Skills Framework. By identifying skill sets (sounds, words, sentences, and paragraphs), the student can more easily focus on specific skills within each skill set. Students who have only limited language may first need to learn a more basic vocabulary before they are taught the vocabulary for the structures of language.

***Educational Objectives and Strategies for Sounds*** The student may need instruction and support to improve her or his phonological awareness and articulation. He or she may need support to improve his or her capacity to hear, discriminate between, and produce speech sounds. The strategy used to teach about speech sound can be selected by the speech pathologist. Speech-sound discrimination and production can be taught through direction instruction or through natural contexts. Strategies might include identifying and then imitating the speech sounds produced by a speaker. The speaker can be an adult or a peer, or the sounds can be taken from an audioclip/videoclip. If the student is learning how to read, the same strategy can be paired with printed words or letters. Speech-sound production by the adult might need to emphasize only the beginning sounds of words or only the ending sounds of words. Early instruction may need to focus on sounds and words that are very different from one another (high phonemic contrast), before teaching about sounds and words that are similar or the same (Zupran & Dempsey, 2013). Speech-sound production can be taught to students with a hearing impairment, along with teaching sign language (Easterbrooks, 1999, 2008). The teacher may need to attend carefully to the quality of the acoustic signal when teaching a student with a hearing impairment. See Chapter 2 for more information about how to ensure a quality auditory signal, and consult with an audiologist whenever possible.



***Educational Objectives and Strategies for Words*** Students with a cognitive impairment may need to master a very basic vocabulary. It is typically useful to start with concrete words before teaching abstract words. For example, instruction might focus on teaching nouns and verbs associated with everyday activities (e.g., *desk, chair, hallway, sitting, standing, eating, dressing*) before teaching adjectives, such as color terms (e.g., descriptors such as blue, yellow, green), quantity terms (e.g., concepts such as bigger, smaller, heavier, lighter), or adverbs (quickly, slowly, carefully). It also may be useful to teach position concepts (under, over, behind). Later the student may be ready to learn about categories of nouns (animals, foods, machines), categories of verbs (cleaning, dressing, cooking), or words associated with grammatical structures. Some students, such as those with hearing impairment, may also need this type of instruction. They would typically benefit from oral language instruction delivered alongside sign language instruction. A teacher of the hearing impaired can help select the best strategies, including how to make the best use of sign language during oral language instruction. Auditory-verbal instruction that is accompanied with visual supports (either pictures or sign language) can also be helpful for students who may have severe cognitive impairments and/or very limited language skills. Students with more fluent language skills may be ready to learn technical terms, such as terms associated with the general education curriculum. Objects, pictures, stories, and videoclips are useful strategies for teaching new vocabulary. Progress monitoring can occur through language samples (measuring whether or not a student uses new vocabulary in conversations or during narrative tasks), by counting the number of words that the student comprehends and uses, by assessing the student's ability to define and use vocabulary related to the general education curriculum, or by asking the speech pathologist to administer standardized vocabulary measures.

***Educational Objectives and Strategies for Sentences*** For some students with language difficulty, the goal may be to improve understanding and use of morphemes and word order. Students with a language-based learning disability are likely to need some instruction in this area. With the help of the speech pathologist, educators can compile a list of the morphemes that the student needs to master and can design instruction accordingly. Exposure to correctly spoken English at the sentence level is one way to teach about morphemes and syntax. Lessons can also include visual supports to help the student focus on the specific morpho-syntactic structures to be taught. Teaching about morpho-syntax can occur with picture stimuli and stories and during conversations with adults and peers. Language sampling can help measure progress. For any given language sample, professionals can look at factors such as whether the student understands and uses morphemes and word order successfully. The sample can also be analyzed to consider changes in the length of the sentences that the student understands and/or produces.

***Educational Objectives and Strategies for Paragraphs*** Teaching staff can develop educational objectives for understanding and producing narrative. A starting goal could be that the student understands and generates narratives of one to three sentences in length, moving to much longer narratives as the student makes progress. Narrative production skills can be developed by having the student listen to and retell a spoken narrative. School professionals can also ask the student to tell a narrative in response to a sequence of pictures or a single picture or to produce a narrative based on a personal event. Another easy starting point might be for the student to produce an oral narrative about a recurring personal event ("Tell me about what you and your family do on weekends.") or an especially interesting personal event ("Tell me about your weekend at the beach."). As narratives get longer, the practitioner can pay more attention to the sequencing of information in the narrative, how successfully the student creates links between the elements and events in the narrative, and how well the student creates subplots or makes use of descriptors.

Within any given narrative task, the student may need to focus on more specific objectives. For example, the teacher may ask the student to produce longer oral narratives (five to seven sentences). The objective might be for the student to generate a narrative that includes more persons, places, events, or interrelationships between all these elements. The objective might be to clarify the goal path by using more linking devices. Student progress can be assessed by making multiple observations and by measuring how successfully the student produces oral narratives with these added elements. These measures can be taken from narrative tasks that are already a part of the student's curriculum for grade, from narrative tasks that are specifically designed for the student, or through use of standardized measures. Oral narrative objectives such as these serve the role of supporting writing skills. See Chapter 10.



## Accommodations for Formal Language Skills

Although accommodations are not designed for teaching new skills, they can facilitate learning new skills if used judiciously. Accommodations for language can be developed to enhance the student's listening comprehension. They also can be designed to reduce demands on the student, for example, by asking the student to create linguistically simple responses or by using picture supports. School professionals can consider the accommodations outlined in the following sections:

***Accommodations for Sounds*** To accommodate for difficulty hearing sounds, educators should articulate and enunciate their speech more carefully. This is a good approach for many different students, including those who might have difficulty discriminating sounds in words (phonological awareness) and students who may have a hearing impairment. Expressively, a student might have an educational objective of producing more accurate speech sounds. However, for some lessons, the teacher may decide not to provide feedback about articulation errors if the purpose of the lesson is to focus on other skills.

***Accommodations for Words/Vocabulary*** When students do not have a strong vocabulary or word bank, educators may need to repeat words, provide definitions of words, or check in with the student to ensure comprehension. For example, the educator can ask, "Did you understand that? Can you show me what I just said? Do you need me to say it another way?" Word-prediction software and/or a thesaurus can be used to help the student find new words or more precise words for both speaking and writing.

***Accommodations for Sentences*** When students have difficulty understanding a large amount of language, educators can simplify the language load in several ways. They can reduce the length of the sentences, reduce the number of grammatical markers by speaking in phrases, and reduce the language load by simplifying the communication to one or two words only. It is best to start out with a full sentence spoken in correct English before reducing the sentence(s) to one-clause sentences and/or reducing sentences further to only the most important words. These strategies can also be used when asking the student to produce language. If the focus of the lesson is not to teach sentence-level speech production, then single words or phrases may be sufficient as responses.

***Accommodations for Narrative*** If students have difficulty understanding narrative, educators can use some of the strategies listed in the educational objectives sections of the IEP Builder. For example, even if same-age peers are expected to understand and retain information from a spoken narrative, a student with a language-based learning disability may need the narrative repeated or may need picture supports to understand the narrative. Even if same-age peers are expected to produce a narrative from memory, the student with a language-based learning disability may initially need to develop narratives that are shorter, with fewer elements and more limited evaluation, before moving on to written narratives that are more elaborate and more appropriate for age or grade.



## CASE EXAMPLE

Leonard is a kindergarten student identified as having a language impairment. He is a friendly boy who is interested in many of the activities presented in his kindergarten class. A review of Leonard's report card revealed challenging behaviors in classroom participation. His teacher rated his performance as "progressing toward the standard" for behaviors such as "understands and follows directions" and "verbal participation in class." Receptively, Leonard is able to make choices when given options and is able to follow instructions when these are delivered one at a time. During circle time, he often appears not to be listening. He often does not follow instructions when they are delivered to the class as a whole.

When considering his expressive language skills, Leonard usually does not participate in classroom discussions. He typically cannot express himself clearly and does not usually volunteer any information unless specifically asked to do so. Leonard often plays on his own. His teacher wondered whether he might be uninterested in socializing, but also noticed that he socializes very well with adults who can take the time to speak more slowly with him and ensure good comprehension. Leonard has an IEP and receives speech-language therapy from the district speech pathologist.

To understand Leonard's profile, a language sample was taken as part of a classroom observation. The language sample in the section that follows was obtained from Leonard in response to a six-picture stimulus that makes up the story "The Fisherman and the Cat." This assessment task is taken from the Autism Diagnostic Observation Schedule (ADOS), a tool commonly used in clinical settings (Lord & Rutter, 2012). It was used to examine Leonard's social awareness and social abilities, but it also revealed important information about his formal language skills. Leonard's performance on the picture narrative task is the only portion of the assessment (ADOS) that is presented here. Other aspects of his communication skills are discussed in Chapter 5.

During the observation, Leonard had to look at each picture and provide a description of what he saw. After doing this, the pictures were taken away, and he had to produce a narrative retell of what he had just seen and discussed. By taking this approach, Leonard showed that he was able to provide sentence-level language samples in response to single pictures. In the retell portion of the task, he provided (or attempted to provide) a narrative-level language sample for all the pictures.

The pictures tell the following story: The fisherman is first seen catching a fish. His cat is watching him from only a few feet away. The fisherman puts the fish into a bucket and returns to continue fishing. The fisherman's cat steals the fish from the bucket while the fisherman's back is turned. In attempting to hide the fish, the cat mistakenly places the fish into a pelican's open beak. The pictures are designed to make this element of the story ambiguous, because the pelican's open beak is not fully visible until the next picture in the story is revealed. In that picture, the cat notices his error and looks surprised. The pelican flies away with the fish, and the cat is left stranded on the wharf without his prized fish, angrily shaking his fists at the pelican.

The italicized text below is a transcript of what Leonard said. Regular type-written text is a transcript of the prompts provided to Leonard by the examiner.

## Sentence-Level Language Samples Provided by Leonard

- Picture 1. *The cat and the boy are trying to get fish. And the cat is worried.* Why is the cat worried? *He wanted to fill in the sea.* He wanted to fall into the sea, or he was scared to fall in the sea? *Scared to fall in the sea.*
- Picture 2. *He's holding a fish. The fisherman caught a fish.*
- Picture 3. *Oh oh! The cat is gonna eat the fish. And he's going to grow bigger, until he burps.*
- Picture 4. What did the cat do? *It's want to grab the fish.*
- Picture 5. Where did the cat drop the fish? *In the sea.* No, look, he dropped it here. (The examiner points to the pelican's beak.) *It's a fish cloud!* Leonard proceeded to then show the examiner the clouds in the background of the picture.
- Picture 6. *The pelican hurt the cat!* Did he? *No more eating the fish! It's not for the cat, it's for the pelican!*



## Narrative Language Sample Provided by Leonard

Tell me what happens in the story: *You never be . . . you not happy! You are worried!* Examiner provides some prompts, as follows: Remember, at the beginning of the story, the fisherman catches a fish. What happens next? *The cat got the fish on the bucket.* What happened after that? *And he dropped it in the pelican's mouth. And no more eating the fish! "That's not for you," said the cat. "Only I can eat the fish."*

## Case Analysis and Interpretation

The language observations provided by Leonard provide descriptive evidence for his language impairment. Before reading the analysis that follows, take a moment to decide what types of language difficulties Leonard seems to have. For example, does he have language performance problems in sounds and sound production? Words/vocabulary? Sentences? Paragraphs? Even though Leonard's language performance difficulties are very apparent, it's only by doing a step-by-step analysis that the observer will be able to describe the language performance difficulties. The analysis is also needed to decide what types of educational objectives and strategies are most likely to be helpful. Only with repeated observations over time can the observer be certain about which components of language are the most affected. In reading the analysis, think about what next steps Leonard might be ready for, so that he can improve his language skills.

### *Leonard's Sound Production Skills: Phonological Awareness and Articulation*

Leonard did not show any difficulty in the production of sounds. His articulation was 100% intelligible.

### *Leonard's Word Retrieval/Word Production Skills: Vocabulary/Semantics/Lexicon*

When Leonard said, "He wanted to fill in the sea," he produced a grammatically correct sentence, but the word choice was poor. The sentence does not make sense. It's hard to know what he actually wanted to say. Leonard corrected himself when the examiner prompted him to clarify what he meant. His intention might have been to use another word. His incorrect word use might therefore reflect a limited word bank or limited vocabulary.

#### *Leonard's Sentence Production Skills: Grammar, or Morphemes and Syntax, or Morpho-syntax*

Leonard was able to produce many sentences successfully. Leonard is only 5 years old, so it is expected that he can still make some grammatical errors. However, the language sample provided by Leonard reveals very underdeveloped use of morphemes and syntax. Midway through this exercise, he said, "It's want to grab the fish" instead of saying, "It [the cat] wanted to grab the fish," or more appropriately, "She wanted to grab the fish" or "She's grabbing the fish." When he said, "The cat got the fish on the bucket," he used good word order, but he did not use the correct morpheme (he said "on" instead of "out of").

#### *Leonard's Paragraph Production Skills/Narrative Skills*

When prompted to describe what happened in the story, Leonard says, "You not happy! You are worried!" What he appeared to have done here is to recite the last thing he remembered, which is the emotion experienced by the cat at the *end* of the story. In other words, he started his narrative at the end and not at the beginning. When prompted to start the narrative over again, he was able to revert to a more logical sequence starting at the beginning. However, he continued to need prompting from the examiner to complete his story. He had some difficulty generating a full account of all the events in the story. In addition to generating a full account of all the events, a narrative requires sentences to be linked with one another. Leonard did this by using the word *and* twice, to show that there was an order to the events. However, his sentences were not linked causally. Preschoolers and young school-age children are likely to deliver clusters of sentences that are not causally linked with each other, even if they deliver the sentences in the right order. A more successful performance from another peer at this age might have looked something like this, "The cat got the fish out of the bucket. And then he dropped it into the pelican's mouth. And then the cat got mad, because he made a mistake. And then he said, 'That fish is not for you! That fish is for me!'"

Not all of Leonard's language difficulties can be identified using one language sample. Repeated observations over time are needed to give a full picture of his language difficulties. A standardized measure, conducted by an expert, can also help in determining where his language performance difficulties lie. That said, the history and observation are both consistent with language impairment. There were several aspects of classroom participation that were affected, and the language sample provided some clear examples of areas of difficulty. The sample is a good start for generating ideas about what next steps Leonard might need to work toward. The majority of Leonard's language interventions should be at the word, sentence, and paragraph levels. Intervention and teaching at the level of sounds is not needed, because his articulation is clear.

### Educational Objectives and Strategies for Teaching Leonard Language Skills

#### *Educational Objectives and Strategies for Teaching Vocabulary*

Leonard is mastering sentence-level speech but may also benefit from expanding his vocabulary. Vocabulary can be expanded through exposure to more language, for example, by discussing the names of objects, labeling actions by discussing position concepts and quantity concepts during everyday activities, and through stories.

### *Educational Objectives and Strategies for Teaching Sentence-Level Speech*

The district speech pathologist was helping Leonard develop a variety of language skills, especially by increasing his use of correct grammatical markers. Corrective feedback is a commonly used strategy to help students improve their use of morphemes and word order. Language activities as developed by a speech pathologist could help determine which morphemes Leonard uses consistently and which ones he does not use consistently. This information can then be used to inform which morphemes Leonard needs to work on mastering. Leonard could also work toward a longer mean length of utterance.



### *Educational Objectives and Strategies for Teaching Narrative Skills*

Leonard has difficulty with narrative. The case history suggests that he responds to conversational demands with single-sentence responses. His sentences are often five or six words in length. At this age, one- to three-sentence responses would be a good objective for him. When delivering a narrative with picture supports or when retelling familiar information, the expectation for his narrative length could be higher. Leonard may also be ready to produce more links in his narrative, so that the sequence of events and the cause-and-effect relationships in the narrative are also clearer.

## Accommodations for Leonard's Language Skills

In addition to enhancing his expressive language skills, Leonard's teacher can provide accommodations for his language. She can speak with him directly—one to one while making eye contact. She can repeat instructions and repeat elements of stories when reading to the class. In doing this, the teacher is reducing demands on Leonard's working memory and attention. She also can simplify language output by repeating herself in shorter sentences and by emphasizing certain words or phrases when she repeats herself. By using these strategies, Leonard is likely to understand language better and to participate more successfully.

## Working With Culturally and Linguistically Diverse Learners

It can be challenging to assess the language skills of a learner who is exposed to more than one language on a regular basis. The constant question is: "Does the learner have language performance difficulties due to a language impairment?" or "Is this child going through the process of learning a second language, and mastering conversational and academic English?" A minimum of 20% of the United States population speaks a language other than English in the home. The first step is to determine whether the learner comes from a home environment where they interact with more than one language. To get started on assessing an English language learners' skills, consider the following approaches:

### *Complete a Home Language Survey*

Most schools in the United States require families to complete a home language survey as part of the registration process. A home language survey is a brief questionnaire intended to determine what language(s) the child has been exposed to. School professionals should review the responses to the survey and then identify a valid and reliable assessment to further assess that student.

### *Conduct Appropriate Assessment*

To learn more about a linguistically diverse learner's language development, school profesionals should implement an assessment instrument normed in the student's heritage language.

Further, whenever possible, language assessors should be fluent in the learner's dominant language. For example, to assess a child's Spanish language development, the assessor should have professional qualifications and Spanish fluency, coupled with an age-appropriate language development instrument written in Spanish and normed on Spanish-speaking learners. A student with language impairment will show that impairment in both languages, not just in English.



## CONCLUSIONS

This chapter reviewed formal language skills and the forms of language. It discussed how sounds are put together to produce words, how words are put together to produce sentences, and how sentences are put together to produce a narrative and other types of discourse. To understand these patterns more fully and to identify difficulties in formal language skills, it is important to obtain and analyze language samples frequently and at routine intervals. Repeated observations can help to measure progress in the student's skills and assess the student's responsiveness to the interventions that are developed by the teacher and the team.

A language sample highlights the student's strengths and needs in a way that a description of that student's language cannot do. Any discussion of a student's strengths and needs is more valuable when actual work samples are shared. In this case, the "work sample" is an oral language sample. A language sample can highlight all the difficulties that a student may have and can make it easier for other team members to understand the types of accommodations or strategies that the student may need.

As discussed at the beginning of the chapter, there is more to language than just its forms. Language goes beyond good comprehension, good articulation, a good word bank, correct use of grammar, and a well-structured narrative. Language must serve the purpose of communication. Effective communication can occur only when the speaker takes into consideration the listener's needs. These needs always occur in a social context. The next chapter looks at how to use formal language for successful communication and focuses on how language forms are influenced by the social context.

## REFERENCES

American Speech-Language-Hearing Association (ASHA). (1993). *Definitions of communication disorders and variations* [Relevant Paper]. Retrieved from www.asha.org/policy/rp1993-00208/

Appleby, A. N. (1978). *The child's concept of story.* Chicago, IL: University of Chicago Press.

Balason, D. V., & Dollaghan, C. A. (2002). Grammatical morpheme production in 4-year-old children. *Journal of Speech, Language, and Hearing Research, 45*(5), 961–969.

Bloom, D. (2003). Language and education. In J. Guthrie (Ed.), *Encyclopedia of education* (2nd ed., p. 1388). New York, NY: Macmillan Reference.

Boudreau, D. (2008). Narrative abilities: Advances in research and implications for clinical practice. *Topics in Language Disorders, 28*(2), 99–114.

Brown, R. (1973). *A first language: The early stages.* London, United Kingdom: George Allen & Unwin.

Chapman, R. S. (2000). Children's language learning: An interactionist perspective. *Journal of Child Psychology and Psychiatry, 41*(1), 33–54.

Clark, E. V. (2004). How language acquisition builds on cognitive development. *Trends in Cognitive Sciences, 8*(10), 472–478.

Crystal, D. (1997). Discourse and text. In *Cambridge encyclopedia of language* (pp. 82, 162). Cambridge, United Kingdom: Cambridge University Press.

Dockrell, J. E., & Marshall, C. R. (2015). Measurement issues: Assessing language skills in young children. *Child and Adolescent Mental Health, 20*(2), 116–125.

Easterbrooks, S. (1999). Improving practices for students with hearing impairments. *Exceptional Children, 65*(4), 537–554.

Easterbrooks, S. (2008). Knowledge and skills for teachers of individuals who are deaf or hard of hearing. Initial set revalidation. *Communication Disorders Quarterly, 30*(1), 12–36.

Farmer, S., & Mendoza, M. (2007). Language assessment. In C. Reynolds & K. Vannest (Eds.), *Encyclopedia of special education* (Vol. 2, p. 1486). New York, NY: Wiley.

Feldman, L. B., & Aronoff, M. (2005). Morphology. In P. Strazny (Ed.), *Encyclopedia of linguistics* (p. 715). London, United Kingdom: Routledge.

Gagne, C. (2005). Lexicon: Overview. In P. Strazny (Ed.), *Encyclopedia of linguistics* (p. 623). London, United Kingdom: Routledge.

Garnet, K., & Farmer, K. (2007). Language therapy. In C. Reynolds & K. Vannest (Eds.), *Encyclopedia of special education* (Vol. 2, p. 1489). New York, NY: Wiley.

Golinkoff, R. M., Hoff, E., Rowe, M. L., Tamis-Lemonda, C. S., & Hirsh-Pasek, K. (2018). Language matters: Denying the existence of the 30-million-word gap has serious consequences. *Child Development.* Advance online publication. doi:10.1111/cdev.13128

Grizzle, K. L., & Simms, M. D. (2009). Language and learning: A discussion of typical and disordered development. *Current Problems in Pediatric and Adolescent Health Care, 39*(7), 168–189.

Hadley, P. A. (2014). Approaching early grammatical intervention from a sentence-focused framework. *Language, Speech, and Hearing Services in Schools, 45*(2), 110–116.

Harrison, L. J., McLeod, S., Berthelsen, D., & Walker, S. (2009). Literacy, numeracy, and learning in school-aged children identified as having speech and language impairment in early childhood. *International Journal of Speech-Language Pathology, 11*(5), 391–403.

Hedburg, N. L., & Stoehl-Gammon, C. (1986). Narrative analysis: Clinical procedures. *Topics in Language Disorders, 7*(1), 58–69.

Hoff, E. (2006). How social contexts support and shape language development. *Developmental Review, 26*(1), 55–88.

Lahey, M. (1994). Grammatical morpheme acquisition. *Journal of Speech, Language, Hearing Research, 37*(5), 1192–1194.

Lord, C., & Rutter, M. (2012). *Autism diagnostic observation schedule* (2nd ed.). Los Angeles, CA: WPS Publishing.

Macroy-Higgins, M., & Kolker, C. (2017). *Time to talk* [ebook edition]. New York, NY: AMACOM.

Simms, M. D. (2016). Language development and communication disorders. In R. M. Kliegman, B. F. Stanton, J. W. St. Geme, & N. F. Schor (Eds.), *Nelson textbook of pediatrics* (20th ed., pp. 307–316). Philadelphia, PA: Elsevier Saunders.

Strazny, P. (Ed.). (2005). *Encyclopedia of linguistics.* London, United Kingdom: Routledge.

Thompson, S. (2003). Functional linguistics. In W. Frawley (Ed.), *International encyclopedia of linguistics* (2nd ed., Vol. 2, p. 53). New York, NY: Oxford University Press.

Wolf, N. (2011). Developmental language disorders. In D. R. Patel (Ed.), *Neurodevelopmental disabilities* (pp. 173–191). New York, NY: Springer.

Zupran, B., & Dempsey, L. (2013). Facilitating emergent literacy skills in children with hearing loss. *Deafness and Education International, 15*(3), 130–148.

APPENDIX 4.1 **Formal Language Skills Framework**

The Formal Language Skills Framework is summarized here. School professionals can use this form as a quick reference for the skill sets and skills that need to be taken into consideration when making observations and developing an intervention plan.

| Skill sets | Functions and skills | Examples of functions and skills in action | Sample performance difficulties | Potential strategies, accommodations, or educational objectives |
|---|---|---|---|---|
| Sounds | Phonemes and phonological awareness<br><br>Articulation | The student is able to hear and discriminate all of the sounds of English. The student is able to hear and discriminate similar-sounding words and understand their meaning.<br><br>The student is able to produce all of the sounds in English in speech; the student's articulation is secure, and listeners can fully understand the student's speech. | The student is not able to differentiate all of the sounds of English and can make comprehension errors as a result of not hearing and/or discriminating the sounds successfully.<br><br>The student's artculation is poor.<br><br>The student makes articulation errors that interfere with intelligibility of her or his speech. Many students with articulation difficulties have difficulties in their phonological awareness.<br><br>Difficulties in phonological awareness are associated with problems mastering phonics. The student may present with reading decoding difficulties. | The student may need the assistance of an amplification system when hearing difficulty is the cause.<br><br>The student may need explicit instruction in hearing and differentating all of the sounds of English.<br><br>The student may need explicit instruction in producing all of the sounds of English in her or his speech. |
| Words | Receptive vocabulary<br><br>Expressive vocabulary | The student is able to understand and follow instructions successfully.<br><br>The student is able to participate in age-appropriate conversations. | Some students have an impairment in acquiring vocabulary. Their vocabulary is below the level expected for age. They may have comprehension difficulties. Separate from comprehension of vocabulary, students also can have difficulty using or retrieving their vocabulary in expressive language. Their speech may be too simple. They may end up using imprecise words, filler words in their speech (e.g., "um" or "the thing"). They may produce poor sentences and paragraphs in their writing. | Students functioning at an early development stage may need explicit instruction in vocabulary so that they can label all of the objects and activities related to daily routines. Students who already have mastered a basic vocabulary may need to expand their vocabulary through literacy activities or by having more opportunities to converse with adults who can share a rich vocabulary with them. |
| Sentences | Morphology and syntax | *Morphology:* The student understands and uses prefixes, suffixes, joining words, possessives, pronouns, prepositions. The student shows an understanding of English grammar.<br><br>*Syntax:* The student can understand and use simple sentence structure, compound sentence structure, sentences with subordinate clauses, and sentences of different lengths. | The student makes excessive errors in grammar because of incorrect use of morphemes. For example, the student may not yet have mastered correct use of suffixes in past tense and possessives, or the student is not yet using prepositions correctly. Sentence structure may be too simple for age. For example, the student might speak in single-clause sentences or be unable to vary sentence structures in spoken or written English. | Teach all the morphemes of English and their function in the sentence. See summary in this chapter.<br><br>Provide corrective feedback or ask the student to identify her or his own grammatical errors, and then correct them in spoken and written language.<br><br>Expand the student's ability to speak in more complex sentences, such as sentences with a subordinate clause, compound sentences. |

*(continued)*

| Skill sets | Functions and skills | Examples of functions and skills in action | Sample performance difficulties | Potential strategies, accommodations, or educational objectives |
|---|---|---|---|---|
| Paragraphs | Narrative and discourse | Narrative applies to both fiction and nonfiction and consists of multi-sentence paragraphs in spoken language.<br><br>The student is able to deliver a narrative that includes the following skills: Shares sufficient information about a topic by including all of the key elements; shares the information in a logical order or sequence; makes connections between each aspect of the narrative (e.g., use linking words such as *because, as a result, and then, before that*). As narrative skills improve, the student can include more elements (i.e., more topics, characters, settings, problems to solve, etc.). | Student may share information out of order. The narrative may be difficult to understand because of missing information, or because of an absence of linking devices, making it difficult to understand the cause-effect relationships in the story or in the information shared. | Teach about the components of narrative, including chronological ordering, identification and description of characters, events, places, or terms needed to understand the story or the information being shared<br><br>Ask the student to review her or his own performance using audioclips or based on memory.<br><br>Use explicit questions about which elements of the spoken narrative could be improved so that the narrative has a more logical sequence, so that cause-effect relations are more clearly established, so that extraneous information is removed, or so that the listener understands the information more successfully.<br><br>Teach the student how to expand upon the number of elements in the story. |

APPENDIX 4.2 **Formal Language Skills Observation Sheet**

| Skill sets | Functions and skills | Example skills or deficits in this student | Potential strategies, accommodations, or educational objectives |
|---|---|---|---|
| Sounds | Phonemes and phonological awareness<br><br>Articulation | | |
| Words | Receptive vocabulary<br><br>Expressive vocabulary | | |
| Sentences | Morphology and syntax | | |
| Paragraphs | Narrative and discourse | | |

5

# Pragmatic Language Skills



## INTRODUCTION AND GENERAL DEFINITIONS

The prior chapter presented the framework for formal language skills. Although an understanding of formal language skills is necessary for good communication, well-structured sentences and paragraphs are not always sufficient for successful communication. The speaker has to choose the right language forms (the right words, sentences, and paragraphs) for the situation—the words need to influence the listener as intended. The right forms for the situation vary by person and by context (Crystal, 1997a, Chap. 21). The most appropriate language forms depend on whether the listener is a real person, an imaginary friend, a child, or an adult. The forms likewise vary depending on whether the audience is listening to spoken language or reading printed text. The best language form also varies by social context. Language forms differ depending on whether the speaker is in a classroom setting, at a family dinner, or on the playground. This chapter is dedicated to the successful use of language in a variety of situations. We presented the concept of language use in Chapter 4. Successful use of language is referred to in this chapter as pragmatic language skills. They are a collection of skills that allow for the successful expression and recognition of intentions (Grice, 1957, 1969). Using pragmatic language skills means selecting just the right form to express the intentions of the speaker while also ensuring the intended effect on the listener (Soames, 2003). Pragmatic language skills are the subject of this chapter's framework.

When students cannot express their intended meaning or do not respond to the message as intended, there is a failure of pragmatics. This concern is present in all types of communication and has important implications for learning and for social interactions, both inside and outside the classroom. Pragmatics are commonly discussed in teaching language and literacy (Hyland, 2017) and in teaching foreign languages (Ishishara and Cohen, 2010; LoCastro, 2012), and they are important enough to consider as a necessary component of teacher training (Melguizo Moreno, 2017). Pragmatics affect how a teacher delivers content information to the class and influence how students receive and understand the information as delivered. Excellent teaching is excellent in part because of pragmatics. However, pragmatics are important in all human interactions. They are important to consider in settings outside of school as well.

Outside the classroom, for example, nonverbal communication, such as facial expressions, gestures, and tone, are critical to successful parent–child interactions. They can enhance learning and compliance of the child. Importantly, these nonverbal aspects of parent–child communication are often underemphasized in interventions designed to improve parent–child interactions (Colegrove & Havinghurst, 2017). The same issue is at stake in physician–patient interactions and has implications for health. When physicians do not communicate effectively, patients do not understand and might not follow medical instructions successfully. Effective physician communication depends on successful use of nonverbal communication skills such as turn taking, posture, tone of voice, and affect (Matusitiz & Spear, 2014). These variables apply to physician communication with both adults and children (Kodjebacheva, Sabo, & Xiong, 2016; Tates & Meeuwesen, 2001). Pragmatic language skills have a profound impact on everyday human functioning and in everyday relationships.

## HOW THIS FRAMEWORK WAS CONSTRUCTED



The study of pragmatic language skills does not represent a coherent field (Mey, 2005; Schneider, 2005). This lack of coherence posed challenges in the construction of the Pragmatic Language Skills Framework, because the collection of skills that are normally included under the term *pragmatic language skills* varies by author and researcher. A first important distinction in defining pragmatic language skills is that communication is both verbal and nonverbal. Some authors (e.g., Crystal, 1997b, Chap. 43) only include linguistic or verbal aspects of communication, such as conversational skills and other types of discourse, when they discuss pragmatics. They argue that nonverbal aspects of communication should not be included in the study of pragmatics, because these aspects of communication are not expressed linguistically (Cummings, 2007). Conversely, current thinking about social communication disorders and language pragmatics includes both verbal and nonverbal components of communication (Baird & Norbury, 2016). Tools used to assess language pragmatics commonly assess both nonverbal and verbal skills (Adams, 2002; Norbury, 2014; Russell & Grizzle, 2008).

This chapter considers pragmatic language skills to include both verbal (linguistic) and nonverbal (nonlinguistic) aspects of communication. Linguistic components are the correct or the most successful forms for the given situation (i.e., the right words, sentences, paragraphs). Nonlinguistic components are the correct or the most successful nonverbal forms of communication, such as facial expressions, gestures, body posture, and changes in tone of voice. For any communication, the linguistic and nonlinguistic forms used must reveal the speaker's intentions, desires, emotions, and/or beliefs, and should influence the listener as intended.

There is significant overlap between pragmatic language skills and several of the other frameworks discussed in this book. Pragmatic language skills are used to express intentions, desires, emotions, and beliefs. Pragmatic language skills are therefore affected by social cognition and social skills, affect and self-regulation skills, and executive skills. As such, the concepts presented in this chapter will be returned to and expanded on in Chapters 6, 7, and 8.

## HOW CAN THIS FRAMEWORK HELP ME?

The framework presented in this chapter is designed to provide the practitioner with a robust understanding of language pragmatics that are necessary for successful classroom participation and are an essential aspect of communication in any context. Students need to be able to express their intended meaning to their listeners and to respond to messages as intended by the speaker. These skills have to be developed in their communication with different speakers in different settings and about different topics. These skills have important implications for learning and for social interactions, both inside and outside the classroom.

This chapter begins with a discussion of the terms and definitions related to pragmatics. This discussion can help school professionals identify and describe observable behaviors as shown in this framework. The chapter highlights what successful pragmatic language performance looks like, as well as how performance difficulties in pragmatics can present. Professionals will learn to observe, analyze, and discuss a student's performance in pragmatic language skills with their colleagues, with the student, and with the student's family. Using strengths-based language, the chapter then offers the IEP Builder to help educators and other school professionals develop goals and objectives for building a student's pragmatic skills.

## PRAGMATIC LANGUAGE SKILLS FRAMEWORK: TERMS AND DEFINITIONS

The Pragmatic Language Skills Framework includes both nonverbal and verbal/linguistic aspects of communication. The first three skills sets of the Pragmatic Language Skills Framework describe the nonverbal aspects of pragmatic language. The next three skill sets include verbal or linguistic aspects of pragmatic language.



The Pragmatic Language Skills Framework is outlined as follows:

1. Facial expressions
2. Gestures and body posture
    a. Simple gestures
    b. Complex gestures
3. Auditory and musical features of speech
    a. Prosody: Accent on the right syllable
    b. Intonation: Emphasis on individual words
    c. Emotional expressiveness
4. Communicative functions
    a. Declaratives
    b. Imperatives
    c. Direct speech, indirect speech, ambiguous speech
5. Conversational skills
    a. Turn taking
    b. Contingency and topic maintenance
    c. Topic elaboration
    d. Conversational repair
6. Narrative skills
    a. Adjusting the complexity of the language (linguistic and syntactic complexity)
    b. Explaining referents
    c. Adjusting the volume of information

Each of the skills sets in this framework is defined and examined in the sections that follow. The nonverbal components of pragmatic language are explained first. The framework is also summarized and available in Appendix 5.1 for quick reference.

## Facial Expressions

Facial expressions are key to effective communication, as they can indicate the emotions contained in a word, phrase, or sentence and can change the meaning of the words. The sentence "I'm so happy that Julia got married" can mean something quite different when delivered with a bright affect (raised eyebrows and a smile) as opposed to a sad affect (eyebrows and mouth turned downward). The recipient of this communication would typically understand the difference instantly, as long as he or she noticed the facial expression. However, it is often difficult for listeners to describe how they know what the speaker intended to communicate. The words indicate something that is positive, whereas the facial expression (and the intonation, see next section) may indicate something different. One reason why it can be difficult for the recipient to describe the intended or underlying message is that a portion of the communication occurred nonlinguistically. It is separate from the verbal exchange. In fact, there are two messages being delivered simultaneously. A positive or negative affect is being conveyed through the facial expression, whereas the words on their own only convey a positive message. To add to the listener's confusion, the speaker may or may not intend to deliver more than one message. The speaker might not even be aware of the message transmitted nonverbally. Another potential reason for a listener's confusion is that facial expressions can change so quickly, often making them hard to notice or describe adequately. The listener may not truly know whether the speaker is happy or sad, especially if not familiar with the speaker.



Facial expressions are often described using general terms such as *happy, mad, scared,* or *sad.* As discussed, these different facial expressions of emotion have a strong influence on the linguistic message that the speaker delivers. However, these emotion terms are actually interpretations of facial expressions more than they are an observation of the facial expression. To understand pragmatic language skills properly, it is important to make objective observations first, and then make an interpretation. The description of the communication should first include details about the movements of different parts of the face. Only then should the observer make an interpretation of the underlying or nonverbal message. Some of the important variables that indicate changes in facial expression include raising or lowering the eyebrows, furrowing the eyebrows, opening the eyes wider or narrowing the eyes, raising the nostrils and the upper lips, lowering the lower lips, and showing the teeth versus keeping the mouth closed. Each of these implies a certain emotional valence or emotional tone.

Buck (1999) states that the facial expression of emotions can be either nonsymbolic or symbolic. Facial expressions that are nonsymbolic occur as a spontaneous expression of one's emotions. Symbolic facial expressions occur through the intentional or conscious manipulation of the muscles of the face. These two aspects can occur simultaneously. For instance, people can express pleasure spontaneously and unconsciously while also expressing their pleasure consciously and purposefully. A person who enters into a room and is greeted by a group of well-wishers who just organized a surprise birthday party might suddenly break out in a big smile. This is an example of a spontaneous expression of happiness or pleasure. As the party progresses, the same person might continue to show bright affect, communicating her ongoing pleasure about the party in a more conscious or purposeful manner. She might even exaggerate the facial expressions as she runs into people whom she is not pleased to encounter, thereby expressing pleasure when she might not actually be experiencing any. The first facial communication occurred instantaneously and was not associated with any intention to communicate information. The latter facial communications occur over a slightly longer time interval and are more conscious or purposeful. They include an intention to communicate a specific kind of emotion. The distinction between spontaneous and intentional facial communication is important to keep in mind for all the nonverbal components of communication. Not all nonverbal communication is intentional.

It is important to notice whether the facial expression (or any nonverbal communication) is congruent with the content of the words that accompany it (Grebelsky-Lichtman, 2014a, 2014b).

Assessing for the congruency between verbal and nonverbal communication is one way to assess the intentionality of the communication. For example, the communication of toddlers is usually congruent. Toddlers are typically not able to manipulate their facial expressions to indicate their intentions. The facial expression of happiness or anger matches the toddler's internal state, even if there are no words to verify this. Preschoolers also generally show congruence between their facial expressions and their words. If they state that they are happy or mad or sad, their facial expression will most likely align with their words. An example of their difficulty in manipulating their facial expressions can occur when a parent asks the preschooler to thank an aunt or uncle for a birthday gift he or she did not especially like. The preschooler can almost certainly comply with the request and say, "Thank you," but the accompanying facial expression is not likely to be congruent with the verbal message. In contrast, school-age children are able to manipulate their facial expressions to augment their communication with adults and peers, especially starting in elementary school. They may use facial expressions in a purposeful and symbolic manner by augmenting or exaggerating their facial expression to communicate an emotion. The school-age child might be able to express pleasure about the aunt's or uncle's gift (regardless of the actual emotion), while also saying, "Thank you!"

## Gestures and Body Posture

Gestures are body movements that serve the purpose of communication. Gestures involve the head, neck, arms, and hands and include the body and bodily posture. As is the case for facial expressions, some gestures reflect a spontaneous communication of a person's internal state and emotions. The same gestures can also be used purposefully or symbolically to augment or reinforce the content of the communication.

For the purposes of the Pragmatic Language Skills Framework, there are two key aspects to consider when making observations of student gestures. First, school professionals should consider whether the gesture is a spontaneous expression of a person's internal state, or whether the gesture is a symbolic representation, and is purposeful or intentional. Second, they should note whether the gesture is simple or complex. Simple gestures consist of one posture or one body movement, whereas complex gestures consist of combinations of posture and body movements that are linked and might take many seconds to deliver.

***Simple Gestures*** Simple gestures can be either spontaneous or symbolic. A simple spontaneous gesture occurs without the conscious awareness of the communicator and includes gestures such as covering the mouth with a hand to communicate surprise or fear. Simple spontaneous gestures can provide information about the communicator's internal state but might not be associated with any intended communication. Just as commonly, simple gestures can be symbolic and can be used in a purposeful manner. A simple symbolic gesture used for communication purposes is that of a person putting her hand on her stomach to indicate pain or hunger or raising her fists to indicate anger or the intention to fight. These gestures are relatively conventional, because they are commonly used by English language speakers and are readily understood in English language cultures. Some simple symbolic gestures are used conventionally, such as nodding the head to indicate yes and shaking the head or an index finger to indicate no. Other simple symbolic gestures include lifting the shoulders upward to shrug, indicating "I don't know" or "I don't care," or using the curled index finger to indicate "Come here." Gestures such as these usually have an obvious meaning that can be summarized by one word or phrase. They can express an emotion, a desire, an intention, a word, or set of words. As is the case for any nonverbal component of communication, their meaning is clearer when accompanied by spoken words. However, they can sometimes communicate an idea clearly even when observed in isolation. Cultural differences play a role. The gestures just described are readily understood in Western culture but might mean something quite different in other cultures.

***Complex Gestures*** Complex gestures are delivered over a longer time span than just a few seconds. They are symbolic, require more interpretation than a simple gesture, and serve the purpose of communicating more complex ideas. For example, tapping the hands on a surface to indicate "put that here" is a gesture that has to be interpreted within a context. The gesture might not be obvious unless the recipient of the communication is also told, "Put that here" or, even more important, "You, put that here." The context (the speaker, the environment, and the fact that the gesture was produced by an adult in a position of authority) all influence how the tapping is interpreted. When accompanied by different words and performed by a different speaker, the gesture of tapping on the table can end up meaning something very different. The person performing the gesture, the recipient of the gesture, and the location of the gesture all influence how the gesture is interpreted. For example, tapping as performed by a toddler has a very different emotional tone. Similarly, the same tapping by an adult without any accompanying words could indicate that the speaker or performer is utterly bored, especially when the adult is looking away from the observer and is staring out of the window. The tapping might even indicate a person's delight in making an interesting sound, especially when the performer holds her ears close to the tapping and experiments with tapping on different surfaces.



Another form of complex gesture, the demonstrative gesture, is used to indicate how something is made or how something is done. Demonstrative gestures could include motions such as a brushing motion to indicate painting a picture or brushing teeth. Often, there are several steps to making the meaning of the demonstration clear. Mime is a highly evolved form of gesture (and also of facial expressions) that can communicate an entire story or scene. American Sign Language consists of highly symbolic gestures that have very specific forms that represent specific words and grammatical structures, akin to the language forms discussed in Chapter 4.

## Auditory and Musical Features of Speech

The sections that follows provides several examples of how changes in volume, pitch, and rate can change or influence verbal meaning. It is not always easy to describe these auditory aspects of speech to learners. In some cases, it may be easier to describe them by imitating them. The sections that follow offer a basis for thinking about and describing auditory and musical aspects of speech, as manifest by changes in prosody and intonation.

***Prosody: Accent on the Right Syllable*** Prosody requires putting the right accent on the right syllable. For example, the word *present* means one thing when the accent is placed at the beginning of the word ("a gift" or "to be in attendance"); when the accent is at the end of the word, it means "to introduce someone or something." Accent is produced by making changes in volume and/or pitch. Toddlers and preschoolers may or may not use prosody successfully, because of their limited vocabulary and their limited ability to express more than one idea for any given word. The same holds true for nonnative speakers of English who are learning how to pronounce words in English and have only learned one meaning for a given word. As children grow into the school-age years, their vocabulary grows. They learn to pronounce the same (spelled) word differently to indicate a change in meaning. School-age children can make use of these differences to ensure correct communication. Most children and youth pronounce words correctly in their heritage language, once they have understood the meaning of those words. Linguists normally consider prosody as a formal language skill because the prosodic change indicates a different word and (often) a historically different word root. For the purpose of convenience, all of the different types of auditory and musical variations in speech are included in the Pragmatic Language Skills Framework.

***Intonation: Emphasis on Individual Words*** Intonation refers to how a speaker places emphasis on certain words within the phrase or sentence. Emphasis is produced by changing the volume and/or the pitch. The meaning of the sentence can change depending on how words are emphasized (or not emphasized) within the sentence. For example, the sentence "Give me that" varies in meaning, depending on whether the word *give*, *me*, or *that* is emphasized. If the speaker emphasizes the word *give*, the sentence suggests frustration about the fact that the listener is not supposed to have the object in his or her possession (and might be withholding the object intentionally). If the speaker emphasizes the word *me*, the sentence suggests that the speaker is making a distinction between handing the object over to the speaker as opposed to another person. If the speaker emphasizes the word *that*, the sentence suggest that the listener does not understand which object to hand over, and the speaker is clarifying the instruction for the listener. Preschool-aged children can use emphasis to enhance the meaning of their sentences but are not likely to consciously manipulate emphasis to change meaning, as described here. In contrast, school-age children can manipulate emphasis to change the meaning of their communication.

***Emotional Expressiveness*** Emotional expressiveness can be conveyed by changes in emphasis of phrases and sentences as a whole. Emotions are expressed through intonation, but also by making changes in the rate of speech. When a sentence is spoken loudly (high volume), quickly (high rate), and with a high pitch, it can convey an emotional tone, such as anxiety or urgency. When a sentence is spoken more slowly, with a lower pitch, it can indicate anger or another emotion.

## Summary of Nonverbal Communication: Facial Expressions, Gestures, and Auditory and Musical Aspects of Communication

The previous sections discussed facial expressions, gestures, and auditory and musical features as distinct aspects of nonverbal communication. Before moving to the verbal and linguistic aspects of pragmatic language skills, it is useful to reflect on the prior discussion. Although the elements discussed so far can be analyzed separately, the nonverbal aspects of communication typically or usually are expressed together.

When the nonverbal (nonlinguistic) aspects of communication are congruent with the verbal (linguistic) aspects, the meaning of the communication is often clearer, and the communication can convey an emotional tone. Communication that is clear and that conveys emotion is typically much more intriguing to the listener. The listener is more likely to pay attention and is also more likely to understand what the communicator intended to convey. As an example, when a speaker says, "He did that" in a flat tone of voice, the speaker expresses more than one possible idea. The sentence might be a statement or a question. The sentence might be saying something positive, negative, or neutral. It's not clear who *he* is or what *that* refers to. In contrast, When the speaker says, "He did THAT?" both emphasizing the word *that* (increased volume) and raising the pitch (higher tone of voice) at the end of the sentence, the listener knows that the sentence is a question and that the speaker is probably expressing surprise or frustration. The listener also knows that whatever was done was probably unexpected or noteworthy. The emotion behind the statement might be clarified by the speaker's raised eyebrows (indicating surprise) or furrowed brow (indicating anger or frustration). When the speaker adds a gesture, for example, by pointing at whatever was done, the listener now knows to what the speaker is specifically referring. The listener can then make an even more accurate interpretation about the speaker's emotion. The emotion might be outrage (about spilled paint on the floor) or delight and amazement (about the astonishing skill behind a piece of artwork).

With each added nonverbal component, the meaning of the sentence "He did that" becomes more and more specific. The listener now not only understands something about the emotion of the speaker (e.g., frustration, delight); he or she now also probably knows something about what the speaker is going to do next (e.g., fix the problem, deliver a reprimand, provide praise). Words therefore become more differentiated when they are accompanied by nonverbal communication, as shown here. Recall the use of the word *differentiation* in Chapter 3. When a motor skill is more differentiated, it can be used in a greater variety of settings, for different circumstances, and under different conditions. Here, the words *He, did,* and *that* are also more differentiated. The same words, when accompanied by changes in volume, pitch, or rate and when accompanied by gestures and facial expression, can be used to convey much more specific meaning. The communication is more highly differentiated as a result of the nonverbal additions. When nonverbal and verbal communication are paired in this way, the speaker ends up generating more interest through the emotional tone and can convey more precise and more complex meaning.

Communication that is more precise and that conveys an emotion is typically more arresting to a listener. The listener understands more about the speaker's intentions, desires, and/or emotions. As a result, the listener can also respond to the speaker in a more precise or more successful manner. In the example here, the listener might spontaneously help out by cleaning up, learn from the skills of the art student to improve their own painting skills, or assume that the art teacher thinks less highly of their own work in comparison and feel let down.



Sometimes, the nonverbal and linguistic aspects of the communication are not aligned. The speaker might not use any nonverbal communication or might use contradictory nonverbal communication. When facial expressions, gestures, intonation, and emotional expressiveness are not congruent with the linguistic aspect of the communication, the communication becomes more difficult to decipher. The lack of congruency can result in a confusing or contradictory message and may require further clarification. However, even though noncongruence affects clarity, it can generate interest through ambivalence. The listener can be led to wonder about the underlying feelings of the speaker and their true intentions in delivering the message. Very often, people interpret the nonverbal aspects of the communication as expressing the speaker's true intentions, desires, or emotions. They use their interpretation of the *nonverbal* aspect of the communication to determine the meaning of the *verbal* aspect of communication. An interpretation such as this is more likely to be accurate if the nonverbal communication is not symbolic and occurred spontaneously. That said, some communication is purposefully ambivalent. For example, sarcasm and humor often contain more than one meaning. In these cases, the speaker intentionally conveys ambivalence by delivering two different messages, verbal and nonverbal, at the same time.

## Communicative Functions

A communicative function consists of a single word, a phrase, or a short sentence. As is true for all pragmatic language skills discussed in this chapter, a communicative function reveals something about the speaker's emotions, intentions, beliefs, or desires. In addition to conveying an intention, a communicative function also has to influence the listener. A commonly used way to categorize communicative functions is to divide them according to their intention. Communicative functions can be divided into imperatives and declaratives. An imperative communicative function makes a demand on the listener. The speaker asks the listener to change his or her behavior in some way, for example, to perform an action. In contrast, a declarative communicative function does not make a demand on the listener other than to alert the listener's attention to something or someone or to share a topic or experience or activity of interest. An imperative communicative function might be, "Give me that book!" A declarative communicative function might include a sentence such as, "I have some information I'm going to share with you." Communicative functions can serve a very large number of social purposes. These include making a request, giving a direction, sharing something of interest, or enhancing a social interaction. However, all communicative functions serve the purpose of either alerting or orienting the listener to something or facilitating or forcing a change in the listener's behaviors in some way. In order to influence the listener, the words and the nonverbal accompaniments to those words must not only convey the speaker's intentions (imperative or declarative), but also influence the listener's understanding or the listener's behaviors. When a speaker says to the listener, "Give me that!" the listener might not comply, because he or she is offended by the tone. The intention of the communication is clear, but the listener does not respond as desired or intended by the speaker. In contrast, when the speaker changes the communication to say something like, "Would you be so kind as to give me that?" the listener is more likely to comply. The speaker may have greater success in influencing the listener as intended. The study of communicative functions therefore emphasizes not only the words used by the speaker to accurately communicate her or his emotions, intentions, desires, or beliefs; it also takes into consideration the success with which the speaker influences the listener.

Nonverbal communication can sometimes serve a communicative function. A speaker can choose not to speak at all and instead use a gesture or a facial expression to communicate something. A well-timed frown can sometimes speak volumes to the person who is intended to see it. In certain circumstances, nonverbal communication is much more effective in influencing the recipient than if words were exchanged. Nonverbal behaviors that represent a communicative function are certainly important to take into consideration. For the purposes of this chapter, however, a communicative function is expressed linguistically. It is the words that define a communicative function, not the nonverbal accompaniments of the communication.

The words chosen to communicate an idea or to make a request have to be tailored to the situation to be pragmatically successfully. The previous section provided an analysis of the sentence "He did that" and discussed how accompanying nonverbal communication differentiated the meaning of the words. The same type of differentiation can be generated using words alone. By adding to or modifying the sentence "He did that," the emotions, desires, and intentions of the speaker can be expressed differently. Modifications and additions in word choice are especially useful in written text, where nonverbal communication is missing. For example, the speaker might transform the sentence into a simple declarative designed to share something of interest ("Why, take a look at that!"). The speaker can make a judgment ("I can't believe it . . . take a look at THAT"). The speaker can make a polite request ("Would you take a look at that, please?"), an indirect or ambiguous request made as a statement ("I'm looking at that"), or a direct imperative ("Look at that!"). Each example uses the words *look, at,* and *that.* However, each sentence also conveys a different set of emotions, intentions, desires, and beliefs. The phrase "look at that" has become more differentiated because of the other words surrounding or accompanying the signal phrase.

Regardless of the choice of words (and the associated nonverbal behaviors), a communicative function is only functional, useful, and effective when it influences the listener as intended. The communicative function has to be just the right function for the situation and has to be more highly differentiated to serve the purpose of the situation. How to create just the right communicative function for a given situation depends on the social context and therefore requires some social thinking. Each of the examples above are the right message for only one or a few situations, not for all situations. These examples would be understood differently (and would result in a different response) depending on whether the listener was a young child, a peer, a superior, or a lecture hall filled with adults.

Toddlers, who have more limited language skills than older children, would typically not be able to express the same idea in more than one way. Communication in toddlers is not highly differentiated, and their pragmatic language skills are more limited. In contrast, the preschooler who already speaks in sentences is able to modify communication for the purpose of the social context. The preschooler is interested in influencing adults and peers, whether the intention is to provoke an emotional response, or whether the intention is to influence the peer's thoughts or behaviors. For example, a preschooler can express his desire for cookies by slyly making an indirect request ("Those cookies look really good!"), knowing that a direct request that signals the same desire ("I want a cookie") might not be the most effective way to influence the listener. Similarly, negotiating which game to play with a peer might require more judicious word choice than a simple command. Social conventions, such as using the words "please" and "thank you," also change the tone of a communication and can enhance the attention and respect given to the speaker. Both linguistic and nonlinguistic forms of communication can be used to produce a more highly differentiated communication. Although preschoolers can vary their word choice in some contexts for social purposes, consciously manipulating words for an intended effect is more likely to occur in children who are older. This skill continues to develop into adulthood.

## Conversational Skills



The pragmatic language skills discussed thus far do not only apply to single phrases or sentences. They also apply to longer types of discourse, such as conversations (discussed here) and narrative (discussed in the next section). As is the case for communicative functions, conversational skills require the speaker to convey her or his emotions, intentions, desires, beliefs, and thoughts. The speaker also has to influence the listener, either by alerting the listener to something or by influencing the listener's behaviors. One way to think about conversational skills is to think of a conversation as a set of verbal exchanges. Each verbal exchange consists of one or several sentences. Each sentence has to serve the function of communicating a person's emotions, intentions, desires, beliefs and/or thoughts. Each sentence also has to have an impact on the listener. In turn, the listener has to respond. The sections that follow examine these components in greater detail.

***Turn Taking*** During conversations, a student must be able to take turns speaking and listening. The most important and most basic conversational skill is the skill of waiting until the other person has finished what he or she has to say. Waiting is an impulse control skill that is discussed in more detail in Chapter 7. Turn taking in a conversation can occur as early as the toddler years but is more properly a preschool-age or kindergarten skill. What toddlers and preschoolers do not do consistently, especially over longer conversational exchanges, is to produce contingent responses.

***Contingency and Topic Maintenance*** When responding to a speaker, the response must be contingent on the speaker's statement, meaning the listener has to produce a response that is related to what the speaker just said. Subsequently, the listener and speaker both have to maintain the topic (topic maintenance) over more than one conversational turn. Being able to maintain a topic over the course of several sentences is a skill that is acquired with age. Typically developing toddlers and preschoolers do not usually show this skill. They often have finished the conversation after responding just once. For example, if a parent says, "Look at the train!" the typically developing toddler might say, "Look at the rooster!" failing to produce a contingent response. In contrast, a typically developing preschooler might produce a contingent response by saying, "It's a red train!" Both of these conversational behaviors are expected for age. Topic maintenance, the ability to maintain contingency over several conversational turns, is present by kindergarten. School-age children expect peers and adults to stay on topic, and they are also able to stay on topic, at least over short intervals. Peers who do not show contingency and topic maintenance by this age can be a source of frustration to the school-age child. School-age children enjoy having conversations and expect to be listened to and understood.

***Topic Elaboration*** As a conversation continues, both speaker and listener may decide to discuss the first topic in more depth or may expand the conversation to other topics. This is referred to as topic elaboration. Kindergarten and older children can participate in longer conversations. During a conversation that lasts for more than a minute or two, the topic might shift away from the topic that initiated the conversation. As children age, their attention span may be the factor that influences how long they maintain a topic and how long they continue any conversation.

***Conversational Repair*** Both speaker and listener need to be aware that conversations sometimes break down. A communicative function sometimes does not end up serving the intended goal. The listener might unexpectedly start a new topic, fail to understand what was just said and respond with an off-topic comment, or simply look puzzled. Conversational breakdowns such as these necessitate conversational repair. If the speaker notices that the listener went off topic, one strategy is to reiterate the original topic and/or to provide additional information. Preschoolers tend to repeat verbatim what they said when they notice a conversational breakdown, whereas school-age children might both repeat what was said but change the choice of words, add gestures, or change their tone of voice to make sure that the listener responds in the expected or intended way.



### Narrative

Narrative refers to speaking in paragraphs. The formal aspects of narrative were discussed in Chapter 4. The delivery of a successful narrative depends very heavily on the formal language components of narrative. However, narratives are an important aspect of conversations. Many conversations consist of narratives, each serving a communicative function or set of functions, just as a sentence might do so. Narratives can also be delivered on their own as a monologue, such as might occur in a lecture hall or during a comedy act. The pragmatic language needs of the narrative change depending upon the context. For example, the narrative may include accompanying nonverbal communication behaviors (facial expressions, gestures, changes in intonation, emotional expressiveness) to signal dialogue or to express emotions.

A narrative may need to be modified in other ways in order to function effectively. Speakers have to use just the right words, sentences, and information to deliver a successful narrative. For example, a narrative may need to be shorter or longer, deliver less information or more information, or use simpler or longer sentences, depending on the audience. A narrative for children typically has fewer, shorter sentences than a narrative for adults. A narrative that makes reference to persons or places that are unfamiliar to the listener will require the narrator to provide additional information. A narrative that has technical terms will require the speaker to explain them or provide examples. As is the case for all skills discussed in this chapter, narratives can reveal information about the emotions, desires, intentions, beliefs, and thoughts of the speaker. What constitutes a successful narrative depends on the intentions of the speaker and the success with which the speaker's intentions influence the listener. The intentions of the speaker might be to alert or inform the listener about something, to share an emotional experience, or to make a demand. To be successful, it must also cause the listener to listen, to remember, and/or to respond in some way.

## PERFORMANCE DIFFICULTIES IN PRAGMATIC LANGUAGE SKILLS

Pragmatic language impairment can affect a variety of classroom participation behaviors and can be evident academically. The following classroom participation behaviors were selected from report cards for students in kindergarten through fourth grade:

1. Answers questions from adults/peers
2. Listens carefully and follows directions from adults
3. Asks and answers questions to seek help, get information, or deepen understanding

4. Listens attentively in small groups; listens attentively in large groups
5. Follows rules for group discussion; participates in group discussions; participates in discussions by listening actively and contributing knowledge and ideas; stays on topic during discussion
6. Produces complete sentences when appropriate to situation
7. Expresses self clearly utilizing appropriate grammar
8. Demonstrates understanding of a text read aloud or information presented orally
9. Retells information from a story; describes people, places, things, and events with relevant details



Although all the skills listed require formal language skills, they also each require pragmatic language skills. Pragmatic language skills are key to successful receptive and expressive communication in the classroom. When a student does not notice or is not able to interpret all the information provided by a speaker (i.e., words, facial expressions, gestures, intonation, emotions), that student is more likely to misunderstand the communication. Similarly, if the student does not carefully select the words, facial expressions, gestures, or prosody needed to communicate an idea, he or she may not be able to communicate ideas successfully to others.

There are multiple reasons why students struggle with understanding pragmatic language skills (receptive pragmatic language skills). For example, young children often need speech spoken slowly and clearly and accompanied by facial expressions, gestures, intonation, and emotional expressiveness before they follow instructions. These behaviors are required to ensure optimal acoustics, orient them to a communication, and also to deliver the same message more than one way. Similar speaker behaviors are needed when working with English language learners. Lack of familiarity with the sounds and words of English requires the use of nonverbal behaviors such as these.

Performance difficulties in pragmatic language also occur in students with disabilities. For example, many students with autism fail to understand and use nonverbal communication such as facial expressions, gestures, changes in intonation, or emotional expressiveness. Sometimes, students with autism use nonverbal communication in an exaggerated or theatrical manner, as if pre-rehearsed, making it difficult to interpret their actual emotions or intentions.

Students other than those with language impairment or autism can also show difficulty with pragmatic language skills. For example, the student with difficulty managing impulses might say the first thought that comes to mind, provoking frustration or sadness in a peer. Before stopping and thinking about what to say, the student might exclaim, "You're fat!" The intention might be to share an observation, though the effect might be something very different. The student with underdeveloped executive skills and associated difficulty sequencing information might not produce a narrative in a logical manner and might jump from one idea to the next. The student might fail to include important information in the narrative, not having taken into consideration the listener's prior knowledge base or familiarity with the topic. Students who show extremes of emotion can sometimes also appear to have pragmatic language difficulty. Students who struggle with anxiety may fail to make eye contact, may show fewer changes in facial expression, and may speak in a very soft voice. The missing nonverbal aspects of their communication make it more difficult to understand them. When analyzing a student's pragmatic language performance, school professionals may need to consider several underlying reasons for any difficulties identified. Students can show difficulty with pragmatic language skills when they have a language impairment, a pragmatic language impairment, or difficulties with executive skills and when they struggle to regulate their emotions.

## HOW TO SET UP AN OBSERVATION OF PRAGMATIC LANGUAGE SKILLS

Chapter 4 presented options for setting up an observation of formal language skills. The suggestions for observing formal language also apply to pragmatic language. Pragmatic language skills can be observed during communication with a social partner, which can be elicited by asking a student to share a narrative, to participate in a conversation about a preferred topic, or by participating in a play interaction with props, toys, dolls, or puppets. The observer of the student's pragmatic language skills should consider both receptive and expressive components. The student's comprehension of facial expressions, gestures, intonation, and emotional expressiveness are just as important as the student's capacity to use them in social contexts. The observer should also consider linguistic aspects of communication, such as the student's ability to produce varied communicative functions, take turns and produce contingent responses, or tailor the delivery of information to suit the needs of the listener(s). See Appendix 5.2, the Pragmatic Language Skills Observation Sheet, for a brief tool to use in conducting effective pragmatic language skills observations.



### Select the Student

To set up the observation, school professionals should first identify a student whose pragmatic language requires an analysis. Consider reviewing the student's report card, if available, as it will likely note performance difficulties with pragmatic language skills. Some of the classroom participation behaviors that are not yet at grade level may be the result of a pragmatic language impairment.

### Obtain a Language Sample

The observation should be designed to obtain a language sample that displays the student's pragmatic language skills. Practitioners should review the classroom participation behaviors listed in Chapter 4, as they provide a good source of language samples. They may be especially useful because they can often be gathered without the student's awareness. Longer sampling may be required and can be obtained by having a conversation with the student, using toys, pictures, books, or peers. The language sample can be obtained by having the student generate a narrative by looking at a picture, a pictures series, or by retelling key components of a story just heard. As with the formal language observation, the observer should make audioclips or, preferably, videoclips and should create a transcript from this documentation. The observer should also document how nonverbal communication occurred during the language sample. The transcript should say exactly what the student said and did, even if it is only a very short segment. Because these language samples are less spontaneous and may make the student feel self-conscious, they can interfere with the student's communication behaviors. The observer may need to make more observations at other times to ensure good samples.

### Analyze and Interpret the Observations

After making the observations, the practitioner should summarize some of the language difficulties witnessed during the observation. Consider some of the communication behaviors outlined in the following sections.

***Analysis of Facial Expressions*** Practitioners should make observations about any changes in the student's facial expressions, across settings. Making observations in a different context can be useful, as a lack of expressiveness in one setting may be due to anxiety or boredom. A more motivating or less anxiety-provoking environment may encourage greater use of facial expressions. When changes in facial expressions are noted, it is important to notice what types of emotions were conveyed, and whether or not they augmented the observer's comprehension.

Consider facial changes such as a smile (happy), furrowed eyebrows (mad), mouth turned downward (sad), eyes wide open (scared). The facial expressions may be conveyed spontaneously, or they may be contrived or symbolic. Notably, facial expressions do not need to be extreme. Even subtle changes in the size of the eyes or subtle changes in the direction of gaze can be sufficient evidence that facial expressions are present and make up a portion of the communication.

***Analysis of Gestures*** Verify whether the student uses any gestures. Note what the gestures are, and whether they serve to augment or enhance the communication. The observations and analysis should consider conventional gestures, such as nodding or shaking the head to indicate *yes* or *no*. The observer should also consider symbolic gestures, such as shrugging the shoulders and raising the hands to express doubt. The observer can ask the student to produce complex gestures, such as by asking the student to demonstrate a plane flying or to show how someone opens up a jar.



***Analysis of Auditory and Musical Features of Speech*** Make note of any features of the student's intonation that indicate normal or atypical use of volume, pitch, or rate. Correct pronunciation of words (prosody) is an important first observation to make. Most native speakers of English will not show any difficulty in the correct pronunciation of words, regardless of disability status. What is sometimes more difficult to identify is how the student changes volume, pitch (high or low), and rate (speed) as part of the communication. Auditory changes such as these can convey sadness, doubt, anxiety, anger, and other emotions or feelings. If the student sounds too monotone or not quite right, consider the volume, pitch, and rate separately. There may be no emphasis on any words in the word stream. The student might speak too loudly or too quietly. The rate of speech might be too consistent and unchanging. In contrast, some students exaggerate the auditory aspects of their speech. They can be too emotional or too expressive and sound too theatrical, dramatic, or scripted.

***Analysis of Communicative Functions*** Analyze the choice of words the student used. Verify that the student's sentences fit into the conversation. The information shared should be related to the conversation that the student is holding with her or his conversational partner (i.e., contingent). The student should be able to use phrases or sentences to communicate wants and needs to others or to influence the attention, interest, or actions of adults or peers. Students who have limited formal language skills can appear to be deficient in this area. In some cases, notice whether or not the student can make up for limited language production through the use of nonverbal communication.

***Analysis of Conversational Skills*** Verify whether the student has the ability to take turns in the conversation. Each turn in the conversation should be a contingent response, a linguistic response that matches the topic or fits into the conversation. The student should be able to maintain the topic for more than one turn. Notice how long the student is able to maintain the topic or to maintain contingency. Without always realizing it, adults often provide the support needed to ensure continued turn taking and topic maintenance when they speak with children and youth. Adults sometimes do this by asking questions that the student can answer. Alternatively, they might respond spontaneously and automatically to fill in the blanks. They may not even realize how often they are supporting the conversation or that they are responding to intonation in one case, to facial expressions in another, and to the words in yet a different situation. Whereas adult support of this type is appropriate for social encounters with students and to assist with learning, excess adult support can interfere with the successful observation and analysis of the student's skills. The analysis here is to verify the student's spontaneous capacity for producing conversation. The student has to be able to contribute with questions and responses that keep the conversation moving forward, not just respond to the adult. Notice how many conversational turns the student is capable of making. Notice whether the student shows conversational repair skills. If the student over relies on the adult to keep the conversation going, consider observing the student during interactions with peers.

***Analysis of Narrative*** Verify the student's capacity for narrative. Consider the aspects of narrative discussed in Chapter 4, which are relevant for almost any listener. Then consider how the student adjusts narrative to the specific context. Notice whether or not the student can find and maintain a topic that the listener is likely to be interested in and can understand. Notice whether or not the student tailors the amount of information provided for the target audience. For example, the narrative might be too long or too short. There may excessive detail or not enough detail. The student may or may not change the topic even when the listener appears bored or does not appear to understand. When making observations, the practitioner should keep in mind that most children have difficulty with producing a well-structured and coherent narrative and are still developing these skills well into the elementary school years.



## Discuss Findings With Colleagues

After analysis, the observer should discuss the student's performance with other members of the student's team and especially with the speech pathologist. These individuals can review the transcript and video- or audioclips and analyze the different aspects of pragmatics discussed here. The group should discuss which pragmatic language skills the student has developed and what challenges the student faces in this area. The goal of the analysis is to understand all of the nonverbal and verbal pragmatic skills that the student brings into their communication. The discussion should include some decisions about what to do next by way of formal evaluation; updated goals and objectives; or new supports, interventions, or accommodation.

The IEP Builder flows naturally from the observations made of the student's performance and serves to help school professionals choose educational objectives and strategies for students with pragmatic language difficulties. For some students, the choice of objectives and strategies will be very straightforward and may not require substantial observations. For other students, only through the observations will it become clear what types of educational objectives or strategies might be the most appropriate. This section opens with general steps to begin teaching about pragmatic language skills and then moves on to more specific examples.

## Decide Whether to Focus on Verbal or Nonverbal Pragmatic Language Skills

To determine what types of pragmatic skills on which the student should focus, professionals should first separate nonverbal and verbal aspects of pragmatic language. Many students need instruction in both, but some students will benefit from instruction that emphasizes one over the other.

## Use the Social Context for Teaching

It is important to provide learning opportunities in the situations and environments where pragmatic skills matter the most. Pragmatic language skills inherently involve a social partner. They are intended to communicate a speaker's emotions, intentions, desires, beliefs, and/or thoughts and to make an impact on the listener. As such, pragmatic language skills must be taught in a social context. Educators and other school professionals should use naturally occurring situations in which to teach pragmatic language skills. All routine interactions with students have the potential for teaching language. Pragmatic language skills need to be taught as a part of conversations between the student and the teacher, between the student and her or his peers, and during storytelling tasks or exercises. The broader system of teachers, peers, and family should therefore be engaged. Teachers and therapists can make use of spontaneous or recurrent social situations for teaching pragmatic language skills. In some cases, the student and teacher can make a joint decision about which social contexts to use for teaching pragmatic language skills and can even set goals mutually (Wolf, 2011).

## Provide the Student With a List of Objectives

Before teaching pragmatic language skills, a list of pragmatic skills and objectives should be generated and then shared with the student. By learning the terms and definitions discussed in this chapter, the student will remember more easily all of the different components they may need to master: Facial expressions, gestures, intonation and emotional expressiveness, communicative functions, conversational skills, and narrative skills. The student can then practice identifying, understanding, and using one or the other skill set in real-time situations.



## Educational Objectives and Strategies for Developing Pragmatic Language Skills

Educational objectives for pragmatic language skills can be built from the Pragmatic Language Skills Framework. Each of the skill sets of the framework can be used to generate objectives for nonverbal and linguistic aspects of pragmatic language. Consider the examples in the sections that follow.

***Educational Objectives and Strategies for Facial Expressions*** Therapists and teachers can help students understand different facial expressions and how to interpret them. The teacher and student can make observations of other students or teachers during real-time interactions. Videoclips and still photographs are also useful in learning about different facial expressions. The teacher and student can experiment with making different kinds of facial expressions for different situations. One way to measure progress is to assess the student's knowledge about facial expressions and how to interpret them, for example, from photos, videos, or in real time. For example, document how many elements or features the student is able to describe. Document how many different interpretations the student is able to generate for a given situation. Discover with the student whether the facial expressions are congruent or noncongruent with the words uttered by the speaker. Another way to assess progress is to watch the student practicing different facial expressions.

***Educational Objectives and Strategies for Gestures*** As with facial expressions, the teacher or therapist can teach about different gestures and how to interpret them. The student can learn about conventional, symbolic, nonsymbolic, simple, and complex gestures. The teacher and student can spend time looking at other students or teachers in real time and describe gestures that are used in everyday situations. Videoclips or still photographs are also useful here. Along with identifying gestures, the student and the teacher can think together about the interpretation of those gestures. Notice whether the gestures are congruent or noncongruent to the situation. Experiment with the student by asking him or her to produce different kinds of gestures. One way to measure progress is to take measures of the different gestures that the student understands and is able to use. Using photos, videos, or real-time situations, discover how many different types of gestures the student is able to identify, how many different emotions the student is able to identify from the gesture, and how many different types of communication the student is able to identify from the gesture.

***Educational Objectives and Strategies for Auditory and Musical Features of Speech*** Teachers and therapists can provide instruction about how changes in intonation can change the meaning of words and sentences. Use audio and video for teaching purposes to help the student listen to and notice differences in intonation and emotional expressiveness, to describe them in the speech of others, and to practice using them. For example, the student can learn about how changes in intonation in the same sentence change its meaning. The teacher can ask the student questions: "Which word is emphasized the most? What would happen if you emphasized different words in this sentence? What would you think if the speaker spoke this sentence more quickly with a loud voice [higher volume]? What would you think if the speaker spoke with a high-pitched voice?" Similarly, the teacher can teach the student about emotional expressiveness. Emotional expressiveness depends upon volume, pitch, and rate of speech. Emotions expressed through these tonal changes are often accompanied by change in facial expression, gestures, or posture.

***Educational Objectives and Strategies for Communicative Functions*** The teacher and student can analyze sentence-level speech in social situations, from video, audio, or printed text read aloud. Ask the student to identify the communicative functions contained within the language sample and to identify if the speaker is making a declarative or imperative statement. Ask the student for an interpretation of the emotion, intention, or desire that the speaker is communicating. The teacher can ask questions such as, "Does the speaker just want to share some interesting information? Or does the speaker want to change the listener's behaviors? Is the communication direct or indirect?" One way to measure progress is to discover how often the student can provide a reasonable or logical interpretation of a communication. Another way to measure progress is to see how successfully the student is able to make changes in communication to suit the context. For example, the teacher could ask, "How would you say that if you were speaking to a younger child? How would you say that if you were speaking to the school principal?"



***Educational Objectives and Strategies for Teaching About Ambiguity in Communication*** Discover and discuss how words, sentences, and paragraphs can have more than one meaning depending on factors such as those described above. For example, the teacher can guide the student by analyzing all of the different components of communication that might be occurring simultaneously: Words, facial expressions, gestures, and changes in prosody. By identifying each of these components, it becomes possible to verify whether linguistic and nonverbal aspects of communication are congruent or not. When noticing ambiguous communication, it's useful to decide if the ambiguity is intentional or nonintentional. The spontaneous expression of delight or fear in a person's nonverbal communication looks different from the expression of the same emotions in someone who is making a joke or being sarcastic. Using real-time social interactions, audioclips, or videoclips, the teacher could say, "Tell me everything that you noticed about that sentence [or about that story]. Which words were emphasized? What facial expressions, gestures, or changes in prosody [emphasis] did you notice? Now, what do you think the speaker was saying? What's funny or unexpected about what the speaker said or did? What's contradictory?" One way to measure progress is to see whether the student's responses become more detailed or more comprehensive.

***Educational Objectives and Strategies for Conversational Skills*** Conversational skills have several components, including the capacity for turn taking, producing a contingent response, maintaining the topic, and elaborating on the topic. The student's progress can be measured by making observations of videoclips or by making real-time observations and asking the student to identify the following: Successful turn taking, when turn taking was not respected, when someone was off topic, when the topic changed, and conversational breakdowns and repair. It is easier to identify all the different features just discussed when making observations of others, but it is also important to teach students how to make these observations within their own conversations. Students can learn about these skills by observing conversations between others or by observing videotaped conversations they held with peers or adults. Some of the instruction can occur as peer-mediated instruction, with peers identifying the components above and providing positive feedback or corrective feedback, as appropriate.

***Educational Objectives and Strategies for Narrative Skills*** Teachers and therapists can provide instruction about all the components of narrative as described in this chapter. Narrative instruction can be delivered with accompanying picture supports for developmentally younger children. This can help them remember and sequence the elements of their story. Developmentally younger children may need to work on aspects of narrative discussed in Chapter 4. For example, they may need to develop their capacity to produce complete sentences and then deliver those sentences in a logical sequence. They may need to develop their narrative skills by increasing the number of elements in the story and by making better use of linking devices.

Developmentally more advanced students may need less visual (picture) support and may be ready to work on the pragmatic aspects of narrative discussed in this chapter. For example, students in middle school or high school can work toward adjusting the volume of information or adjusting the complexity of the language to meet the needs of the audience. These skills apply to both oral and written narratives. For oral narrative specifically, students should learn how to use nonverbal communication to their advantage. One way to measure progress is to present students with a list of the skills discussed in this chapter and in the previous chapter and to use the list to rate narrative performance. Students can rate real-time or videorecorded performances of themselves, peers, or an actor in a prepared videoclip. Progress monitoring can occur by asking students to identify all the skills discussed in this chapter and to provide examples of how a narrator used or did not use these pragmatic language skills. Another way to measure progress is to see whether students can use the skills listed in this chapter.



### Accommodations for Pragmatic Language Skills

School professionals can accommodate for a student's difficulty understanding language by reducing the volume of language delivered. Repetition, use of simpler sentences, and the addition of exaggerated nonverbal communication can assist with comprehension. Prior to speaking, the adult should get the student's visual attention, so that the student notices changes in the speaker's facial expression and gestures. The adult should also get the student's auditory attention so that the student notices changes in intonation or in emotional expressiveness. Chapter 4 discussed how important it is to repeat spoken sentences, to shorten them, or to emphasize certain phrases or words for students with a language impairment. The same process may be true for pragmatic language skills. School professionals can repeat facial expressions, gestures, or intonation (or just exaggerate them). They can also repeat communicative functions, change the choice of words, and emphasize the nonverbal aspects of communicative functions to enhance the student's comprehension.

## CASE EXAMPLE

Leonard was introduced in Chapter 4. The case material presented for Leonard will be amplified here, so that the reader can make connections between the verbal and nonverbal aspects of Leonard's performance. At the time of the observation described in Chapter 4, there was a concern not only about Leonard's formal language skills, but also about the difficulty in his pragmatic language skills. The observations made therefore included observations of his pragmatic language. Leonard did not use eye contact consistently. He played on his own and appeared uninterested in socializing. It was often difficult to interpret his nonverbal communication, because he communicated less often than other students and often did not make eye contact with others.

Leonard's report card provides limited information about his nonverbal communication, but it does provide information about his communicative functions and his conversational skills. Leonard performed "below grade expectations" in the following skills:

- Communicates effectively in order to seek help, gain information, or deepen understanding of an academic task (Communicative functions)
- Controls unnecessary talking (Turn taking)
- Stays on topic (Topic maintenance)
- Participates in discussions by listening actively and contributing knowledge and ideas (Contingency)

To understand Leonard's pragmatic language more comprehensively and to better understand his nonverbal communication skills, more detailed observations were undertaken. See the Case Example in Chapter 4 to review Leonard's language samples and the linguistic aspects of his language performance. What follows is an analysis of the pragmatic language features of the observation.



## Leonard's Facial Expressions

Leonard used facial expressions to reinforce what he was saying. One example occurred at the end of the story "The Fisherman and the Cat," when he furrowed his eyebrows and showed his teeth by making a grimace with his lips while saying, "'That's not for you,' said the cat. 'Only I can eat the fish'." His facial expression communicated "I'm angry!" Leonard's ability to express anger with his facial expressions during this narrative task was a signal that he can express emotions. This skill was important for his teacher to verify, because his limited eye contact made it difficult to interpret his facial expressions much of the time.

## Leonard's Gestures

At one point, Leonard pointed at the cloud in the picture when he said, "It's a fish cloud!" and he made eye contact with his teacher. The gesture of pointing at the cloud said (nonverbally), "Look at the cloud." When he said, "It's want to grab the fish," he made a grabbing motion with his right hand, reinforcing the word *grab*. Later, in his narrative retelling, he raised his fisted hands in imitation of the cat. The act of raising his hands said (nonverbally), "I'm angry!" In other words, Leonard is able to use gestures to reinforce the meaning behind his verbal/linguistic performance. Nonverbal and verbal performances were congruent.

## Leonard's Intonation

When Leonard first started his narrative retelling, he used an expressive tone when he said, "You never be . . . you not happy!" He used an even, loud tone for each word in the sentence. His tone reinforced the fact that the cat was frustrated. At the end of the story, he also used a frustrated tone of voice (higher volume), when he said, "That's not for you," a more neutral tone of voice when he said, "said the cat." He reverted to a frustrated tone of voice when he then added: "Only I can eat the fish." He both used stress (changed the volume and pitch) and purposefully did *not* use stress in this sentence. In so doing, he indicated when the cat was speaking and when the narrator was speaking.

To summarize, Leonard used nonverbal components of communication successfully during this observation. Facial expressions, gestures, and intonation all suggested emotions experienced by the cat (e.g., frustration). He also used gesture to augment the meaning of his words (e.g., raising his fists, making a grabbing motion while using the word *grab*). Verbal and nonverbal communication acted congruently to reinforce meaning. In some respects, Leonard's nonverbal communication was more secure and richer than his linguistic skills. He was able to partially make up for limited formal language by augmenting his communication with nonverbal behaviors.

## Leonard's Communicative Functions and Narrative Skills

Leonard has difficulties with formal language skills. He has a limited vocabulary and errors in grammar that prevent him from using language as successfully as a peer might. That said, he used nonverbal communication successfully, because he communicated the intentions of the cat successfully. Although the sentence "It's want to grab the fish" might not be meaningful on its own, the accompanying grabbing motion made his meaning clear.



## Educational Objectives and Strategies for Teaching Leonard Pragmatic Language Skills

The following paragraphs are divided by skill. One basic decision for any school professional is to divide the educational objectives of nonverbal and verbal aspects of pragmatic language. Because of Leonard's limited formal language and because of his age, teaching for linguistic pragmatic skills is more limited than might be the case for an older student with more advanced formal language skills.

### *Educational Objectives and Strategies for Teaching Nonverbal Communication Skills*

Leonard needs to use eye contact more consistently, so that his facial expressions are more visible to the listener. He is also ready to learn to identify many different types of nonverbal communication acts in others (facial expressions, gestures, intonation, and emotional expressiveness). He can also learn to enhance the use of nonverbal communication and to pair it with verbal communication. In doing so, his social partners will understand his communication better.

### *Educational Objectives and Strategies for Teaching Communicative Functions*

Leonard needs to expand his repertoire of sentences and communicative functions. He also needs to produce contingent responses. Given that he is still mastering basic morpho-syntax and given his age, he might not be ready to focus his learning on different ways to deliver the same message (different types of communicative functions for the same context). A reasonable goal would be for him to master a variety of communicative functions that he could use in different contexts. Notice that by teaching Leonard communicative functions for use in a social context, the therapist or teacher is also teaching him about morpho-syntax in general.

### *Educational Objectives and Strategies for Teaching Leonard Conversational and Narrative Skills*

Leonard can be taught verbal pragmatic language skills, such as developing contingent responses and maintaining a topic during a conversation. He may have difficulty remembering enough information about a conversation to be able to generate a new sentence and maintain the topic with each conversational turn. Similarly, he would be expected to have difficulty generating narrative as part of his conversations. For example, he showed during the observation that it is difficult for him to produce multiple sentences to deliver a narrative. He needed some adult support to do so. Therefore, contingency, topic maintenance, and narrative are all good skills to be teaching him. However, the objectives may need to be small, and he may need adult scaffolding and/or visual supports (pictures) in order to develop these skills.

### Working With Culturally and Linguistically Diverse Learners

Nonverbal communication varies between different cultural and linguistic groups. School professionals should keep the following differences in mind when working in diverse classrooms:

#### *Eye Contact and Respect*

The cultural norms for eye contact, for example, are not the same amongst many Anglo children and many Spanish-speaking children from Mexico. Native Spanish-speaking children are far more likely to avoid direct eye contact with adults as a manner of respect. Other cultures also have different norms or expectations for eye contact.

#### *Nods*

Nods are a very common nonverbal response. Nods mean different things for different cultural groups. In some cultures, nods are used to indicate a positive or affirmative response to a question. In other cultures, it may simply be a sign of respect. For example, you may ask someone to do something and they smile and nod. Later you discover that what you asked has not been completed. The individual nodded to indicate that they were listening and respecting you rather than agreeing to do something for you.



## CONCLUSION

This chapter presented several sets of pragmatic language skills. It discussed the nonverbal components of communication (facial expressions, gestures, intonation, and emotional expressiveness), as well as the verbal or linguistic aspects of pragmatic language (communicative functions, conversational skills, and narrative). To understand these aspects of communication, it is important to make frequent observations. It is especially important to make good observations of the nonverbal aspects of communication, because these aspects have such a strong influence on how a listener-observer interprets a speaker's words. By enumerating the different components of nonverbal communication, the listener-observer can make observations of communication more systematically and more accurately. Educators and other school professionals should practice describing nonverbal aspects of communication when discussing a student's classroom performance and organizing the descriptions using the terms outlined in this chapter.

The same process applies for enumerating linguistic or verbal aspects of pragmatic language. It can be time consuming to do a detailed analysis of the verbal/linguistic aspects of communication as proposed in this chapter. School team members may wish to ask the district speech pathologist for assistance. That said, it's important for all team members to understand all of the skills discussed in this chapter. When pragmatic language difficulties emerge, any adult working with the student can then identify and discuss the skills that the student needs to develop further.

For the advanced reader and for the expert, we wish to acknowledge briefly the difficulty we faced in separating pragmatic language skills from the skills that will be presented in other chapters in this book. Remember that pragmatic language skills are used to enhance communication and comprehension in a social context. Successful comprehension and use of pragmatic language skills requires both the speaker and the listener to think about the intentions, desires, emotions, and beliefs of others. Identifying intentions, desires, emotions, and beliefs is a critical aspect of social cognition (Sperber & Wilson, 2002). Pragmatic language skills are therefore not separable from social cognition (Norbury, 2014; Russell, 2007). The Pragmatic Language Skills chapter thus provides a logical transition to the social skills chapter which follows. Good formal and pragmatic language skills enhance social interactions. The skills discussed in the next chapter provide a larger context within which to understand formal and pragmatic language.

## REFERENCES


Adams, C. (2002). Practitioner review: The assessment of language pragmatics. *Journal of Child Psychology and Psychiatry, 43*(8), 973–987.

Baird, G., & Norbury, C. F. (2016). Social (pragmatic) communication disorders and autism spectrum disorder. *Archives of Disease in Childhood, 101*(8), 745–751.

Buck, R. (1999). The biological affects: A typology. *Psychological Review,* (106)2, 301–336.

Buck, R., & VanLear, C. A. (2002). Verbal and nonverbal communication: Distinguishing symbolic, spontaneous, and pseudo-spontaneous nonverbal behavior. *Journal of Communication, 52*(3), 522–541.

Colegrove, V. M., & Havighurst, S. S. (2017). Review of nonverbal communication in parent–child relationships: Assessment and intervention. *Journal of Child and Family Studies, 26*(2), 574–590.

Crystal, D. (Ed.). (1997a). *The Cambridge encyclopedia of language* (2nd ed., p. 248). Cambridge, United Kingdom: Cambridge University Press.

Crystal, D. (Ed.). (1997b). Pragmatic development. In *The Cambridge encyclopedia of language* (2nd ed., p. 120). Cambridge, United Kingdom: Cambridge University Press.

Cummings, L. (2007). Clinical pragmatics: A field in search of phenomena. *Language and Communication, 27,* 396–432.

Grebelsky-Lichtman, T. (2014a). Children's verbal and nonverbal congruent and incongruent communication during parent-child interactions. *Human Communication Research, (40)*4, 415–441.

Grebelsky-Lichtman, T. (2014b). Parental patterns of cooperation in parent-child interactions: The relationship between nonverbal and verbal communication. *Human Communication Research, (40)*1, 1–29.

Grice, H. P. (1957). Meaning. *Philosophical Review, 66*(3), 377–388.

Grice, H. P. (1969). Utterer's meaning and intention. *Philosophical Review, 78*(2), 147–177.

Hyland, K. (2017). Metadiscourse: What is it and where is it going? *Journal of Pragmatics, 113,* 16–29.

Ishihara, N., & Cohen, A. D. (2010). *Teaching and learning pragmatics: Where language and culture meet.* London, United Kingdom: Routledge.

Kodjebacheva, G. D., Sabo, T., & Xiong, J. (2016). Interventions to improve child-parent-medical provider communication: A systematic review. *Social Science & Medicine, 166,* 120–127.

LoCastro, V. (2012). *Pragmatics for language educators.* New York, NY: Routledge.

Matusitz, J., & Spear, S. (2014). Effective doctor–patient communication: An updated examination. *Social Work in Public Health, 29*(3), 252–266.

Melguizo Moreno, E. (2017). A proposal for the study of pragmatics in the primary education degree. *Porta Linguarum,* 87–101.

Mey, J. L. (2005). Pragmatics: Overview. In K. Brown (Ed.), *Encyclopedia of language and linguistics* (2nd ed.). New York, NY: Elsevier.

Norbury, C. (2014). Practitioner review: Social (pragmatic) communication disorder conceptualization, evidence, and clinical implications. *Journal of Child Psychology and Psychiatry, 55*(3), 204–216.

Russell, R., & Grizzle, K. (2008). Assessing child and adolescent pragmatic language competencies: Towards evidence-based assessments. *Clinical Child and Family Psychology Review, 11*(1–2), 59–73.

Schneider, K. (2005). Pragmatics. In P. Strazny (Ed.), *Encyclopedia of linguistics* (pp. 869–872). Taylor and Francis e-library.

Soames, S. (2003). Pragmatics and contextual semantics: Overview. In W. J. Frawley (Ed.), *International encyclopedia of linguistics* (2nd ed., p. 379). Oxford, United Kingdom: Oxford University Press.

Sperber, D., & Wilson, D. (2002). Pragmatics, modularity and mind-reading. *Mind and Language, 17*(1–2), 3–23.

Tates, K., & Meeuwesen, L. (2001) Doctor–parent–child communication. A (re)view of the literature. *Social Science and Medicine, 52,* 839–851.

Wolf, N. (2011). Developmental language disorders. In D. R. Patel (Ed.), *Neurodevelopmental disabilities* (pp. 173–191). New York, NY: Springer.

## APPENDIX 5.1 Pragmatic Language Skills Framework

The Pragmatic Language Skills Framework is summarized here. School professionals can use this form as a quick reference for the skill sets and skills that need to be taken into consideration when making observations and developing an intervention plan.

| Skill sets | Functions and skills | Examples of functions and skills in action | Sample performance difficulties | Potential strategies, accommodations, or educational objectives |
|---|---|---|---|---|
| Facial expressions | Spontaneous facial expressions<br>Contrived facial expressions | The student spontaneously shows changes in facial expression that provide information about underlying thoughts or feelings.<br>The student is able to interpret the facial expressions of others.<br>The student is able to coordinate the emotions expressed by facial expressions with the words used in verbal communication to produce a desired effect. The facial expression can augment and support the meaning of the words, send the opposite message conveyed by the words, or communicate another idea in addition to the idea(s) communicated by the words. | The student does not produce facial expressions spontaneously.<br>The student has difficulty interpreting the facial expressions of others,<br>The student uses facial expressions in communication, but they appear contrived or theatrical and do not seem to match underlying feelings or thoughts. | Teach the student about the interpretation, production, and effective use of facial expressions. |
| Gestures and posture | Conventional gestures<br>Demonstrative and symbolic gestures | The student spontaneously shows conventional gestures such as nodding or shaking the head to indicated yes/no or a shoulder shrug to indicate "I don't know." These spontaneous gestures provide information about the student's underlying emotions or thoughts.<br>The student is able to use conventional, demonstrative, and symbolic gestures alongside words to produce a desired effect. The gestures can augment and support the meaning of the words, send the opposite message conveyed by the words, or communicate another idea in addition to the idea(s) communicated by the words. | The student does not produce spontaneous gesture in communication.<br>The student has difficulty interpreting the gestures produced by others or identifying differences between what is communicated through gesture and what is communicated through words.<br>The student has difficulty producing gesture in communication even when given time to do so. | Teach about gestures and their different meanings.<br>Teach how to produce gestures in communication. |

(continued)

| Skill sets | Functions and skills | Examples of functions and skills in action | Sample performance difficulties | Potential strategies, accommodations, or educational objectives |
|---|---|---|---|---|
| Auditory and musical features of speech | *Prosody:* Accent on the right syllable in each word<br>*Intonation:* Stress on a word in the sentence<br>*Emotional expressiveness:* Emphasis or stress on a phrase or sentence as a whole | The student correctly pronounces words in English and/or in other languages.<br>The student recognizes differences in meaning as expressed through differences in intonation, such as by changing the stress applied to each word in a sentence.<br>The student uses intonation to augment or alter the meaning of sentences.<br>The student recognizes differences in emotional expressiveness in the communication of others.<br>The student uses volume, pitch, and rate to indicate an emotion to augment or alter the meaning of sentences or narratives. | The student is not able to hear, recognize, or produce correct pronunciation of words in English or in another language.<br>The student has difficulty recognizing and showing differences in meaning as expressed through intonation.<br>The student has difficulty recognizing and showing emotional expressiveness as expressed through volume, pitch, or rate of speech. | Teach correct pronunciation in English or in another language.<br>Teach how to recognize and produce changes in intonation to influence or change the meaning of sentences.<br>Teach how to recognize and use changes in volume, pitch, or rate to indicate an emotion. |
| Communicative functions | A word, phrase, or short sentence that communicates an idea or intention and has the intended effect on the listener. The communicative function influences the listener in some way. | The student uses a variety of words, phrases, or sentences to communicate a demand or imperative, which influences the listener's behaviors.<br>The student uses a variety of words, phrases, or sentences to communicate an idea or to make a declarative. The declarative influences the listener's attention or changes the listener's point of view.<br>The student can use communicative functions to express more than one idea and can be intentionally ambiguous. | Students with difficulty in this area may use language that does not communicate any intention clearly (e.g., noncontingent responses). The communicative function is not effective in influencing or changing the behaviors of others.<br>The student's communicative function serves only limited purposes, such as getting personal needs met. The communicative functions may be scripted, and the student comes across as overly demanding or awkward.<br>The student may have difficulty interpreting and/or producing communications to suit different social contexts.<br>The student may not be able to understand or produce communication that has more than one meaning or that is ambiguous. | Teach the student basic communicative functions, such as how to communicate different needs, wants, desires, or beliefs.<br>Teach the student to produce communication that is contingent on and related to the context.<br>Teach the student to assess the responsiveness of the listener and to adjust the communication if needed.<br>Teach scripted communicative functions for commonly encountered situations (e.g., greetings, apologies, thank you).<br>Teach the recognition and use of different types of communicative functions, such as direct, indirect, and ambiguous functions. Teach how communicative functions have to change, depending on the social context.<br>Teach the student scripted responses for commonly required communicative functions; teach options for changing communicative functions for the same context. |

| Skill sets | Functions and skills | Examples of functions and skills in action | Sample performance difficulties | Potential strategies, accommodations, or educational objectives |
|---|---|---|---|---|
| Conversational skills | Turn taking | The student can take turns in a conversation and waits for the social partner to finish saying what he or she wants to say before speaking. | The student often interrupts others or does not respond to their conversational bids. | Teach about turn taking. |
| | Contingency and topic maintenance | The student produces a response that is related (contingent) to the previous utterance and can maintain the same topic for several conversational turns. | The student produces responses that are not contingent on the prior utterances. The student is not able to maintain the topic of the conversational partner and instead inserts topics of his or her own interest. | Teach strategies to improve contingency and topic maintenance. |
| | Topic elaboration | The student can then go on to elaborate on the topic and shift to a new topic. | The student is not able to follow a conversation once the topic changes. | Teach how to recognize and participate in topic elaboration. |
| | Conversational repair | The student recognizes when the social partner(s) failed to understand something and makes an attempt to correct the misunderstanding. | She or he does not recognize and/or does not know how to repair conversational breakdowns. | Teach how to identify and repair conversational breakdowns. |
| Narrative skills | Adjusting the complexity of the language (linguistic and syntactic complexity) to suit the needs of the listener | The student is able to adjust the complexity of language to suit the needs of the listener (e.g., by using simple words for a younger peer). | The student uses excessively complex or overly simple words or sentence structures that do not match the needs or interests of the audience. | Students with difficulty in producing narrative often benefit from instruction in the formal aspects of narrative. See Chapter 4.<br>Students need instruction in how to anticipate the needs of their audience. Provide instruction about the level of language that is best, the knowledge base of the audience, the amount of key information to share, and how to maintain the topic without introducing too many related or unrelated topics. |
| | Explaining referents to ensure comprehension of the listener | The student is able to explain her or his referents (e.g., the topic or subject of discussion). The student anticipates how much the listener might know about a topic and can explain referents or introduce the topic by providing key background information as needed. | The student fails to recognize the needs of the audience and therefore fails to introduce the topic or to explain referents by providing key background information. | |
| | Adjusting the volume of information to suit the needs of the listener | The student is able to maintain the topic and share the right amount of information for the intended audience. | The student speaks about too many topics and/or goes off topic, leaving the audience confused about the content of the narrative. | |

APPENDIX 5.2 **Pragmatic Language Skills Observation Sheet**

| Skill sets | Functions and skills | Example skills or deficits in this student | Potential strategies, accommodations, or educational objectives |
|---|---|---|---|
| Facial expressions | Spontaneous facial expressions<br><br>Contrived facial expressions | | |
| Gestures and posture | Conventional gestures<br><br>Demonstrative and symbolic gestures | | |
| Auditory and musical features of speech | *Prosody:* Accent on the right syllable in each word<br><br>*Intonation:* Stress on a word in the sentence<br><br>*Emotional expressiveness:* Emphasis or stress on a phrase or sentence as a whole | | |
| Communicative functions | A word, phrase, or short sentence that communicates an idea or intention and has the intended effect on the listener. The communicative function influences the listener in some way. | | |
| Conversational skills | Turn taking<br><br>Contingency and topic maintenance<br><br>Topic elaboration<br><br>Conversational repair | | |
| Narrative skills | Adjusting the complexity of the language (linguistic and syntactic complexity) to suit the needs of the listener<br><br>Explaining referents to ensure comprehension of the listener<br><br>Adjusting the volume of information to suit the needs of the listener | | |

# Social Skills



## INTRODUCTION AND GENERAL DEFINITIONS

Social skills are the capacity to think and act socially. Social skills consist of a complex collection of skills. In this framework, social skills consist of two important skill sets: Social cognition and knowledge of social conventions.

The first skill set, social cognition, consists of information processing about people and knowledge of the norms and procedures of the social world (Beer, Mitchell, & Ochsner, 2006b). Social cognition is about the mental capacity to represent (to imagine or think about) the minds of others. Social cognition can be considered as the act of thinking about what other people are thinking. It includes knowledge about how people normally behave. When observing people, it is not always possible to know what they are thinking or feeling or to understand why they behave the way they do. To consider what others are thinking, interpretation is often required. For example, people make use of the nonverbal aspects of communication, discussed in the prior chapter, in order to interpret or think about the minds of others. Social cognition is difficult to separate from the formal and pragmatic language skills discussed in the last two chapters. However, Social Skills Framework diverges from Formal Language Skills and Pragmatic Language Skills Frameworks because the skills discussed here are more purely social in nature. They are not linguistic and not even necessarily related to communication.

The second factor, social conventions, refers to the rules, customs, or customary behaviors that govern how people interact with one another. Beer et al. (2006b) refer to these as the behavioral norms and procedures of the social world. Saying hello, please, and thank you; waiting in line at a store; or asking about another person's health are examples of such customs, rules, or norms. Other social conventions relate to expected behaviors, such as those expected at meal times, during a play date, or during classroom participation. These conventions are important to master and use because they facilitate social interactions. Once mastered, such behaviors are often performed somewhat automatically. The application of social conventions does not usually involve much social cognition. People typically think about social conventions only when they notice that others do not share them (e.g., when encountering someone from a different culture or in a new situation where the social norms are uncertain). Social conventions are learned. They do not emerge spontaneously as a natural part of child development. Through imitation, modeling, and explicit instruction, they are acquired as part of child development. The Social Skills Framework presents key aspects of social cognition in a developmental hierarchy that mirrors typical child development, proceeding from least complex to most complex. The terms presented in this chapter help in interpreting students' social cognition and social skills.

## HOW THIS FRAMEWORK WAS CONSTRUCTED

As with many of the skills discussed in this book, the study of social skills lacks a unifying terminology. There is no formally agreed-on definition of what constitutes social skills or social cognition (Beer et al., 2006a). The lack of conceptual clarity in the social skills domain affects assessment and intervention (Halle & Darling-Churchill, 2016; Jones, Zaslow, Darling-Churchill, & Halle, 2016) and therefore also affects the terms and behaviors included in this chapter on social skills. As discussed in Chapter 5, social skills cannot be separated easily from other types of developmental skills. For example, social thinking requires understanding communication. The observer has to understand a person's communication by listening and by looking at nonverbal aspects of communication. Social thinking is therefore difficult to separate from communication (Russell, 2007; Sperber & Wilson, 2002). Social cognition includes being able to identify and interpret another person's emotions (Halberstadt, Denham, & Dunsmore, 2001). As discussed in the pragmatic language skills chapter, interpretation of emotions has to occur for those emotions that are expressed intentionally and verbally, as well as those expressed unintentionally and nonverbally.

The framework proposed in this chapter takes into consideration the very close interrelations among language, pragmatic language, emotional awareness, and expression of emotion. At the same time, this chapter separates, as much as possible, those aspects of social cognition that overlap with other developmental domains, such as executive skills (Aboulafia-Brakha, Christe, Martory, & Annoni, 2011; Devine & Hughes, 2014; Moriguchi, 2014), emotions (Mitchell & Phillips, 2015), or language (Spanoudis, 2016). Those topics are discussed in Chapters 4, 5, 7, and 8. The reader should review these other chapters for a better understanding of the breadth of social skills. The chapter borrows conceptual frameworks as proposed by Frith and Frith (2012), Happe and Frith (2014), Beauchamp and Anderson (2010), and Lieberman (2007).



## HOW CAN THIS FRAMEWORK HELP ME?

This chapter discusses key terms related to social skills and can help readers to deepen their understanding of social cognition and social skills. The framework is designed to help school professionals identify successes in social thinking and social performance. The terms and skills presented here will help professionals accurately describe social behaviors and social difficulties to colleagues and with students. Using a description of a student's social difficulties, school teams will be able to develop a successful intervention plan.

Educators and other school professionals should help students understand and use social skills not only because they are important in building friendships, but also because they are so critical for successful teaching and learning experiences in the classroom (Caemmerer & Keith, 2015; Denham & Brown, 2010; Frith & Frith, 2012). These skills are also essential for successful work interactions in vocational training programs for students with and without disabilities (National Center for Education Statistics, 1992; Smith, Atmatzidis, & Capogreco, 2017).

## SOCIAL SKILLS FRAMEWORK: TERMS AND DEFINITIONS

The Social Skills Framework provides a set of terms to describe and discuss concepts related to social cognition. The terms are designed to provide a common understanding among team members, so that they can actively discuss students' capacities in the social domain. This discussion should facilitate the team's capacity to think proactively about educational objectives to improve students' abilities to perform successfully in social situations.

The Social Skills Framework consists of the following skills sets and skills:

1. Attachment
2. Empathy
3. Imitation
4. Social attention
5. Joint attention
6. Theory of mind
   a. Intentions, desires, emotions, and beliefs
   b. False beliefs
   c. Ambiguous and difficult-to-interpret situations
7. Social conventions



The majority of the skills listed above fall under the category of social cognition. Social conventions, the last of the skill sets, is considered separately. The first two components of the framework, attachment and empathy, pertain to the emotional aspects of social cognition. As such, they overlap substantially with affect and self-regulation skills. These two skill sets are often referred to as social-emotional skills, highlighting the important connection between social interactions and emotions.

Two subsequent components of the framework, social attention and joint attention, are difficult to separate from attention span in general. Attention span and its components are revisited in Chapter 7. The next to the last skill set in the framework, theory of mind, is difficult to separate from cognition in general. The sections that follow describe each component of the Social Skills Framework in more detail. The framework is summarized in Appendix 6.1 for quick reference.

## Attachment

Attachment refers to the personal relationship between an infant, toddler, or child and his or her primary caregivers. Attachment behaviors are intrinsically emotional, but also intrinsically social. A secure or healthy attachment is one where a child recognizes a feeling of security and comfort with primary caregivers. It serves as a foundation for the later discrimination and understanding of the emotions and intentions of others (Sherman, Rice, & Cassidy, 2015). Attachment serves as a foundation for later competence in both emotions and social cognition.

Attachment is identified by observing the behaviors of infants and young children as they seek out a parent figure for comfort when stressed (Fearon, 2011). Successful attachment means that the infant or toddler is able to recognize who is a primary caregiver, knows where the caregiver can be found, has memories of interactions with the caregiver, and is able to predict how the caregiver is likely to respond in different situations. These criteria can be met only when the caregiver responds in a soothing and predictable manner. When caregivers are inconsistent in their behaviors or do not provide soothing to the emotional infant or toddler, the child is then much less able to predict caregiver behaviors. An inability to guess at or know how the caregiver will respond can interfere very substantially with the development of attachment.

Healthy attachment behaviors for toddlers and young preschoolers include signaling behaviors (signaling to the primary caregiver by vocalizing or gestures, with the intention of gaining caregiver attention), proximity behaviors (staying close to the caregiver), and distress when faced with strangers (Fearon, 2011). The duration of proximity behaviors (e.g., number of minutes) can help identify healthy attachment. Proximity behaviors that are maintained only fleetingly do not suffice for identifying a healthy attachment, just as prolonged duration of proximity behaviors may be a sign of an unhealthy or unsuccessful attachment (e.g., when associated with anxiety or clinginess). Healthy attachment in toddlers and preschoolers also includes not showing excess proximity behaviors or affection to unfamiliar adults. As children age, attachment behaviors change. Children show greater security with unfamiliar adults, especially when sanctioned by their primary caregivers. They still preferentially seek out primary caregivers for important emotional exchanges, including soothing, but they can defer their contact with primary caregivers for longer periods of time. They may be able to seek soothing with adults other than primary caregivers, albeit with familiar adults.

## Empathy



Empathy is the experience of sharing feelings and emotions with another person. The shared feelings manifest as an emotional reaction in the observer. Both members of a social pair might experience the same emotion at the same time, such as happiness, excitement, anger, or sadness. When faced with intense emotions in another person, the observer might feel a similar emotion and might feel it just as intensely. Empathy can also be experienced less reflexively (and usually less intensely) when the observer responds with sympathy or understanding. The observer may notice an emotion in another person and may even be able to identify the emotion correctly. However, the observer understands that the emotion does not have the same implications in the self as it may have in the observed.

Empathy does not necessarily include an emotional response. Through experience and cognition, an observer can reflect empathically on the emotions of another person even while not being emotionally affected by the observation. Even if the actual emotion is not shared, the observer can still respond in a socially appropriate and empathic manner. Psychotherapists working with clients often are able to help their clients more successfully when their responses remain sympathetic and when they do not experience too deeply the emotions experienced by their clients.

Empathy therefore consists of two types of responses. It can consist of an automatic response that is not voluntary and outside of the observer's control. The response is emotional, is shared with the person being observed, and can be intense. Empathy can also be more cognitive and reflective. The observer may have thoughts about the emotion. The thoughts might consist of ideas or interpretations of why the person being observed is experiencing an emotion. These thoughts make up the cognitive aspect of empathy, sometimes referred to as an appraisal; this consists of identifying the emotion by name and then thinking about its causes and consequences.

Empathic responses can therefore be elicited directly, by witnessing the emotional reactions of others and sharing in the emotional experience. Empathic responses can also be elicited through cognition, for example, by hearing stories that include an emotional theme or story (de Vignemont & Singer, 2006). Empathic responses are therefore made up of direct emotional reactions as well as an appraisal of an emotional situation. The extent to which each plays a role depends very much on the context. The observer will have a lesser or greater emotion depending on the relevance of the emotion stimulus to the observer, the observer's internal context such as mood and attention span, the relationship of the observer and the observed, or the type of emotion being experienced (de Vignemont & Singer, 2006). Similarly, the observer will have a lesser or greater number of cognitive appraisals about the emotion-eliciting event or situation, depending upon all of the same factors just discussed.

Empathy develops and expands with age. As children develop, there is a general trend of moving from direct emotional reactions that occur with others toward a less reactive, more reflective, and more cognitive experience of the emotion that the observer experiences as sympathy or as understanding. Younger children tend to react to and react with the emotions of others. Babies and toddlers instinctually and automatically share in a variety of emotions of others. A baby may start to cry in reaction to another baby's crying. Toddlers can recognize and have an automatic empathic response to pain (a physical sensation) and also to emotions, such as sadness, joy, or anxiety. These automatic responses can be referred to as bottom-up processes (Decety, 2010). They occur reflexively, through activation of arousal processes or through automatic or learned imitation (Bastiaansen, Thioux, & Keysers, 2009).

As toddlers develop greater cognitive abilities, they can recognize that an emotion is occurring in another person instead of just reacting to the emotion. They can opt to join the other person in this emotional experience (e.g., if it is laughter or joy) or try to help the other person by offering soothing activities (e.g., if the experience is sadness or distress). The toddler might imitate the happy or excited facial expression when exposed to happy or excited peers or adults, with the goal of joining a positive social experience. The toddler may show a sad facial expression and approach the peer or adult with a preferred toy or blanket, giving it for the purpose of soothing (Decety, 2010). These latter examples of empathy involve some cognition. They involve some conscious reflection about where the emotion came from (causation) and choice-making about how to best respond to the emotional situation (consequence).

The experience of empathy facilitates learning. Through imitation, toddlers and preschoolers learn about how other people feel. They can learn about which emotion is the right one for any given situation. Instead of being fearful of an exciting event such as fireworks, they can instead notice that peers and adults are not fearful. By noticing the excited emotion of others, they can choose to join empathically with others. Instead of showing fear, they can choose to show pleasure in imitation of those peers and adults. They can now respond with others instead of just reacting with others. They can share the experience both emotionally and cognitively.

Children, adolescents, and adults show empathic responses that include more thinking about the other person's experiences and more complex behaviors in response to the emotions (or perceived emotions) of others. These responses can be referred to as top-down responses. For example, they can show more complex behaviors to indicate that they are sharing an emotional experience by sharing a story about a similar experience. They might say, "That reminds me of a time when I was feeling the same way." They may also propose more complex behaviors to participate in or regulate the emotion, saying something like, "You know what we could do that would be even more fun . . .?" Or, they might say, "When I was feeling that way, what I did was . . ." Empathic responses can be both altruistic and egocentric. Empathy can emerge from a genuine feeling of connection with others and can result in behaviors that occur for the benefit of others. The observer may perform an action to help soothe the social partner who is distressed or anxious, for example. Empathic responses can also occur for the benefit of the self. A person might feel an empathic response to someone's distress and then make a plan to avoid the same situation going forward. The observer might also join in on the excitement experienced by the social partner, such as in the case of the fireworks, discussed above. Here, the empathic response is used in the service of learning. The phenomena just described highlight the fact that empathy consists of both emotional responses and cognition, within and between people. They can occur for a variety of emotions, not just for distress or sadness. They can involve a variety of cognitive appraisals about the causes of the emotion and the consequences that can or should follow. All these interactions between emotion and cognition can change the thoughts, feelings, and behaviors of both the observer and the observed (Preston & de Waal, 2002).

## Imitation

The next skill in the Social Skills Framework is imitation. Imitation has parallels to empathy. Like empathy, imitation can occur spontaneously and automatically. Spontaneous imitation may occur because of the presence of mirror neurons, parts of the brain and nervous system that help humans imitate the motor actions of others. The motor actions can be very simple (e.g., a change in facial expression such as sticking out the tongue) or highly complex (the series of motor actions required to tie one's shoelaces or to repair a broken bicycle). On its own, the capacity to observe others and imitate others is not a highly complex skill. Imitation also does not reflect a highly complex way of understanding others. Many young children imitate others without showing any understanding of the behavior that they have just imitated.

In more fully developed imitation, humans do not just copy an action. They also think about the purpose or the intention that the person had when performing the action and the relevance of action to the self (Oztop, Kawato, & Arbib, 2013). This means that, like spontaneous empathy, spontaneous imitation can result in an appraisal of a situation. In more fully developed imitation, the spontaneous capacity to imitate others is combined with an understanding of the intentions, beliefs, and/or purpose that underlie human actions and behaviors. Spontaneous imitation is combined with cognition about others in order to be meaningful (Jacob & Heannerod, 2005). Through imitation, humans learn to express emotions, to speak and use language, and to socialize (Iacoboni & Daprettto, 2006). For example, a toddler starts out life by imitating the actions of parents and peers. The imitating toddler learns about drinking, playing, and household routines by imitating those activities. All of these different activities provide information about the persons whom the preschooler has imitated. These new skills present opportunities for socializing (when the activity is fun) and challenges to avoid (when the activity is difficult or boring). In the process, the imitator learns about the world and others. Imitation is an important foundation for learning.



## Social Attention

Social attention refers to behaviors such as noticing, paying attention to, and/or being interested in other people. Social attention begins at birth and can be receptive and expressive. For example, a baby may gaze for long periods at a primary caregiver. This behavior suggests social attention, especially if there is shared eye gaze. In older infants and toddlers, social attention is assessed by observing the child's responsiveness to social stimuli and by observing the child's capacity to elicit social responses from others. Social attention can be passive. The infant, toddler, or preschooler may simply pay attention to the actions of others, or might imitate others, without taking the social thinking process further than this. In contrast, an infant, toddler, or preschooler might make a social bid. A social bid is an observable behavior that is designed to elicit a social response and is important to notice and document when assessing social attention. As infants and toddlers age, they are more purposeful in seeking out social attention through social bids. The behavior may be nonverbal or verbal and can include behaviors such as squealing or making another kind of vocalization, changing facial expression, pointing, showing something, saying something, asking about something, and telling someone about something. These same behaviors may occur in response to a social bid from another person.

Eye contact is one of the most important observable behaviors associated with social attention. Shared eye gaze declares the social nature of a social bid, especially when the social bid is nonverbal. Social attention can be measured by assessing how often eye contact or shared eye gaze is present, the duration of the eye contact, and whether there is joint attention (see next section) (Salley & Colombo, 2016). Social attention is a necessary aspect of all social behaviors and social learning, such as attachment and imitation (discussed in this chapter) and communication (discussed in Chapters 4 and 5).

## Joint Attention

Whereas social attention refers to the general behavior of an individual paying attention to other individuals, joint attention refers to simultaneously paying attention to a person and to an external object, event, other person, or conversational topic. Joint attention, or shared attention, is social attention that includes directing attention *away* from the social partner. The person who initiates joint attention has to make eye gaze with the social partner, look away from the social partner in order to indicate a shared object or person of interest, and then return eye gaze to the social partner (Klein & Shepherd, 2009). In toddlers, joint attention is most clearly manifest when the toddler shows shared eye gaze with an adult and uses a pointing finger to indicate to the adult where to look, after which both the toddler and the adult shift their eye gaze from each other to look at the object, event, or person of interest. The toddler and the caregiver know that that they are both looking at the same object at the same time.

Less mature manifestations of joint attention emerge earlier in life. For example, an infant, perhaps at age 10 months, might notice that the caregiver looked out the window and might then look in the same direction. The infant or toddler might notice that the caregiver is pointing at something and might then look in that direction. These behaviors indicate that the infant or toddler understands something about the adult's eye gaze and attentional focus. Mature joint attention, in contrast, is initiated by the child. It emerges in typically developing children by age 18 months. After age 18 months, joint attention is no longer fleeting. As the duration of joint attention increases, the toddler and the adult might be able to have a conversation or discussion about the shared object or person of interest. The joint attention might last a minute or two, in the case of the toddler or preschooler, or for much longer intervals in older children and youth. Joint attention is a critical developmental milestone. It identifies the toddler or child who has understood that other minds can have shared interests.



## Theory of Mind

Joint attention is the first evidence that a toddler or young child has a theory of mind (Klein & Shepherd, 2009). Once a toddler understands that interests can be shared with another person, he or she can also start to show curiosity about the minds of others. The capacity to think about the minds and the mental states of others is referred to as theory of mind. In this chapter, the discussion of theory of mind will be limited to a discussion of the intentions, desires, and beliefs of others (Premack & Woodruff, 1978), including understanding mistaken beliefs (Flavell, 1999; Flavell, Mumme, Green, & Flavell, 1992). Other authors, such as Slaughter (2011); Schaafsma, Pfaff, Spunt, and Adolphs (2015); and Beauchamp and Anderson (2010) include aspects of theory of mind not elaborated upon here.

Understanding mental acts is dependent on observing and correctly interpreting the behaviors of others. Theory of mind depends on general knowledge about how people are likely to behave and knowledge about social conventions that people normally show. Theory of mind sometimes also depends on more specific knowledge, such as knowledge about familiar people and how they usually behave. Theory of mind refers to making observations of others and linking those observations with an interpretation of the underlying intentions, desires, and beliefs of others.

When people apply theory of mind skills to understanding the minds of others, they have to rely on observable behaviors and general knowledge about the intentions, desires, or beliefs associated with those behaviors. They do not necessarily have access to the emotions or the internal thoughts of the person being observed. Internal information is usually a more accurate source of information about the person's intentions, desires, or beliefs (Pronin, 2008). For this reason, theory of mind is just that: A theory or set of theories. Unless the person being observed can communicate his or her intentions, desires, and/or beliefs, the observer's theories about that person can be faulty or flawed.

Although theory of mind is more typically applied to knowledge of others, it can also be applied to knowledge of the self (Schaafsma et al., 2015). These two uses of theory of mind depend on somewhat different types of knowledge. Theories about one's own mind are typically restricted to one's internal thoughts and feelings. A theory of one's own mind does not usually take into consideration awareness or knowledge of the behaviors that are observable to others, such as one's changes in facial expression, gesture, or body language at a given point in time or as part of a pattern that repeats itself over time. People can develop a much richer and much more accurate theory of mind (their own mind, as well as the minds of others) when they have access to both types of information: Observable (external) behaviors, as well as (internal) feelings and thoughts. For people to understand one another, both types of information need to be accessible. In some situations, both types of information need to be gathered over time in order to ensure accuracy.

People's theories about others' minds can change when both externally observable and internally experienced information is shared. For example, a child may generate a theory that her mother is mean because she makes her turn off her iPad. If she does not pay attention to her mother's predictable pattern of setting limits and enforcing rules of various kinds (behavioral observations over time), she may have only one theory about her mother's mind: "My mother is mean." By sharing information about observable behaviors and by sharing internal information, the child's mother can transform her daughter's theory of mind. She might say something like the following: "As your mother, I have to make and enforce rules. I need to teach you how to manage frustration when fun things come to an end. I also need to teach you how to manage frustration when I ask you to do boring tasks. We all have to do things that are frustrating or boring. But don't worry. After a while, it won't seem so frustrating anymore." By communicating the intentions that underlie her behaviors, the mother teaches the child a more complex way of understanding the behaviors of her mother. The child learns to take into consideration multiple observations over time and also learns about the internal thinking process of the person being observed. The child may still not prefer her mother's behaviors, but at least she understands the true intentions behind those behaviors.

When adults and children can communicate with each other in this manner, the adult not only transforms the child's theory about the adult's mind. The adult also transforms the child's theory of her own mind. When the adult explains her behaviors to the child, the child starts to understand minds in a more complex way. The child might start to look for patterns of behavior in others. She might also become more purposeful in asking about the intentions, desires, and beliefs of the behaviors of others. By gathering more information first, she can more accurately identify true intentions, beliefs, and desires. Over time, the child can see herself as an observer of human behavior who can start to make predictions about how her mother (and others) will behave in certain situations and can plan accordingly.

As another example, consider the adolescent who exclaims that he is "not at all interested" in a female peer, but he turns red, looks downward, cannot make eye contact with her and speaks more quickly whenever she is nearby. He might truly believe that he is indifferent to her. However, his observable behaviors tell another story, especially if they are recurrent or persistent. The adolescent needs information about his observable behaviors, as well as his intentions, desires, and beliefs, in order to create a coherent theory of his own mind. An empathic adult can help the adolescent understand his own mind and can help the adolescent expand his theories about his own mind through the conversation. The adolescent might then come to a realization of the attraction that he feels and can then make more coherent decisions about how he would like to behave going forward.

A good theory of mind requires making good observations of the person being observed. It also requires good information about the internal experience of the person being observed. Both types of information need to be gathered over time. Much of the time, when developing a theory of mind about a particular person, people fail to make good observations over time. Perhaps more commonly, people fail to ask about the other person's internal experience(s). In social skills training, it is important for children to think about both aspects of theory of mind. Both observable and internal types of information matter to a person's theory of the minds of others, as well as the person's theory of his or her own mind. Videorecording is one way to help the learner see him- or herself in action.

***Intentions, Desires, and Emotions*** Internal states, such as intentions, desires, and emotions, underlie people's behaviors. This important insight develops late in infancy, when babies show understanding for intentionality. They understand people have intentions, whereas objects do not. For example, past the age of 6 months, infants respond differently to moving objects as opposed to moving people. They understand that people can propel themselves (e.g., move from one place to another), but objects cannot do so. If a ball suddenly starts to move on its own, the infant will show surprise. When a person suddenly starts move on his or her own, the infant does not show this type of surprise. Past the age of 1, toddlers develop an understanding of internal states such as desires. For example, the toddler understands internal states, such as feeling hungry or tired. The toddler also understands the predictable behaviors that people show when hungry or tired. For example, a 2-year-old knows that when people are hungry, they will likely go to the kitchen or go to the refrigerator but not to the bathroom. When tired, people go to bed, not outside for a walk.

Another important development in children's understanding of internal states is the ability to identify emotions. Toddlers and preschoolers learn that emotions are a key driver of human behavior. Initially, toddlers and preschoolers identify emotions in others based on their facial expression or other verbal and nonverbal behaviors. They then learn to describe those emotions in the self. Later, toddlers and preschoolers learn about how emotions influence intentions and desires. For example, sadness and fear lead to a desire for soothing from a trusted adult. Fear can lead to avoidance behaviors, such as running away from a big dog. Other developments in understanding emotions and their influence on behaviors are discussed in Chapter 8. The main idea to share here is that toddlers and preschoolers learn to identify emotion and the connection between emotions and behaviors in the self and in others.



***Beliefs*** Older toddlers and preschoolers understand beliefs. First, they learn about certain common patterns in the world. For example, preschoolers know that cookies are usually found in the kitchen and not in the bathroom. If asked by an adult, "Where would you look if you wanted to eat a cookie?" they will inform the adult that they will look for cookies in the kitchen. If asked where another child would look if that child wanted to eat a cookie, they would provide the same response. Preschoolers who respond successfully to this question show a dual awareness. They know that common knowledge or commonly held beliefs about where cookies are located will dictate their own behavior, as well as the behaviors of others. They also assume that this common knowledge or commonly held belief is shared with others.

There are other ways that adults can elicit a toddler's or preschooler's understanding of desires and beliefs. For example, an adult can ask a child or student to describe another person's beliefs based on a photo of people and by asking what the people in the photo might be thinking, feeling, or planning to do in response to a situation. The adult might show the child a photo of students sitting in circle time in a classroom or families shopping at a grocery store. The child is then asked what is currently happening and what the people in the photo might do next. The responses of the child depend on what the child knows to be commonly true. Commonly shared desires, emotions, and beliefs will dictate what people usually or normally do and will also dictate the child's responses to questions such as this.

The knowledge and skills discussed above have their limitations. For example, if a child sees an adult open the refrigerator door, he or she might conclude that the adult is hungry and wants to get something to eat. The child might not realize that the adult who opened the refrigerator door did so to replace the light bulb. Thus, to have an accurate mental representation of the minds of others, children have to consider nonhabitual intentions, desires, and beliefs, not just conventional ones. Careful observation is needed to notice what might be nonhabitual in the scene laid before them. The child can generate a good theory about the mental processes of others only by taking into consideration all the observable information. A child may have a false belief if he or she fails to notice the screwdriver or the light bulb in the adult's hands. When they do observe these aspects of the social scene, they can theorize more effectively.

The examples just discussed are examples of a belief-desire psychology. The child interprets the behaviors of others based on shared knowledge that most people hold about human behaviors. Some of the time, because of missing information or because the child is in a novel situation, the child's mental representation of the minds of others is incorrect or false. Understanding that people (the self and others) can have false beliefs about a situation is a separate developmental accomplishment.



***False Beliefs*** An important development in theory of mind occurs when preschoolers understand that a person can have a false belief. Two people might not share the same information, knowledge, or beliefs. Sometimes, people act out of a false belief or a false understanding of a situation. Understanding that not all people share the same information, knowledge, or beliefs is a developmental accomplishment that emerges during the preschool years, usually age 3–4 years. At this age, children learn that two people can have different knowledge about a situation and can therefore have a false belief about that situation. This accomplishment is measured by the false belief task (Wimmer & Perner, 1983), in which a student is told a story about a person (usually another child) who mistakenly believes something to be true. The child in the story might have a mistaken idea about the location of a candy bar inside the house. The student being tested is told about the true location of the candy bar and is also told that the protagonist in the story believes the candy bar to be located somewhere else. The student being tested is then asked to predict the behaviors of the child portrayed in the story. The examiner might ask the student where the child is likely to look for the candy bar. Children who have not yet developed an understanding of false beliefs will interpret the story based on their knowledge of the actual situation (the actual location of the candy bar), not based on the protagonist's knowledge of the situation (the false belief held by the protagonist). In contrast, older preschoolers will understand the false belief held by the protagonist in the story and can more accurately interpret the protagonist's likely behaviors. See Box 6.1 for an illustration of this important concept. False belief tasks are one way of establishing the capacity of children to interpret the mental states of others. They are considered to be a good test of theory of mind, because the child has to correctly identify a belief held by another person that the child does not share.

**BOX 6.1. Theory of Mind and the False Belief Task**

The false belief task is a developmental assessment task that establishes the presence of early theory of mind skills. Typically developing 3-year-old children usually do not pass this test, whereas typically developing 4-year-olds do. In this task, the child being tested has to separate what she or he knows to be true from what another person believes to be true. The child has to reason logically from the perspective of another person's mind. Two common theory of mind tasks follow. Both highlight a situation in which a person or a character in a story has a false belief.

**False Contents Task**
A child named Marianne is shown a box that shows a picture of candies and that is labeled *candies*. Marianne opens the box and discovers that the box contains crayons, not candies. The examiner then asks Marianne what she was expecting to find in the box. If Marianne is a typically developing preschooler, she will state that she was expecting to find candies. The examiner then closes the box. Subsequently, the examiner asks Marianne, "If I show this box to your friends, what will they say is inside the box?" If Marianne is a typically developing 3-year-old, she is likely to say that her friends will say that there are crayons in the box. If Marianne is a typically developing 4-year-old, she is likely to say that her friends will say that there are candies in the box. Between the ages of 3 and 4 years, there is a developmental shift, and children are able to switch perspectives between self and other. They can distinguish between what they know to be true and what others believe to be true. They can start to reason logically about the behaviors of others as based on their perspective instead of reasoning from the perspective of the self.

**Hidden Object Task**
In the hidden object task, the examiner tells Marianne a story about a boy named Matt. The examiner can tell the story with the assistance of pictures if desired. Matt hides his Halloween candies inside a drawer in the kitchen while Matt's sister is secretly standing outside the kitchen watching him. When Matt leaves the kitchen, she takes the candies out of their hiding place and puts them into the cookie jar, unbeknownst to Matt. The examiner then asks the child, "When Matt comes back to the kitchen to look for his candies, where will he look?" If Marianne is a typically developing 3-year-old, she will guess that Matt will look in the cookie jar. If Marianne is a typically developing 4-year-old, she will guess that Matt will look in the kitchen drawer. Four-year-olds are able to reason from Matt's beliefs and Matt's knowledge, not from their own knowledge of the situation. The 4-year-old understands that Matt's beliefs dictate his behaviors. It is not the knowledge held by the observer that dictates Matt's behaviors, but rather the knowledge held by Matt that dictates his behaviors.

**Limitations of Standardized Theory of Mind Tasks**
The limitations of testing situations for theory of mind apply to testing situations in general. Whether the child passes or fails the task needs to be interpreted in context. A child can pass a theory of mind task but still have difficulty with theory of mind skills in real-time social situations. Conversely, a child can fail a theory of mind task (e.g., because he or she misunderstood the instructions or was confused by the pictures) but could still perform well socially.



***Complexities in Theory of Mind*** The theory of mind demands of everyday life are usually much more complex than a theory of mind task or any of the belief-desire examples discussed above. To theorize about the behaviors of others, people have to gather, synthesize, and integrate a lot of information about the intentions, desires, beliefs, and knowledge that others may have. Differences in the knowledge and beliefs of people are usually much more complex than the differences that a false belief task can measure. In order to theorize successfully, people have to compare whatever they know to be generally true about most people against what they generally know to be true about a familiar person. They have to then map observable behaviors of the person they are theorizing about with what they know about the person. The observer may need to take into consideration a lot of information before it is possible to guess accurately at what another person might be thinking or feeling.

People commonly encounter contradictions or difficulties when they theorize about others. A person might express interest or enthusiasm with words, but at the same time use a facial expression, a gesture, or a tone of voice that suggests a lack of interest or a lack of enthusiasm. Sarcasm and ambivalence can be expressed this way. The true intentions or desires of the speaker can be difficult to interpret. Difficulties in theorizing can also occur because of missing information. For example, the observer of a social situation might not notice a change in facial expression, might fail to hear what was actually said, or might be missing important background information about that person or about the situation. Missing information increases the chances of making errors. Most often, mistakes occur when the theorizer relies on behavioral observations alone and cannot supplement behavioral observations with direct information about the person's thoughts or feelings. Theory of mind is therefore not a skill that one either has or does not have. It is a skill set that requires gathering information and behavioral observations over time and verifying one's theory by asking for internal information from the person being observed. There are many possible reasons why people fail to theorize successfully about the minds of others.

## Social Conventions



Social conventions are another important component of social skills. As presented at the beginning of the chapter, social conventions are the rules, customs, or customary behaviors of others. Social conventions are identified through observable behaviors. These behaviors often consist of rehearsed or scripted communicative functions and rehearsed or scripted nonverbal communication behaviors. These scripted or memorized behaviors facilitate social interactions. Social conventions are a type of knowledge but are also a set of skills. Making a greeting, smiling during the greeting, holding the door open for an older person, or using eating utensils properly are all behaviors that are learned through convention and are applied in a rote manner. Although they often do not involve much thought, the rote application of social conventions helps to facilitate social success. They communicate positive desires, intentions, and beliefs about the social interaction. Smiling at someone or holding open the door suggests respect, while eating neatly using eating utensils is more pleasant for others and is also a sign of respect.

Although social conventions usually consist of rote and scripted behaviors, they cannot always be used in a rote manner and they sometimes require interpretation. Sometimes, social conventions have to be modified for the situation. For example, showing polite eating behaviors is more important in some settings than in others. It takes some judgment and experience to decide when a social convention is required and when it is not required. Social conventions do not necessarily provide any information about the underlying intentions, desires, or beliefs of the person who is showing the conventions. At times, the positive intentions, desires, or beliefs that are communicated by a social convention are not actually held by the person performing the convention. It takes observation and experience to understand the difference between the two.

Knowledge about and use of the social conventions of one's heritage culture is only one aspect of understanding and using social conventions successfully. It is just as important to understand how social conventions can differ across cultures. Knowledge of different types of social conventions helps people to socialize with people from other cultures. This knowledge can also enhance one's theory of mind! Knowledge of other cultures helps to interpret the social behaviors of people from other cultures and serves as a reminder of the intention of social conventions. Social conventions help people to feel respected, understood, included, and treated fairly. The rote application of social conventions is not always successful in meeting these important social goals. In order to be socially successful, it is always important to show behaviors that communicate respect, understanding, social inclusion, and a desire to offer fair treatment. The most appropriate behaviors, including the most appropriate social conventions, depend upon the situation or context.

## PERFORMANCE DIFFICULTIES IN SOCIAL SKILLS

Social difficulties can be evident in a variety of classroom participation behaviors. Students with social skills challenges may experience the following:

- Difficulty with peer-mediated learning (students learning from one another) and difficulty socializing
- Difficulty maintaining the topic during conversations or during classroom discussions
- Difficulty asking questions and responding to questions from adults or peers to seek help, get information, or deepen understanding
- Difficulty reading, comprehending, and retelling narrative text
- Difficulty establishing friendships

The Social Skills Framework and its terms are relevant to all of the classroom performance difficulties in the list. In some instances, the performance difficulties are caused by factors other than those related to social cognition or theory of mind. Performance difficulties in language skills, executive skills, and emotion-management skills can explain social difficulties. Each of these is examined in other chapters. The sections that follow present examples of social impairment not captured by the classroom participation behaviors listed above. They also offer examples of how atypical social cognition manifests in children and youth.



### Atypical Attachment Behaviors

Atypical attachment behaviors are observable in young children. These behaviors are most likely to occur in children who have experienced trauma, neglect, prolonged lack of access to caregivers, or abuse. Young children with atypical attachment may be indifferent to the primary caregiver. Such a child would not be interested in greeting the primary caregiver and would not show proximity behaviors, such as staying near the caregiver. Alternatively, the child might show contradictory behaviors when in the presence of the primary caregiver. For instance, the child may exhibit distress when reunited with the caregiver or might vacillate between emotional extremes (affection and anger). Young children with attachment disorders can also show their affection for all adults indiscriminately, as though all adults have the same emotional importance as the primary caregivers.

Attachment can develop in an atypical manner in children who have not been abused or neglected. For example, students with autism spectrum disorder typically exhibit healthy attachment behaviors, but these behaviors may develop at a later age. Instead of showing healthy attachment behaviors prior to the first birthday, they may only do so in the months or years that follow. The child's degree of cognitive impairment can affect the emergence of attachment behaviors.

As children with atypical attachment age, it is harder to identify their social and emotional responses as being caused by attachment problems. With age, atypical attachment may only be identifiable as atypical emotion regulation. Older children or adults with atypical attachment may be emotionally volatile in situations in which a more reasoned response is expected. Verbal children with atypical attachment may be able to describe inconsistencies in the caregiving that they received and may state that they do not have a family or do not having a meaningful connection to others as would be expected from family members.

### Difficulties in Social Attention

Atypical social attention may present as a lack of responsiveness to social bids from others, or an absence or reduction in social bids toward others. The student with atypical social attention might not show any responsiveness to the social bids of others. Alternatively, the student might respond to the social bid, but might do so without making eye contact or by making a noncontingent or off-topic comment. If the student does make social bids, these might appear atypical. For example, the social attention may manifest through proximity behaviors only and without eye contact. Or the student might make a social bid by touching a peer or even pushing or hitting a peer as a means to gain peer attention. Finally, students with atypical social attention might make social bids only for the purpose of getting personal needs met. For example, a student would make social bids to obtain food but would not make social bids for the purposes of play or conversation. Even when some social bids or social responses appear to be typical, they may occur too infrequently or be too fleeting. At times, students show no social attention behaviors at all and seem content to play alone even while surrounded by peers. Atypical social attention is usually seen in students on the autism spectrum, though it can also be seen in students with attachment disorders and/or anxiety.

### Performance Difficulties in Theory of Mind



Many of the behaviors listed above also emerge in children who do not have a fully developed theory of mind. Students who have difficulty with theory of mind might not be able to interpret basic social behaviors in others, such as the intentions, desires, or beliefs of others in given situations. Some students have difficulty with theory of mind because they cannot interpret accurately the facial expressions, gestures, or tone of voice of a social partner. They might think that the person is happy when, in fact, the person is angry. Even if they can interpret nonverbal communication correctly, they may or may not be able to imagine what the other person is thinking or what the other person might do in a given situation. Understanding the perspective of the other person is difficult for some students, especially when the student has to identify or respond to a person who has misunderstood something or who has a false belief about something. One of the conversational skills discussed in Chapter 5 included conversational repair. Not all students are able to identify conversational breakdowns and/or repair them.

Students with difficulty in theory of mind may make incorrect attributions about the intentions or beliefs of others, even those that seem very basic. They might not be able to guess or know about basic human drives, such as how to identify if someone is hungry, thirsty, or tired. In a social context, they may not know how to distinguish a social bid from teasing or bullying. Students on the autism spectrum may be especially vulnerable to situations such as this. However, many children with a variety of disabilities show difficulties with theory of mind skills. In some of these students, theory of mind skills appears to be intact in testing situations or when reading a story. However, they may show difficulty applying theory of mind skills to real-time social situations. Language impairment, a short attention span, or emotional dysregulation can all interfere with successful information processing in real-time social situations and can result in misinterpretations or misunderstandings.

## HOW TO SET UP AN OBSERVATION

The observations section is designed for the practitioner to put knowledge into practice. For the Social Skills Framework, the observations will be analyzed using information and knowledge about the social thinking skills of children and youth.

### Preliminary Considerations

The ability to demonstrate the skills discussed in this chapter, which include attachment, empathy, imitation, social attention, joint attention, and theory of mind, are dependent on several factors. First of all, these skills can only be assessed during a social interaction. The student needs social partners who are temperamentally or developmentally similar or who have shared interests. Second, a social interaction requires paying attention to multiple variables, such as formal language (words), pragmatic language (words, as well as nonverbal communication behaviors), and context (formal or casual situation, same-age peer or differently aged peer). Observers should keep in mind all of the different factors that might interfere with the student's social skills. Failure to socialize successfully can occur for reasons other than underdeveloped social cognition. Information from other chapters should be considered in analyzing the reasons for the student's socializing difficulties.

## Select the Student

As is true for all of the frameworks in this book, it is as important to observe students who are performing successfully as it is to observe students who have performance difficulties. One option when first making observations in the social skills domain is to make observations of a student who is socially more able than her or his peers. Observations of students who perform successfully in social situations are sometimes easier to do and can help set the stage for making observations of students who are socially less able. Students with difficulties socializing can then be selected for an observation. These students are likely to have difficulties in many of the classroom participation behaviors listed in a report card. These difficulties can become a reason for observing social skills more carefully. For example, difficulties in social skills can manifest as difficulty in listening to and following instructions, paying attention in class, participating successfully in class discussions, or performing successfully during peer-mediated learning. Performance difficulties in these areas can be due to difficulties in the social skills discussed in this chapter, because the student may be confused, indifferent, or unaware of social interactions in general. Language impairment and difficulties in executive skills (discussed in Chapter 7) can also explain these performance difficulties. By making multiple observations and considering multiple causes, the practitioner can separate out difficulties in social cognition from social difficulties related to formal language, pragmatic language, executive skills, or affect and self-regulation skills.



## Obtain Samples of Social Behaviors

Setting up an observation for social skills and social cognition is very similar to setting up an observation for formal and pragmatic language. See the description of how to set up an observation in Chapters 4 and 5. School professionals can also use Appendix 6.2, the Social Skills Observation Sheet, to set up and guide their observation of social skills. The observer should choose an activity that is socially expected for age or grade or that is likely to be interesting to the student. The activity could be a narrative task, a play activity, or a conversation. Play activities are especially useful for observing social skills in young children and in students who have limited formal and/or pragmatic language skills. See Box 6.2 and select an activity that would have the most appeal for the situation.

Another option to consider for making an observation is not to set up a specific task or activity and instead choose to observe social interactions that occur naturally throughout the day. The observer might start out by watching spontaneous social behaviors the student shows with peers. The observation might also include watching the student during peer-mediated learning activities. Whenever possible, the observer should include observations of comparison students who have typically developing social skills.

**BOX 6.2. A Hierarchy of Play Activities**

Play activities are very useful to use when assessing social skills. Play activities do not require too much language and can help facilitate a social interaction for students whose language is underdeveloped. The hierarchy shown here describes play skills proceeding from least complex to most complex. The hierarchy starts with sensory-motor activities. These activities are enjoyable and can facilitate a social interaction for this reason. However, on their own they do not reveal much information about social cognition. Play activities that are higher up in the hierarchy typically yield more information about a student's social skills. For any observation, the student has to be comfortable and must find the activity engaging. You will have more difficulty obtaining good observations if the student feels reticent, frustrated, anxious, or embarrassed.

**Sensory-Motor Play**

Sensory-motor play consists of repetitive actions and often includes gross motor activity. Cause-and-effect toys, rocking and spinning behaviors, running in circles, swinging and gross motor play on a playground are examples of sensory-motor play. Sensory-motor activities are repetitive and do not require any social interaction. As such, sensory-motor play activities are not always useful for observing social skills. However, sensory-motor activities can be social when they occur with peers. An observer can start out with sensory-motor activities to capture the student's interest. The observer can then try to build up a more complex interaction by introducing more advanced play activities. For example, the sensory-motor activity can be made more social by introducing turn taking, by introducing some conversation, or by adding more complex features of play such as the ones listed in the paragraphs that follow.



**Functional Play**

Functional play refers to play with real-world objects. Sometimes, those objects are toys that look real, and sometimes the objects are real. One of the most common examples of functional play is use of a telephone or cell phone. Almost all children know how to use a telephone, and most children can be engaged to use one as a prop. Plastic forks, spoons, and cups also serve the purpose of functional play, as do other household objects such as a comb or toothbrush. If the child uses the objects for their intended purpose, then they are revealing to the observer that they have learned through social imitation and that they have at least a rudimentary understanding of the behaviors of others. Other examples of functional play include manipulating toy trains, trucks, and cars. Even though children understand that these toys are not real cars, trucks, or trains, they know how to use them functionally. The same is true for play with imaginary tools, blocks, or Legos. The types of play activities children can do with these objects are fairly predictable. Even though these toys are functional in nature, they can also be used for imaginary play. The child's verbal description of his or her play can help the observer identify when the toys are being used in an imaginary manner.

Appropriate play with toys and objects such as those discussed here signal some social learning. However, play with these objects may or may not result in a social interaction and might not result in a good observation of the social skills discussed in this chapter. One way to create a social interaction during functional play is to sit down with the child and let him or her engage with the objects. After a time, the observing adult can comment on the child's actions, imitate the child's actions, make suggestions for new actions, start a different play activity alongside the child, or interfere with the child's play. These adult behaviors serve the purpose of inviting social responses from the child. If the child is not comfortable playing with the adult and purposefully ignores the observer, it may be worthwhile finding an adult or peer who is more familiar and to see whether social responsiveness is greater with someone else.

**Imaginary Play**

Imaginary play consists of play with functional or imaginary objects. Imaginary play items are different from functional objects because it is clear that they are not real-world objects, persons, or animals. The most common examples are dolls or toy animals. Imaginary play items can also include miniature doll houses, miniature food items, and miniature cars and trucks. Unlike functional objects, some imagination is needed to play successfully with imaginary objects. The child has to be able to imagine that the object being used represents a real-world object. A good example of imagination occurs when a child uses one object to represent another object. For example, a child might not have any toys that look like a telephone and will use a block to pretend speaking on the telephone. The child might use blocks or pieces of paper as pretend food. In even more highly imaginative play, a child might use a doll, a spoon, or a block to represent a human figure or an animal. The play might be to enact the activities or interactions that occur between people, such as household activities, social activities, or learning activities at school. The play might be a re-enactment of a story or event from the child's prior exposure to books, movies, or a life circumstance.

What makes imaginary play more social than functional play is that imaginary objects are given attributions that they do not (inherently) have in real life. The toys are used to act out social or other functions. Inanimate objects are made to have human thoughts, desires, beliefs, and intentions. Children show these human attributions by interacting directly with the toys or by making the toys interact with each other. For example, the child may speak to the toy or might pretend that the toy is speaking to them. The child might perform actions on the toy, such as feeding, dressing, or playing, or might make one toy speak with another toy. The play behaviors performed by the child may mimic attachment behaviors between a child and her or his parents. The play behaviors may also mimic social attention, such as turning the dolls/animals to face each other (eye contact), making social or conversational bids, or responding to social/conversational bids. Imaginary play, when observed, can provide a lot of information about the child's understanding of social relations. Imaginary play is a very good way to interpret aspects of the child's social cognition, especially if the play is flexible (changes from one day to the next) and not over-rehearsed or repetitive.

**Dramatic Play**

Dramatic play is defined as play that involves acting. When a child pretends to be a character or another person (e.g., a parent, teacher, movie star, or comic book character), they are showing dramatic play. The play might involve dressing up, the use of functional or imaginary objects, or symbolic play and might be solitary or with one or more peers. The play can occur spontaneously or might consist of a script that was previously heard or learned from a videoclip. Adults do not often dress up, but they can, to the delight of children. Like imaginary play, dramatic play involves pretense. It can also provide information about a child's social cognition. The observing adult can gain insight into the child's social cognition by observing which characters the child chooses to play, how easily and how often the child chooses different characters, how flexibly those characters engage in dialogue with other characters, and how easily the child makes up novel dialogue, as opposed to using scripted (previously memorized) dialogue only.

*(continued)*

**BOX 6.2.** *(continued)*

**Rule-Based Games**

Rule-based games include card games, board games, or sports activities such as baseball, soccer, or basketball. The structure of the game can be a good way to observe social interactions and other aspects of social behavior. Sometimes, rule-based games are a good way to make observations of a student's social cognition. The game provides the motivation to socialize. The rules and the structure of the game provide the platform within which social interactions can occur. In fact, playing with peers while following a rule-based game can facilitate the student's socializing. When children have a set of rules to follow, they sometimes feel more comfortable interacting with peers because they do not need to use as much social cognition. The game provides the shared focus of interest and can allow for conversations and interactions.



To understand the student's social cognition and social skills fully, observers should make multiple observations across different settings and should obtain observations from other adults. The input from multiple observations over time and from other adults who work with the student allows for a more accurate description of the student's social behaviors and social skills.

***Sample Observations for Attachment Behaviors*** Typical attachment behaviors early in life consist primarily of proximity behaviors and positive emotional exchanges with adults who are important in the student's life. To comment on attachment behaviors, the observation should include an interaction between the child and his or her parent(s) or caregiver(s). This observation might occur when the parents are dropping off or picking up their child at the beginning and end of the school day. School professionals can also ask parents about whether their child shows expected proximity behaviors. In typical attachment, young children usually stay near the primary caregiver or parent, especially in unfamiliar settings.

Attachment behaviors can also be observed through the emotional exchanges between the child and her or his parents, or other primary caregivers. For example, the observer can make a note about whether the child is happy, anxious, or angry about seeing the caregiver. The observer can notice whether the child seeks out the primary caregiver for soothing and how successfully the caregiver is able to carry out a soothing function. Emotional exchanges between a child and a primary caregiver should be generally positive, not generally negative. The child should typically be eager to share information with the primary caregiver or to stay near to the primary caregiver. Before drawing conclusions too quickly about difficulties in the attachment, the observer should be sure to verify concerns by asking about the child's behaviors in different settings or by asking other adults familiar with the child to provide their perspectives. As children age, it is possible to ask them directly about attachment behaviors. For example, a teacher or guidance counselor might ask questions such as, "Who do you feel the most comfortable with?" or "When you're in distress, who do you trust most?" School professionals should only ask questions such as these if they have the training needed to interpret the responses that the student might subsequently share. The school psychologist or guidance counselor can assist in conversations of this kind, can help ensure that the child's confidentiality is respected, and can help decide if the child needs to access mental health or child protection services.

***Sample Observations for Empathy*** Spontaneous empathic sharing of an emotion may not come up during any given observation. Before deciding that a student either does or does not have a capacity for empathy, the observer should be sure to make observations during multiple social interactions. One episode of showing empathy (or failing to show empathy) is likely not sufficient to draw a meaningful conclusion. If the observer is familiar with the student, it may be possible to consider information from prior interactions with the student. Empathic responses might come up during routine classroom activities, on the playground, or in response to an event that occurred to a student at school or at home. The student might show helping behaviors toward another student in distress or show enthusiasm for shared interests. If it is not clear whether the student has a capacity for empathic responses, a structured task can be implemented to elicit empathy. For example, the observer could tell a story about a peer who is having an emotional reaction to a situation, using photos or props (toys, puppets) if desired. Recall that empathy includes both an immediate emotional or feeling component as well as a cognitive appraisal of the emotion or feeling. The immediate, emotional response provides information about capacity for reacting or responding to another person's emotions in real time. With subsequent discussion, the cognitive appraisal can be elicited. The observer can start out by asking the student to respond to a predictable or familiar event, such as the emotions that occur when a student is bullied by a peer or the emotion that occurs when a parent gives a nice birthday present to the child. The practitioner can also share a story about a novel or unfamiliar event. After telling the story, the observer can discuss with the student how she or he understands the emotions in the story. The observer might ask, "What type of emotion do you think the person in the story is having?" and "Why would the person feel that way?" Or, "How would you feel and what would you do if the same thing happened to someone you know?" Toys, pictures, and photos used during the observation can help reduce the language demands. It is important to differentiate the student who has a good answer to a common or standard test question about emotions from the student who can spontaneously empathize with a novel situation and then also analyze or interpret the emotions in that situation successfully.



***Sample Observations of Imitation Behaviors*** Imitation is a very early emerging skill and should not be difficult to identify. Very few students are not capable of imitation. A student with very substantial cognitive impairments may not show imitation skills, as may be true for a student with a vision impairment. A student with autism may also show limited imitation skills long after the typically developing child has started to show them. When assessing imitation, observers should keep in mind that imitation can be identified as both immediate and delayed. For the purposes of learning, the imitation has to occur in response to a social prompt. To assess immediate imitation, the student can be prompted to copy facial expressions, copy motor actions, or repeat words spoken to them. The observer should watch the student's behaviors and verify that imitation is occurring. A task that does not place demands on the student's language skills is also a good choice. The practitioner might ask the student to copy the actions required to fill a container with beads or to make a drawing of a house. Instructions to perform these actions can occur by modeling. The student who has social attention and imitation skills should be able to understand the instruction even if there is no accompanying verbal instruction. Be sure to elicit social attention prior to assessing imitation skills. Some students with autism, especially those who are still functioning at an early cognitive stage, can have difficulty with a demand such as this. The fact that the same student shows imitation of other activities, such as imitating scripts, songs, or actions after watching a videotape, is not the type of imitation that is being assessed here. Imitation of this sort has limited social value and typically is not associated with developing new skills. The capacity to imitate in real time has important implications. Without socially motivated imitation, students have much greater difficulty learning in general.

***Sample Behaviors for Social Attention*** Social attention is generally easy to identify, whether the student interacts with peers or adults. Shared eye gaze is so critical to social attention that it merits special consideration. The observer should notice the student's eye contact, and particularly the shared gaze, between the student and the observing adult or between the student and a peer. Eye gaze sometimes serves the purpose of inspecting another person and does not always serve the purpose of socializing. When shared (social) eye gaze is present, it includes subtle changes in the movements of the eyes, movements of muscles around the eyes, and other facial movements or changes in facial expression. In order to make the distinction between shared eye gaze that is social versus eye gaze initiated for other reasons, the practitioner should make observations that span 10–15 minutes. This allows the observer to notice all the different components of the social attention.

Even though social attention is typically recognizable through shared eye gaze, it does not have to include eye gaze. Social attention can also be identified through a student's verbal responses or through nonverbal communication. Verbal or nonverbal responsiveness to questions and socially motivated imitation skills and learning are examples of social attention as well. They can occur without any shared eye gaze. That said, some shared eye gaze is expected, certainly for students with intact vision. Finally, the observer should take into consideration how often the student produces social bids, how many social bids the student is able to respond to, and for how long the social attention typically lasts. Social attention that occurs intermittently or is not sustained may signify that it is not as developed as it should be. Social attention that is not integrated with language and play skills is not as fully developed and is more likely to require intervention.



***Sample Behaviors for Joint Attention*** During the observation for social attention, the observer should look for joint attention. The classic triad of joint attention consists of looking at the social partner, pointing at and looking at a shared object or event of interest, and then returning the eye gaze to the social partner. This triad is especially useful to assess in developmentally younger students, because it is such a critical milestone. If a student does not produce an example of joint attention spontaneously (expressive joint attention), the adult can provoke joint attention by urging the student, "Look at that!" while pointing at an object or person of interest, and then noticing whether the student looks in the direction of the object/person (receptive joint attention). Older and socially more able students will not always show the classic triad of behaviors, even though they may have very secure joint attention. As children become older, they can rely on verbal and nonverbal communication behaviors to identify that their social partner is truly sharing their attention. Staying on topic in a conversation is an example of joint attention that does not necessarily include shared eye contact or shared eye gaze at an object.

***Sample Behaviors for Theory of Mind*** When making observations of a student's theory of mind skills, it is important to have a set of interview questions, sample stories, sample videos or photos, or sample situations to discuss with the student. Recall that theory of mind includes knowledge not only about people in general but also about specific people. Theory of mind skills follow a developmental hierarchy of understanding intentions, desires, beliefs, and false beliefs. The questions or social scenes that the practitioner develops for making observations can keep these concepts in mind. The interview questions or stories can be used to probe the student's understanding of each of these different types of social knowledge. If preferred, the conversation can occur in a group setting. By using a group, the observer can make more naturalistic observations of the target student, while also using other students as a comparison.

For developmentally younger children, toys, dolls, and puppets can be used to act out simple social scenes, such as a family eating a meal or going on an outing. The student's play behaviors can indicate the student's degree of social awareness or interest. A child can show their awareness by acting out conventional social scenes such as the ones just listed. Some students might show only the most basic types of social awareness through the props, and the actions may be limited to one or two components or appear scripted or copied from a television program or video. Other students might produce very elaborate social scenes that have multiple components or that tell a longer story. The observer can ask the student questions about the emotions of the characters in the play activity.

If using play activities, the observer can make a doll, puppet, or action figure interact and converse with the toys that the student is already playing with. For example, the adult can imitate the child's play behaviors, such as role-playing household activities using dolls and a dollhouse, or by copying or extending a battle while playing with action figures. The adult might make the doll say: "I have a lot of cleaning to do!" and see what the student makes their doll say in in response. The adult might hold an action figure, doll, or puppet, turn it towards the student or the student's toy, and start a conversation. The goal is to see whether the student can respond to the conversational bid and can maintain the topic for one or more conversational turns. All of these play actions reveal aspects of the child's understanding of intentions, desires, and beliefs. Not all students are comfortable playing with adults and some might not wish to play with the adult at all. The practitioner may have greater success allowing the student to play with peers, while the adult watches from farther away.

Theory of mind skills can also be elicited through interviewing. The practitioner should use the hierarchy presented earlier in the chapter. Theory of mind skills can be very basic, such as producing a contingent response in a conversation or play interaction or identifying basic emotions (happy, mad, scared, sad) and desires (hunger, fatigue, desire to be soothed) in photos and stories. The observer can ask questions such as: "What things make you or other people feel happy? What makes people feel sad?" Taking the conversation a bit further, the observer can ask, "What is the person in this photo feeling? Why do you think the person feels that way? What do you think just happened? What do you think will happen next?" In responding to the questions just listed, the child or student might be able to describe social situations that elicit emotions and how to respond in the situation. The awareness of emotions includes a cognitive awareness of the causes and consequences of emotions. See Chapter 8 for more information about basic and complex emotions and the relationship of emotions to cognition.

As theory of mind skills become more sophisticated, the student should be able to show that he or she is taking more information into consideration and is able to interpret ambiguous situations. For example, the observer could ask questions why students and adults do not always behave as expected. The observer might describe a situation in which a friend expresses that they are interested in doing something by saying "Sure, let's do that!" but then never returns a phone call to set specific plans. In this case, the friend's nonverbal communication behaviors or subsequent actions tell another story. Alternatively, the practitioner could tell a story about the verbal and nonverbal behaviors that might arise when a child receives an undesired present for her or his birthday: The behaviors that the child is expected to show, the thoughts or feelings that the child might actually have, and the conversation that the child might have with parents after the birthday party is over. Responses to questions about social behaviors such as these require more advanced theory of mind skills and also require the language skills to support the description.

***Sample Behaviors for Social Conventions*** Many classroom activities require knowledge of social conventions, such as raising one's hand before speaking, lining up before going outside, understanding what behaviors are expected at a birthday party, or respecting social conventions in community settings. One way to assess the student's knowledge and awareness is to monitor whether the student practices classroom social norms. Alternatively, the practitioner can ask the student to share their knowledge of social conventions for the school building and elsewhere. Other ways of eliciting knowledge about social conventions might be to ask the student about how to make greetings, what types of behaviors to show during meal times, and how to respond when someone offers a gift. A group of students could discuss social conventions in other cultures. Students could share how holidays or special events are celebrated in different cultures and what constitutes socially appropriate behaviors in those different contexts. When the discussion also asks the students to take into consideration why social conventions are important, the practitioner will simultaneously learn about the student's theory of mind skills.



## Analyze and Interpret the Observations

By making the kinds of observations discussed above, the practitioner can review all of the components of the Social Skills Framework and make some guesses about the skills that the student has developed thus far. Social difficulties in the areas of attachment are often evident from historical information that the school team may have about the child's home circumstances. Chapter 8, on affect and self-regulation skills, shares information about the emotional impact of attachment disorders. What is important to highlight here is that difficulties in attachment can have a range of effects on all of the social skills discussed in this framework. Difficulties in the skills of empathy and imitation are common in students who have limited social attention or who lack joint attention. The most commonly identified social difficulties occur in the realm of theory of mind. Practitioners may commonly associate theory of mind deficits with students on the autism spectrum. However, difficulties in theory of mind affect a broad range of students. Not only do all of the social skills listed earlier in the framework need to be in place for secure theory of mind (i.e., empathy, imitation, social attention, joint attention), but other skills, such as formal and pragmatic language skills, executive skills, and affect and self-regulation skills, also influence the student's performance. The practitioner may need to look to some of the other frameworks presented in this book in order to make accurate judgments about a student's theory of mind skills. Theory of mind can be impaired or affected for more than one reason, and not only for reasons related to social cognition. These distinctions are important for developing an intervention plan. A student who is not socializing successfully because of impairments in language, executive skills, or affect and self-regulation skills will need a different intervention plan from the student who has impairments related to social cognition.

## Discussion of Findings With Colleagues

After completing the observation and analyzing the results, the observer should discuss the student's performance with colleagues. The discussion may occur with the student support team, the special education team, the school psychologist, or professionals trained in mental health. The group can discuss the social abilities and social difficulties for the student. The discussion should decide whether formal evaluation is needed and what other steps should be taken.

Teaching social skills is a broadly based task and involves teaching many different types of component skills. The Social Skills Framework alone does not cover everything that may need to be taught when teaching social skills. When teaching students how to socialize and how to think socially, school professionals should consider other frameworks from this book, including those chapters on executive skills, affect and self-regulation skills, and formal and pragmatic language skills. All of them discuss skill sets and skills that are important to master as a part of socializing successfully.

## Educational Objectives and Strategies for Teaching Social Cognition and Social Skills

Suggested educational objectives and instructional strategies for teaching students with social skill difficulties are discussed in the sections that follow. They are broken down into the skill sets and skills discussed in this chapter. As is true for many of the frameworks in this book, several skill sets and skills from within the Social Skills Framework can be taught simultaneously. Educators and therapists can choose one or several different types of activities to serve as the platform for teaching. Within that activity, the teaching approach should be organized to ensure that the student knows which specific social skills are being taught. The activity might focus on empathy and emotions or it might focus on thoughts, beliefs, and false beliefs. It is useful to be explicit with the student about the skill set being discussed. This can help to focus the student's learning and can also help in measuring progress.

***Educational Objectives and Strategies for Teaching Attachment*** Teaching appropriate attachment behaviors involves teaching both the child and the primary caregiver(s). It requires teaching the caregiver(s) how to become attuned to the behaviors of the child and how to respond empathically to the child's behaviors and emotions. Both the child and the parents or primary caregivers have to become attuned to one another. The work of teaching about attachment is typically conducted by skilled therapists working in a clinical setting and would typically not be included as part of the student's educational program.

***Educational Objectives and Strategies for Teaching Empathy*** Empathy is partly a spontaneous act of sharing an emotional experience with another person. The spontaneous experience of empathy is difficult to teach if it is not already present. However, it can still be discussed and taught as an experience that most people share. Empathy also includes thinking about the emotions of others, not just sharing in their emotional experiences. Students can be taught about the emotional experiences that people can have and how one should or could respond to them. As students develop the ability to make cognitive appraisals, they may also learn how to respond to emotion-eliciting events more successfully.

For developmentally young children, objectives may be best limited to recognition of basic emotions, in facial expressions, in gestures, and as part of intonation. From here, objectives might proceed to recognizing and responding to emotions expressed through words and emotions that recur in others. The teaching can be extended to include a discussion about the causes and consequences of emotions. See Chapter 8. For example, when a person experiences a loss, adults and peers should normally respond with sympathy and can discuss the sad feelings associated with the loss. When a person experiences a success, adults and peers would normally provide congratulations and share or discuss the happy feelings associated with the success. By discussing different types of life situations, students can learn about different emotional reactions that humans can experience. They can also learn about how they should respond when they notice emotions in others.

***Educational Objectives and Strategies for Teaching Imitation*** As with spontaneous empathy, it is difficult to teach imitation skills if spontaneous imitation is not already present. One approach is for the practitioner to imitate the student. Through imitated actions, the student who does not imitate spontaneously may start to do so. Much of the time, the student who does not imitate spontaneously will need instruction with substantial verbal and physical prompts and supports.

***Educational Objectives and Strategies for Teaching Social Attention*** Teaching students about social attention may require the practitioner to address the reason that underlies lack of attention. Some of the time, social attention is lacking because the student is unaware of others, is not interested in socializing, and/or has marked difficulty interpreting others. This type of barrier to social attention is common for students on the autism spectrum and is more difficult to overcome. Other students may fail to show social attention because of difficulty regulating their attention span or for emotional reasons such as anxiety. In these students, medical or mental health professionals working outside of school may need to address the underlying attentional or emotional issues and in so doing assist educational professionals to teach social attention.

Social attention can be taught by expanding the student's repertoire for making social bids. For developmentally young students with limited language, social attention can be developed by teaching the student how to use a gesture such as touch, sign language (e.g., the sign for *more*), or a picture from a picture exchange system, to make a social bid. Social bids can be separated into those that are designed to help the child meet personal needs and those that are designed for socializing. The student will need to learn about eye contact in teaching about social attention and when making social bids. For developmentally older students who have language skills, the student can learn about other components of social attention. For example, the student can learn to use eye contact, facial expressions, gestures, and words to make a social bid and to practice making these social bids more often. Many students who do not make social bids often enough or successfully enough benefit from scripts that can be used to make social bids and that serve as conversation starters. A script is a verbal communicative function or nonverbal communication behavior that is rehearsed, memorized, and applied in real-time social situations. It can consist of a question or a statement, such as saying, "How are you?" or by saying, "I like your dress." Scripts can also be useful for prolonging an interaction. For example, when a communication breakdown occurs or when the student seems to have difficulty following the social interaction, the student can learn to use a script such as, "I didn't catch that; can you repeat what you said?" Educators can measure student progress by measuring how often the student makes social bids spontaneously, how often the student makes social bids with prompting, how often the student makes use of social scripts to make social bids, how long the student continues to make social bids to keep a social interaction going, and whether the student generates novel scripts or behaviors when making social bids.



***Educational Objectives and Strategies for Teaching Joint Attention*** Teaching students about joint attention builds upon the teaching done for social attention. The student can learn to use shared eye gaze, shared gaze upon an object of interest, and shared communication about a subject of interest (joint attention). For students with limited social attention, a prompt from an adult to remember about shared attention can improve the chances that the student is paying attention to the right object, event, person, or topic.

***Educational Objectives and Strategies for Teaching Theory of Mind*** Teaching students about theory of mind shows them how to interpret or predict the intentions, desires, emotions, beliefs, and thoughts of others. For students who are socially less aware, teaching about cause-and-effect relations is one way to help the student make connections. For example, students with developmental delay can learn to predict the behaviors of adults by use of a visual schedule. Based on the time of day and based on the number of events that have already occurred in the schedule, an adult can ask the student, "What will your teacher/your peers do next?" or "What is on your teacher's mind now?" Some students may be ready to learn about theory of mind by listening to stories, looking at pictures, or watching videoclips or movies. When the story or videoclip is repeated or when the pictures are shown a second time, the student can take the time needed to make attributions about characters or events, predict subsequent behaviors, and can potentially also predict subsequent behaviors not included in the picture or the story. In so doing, the student can learn about intentions, desires, emotions, and beliefs in others. Teaching should first occur for routine and conventional situations before moving to novel or unconventional situations.

Students should also have the chance to develop their theory of mind skills for conventional and nonconventional situations that occur in real time. By examining or observing peers, students can learn to think about the emotions, desires, intentions, and beliefs of others. They can participate in this learning based on prior observations or based on real-time observations. The learning is more challenging because the social scene cannot be repeated. It requires students to think on their feet. After the student has provided a description of the behaviors he or she observed, the instructor can ask the student to predict subsequent behaviors based on the student's analysis. Videotaping of the self is another way to facilitate learning for a student or for a group of students. Watching one's own performance can be a very informative format for learning.

One way to measure progress is to document whether the student is able to provide a simple or complex interpretation of a social situation. For example, the student can be asked to describe a social interaction he or she just observed or to repeat a conversation that was just held. After summarizing what the student saw or heard, they can make an interpretation of underlying emotions, intentions, desires, and beliefs or thoughts. Both the summary of the social scene, and the detail of the interpretation, can be analyzed for their complexity. The teacher or therapist can measure progress by documenting the number of nonverbal communication behaviors the student identified (facial expressions, gestures, intonation), whether the student could repeat the words exchanged during the interactions, and whether the student could identify relevant contextual information such as the age of the social partners or the location of the social interaction. See Box 6.3 for a framework for speaking with the student that can help assess the student's performance.



**BOX 6.3. A Checklist of Questions for Social Skills Instruction**

1. Verbal communication. "Repeat the words that you heard."
2. Nonverbal communication. "Describe the facial expressions, gestures, or changes in tone of voice that you noticed."
3. Contextual information. "Where is this interaction occurring?" Who is present? What are they doing? Where did they just come from, and where are they going to go after this scene is completed? What do these people need to do next?
4. Links. How successfully does the student link observable behaviors with intentions, desires, emotions, or beliefs? "What do you think the person is thinking or feeling?"

***Educational Objectives and Strategies for Teaching Social Conventions*** Developmentally younger students should learn about routine and commonly required social conventions. A student's educational objective may be to learn social conventions, such as greeting peers, asking about other people's health, taking turns in a conversation, respecting classroom participation behaviors, or eating with one's mouth closed. Social conventions are often taught as scripts (verbal and nonverbal communicative functions) or rote behaviors. Older students can learn about social conventions in different settings (a medical office, a formal event) or in different cultures. School professionals can create a list of social conventions appropriate for age and for the student's environment and can measure progress by determining how often the student uses those scripts or behaviors. Progress measures should also consider how often the student does or does not need a verbal reminder to use social conventions successfully. Progress measures could also consist of assessing the student's knowledge of social conventions.

***Accommodations for Social Cognition and Social Skills*** When students have difficulty understanding and responding to social demands, adults may need to provide accommodations to simplify those demands. Accommodations for social interactions could consist of slowing down social interactions with the student, taking pauses during social interactions to ensure that the learner is capturing all the information needed to participate socially, or providing more explanation of and coaching about what is happening during the social interaction. The student may need help focusing attention on all the components of a social interaction: Nonverbal communication, verbal communication, context, general knowledge about people, and knowledge about a specific person. An adult or peer mentor could use a checklist such as the one in Box 6.3 to remind the student about aspects of social interactions and then hold a brief discussion about how to respond.

Peer-mediated instruction and reverse inclusion may be very good ways to accommodate the learner whose social interactions are more limited. In reverse inclusion, peers who are socially more able are used to model socially appropriate behaviors to their socially less able peer. Because children and youth are typically more motivated to learn from peers rather than from adults, peer-mediated instruction and reverse inclusion can be useful strategies.



## CASE EXAMPLE

Eric is a kindergarten student who currently receives specialized instruction for his previously identified diagnosis of autism spectrum disorder. Eric participates successfully in his kindergarten inclusion program. His mid-year report card reveals age- and grade-appropriate acquisition of counting, spelling, and reading decoding. His teacher commented that his narrative skills are still developing. Classroom performance for getting work done and following classroom rules are areas of relative strength for him. However, his report card reveals some characteristic difficulties for children with autism in the areas of speaking and listening, playing cooperatively with peers, and following directions. The skills listed below were left unrated on his report card because his skills are too low:

- Communicates effectively in order to seek help, gain information, or deepen understanding of an academic task
- Controls unnecessary talking
- Stays on topic
- Participates in discussions by listening actively and contributing knowledge and ideas
- Listens attentively

In the comments section of his report card, Eric's teacher noted that he rarely uses eye contact when interacting with either peers or adults. The teacher also noted that unless he is specifically prompted to do so, Eric usually does not socialize with peers or adults. He prefers to play on his own. Social skills are therefore present only with adult support. Eric's language is limited, as shown in the language sample below.

### Social Behaviors Shown by Eric During Language Sampling

Eric's teacher made some observations of his social skills during a language sampling task. Eric participated by completing the same task that was administered to Leonard in Chapter 4 (the story "The Fisherman and the Cat"). By using the same activity with different students, Eric's teacher has learned about the similarities and differences that students bring to this task, even if they are all the same age. Although it provides preliminary information only, the narrative task allows the teacher to make observations of skills such as empathy, social attention, and joint attention. As discussed below, the formal language sample itself provides insight into Eric's theory of mind. The narrative sample also provides a way to observe other spontaneous social behaviors such as social attention.

### *Observations of Eric's Spontaneous Social Behaviors*

Eric almost never made spontaneous eye contact with his teacher as she discussed the narrative with him. He did respond to social bids from her by making eye contact some of the time. Eric's limited eye contact is a very consistent finding across settings and across adults. According to his teacher's report, Eric usually does not make any social bids. Even when interested in an object or an activity, he never shares his interest with peers or even familiar adults. This was also true during the observation. Prior to starting the narrative task, Eric was playing with a toy car that wouldn't roll because it had a broken wheel. Eric did not make use of the opportunity to show the broken toy to his teacher to request assistance (i.e., making a social bid to get personal needs met).



### *Observations of Eric's Responsiveness to the Examiner's Social Bids*

When Eric responded to social bids, he did not use nonverbal aspects of communication very well. For example, when his teacher said to him, "Eric, I have some pictures that I want to show you," he did not respond with eye contact, even though he stopped playing and sat in readiness when she sat down next to him.

### *Observations of Nonverbal Communication Behaviors*

Eric showed a very limited variety of facial expressions and gestures. He usually stared only at the pictures and did not turn his head or his eye gaze to his teacher. His intonation was unusual, sounding a bit wooden or monotone, because he did not emphasize any words within the sentence. They were all spoken with the same volume and at the same pitch. The overall result of these nonverbal communication behaviors was that his narrative did not convey any emotional tone. He showed neither delight nor annoyance in response to the interruption or during the narrative task. It was difficult to know whether Eric found the interaction enjoyable, neutral, or frustrating. Eric did not show any joint attention during interactions, even though he was able to follow instructions and produce contingent responses some of the time.

### *Sentence-Level Language Sample for Analysis of Theory of Mind*

The following language sample was obtained. The reader is invited to review Chapter 4 for a description of the story line. Before reading the analysis that follows, read the following sentences and decide what they reveal about Eric's understanding of desires, emotions, and/or beliefs of the characters in the story. Eric's language sample was as follows:

1. He got the fish out of the water.
2. He put it in the bucket.
3. He kissed it. Angry look at him.
4. He put him in a bucket.
5. Then the bird.
6. Then he flapped away.

### *Narrative-Level Language Sample for Analysis of Theory of Mind*

After Eric had a chance to discuss each picture, Eric's teacher asked him to retell the story without the support of the pictures. His teacher prompted him by saying, "Now, tell me the whole story but without looking at the pictures." The italicized text below is a transcript of what Eric said. Regular font indicates prompts provided by his teacher:

1. *Keep the fish out.*
2. *Then he puts it in the bucket. Then he eats it.*
3. Anything else? *Yup.* What? *And . . . a bird came and flapped away.*

Eric's language sample merits an analysis using the Formal Language Skills Framework in Chapter 4. The interested reader is encouraged to do so, given Eric's difficulties with both sentence-level speech (morpho-syntax) and the structure of his narrative. However, even when considering his language impairment, it is clear that Eric also shows an impairment in social cognition.



## Case Analysis for Eric

The following analysis was developed by Eric's teacher and her colleagues. The analysis was carried out using the Social Skills Framework. Based on this very short observation, it is not possible to draw firm conclusions. All the same, the observation does provide very valuable information about Eric's social skills. It is also useful for identifying educational objectives.

### *Eric's Attachment*

No comments were made about Eric's attachment based upon this observation.

### *Eric's Empathy*

Empathy, the spontaneous emotion experienced when faced with the emotions of another person, was not formally tested in the observation sample obtained above. Given Eric's limited social attention (see the section below), he would be expected to show empathy less often or have greater difficulty experiencing an empathic response along with others. As his social attention improves, he may show more clear evidence of empathy. An indirect measure of empathy could be to assess whether Eric can make an appropriate attribution of the emotions of the characters in the story.

### *Eric's Imitation Skills*

Imitation skills were not tested in the observations made above. Eric understood and followed the teacher's instructions very quickly. His behavior shows that he understands classroom expectations and did not need any modeling in order to participate in the narrative task. He participated in the task based on a verbal prompt to do so. There are no concerns about Eric's capacity for imitation, except that teachers and other professionals have to secure his social attention so that he can learn through imitation.

### *Eric's Social Attention*

Eric's social attention and joint attention are both underdeveloped for his age. He did not make spontaneous eye contact with the teacher. His teacher had to direct his attention to the book, which Eric also did not do spontaneously. Eric was able to make eye contact when prompted.

### *Eric's Theory of Mind*

Eric's understanding of intentions and desires is limited. For example, when Eric looked at the picture of the cat sticking out his tongue, his interpretation was that the cat was "kissing" the fish. The cat's desire (hunger and a desire to eat) are obvious from the content of the pictures, but Eric was not able to identify this desire or the cat's intention to eat the fish, at least not initially. In his narrative retell, Eric stated that the cat ate the fish (which is not true), though his error suggests that he later did understand the cat's intention. More striking about the story is the fact that Eric persisted in not understanding the most important social element of the story, which is the cat's false belief that he was hiding his fish and would be able to eat it later. To improve his performance for the narrative retelling, the examiner provided extra prompts to help Eric understand this segment of the story. She said, "Look here; the cat wanted to eat the fish later. He wanted to put the fish in a hiding place. But then, he had a big surprise! He didn't realize he made a mistake when he put the fish into the bird's mouth! That's why the bird got away with the fish!" With this very explicit prompting, Eric showed that he understood the cat's intention of eating the fish during the retell. However, he was still not able to describe the cat's false belief—that the cat was hiding his fish in a safe place for later retrieval. Contrast this performance with Leonard's performance. Even though, like Eric, Leonard's language performance is weak for his age, Leonard's narrative sample shows that he understood correctly the cat's dilemma. Leonard said, "And he [the cat] dropped it in the pelican's mouth. And no more eating the fish!" Leonard understood that the cat did not get to eat the fish because of the mistake he made in putting the fish into the pelican's beak.



## Educational Objectives and Strategies for Eric

Eric is at an early stage of developing his social cognition. Many of the skill sets and skills discussed in this chapter are appropriate areas for instruction. The Social Skills Framework is applied below to organize thinking around Eric's needs and objectives.

### *Educational Objectives and Strategies to Develop Eric's Attachment*

Eric's performance for attachment was not tested in this observation. Attachment was not an area of concern based on the observations or on the history available. Most students with autism develop secure attachment skills, though they may do so later than expected for their chronological age.

### *Educational Objectives and Strategies to Develop Eric's Empathy and Imitation Skills*

Eric would be expected to show reduced empathy and reduced imitation of others. When a student shows such limited social attention, as is the case for Eric, he will also show much less empathy and imitation. That said, when Eric is paying attention to others, he imitates them more often and may also show more empathy toward their emotions. The primary way to access his capacity for empathy and imitation is to secure his social attention and to teach him about how to observe others and learn about them through their behaviors.

### *Educational Objectives and Strategies to Develop Eric's Social Attention*

The primary area of difficulty for Eric is his limited social attention. Social attention is a challenging skill to build when a student starts out with a low level of social motivation and does not spend much time observing others. Eric is a student who behaves this way. He does not spontaneously look toward others or seek out the company of others, preferring to engage in his own activities. Eric needs to learn to develop more social attention (observe others more often, make eye contact more often, make social bids more often). He also needs to be able to respond to social bids from another person. Many social responses that young children need to learn are scripted and/or represent social conventions. He can learn how he should respond to classroom routines, such as lining up before going outside, how to respond to routine teacher requests, and how to respond to requests from peers. By teaching about these situations, Eric can expand his understanding of and performance in social situations. He can also learn some verbal scripts and learn how to increase his eye contact.

One way of enhancing Eric's social attention is to increase his motivation. By pairing social attention with rewards and privileges, Eric may become more motivated to show social attention. By following rules and routines, he may be allowed access to privileges, for example. By teaching Eric these social conventions and pairing them with rewards, he may also show more spontaneous social attention. One way to measure progress is to see how often Eric responds successfully to routine classroom expectations, how often he responds to social bids from others, which verbal and nonverbal behaviors he shows, and how often he shows spontaneous social attention.



### *Educational Objectives and Strategies to Develop Eric's Theory of Mind*

In addition to expanding his social attention, Eric can be invited to develop his theory of mind. By expanding his capacity for theory of mind, Eric is likely to understand social interactions around him more fully and might be able to respond more successfully to social demands. The narrative task that was used to make observations of Eric can serve as a platform for teaching. The narrative task required him to look at human and animal behavior (e.g., fishing, stealing a fish, eating a fish, flying away) and then look at or discover the emotions, desires, intentions, and beliefs that underlie those behaviors. Other sources, such as videoclips, photos, or listening to stories, can serve the same purpose. Real-time observations of classroom routines or social interactions can serve as a platform for teaching and learning. These may be more difficult for a child such as Eric. However, real-time social interactions between other peers and/or adults can be video recorded, if appropriate permissions are obtained first. Video recordings are useful because they allow for a second look at the interactions. Eric could benefit from instruction of this sort, because the persons and objects in the video would be familiar to him.

Eric can also learn about theory of mind in real-time social interactions in which he plays a part. For example, a teacher or therapist can ask him to help out with an important job. The teacher might say, "I have a new job that I need you to do. Take a look at these papers. Someone in the main office needs them." Or, the teacher might say, "We're going to play a new game. We need two classmates who can play the game with you." Without adding any new information, the teacher or therapist can then observe for socially appropriate behaviors to this (indirect) social demand. The adult can also ask Eric what he is supposed to do in response to the social demand. The teacher can then ask leading questions (e.g., "What do you think I'm going to ask you to do now? What do you think you should do next?"). If Eric is able, he should identify the emotions, desires, intentions, or beliefs and thoughts that are associated with this demand and link his understanding of theory of mind with the desired behaviors. He can be encouraged to ask clarifying questions if needed. When asking a student such as Eric to respond to a new demand, the teacher or therapist will have to observe carefully for evidence that Eric is using knowledge of emotions, desires, intentions, and beliefs or thoughts of others in his social responses. He should certainly be asked to identify or describe those elements of theory of mind if he is able.

One way to measure Eric's progress in theory of mind skills is to measure how many elements he can bring into his analysis of social behaviors. For example, the teacher can help him to remember the words used during the social exchange, the nonverbal communication behaviors that occurred, and the context of the social interaction. By using questions, the teacher can help Eric think about the social situation more systematically. Given that Eric's language skills are still underdeveloped, it may be some time before Eric is able to respond to questions related to theory of mind. However, he may still show that he is socially more able through his responsiveness to social bids. By observing his subsequent behaviors, Eric may show (nonverbally) what he knows. It is always useful for the teacher or therapist not only to follow up on his performance and praise him for social successes, but also to describe to him what he did successfully. For example, the teacher could say, "You knew that you had to take the papers from me. How did you figure that out? When you got to the office, you knew that you had to give them to the secretary. How did you know? Now, do you think that the secretary knows who the papers are for? How is she going to figure it out?" To answer these questions, Eric would have had to identify the teacher's desire or intention to have him bring papers to the office, as well as the secretary's belief or understanding about what to do with those papers.

#### *Educational Objectives and Strategies to Develop Eric's Social Conventions*

Eric can improve his social skills by learning rote social conventions. Using simple cause-and-effect sequences, he can learn what he is supposed to do or say in predictable social situations, such as when meeting someone new or going to the grocery store or to the doctor's office. Many social responses that young children need to learn are scripted and/or represent social conventions. They can be taught as so-called social stories. Some of Eric's social skills training can be embedded into the master classroom routine and school rules. By learning rote scripts and other social conventions, Eric can expand his understanding of and performance in social situations. His teacher can measure progress by measuring how successfully Eric shows social skills by rote (e.g., how successfully he follows social conventions of the classroom, how often he uses eye contact, how often he makes use of a script to clarify what someone wants or needs from him). Progress measurement can also consider how often he performs successfully (verbally or nonverbally) in response to a social demand.



### Accommodations for Eric's Social Skills

Accommodations for Eric will likely consist of adult prompting. Adults will likely have to slow down the pace of social demands and prompt him to use eye contact (both to secure his attention and to reinforce the need for social attention). They also will need to deliver instructions more explicitly by using repetition and more nonverbal communication behaviors. Demonstrative gestures are especially useful. Adults will likely have to take extra time to allow him to solve social problems by asking him questions and helping him to think about the best response for a given situation. Adults and, at times, peers can help Eric by explaining social demands a second time, perhaps in a different way.

### Working With Culturally and Linguistically Diverse Learners

School professionals should consider cultural and linguistic diversity when assessing social skills; different cultures and languages have different rules about appropriate social behaviors. As such, assessing social skills in students who are culturally and linguistically diverse can be challenging; assessors must be sure to distinguish social differences from social performance difficulties. For example, native Spanish-speaking children are often not expected to have as much direct eye contact with adults as native English-speaking children. Thus, it is necessary to determine if a native Spanish-speaking child's lack of eye contact can be attributed to cultural differences or if the child

*(continued)*

is having difficulty with social skills. When assessing limited or non-English proficient learners, it is useful to have a trained assessor fluent in the student's dominant language and familiar with the child's cultural background conduct the assessment. If a bilingual assessor is not available, it may be useful to use the following strategies:

- Ask professionals making the referral to compare the student's social skills to other learners from the same cultural and linguistic background.
- Ask parents and other family members to describe the student's social skills in comparison to other family members or individuals from their cultural and linguistic background.



## CONCLUSION

This chapter examined several important aspects of social cognition. The Social Skills Framework begins with the most basic understanding of social interactions and the most basic connections between humans. These include the skill sets of attachment, empathy, and imitation. The chapter then described social attention and joint attention. From there, it further showed how these foundations of social skills can be elaborated on by using social thinking. Social thinking, social cognition, and/or theory of mind require an understanding of human emotions, intentions, desires, and beliefs. The framework introduced the important concept of the false belief and other examples of what constitutes a more fully developed theory of mind. Theory of mind integrates all the skills that precede it. Theory of mind is critical for social success, along with the social conventions that people use to facilitate and improve their social interactions. The next chapter adds more components to the discussion of neurodevelopmental foundations in learning. We will discover links between executive skills and social skills. However, we will also expand our understanding of executive skills into other aspects of learning across multiple frameworks.

## REFERENCES


Aboulafia-Brakha, T., Christe, B., Martory, M.-D., & Annoni, J.-M. (2011). Theory of mind tasks and executive functions: A systematic review of group studies in neurology. *Journal of Neuropsychology, 5*(1), 39–55.

Bastiaansen, J. A., Thioux, M., & Keysers, C. (2009). Evidence for mirror systems in emotions. *Philosophical Transactions of the Royal Society of Biological Sciences, 364*, 2391–2404.

Beauchamp, M., & Anderson, V. (2010). SOCIAL: An integrative framework for the development of social skills. *Psychological Bulletin, 136*(1), 39–64.

Beer, J., Mitchell, J. P. S., & Ochsner, K. (2006a). Multiple perspectives on the psychological and neural bases of social cognition. *Brain Research, 1079*(1), 1–3.

Beer, J., Mitchell, J. P. S., & Ochsner, K. (2006b). Social cognition: A multi-level analysis. *Brain Research, 1079*(1), 1–3.

Caemmerer, J. M., & Keith, T. Z. (2015). Longitudinal, reciprocal effects of social skills and achievement from kindergarten to eighth grade. *Journal of School Psychology, 53*, 265–281.

de Vignemont, F., & Singer, T. (2006). The empathic brain: How, when and why? *Trends in Cognitive Sciences, 10*(10), 435–441.

Decety, J. (2010). The neurodevelopment of empathy in humans. *Developmental Neuroscience, 32*, 257–267.

Denham, S. A., & Brown, C. (2010). "Plays nice with others": Social-emotional learning and academic success. *Early Education and Development, 21*(5), 652–680.

Devine, R. T., & Hughes, C. (2014). Relations between false belief understanding and executive function in early childhood: A meta-analysis. *Child Development, 85*(5), 1777–1794.

Fearon, P. (2011). Attachment theory: Research and clinical implications In D. Skuse, H. Bruce, L. Dowdney, & D. Mrazek (Eds.), *Child psychology and psychiatry: Frameworks for practice* (2nd ed., pp. 85–91). New York, NY: Wiley.

Flavell, J. H. (1999). Cognitive development: Children's knowledge about the mind. *Annual Review of Psychology, 50*, 21–45.

Flavell, J. H., Mumme, D. L., Green, F. L., & Flavell, E. R. (1992). Young children's understanding of different types of beliefs. *Child Development, 63*(4), 960–977.

Frith, C. D., & Frith, U. (2012). Mechanisms of social cognition. *Annual Review of Psychology, 63,* 287–313.

Halberstadt, A. G., Denham, S. A., & Dunsmore, J. C. (2001). Affective social competence. *Social Development, 10*(1), 79–119.

Halle, T. G., & Darling-Churchill, K. E. (2016). Review of measures of social and emotional development. *Journal of Applied Developmental Psychology, 45,* 8–18.

Happe, F., & Frith, U. (2014). Annual research review: Towards a developmental neuroscience of atypical social cognition. *Journal of Child Psychology and Psychiatry, 55*(6), 553–577.

Iacoboni, M., & Dapretto, M. (2006). The mirror neuron system and the consequences of its dysfunction. *Nature Reviews, 7,* 942–951.

Jacob, P., & Heannerod, M. (2005). The motor theory of social cognition: A critique. *Trends in Cognitive Sciences,* 9(1), 21–25.

Jones, S. M., Zaslow, M., Darling-Churchill, K. E., & Halle, T. G. (2016). Assessing early childhood social and emotional development: Key conceptual and measurement issues. *Journal of Applied Developmental Psychology, 45,* 42–48.

Klein, J. T., & Shepherd, S. V. (2009). Social attention and the brain. *Current Biology, 19*(20), R958–R962.

Lieberman, M. D. (2007). Social cognitive neuroscience: A review of core processes. *Annual Review of Psychology, 58,* 259–289.

Mitchell, R. L. C., & Phillips, L. H. (2015). The overlapping relationship between emotion perception and theory of mind. *Neuropsychologia, 70,* 1–10.

Moriguchi, Y. (2014). The early development of executive function and its relation to social interaction: A brief review. *Frontiers in Psychology, 5,* 1–6.

National Center for Education Statistics. (1992). *Public secondary school teacher survey on vocational education. Competencies contributing to students' grades* (NCES Report No. 94409). Retrieved from nces.ed.gov/surveys/frss/publications/94409

Oztop, E., Kawato, M., & Arbib, M. A. (2013). Mirror neurons: Functions, mechanisms and models. *Neuroscience Letters, 540,* 43–55.

Premack, D., & Woodruff, G. (1978). Does the chimpanzee have a theory of mind? *Behavioral and Brain Sciences, 1*(4), 515–526.

Preston, S. D., & de Waal, F. B. M. (2002). Empathy: Its ultimate and proximate bases. *Behavioral and Brain Sciences, 25,* 1–72.

Pronin, E. (2008). How we see ourselves and how we see others. *Science, 320*(5880), 1177–1180.

Russell, R. (2007). Social communication impairments: Pragmatics. *Pediatric Clinics of North America, 54,* 483–506.

Salley, B., & Colombo, J. (2016). Conceptualizing social attention in developmental research. *Social Development, 25*(4), 687–703.

Schaafsma, S. M., Pfaff, D. W., Spunt, R. P., & Adolphs, R. (2015). Deconstructing and reconstructing theory of mind. *Trends in Cognitive Sciences, 19*(2), 65–72.

Sherman, L. J., Rice, K., & Cassidy, J. (2015). Infant capacities related to building internal working models of attachment figures: A theoretical and empirical review. *Developmental Review, 37,* 109–141.

Slaughter, V. (2011). Development of social cognition. In D. Skuse, H. Bruce, L. Dowdney, & D. Mrazek (Eds.), *Child psychology and psychiatry: Frameworks for practice* (2nd ed., pp. 51–55). New York, NY: Wiley.

Smith, D., Atmatzidis, K., & Capogreco, M. (2017). Evidence-based interventions for increasing work participation for persons with various disabilities: A systematic review. *OTJR: Occupation, Participation and Health, 37*(Suppl. 2), 3S–13S.

Spanoudis, G. (2016). Theory of mind and specific language impairment in school-age children. *Journal of Communication Disorders, 61,* 83–96.

Sperber, D., & Wilson, D. (2002). Pragmatics, modularity and mind-reading. *Mind and Language, 17*(1–2), 3–23.

Wimmer, H., & Perner, J. (1983). Beliefs about beliefs: Representation and constraining function of wrong beliefs in young children's understanding of deception. *Cognition, 13*(1), 103–128.

## APPENDIX 6.1 Social Skills Framework

The Social Skills Framework is summarized here. School professionals can use this form as a quick reference for the skill sets and skills that need to be taken into consideration when making observations and developing an intervention plan.

| Skill sets | Functions and skills | Examples of functions and skills in action | Sample performance difficulties | Potential strategies, accommodations, or educational objectives |
|---|---|---|---|---|
| Attachment | The sense of security and safety that a child develops in response to primary caregivers | The student is able to identify primary caregivers.<br><br>The student shows appropriate stranger anxiety or social reservation with strangers.<br><br>The student appropriately modifies behaviors in response to familiar versus unfamiliar peers or adults. | The student responds no differently toward primary caregivers than toward other adults; might show excess affection or familiarity to unfamiliar adults. | Attachment therapy can help to teach children about their safety and security in proximity with primary caregivers. It is typically not within the purview of school professionals to provide this type of therapy.<br><br>Provide psychoeducation about differences between familiar and unfamiliar people and how to respond to each. |
| Empathy | Capacity to experience the same emotions as others when exposed to those emotions in others | The student has the capacity to experience the same emotions as those experienced by others while also being able to label or articulate the emotion.<br><br>The student shows the capacity to reflect on and discuss the emotional experiences of others without necessarily experiencing the emotion at the same time (sympathy). | The student does not show reactive or spontaneous empathy toward the emotional experiences of others (e.g., lack of fear, distress, anger, or excitement even when faced with these emotions in others).<br><br>The student shows reactive empathy toward the emotional expression of others and becomes dysregulated but is not able to identify the source of the emotional reaction.<br><br>The student is not able to describe, identify, or anticipate the emotional experiences in others.<br><br>The student can identify emotions in others, but only for predictable emotion-eliciting situations or when provided with explicit instruction. | Reactive or spontaneous empathy are difficult to teach but normally develop with exposure and over time.<br><br>Teach about emotions that occur in the self, then teach about these same emotions in others.<br><br>Teach the student how to identify emotions in others and how to reflect on or analyze those emotions. See affect and self-regulation skills (Chapter 8) for additional examples. |

| Skill sets | Functions and skills | Examples of functions and skills in action | Sample performance difficulties | Potential strategies, accommodations, or educational objectives |
|---|---|---|---|---|
| Imitation | The capacity to learn from others by imitating their actions | The student shows the capacity to imitate the actions of others in a reflexive or spontaneous manner.<br><br>The student shows the capacity to observe and subsequently imitate the actions of others (delayed imitation).<br><br>The student shows the capacity to observe, imitate, and learn from others and use what was learned in other contexts to get personal goals and needs met. | The student is unable to imitate others or fails to pay enough social attention to imitate others.<br><br>The student has the capacity to imitate others but is not able to use the imitation in a functional manner to meet personal goals or needs. For example, echolalia is a form of imitation that is often nonfunctional in nature. | Spontaneous imitation of others is difficult to teach, especially in children with limited social attention. However, instructors can teach students to copy others by physically prompting them to copy the actions of others. For learners functioning at a very early developmental stage, successive approximations of copying can be rewarded through tangibles or praise.<br><br>Integrate copied actions so that the student can see how personal goals and needs get met. |
| Social attention | The capacity to pay attention to others | The student pays attention to the behaviors of others by observing others.<br><br>The student makes social bids toward others and responds to social bids from others.<br><br>The student uses eye contact to regulate social interactions with others. | The student does not notice others or does not seem interested in looking at or copying the actions of others.<br><br>The student does not approach others and/or seems to avoid others.<br><br>The student avoids or is not responsive to eye contact or other social bids from others.<br><br>The student shows proximity behaviors but does not make any social bids.<br><br>The student makes awkward or inappropriate social bids (e.g., shows proximity behaviors only or pushes or is disruptive instead of using a socially more effective bid).<br><br>The student makes an initial social bid but is unable to sustain the bid to participate in conversations or an activity. | Teach the student to make eye contact and to notice the social behaviors of others.<br><br>Teach the student about how to anticipate the actions of others (e.g., by using a visual schedule and teaching the student about the predictable behaviors of others as related to daily routines or other predictable events).<br><br>Teach the student how to make a social bid through conventional scripts or conventional nonverbal behaviors that can facilitate a social interaction. |

*(continued)*

| Skill sets | Functions and skills | Examples of functions and skills in action | Sample performance difficulties | Potential strategies, accommodations, or educational objectives |
|---|---|---|---|---|
| Joint attention | The capacity to share attention and focus on an object or topic of interest | The student uses shared eye gaze while also looking at an object of shared interest with a social partner.<br><br>The student uses shared eye gaze while also conversing about the same topic or while engaged in play activity with a social partner.<br><br>The student shows the capacity to sustain a conversation about a shared topic without necessarily showing shared eye gaze. | The student does not show shared eye gaze.<br><br>The student does not show attention or focus on an object or topic of shared interest.<br><br>The student is not able to show the capacity for sustained conversation on a shared topic of interest. | Teach the student about social attention.<br><br>Teach the student about objects or topics of shared interest. The student may need explicit instruction in identifying the topic, object, or activity that is the focus of shared attention. |
| Theory of mind | The capacity to think about what others are thinking: Their intentions, desires, emotions, and beliefs | The student is able to identify the intentions, desires, and beliefs that people commonly hold in common situations.<br><br>The student is able to theorize about the desires and beliefs of others even in a nonconventional or atypical situation.<br><br>The student is able to identify or theorize about the desires or beliefs in others that the student does not share with the others; the student shows an understanding of false beliefs and can theorize about the actions of others that may be the result of a false belief.<br><br>The student is able to theorize about the desires, beliefs, thoughts, and/or emotions of others in real-time social interactions.<br><br>The student is able to theorize about the intentions, desires, beliefs, thoughts, and emotions of others even when the social situation is ambiguous and when information is missing.<br><br>The student recognizes that her or his own theory may be false and that inquiry and repeated observations may be needed to develop a more accurate theory of mind of others. | The student has difficulty theorizing about the intentions, desires, beliefs, thoughts, or emotions of others. The student may appear to be confused by facial expressions, gestures, or words shared by others.<br><br>The student may not understand that intentions, desires, and beliefs are not always shared. The student may not recognize that other people may have different beliefs or false beliefs. They are not able to reason logically from the beliefs held by others to guess at subsequent behaviors.<br><br>The student may understand intentions, desires, and beliefs in others in a narrative or a story but be unable to use their theory of mind skills successfully in real-time social interactions. | Teach the student about the intentions, desires, beliefs that people commonly have in conventional situations.<br><br>Teach the student how to identify emotions and desires in others by observing their facial expressions and gestures and listening to their words.<br><br>Teach the student more complex social thinking skills such as understanding false beliefs and the behaviors that can flow from a false belief.<br><br>Teach the student how to use theory of mind skills in real-time social situations.<br><br>Teach the student to anticipate mistakes or failures in theory of mind, as many social situations are ambiguous and can be difficult to interpret.<br><br>See also Chapter 5 (pragmatic language skills) and Chapter 8 (affect and self-regulation skills) for additional examples of how to teach students about people. |

| Skill sets | Functions and skills | Examples of functions and skills in action | Sample performance difficulties | Potential strategies, accommodations, or educational objectives |
|---|---|---|---|---|
| Social conventions | The capacity to identify and understand scripted behaviors and communicative functions that facilitate social interactions | The student is able to show conventional social behaviors, such as greetings, appreciation, socially appropriate eating habits, in the heritage culture.<br>The student can modify social conventions depending on the context (e.g., formal and informal), conventions with adults versus conventions with peers<br>The student is able to identify differences in social conventions in cultures other than the heritage culture.<br>The student can learn new social conventions as the need arises, including new social conventions as dictated by other cultures. | The student has not yet learned social conventions in the heritage culture and may not use scripted behaviors or communicative functions effectively in the heritage culture.<br>The student has not yet learned that social conventions have to be modified depending on the context.<br>The student has not yet learned that social conventions vary depending on the culture. | Teach social conventions appropriate to the heritage culture (e.g., eating behaviors, behaviors expected in the school building, behaviors expected in the home setting).<br>Teach how to modify social conventions, depending on changes in context.<br>Teach about social conventions in other cultures.<br>Teach about the underlying purpose of social conventions, which is to convey a message of respect, understanding, social inclusion, and fair treatment. |

APPENDIX 6.2 **Social Skills Observation Sheet**

| Skill sets | Functions and skills | Example skills or deficits in this student | Potential strategies, accommodations, or educational objectives |
|---|---|---|---|
| Attachment | The sense of security and safety that a child develops in response to primary caregivers | | |
| Empathy | The capacity to experience the same emotions as others when exposed to those emotions in others | | |
| Imitation | The capacity to learn from others by imitating their actions | | |
| Social attention | The capacity to pay attention to others | | |
| Joint attention | The capacity to share attention and focus on an object or topic of interest | | |
| Theory of mind | The capacity to think about what others are thinking: Their intentions, desires, emotions, and beliefs | | |
| Social conventions | The capacity to identify and understand scripted behaviors and communicative functions that facilitate social interactions | | |

# 7 Executive Skills

## INTRODUCTION AND GENERAL DEFINITIONS



Thus far, Section II of this volume has introduced three developmental frameworks: Formal language skills, pragmatic language skills, and social skills. This chapter expands on those topics through a discussion of executive skills, which affect all the skills discussed in this book and have a particularly close relationship to affect and self-regulation, discussed in Chapter 8. Executive skills are not truly separable from any of the skills listed in this book. They influence every skill that students have to master in school settings. They are at the heart of learning and academic performance, classroom participation, social interactions, motor performance, and more.

Executive skills can be thought of as the supervisory functions of the brain. These skills develop slowly. Children require adults to provide supervision for many years until they integrate and master these skills and can perform independently. As examples, adults devote a lot of their time telling children and youth what they need to do and how to do it. After giving instructions to children and youth, adults then have to monitor and supervise the child or adolescent to make sure that the instructions are followed. After that, the adults have to review the outcome to make sure that it is satisfactory. All of these supervisory behaviors are examples of executive skills. A primary reason that children and youth need so much supervision is because of their underdeveloped executive skills.

The definition of *executive functions* (or *executive skills*, the term preferred in this chapter) is not straightforward. There is a lack of consensus about the definition of executive functions and executive skills. Executive skills can be defined as those components or aspects of cognition that allow for self-regulation (Nigg, 2017). *Self-regulation* is a broad term that refers to regulating or changing one's behaviors in response to environmental demands and choosing the best behavior for the situation. It includes regulating or changing one's emotions. A narrower definition of executive skills proposes that executive skills reflect the capacity of humans to shift from external to internal thinking (Barkley, 2000). As executive skills develop, human behavior no longer consists of reacting to environmental stimuli. Rather, people learn to respond strategically to environmental stimuli and environmental demands. Executive skills therefore allow for internalized behavioral control or self-control.

Suchy (2009) provides a more succinct definition, stating that executive skills are purposeful, goal-directed, and future-oriented behaviors. This definition is the starting point for the

Executive Skills Framework. As proposed by Suchy, individuals use executive skills successfully when they do the following:

1. Create or have a goal in mind
2. Plan the steps needed to reach that goal
3. Maintain attention and focus on the goal as the steps get carried out
4. Reflect on their performance to see whether the goal was reached
5. Change behaviors, if needed, to continue to reach the goal

A goal, as defined above, can be very small or very large. A small goal might be to get dressed or participate in a conversation and might be reached within minutes. The goal might be larger and take more time to complete, such as finishing homework, cleaning out the garage, or writing an essay. These larger goals are defined as being more distal because they take longer to reach, perhaps hours or even days or weeks. The goal can be more distal still, such as improving grades by the end of the school year, improving one's soccer skills to make the varsity team, or taking preparatory courses for entry into college. Goals such as these might take months to years to reach. Executive skills allow us to imagine and reach goals, regardless of the number of steps or the time needed to complete them. As will be discussed later in the chapter, the temporal aspect of distal goals is a critical factor for children and youth. Because they have had much less experience with the passage of time, children and youth are less capable of judging the time needed to complete steps and reach longer term goals.

Goal-directed behavior is such a fundamental component of human behavior that it is sometimes easier to recognize it as a phenomenon when it is absent. Persons with goal neglect, such as patients with frontal lobe injuries of the brain, illustrate this point. Persons with goal neglect do not reach their goals, or they do not reach them consistently or successfully. Goal neglect can manifest as behaviors that are perseverative and rigid, impulsive, disinhibited, or passive (Duncan, Emslie, & Williams, 1996). Instead of remaining focused on a goal, the person with goal neglect might get stuck on one step or might get distracted and focus attention elsewhere. Some people with goal neglect are not oriented toward a goal at all and remain passive without initiating any goals. Persons with these behaviors may need a substantial amount of supervision, guidance, and prompting to follow through on a plan and reach a goal.

Children and youth with impairments in their executive skills can show these same behaviors. They can present as being inattentive and disorganized and may be unable to complete tasks or chores. They may present as careless because of the many errors they make, and they seem to be breaking the rules in social situations because of impulsive behaviors. Others may present as unmotivated, because they do not initiate tasks, and still others might present as rigid and inflexible. Children and youth with these difficulties typically need more reminders, prompts, and supervision to identify goals, to start a task or activity that will lead to reaching a goal, to stay on task, and to complete tasks successfully and accurately. Think of the student who always forgets to brush his or her teeth in the morning before leaving for school or repeatedly fails to put belongings into their right location and is subsequently unable to find them. Consider the student who does not follow classroom rules consistently, even though capable of reciting them accurately. Think of the student who constantly bothers peers by not taking turns in a conversation or in a game. The supervisory functions of the brain, also known as the student's executive skills, are needed for successful performance in these kinds of activities. Underdeveloped executive skills lead to these types of performance difficulties.

## HOW THE FRAMEWORK WAS CONSTRUCTED

As was the case in previous chapters, researchers, clinicians, and therapists can use somewhat different terms to discuss the same or similar ideas surrounding executive skills. Terms such as *self-regulation, effortful control,* and *executive functions* all relate to executive skills (Zhou, Chen, & Main, 2012). The framework presented here separates the term *executive skills* from the broader term *self-regulation,* a topic discussed in the next chapter. The goal of this chapter is to be targeted and specific in its use of terms, to develop coherence and a shared terminology for a school team.

The authors of this book decided to use the term *executive skills* instead of *executive functions,* despite how commonly the terms *executive functions* and even *executive functioning skills* are used elsewhere. Our rationale is that executive functions are biologically preprogrammed and emerge over the first years of life through normal growth of the brain. They develop because of the maturation and specialization of neurons, pertain to bodily structures and functions (see discussion in Chapter 1) and are often considered to reside in the frontal lobes of the brain (Alvarez & Emory, 2006). In contrast, executive skills express the influence of nurture on nature. They reflect how executive functions expand and develop through nurture and are the result of modeling, experience, and formal instruction (Klingberg, 2016). Executive skills are therefore learned behaviors, consisting of a set of skills that are used to enhance and refine goal-directed behavior. Their emergence reflects changes in multiple neurological networks of the brain (Stuss & Alexander, 2000).

The Executive Skills Framework was constructed based on a review of literature as shown throughout this chapter. The chapter takes into consideration the most common and relevant skills, such as remaining focused, remembering all the steps needed to reach a goal, completing the steps in the correct order, monitoring for accurate completion and making corrections if needed, and modifying the order if barriers or unexpected interruptions occur.

Clinicians and researchers commonly use terms such as *working memory, inhibition and interference control, cognitive flexibility,* and *selective attention* to describe the behaviors and skills listed above (Diamond, 2013). Other relevant terms include *planning, organization, follow-through,* and *sequencing* (Best, Miller, & Jones, 2009; Suchy, 2009; Zhou et al., 2012). The concept of metacognition, which means thinking about one's own thinking, is also included in the topic of executive skills (Fernandez-Duque, Baird, & Posner, 2000). Zelazo and Cunningham (2007) make a useful distinction between cool and hot executive functions. *Cool* executive functions are more cognitive in nature, whereas *hot* executive functions include a motivational or emotion-regulation component. Hot executive functions control the arousal system and control or modify emotions. This distinction was instrumental in the construction of this framework. The Executive Skills Framework is based primarily on the definitions of cool executive functions. The discussion of self-regulation, self-control, and their relationship to hot executive functions is found in Chapter 8.



## HOW CAN THIS FRAMEWORK HELP ME?

This chapter will summarize key concepts embedded in the term *executive skills* and explain the relevance and importance of executive skills to learning in general. The information shared in this chapter helps describe the capacity for reaching goals successfully. It will also help school professionals think about how to break down learning tasks so that students can reach goals more successfully. The chapter will provide some strategies for how to redefine the terms *goal* and *task* and how to apply these terms to a variety of school demands, such as following classroom rules, socializing successfully, completing formal learning activities, and participating in recreational activities, among others. The discussion presented in this chapter is designed to help educators and other school professionals understand the oftentimes challenging behaviors of students in new ways. Many students with underdeveloped executive skills struggle to participate successfully in school. Challenging and disruptive behaviors are not always intentional or goal-directed. They are commonly a reaction, not a response, to environmental demands. They often reflect underdeveloped self-control and executive skills. School professionals should always consider skill gaps to help explain why a student might appear unmotivated or does not seem to take responsibility. Underdeveloped executive skills more likely explain why some students break classroom rules, make careless mistakes in school work, or struggle to socialize successfully. In explaining the source of these behaviors, the Executive Skills Framework invites school professionals to think about their students in a new way. By using the terms presented in this chapter, school professionals can discuss challenging or disruptive behaviors in more constructive ways, with colleagues, with the student, and with the student's family. By learning to make observations of student behaviors as presented in this chapter, practitioners can develop a more accurate oral and written description of student behaviors, develop a more clearly articulated intervention plan, and also measure progress more accurately.

## EXECUTIVE SKILLS FRAMEWORK: TERMS AND DEFINITIONS

The Executive Skills Framework begins with a detailed discussion of relevant terms to be used in discussions with colleagues. The terms will help school professionals think about how to build the student's executive skills using a wide range of possible tasks or activities. Some readers may recognize several of the terms used in this chapter from a commonly used behavioral rating scale (Gioia & Isquith, 2013). However, the terms are also taken from other references.



There are two skill sets in in the Executive Skills Framework:

1. Basic (first-order) executive skills
    a. Orientation
    b. Initiation
    c. Inhibition
    d. Shifting cognitive set
    e. Working memory
2. Advanced (higher order) executive skills
    a. Planning
    b. Organization
    c. Metacognition

Basic or first-order executive skills are the first five skills of the framework: Orientation, initiation, inhibition, shifting cognitive set, and working memory. Advanced or higher order executive skills consist of the subsequent three skills: Planning, organization, and metacognition. Even though the two skill sets are highly interdependent, the critical difference between basic and advanced executive skills is that no planning is required in the former. When a student only has to use basic executive skills, it is because the task or activity has been planned by someone else, such as an adult or a peer. Most students who do not develop their executive skills successfully have difficulty with first-order or basic executive skills. Basic executive skills serve as a prerequisite to developing more advanced or higher order executive skills. Both types of executive skills are discussed in the sections that follow. The summary of the Executive Skills Framework is available in Appendix 7.1 for quick reference.

## Basic Executive Skills

For students to perform successfully, they have to develop basic executive skills for both familiar goals and new goals. Basic executive skills are those skills needed to reach a goal that does not require any planning. Goals that are achievable without planning are very simple goals (e.g., reaching for a cup), goals that have been planned by a teacher ("Do this work sheet. Start at number 1 and then finish at number 10"), or goals that have been rehearsed and previously memorized ("Get ready for school," "Put your toys into the toybox"). A very substantial amount of learning, especially for young children and for novel tasks, requires the use of basic executive skills only. The adult dictates the goals, identifies the necessary steps, sequences the steps (puts them into the right order to reach the goal), and explains to the student what to do. For some of the tasks, the order of the steps may not even matter, and the student only has to remember the steps, and stay focused on the goal. The adult verifies that the goal was reached successfully and helps out when the student runs into a barrier.

Young learners need to master basic executive skills, many of which can be taught by asking students to complete tasks by rote. Think, for example, about how children learn safety rules or classroom participation behaviors. The expectation is that the student follows the plan as dictated by the adult. The student learns to follow the plan successfully through frequent practice. The same holds true for following classroom routines, and even for many reading, spelling, and early math skills. A student's capacity for basic executive skills can be observed as they participate in activities and tasks that are either very simple, familiar, rehearsed, or planned by the adult. The following sections provide definitions and examples of basic executive skills.

***Orientation and Initiation*** Orientation and initiation are the most preliminary components of executive skills. They are necessary, but they are not sufficient for reaching goals. Orientation refers to directing one's attention to a stimulus or to a goal. Orienting behaviors are present at the beginning of life. In the first weeks of life, they manifest as alerting to a stimulus, either by looking or turning toward that stimulus or by quieting in order to listen to a stimulus. The stimulus may be a sound, the face of a caregiver, or an interesting object. Orientation may also be defined as being focused on a goal, such as having the goal to speak with a peer, to get out of the house on time to get to school, or to complete writing an essay. Orientation only refers to the stimulus or the goal to which the person is paying attention. Orientation may or may not lead to initiation.

Initiation is the very first step taken toward a goal. In infancy, initiation emerges in the first months of life and might manifest as swatting a mobile or taking a first step toward an interesting stimulus. In toddlers or preschoolers, initiation might manifest as reaching for a toy to start to play with it. In school-age children, initiation could manifest by reaching for a book needed for a homework assignment or picking up a pen to take notes or start an assignment. Initiation might even involve asking a question to clarify what the instructions were to start a task successfully and reach the goal. Whatever the task or activity, orientation is the focus and initiation is the first step that leads toward a goal. The main purpose in writing about orientation is to remind the reader of an obvious but important point: Adults need to ensure that the student is oriented to the right activity before any initiation or participation will occur. The importance of orientation and initiation is discussed later in this chapter, in the section dedicated to performance problems.

***Inhibition*** Inhibition skills allow people to sustain their focus (sustain their orientation) toward a goal that can give them satisfaction later. Inhibition skills are important for reaching goals, because they prevent distractions from changing the goal orientation. Inhibition refers to suppression. When inhibition skills are present, higher order cognitive or mental processes are used to suppress interferences (such as a distractor) and allow sustained orientation toward a goal.

Very often, adults think about the importance of inhibition skills because the absence of inhibition skills prevents children and youth from following adult instructions successfully and reaching (adult-desired) goals. For example, the adult might say, "Stop talking with your peers and focus on your work." The adult is asking the child or adolescent to inhibit the desire to socialize and instead to focus on (orient attention to) classroom work. At home, a parent might ask their child or adolescent to maintain orientation on a task such as cleaning up the bedroom and inhibit the desire to play with preferred toys or send a text message to a friend. Adults will typically want to see the child or adolescent maintain orientation to a task even if a distractor arises, such as a peer or sibling who invites them to play. Adults sometimes use consequences and rewards to help children and youth develop their inhibition or impulse control skills and teach them to focus on adult-preferred goals.

The fact that adults offer rewards to children for their compliance is an indicator of how valuable the task is to the adult, not necessarily to the child. The value of developing inhibition skills is not so that children can behave better in the service of adults. Rather, from the child or youth's perspective, the value of developing inhibition skills is that doing so offers choices. Inhibition allows the child or youth to make decisions that will improve or enhance long-term outcomes. When children and youth use inhibition skills to suppress distractors, the environment no longer determines the child's orientation and initiation. Instead, the child shifts from external to internal thinking (Barkley, 2000). The child can now use inhibition to maintain orientation and attention on a goal and not shift away from that orientation because of a distractor. Not all of the stimuli that need to be suppressed come from the environment. The distractors can also be internal, such as a thought or a memory that then interferes with the task at hand. With inhibition skills in place, tasks get done and goals get reached. Arrival on time at school is possible, classroom work gets done, the room gets cleaned. The reward may be good grades at school and a sense of academic success or more time for playing and socializing. In the process, children develop a sense of mastery and personal control. The goals that children work toward may be determined initially by adults. However, the ultimate purpose of building inhibition skills specifically, and executive skills more generally, should be that they allow children and youth to pursue their own goals.



Inhibition skills are sometimes categorized into different types, based on differences in the type of distractor and based on the behavior used to exhibit inhibition skills (Barkley, 2001; Nigg, 2000). The two most common categories of inhibition skills are *impulse control* and *interference control*. Impulse control allows for deferred gratification and prevents acting before thinking. Interference control consists of the repeated inhibition of distractors over longer time intervals to maintain orientation to a goal.

For the purposes of the Executive Skills Framework, the main difference between impulse control and interference control is a difference of degree rather than a difference of kind. Deferred gratification and sustained attention require the same type of inhibition. However, the behavioral manifestation of the inhibition looks different when it has to occur over a shorter rather than a longer time interval. It can also look different when the distracting stimulus is weak rather than very salient or especially interesting.

For children and youth, exciting or arousing stimuli might include access to chocolate or preferred sweets, the thought of going outside to play, or the frustration felt when teased by a sibling. A less arousing but still salient stimulus might include a conversation between two classmates at the back of the classroom. A low-level distracting stimulus might be the hum of the air conditioner. For any given stimulus, the intensity and duration of the stimulus will influence the student's success at inhibition. A highly salient stimulus (e.g., a clown enters the classroom) will not be ignored very easily. For some students, the conversation between peers on the other side of the room might be a high-intensity stimulus that is difficult to ignore, while other students may suppress this distractor more easily. The distraction of the hum of the air conditioner can be suppressed by most students. The main point is that inhibition skills must be applied in a variety of situations, and require varying strength, depending on the stimulus and how long or how often the inhibition skills are needed. Box 7.1 provides another model to help in understanding the same distinction. Children can show inhibition skills for longer time intervals and for more varied types of distractors as they age.

**BOX 7.1. Hot and Cool Inhibition Skills**

Several of the inhibition examples cited in the text could be categorized as examples of self-regulatory control or as hot executive skills (Hongwasnishkul, Happaney, Lee, & Zelazo, 2007; Zelazo & Cunningham, 2005). Hot inhibition skills are needed in emotionally more exciting situations. For example, not responding to a criticism from a peer is a hot form of inhibition. Not responding to a clown who suddenly enters the classroom is a hot form of inhibition.

In contrast, cooler inhibition skills are required to suppress a response to less arousing or less interfering stimuli. Inhibition that is applied for longer time intervals or in the service of academic tasks is considered to be cooler. Impulse control is a hot type of inhibition, whereas interference control is cool. Hot inhibition skills and their role in suppressing arousal and emotions are discussed in Chapter 8.



*How Inhibition Develops With Age: Infants and Toddlers* Inhibition skills develop and expand throughout childhood. Early in development, infants are distracted very easily, respond somewhat indiscriminately to all the different stimuli that might catch their interest, and do not have inhibition skills. Their orientation shifts quickly and often. As infants become toddlers, their inhibition skills start to develop. Toddlers can ignore some stimuli to focus on others that are especially interesting or important to them. For example, they can ignore background noise, while engaged in a play activity, and can also ignore adult requests (e.g., "Come here") and persist in what they are doing instead of following the adult's directive. Although this type of inhibition skill can be a source of frustration to the parents (because the toddler now has a mind of her own), the emergence of this skill is an important developmental accomplishment.

The toddler's inhibition skills are fragile, and their somewhat improved attention span has developed because they can orient toward an activity that is preferred, interesting, or exciting. That said, as soon as another interesting stimulus comes along, the toddler is liable to become distracted and change his or her orientation again. Even though toddlers have a longer attention span than in infancy, they are still largely stimulus bound and will respond to the stimulus that is the most arousing.

*How Inhibition Develops With Age: Deferred Gratification in Preschoolers* The next accomplishment to emerge is the capacity to suppress an exciting or interesting stimulus to focus attention on something that is less exciting or interesting. Inhibition skills of this sort are evident in the preschooler's capacity to follow rules. The preschooler learns to follow rules such as "first-then," "First, put your shoes on, then go outside." The preschooler inhibits the desire to do the second activity immediately and can instead focus on the first activity as a prerequisite to participating in the second activity later. When preschoolers follow this rule independently, they are showing impulse control skills or deferred gratification skills. It is hard work for a preschooler to wait until later to do the exciting thing that they want to do right away. Most of the time, the duration of inhibition required is very short, and the preschooler is only required to show deferred gratification over short time intervals. Substantial adult support may still be needed to prevent the preschooler from becoming distracted.

Inhibition skills and deferred gratification develop further when preschoolers and kindergarten students learn to follow rules of conduct. To follow rules, students not only need to know the rule ("raise your hand before speaking," "line up before going outside"), they also need to suppress the immediate desire to speak out or to rush outside when the recess bell rings. Many classroom participation behaviors or classroom rules require this type of inhibition. The developmental difference over this age range lies in the child's capacity to show inhibition skills consistently and with less immediate adult support.

*How Inhibition Develops With Age: Sustained Attention in School-Age Children* As children enter the school-age years, inhibition skills become more secure and more highly differentiated. They can show deferred gratification multiple times over the course of an hour or over the course of a day. Deferred gratification and the ability to follow rules is more consistent, occurs more often, and occurs in different settings and under different circumstances. Sustained attention requires ongoing suppression or ongoing inhibition. When inhibition skills become more secure, attention to task gets longer. A practical way to look at how inhibition skills improve with age is to measure improvements in a child's attention span. By the time children enter into first grade, they are required to sustain their attention for 20–30 minutes, something that was not possible when they were younger. They can do this because they are able to defer gratification for longer, and because they can continuously inhibit minor distractors for longer periods of time. Ongoing inhibition requires ongoing "don't do" skills (e.g., "Don't go outside," "Don't play with your toys," "Don't speak with your neighbor"). Box 7.2 provides corollary information by discussing the importance of developing "do" skills.



### BOX 7.2. Inhibition Skills, Attention Span, and Attention-Deficit/Hyperactivity Disorder

As discussed in the main body of the text, inhibition skills are a key factor in a child's developing attention span. However, a longer attention span actually requires more than just inhibition skills. Language skills, other executive skills discussed in this chapter, and general knowledge all interact and help the student remain oriented to task. Multiple skills therefore help the student sustain attention to task, not just executive skills (Verte, Geurts, Roeyers, Oosterlaan, & Sergeant, 2006). One aspect of a student's new capacity for sustained attention is his or her ability to focus attention on "do" skills (e.g., "Do keep your attention on your deskwork," "Do finish your math problems") (Kochanska, Coy, & Murray, 2001). This skill is just as important as the suppression or inhibition skill of "not" paying attention or "don't do" skills. "Do" skills are needed when children need to pay attention to something that is not especially interesting or important to them.

Experience and general knowledge help children to prolong their attention span. As they age, children learn to focus attention on tasks and activities that are less immediately gratifying. They can do this because they have experienced feelings of mastery and success with those (less salient) tasks in the past. Math or spelling become meaningful when they have experienced success and can see how math and spelling skills are relevant to goals or activities outside the classroom. It is easier to inhibit distractors for longer periods of time when the task or activity becomes its own source of satisfaction. The more successful the student is, the higher the potential becomes for a prolonged attention span.

Commonly, professionals assume that a short attention span is a sign of attention-deficit/hyperactivity disorder (ADHD). However, a short attention span in any given student requires thorough analysis. Not all students with a short attention span have ADHD. Children can appear inattentive for a number of different reasons (Roberts, Martel, & Nigg, 2017). First, all three of the basic executive skills (inhibition, shifting cognitive set, and working memory) are required for sustained attention. When a student is inattentive, it could be due to difficulties in one or all three of these skills. Affective processes and emotion regulation are also implicated (Martel, Nigg, & von Eye, 2009). Attention and focus improve when several executive skills interact with one another and with affect and self-regulation skills. Attention and focus also improve as children develop all of the other skills discussed in this book. When working with children who may have a short attention span, educators and therapists have to consider multiple reasons for the students' difficulty with attention. Multiple domains for skills building should be considered to help build the students' attention span and successful orientation to task. A medical evaluation is often necessary and can help to verify that the short attention span is related to difficulties with inhibition and impulse control.

*How Inhibition Skills Develop With Age: Interactions Among Inhibition Skills, Cognitive Flexibility, and Working Memory* As children age into elementary school–age years and beyond, inhibition skills are applied to cooler decision-making situations. With maturation, children need to hone their inhibition skills to activities with the same or similar emotional salience or level of interest. When playing with peers, for example, children have to choose between different types of play. When asked to complete tasks in the classroom, they can choose to do one task before the other. Within academic tasks, students can approach a math or writing problem one way or another. Cooler inhibition skills are needed to make choices such as these, and students commonly require the skills discussed next—shifting cognitive set and working memory.



***Shifting Cognitive Set*** Shifting cognitive set refers to the mental capacity to shift from one task, activity, or idea to another. Shifting cognitive set is also referred to as mental flexibility or cognitive flexibility. Shifting cognitive set requires inhibition. As students shift from one activity to the next, they have to suppress or inhibit their orientation to the first activity in order to shift their orientation to the new activity. The same shifting has to occur when children shift mind-set and when youth and adults have to shift their perspective or point of view. The sections that follow outline some of the developmental accomplishments that children show in their capacity to shift cognitive set.

*Transitions: Shifting Between Two Familiar Activities* A basic example of shifting cognitive set is the capacity to transition or shift between activities. During infancy and early toddler years, set-shifting difficulties are not apparent because inhibition skills have not yet developed. Infants and toddlers shift their orientation and focus all the time, in response to environmental stimuli. After the first year of life, toddlers develop just enough inhibition skills to focus on a preferred activity. As a result, they do not shift orientation to a new stimulus as easily. An adult's request for a transition (e.g., "Time for supper!") does not interrupt the toddler's orientation and focus as quickly. Toddlers often need more than one reminder or need time to shift their orientation. The child now has the inhibition skills needed to make choices about whether to focus upon or ignore a stimulus. In other words, the issue of set-shifting first emerges as a *lack* of ability to shift smoothly or efficiently. In toddlers, set-shifting demands such as the one described here are often associated with an emotional outburst or protest. Although the sluggishness and resistance that toddlers can show are sometimes a source of frustration to the child's parents, the emergence of these behaviors is a developmental accomplishment.

Set-shifting improves as inhibition skills improve. When the preschooler becomes more skilled at suppressing interesting and exciting stimuli, it is easier for them to shift attention to activities and demands that are less interesting and less exciting. For example, when told, "Come for supper," a preschooler or kindergartener should be able to follow the adult's directive and suppress the desire to continue playing. Greater familiarity with the many transition demands of the day, and better understanding of time intervals, help to make inhibition and set-shifting demands easier for the young child to manage. When preschoolers have the memory that "play time will occur again after supper" or that "TV time will happen again tomorrow," it is easier for them to tolerate the frustration of being told to stop playing or to turn the television off. With increasing familiarity of the routines of the day, shifting occurs more quickly and protesting diminishes. The developmental accomplishment here is related to improved inhibition. Improvements in inhibition facilitate set-shifting.

*Shifting Between a Familiar and an Unfamiliar Task or Activity* A less commonly noticed type of set-shifting demand occurs when adults ask students to shift from a task or activity that is familiar to a task or activity that is not familiar. This developmental accomplishment emerges during the preschool years. For instance, toddlers and young preschoolers often prefer familiar plans or routines. The bedtime routine is perhaps the best example. It is common for toddlers to insist on carrying out their bedtime routines in a rigid manner before they are willing to settle into bed. They may show the same rigidity with mealtime or classroom routines and with certain play activities. For example, bedtime activities might need to occur in a specific order, mealtimes may require a specific set of dishes, or a play activity may need to be acted out in a specific way. When adults or peers do not adhere to the usual routine, the child may protest.

Difficulty with shifting in toddlers and preschoolers relates to difficulty shifting between what is familiar and what is not familiar. As preschoolers learn more about how the world works, they can tolerate changes in routines more easily. They develop an awareness that goals can be reached more than one way. The bedtime routine can be had with a teddy bear, just as it can occur with a favorite doll. A meal can be had with the blue cup instead of the red cup. In spite of this increased awareness, rigidity and inflexibility remain common in preschoolers. Young children stick with what is familiar, something that is not always easily inhibited or suppressed. They have difficulty shifting their orientation away from what they normally do to shifting their orientation toward doing an activity a new way. Anxiety and confusion about what is new and unfamiliar may be one way to understand the preschooler's rigid behaviors. A very specific example of developmental growth in cognitive flexibility emerges by the time a preschooler becomes a kindergarten student. It has to do with shifting from a prepotent response. See Box 7.3 for a more detailed explanation.



**BOX 7.3. Card-Sorting Tasks: A Measure of Set-Shifting Skills**

One of the most well-developed neuropsychological tasks is the card-sorting task (Grant & Berg, 1981). Card-sorting tasks measure how set-shifting improves with age. In a classic card-sorting task, a preschool-age child is asked to classify cards that have different colors (e.g., red or blue) and different shapes (e.g., square or circle) (Zelazo, Frye, & Rapus, 1996). The tester gives the child one of two instructions: "Sort the cards by shape" or "Sort the cards by color."

After the preschooler has sorted the cards by one rule, the tester asks the child to sort the cards by the other rule. The first rule chosen by the tester does not matter, because preschoolers are capable of following either rule equally well. However, when asked to shift to the new rule set, 3-year-old children typically persist in sorting according to whatever rule they were given first. In fact, some 3-year-old preschoolers will recite back the new rule dictated by the examiner, while performing the old rule. They correct their error only when the tester reminds them once or twice what they are supposed to do and after they have made one or two attempts to sort correctly. In contrast to 3-year-olds, most 4-year-olds switch rules successfully at the first attempt. Five-year-olds perform very securely and smoothly when given this task and are able to perform the new rule while suppressing the old rule.

The card-sorting task is an easy way to reveal a neurodevelopmentally based difficulty with flexibility. The difficulty that the young preschooler faces in this task is a difficulty in inhibiting the prepotent response, meaning the response that is familiar or usual. The preschooler's capacity to shift is dependent on inhibition of the prepotent response. Mental effort is required to shift away from the prepotent response and to orient toward a different kind of response.

An important development in set-shifting, therefore, occurs between the ages of 3 and 5 years, allowing the older preschooler to show greater flexibility. However, just because 4- and 5-year-olds can switch rules sets in a card-sorting task does not mean that they are especially flexible in real life! Cognitive inflexibility persists well into the school-age years. For example, in the early school years, a teacher might give the class a worksheet and ask the students to add all of the numbers on one side of the page and subtract all the numbers on the other side of the page. Young school-age children can often make the error of not switching rule sets and make mistakes even though they understand both adding and subtracting. Such inefficiencies persist for several more years.



Improvements in inhibition skills and in working memory both serve to improve cognitive flexibility. As preschoolers become more familiar with different types of routines, and as their capacity to remember more steps improves, they can shift their orientation between different activities more easily. They also develop the capacity to shift their orientation between or among two or more different ways of carrying out the same activity. As their working memory, inhibition, and set-shifting skills improve, they show greater flexibility in choosing which activity to initiate and how that activity will get carried out. Inhibition skills are now applied to cooler tasks. Improved working memory allows the preschooler to remember and keep track of different ways to carry out tasks. The preschool or kindergarten-age student is no longer bound to the one way that he or she knows how to complete a task or activity. The improvements in flexibility just described are not only the result of improved inhibition skills. They are also the result of improvements in working memory (Best & Miller, 2010; Zelazo et al., 2003) With a stronger ability to remember what the options are and to remember different ways of reaching the same goal, set-shifting and cognitive flexibility improve.

***Working Memory*** Working memory refers to retaining or remembering multiple pieces of information that are needed to reach a goal. Each piece of information is held in memory for immediate use as needed. The capacity to remember several pieces of information simultaneously is possible partly because of developing inhibition skills, which prevent distractors from deleting or replacing the information that is currently being held. Researchers estimate that approximately four units of information can be held in working memory at a given time (Cowan, 2001). The items or pieces of information held in working memory are prioritized and reprioritized depending on which piece of information is needed most. The information held in working memory is also updated and modified with new information when old information is no longer needed for immediate purposes. Working memory is therefore not only a measure of how much information is held in memory. It includes the phenomenon of how information is manipulated and modified while it is kept in mind for immediate use for the task at hand. As such, working memory skills cannot be separated from other executive skills such as inhibition and shifting cognitive set. Working memory is available and usable because inhibition skills (preventing distractors) and shifting between the available options (set-shifting skills) are both supporting working memory.

Just as working memory cannot be separated easily from inhibition and shifting cognitive set, it also cannot be separated easily from long-term memory. Information stored in long-term memory may compete for space in the working memory circuit and may be needed in the immediate term to perform tasks and reach goals (Bledowski, Kaiser, & Rahm, 2010). The information held in working memory can be either in verbal, visual, or kinesthetic (motor) form. Early in development, working memory is primarily visual and motor rather than verbal. After approximately age 4 years, improvements in language skills allow for verbal working memory to become more prominent. The model of two modes of working memory, visual-spatial and phonological, was proposed by Baddely (2003; Baddely & Hitch, 1974), and remains a prominent model today. That said, verbal working memory generally replaces other forms of working memory as children age, because it is usually the most efficient way of storing and manipulating information. The following sections highlight the importance of verbal working memory.

*Developments in Working Memory* Prior to the development of language (and even for some time afterward), children often depend on memorized rote sequences to complete tasks. They can initiate and complete tasks as long as there are no interruptions and the steps are carried out in the right order. For example, a young preschooler who has just learned how to get dressed can do so without parent support. If not interrupted, the preschooler may be able to accomplish the task successfully and smoothly. Yet if interrupted by her own distractors, or by a sibling who asks a question, the preschooler may need to start the process all over again or may need guidance about how to continue. She may not be able to simply pick up from where she left off. In this example, the preschooler's working memory for dressing is stored in motor and visual circuits in the brain. In contrast, once children have language, they can remember the steps using words. If the child is interrupted, she can use words to recite back the sequence and then pick up where she left off. The child might say to herself, "First underpants, then pants. I did pants. Next, shirt." The use of songs and rhyming games in this age group are used partly because they facilitate working memory skills by linking words with musical cues. As verbal working memory improves, so too does cognitive flexibility. In the example here, the preschooler can shift her orientation from the task, to a distractor, and then back to task. Interruptions or distractors no longer prevent her from reaching goals.



During late preschool and early school-age years, children can often be heard talking themselves through a task, a first sign that they are using verbal working memory to complete tasks or carry out a sequence. When following adult-directed tasks, young children typically remember the steps only over a short time interval (e.g., right after receiving the instructions) and are likely to forget what they were supposed to do if an interval of a few minutes passes between the time that an instruction was given and when it is actually carried out. Over time, working memory improves and allows the child to remember instructions over a longer time interval. Older children and adults generally use verbally mediated working memory to remember all the units of information needed to reach immediate goals.

Children are able to remember more units of information as they age. Improvements in working memory occur at least into adolescence and are supported by improvements in inhibition and shifting cognitive set (Best & Miller, 2010). The three skills are difficult to distinguish from one another in formal measures, as they are highly interdependent (Miyake, Friedman, Emerson, Witzki, & Howerter, 2000; Verte et al., 2006). The interdependence of inhibition, shifting cognitive set, and working memory is relevant to many tasks. The reader is invited to review Chapter 11 on math skills for specific examples of these interrelationships. Inhibition skills, shifting cognitive set, and working memory are all important in the cool task of math problem solving.

## Advanced Executive Skills

As discussed above, basic executive skills are those skills that children and adolescents need to use when following adult-developed plans. Frequently, the adult selects the goal and ensures that it is achieved correctly. While it is certainly important for children to be able to carry out and complete tasks imposed by adults, children and youth need to be able to do much more than that. They need to be able select their own goals and to reach those goals successfully by developing their own plan. Ideally, they should learn to do so without adult supervision. The subsequent sections discuss how children and youth learn to set their own goals and make their own plans. These skills greatly enhance the student's independence. The advanced executive skills discussed here include planning, organization, and metacognition and are required for the student's future independent functioning.

***Planning*** Planning refers to creating the correct sequence of steps needed to reach a goal successfully. For any task or activity, the student has to be able to break the task down into a set of steps, and the steps need to be carried out in the correct sequence. Young children engage in many different types of plans, even though they may not have any planning skills. For example, they can carry out plans that are developed by adults relating to daily routines, such as completing the steps needed to get to school in the morning and completing classroom entry routines upon arrival at school. The same holds true for many play activities. Children rely on scripts and general event knowledge to make up play activities. For example, there are scripts or routines that children follow when they pretend to go to the store, or when they engage in playing pirate ships. The child carries out familiar sequences and routines by modeling real-life experiences or by imitating what they may have seen in a movie or read in a book. As imaginary play develops, children can appear to be creating novel sequences. Often, however, they end up using one or more rehearsed or memorized plans that they carry out one after the other. This skill of cutting and pasting previously learned plans is called proto-planning (Hudson, Sosa, & Shapiro, 1997). Most of the planning undertaken by young children consists of proto-planning.

True planning is different from proto-planning and requires breaking a task down into its component parts and independently sequencing the steps needed to reach a goal. True planning requires the basic executive skills discussed earlier in this chapter. However, it also requires two additional skills: Making or having a goal (a vision or expectation of how something will be in the future) and understanding temporal sequences (how steps are carried out over a time interval) (McCormack & Atance, 2011). True planning skills are not commonly seen in young children and emerge after the preschool years in typically developing children. Even adults use rehearsed plans and scripts much of the time.

Creating future goals, understanding sequences, understanding temporal aspects of a sequence, and understanding the concept of a new future state are skills that emerge with participation. Getting dressed for school and leaving the house on time and completing a grocery shopping trip are examples of plans that have a temporal sequence and result in a changed future state. Initially, children understand temporal sequences and a future state through memorized and familiar plans or activities such as these. They know that, by carrying out a familiar set of steps, the end result will be that one is fully dressed or that the kitchen will be restocked with groceries. However, they do not necessarily understand temporal sequencing as a general concept that can be applied to different kinds of activities. They do not understand that any task can be broken down into component steps and that by completing the steps in the right order a new future state is realized.

A practical example of a true planning demand occurs when a child encounters a mishap or barrier that needs to be overcome. They might know how to get dressed but may not know what to do if a piece of clothing is missing. The barrier of missing clothing requires knowledge and sequencing of steps, so that the problem can be solved. The missing clothing might be in the dryer or a drawer, and a plan needs to be developed to retrieve the clothing and reach the desired future state of being fully dressed. During play activities, for example, the child may have a goal to play with props as part of a dress-up routine and then discovers that a necessary toy is broken or that props are missing. Not all children know how to resolve mishaps or barriers such as these, and many would call for adult assistance. In contrast, the child who has developed planning skills can develop and carry out a plan to find missing clothing or props or fix the broken toy. He or she is able to use a desired future state as the goal for planning a sequence and overcoming the barrier. The child who is capable of planning might say, "There are three places that I can think of where that missing piece might be. I'll look in my brother's room first."

Children often mix memorized sequences, proto-plans, and novel plans in their play and other activities. As they age and as they understand time intervals better, they participate in plans that take longer to carry out. For example, they might start a project, such as planting seeds or building a Lego construction, both of which might require several days (or longer) to complete. Each day, an additional portion of the sequence is completed to reach a more distal goal (a more distal future state). In elementary and middle school, students write essays and complete science and social studies projects, and the steps involved are carried out over several days or weeks. In another planning situation, students receive a report card with low grades and then decide to change their study habits in order to improve their grades. This goal may need to be pursued over several months. In high school, students have to choose their own courses, keeping in mind distal goals such as college admission or vocational aspirations. All of these tasks and activities involve selecting goals for an altered future state and using temporally defined sequences to reach those goals.



Learning how to plan is embedded in school activities and expectations. As noted earlier in this chapter, students typically follow highly prescriptive plans as developed by teachers in their early school years. An important shift occurs in how teachers interact with students when they enter elementary school, occurring in fourth grade and later. Although learning goals are still selected by the teacher, students are given increasing responsibility for planning. This is a critical step in their development. Instead of just acquiring skills by rote (e.g., reading, spelling, math facts), they now have to apply them strategically in ways that allow for more complex learning. When first learning about how to plan their own educational activities, students are likely to need some explicit instruction. For example, when shifting from learning to read to reading to learn, students should receive instruction about how to read a chapter book strategically (reading strategy instruction). The same type of strategy instruction should take place when students shift from learning to print and spell to learning to write a composition. Strategy instruction teaches students to approach tasks in a planful manner by setting up sequences that contain some predictable steps. There may be several components to the steps, each of which may take hours or days to complete. To read strategically, students have to remember key information and may need to use strategies such as underlining or repeating the text, thereby ensuring good comprehension before attempting to answer comprehension questions. In writing, the student may need to follow the right sequence of steps, including researching, taking notes, writing a first draft, and writing a final draft. See Chapters 9 and 10 for a more detailed description.

In elementary school and higher grades, learning is no longer just about completing or following an adult-created plan. The adult now begins to help the student make her or his own plans. Teachers have to show students how to manage their homework assignments by showing them how to create a list, create a plan of action (sequence), and carry out the plan to reach the goal of finishing all of their homework. By middle school, students are expected to manage more complex tasks, such as a daily or weekly schedule with several teachers, a larger number of homework assignments, and larger and longer learning activities such as book reports and projects. All these learning activities require the student to make plans. They have to be broken down into its component steps. Those steps then have to be sequenced successfully in order to reach the goal.

As students age into middle school and high school, learning and personal goals both become more distal. Learning activities include many more steps and the goal takes longer to reach. It is no longer sufficient to develop a plan for one learning task at a time or to develop a plan for getting today's work done in time for tomorrow. As greater numbers of tasks and activities are included in the plan, and when the plan takes days or weeks to complete, the planning process becomes more complex. It requires the student to create subgoals, each of which may require its own plan and each of which may need to be carried out in the right order. Whereas one goal requires one carefully developed plan, multiple goals require multiple carefully developed plans that may need to be coordinated with one another. Examples might include purchasing or replacing broken hockey equipment and practicing in the rink for the next three weekends in anticipation of the tryouts for the team, making some telephone calls to friends to see what they are doing for transportation options, and speaking with one's boss at the bicycle repair shop to get the time off that's needed for the tryouts a month in advance. Another example might include setting up the weekly schedule to be sure that there is enough time to complete a project that is due the following Monday, planning to take time away from studying on the weekend in order to attend a friend's birthday party, and setting time aside to purchase a birthday gift. Each situation consists of more than one goal and may occur alongside independent (unrelated) plans or may require intermediate and dependent plans. To accomplish multiple goals such as the ones listed, students can no longer relying on planning or temporal sequencing skills alone. Rather, they now must use organizational skills.

***Organizational Skills*** Organizational skills are about the planning of plans. Recall that a plan only refers to the steps and the sequence needed to reach a goal. Organizational skills, in contrast, require students to plan goals. Each goal may consist of a plan. The plans may need to be coordinated with one another in a specific order, may require a plan to prevent mishaps or barriers, and need to take into consideration time constraints (efficiency). The result of good organizational skills is that a larger number of more distal goals (e.g., goals that might only be realized hours or days into the future) can all be reached successfully. The following sections illustrate these concepts and are synthesized from the references listed here: Friedman & Kofsky, 1997; Goswami, 1998; Haith, Benson, Roberts, & Pennington, 1994.



*Planning Against Mishaps: Coordinating Dependent Plans* One example of organizational skills is the skill of planning against mishaps. Mishaps can be expected or unexpected. For instance, in the prior example of a child who developed a subplan to address a mishap (a toy was broken and not available for dramatic play), the child created a new plan in the moment, solved the problem of the broken toy, and then continued with the original plan of engaging in dramatic play after repairing the toy. This example includes simple planning alone and would be typical for many or most children and youth. In contrast, a child with organizational skills would have prevented the mishap from occurring. By thinking ahead, the child might have said, "Tomorrow, I'm having a play date, and I'm going to need specific toys. I'd better make sure that I know how to find them, and that they are in good shape. I'll fix anything that's broken today, so that I can spend my time playing tomorrow." For most children and youth, the frequency and consistency of making contingency plans such as this are low. Most children and youth do not show organizational skills of this sort or would show them only if prompted or reminded.

*Coordinating Goals, Subgoals, and Nondependent Plans* In addition to coordinating dependent plans to ensure that distal goals are reached, being organized also requires coordinating plans that are not dependent on one another. For example, a student might have the goal of completing a book report and might have created steps in a plan for reaching this goal, such as research the topic, take notes, write initial draft, and write final draft. They might even have sequenced the plan, noting the hours that the public library is open and planning ahead for the upcoming holiday closure by taking out a necessary book before actually needing it. Accessing the library is an example of a dependent plan that includes its own set of steps, such as arranging for transportation and identifying the right book that needs to be checked out. The dependent plan needs to be carried out before the overall plan of writing a book report can be carried out. The goal of writing a book report has to be temporally coordinated with other activities. Because of the everyday demands of school, meals with the family, and recreational interests, only a few pockets of time remain in the schedule for working on the book report. Competing goals and competing plans can therefore interfere with the goal and plan of writing a book report. Careful consideration all the available times between the start and finish dates will be needed to reach all of the goal of writing the book report while also reaching other goals.

*Efficiency: Carrying Out Plans in the Least Amount of Time Possible* To be efficient and manage time effectively, students must identify all the goals that need to be met within a time interval (e.g., over the course of a day or week) and coordinate goals and subgoals so that enough time is dedicated to each of the plans needed to reach each of the goals. Organizational skills are easier for a student to master when all goals can be reached over a short time interval (e.g., a morning plan with several dependent plans including plans for potential mishaps) as opposed to goals that may need to be reached over the course of a few days or weeks. In elementary or middle school, a student might be able to plan a social event with a friend to occur later in the week and decide on the order of events within the social event. The students might be able to coordinate tasks of the day with one another and also in relation to the social event occurring later in the day. In high school, the student may be able to independently coordinate his or her school schedule with events that occur outside regular school hours and that all occur within a week or so. In these instances, students may need to prioritize, as well as coordinate plans with peers.



*How Organizational Skills Develop With Age* There are no norms for when children or adolescents develop organizational skills. Factors that influence a student's organizational skills depend on the student's level of enthusiasm for the activity, familiarity with the activity, and ability to understand and estimate the time needed for the activity. With these factors in mind, adults can make estimates about what to expect from children and youth. An elementary school student can be expected to reach a distal goal (e.g., by the end of the week), after she or he has been shown the sequence. The plan can be carried out over a day or several days and might need to be coordinated against competing goals, subgoals, and nondependent plans. For example, a student who wants to reach the goal of writing an essay may require adult prompting if he or she forgets to return to the initial goal.

A middle school–age student can be expected to modify previously learned plans related to schoolwork and apply them to similar learning demands in new contexts. The student may have developed a plan for writing an essay and use it to write different types of essays or apply those planning skills to completing a science project. That student may start to brainstorm with parents about how to organize competing plans related to the daily or weekly schedule. He or she can learn how to coordinate recreational interests or family obligations with writing the essay or completing the science project. In high school, increased demands can be placed on the student to organize her or his own schedule and solve problems such as prevention of mishaps, coordinating unrelated goals and subgoals with one another, and efficiency. However, many high school students and even young adults continue to need guidance and supervision from adults to prevent mishaps from interfering with important personal goals, to coordinate competing goals and their associated plans, and to carry out plans out efficiently.

***Metacognition*** The literature of metacognition, like the literature on executive skills, consists of varying definitions and interpretations of its scope. All the skills discussed in this chapter naturally lead to and support metacognition. *Metacognition* can be defined as thinking about one's own thinking. It is the act of thinking about one's goals, how to reach those goals, and how to change one's behaviors to reach goals successfully. Metacognition as related to executive skills depends on an understanding of goals, plans, and organization of plans. This chapter focuses on metacognition as it relates to executive skills specifically. Metacognition is also discussed in Chapter 8 on affect and self-regulation, because it is an important component of the overall phenomenon of behavioral self-regulation. It involves changing one's behaviors to suit environmental demands and reach personal goals successfully.

Metacognition refers to thinking about one's own thinking and about one's behaviors. It is part of the broader phenomenon, theory of mind (Flavell, 2004), which was discussed in Chapter 6. An influential definition of metacognition was proposed by Flavell in 1979, who defined *metacognition* as cognition about cognitive phenomena.

There is both a static and an active component to metacognition. Static or factual knowledge includes knowledge about what and how people think; about the goals, tasks, and activities that people undertake; and about the strategies that people use to reach goals or participate in tasks and activities. The word *people* includes the self. Metacognition also includes active monitoring of the above knowledge as it is applied in-the-moment to activities, tasks, and plans of the day. The active monitoring aspect of metacognition includes changing behaviors to suit current needs. Metacognition is both an activity and a skill.

Flavell (1979) identified four factors under the active part of metacognition:

- Monitoring one's knowledge as it gets applied to the activities of life
- Monitoring one's experiences (e.g., one's feelings) as the activities of life occur
- Monitoring what the goals, tasks, and activities of life are as they unfold
- Monitoring the strategies being used to carry out the activities of life

As highlighted throughout this chapter, the purpose of executive skills is for children and youth to be able to reach goals. Goals can be reached only if people actively change their behaviors in response to environmental barriers and demands. This requires using the knowledge and monitoring just described. Metacognition changes how people understand prior (static) knowledge, how they change behaviors to reach goals, and also how they change the goals that they initially chose to pursue (Donker, de Boer, Kostons, van Ewijk, & van der Werf, 2014). Other authors share similar and overlapping perspectives, and associate metacognition with the broader concept of self-regulation (Dinsmore, Alexander, & Loughlin, 2008; Fernandez-Duque et al., 2000; Follmer & Sperling, 2016). Only those aspects of metacognition that relate to executive skills are discussed in this chapter. Metacognition is defined in relation to externally imposed expectations or goals. The broader concept of self-regulation is discussed in Chapter 8. In that chapter the subject of metacognition is revisited in terms of a student's personal goals, beliefs, and standards.

*Metacognition and Performance Standards* Children do not have very secure metacognitive skills when they are young. They need adult support because they are not able to see their own performance and can fail to reach important goals. One early emerging metacognitive skill is that of error detection and error correction. It emerges in kindergarten or grade one when students learn about performance standards, and they start to judge their performance against external standards. They notice whether classroom rules are followed successfully. The learn from teacher feedback whether or not academic standards are reached. The metacognitive awareness of performance standards can be applied to any type of goal or activity: Completing classroom work, following classroom rules, or participating successfully in play activities.

The skill of metacognition can also be explained by considering the developmental shift that occurs in young children who at first do not have metacognition and then develop it. For example, preschool-age children typically do not hold themselves to specific goals or specific performance standards. They are content *not* to judge their work samples in the way described above. A preschool-age child may set out to draw a picture of a house and instead produces a picture that looks like a horse, proudly showing the drawing to a cherished adult, and perhaps even stating that they were intending to draw a horse all along. In contrast, the school-age child is no longer content merely to have produced a drawing of any sort and will become upset if the expected goal is not reached. This new behavior suggests not only that the child created his or her own goal but that the child also monitored whether the outcome was as expected. Not having met the expected outcome or the expected performance standard, the child regulates his or her behaviors differently from the preschooler and starts the process of drawing again.

Although able to set their own performance standards in some situations, school-age children use most of their metacognition to judge their performance against adult-imposed standards. Not until elementary school and higher grades do children become more consistent in generating their own goals and performance standards, and then regulating their performance in response to those standards. Judging one's performance against a performance standard is just one component of metacognition, albeit an important one. Without this ability, it is difficult to change behaviors to reach different types of goals, which in turn makes it harder to acquire new skills and to develop more new goals. In other words, the capacity for judging one's performance against a performance standard (an early emerging type of metacognition) is a critical skill that allows learners to continuously grow and expand their knowledge and their skills. The challenge for adults is how to make the experience of judgment a positive one, kindling the desire for more for mastery of more new skills and for developing new kinds of goals. The judgment should not result in the child feeling criticized and feeling incapable of meeting new performance standards or creating new goals.



*Comparing the Past With the Present* An important aspect of metacognition is its relationship with time. Metacognition involves a comparison of the past with the future. It allows the student to compare past goals, plans, and outcomes with those in the future. People constantly compare the past (prior knowledge) with the present (what is happening now) and then make a plan accordingly. For example, when a person encounters an unexpected behavior in a peer or colleague, the person has to consider their past observations or interactions, compare them with the current behavior, and then make a plan about how to socialize going forward. If the peer was friendly in the past but looked bored or indifferent today, it might require a change in expectations of behaviors going forward. This might result in a decision to consider a different social activity, or to consider socializing with someone else. Considering the past, observing the present, comparing against a future state or goal, making a plan, and then reviewing outcomes are critical aspects of metacognition. They pervade all human behaviors.

*Updating and Revising* Metacognition involves updating and revising. Knowledge obtained from the past (e.g., knowledge of rules, preestablished performance standards, prior behaviors in other people) all need to be updated over time. New situations and new environments require a reevaluation of previously acquired knowledge and previously acquired skills. This new information can be used to inspire new types of social activities or might result in finding new people with whom to socialize. Revising previous knowledge and skills applies as much to social skills as it does to anything else. Report-writing skills, research skills, the ability to master new content, and adaptive and recreational skills are but a few of the skills that one might consider here. By noticing and reflecting on what was learned, and by noticing how prior knowledge and prior skills meet (or fail to meet) the expectations of the current environment, the metacognitive thinker can adapt and change. By incorporating new knowledge and new skills, the metacognitive thinker can change how he or she responds to the world. Metacognition implies a continuous process of learning.

## PERFORMANCE DIFFICULTIES IN EXECUTIVE SKILLS

Executive skills affect most of a student's classroom participation and learning behaviors. A student's performance in executive skills can be gleaned by watching the student perform in variety of tasks and across settings. Very commonly, students with performance difficulties related to executive skills struggle with appropriate classroom behaviors, in areas such as listening attentively, following rules, staying on topic, following rules of classroom conduct. Difficulties with these particular behaviors are often a focus for intervention because they can be disruptive to the teacher and the class. However, students who have difficulties in these areas are likely to have challenges in other areas that also require executive skills. Difficulties can show up in social interactions, in doing homework, and in completing tasks and following rules at home. Students with difficulties in executive skills often do not follow instructions successfully because of forgetfulness. They may be sluggish in responding to task demands, or they may be rigid about how they go about tasks. They commonly fail to review their performance to detect and correct errors, further interfering with their ability to perform successfully. The behaviors may not occur consistently but occur often enough that they affect overall performance. The sections that follow offer more specific examples of how performance difficulties in executive skills can manifest in student behaviors.

### Performance Difficulties With Orientation/Initiation

Students with significant neurological impairments may lack the capacity for orientation. They may be unable to orient to the adult's voice or to sustain orientation to a stimulus. Without orientation there is no initiation, a prerequisite for participation. These students may need consistent supervision to orient successfully and may only participate with physical prompting. A more common example of lack of orientation (and accompanying lack of initiation) occurs when a student has the capacity to orient but fails to respond to an adult's instruction. For example, when an adult states that a student "doesn't listen," it is almost always because the student is not oriented to the adult's voice or instruction. By extension, the student is also not oriented toward the adult's goal. There are multiple reasons why students do not orient or initiate successfully. For instance, students who struggle with distractibility, difficulty shifting attention between tasks, and lack of motivation (see Chapter 8) may require adult support to orient and initiate. Educators should provide prompts or reminders to secure a student's orientation to task before making a judgment about the student's initiation to task or about the student's executive skills more generally.



### Performance Difficulties With Inhibition

Underdeveloped inhibition skills are one of the most common manifestations of difficulties in executive skills. The student with underdeveloped inhibition skills might have trouble inhibiting the desire to move about, instead of staying seated. Alternatively, the student may have difficulty staying in their seat and focusing on work because they are too distracted. They may struggle to follow classroom rules and fail to raise their hand before speaking or wait for their turn during a classroom discussion. These students might race to be at the front of the line before going outside, or not line up at all. Students who appear distracted and unfocused commonly have difficulty inhibiting external and internal distractors. Completing homework and ensuring that all materials are ready and available in classroom work are often areas of significant difficulty for students with underdeveloped inhibition skills. They often forget what they are supposed to bring to class and forget to hand in their work, even if it is already completed. Students with performance difficulties in this area may seem not to learn from extra instruction about the rules and plans that they are supposed to follow. They can recite all the rules of the classroom and of social interactions and can even recite the strategies that they are supposed to use to ensure those rules are followed. Yet they often are not able to follow those rules or implement the strategies successfully. Often the students themselves notice the discrepancy between their (secure) knowledge of rules and strategies and their (very insecure) performance. And yet they are unable to explain their repeated performance difficulties. While this kind of student behavior may cause frustration for classroom educators, it is important to consider the frustration that these students experience themselves. At times mystified by their own performance difficulties and often frustrated by a constant stream of corrective feedback from others, these students can show acting-out behaviors and feel socially stigmatized.

## Performance Difficulties With Shifting Cognitive Set

***Transitions*** Students with difficulty shifting cognitive set may appear sluggish or inefficient and may shift between activities more slowly than other students. Whereas other students might transition to a new task or activity within 10–15 seconds, the student with a disability may get stuck and might need one or several minutes to transition. The student may say, "Wait a minute," or "I just need to finish . . ." Even with extended time, the student may work slowly.



***Defiance, Oppositional Behaviors, and Emotional Outbursts*** Students with difficulty shifting cognitive set can present as defiant and oppositional. They may have tantrums and use colorful language as they express their frustration. When faced with an interruption (such as a transition) or an unexpected demand (such as a change in routine or a new task or activity), the student may become resistant and upset. Many students who show defiant and oppositional behaviors are actually compliant and cooperative much of the time, and the transient nature of the defiance is overlooked by the adult. The students' expression of frustration is misunderstood as a refusal to comply, when in fact, they just need more time to organize their thoughts and manage their emotional reaction.

***Shifting Between What Is Familiar and What Is Not Familiar*** Students with difficulty shifting cognitive set can also show the above behaviors when faced with changes in their routines or when asked to approach a task or activity differently from what they were expecting. When unsure about what the (new) plan might be, they are likely to insist on carrying out the plan in a familiar or preferred way. Although this behavior might occur more commonly when adults place demands on the student, it can also occur during interactions with peers. If not allowed to carry out their preferred or familiar plan, children with set-shifting difficulty can become rigid, oppositional, and/or angry. As noted above, it is important to notice that underneath the frustration lies a child who is not able to perform as efficiently, quickly, or smoothly as their peers. Some students who are rigid and inflexible have a coexistent autism spectrum disorder. However, rigidity and lack of flexibility are not limited to children on the autism spectrum. They can also occur in children with disruptive behavior disorders and with developmental delays.

***Repetitive/Perseverative Behaviors*** Students with difficulty shifting cognitive set may show a preference for activities that are repetitive. They may always seem to want to discuss or learn about the same topic of interest. Some may appear socially unaware, not noticing feedback from adults or peers that would otherwise indicate the need to shift to a new topic, because they are stuck in their preferred interests and activities. The set-shifting difficulty can manifest as a problem in social cognition and often occurs in students with autism spectrum disorder.

### Performance Difficulties With Working Memory

Working memory problems commonly co-occur with the performance difficulties discussed above. Distractibility and showing difficulty shifting between tasks are commonly associated with forgetfulness and difficulties with working memory. For example, remembering to bring materials for homework between home and school requires working memory to remember what those items are. Distracted students who also have underdeveloped working memory would be likely to have difficulties with tasks such as this. Working memory difficulties can also interfere with a variety of other daily routines, such as remembering all the steps involved in getting dressed and ready for school in the morning. Working memory skills appear to be especially important in math and may be evident in classroom work that requires remembering important information in active memory (Van den Bos, van de Ven, Kroesbergen, & van Luit, 2013). This topic will be revisited in Chapter 11.

### Performance Difficulties With Planning and Organizational Skills

Basic executive skills need to be in place for planning and organizational skills to emerge. Only rarely do students have difficulty in planning and organizational skills without also having difficulties in the basic executive skills discussed in this chapter (McCormack & Atance, 2011). Some students have difficulty ordering the steps needed to reach a goal, a sign of temporal sequencing difficulties. Lack of time awareness is especially interfering with organizational skills. These students may understand the sequence but lose track of time and end up not reaching important goals for this reason. Some plans need to take time constraints into consideration, especially when the plan has to be carried out alongside other daily or weekly goals and plans. Larger academic tasks, such as writing an essay or doing a science project, may be especially difficult for students who have difficulty understanding the passage of time, are unable to sequence steps into a plan, and are unable to coordinate plans with one another. The longer the time interval between setting and reaching the goal, the more difficulty the student is likely to have.



### Performance Difficulties With Metacognition

Most students with performance difficulties related to executive skills will have performance difficulties in metacognition. Adults typically have to help students judge their performance against the performance standard and detect errors in their performance. Without adult supports or reminders, students with underdeveloped executive skills typically fail to review their performance to detect and correct errors and are also less likely to generate a goal for improving performance in the future. Learning from the past, comparing with the present, and preparing for the future can still occur. However, the capacity to change behaviors in response to past events is reduced when metacognition is not used in a systematic or consistent manner.

## HOW TO SET UP AN OBSERVATION

It is sometimes better *not* to set up a formal observation to learn about a student's executive skills. A structured observation, such as the ones presented in prior chapters, can sometimes interfere with making good observations of a student's executive skills. This is because specific activities, as planned and monitored by the adult, often provide the student with some of the executive support that the student is not able to access on his or her own. Sometimes the presence of the adult provides executive supports by making students more self-conscious and therefore more aware of their current behaviors. Metacognition increases in the presence of the adult. See Box 7.4 for additional information about the challenges inherent in making good observations of executive skills.

### BOX 7.4. Making Observations of Executive Skills: Why Measures of Executive Skills Do Not Always Tell You What You Need to Know

Although executive skills can be measured in testing situations, it is difficult to use controlled testing conditions to get a good understanding of a student's executive skills in everyday life. The following sections provide information about the limitations of tests of executive skills and highlights the importance of making observations of students outside of testing situations.

**Task Impurity**

One important limitation in tests of executive skills is that imposed by task impurity (Burgess, 1997). No single test of executive skills is a pure test of executive skills, because there is no way to measure executive skills in isolation. All tests of executive skills measure other types of cognitive activities at the same time. Executive skills are implicated equally during speaking and listening (language) tasks, writing and reading tasks, social activities, playing soccer, or moving pegs about on a board. The way to identify a student's performance in executive skills is to notice the same or similar performance difficulties across a range of tasks. For example, if a student gets distracted or is forgetful and does not follow plans successfully across a variety of activities, the observer can likely attribute the student's performance difficulties to underdeveloped executive skills as opposed to performance difficulties in the specific task being observed.

**Structure of the Testing Situation**

The second limitation of measures of executive functions or executive skills is that the testing situation itself offers executive supports to the student by providing a plan for the student to follow. Testing situations structure participation and typically occur over short time intervals. They are not able to capture day-to-day variations that can affect a student's performance in real-time situations.

**Ecological Factors That Influence Executive Skills**

When a student passes or fails a measure of executive skills in a formal testing situation, it is hard to know how that performance will map on to activities that are different from the one being tested (Burgess, Alderman, & Forbes, 2006). A student's difficulties with executive skills are likely to be much more apparent in unstructured settings and outside of testing situations (Suchy, 2009), which is referred to as a problem of ecological validity. What is most important to know is whether the student's performance in the testing situation helps to predict the student's performance in everyday settings and situations, and how the student is likely to perform when faced with different types of cognitive demands and different levels of adult support. Differences in the student's level of motivation across tasks are equally important to consider (Anderson & Reidy, 2012).

**Behavioral Rating Scales and Executive Skills**

Behavioral rating scales have been developed to circumvent the ecological validity problem detailed above. Behavioral rating scales allow for a measure of the student's performance in different types of activities over time (Mahone & Scheider, 2012) and can be used to augment one's understanding of the student's performance when using a standardized measure in a formal test situation. Importantly, a student's performance as assessed by behavioral rating scales usually does not correlate very closely with the performance as assessed by a standardized measure (Burgess, Alderman, Evans, Hazel, & Wilson, 1998). The lack of correlation may be related to the difference in the degree of structure provided by each of the measures or may be related to differences in what each instrument measures (Toplak, West, & Stanovich, 2013). A student's performance in executive skills can be understood only if the student's performance is analyzed over time and across different types of tasks and activities. Neither a formal measure of executive skills in a testing situation nor the results of a behavioral rating scale helps the observer draw firm conclusions about the student's executive performance in everyday settings. To get an accurate assessment of a student's executive skills, it is always best to do all three types of measures: Standardized measures, behavioral rating scales, and real-time observations in everyday settings.

## Preliminary Considerations

Instead of setting up a specific task for the student, observations of executive skills should be conducted while the student is engaged in everyday classroom activities, especially those that are not too closely supervised. Fruitful times for observation include tasks and activities that require a sustained attention span. Any desktop work, such as completing worksheets, reading independently, responding to reading comprehension questions, and writing an essay, can serve as an opportunity for observations. Completing daily routines, such as keeping one's belongings tidy or performing routines for entering or leaving the classroom, are a second source of activities to use in the observation. A third set of activities includes peer interactions, either during peer-mediated learning or during social activities with peers. Observers should collect information from all three types of activities on an ongoing basis, rather than during a single lesson or day. Appendix 7.2, the Executive Skills Observation Sheet, can be used as a tool for capturing these data over time.

When conducting observations, professionals should take into consideration the executive demands of the task, as well as the student's motivation to perform. Desktop activities, especially reading and writing at the text level, place substantial demands on the student's working memory and planning skills. However, before drawing too many conclusions about the student's executive skills, the observer also needs to take into consideration the phonics and language demands of reading and writing. Difficulties with phonics or language are very likely to interfere with a student's attention span and ability to complete the task successfully. Classroom routines do not place as extensive demands on the student's cognitive skills or planning skills but do require the basic executive skills of inhibition and working memory. Social activities can lie somewhere in between. Simply following a conversation may not require a lot of working memory or planning (it depends on the conversation), while playing a game of soccer is much more taxing on both.

A challenge often encountered in making observations of executive skills can vary from one day to the next and from one activity to the next. The level of motivation for the activity can affect the student's performance. A higher level of motivation can sometimes mask difficulties with executive skills. In contrast, intense emotions regardless of type (frustration, anxiety, or excitement) tend to reduce already fragile inhibition and working memory skills and can amplify the student's difficulties. The student's level of alertness and the degree of support provided by the environment also influence a student's performance in executive skills. To discover difficulties with executive skills, the observer may need to look for trends or patterns that emerge over the course of days to weeks. When reviewing the student's performance, it may be difficult to arrive at a definitive answer about the student's inhibition, working memory, or planning skills. It can be helpful to consider making observations using Likert scales. For example, the observer can rate the student as reaching a goal "rarely," "not usually," "sometimes," "usually," or "often." The observer can also use a numeric scale to rate distractibility or on-task behaviors. By using rating scales repeatedly, it can be easier to establish behavioral trends, thus improving the chances of making a good interpretation of the behaviors.

Another way of estimating whether executive skills are developing as expected is to take measures of a student's attention span. For example, the observer can document how long the student is able to participate productively in an activity or task. It makes a big difference if the answer is 1–2 minutes, as opposed to 20–30 minutes. The student's attention span might vary by task. Some students may have difficulty accessing their executive skills during independent learning but can perform successfully during whole-classroom learning or during peer-mediated learning. Observers will need to use judgment about any measure of the student's attention span and take into account the nature of the activity and the student's level of motivation. Multiple measures of attention span across tasks and on different days can be helpful, especially when the observations are compared against an age-matched group of typically developing peers.

A thoughtful observer can help ensure that the student's difficulties are not related to other developmental domains. For example, if a student does not listen, he or she may not be oriented to task, may have difficulty inhibiting distractors, or may have difficulty remembering instructions (working memory). However, that student may also have difficulties in hearing or in language skills. For any given behavior, and for any given observation, the observer has to decide whether the behavior (or its absence) is due to underdeveloped executive skills or another cause. When informed by multiple observations, over time and across different activities, the interpretation is more likely to be accurate.

## Select the Student



To set up the observation, school professionals should first identify a student whose executive skills they wish to analyze. The student's report card should be reviewed, as it likely will highlight classroom performance difficulties. Very often, classroom participation behaviors such as listening attentively, following classroom rules of conduct, working independently, and others will be below grade expectations.

## Make Observations

Observers should conduct 5- to 10-minute observations for whole-class learning, peer-mediated learning, independent learning, daily routines, and socializing with peers. Observations should occur in different settings and on different days. For students who are already very familiar to the observer, a careful history of the student's past performance across activities, settings, and time may be sufficient and could negate the need for a new observation. The observer could instead provide a description based on prior observations that have occurred naturally over time. Ideally, a specific observation using the structure proposed below would be included along with the information gathered from prior observations. Observers can consider the following questions and recommendations in setting up their observation.

***Observations for Orientation and Initiation*** The observer should consider whether the student orients and initiates to tasks quickly or slowly. Determine whether the student typically needs an extra prompt or reminder from the teacher before orienting to a task.

***Observations for Inhibition*** To assess inhibition, the observer can note how successfully the student follows classroom rules. The student should be able to raise her or his hand before speaking and not blurt out answers. The student should be able to remain seated for a reasonable or appropriate amount of time. Find out whether the student is able to follow multiple-step instructions. Does the student start a task, but then becomes distracted and off task? Initiating successfully and then getting distracted is evidence of poor inhibition skills. Equally important, the observer should record how long the student can sustain her or his attention. Attention span should be assessed during independent work, peer-mediated activities, routines of the day, and social activities. The attention span might vary, depending on the activity. Document whether the student's attention span is usually 1–5 minutes as opposed to 15–30 minutes. Make a note of differences in the student's attention span as compared with her or his peers. Make a note of differences in the student's attention span across activities or settings.

***Observations for Shifting Cognitive Set*** The student who has difficulty shifting cognitive set can show more than one type of behavior. They might be sluggish in transitions, such as between learning and recess or lunch, or when transitioning from peer-mediated learning to independent learning. The student may also be sluggish in shifting from one independent learning task to the next. Sluggishness may show up as taking excessive time during transitions but can also show up as excess frustration and intense emotional outbursts. Other students with difficulty shifting cognitive set may show frustration when routines are changed. They may wish to complete daily routines, social interactions, or learning tasks the same way each time. They may exhibit repetitive behaviors or be overly perseverative (e.g., the student might talk about the same topic incessantly and have difficulty taking turns in a conversation).

***Observations for Working Memory*** Multiple-step instructions are common in a classroom setting and are a common challenge for students with underdeveloped working memory. When faced with a multiple-step instruction, monitor whether the student seems confused or cannot remember the steps. Some students with working memory difficulty will remember the first or the last step of the instruction, whereas others may forget what they were supposed to do because they got distracted. If the student gets distracted along the way, the observer could intervene and ask, "Do you remember what the task is that you're supposed to complete? Do you remember which steps you've done, and which ones you still have to do?" The student's responses will give an indication of how well he or she remembered the steps of the routine. Multiple observations of this sort may be needed before it is clear whether the student's difficulty is related to underdeveloped working memory or to another factor such as gaps in the language or comprehension skills.

***Observations for Planning Skills*** Many tasks at the elementary school level or higher require some planning, though play activities in younger children may include some planning. The teacher might assign a planning task by asking the student to prepare a longer project such as a book report or essay. The observer should identify whether the student is able to initiate the task and follow instructions that are intended to be carried out over the course of days. The student should know all the steps of the plan and their sequence. The observer could ask the student, "Can you tell me about the plan for your goal? What are the steps? Which step are you doing now? Which steps do you still have to complete?" Alternatively, the observer could also watch how the student performs in social activities, such as engaging in imaginary play or making up a game. Students with underdeveloped planning skills sometimes need their peers to follow their plan, without which they can become confused. At times, they can be perceived as rigid or too dictatorial with their peers, because they are so insistent about everybody following their play preferences. These behaviors can be due to difficulty shifting cognitive set, but they can also be due to underdeveloped planning skills.

***Observations for Metacognition*** If it becomes clear that the student is not performing successfully, the observer can assess metacognition by gently interrupting the student and asking the student questions such as, "What are you currently working toward? What is the goal? How are you going to know if you've reached the goal? How far along are you in reaching the goal?" The observer may discover that the student is confused about the goal, about the steps needed to reach the goal, and/or about the order of the steps needed to reach the goal. These questions can help determine whether the student is able to compare the past (the goal and the plan to reach the goal) and her or his performance in the present (how close or how far the student is from reaching the goal). Another way to assess metacognition is to ask the student to detect and correct errors. For example, the observer can ask the student, "Before you show your work to the teacher, how will you know that you did the job successfully? How will you know whether there are any mistakes? What would a mistake look like? What should you do if you find a mistake?"

Mishaps and surprises can also be a way to learn about metacognition. The observer can create a mishap or problem by introducing a change in the schedule or by introducing a visitor to the room. For the mishap, the observer can then ask the student, "What are you supposed to do? How are you going to get your work done?" The observer could ask the student: "Can you tell the visitor about our schedule? Can you tell the visitor what we are doing right now?" The student's responses will provide some information about understanding routine expectations, performance standards, and how to compare one's performance against the standard. Be sure to take into consideration the student's level of comfort and rapport with the adult. If the student is anxious about speaking with an unfamiliar adult, he or she is less likely to give successful responses. Other examples of metacognition, such as learning to respond to new situations in new ways, cannot be assessed through a single observation and would require multiple observations over time.

## Analyze and Interpret the Observations



After completing multiple observations, the observer can review the results and identify specific executive skills that may be underdeveloped. In order to analyze comprehensively, observers should take into consideration all of the terms discussed in this chapter. The point of the analysis is to identify those areas that are challenging for the student. It will not always be possible to identify the student's performance difficulties in each of the skills listed in the Executive Skills Framework. As discussed in this chapter, executive skills are highly interrelated. Inhibition, shifting cognitive set, and working memory are interrelated and all of them influence and affect planning, organization, and metacognition. The main purpose of the hierarchy and of the observations is to be able to describe behaviors consistently, develop interventions, and monitor progress. The observer can cluster observations together into groups that reflect the framework: Difficulties with orientation and initiation, difficulties with inhibition, difficulties with shifting cognitive set, and so forth. In most cases, it should be possible to identify accurately whether there are problems with basic executive skills, advanced executive skills, or both.

## Discuss Findings With Colleagues

After analyzing the observations, the observer can discuss the observations with colleagues and find out whether other members of the team have noticed similar behaviors in that student. If they have, the observer can be more confident that the student shows difficulties in executive skills. Alternatively, it may come to light that the student's performance is very good in settings where no formal observations were made. When discrepancies occur, the group should discuss why the student sometimes performs better in some activities or settings than in others. Any patterns of successful performance are important to identify because that knowledge can be used to improve the student's performance in settings in which he or she is less successful.

The IEP Builder flows naturally from the discussion above. Using the framework, the IEP Builder categorizes educational objectives, strategies, and accommodations into a logical hierarchy that can be used for a variety of students.

## General Comments About Teaching Executive Skills

After the observation, summarize which executive skills are the most affected in the student. Inhibition skills, shifting cognitive set, and working memory skills are the most likely targets for intervention and instruction. Gaps in these areas tend to show up early in a student's school career and affect performance in all of the higher order or second-order executive skills (planning, organization, and metacognition). Educators and therapists should focus on basic skills before making attempts to teach planning and organizational skills. Metacognition is a useful skill to teach regardless of the task or activity.

As a general rule, students with difficulties with executive skills perform better when provided with a well-defined plan and individualized attention that reinforces the plan. The teacher needs to make sure that the instructions are explicit and are understood by the student and that the student can recite the instructions back to the adult. All students with difficulties with executive skills benefit from a visual summary or graphic organizer of the plan. This helps them when they need to refer to the instructions because they lost track of the next steps needed to complete the task or activity. The visual plan can be a list of typed or written instructions. The visual plan can also consist of photos or pictures that help the student understand the task expectations and can serve as a reminder of what needs to get done. These strategies apply across all types of activities: Independent learning, peer-mediated learning, and whole-group instruction; daily routines that are over-rehearsed and over-learned; and novel tasks that are unfamiliar. Even social activities can be discussed and planned in advance, for students whose social skills are affected by underdeveloped executive skills.

Educators should choose student-friendly terms to explain their choice of educational objectives or what accommodations are being offered for. Phrases such as "staying focused," "waiting your turn," and "following the rules" are all related to inhibition and impulse control. A phrase such as "remember the steps" is related to working memory. Phrases such as "changing activities more quickly," "trying out a new way," and "doing it the old way and doing it the new way" are related to shifting cognitive set. Some students may be ready to learn about the terms presented in this chapter, whereas other students will need the terms simplified and modified to suit the situation. When assessing the student's responsiveness to instruction, be sure that the student is oriented and has initiated the plan as discussed.

Teaching and learning executive skills can be frustrating for both adults and students, especially when there is not a specific block of time dedicated to doing so. It takes just as much thoughtfulness, planning, practice, and time to teach executive skills as it does to teach soccer, reading, or a science module. It is also just as important to take into consideration the developmental hierarchy proposed in this chapter. Just as learning to read full-length text requires the more basic skill of decoding words and learning to read fluently, improving one's executive skills also requires mastering basic skills before moving on to advanced skills. It is very important to help students master inhibition, shifting cognitive set, and working memory skills before asking them to learn about planning and organization. For students who cannot make rapid enough progress in these areas, the focus may need to be on teaching them how to make use of accommodations. Executive skills are not developed at a single point in time. They should be taught frequently over extended time intervals. They should first be taught by using preestablished plans and by providing substantial monitoring. Only when basic skills are in place should students be expected to master advanced executive skills.

## Educational Objectives for Executive Skills

In the examples of educational objectives that follow, the reader will discover how accommodations are used in the service of working toward educational objectives. Here, accommodations are defined as strategies that teaching staff can use to help the student circumvent executive skills difficulties. Teacher accommodations commonly manifest as more teacher supervision and support. At times, teachers may also modify tasks so that students can participate successfully. Accommodations are appropriate to offer to the student, however, no student wishes to be dependent on the support of a teacher over the long term. The focus of the student's education should be on building executive skills and independence.

### *Educational Objectives and Strategies for Teaching Orientation/Initiation to Task*

Adults often need to orient students to task and ensure that they initiate tasks. This might manifest as the teacher saying, "Please look at me!" before making a request. Visual and auditory stimuli, such as ringing a bell, clapping hands, turning the lights off and then on, or touching the student can also help. Educators may need to follow through by observing the student's eye gaze to see whether they are oriented to the desired task or activity. It may also be helpful to ask the student to recite back a set of instructions in order to verify whether they are oriented to task. Do not be surprised if even highly intelligent students need this degree of prompting and orienting! Many students are oriented elsewhere and "off in their own world" when their teacher needs them to initiate a task. Orientation and initiation are often very dependent on adult prompting. Practitioners can measure progress by documenting the frequency of prompting needed for the student to orient and initiate successfully. Practitioners can assess whether or not the frequency of adult support goes down, or if the type of adult support can shift from touch to a verbal prompt, or from an explicit verbal prompt to a nonspecific visual prompt.



### *Educational Objectives and Strategies for Teaching or Improving Shifting Cognitive Set*

When teaching a student to shift cognitive set more flexibly, educators and other school professionals have to carefully consider what type of set-shifting behavior will be targeted and how to measure progress. Some students need help with managing transitions between activities. Some students need help tolerating interruptions and reducing their level of expressed emotion, while others need help shifting away from preferred interests and reducing repetitive behaviors. By making observations over time and in response to instruction, educators can adjust their expectations to match the student's abilities. As demonstrated in the examples that follow, school professionals should discuss set-shifting with the student and create a plan to assist them build cognitive flexibility. The suggestions that follow are paired with sample dialogue or scripts.

*Repetitive Behaviors* An educational objective for the student with repetitive behaviors or perseverative interests might be to constrain the amount of time they spend engaged in repetitive behaviors or to constrain where these behaviors are allowed to occur and at what time. A teacher might say, "I know it's important for you to spend some time on your special interest. I'm going to show you when it's allowed, and when you have to do something else. Let's set up a schedule. If you know when you are allowed to do your preferred behavior, it won't bother you so much when I tell you that it's not the right time."

*Transitions* An educational objective for the student who transitions too sluggishly might be to transition more quickly or smoothly. A first step is to increase the student's awareness of the demand. When setting up the teaching plan with the student, educators should share their expectations with the student. A teacher might say, "Most kids I know don't like it when adults interrupt them. But, there are a lot of things to get done each day! Let me know how I should interrupt you. I can give you a reminder using words, or I can write it down. I can also remind you to look at your schedule. What do you think would work best?"

The teacher might later say, "What I've noticed is that, each time I interrupt you, you always get back to task. Sometimes you need a lot more time than the other students, sometimes you only need a little bit of time. I think that if we practice this together, you're going to get better at this."

Once the student has shown greater understanding of the concept of transitions, the teacher can use some of the strategies that were generated during the prior conversations. During actual interruptions, the teacher can use an indirect prompt: "Look at your schedule and tell me what's next" or "Please look at me. It's time to use your shifting skills. What do you have to shift to now? Tell me your plan." After the interruption, the educator should notice it with the student, acknowledging, "Thanks, now I can see that you are transitioning/shifting. Okay, it took you 30 seconds to shift that time. Let's keep that number in mind." The student with very limited language skills might benefit from a visual acknowledgment of the transition, such as a picture of a smiling face.

Some students protest at times of transition. They may have a tantrum or burst out by saying, "No! I don't want to!" Some students even use inappropriate language and they can be perceived as disrespectful. It is very tempting to try and reduce or control the student's level of expressed emotion and try to teach the student more respectful behaviors. However, even if a protest occurs, educators may at first want to avoid focusing on the protest. Instead of saying, "I need you to calm down," the educator could say nothing at all and simply wait an extra 30–60 seconds. Very often, no response to the emotional behavior actually ends up improving the student's performance the most, because the teacher's nonresponse allows the student to think about what he or she needs to do next. Commonly, the student does follow through on the instruction, even if it takes some time. When the student follows through on the instruction, the teacher can notice the student's success, and say something like: "Great; I can see that you are now moving to the next step." Alternatively, the teacher can withhold comments until later by saying, "Earlier this morning, you said you were not going to do as I asked, but I noticed that when I said nothing, you did follow my instruction. I'm glad about that." The teacher could even go further by saying: "I'm going to keep noticing how long it takes you to follow classroom instructions. I'm pretty sure if we both put our heads together, you'll get better at this." If the frustration persists at the time of the transition and if the student never moves to the next task, the option to intervene with other strategies still exists. Some of these other options are discussed in Chapter 8.

*Changing Plans and Being More Flexible* Most students like to be in charge of their own plan. This may be especially true for students who are rigid and insist upon predictability and routines. However, most students will follow a plan willingly if they understand it. Even those students who appear to be inflexible and rigid can accept changes in a plan, when it is discussed in advance and when they know what to expect. An objective for students such as this might be for them to accept new plans more often or more quickly. One such script might be the following: "I know you like to do things the same way, but I think you won't mind doing things a new way as long as you know how to do it. Let me show you how it works." The same strategy can apply during the student's social interactions. Some students who are inflexible can have difficulty socializing with peers. They would like to socialize, but they always want to dictate what the play activity will be. For these situations, an educational objective could be to become more flexible in social situations. The adult could say to the student, "I know that you really like playing your favorite game, but now your friends want to play something else. I have an idea. Let's talk with your friends and figure out what the plan is. If you know what the plan is, you'll be able to play with your friends and have fun." Peers can be coached to assist the student with set-shifting challenges by setting up their own planning meetings. An educator might coach peers as follows: "Hey everybody, I have an idea. Your friend wants to play with you, but he might need to know what you're going to do before you do it. Why don't you discuss the plan first? I think it will make it work better for everybody." If the peers need more guidance, the adult can say, "Why don't you all create a plan together? Each person chooses an activity, and then you'll decide who goes first, who goes second, and who goes third." By making repeated observations over time, adults can monitor how often the student responds successfully to an adult prompt to be flexible, how often the student responds to an adult nonverbal prompt that is less direct, how often the student responds to prompts from peers, and how often the student becomes flexible without any prompting.

*Measuring Progress in Shifting Cognitive Set* Educators can measure progress by measuring how quickly students transition to new activities or how much frustration they show about the transition.

***Educational Objectives and Strategies for Teaching Inhibition Skills*** Most students who struggle with inhibition are not able to inhibit distractors. Their distractibility occurs so quickly and spontaneously that they are often left puzzled about their performance failures. Educators should approach instruction with an empathic understanding of the student's dilemma and should share that understanding with the student. For example, a teacher could develop a shared understanding of distractibility with the student, by saying, "I have been paying attention to you, and I think I figured something out. You know what you need to do, but some of the time, things still don't get done. Have you noticed that too?" Then, the teacher might add, "I want to make sure that you get everything done, and I want to make sure that you don't have to listen to my reminders. Here are some ideas that I want to share with you." To select specific behaviors for teaching inhibition, consider the hierarchy presented in the section dedicated to the definition of terms. The two examples provided in the section that follows pertain to following classroom rules and routines and sustaining attention span.



*Following Rules of Conduct and Completing Routines* Most students having difficulty with inhibition skills will fail to inhibit distractors. Because they get distracted so often, they either are not oriented to task or become distracted from the task. The challenge for school professionals is that inhibition skills cannot be easily taught. Inhibition skills develop only very slowly in some students, and are difficult to enhance or improve through behavioral or educational interventions. This is especially true in children and youth with ADHD. It is important to frame the educational objectives correctly. The main educational objective here is to teach the student to use compensatory strategies. For example, instead of making it the goal to stay on task or follow all rules, the educator could instead make it the goal to get tasks done while using accommodations for distractions or follow the rules and use a repair strategy when the rule gets broken. The teacher helps the student to notice when they were distracted or when they acted before thinking. For example, a teacher could say, "I want to make sure that you are able to get tasks done and follow rules more consistently. It's going to mean thinking before acting and making good choices. But here's the catch: I'm pretty sure that you are going to get distracted later today, and not get something done. I'm pretty sure that you are going to break the rules that we're working on. It's called acting before thinking. You might even do it later today! Don't worry. We can develop a plan for that too." The goal of the teacher is to enhance metacognitive awareness of the inhibition failures. Failure to inhibit should also be reframed as an opportunity for learning. For example, the teacher could say, "If you find that all of a sudden, without thinking, you did something that you shouldn't have done, you can always go back and make up for your mistake." Educators may need to create a prior agreement with the student about how and when a gentle reminder will be provided. "Let's decide how I should help you, because you aren't always going to notice it when you are acting before thinking. I know that you don't want me to single you out in front of the class. So why don't we come up with a silent signal like touching my ear, that I can use to remind you to 'Stop, think, and then act.' What would work for you?" One way to measure progress is to assess how well the student follows classroom rules and completes routines successfully. Progress can also be measured by tracking how often the student self-corrects after failing to follow a rule or complete a routine successfully.

The practitioner can also assess whether or not the student needs fewer prompts, or less explicit prompting to self-correct.

*Improving Attention Span* To help students focus for longer periods, educators can begin by reducing expectations for focus. For example, a teacher might use a timer to help the student understand how long he or she normally stays on task and over time ask the student to focus just a little bit longer. While it is a good idea to keep increasing expectations, it may only be possible for the student to make small gains over the course of the school year. As discussed in the section above, for most students, it is very challenging to improve attention to task if the performance difficulty is due to a neurological condition such as ADHD. That said, it is still important to help the student notice and understand what distractibility means and how it manifests in the student's own behaviors. Even more important, adults need to help the student notice when inhibition skills are working successfully. "Wow, I noticed that you focused on that work task for 15 minutes," or "I noticed that you followed the rules of the classroom routine really well just now." The adult's positive feedback is especially important right at the moment when the student is being successful. In conjunction with the student, the teacher should set up a plan for providing both corrective and positive feedback. It is very important for the student to recognize success and know what it feels like and looks like when they are being successful. Many adults do not provide positive feedback to children and youth for expectations that they believe the student should have been able to meet a long time ago. School professionals should make efforts to catch the student being successful, as it can be a highly effective method of instruction support.



*Measuring Progress in Inhibition* When a student has underdeveloped inhibition skills, it can be difficult to measure progress. Instead of measuring progress in the skill of inhibition, adults may need to measure progress in other ways. For example, one way to gauge progress is to measure whether the student is able to notice her or his own errors and correct those errors (error detection and error correction). Another way to measure progress is to assess the degree of adult supports required (physical, verbal, nonverbal, directive, or indirect). Using different levels of support, students can develop the skill or habit of reviewing their work or their social performance and correcting errors. Over time, the level of support should decrease.

### *Educational Objectives and Strategies for Teaching and Improving Working Memory Skills*

*Visual Reminder Systems* Most students with executive dysfunctions have difficulty remembering all the steps of a task and can make errors because they forget one or more steps. It is a common outcome for the adult to then step in on behalf of the student, check the student's performance, and provide reminders or corrective feedback. Most students do not appreciate the volume of corrective feedback that they normally receive. What the adult can do instead is provide the student with a visual reminder of the component steps and instructions. The visual reminder can be a set of photographs or pictures, placed in the right order, or a written task list. A highly effective teacher of executive skills in the lead author's community suggests using photos for the student, as a reminder of what needs to get done (S. Ward, personal communication, March 2010). The photo might be of a backpack that contains all the items needed for school, a picture of the desk when it is tidy, or a picture of the student who is dressed and ready to carry all the items needed to go home. The student uses the photos as a visual tool to check and make sure that the task is completed successfully.

When a visual reminder system is first introduced, it is common for students to perform more successfully for 3 or 4 days but then revert to their prior behaviors after the novelty of the strategy disappears. When this happens, educators need to resist the temptation to revert to using corrective (verbal) feedback. Verbal or corrective feedback is very labor intensive for the adult. Adults should instead use their verbal reminders to prompt the student to use the visual reminder system by saying: "Check your reminder system," or "Wait; I think you missed something." Or, "Hmm. That didn't work out. Did you forget anything?" Then, the teacher should encourage the student to check the list, saying, "Take a look at the list. I think I know what you missed. Can you figure it out?" The teacher can also not provide any prompt to use the list, allowing the student to prompt themselves to do so. The teacher's puzzled or quizzical look might be sufficient as a reminder. Once the student can perform successfully with visual reminder systems in place, photos can be eliminated or written task lists can be removed over time to encourage more independent functioning. For other students, long-term independent use of a visual prompting system might be the right goal.

*Measuring Progress in Working Memory Skills* Measuring progress in working memory skills can be accomplished by monitoring how often the student uses his or her own reminder system with prompting, without prompting, and/or completes tasks successfully without use of the visual reminder system at all.

***Educational Objectives and Strategies for Teaching Planning*** All the suggestions listed thus far do not teach independent planning skills. The adult dictates the plan and helps the student carry out the plan successfully. After the student has had some experience completing adult-created plans successfully, the focus of instruction should turn to independent planning. Instruction in planning is not likely to be effective until the student has practiced the basic executive skills of inhibition, shifting cognitive set, and working memory. Practice in these areas, including the use of strategies designed to circumvent performance difficulties, should all be in place before the teacher undertakes instruction in planning.



A simple planning exercise might be for the teacher to teach a task that relies on a straightforward sequence. One way to do this is to take the student aside when there is time and jointly create a visual reminder system (a checklist, a graphic organizer) for the task or activity that needs to be completed independently. A common example in the school setting includes classroom entry and exit routines or a checking system to make sure that all homework items get into the backpack. The teacher can use a basic plan such as this to teach important vocabulary, such as the words: *goal, steps, error detection, error correction,* numeric sequences (*first, second, third*), and potentially other terms. Subsequently, the teacher can use the lessons learned from this simple plan to then develop plans that are longer and have more component steps. For example, the teacher could say: "Now that we've learned about steps and sequencing for homework, we're going to apply the same logic to something that's different. I'm going to teach you how to figure out the sequence for completing your book report/ your science project/ your five-paragraph essay."

Lessons about planning can be used for many different activities. Once the student is aware of the concept of steps and sequences, the adult can use a question-and-answer format to help the student build planning skills. The adult can prompt the student to solve the planning problem by not providing too many instructions. For example, the teacher could say, "The goal is to get a book report done. What does a finished book report look like? How are you going to know that you are done and that you completed the task successfully?" Alternatively, the teacher could say, "The goal is to know all of the assignments that you need to complete for this week. You will also need to know all of the materials needed to complete the work." Once the goal is established, the student can be asked to break it down into component steps. The teacher could say, "Okay, now let's look at each of the components. For the research step of your essay, what are all of the things that you are going to have to do? For the taking-notes portion of the project, what are all of the things that you are going to need to do?" If the student is learning to manage homework assignments, the teacher could say, "Okay, now we know how many classes you have. For each class, how are you going to know what work needs to get done? Where are you going to look?" Some of the planning work that the instructor undertakes with the student will have to take into consideration timing and time. The instructor can plan ahead by asking,

"At what point during the day will you do which step of the plan?" Or, "How much time will you dedicate to this step?" Finally, the component steps have to be sequenced. The teacher can say, "Okay, now, let's think about which step comes first, second, and third." These kinds of prompts promote joint ownership. They enhance and reinforce the working memory and the motivation needed to complete the task. Notice that by speaking in this manner, the teacher is modeling how to use metacognition. By being more fully aware of the goal and the plan, the student now has a performance standard against which the outcome (the student's performance) can be compared.

***Educational Objectives and Strategies for Teaching Organizational Skills*** Organizational skills, as defined in this chapter, involve teaching about planning over an extended time interval and coordinating plans and goals with one another. The extended time interval would typically be on the order of days or weeks. Important concepts when teaching organizational skills are the concepts of time (how long does each task take) and efficiency (how to set up plans so that time is not wasted). Another important concept is that of subgoaling and advance planning for mishaps. This refers to sequencing plans in a logical order, so that dependent plans are completed earlier in the sequence and a distal goal can be reached. Progress measures include the student's level of knowledge about planning and organization, the student's capacity for independent planning and organization, and the student's capacity to complete tasks successfully over extended time intervals.

***Educational Objectives and Strategies for Teaching Metacognition*** Students with executive skills difficulties are commonly unaware of their performance errors in the moment when they are occurring. These students may be distracted, forget steps, lose track of time, and carry steps out in an illogical sequence. All of these performance difficulties end with the same result: Failure to reach important goals. A major function of adults is to help build the student's self-monitoring skills so that executive skills are applied more consistently in real time. One way to introduce metacognition to students is to discuss what constitutes a goal and how to compare actual performance against the intended goal. Another way is to teach about error detection and error correction. Several of the sample conversations provided earlier in this section are designed to improve a student's metacognition, though they also serve the goal of teaching the student to improve working memory and planning skills.

An important facet to teaching metacognition is to ensure that there is a focus on the student's successes rather the student's failures. Students need to see, feel, and notice what it means to reach goals successfully, and what it means when they apply executive skills successfully. See the discussion in earlier sections of the chapter. The feeling and personal discovery of success is critical to success in learning in general. Educators can enhance the student's awareness of personal successes by making statements such as, "I noticed that you waited your turn," "I noticed that you finished your work and started the next activity really quickly," "I noticed that you made a really good plan. Tell me about the steps that you created. Did you reach your goal?"

Corrective feedback, while necessary some of the time, does not typically help the student develop the awareness needed to improve performance. Corrective feedback also does not give the student a chance to reflect on her or his own performance and in the process find her or his own way to be successful. Instead of telling students what they failed to do, it is important to let them discover their errors on their own. For example, instead of saying, "You forgot to . . ." or "Fix that" or "Do the task this way," the adult can say, "I think you forgot something here. I'm wondering whether you can see what you missed." Or, "Let me know how you'd like to fix the error that I noticed." Students need the chance to compare the goal with the outcome and to find ways to self-correct their performance. The correction needed might be for the student to make amends for breaking a rule, to complete missed steps in a routine, or to look carefully at the plan and discover which steps need to be added or re-ordered.

*Measuring Progress* To measure progress in metacognition skills, educators can monitor how often the student is able to identify his or her own successes, how often the student is able to correct errors on his or her own, or how often the student corrects errors with adult prompting.

## Accommodations for Executive Skills Difficulties

Adults often provide accommodations for the student with underdeveloped executive skills. Many or most of the strategies discussed in this section consist of finding a way to step in on behalf of the student to help detect and correct errors. The error could be getting distracted, breaking a rule, or making simple mistakes in a math or spelling problem. Many or most of the strategies could be considered accommodations. However, used judiciously, accommodations can help to build skills and can be used as teaching strategies or interventions.

Error detection and error correction are the most common accommodations. Examples include corrective feedback from adults if a classroom or social rule is broken, a reminder to the student to return to task when she or he gets distracted, and a suggestion to complete a missing step when a task is not completed accurately. Corrective feedback is a fact of life for all children and youth. Even though corrective feedback can ameliorate errors in the short term, it typically does not result in greater independence or more successful functioning over the long term. When used too frequently, corrective feedback can become an accommodation that children and youth rely on. Knowing that adults will step in to detect and correct errors, the student may believe that it is no longer her or his responsibility to do so. Even worse, corrective feedback can lead to frustration with adults and with learning in general.



Students with underdeveloped executive skills may make a considerable number of errors over the course of a day, and it can be challenging for the adult to notice all the errors, to look carefully for any successes, and to provide opportunities for improving the student's performance. Educators have to find the right balance between stepping in on behalf of the student to detect and correct errors (accommodation) versus using errors and performance difficulties as teachable moments (instruction). For many students, some errors may need to go undetected and uncorrected, so that the focus is then on only those few and more important errors that create an opportunity for skills building. One approach is to decide, in advance, how the adult will step in to help correct errors. Monitoring and feedback can be scheduled before instruction. For example, the educator could say to the student, "I'm going to check in with you every 15 minutes," or "I'm going to check in with you at the end of each activity and give you feedback." By reducing the number of times that corrective feedback is offered, by scheduling corrective feedback in advance, and by emphasizing successes, the student may become more receptive to the feedback and learn from it instead of feeling criticized.

An accommodation for underdeveloped executive skills can also be to modify the curriculum's scope and/or the pace of instruction. When tasks are broken down into smaller segments, the student can perform more successfully because the demands on the student's attention span are reduced. Short periods of high-quality work are more likely to result in positive longer term outcomes than asking the student to focus and pay attention for the same length of time as other students, while producing low-quality work. Having students seated close to the teacher may make it easier for the teacher to provide corrective feedback or to notice learning successes. Assistive technology is also important to consider. Using a timer to prompt the student to remember important obligations or to schedule times for error detection and correction may also be helpful.

Teachers can reduce the demands on the student's executive skills by delivering instructions more explicitly and by crafting a clearly defined plan. The instructions should be delivered personally and should be reinforced using visual supports. A step-by-step guide using pictures or words can help reduce the planning demands on the student and increase the chances of a successful outcome. As the student's skills progress, planning itself can become part of the student's lesson plan. The student and the teacher can plan the activity together. By doing this, the student not only learns about a task or activity that needs to be completed, but also learns how to break down that activity into a logical set of steps.

Finally, digital solutions are available for helping student develop their organizational skills. Digital calendars, available on multiple devices, that make use of color coding and graphic representations can be very helpful to many students, not just those with underdeveloped executive skills.

## CASE EXAMPLE

Julie is a fourth-grade student who is well liked by her peers. She is passionate about caring for others and maintains a positive relationship with her parents and teachers. She is always eager to perform well and enjoys positive reinforcement from adults. In spite of Julie's many positive qualities, her parents and teachers are often distressed by her behaviors in class and at home. She can be very forgetful and commonly neglects to check her performance to correct for errors. Errors occur in many different aspects of her day, starting with forgetfulness during the morning routine at home. Her parents always discover one or another missing step, such as not brushing her teeth, not tying her shoelaces, or forgetting to put needed items into her book bag. When Julie enters her classroom, her teacher frequently has to remind her not to socialize until after she has hung her coat on her hook or stowed her bookbag and other belongings in her cubby. Sometimes, the teacher also has to check to make sure that Julie put her items away correctly. When doing independent work, Julie makes many seemingly careless errors in math calculations or spelling, even though she can perform at grade level in all subject areas. Although she is social, Julie also makes mistakes in the social arena. She sometimes speaks her mind too freely, such as asking unfamiliar peers questions that are a bit too personal or making inappropriate comments about their appearance. Whenever she gets corrective feedback from adults, she always apologizes and seems to understand her error.

The behaviors of concern have been present for at least a couple of years. Julie has always needed closer supervision to perform successfully. However, now that Julie is in fourth grade, her parents and her classroom teacher are somewhat more concerned. Her performance now seems immature compared with her peers. Her teacher allows her more motor breaks than normally required by other students. Allowing her to get up and wander was helpful in prior years and resulted in her getting more work done. Unfortunately, the accommodation of allowing more motor breaks is now disruptive for other students, because her moving about the classroom is accompanied by social chatter. Julie recently resorted to lying about getting tasks done and about breaking rules. For example, her mother recently found a stash of granola wrappers under her bed, a treat that she is only supposed to have as an afternoon snack. She denied ever having eaten the granola bars, even though there was clearly no other way that the granola bar wrappers could have found their way into her bedroom. Another example has started to occur with her homework. In consultation with her teachers, her parents recently decided not to provide as much supervision for her homework to see how well she could complete her homework independently. The outcome was that Julie did not complete her homework, and on more than one occasion she stated that she completed her homework when this was not actually the case.

Julie typically does not follow instructions successfully, and her teacher has to repeat instructions to Julie personally, after she has delivered instructions to the class. Without this intervention, Julie tends not to start her tasks or seems confused about what she is supposed to do. This is surprising to her teacher, because when she gets instructions delivered one-to-one, she can initiate tasks very well.

Julie's teacher often checks the quality of her work, knowing that Julie tends to skip steps or make errors. The conversations she has with Julie are always the same: She looks at Julie and asks Julie to show her what is missing or incorrect. When Julie is unsure, she asks Julie to tell her what the instructions were and then asks her to point out what remains incomplete. Julie is always able to respond successfully to this form of questioning and immediately sets out to correct errors and complete anything that is missing. Often, she says, "Oh, I knew that" or "Oh, I was just going to change that," when it was clearly not her intention to correct her errors prior to the teacher's intervention. That said, Julie appears happier when provided with this type of one-to-one attention and can correct her performance very successfully.

Julie's teacher uses the same type of questioning when it is time to check her desk and when it is time for her to put together her bookbag prior to returning home. Only by providing this degree of check-in is Julie able to get her belongings together successfully so that her homework can get done. Julie's teacher is surprised that she has to provide so much support and intervention. "It's almost as if she never graduated from first grade," her teacher said. "She acts like a younger child, even though she can perform at a fourth-grade level." Given how much difficulty Julie is having at school now, her parents decided to pursue medical evaluation and will consider an array of treatment options.



## Case Analysis

Julie presents with very typical behaviors of a student whose executive skills are not developing successfully. The specific behaviors that she shows, across settings and across activities, all point toward executive skills as the underlying area of concern. Her forgetfulness and inaccuracies manifest during over-learned and memorized tasks, such as classroom rules and daily routines as well as learning tasks, such as during homework. They occur across both settings, home and school, but they do not occur 100% of the time. The sections that follow apply the Executive Skills Framework to the analysis of the behavioral observations made above. The analysis is designed to understand Julie's strengths and challenges more fully. A deeper understanding of her behaviors can help generate a more comprehensive intervention plan.

### *Julie's Orientation and Initiation*

Julie is often not oriented to task. The example of her socializing on entry into class, instead of putting her belongings away, is an example of not orienting to the task or activity. Julie often needs a prompt or reminder to orient to and initiate tasks. Lack of orientation here is related to her difficulty with inhibition. Social interactions are too tempting, and she cannot inhibit her desire to socialize and defer the gratification of socializing until a later time. She needs to be reminded to defer gratification by first doing a task and then socializing if time allows.

### *Julie's Ability to Shift Cognitive Set*

No difficulties in shifting cognitive set have been observed. Julie does not show repetitive behaviors, or any difficulty in managing transitions. That said, she is often inefficient in her transitions from one activity to the next, because she so often gets distracted. She often ends up not focusing successfully on transition demands as they arise.

### *Julie's Inhibition Skills*

Most of the behaviors outlined here can be traced back to Julie's underdeveloped inhibition skills. Because she gets distracted often, she often also completes tasks without giving them the full attention that they deserve. It may be tempting to judge Julie for being lazy or for not trying hard enough, given that she can produce good work when she is paying attention. This misinterpretation of her behaviors is very common. The disability of her limited inhibition skills is not apparent to an untrained observer, because she does not show lack of inhibition all of the time. Her inconsistent pattern of performance difficulties is likely to generate an inappropriate interpretation, such as laziness or lack of motivation. In fact, her inconsistent performance is a puzzle to Julie herself.

Underdeveloped inhibition skills lead to problems with working memory and to higher order executive demands such as planning and organization. Because of her difficulty with inhibition, Julie forgets to complete tasks and forgets to check errors. She also cannot always inhibit the desire to break a rule that her parents imposed at home, such as, "Granola bars are only for your after-school snack." Because her inhibition difficulties occur so often, she commonly ends up lying about her performance. Lying about incomplete homework or about breaking a rule is one way for children and youth such as Julie to save face. Students like Julie cannot really explain why it is so hard for them to follow rules. Some of the time, lying also occurs because they truly forget about the rule that they broke. Rule breaking happens so often that even Julie can't keep track of all of the incidents. Julie's behaviors are best understood as a primary difficulty with impulse control and with inhibition skills in particular.

### *Julie's Working Memory*

Julie might perform successfully when she has to participate in a test of working memory, such as remembering digits forward and backward during a psychological test. However, her working memory is not very secure in real-time situations, because she gets distracted so often. When distracted, she seems to forget what she was supposed to do and when reminded, she can correct her performance. Limited working memory, or inconsistent use of her working memory, helps to explain Julie's performance difficulty with the daily routines. Now that she is in fourth grade, Julie has completed daily routines literally hundreds of times, but she continues to forget steps in her morning routine, both at home and at school. This difficulty reflects her limited verbal working memory. When provided with a visual reminder, she can perform much better. Very often, Julie also needs extra reminders and prompts for instructions delivered in class. This is an important limitation. If she forgets the instructions that she was supposed to follow, it is much harder for her to check up on her own performance and correct errors.



### *Julie's Planning Skills*

The case as presented does not give any good examples of Julie's difficulty with planning. However, given her difficulty with basic or first-order executive skills, Julie's teachers and parents should anticipate that she will have difficulties with planning. The issue of her planning skills takes on special importance now that she is in fourth grade. Planning demands are now part of her curriculum, and teachers should expect Julie to have difficulty in this area unless provided with explicit instruction.

### *Julie's Organizational Skills*

Julie would not be expected to have very developed organizational skills, both because of her difficulty with basic executive skills and given her age. Most students in her class still rely heavily on adults to organize their daily or weekly schedules.

### *Julie's Metacognition*

Julie does have metacognition, which is most apparent when her teacher approaches her and asks her to identify her own errors (i.e., error detection and correction). Julie is able to do this quite successfully, especially when the evidence of her errors is visual (e.g., when correcting errors on a worksheet). However, Julie does not access her metacognition consistently. She is often content to focus on whatever might come up that is interesting and struggles to monitor her performance and correct her own errors unless prompted by adults. She typically does not use the metacognitive skills discussed earlier in this chapter: Take the time think about the past ("What was my goal?"), compare it with the present ("What does my performance look like now?"), and plan for the future ("How can I plan ahead to avoid this error in the future?").

## Educational Objectives and Strategies for Teaching Julie How to Improve Her Executive Skills

Therapists and clinicians working with a student like Julie would interpret the majority of her behaviors as evidence of limited inhibition skills. Underdeveloped or inconsistent use of inhibition skills is certainly a good way to understand her behaviors. However, full use of the Executive Skills Framework can illustrate more about the types of interventions that might help improve Julie's performance.

### *Objectives for Improving Julie's Orientation and Initiation to Task*

Julie is likely to orient and initiate tasks that are preferred, because she has difficulty deferring gratification by inhibiting more salient activities (such as socializing), while focusing on less salient activities (such as putting her items into her cubby). Most students like Julie will rely quite heavily on adults, who can remind them to orient to task and to initiate tasks. That said, if distractors are removed and if peers model desired behaviors, Julie might be able to inhibit the desire to socialize and instead get back on track. Some of the suggested strategies listed in the Accommodations for Executive Skills Difficulties section might also be useful. By reducing demands on her short attention span and by developing a strong plan with her about the expectations of the situation, Julie might be able to focus her attention on adult-preferred goals more consistently.



### *Objectives for Improving Julie's Inhibition Skills*

Julie's primary difficulty lies in her inconsistent use of inhibition skills. It may be challenging for students like Julie to accept corrective feedback as often as they usually need to, because the feedback is provided after they have already failed. One option is to try and provide positive feedback and corrective feedback in equal measure. It is just as important, and perhaps more important, to point out to Julie when she is using her inhibition skills successfully. She needs to know what it looks like and feels like when she is deferring gratification successfully, such as when she follows rules successfully (e.g., does not socialize with peers until she has completed tasks), completes a routine successfully (e.g., gets herself dressed and ready for school without reminders), or remains focused on task successfully.

When Julie shows failures, such as leaving tasks incomplete, breaking rules, and lying about having broken the rule, she should still be held accountable for completing an incomplete task. In the case of unfinished homework, her teacher might say, "Well, maybe you can take a look at the homework assignment again. I think there are some items missing. I can help you, or you can check up on your performance on your own, and I'll look at it with you later." For breaking rules, her parents could say, "Oh well, I guess you won't be able to eat any granola bars for after-school snack until it's time to buy a new box." Adults can also ask Julie to identify a repair strategy for the mistake. "Hmmm. Tell me what you could do to make up for this." The dilemma for both Julie and the adult is that infractions or unfinished work commonly persist, in spite of the consequences or repair strategies that the adult and student develop together to address the performance difficulties. It can be very tiring to keep having to check up on unfinished business.

In order to avoid frustration associated with excess feedback, one strategy could be to make a prior agreement with Julie about how often feedback will be provided. For example, her teacher or parents could say, "I think that you might run up against some more situations of forgetting your work or forgetting the rules. How about I check in with you once or twice per hour and review your performance? We'll think about any steps that you might have missed and see what can be done to get your performance back on track." In the home setting, check-ins for error detection and error correction should likely occur much less often than in the classroom (e.g., a few times per day). This increases opportunities for positive feedback, and reduces the number of episodes of corrective feedback. Preserving a positive parent-child relationship is an especially important consideration for children and youth like Julie. Her parents will need to fully understand her limitations and set realistic expectations.

### Objectives for Improving Julie's Performance With Working Memory

Julie often forgets what she is supposed to do. She may show poor working memory because she never actually heard the instructions in the first place. She might sometimes hear instructions successfully, but then neglect to carry them out because of her forgetfulness. Or she might forget what she was told because of limited working memory. Many students like Julie then struggle to complete tasks because they cannot remember what it was that they forgot to do. In these situations, adults can produce preprinted task lists, cheat sheets, or visual reminders. One good point to remember: The student may need to be reminded to use the reminder system!

### Objectives and Strategies for Improving Julie's Planning Skills

Given her age and given her difficulty with basic executive skills, Julie would not be expected to show good planning skills. Planning requires not only deferred gratification but also working memory. Specific instruction in planning is appropriate for Julie, for a variety of activities. Her fourth-grade peers now have to learn to plan their own homework, for example, and are also learning about how to plan written compositions and larger projects. Julie will need the same type of instruction, but she may need it for longer and she may need more details included in her plans so that they are carried out successfully. For example, instead of sharing a writing strategy with only five steps (gather information, take notes, choose the important ideas, order your ideas, and write a paragraph about each), Julie may need much more explicit description for each step. For the first step (gather information) she may need specific guidance about where to look for information, how many notes to take, how many minutes to dedicate to notetaking, when to stop taking notes about one topic and start for another. For the next step, choose the important ideas, Julie may need some specific pointers about how many ideas she is supposed to choose and might need instruction about how to choose ideas that are related to one another. Oral practice with a teacher, prior to choosing her ideas and writing them down, slows the process and can help her to focus on the steps and make better choices. When Julie fails to complete a complex task such as writing a composition, it will be easier to pinpoint specific errors or omissions that she may have committed along the way.

### Objectives and Strategies for Improving Julie's Organizational Skills

Organizational skills can be a topic of discussion for Julie and for her classmates. However, most students at this age are ready to work on planning and will need assistance from adults to acquire organizational skills such as planning against mishaps, planning and coordinating unrelated plans with one another, and planning with time constraints and efficiency in mind.

***Objectives and Strategies for Improving Julie's Metacognition*** Julie has good metacognition. She is able to reflect on her own performance when prompted, and she can identify and correct errors when reminded. However, she does not use her metacognition without reminders. She may need specific reminders, either from a teacher or from a clock with an alarm, to stop, review, detect errors, and correct errors. Julie might benefit from a preprogrammed system such as this.

## Working With Culturally and Linguistically Diverse Learners

School professionals should consider the following strategies when helping culturally and linguistically diverse learners develop their executive skills:

### *Increase Wait Time*

Culturally and linguistically diverse learners may need a few extra seconds of wait time, before responding to or answering questions. This is especially important to take into account when developing or teaching executive skills because it gives them an opportunity to formally "switch" from heritage language and focus in English.

### *Allow for Response in the Wrong Language*

Linguistically diverse learners may occasionally respond in the wrong language. For example, a learner might walk up to someone and say something in Korean and then immediately realize that the individual only speaks English. If this happens occasionally, there is nothing to worry about because it is easily corrected by the individual. If this happens frequently, more specific instruction in English may be needed in areas where the student appears to have persistent communication difficulties.



## CONCLUSIONS

The Executive Skills Framework opened by reviewing the basic executive skills. These include orientation, initiation, inhibition, shifting cognitive set, and working memory. A majority of the time, students who have underdeveloped executive skills will show performance difficulties that are related to these five basic executive skills. Many students with behavioral dysregulation and difficulty completing tasks have difficulties in this area. School professionals should keep this important point in mind when they encounter students who appear to be lazy, forgetful, or defiant. These students typically require extra prompting from adults to monitor, detect, and correct errors across a wide range of activities: Daily routines, social interactions, classroom work, classroom rules, homework. It can feel burdensome for adults to take the extra time needed to check in with students, do a joint analysis to detect errors, and create a joint plan to correct errors. Even though students with difficulties in this area appear to need so much extra time, the amount of time they need from adults is most often seconds and minutes, not hours. School professionals can have a very positive impact if they can understand the struggle that these students face and find a way to connect empathically and discover ways of being supportive to them. The basic skills just listed need to be in place for the student to move to advanced executive skills. Developing the skills of planning and organization should always be the goal for the student, even if these skills rely on the use of accommodations. Students need to have the experience of choosing their own goals, developing their own plans, and organizing those plans to fit into their schedule.

The excitement and satisfaction of choosing one's own goals and experiencing success in reaching them can lead to taking risks in learning by developing new goals and mastering new skills. However, people choose goals based not only on their prior successes but also on prior failures. Past failures can influence whether people attempt to create new goals in the first place. Chapter 8 presents important information about arousal, emotions, and motivation, which influence the goals that people choose. They influence when, why, how, and for how long people apply their executive skills to reach any new goal they may have chosen. These influences are present regardless of whether a student has an impairment in executive skills. It is important to understand why students sometimes apply executive skills successfully, and why students sometimes do not apply them successfully at all. These important aspects of executive skills, and of human behavior in general, are discussed in the next chapter.

## REFERENCES


Alvarez, J. A., & Emory, E. (2006). Executive function and the frontal lobes: A meta-analytic review. *Neuropsychology Review, 16*(1), 17–42.

Anderson, P. J., & Reidy, N. (2012). Assessing executive function in preschoolers. *Neuropsychology Review,* 22(4), 345–360.

Baddeley, A. (2003). Working memory: Looking back and looking forward. *Nature Reviews: Neuroscience, 4*(10), 829–839.

Baddeley, A. D., & Hitch, G. J. (1974). Working memory. In G. H. Bower (Ed.), *The psychology of learning and motivation* (Vol. 8, pp. 47–89). New York, NY: Academic Press.

Barkley, R. (2000). Genetics of childhood disorders: XVII. ADHD, Part 1: The executive functions and ADHD. *Journal of the American Academy of Child & Adolescent Psychiatry, 39*(8), 1064–1068.

Barkley, R. (2001). The executive functions and self-regulation: An evolutionary neuropsychological perspective. *Neuropsychology Review, 11*(1), 1–29.

Best, J. R., & Miller, P. H. (2010). A developmental perspective on executive function. *Child Development, 81*(6), 1641–1660.

Best, J. R., Miller, P. H., & Jones, L. L. (2009). Executive functions after age 5: Changes and correlates. *Developmental Review, 29*(3), 180–200.

Bledowski, C., Kaiser, J., & Rahm, B. (2010), Basic operations in working memory: Contributions from functional imaging studies. *Behavioural Brain Research, 214*(2), 172–179.

Burgess, P. (1997). Theory and methodology in executive function research. In P. Rabbitt (Ed.), *Methodology of frontal executive function* (pp. 81–116). Hove, United Kingdom: Psychology Press.

Burgess, P. W., Alderman, N., Evans, J., Hazel, E., & Wilson, B. (1998). The ecological validity of tests of executive function. *Journal of the International Neuropsychological Society, 4*(6), 547–558.

Burgess, P. W., Alderman, N., & Forbes, C. (2006). The case for the development and use of "ecologically valid" measures of executive function in experimental and clinical neuropsychology. *Journal of the International Neuropsychological Society, 12*(2), 194–209.

Cowan, N. (2001). The magical number 4 in short-term memory: A reconsideration of mental storage capacity. *Behavioral and Brain Sciences, 24*(1), 88–114.

Diamond A. (2013). Executive functions. *Annual Review of Psychology, 64,* 135–168.

Dinsmore, D. L., Alexander, P. A., & Loughlin, S. M. (2008). Focusing the conceptual lens on metacognition, self-regulation, and self-regulated learning. *Educational Psychology Review, 20*(4), 391–409.

Donker, A. S., de Boer, H., Kostons, D., van Ewijk, C. C. D., & van der Werf, M. P. C. (2014). Effectiveness of learning strategy instruction on academic performance: A meta-analysis. *Educational Research Review, 11,* 1–26.

Duncan, J., Emslie, H., & Williams, P. (1996). Intelligence and the frontal lobe: The organization of goal-directed behavior. *Cognitive Psychology, 30,* 257–303.

Fernandez-Duque, D., Baird, J. A., & Posner, M. I. (2000). Executive attention and metacognitive regulation. *Consciousness and Cognition,* 9(2, Pt. 1), 288–307.

Flavell, J. H. (1979). Metacognition and cognitive monitoring. *American Psychologist, 34*(10), 906–911.

Flavell, J. H. (2004). Theory-of-mind development: Retrospect and prospect. *Merrill-Palmer Quarterly, 50*(3), pp. 274–290.

Follmer, D. J., & Sperling, R. A. (2016). The mediating role of metacognition in the relationship between executive function and self-regulated learning. *British Journal of Educational Psychology, 86*(4), 559–575.

Friedman, S. L., & Kofsky, E. (Eds). (1997). *The developmental psychology of planning: Why, how, and when do we plan?* Mahwah, NJ: Lawrence Erlbaum.

Gioia, G., & Isquith, P. K. (2013). BRIEF: Behavior Rating Inventory of Executive Function. Torrance, CA: WPS.

Goswami, U. (1998). *Cognition in children.* London, United Kingdom: Psychology Press.

Grant, D. A., & Berg, E. A. (1981). *Wisconsin Card Sorting Test.* Torrance, CA: WPS.

Haith, M. M., Benson, J. B., Roberts, R. J., & Pennington, B. F. (1994). *The development of future-oriented processes.* Chicago, IL: University of Chicago Press.

Hongwasnishkul, D., Happaney, K. R., Lee, W. S., & Zelazo, P. D. (2005). Assessment of hot and cool executive function in young children: age-related changes and individual differences. *Developmental Neuropsychology, 28*(2), 617–644.

Klingberg, Torkel. (2016). Neural basis of cognitive training and development. *Current Opinion in Behavioral Sciences.* 10. 10.1016/j.cobeha.2016.05.003.

Hudson J. A., Sosa, B. B., & Shapiro, L. R. (1997). Scripts and Plans: The development of preschool children's event knowledge and event planning. In S. L. Friedman & E. K. Scholnick (Eds.) *The developmental psychology of planning: Why, how, and when do we plan?* (pp. 77–102). Mahwah, NJ: Lawrence Erlbaum.

Kochanska, G., Coy, K. C., & Murray, K. T. (2001). The development of self-regulation in the first four years of life. *Child Development, 72*(4), 1091–1111.

Mahone, E. M., & Scheider, H. E. (2012). Assessment of attention in preschoolers. *Neuropsychology Review, 22*(4), 361–383.

Martel, M. M., Nigg, J. T., & von Eye, A. (2009). How do trait dimensions map onto ADHD symptom domains? *Journal of Abnormal Child Psychology, 37*(3), 337–348.

McCormack, T., & Atance, C. M. (2011). Planning in young children: A review and synthesis. *Developmental Review, 31*(1), 1–31.

Miyake, A., Friedman, N. P., Emerson, M. J., Witzki, A. H., & Howerter, A. (2000). The unity and diversity of executive functions and their contributions to complex "frontal lobe" tasks: A latent variable analysis. *Cognitive Psychology, 41*(1), 49–100.

Nigg, J. T. (2000). On inhibition/disinhibition in developmental psychopathology: Views from cognitive and personality psychology and a working inhibition taxonomy. *Psychological Bulletin, 26*(2), 220–246.

Nigg, J. T. (2017). Annual research review: On the relations among self-regulation, self-control, executive functioning, effortful control, cognitive control, impulsivity, risk-taking, and inhibition for developmental psychopathology. *Journal of Child Psychology and Psychiatry 58*(4), 361–383.

Roberts, B. A., Martel, M. M., & Nigg, J. T. (2017). Are there executive dysfunction subtypes within ADHD? *Journal of Attention Disorders, 21*(4), 284–293.

Stuss, D. T., & Alexander, M. P. (2000). Executive functions and the frontal lobe: A conceptual view. *Psychological Research, 63*(3–4), 289–298.

Suchy, Y. (2009). Executive functioning: Overview, assessment, and research issues for non-neuropsychologists. *Annals of Behavioral Medicine, 37,* 106–116.

Toplak, M. E., West, R. F., & Stanovich, K. E. (2013). Practitioner review: Do performance-based measures and ratings of executive function assess the same construct? *Journal of Child Psychology and Psychiatry, 54*(2), 131–143.

Van den Bos, I. F., van de Ven, S. H. G., Kroesbergen, E. H., & van Luit, J. E. H. (2013). Working memory and mathematics in primary school children: A meta-analysis. *Educational Research Reviews, 10,* 29–44.

Verte, S., Geurts, H., Roeyers, H., Oosterlaan, J., & Sergeant, J. (2006). The relationship of working memory, inhibition, and response variability in child psychopathology. *Journal of Neuroscience Methods, 151*(1), 5–14.

Zelazo, P. D., & Cunningham, W. (2007). Executive function: Mechanisms underlying emotion regulation. In J. Gross (Ed.), *Handbook of emotion regulation* (pp. 135–158). New York, NY: Guilford.

Zelazo, P. D., Frye, D., & Rapus, T. (1996). An age-related dissociation between knowing rules and using them. *Cognitive Development, 11*(1), 37–63.

Zelazo, P. D., Muller, U., Frye, D., Marcovitch, S., Argitis, G., Boseovski, J., . . . Carlson, S. M. (2003). The development of executive function in early childhood. *Monographs of the Society for Research in Child Development, 68*(3), 1–151.

Zhou, Q., Chen, S. H., & Main, A. (2012). Commonalities and differences in the research on children's effortful control and executive function: A call for an integrated model of self-regulation. *Child Development Perspectives, 6*(2), 112–121.

# APPENDIX 7.1 Executive Skills Framework

The Executive Skills Framework is summarized here. School professionals can use this form as a quick reference for the skill sets and skills that need to be taken into consideration when making observations and developing an intervention plan.

| Skill sets | Functions and skills | Examples of functions and skills in action | Sample performance difficulties | Potential strategies, accommodations, or educational objectives |
|---|---|---|---|---|
| Orientation | Orient one's attention and focus to a stimulus, task, activity, or goal | Alerts toward a visual or auditory stimulus, such as a person's face or voice<br><br>Alerts toward someone's voice and orients attention to the conversation or instruction offered by the other person<br><br>Orients attention toward an expectation (e.g., orients self to complete the steps needed to get to school on time, to write a book report or essay, to invite a friend for a social event) | Does not orient to a visual or auditory stimulus<br><br>Orients to a visual or auditory stimulus but takes excessive time and needs extra prompting | Students who do not orient easily may need extra attention from adults to ensure that they orient successfully. Extra stimulation may consist of approaching the student to alert the student to a task or activity, provide repetition of the instruction or other auditory stimulus, provide a visual stimulus in addition to an auditory stimulus (e.g., picture cue in addition to an instruction), and/or provide a prompt through touch. |
| Initiation | Take a first step toward completing a task or activity or toward reaching a goal | After orienting to a person's face or voice, or after orienting to a task expectation, the student takes the first step toward completing the task or participating in the activity.<br><br>Initiation might manifest as asking a clarifying question, making a comment to participate in a conversation, opening the closet door to choose clothing to get ready for school, opening a book to take notes that will lead to writing a book report, or finding the phone number to call a friend. | After orienting to a task or activity, the student shifts focus or attention and fails to initiate the task or fails to take a first step toward participation. Instead, the student orients to something else. | Students who do not initiate tasks are typically not oriented to task. The strategies listed previously can be useful for orienting the student and to making sure that an initial step is taken. The student may benefit from a physical prompt to initiate the task. For example, the adult might open the closet door, open a book or hand the student a pen, or find the phone number and hand the phone to the student. |

*(continued)*

| Skill sets | Functions and skills | Examples of functions and skills in action | Sample performance difficulties | Potential strategies, accommodations, or educational objectives |
|---|---|---|---|---|
| Inhibition, interference and impulse control | Inhibition of distractors to maintain focus on a task, activity, or goal | The student is able to maintain focus on an interesting or especially salient task, activity, or goal and inhibit interferences coming from elsewhere. For example, the student can continue playing a game and not get distracted by a person calling her or his name or otherwise trying to attract the student's attention. | The student gets distracted too quickly. The student shifts orientation, attention, and focus whenever a new stimulus presents itself, regardless of stimulus type. | It is difficult to teach the ability to inhibit stimuli and/or to teach the student how to inhibit stimuli selectively in order to reach a goal. Frequent adult monitoring is needed, and extra adult time needs to be put aside to serve the function of reorienting the student to task when distracted.<br>For many students with underdeveloped inhibition or impulse control skills, learning inhibition and self-control starts with repair strategies. For example, after failing to inhibit irrelevant stimuli and not getting a task done, the student is reoriented to task and is required to complete that task. After breaking a classroom or social rule, the student is prompted to do a repair strategy, such as raising the hand prior to speaking and waiting for the adult to solicit the response or apologizing and restating a socially inappropriate comment so that it is socially more appropriate.<br>All students with problems with impulse control are at risk for very frequent corrective feedback from adults. Strategies should be put into place so that the student understands why the corrective feedback is needed. Preferably, the student should strategize with the adult so that corrective feedback is not perceived as excessively critical or negative. It is especially important for the adult to share feedback about the successful use of inhibition skills.<br>Inhibition skills do improve with age and practice, but their development can be slow in some students. |
| | Defer gratification by inhibiting attention toward an interesting stimulus, and instead focus on a less desired or less interesting activity first | The student is able to maintain focus on a less interesting task, activity, or goal and not get distracted by a more interesting or more salient activity or goal. For example, the student can first complete a boring task ("put on your shoes") before going outside. | The student is able to sustain focus on interesting or salient tasks and activities but is not able to get through less salient or more time-consuming tasks or activities without getting distracted. For example, the student can focus on a game or interesting activity but not on a less interesting activity. | |
| | Interference control and ability to sustain attention | The student can maintain orientation and attention to a learning activity and not get distracted by a conversation occurring on the other side of the classroom.<br>The student is able to suppress irrelevant information in a math word problem while identifying the essential steps in that problem and also solving the math problem. | The student fails to complete familiar or daily tasks and activities because of an inability to sustain orientation and attention or to inhibit distractors for long enough to get the task done. Tasks typically do not get started and/or do not get completed because of excessive distractibility. | |
| | Temporary suppression of an emotion in order to think and reflect before acting | The student is able to follow rules ("raise your hands before speaking"). The student is able to wait his or her turn in a game.<br>The student is able to suppress the immediate impulse to make a socially inappropriate statement and instead not say anything at all or say something that is socially more appropriate.<br>The student is able to use inhibition to suppress emotions in the service of self-regulation; see Chapter 8. | The student fails to follow common rules of conduct and often breaks social expectations in the classroom or at home (e.g., blurts out an answer instead of first raising her or his hand, makes socially inappropriate statements that later have to be detracted). | |

| Skill sets | Functions and skills | Examples of functions and skills in action | Sample performance difficulties | Potential strategies, accommodations, or educational objectives |
|---|---|---|---|---|
| Shifting cognitive set | The capacity to shift orientation, attention, or focus between different activities, tasks, or goals or between steps within a task or activity | The student is able to transition easily between tasks and activities over the course of the day. For example, the student can transition between two activities that are equally salient ("stop doing math; we are going to do reading now") or even between a more salient and a less salient activity ("stop playing now; it's time to get back to work").<br><br>The student shows flexibility. The same task or activity can be approached more than one way. For example, clean-up routines or bedtime routines at home and play activities with peers can all be completed in a different order, using different props, and accompanied by different adults or peers.<br><br>The student shows cognitive flexibility in approaching academic tasks and can shift between rule sets. For example, the student can shift back and forth between solving addition and subtraction problems without getting confused. | The student does not transition easily between activities, regardless of salience or level of personal interest. The student may protest and refuse to carry out the transition. When the transition occurs, it occurs sluggishly.<br><br>The student is inflexible with daily routines at home and at school and insists that certain routines or rituals be respected.<br><br>The student is inflexible with peers and insists that play activities have to occur according to her or his wishes.<br><br>The student makes mistakes in learning activities because of difficulty in switching rule sets. | Extra adult support and time are needed for students who are rigid or who transition sluggishly. Provide advance warning about transitions. Include the student in the decision-making process about how transitions will be announced and how much time will be allowed to carry out the transition. Transitions between activities should normally be possible within a minute or two.<br><br>Be sure to focus on the transition instead of on the protest. Many students who protest about transitions are considered to be noncompliant. However, when given a bit of extra time, they can show their compliance quite successfully.<br><br>Transitioning without protesting should be a secondary goal and is not always possible when first teaching about transitions.<br><br>Inflexible students may need not only advance warning but also a well-defined plan. The plan has to show the student that the same goal can be met in more than one way. With a clearly defined plan in place, she or he can transition more easily and can also show greater flexibility. |

*(continued)*

| Skill sets | Functions and skills | Examples of functions and skills in action | Sample performance difficulties | Potential strategies, accommodations, or educational objectives |
|---|---|---|---|---|
| Working memory | The number of units of information that can be kept in memory in real time and be used to complete tasks, participate in activities, and reach goals | The student is able to remember all of the steps needed to complete a familiar routine (e.g., home routines, such as how to get ready for school, or classroom routines, such as where to put one's belongings upon arrival at school and the first steps needed upon entry into the classroom).<br><br>The student is able to remember several novel instructions and to carry them out successfully. For example, the student can remember the instructions delivered at the beginning of the task for an in-class art assignment.<br><br>The student is able to remember the rules of math (e.g., "do multiplication before you do addition") while solving multiple-step math problems and can also remember answers to intermediate calculations while solving a longer multistep calculation. See Chapter 11.<br><br>The student can read and remember key pieces of information in the early part of a text and can keep available and use this information to comprehend later portions of the text. See Chapter 10. | The student is unable to remember all of the steps needed to complete a familiar routine. The student commonly misses one or more steps and needs reminders from adults to complete the routine successfully. For example, when dressing in the morning, the student forgets to put on her or his socks. When entering the classroom, the student does not put her or his homework into the basket on the teacher's desk.<br><br>The student is unable to remember novel instructions and commonly follows only the first or last instruction from a set of instructions. The task does not get completed successfully.<br><br>The student is unable to remember key information about math rules or the answers to intermediate calculations when asked to carry out longer math problems; more errors occur when solving multistep math problems.<br><br>The student is unable to remember key information about a text when asked to respond to comprehension questions about a longer text. | Difficulties with working memory are related to difficulties with inhibition and shifting cognitive set. The three skills interact with and support one another. The strategies listed previously for inhibition and shifting cognitive set will apply equally to the student with working memory difficulties.<br><br>Students with working memory difficulties need extra support from adults to complete tasks successfully. Extra support can take the form of corrective feedback, which then allows the student to correct missing steps or correct errors.<br><br>The adult working with the student should engage the student and be strategic about how to deliver corrective feedback. One way to do this is to create a system for detecting and correcting errors. The student is provided with a written list of the steps needed to complete a task, the rules needed to solve math problems, or the strategies that one can use to remember key information. The adult can set up a prescheduled time to verify that the student has completed the task or activity successfully and to discover errors. Preferably, the student is invited to use the visual reminder system to notice her or his own errors. The student is then also invited to correct those errors. Using a strategy such as this is time consuming when it is first implemented but can serve the longer-term goal of reducing the student's overreliance on others to detect and correct errors. Students commonly protest about visual reminder (error detection and error correction) systems. However, the choices are limited. Either the adult serves as the reminder system or the student develops a self-reminding system. Error detection and error correction procedures also serve to foster development of metacognition (see below). |

| Skill sets | Functions and skills | Examples of functions and skills in action | Sample performance difficulties | Potential strategies, accommodations, or educational objectives |
|---|---|---|---|---|
| Planning | The capacity to break tasks, activities, or goals into component steps, to sequence the steps, and to complete the steps to reach a goal. | The student can add a familiar or previously memorized plan to other previously memorized plan (proto-planning).<br><br>The student can create a goal, such as to build a mobile, to leave school every day with all needed homework items in the bookbag, to write an essay, to repair a bicycle, or to host an anti-bullying event at school. The student is able to break individual goals into subgoals or component steps, sequence the steps in a logical order to ensure that the goal is reached, and complete all of the necessary steps to reach the goal. Here, planning is applied to goals, tasks, and activities that can be reached or completed over the course of hours or days. | The student may have difficulty completing memorized and familiar plans due to difficulties with the executive skills listed previously.<br><br>The student may be able to identify a goal and identify component steps to reach the goal but need adult assistance to sequence the steps into a logical order and to make sure that each step is completed accurately. Without adult support, the student is liable to get lost along the way and/or lose his or her place in the sequence. | All of the strategies listed previously are important to keep in mind when teaching a student about planning. Teach lower-order executive skills before attempting to teach planning skills.<br><br>Teach the student about sequencing (ordering) steps. Apply these terms to a variety of different planning demands so that the student can recognize similarities in sequencing no matter what the task might be (cleaning up the bedroom or classroom, writing an essay, repairing a bicycle, hosting an event).<br><br>Provide a schematic or an outline for a larger project (such as writing an essay) and have the student practice identifying component steps for each segment of the outline.<br><br>Provide strategy instruction in reading and writing. See Chapters 9 and 10. |

*(continued)*

| Skill sets | Functions and skills | Examples of functions and skills in action | Sample performance difficulties | Potential strategies, accommodations, or educational objectives |
|---|---|---|---|---|
| Organizational skills | The capacity to coordinate plans with one another. Organizational skills include the development of plans that respect time constraints, promote efficiency, and prevent the occurrence of mishaps or goal conflicts. | The student is able to coordinate familiar as well as novel plans with one another so that multiple goals can be reached over an interval of days or a week or two. The student is capable of scheduling times for homework, for recreational activities, and/or for family events. These several goals do not conflict with one another because time was dedicated for each in the weekly schedule. Organization of these plans includes creating a contingency plan when needed, such as scheduling extra time in case a homework assignment takes longer than expected, scheduling extra time or alternate activities if bad weather interferes with recreational activities, or scheduling a visit to the library well in advance of necessary to accommodate an upcoming holiday when the library might be closed. | Many students have difficulty with organizational skills, especially when the executive skills listed previously are not yet in place.<br><br>Even students who show planning skills may have difficulty coordinating plans with one another and may be unable to reach multiple goals over time intervals. Goals come into conflict with one another because of mishaps or because advance scheduling was not undertaken successfully.<br><br>Goal conflicts become apparent when it is too late to rectify the conflict. As examples, only at the last minute does the student realize that missing reference material cannot be obtained because the library is closed. Only at the last minute does the student recognize that the extra soccer practice scheduled this week because of last week's bad weather now conflicts with the studying time needed for the next day's test. Some of the student's goals are not reached because of lack of organizational skills and associated goal conflicts. | Teaching organizational skills can occur when the student has mastered many or most of the skills listed previously. Time constraints (estimating the amount of time needed and finishing on time), efficiency (getting as many goals reached in the shortest time interval), and prevention of mishaps are key concepts to teach. With practice, students learn how organizational skills help them to meet their personal goals or how those goals fail to get met because of problems in organizing their plans<br><br>It is important to teach how the key concepts listed here apply to all of the different types of goals that a student may have (academic, recreational, personal, social, etc.). |

| Skill sets | Functions and skills | Examples of functions and skills in action | Sample performance difficulties | Potential strategies, accommodations, or educational objectives |
|---|---|---|---|---|
| Metacognition | The capacity to review one's performance against a performance standard to detect and correct errors<br><br>The capacity to judge one's past performance against current expectations<br><br>The capacity to adjust past knowledge and skills in order to be able to meet current expectations successfully<br><br>Metacognition used in the service of self-regulation is discussed in Chapter 8. Self-regulation refers to adjusting goals in response to personal standards or beliefs. | The student can review her or his own performance, compare against a performance standard, and detect and correct errors.<br><br>The student can review her or his performance and modify behaviors so as to reach goals more accurately or more successfully when the same or a similar goal has to be met in the future.<br><br>The student can review her or his performance and can use this information to adjust behaviors to meet new goals and new expectations.<br><br>The student can compare past successes and difficulties and can use this information to revise and update current knowledge and skills. In turn, the student can adjust behaviors as new goals and new expectations have to be met. | The student does not take the time to review her or his performance against a performance standard and does not detect or correct errors.<br><br>The student does not review her or his performance and therefore does not modify behaviors when the same or a similar goal presents itself in the future, resulting in repeated performance difficulties.<br><br>The student does not review her or his performance and does not use this information to adjust previous behaviors to successfully meet new goals and new expectations. In turn, the student has difficulty reaching new goals and meeting new expectations.<br><br>The student does not review past successes and difficulties and/or does not use this information to revise and update knowledge and skills. In turn, the student has difficulty reaching new goals and meeting new expectations. | All of the strategies, accommodations, and objectives listed previously assist in the development of metacognition.<br><br>Adult support should be provided to assist the student in reviewing her or his performance. Adults need to anticipate the resistance that students with executive dysfunctions often show when asked to review their performance. The performance review is commonly accepted as a form of corrective feedback and as a reminder of their failures. It is important to highlight successes as part of the review.<br><br>Adult support is needed to help the student learn from past successes as well as past difficulties, and to plan strategically her or his behaviors and responses to new goals and new expectations.<br><br>Adult support is needed to guide the student to learn from past successes and difficulties and to help the student update and revise prior knowledge and skills. |

APPENDIX 7.2 **Executive Skills Observation Sheet**

| Skill sets | Functions and skills | Example skills or deficits in this student | Potential strategies, accommodations, or educational objectives |
|---|---|---|---|
| Orientation | Orient one's attention and focus to a stimulus, task, activity, or goal | | |
| Initiation | Take a first step toward completing a task or activity or reaching a goal | | |
| Inhibition and impulse control | Inhibition of distractors to maintain focus on a task, activity, or goal<br>Defer gratification by inhibiting attention toward an interesting stimulus, and instead focusing on a less desired or less interesting activity first<br>Capacity for sustained attention | | |
| Shifting cognitive set | The capacity to shift orientation, attention, or focus between different activities, tasks, or goals or between steps within a task or activity | | |
| Working memory | The number of units of information that can be kept in memory in real time and used to complete tasks, participate in activities, and reach goals | | |
| Planning | The capacity to break tasks, activities, or goals into component steps, to sequence the steps, and to complete the steps to reach a goal | | |
| Organizational skills | The capacity to coordinate plans with one another. Organizational skills include the development of plans that respect time constraints, promote efficiency, and prevent the occurrence of mishaps or conflicts | | |
| Metacognition | The capacity to review one's performance against a performance standard to detect and correct errors<br>The capacity to judge one's past performance against current expectations<br>The capacity to adjust past knowledge and skills in order to be able to meet current expectations successfully | | |

# Affect and Self-Regulation Skills



## INTRODUCTION AND GENERAL DEFINITIONS

The previous chapter concluded with a discussion of metacognition and how people choose goals. Although metacognition is essential to reflecting on one's performance, human behavior depends on much more than just monitoring one's performance, making sure that tasks get done, and that errors are detected and corrected. Executive skills alone are not enough to explain successful human behavior. Although executive skills and metacognition help humans to choose and work toward different types of goals, it is important to consider what influences the choices and goals that people make in the first place, the motivation or the drive that leads to choosing one goal versus another. This chapter discusses how affect influences the goals that people choose and expands the conversation to the broader topic of self-regulation. This chapter is interested in successful self-regulation: How affect influences people to choose the right goal for the right situation. The chapter begins with some general definitions of *affect* and *self-regulation,* which sets the stage for understanding the other terms presented in this chapter.

### Definition of *Affect*

*Affect* is a very general term that refers to the experience of feelings and emotions. Feelings and emotions have several components, which are discussed in more detail later in this chapter. Feelings can be physiological (e.g., bodily sensations, referred to as arousal) and emotional (e.g., being angry, sad, or happy). Even though affect consists of internally experienced feelings and emotions, it can be observed and measured as physiological phenomena, such as changes in heart rate or blood pressure. More typically, affect is noticed through behaviors such as changes in facial expression, changes in tone of voice, and changes in body posture or activity level. Some of these behaviors were discussed in Chapter 5. Affect may present itself using language as well. For example, a person might say, "I'm tired!" or "I'm really angry!" while at the same time showing a tired or angry facial expression. Nonobservable features of affect are those that are experienced internally by the individual and are apparent to the observer only if the person experiencing the affect describes them. Nonobservable features could be sensations such as a tightening of the stomach when anxious or an elated feeling when something good happens.

Internally experienced sensations influence how goals are selected and how people subsequently behave. When people decide upon a course of action for any given situation, affect is a major consideration. For example, if too tired or too anxious, a person may avoid pursuing certain goals. If very excited or angry, a person may also pursue certain kinds of goals. In both of these instances, affect influences choices and thereby shapes subsequent behaviors. When adults observe students in the classroom, they often make guesses about affect and how it motivates certain behaviors.

Affect is often most noticeable when it is dysregulated, or out of balance. In the classroom, the observing adult might be especially prompted to think about affect and its influence when the student's behaviors fall outside of expected norms. For instance, if a student is experiencing hunger and seems irritable, or when a student is very tired and looks sleepy, adults are more likely to notice their affect. Similarly, when a student shows significant anger, anxiety, or unhappiness through facial expressions, tone of voice, behaviors, or words, adults may also notice the affect and how it interferes with learning. Any excess or intense emotion, including excitement or happiness, can be disruptive to learning. Once the reasons for the affect are identified, adults can seek solutions to diminish or change the affect so that the student can learn more successfully.

Diminishing or changing affect that is interfering with student participation is certainly an important goal. However, affect is not something that is bad and it is not necessarily disruptive. In fact, affect is the driving force behind all action in the world. Affect supports learning (Blair, 2002; Denham, Ferrier, Howarth, Herndon, & Bassett, 2016; Garner, 20010; Valiente, Swanson, & Eisenberg, 2012) and is part of what a student needs to learn successfully. All students should learn about how affect influences behavior and how it can be harnessed as a resource to impact behavior in positive ways. Understanding affect can help all people reach important personal goals.

Like metacognition, competence in affect consists of both a base of knowledge and a set of skills. To become competent in affect, students must have knowledge about their own affect and about affect in others. For example, it is important to know what types of behaviors reveal what types of affect. It is also important to know how people describe the internal experience of affect and to have knowledge about what types of goals people are likely to pursue when they experience a given type of affect. These examples highlight general knowledge about affect. Competence in affect also requires the successful expression of affect. When people do not express affect successfully, those around them can make false assumptions about their intentions, desires, beliefs, and thoughts. One must be capable of using the right facial expressions, gestures, tone of voice, and words to express the internal experience(s) accurately and to explain one's choice of behaviors or goals. This does not mean that affect should always be expressed. What it does mean, however, is that students and adults alike need to know the difference between how affect is expressed externally, how it is experienced internally, how often the two are aligned, and what the impact can be when the two are not aligned.



## Definition of Behavioral Self-Regulation

Behavioral self-regulation, like affect, consists of both observable and nonobservable phenomena. Hofmann, Schmeichel, and Baddeley (2012) defines *self-regulation* as the capacity to reduce the discrepancy between one's personal goals, beliefs, or standards and the actual state of one's behaviors. When a person engages in successful self-regulation, there is an alignment among affect: Its internal experiences, its external behaviors, and the person's stated goals, beliefs, and standards.

A simple example of the need for alignment might occur when a person receives an undesired a birthday present and responds by laughing or making an inappropriate or negative comment. Upon reflection, the receiver of the gift then needs to decide which external behaviors to show next. They could continue in the same vein, making fun of the gift, getting angry, or ignoring the gift giver. These behaviors may be consistent with the internally experienced affect (the frustration or upset that the receiver experienced) but are not necessarily consistent with the desire to maintain positive social relations (goals or standards). Once the recipient recognizes underlying affect and the simultaneous desire to maintain positive social relations, he or she can then modify the behaviors through self-regulation. For example, he or she could say, "Thank you for this lovely gift," a response that is consistent with their desire to maintain positive social relations, even if it is not aligned with their internal experience of the affect. Taking the example a step further, the receiver of the gift might choose to change (regulate) the underlying affect by focusing on the positive intentions of the gift giver. By identifying the right internal experience of affect (e.g., the receiver of the gift might find a way to feel thankful or grateful), it is easier to find the right words and to show the right behaviors. With this self-regulation, the behaviors and the affect are also in line with personal standards of maintaining friendship and are now both in line with the person's internal standards, beliefs, and goals.

Depending on the type of friendship between these two people, the receiver of the gift could take self-regulation further. The recipient could speak with the giver of the gift by talking about gifts and friendship more generally. For example, he or she could say something like, "Thank you so much for the gift; it means a lot that you thought of me. At some point, I would like to talk about what kinds of gifts we should be exchanging." The experience of the gift now becomes an opportunity for the friendship to deepen. Self-regulation has now been taken further and is no longer just about preserving the friendship. It improves the chances of a positive, long-term outcome for both the receiver and the giver of the gift.

*Self-regulation*, as defined in this chapter, refers to making an alignment among the internal experience of affect, the external expression of affect, and getting important long-term needs met. Successful self-regulation is not an all-or-none phenomenon. Commonly, self-regulation is an iterative and even repetitive process that strives to improve both short- and long-term outcomes.

As is the case for affect, competence in self-regulation requires both knowledge and skills. Successful self-regulation requires general knowledge about how people, familiar and not familiar, select goals that are worth pursuing and the types of behaviors that help people reach those goals. Self-regulation is also a set of skills that involves actively choosing the right goals and the right behaviors for the situation. Unless a person engages in some self-regulation of the internally experienced affect, the choice of goals and behaviors is more constrained. As in the case above of someone who receives a gift, a lack of reflection on affect can lead somewhat automatically to behaviors that end up not serving personal long-term goals. The right goals and behaviors for a given situation should end up serving important values, beliefs, and standards and should enhance the chances of a positive long-term outcome.

What makes humans different from animals is that humans not only can use metacognition to choose different goals and behaviors but also can change the affect that influences the goals and behaviors that they choose (Denham et al., 2016). Stated another way, humans can choose how to act. By practicing self-regulation, they can also choose how to feel. By changing feelings, it is possible to choose from a wider range of behaviors that support a wider range of goals. The ability to choose both how to feel and how to behave is an inherently human skill.



## HOW THIS FRAMEWORK WAS CONSTRUCTED

The scientific literature is not yet clear about how to define, distinguish, and discriminate among terms such as *bodily sensations*, *feelings*, *emotions*, and *motivation*, and it is also not clear how to separate these (internal) feelings from their associated behaviors. Definitions vary within and among researchers and clinicians (Dinsmore, 2008). For example, one definition of emotions states that they include arousal processes, motivational processes, and behaviors (Izard, 2010). The framework presented here uses similar terms but takes a different approach. The terms *arousal*, *emotions*, and *motivation* are considered separately and subsumed under the umbrella term *affect*. By separating the terms, it is easier to understand the similarities, differences, and overlap among them. It is also easier to develop more targeted intervention strategies.

This framework separates the term *self-regulation* from *affect* by focusing on successful self-regulation (i.e., how affect is expressed and then either used or changed so that subsequent behaviors lead to positive outcomes). It also differentiates the term *self-regulation* from the terms *metacognition* and *executive skills*. In the previous chapter, the term *metacognition* was identified as a means to evaluate whether a goal was reached. In self-regulation, metacognition is not only applied to understanding whether a goal was reached. It is extended to take into consideration the motivation, emotions, and arousal that influence how humans choose goals and behaviors in the first place. It asks how motivation, emotions, and arousal can be altered or changed, so that new goals and behaviors become possible. It requires an understanding of how people choose goals, why their choices are not always aligned with their values, and how they can change how they feel so that affect, goals, behaviors, and values can all be aligned.

This chapter will focus on the phenomena of affect and self-regulation as they arise in response to everyday situations. While most of the examples are related to classroom activities, affect and self-regulation can occur in patterns or trends that are not specific to school or other day to day situations. *Moods, temperament*, and *traits* are terms that refer to affect that is continuous or consistent within a person regardless of the setting. For example, a person can be generally sad or happy and can respond to many or most situations with the same affect. Having a general propensity to feel a certain way can result in habitually behaving in a certain way. This in turn results in a person having a reduced behavioral repertoire that constrains the number of goals that get chosen. Features such as these are often considered personality characteristics and do not change easily or quickly. They are also important to identify and understand. Traits, temperament, moods, and personality characteristics are not typically within the purview of school professionals to identify or to help manage. For this reason, these aspects of affect are not discussed at length in this chapter. The goal of this chapter is to introduce basic components of *affect* (arousal, emotions, and motivation) and *self-regulation* and to show how this information can lead to greater understanding of student behaviors and to intervention planning that enhances school performance.



## HOW CAN THIS FRAMEWORK HELP ME?

The terms presented in this chapter can be used to discuss student performance with students, family members, and professionals. The Affect and Self-Regulation Skills Framework can help school teams describe the important components of affect and how a student's behaviors are related to affect. When adults understand the affect that underlies student behaviors, they can also help students to shift affect and to choose different behaviors to reach a broader set of goals.

Teachers understand that attending to the affect of their students can enhance learning (Blair, 2002; Denham et al., 2016; Garner, 2010; Valiente et al., 2012). Members of school teams are likely to find this chapter useful primarily for students who have difficulty managing intense or disruptive affect (e.g., aggression and anger, anxiety, or inattention due to arousal processes). These students may be identified as being willful, disobedient, scared, or lacking in motivation, and they often do not receive the services or supports that they urgently need (Forness, Freeman, Paparella, Kauffman, & Walker, 2012). An important intention of this chapter is to encourage school professionals to think differently about students who show extremes of affect and to use the terms and concepts discussed in this chapter to enhance the student's ability to change affect, align affect with behaviors, and align behaviors so that they are consistent with the academic and social goals of school.

This chapter is also designed to help the reader hold conversations with students for whom managing affect is not an area of difficulty. All students need to know about how affect underlies all of their behaviors, in ways that are positive as well as not positive. To understand the role of arousal, emotions, and motivation in education and to harness them for successful participation at school, students and professionals need to focus on circumstances in which the student is not performing successfully but also include those in which the student is performing well. The intention of this chapter is to help educators and their colleagues think flexibly and creatively about student behaviors and underlying affect, both when it disrupts and when it facilitates learning.

## AFFECT AND SELF-REGULATION SKILLS FRAMEWORK

The foregoing discussion offered an overview of the concepts that underlie affect and self-regulation. The Affect and Self-Regulation Skills Framework that follows provides a breakdown of these concepts with more details. It will help the reader accurately describe affect and successful self-regulation and choose interventions in a more targeted manner.

Affect and self-regulation consist of the following components:

1. Arousal
   a. Intensity: High and low
2. Emotions
   a. Intensity: High and low
   b. Valence: Positive and negative
   c. Type: Basic emotions, social emotions, and complex emotions
3. Motivation
   a. Motivation and its primary goals: A hierarchy
   b. Motivation and its associated behaviors: Approach and withdrawal
   c. Motivation and goal persistence
4. Self-regulation
   a. Regulation of affect
   b. Regulation of goals and associated behaviors

The framework, discussed in the sections that follow, is also summarized and available in Appendix 8.1 for quick reference.

### Arousal

Arousal is a broad concept that encompasses several phenomena. It refers to changes in alertness related to sleep and wakefulness and to the level of activity in physiological functions such as heart rate, respiratory rate, digestive activities, and the motor system. It also refers to the level of cognitive activity, the alertness and attention given to cognitive processes. The arousal system is designed to support animals and humans to help them engage successfully in goal-directed behaviors required for behavioral adaptation and survival (de Leceal, Carter, & Adamantidis, 2012). Changes in arousal level occur in response to external sensory inputs (sights, sounds, touches, smells, and tastes), as well as internal sensory inputs (feeling tired, feeling unwell, feeling hungry or sated, feeling bowel/bladder needs, having sexual appetites or urges). Arousal is considered to be at a higher level when a person is more alert to sensory inputs, shows a higher activity level, and shows greater emotional reactivity. Arousal is considered to be at a lower level when a person looks sleepy or tired, has a low activity level, and does not show much emotion. In fact, it can be defined on the basis of these three phenomena (Pfaff, 2006). The right level of arousal needed to help people function successfully depends on the function or activity that is most important at any given moment. Arousal processes help to ensure safety by avoiding danger through fight-or-flight responses, and in the larger context of evolution ensure long-term survival through sexual and reproductive processes. Overall, levels and types of arousal need to match specific circumstances and goals to ensure physical safety and well-being.

In the classroom, arousal levels need to be optimized so that the student is alert to learning and primed for classroom participation. The level of alertness depends on intrinsic factors such as the student's capacity to remain alert for learning as well as the level of stimulation provided by the environment. Both too little or too much arousal can result in a decreased level of attention for learning. This relationship is referred to as an inverted U-shaped curve (Blair & Raver, 2015; see Figure 8.1). The optimal or "just right" level of arousal lies at the top of the curve. Optimal arousal means that there is enough arousal to sustain attention and energy on an important task or activity but not so excessive that attention and energy toward the task or activity starts to diminish again.

Since arousal involves complex neurological and hormonal systems, it is only possible to measure with precision in laboratory and highly controlled research settings. Measuring levels of arousal in the classroom setting is done indirectly, based on adult reports of student levels of alertness, attentiveness, and participation. Excess activity levels suggest a high level of arousal, whereas sleepiness and a low activity level suggest a low level of arousal.

***Arousal and Its Effects on Behavior*** Fight-or-flight responses are dictated by arousal processes. They are predictable and automatic behaviors that are helpful for preserving physical safety and security, are produced in a largely reflexive manner, and are not very flexible (Levenson, 1999). The higher the arousal level, the more rigid and the more predictable the resultant behavior will be. Withdrawal from pain, such as after touching a hot stove, is a good example of an automatic and predictable behavioral response to an arousal state.



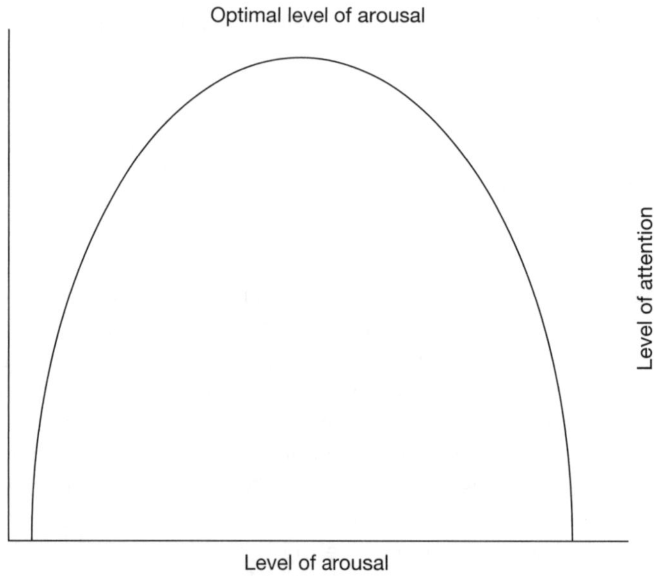


**Figure 8.1.** To facilitate learning, arousal should be at the "just right" or optimal level. This inverted U curve highlights that relationship between attention and arousal.

Analyzing brain–behavior relationships, including learning behaviors, requires taking into consideration the person's arousal processes. When arousal is directed toward addressing bodily or safety needs (hunger, pain, discomfort), classroom participation and learning decrease. Flexible thinking and the pursuit of varied goals, so critical for learning, are generally not available to the student when arousal is dedicated to these other functions.

In the classroom, optimal arousal requires the student to not be "too anything": Not too tired, hungry, energetic, or excited. Optimal arousal means not being overly tired or too energetic or too excited. Optimal arousal means being engaged, but not overwhelmed by the sensory stimulation of the classroom. It is also needed to regulate emotions, not just to learn successfully. For example, when people are hungry or tired, they tend to tolerate frustration poorly and might even feel depressed or sad. It is more difficult to regulate emotions when basic arousal processes have not been addressed first. Physiological processes and the student's safety and security need to be addressed successfully so that arousal can be dedicated to the regulation of emotions, to learning, and to classroom participation.

## Emotions

Arousal is closely tied to emotions. When arousal levels are high, emotions are experienced as more intense. Like arousal, emotions consist of bodily sensations and have neurobiological components. However, emotions are also experienced cognitively and through language (Barrett, Mesquita, Ochsner, & Gross, 2007). There are many facets to what constitutes an *emotion*, and researchers are not yet in agreement on the definition of this term. It can include the concepts of arousal, motivation, and self-regulation (Izard, 2010). The fact that so many concepts are subsumed under the term *emotion* highlights how difficult it is to separate the term from the other terms discussed in this chapter. Normally, when people think about emotions, they think of specific emotions such as feeling happy, angry, sad, or scared. The framework in this chapter recognizes the importance of types of emotions such as this, but starts by discussing the concepts of intensity and valence first.

***Intensity of Emotions*** Emotions are either intense or subdued, associated with high or low levels of arousal. Young children tend to experience emotions intensely. The intensity of the emotions wanes with age and with greater perspective, and their emotional experiences are no longer perceived as being so intense. This may occur because the experience is less novel, thus provoking a lower level of interest and alertness. For example, the anger in a toddler or preschooler who is told to turn off a screen-based toy is replaced over time with a more subdued expression of anger (it might be called frustration or annoyance), because the child knows that screen time can occur again later in the day. Likewise, the excitement of having a parent come home from work is replaced over time with a more subdued expression of happiness or contentment, because the child is familiar with the pattern and knows that parents come home every day.

Like arousal, emotions must have just the right intensity for the situation. Intense emotions are likely to interfere with successful action in the world, but so too are emotions that are not felt intensely enough. Excessive anger that leads to aggression will usually not result in a positive outcome. Similarly, excessive excitement that leads to impulsive behaviors or an inability to follow instructions can also interfere with a successful outcome. At the same time, someone who experiences no anger at all when faced with an unkind remark from a peer may become a target for bullying or be at risk for not building healthy relationships. The child who is not excited enough by the activities of school might not engage successfully and underperform for this reason.

Emotions have to be just right for classroom participation and for learning. When a student is not concerned enough about an upcoming exam, for example, they might not study enough and end up performing poorly. At the same time, excess anxiety about an exam can interfere with the quality and duration of studying, resulting in difficulty remembering important details or an inability to focus. Similarly, feeling proud of one's academic accomplishments can contribute to success ("I want to make sure I keep getting good grades, so I better study"), or, if misappropriated, can result in no studying at all ("I don't need to worry, I'm a good student and I never fail tests. I don't need to study"). An optimal level of emotions is needed for successful learning, social interactions, adaptive tasks, classroom participation behaviors, and more. To function effectively, the intensity of emotions needs to be just right.

Extremes of emotions are easy to notice and can be particularly disruptive in school settings. As such, it is important for students and education professionals to discuss and agree upon the just right level of emotions that can result in successful learning and behavioral outcomes.

***Valence of Emotions*** The second way that researchers and clinicians discuss emotions is to consider the extent to which they are pleasurable or non-pleasurable, known as *valence*. Emotions can be assigned valence by placing them on a continuum of being either positive or negative (Barrett et al., 2007). For example, sadness and anxiety are typically considered negative emotions, whereas happiness and excitement are considered positive ones. See Table 8.1. Differentiated and complex emotions, discussed later in this section, are made up of combinations of basic emotions, each of which may have its own intensity and its own valence.

Valence is not observable in isolation but can be identified by asking the person to reflect upon whether what they feel is or is not pleasurable. The answer to this seemingly simple question is not always that straightforward, because the valence can be mixed. For example, anger most often presupposes negative valence but can be associated with pleasure when people experience it with feelings of power or control. Emotions are more likely to include a mixture of positive and negative valence when more than one emotion is experienced at the same time. For example, a student could simultaneously feel embarrassment (a negative emotion) and humor (a positive emotion), when he or she inadvertently makes a statement that causes everybody to laugh. The positive or negative valence of an emotional experience will depend on the circumstances. Valence is a useful concept, because it helps in discovering the richness and complexity of the emotion. Educators and therapists can practice having conversations with students about the valence of their emotions, so that they learn how to make distinctions such as these.

*Valence and Associated Behaviors* People typically enjoy positive emotions more than negative emotions. They seek out positive valence and try to avoid or diminish negative valence. When classroom participation and learning are associated with positive emotional valence, a student is likely to seek out more classroom participation and deeper learning experiences. Valence associated with social behaviors can be mixed and more complex. For example, it can be pleasurable to maintain positive social connections with peers and experience happiness or contentedness but can also be pleasurable to engage in teasing or bullying behavior, which may be associated with anger or disgust. Both of these social behaviors are associated with positive valence, even though anger and disgust are not typically considered to be positive emotions. Only by discovering the experienced valence of an emotion can the observer learn about why a student may have behaved in a certain manner.

**Table 8.1.** Examples of basic emotions

| | Positive emotion | Negative emotion |
|---|---|---|
| Basic emotions | Contentment<br>Happiness<br>Desire<br>Anticipatory pleasure | Fear<br>Anger/frustration<br>Disgust |
| Social emotions | Pride | Jealousy, embarrassment, shame, guilt |

***Specific Types of Emotions*** The third way that researchers describe and discuss emotions is by using specific words, such as *happy, sad, angry,* or *scared.* The Differential Emotions Theory (DET) ascribes specific labels to specific emotions (Abe & Izard, 1999). The specific emotion labels shown in Table 8.1 are commonly used as a starting point when discussing emotions with students. Some debate persists about whether emotions can be categorized as discrete experiences or discrete types (Barrett, 2006a, 2006b). One limitation of labeling emotions is that they are not descriptive enough. For example, basic emotions become more differentiated as they are experienced in different circumstances. They can have more than one valence and intensity, especially when basic emotions combine with one another. Any one of the emotions listed in Table 8.1 can be experienced differently depending on the associated level of arousal and on the valence for the person who is experiencing the emotion.

An example of how the same emotion can be experienced differently is to consider the emotion of anger. A child can be angry when told to turn off the television or when a friend says that he cannot go to the zoo as planned because he made other plans at the last minute. Whereas both of these situations might trigger feelings of anger, the nature and intensity of these emotional experiences could be very different (Cacioppo & Gardner, 1999). The experience of anger can also be different when it is associated with other emotions, such as when a child misses out on a playdate because a friend is ill. Here, the emotion of anger or frustration might also be associated with empathic concern or sadness. When emotions are associated or blended with one another, both their intensity and valence change. The actual experience of an emotion is never fully captured by just one word or even by a few words (Kreibig, 2010; Rottenberg & Gross, 2007). See also the Basic Versus Complex Emotions section, below.

***Mapping Valence, Intensity, and Type*** Figure 8.2 shows the relationships of the different types of emotions by mapping them on two axes. The X-axis reflects valence (negative and positive), whereas the Y-axis reflects the person's state of arousal (high versus low intensity). Any discrete emotion can be placed on the Y- or X-axis based on these two features (Russell, 1980). All the terms discussed thus far and listed in the table can be placed on the graph in Figure 8.2.

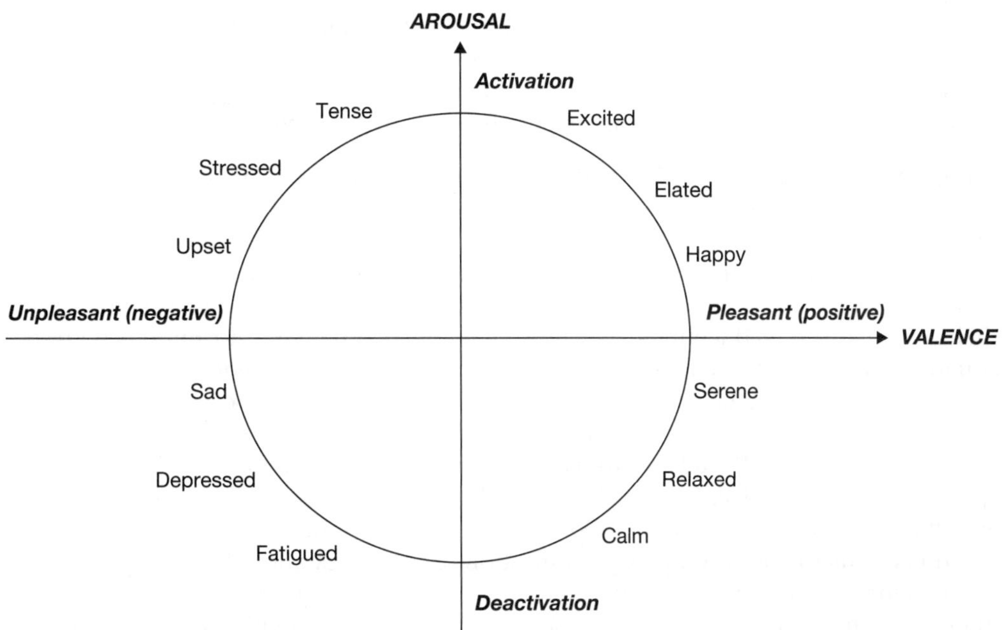


**Figure 8.2.** Russell's (1980) model of affect, which shows the relationship between different emotions based on their level of affect and valence. (From Lanata, Valenza, & Scilingo [2012].)

The figure serves to integrate the concepts of positive and negative valence, intensity, and specific types of emotion. By seeing emotions mapped out in this way, educators and therapists can develop questions and speak more comprehensively about emotions with their students, helping them to develop a richer description. As discussed later in the chapter, a good description of emotions facilitates successful self-regulation. Each of the terms used to describe emotion (intensity, valence, and type) can help educators and therapists choose the right strategy for regulating the behaviors that follow.

***Basic Versus Complex Emotions*** A fourth way to conceptualize emotions is to think of them as either basic or complex. Basic emotions are those of happiness, sadness, fear, and anger. They can also be referred to as fundamental, foundational, or first order and can be experienced without much cognition. These emotions are associated with simple motivations and behavioral outcomes (Izard, 2011) and are identified early in life, typically during the toddler years. Emotions tied to social interactions and social relationships, such as jealousy, shame, guilt, and pride emerge soon after in older toddlers and preschoolers. Early in life, the basic emotions are experienced as single entities that may follow one another. They are not experienced as blends of two or more emotions, and they are not highly differentiated. Each of the emotions is experienced in largely the same way, regardless of the inciting event.

As children age into the school-age years, emotions become more differentiated and more complex. In any given emotion-eliciting event, there can be more than one type of emotion, each varying in valence and intensity. For example, children at this age understand that one can feel sadness (a negative emotion associated with low arousal) and happiness (a positive emotion associated with high arousal) at the same time. The young student can be sad if her or his goldfish died but can at the same time feel happy because the student's grandparents are coming for a visit. Similarly, students can learn that anger can be associated with pleasure as well as with fear. A child or adolescent can experience anticipatory pleasure when plotting revenge against a sibling but might at the same time be fearful of a punishment that could occur after the revenge is carried out. Experiencing blends of emotions such as this is possible as children recognize how different situations can provoke different kinds of emotions. Complex emotions by definition include more complex thinking. As children and adolescents age, their emotions include more thoughts. They start to map their emotional experiences onto memories of past experiences and blend information about their emotions with how they perceive emotions experienced by others. They learn to describe emotions using a richer set of terms and understand how those emotions are experienced in different circumstances.

***Emotions, Cognition, and Behaviors*** Emotions are a more complex phenomenon than arousal. Arousal processes tend to influence behaviors in a predictable manner, especially when the arousal is dedicated to physiological functions and survival needs. In contrast, emotions affect behaviors in a more complex manner and are associated with more complex thinking. As children age, their emotions include memories and general knowledge. When they learn about their own happy or sad feelings, they almost automatically make attributions with the event or situation out of which the feeling arose. Once an attribution is made ("I'm feeling sad because of . . ."), a consequence also emerges ("Because I'm feeling sad, I'm going to . . ."). In other words, having and noticing an emotion sets up a chain of thinking: Where the emotion came from and where the emotion will lead. For this reason, emotion can be defined as "motivated cognition" (Izard, Fine, Mostow, Trentacosta, & Campbell, 2002). Emotions correspond to the motivational aspect of cognition (Barrett et al., 2007; Zelazo & Cunningham, 2007). A simple description of emotions leads to a less complex identification of its causes and a less complex set of possible consequences (resultant behaviors or choices). A rich description of emotions reflects a richer understanding of the causes of the emotions and has the potential to result in more complex behaviors (Izard, 2011). How a child (or adult) behaves in response to an emotion-eliciting event depends on the number and type(s) of emotions involved, their intensity, and their valence.

***Emotions, Cognition, and Classroom Behaviors*** Positive and negative emotions play varying roles in how they influence classroom participation behaviors and learning. The Arousal section of this chapter discussed the fact that arousal is neither bad nor good, and that successful functioning requires just the right level of arousal. The same applies to emotional valence. It is not the positive or negative valence of the emotion that determines the impact it has on learning, but how the emotions support or fail to support learning. Positive and negative emotions support learning differently. For example, negative emotions narrow the perceptual (thinking) field and restrict the amount of information that is taken into consideration. In contrast, positive emotions broaden the perceptual field and increase the amount of information that is taken into consideration (Izard et al., 2002). So-called negative emotions, such as fear or anger, are associated with detail-oriented learning. They narrow the focus to central aspects of a task, simultaneously reducing the focus on peripheral aspects of a task. Learning and task completion are less flexible and more linear when negative emotions underlie the learning behavior. The type of thinking described here is associated with greater memory accuracy and greater goal directedness (Levine & Edelstein, 2009). As an example, pre-exam anxiety often facilitates memorizing key information in preparation for a test and prevents the broad type of thinking needed to make new links with associated topics.

In contrast, positive emotions can promote a widening of one's attentional focus. Positive emotions allow the learner to make links among disparate aspects of a problem or learning task and potentially allow for the creation of new solutions to a problem or new ways of completing tasks. Positive emotions are required for tasks that require creativity. In creative thinking, the outcome often matters less than the discovery or exploration of ideas and options. This type of thinking is more flexible and less linear than the type associated with negative emotions.

The impact of emotions on classroom behaviors depends on the intensity of the underlying arousal, not just on whether the emotion is positive or negative. The arousal that underlies the emotion gives it force. Emotions that are too intense and not intense enough both interfere with classroom participation. The student who experiences no anxiety at all about studying could be just as unproductive as the student who is excessively anxious. Productive learning, as well as flexible and creative thinking, all require just the right level of arousal, and just the right mixture of both positive and negative emotions. A rich description of the causes and consequences of emotion helps identify a wider range of behaviors to support successful action in the classroom and elsewhere.

***Emotions: Conclusions*** The terms and concepts outlined above are useful in describing and discussing emotions with students. When teaching students about emotions, educators can think about teaching the words needed to define the intensity of the emotion (arousal), the valence of the emotion (positive or negative), and the type of emotion (such as happiness, jealousy, pride, anger, sadness). Further discussion with students can reveal whether the emotion is complex or basic. In obtaining a rich description, students and adults can work together to describe the causes and consequences of emotion in a richer and deeper way. This opens up the possibility of richer and deeper behavioral repertoire and improved self-regulation, inside and outside the classroom.

## Motivation

*Motivation* refers to how people orient attention toward goals and how they sustain the energy needed to meet those goals. As is the case with other key terms presented in this book, there are differences of opinion about how best to define *motivation*. One approach defines it as a predecisional impulse toward a goal (Heckhausen & Kuhl, 1985). Motivation that does not include any reflection on underlying arousal and emotions fits into this category. The associated behaviors are somewhat automatic responses that are not subject to prior planning or any intentional thought by the individual (Ball, 1982). Arousal processes dedicated to physiological functions fit this description, as do basic emotions, such as lashing out in anger or running to greet a cherished parent. Whatever reflection may occur does not result in highly complex behaviors. The motivation is to get immediate needs met, without reflection about what might be best for a positive long-term outcome.

The term *motivation* is also used to refer to more complex behaviors that are designed for positive long-term outcomes. Motivation can refer to broader human values, not just to getting one's immediate needs met (Botvinik & Braver, 2015). This chapter uses the term *motivation* in that broader way and includes four categories of values: Physical safety and sensory-motor needs; social needs including group membership, social attention, and social connectedness; self-efficacy; and altruism. As will be discussed later in this chapter, successful self-regulation depends on the success with which people choose goals and behaviors that will help to fulfill all these motivations, over the long term, for oneself and for others. When motivation is defined in relation to fundamental human needs and values, it is easier to start to think more systematically about why students (and people in general) behave one way or another. This definition reflects a belief that there are certain universal needs that are felt by all people and that drive all human behaviors. These universal needs are important to consider in the classroom as much as elsewhere.

The hierarchy presented below separates the concept of motivation from the behaviors used to fulfill those motivations. By separating these concepts, it is easier to identify observable student behaviors as separate from their motivations. By framing the subject this way, the topic of motivation can be used to understand student behaviors. It also paves the way for the discussion later in this chapter on successful self-regulation.

***Motivation: A Hierarchy*** Over the course of evolution, the motivations that drive human behaviors have become more complex than the arousal system and its associated fight-or-flight responses. An evolutionary and developmental shift in motivation (Heckhausen, 2000) has resulted increasingly complex human behaviors. Motivation starts with the desire to meet immediate, physical, physiological, and sensory needs. These needs are met by the environment and are outside the individual. Physical and safety needs are also met through a person's social interactions and group membership. This is referred to as *extrinsic motivation*. With evolution, and when people know that they can meet their survival needs consistently, motivation shifts toward being more intrinsic. For example, the (extrinsic) motivation for group membership and its association with physical safety and well-being shifts toward the (intrinsic) psychological need for social attention, approval, and friendship. Next, motivation shifts toward the need for a sense of personal competence or self-efficacy (Ryan, 2012; Wolters, 2003). It includes a desire to pursue goals and to have an impact on the environment and on others. Finally, motivation is oriented toward altruistic goals, where people desire to be helpful toward others and to leave the world a better place.



Many human behaviors can be attributed to more than one motivation at a time. For example, people can strive to ensure their own safety and physical well-being while simultaneously promoting the safety and well-being of their family and the larger social group. They can show behaviors that help ensure their psychological need for social approval, such as obtaining praise from superiors or peers or the approbation that comes from being considered worthy of group membership. People can also show behaviors designed to fulfill their need for a sense of personal competence and to fulfill the (altruistic) need to be helpful to others and to make the world a better place. All these motivations are present in most or all people. The discussion that follows explains these four categories of motivation in greater detail. The categories are synthesized from diverse disciplines and resources (Braver et al., 2014; Heckhausen, 2000; Ryan, 2012; Wolters, 2003). They are listed in an overlapping hierarchy, moving from motivational drivers at the lower end toward a continuum of motivational incentives at the upper end (Berridge, 2004).

*Sensory-Motor Needs* Sensory-motor needs include meeting physiological needs and maintaining bodily health (e.g., food, shelter, rest, protection from harm). They are critical for physical safety and security and are also related to pleasure. Motor experiences, hearing and seeing, being touched by others, intimacy, and recreational interests all have a sensory or sensory-motor aspect. They confer benefits through the sensory stimulation that they provide, and while not always associated with survival they are important for a sense of physical well-being.

*Social Needs* Social interactions are needed for basic survival. Interactions with primary caregivers include having physical contact and having a sense of physical safety. A person's social group ensures survival by ensuring access to water, food, and shelter. Group membership, social approval, and social attention also fulfill the need for a sense of belonging. These social needs are considered psychological in nature and are more intrinsic than the basic social needs.

*Personal Efficacy* Personal efficacy needs are fulfilled by having a sense of competence. Positive feelings of competence, mastery, and the capacity to exert some control over the environment come with getting one's personal needs met. They also come with some social approval or social attention and recognition. Personal efficacy can come from being skilled at a service or activity that is useful to others, such as teaching or cooking. It can be related to a specific skill or skill set, such as being able to draw, dance, or play sports. When a person is competent in a vocation or skill set, they not only gain social attention and social approval, but also can use those skills to fulfill the need for altruistic acts, the desire to be helpful to others.

*Altruism* With advancing age, and as lower order needs are consistently met, people become better able and more interested in meeting the needs of others. The need for physical safety and well-being, and the need to belong to a social group, never go away. However, with age, people can start to see how other groups also have the same needs and can appreciate the interrelatedness of their own needs and the needs of others. The desire to ensure that personal needs are met can now be paired with meeting the needs of the social group and/or meeting the needs of the larger community. Altruism, the desire to be of service to others and the desire to leave the world a better place, is also a deeply felt motivation.

***Motivation and Associated Behaviors: Approach and Withdrawal*** The behaviors associated with motivation can be highly variable and are sometimes very complex. When adults observe student behaviors, they need to do a careful analysis to infer the motivation that underlies the observable behaviors. To decipher the motivations that underlie human behaviors, it is useful to understand the motivational hierarchy discussed above. It is also useful to know that human behaviors can be divided into two types: approach and withdrawal.

Motivational systems are based on behaviors that are designed to approach incentives and avoid threats. They can be called survival behaviors, fight-or-flight behaviors, or approach-withdrawal behaviors (Carver & Harmon-Jones, 2009; Levenson, 1999). All behaviors are associated with motivation, and all behaviors consist of approach behaviors, avoidance-withdrawal behaviors, or a mixture of the two. The polarity between approach and avoidance/withdrawal are related to somewhat separate neurological circuits in the brain (Carver & Harmon-Jones, 2009).

Approach behaviors are those designed to gain access to something or to fulfill a need. Avoidance behaviors are designed to prevent the loss of access to something or to prevent situations in which access might be denied or curtailed. Approach behaviors help to ensure physical safety and security, expand social opportunities, expand one's personal efficacy, or perform more altruistic acts, whereas withdrawal behaviors are designed to avoid the loss of those same needs. Approach behaviors used to meet personal needs might include being physically aggressive and stealing someone's lunch, while a withdrawal behavior that serves the same goal is to withdraw from a bully to hide one's lunch and prevent the bully from stealing it. Both behaviors are related to getting one's physical needs met. Similarly, an approach behavior toward getting social needs met might include striking up a conversation with a peer during recess, while an avoidance behavior is to stay home from school because of not having completed a homework assignment that is up for class discussion the next day and the anticipated embarrassment of having one's classmates find out. In any situation, the underlying motivation is always related to one or more of the four needs listed in the hierarchy. The challenge for the observing adult is to describe the observable behaviors and to connect them with their associated motivations.

Human behavior is complex, and the above analysis will not always tell the whole story. In addition to considering the four categories of motivations and the concept of approach-withdrawal behaviors, adults may also need to think carefully about which motivation in the hierarchy seems to have the strongest influence on the student's behaviors. For example, a student may be interested in playing outside and speaking with friends after school, with the underlying motivation being to get social needs met. The student may also be interested in doing homework and getting praise from the teacher, the motivation being to enhance their sense of personal efficacy. The specific behaviors that the student chooses at any point reflect which motivation is the strongest at that point. The student may head outside to get social needs met or may stay indoors and do homework to get personal efficacy needs met. The motivation that is the strongest or the most important is the one that gets addressed first, sometimes at the expense of the other. Researchers use the term *incentive value* to describe the strength of a motivation, which helps to identify what motivates a person to behave a certain way in a given situation (Braver et al., 2014). The actual behaviors that stem from competing motivations depends on adding and subtracting the incentive value of the two. The motivation with the highest incentive value is the one that will dictate the subsequent behaviors (Braver et al., 2014).

When adults make attempts to understand the behaviors of students (or of other adults), they use the concept of incentive value, without necessarily realizing that they are doing so. Incentive value cannot actually be measured, but it is still a useful term when analyzing the behaviors of others. One way to think about incentive value is to consider the arousal or the emotions that underlie observable behaviors. Arousal gives behaviors force or intensity. The positive or negative valence of the emotion gives behaviors direction (e.g., approach-withdrawal). An intense level of arousal or an intense emotion leads to a stronger likelihood that one motivation will be chosen over another. For example, the student who has only just recently made some new friends may be much more excited about the idea of getting social needs met and will go to the playground to find the peers instead of studying. In contrast, the student who just failed an important exam might instead be highly motivated to improve her or his grades and will go home to complete homework and will seek extra help from a teacher to address personal efficacy needs. The first set of behaviors is an approach behavior related to the excitement of socializing and social approbation. The second is a withdrawal behavior related to a desire to avoid the shame of failure and to preserve a sense of self-efficacy.

The hierarchy can be used to understand a variety of student behaviors, both those that seem to advance the student's personal goals and those that seem to pose barriers to the student's goals. Motivation results in sensory-seeking behaviors, social-seeking behaviors, self-efficacy-seeking behaviors, or altruism-seeking behaviors. Table 8.2 shares examples of approach and avoidance behaviors that may be observable in the classroom. It focuses on common off-task behaviors that are not aligned with the behavioral expectations and does not include examples of behaviors that are associated with success at school. The table is simplified, because it relates only to arousal and emotions. It does not take into consideration the personal and environmental resources that are needed for goal persistence, discussed in the next section.

The examples in the table describe the immediate types of factors that influence a student's decision to behave one way or another. These factors provide the original thrust or inspiration for the student's behaviors. However, there is another factor that also needs to be considered when analyzing student behavior: Goal persistence and how a motivation is maintained over time. Only with goal persistence, and only with persistent behaviors, do students truly get their needs met.

***Motivation and Goal Persistence*** The motivation with the highest incentive value influences or directs behaviors toward certain kinds of goals. However, the incentive value alone

**Table 8.2.** Example behaviors and their underlying motivation and goal orientation

| Motivation | Approach behaviors | Withdrawal behaviors |
|---|---|---|
| Meet sensory motor needs, physical safety and security, physical pleasure | Exhibits food-seeking behaviors such as sneaking food from peers because of actual hunger or a worry about getting hungry in the future<br>Steals items because of an actual or perceived need for the item<br>Prefers to play video games instead of working, or to engage in motor activities or motor behaviors because it is more fun or more pleasurable or because of a greater sense of personal efficacy when engaged in these behaviors | Hides food or hides belongings because of actual or perceived threat of loss<br>Has difficulty sharing toys or classroom items because of actual or perceived loss of physical needs<br>Uses video games to feel better and avoid negative emotions related to losses in other aspects of life |
| Meet social needs: The need for security through group membership; the need for social approval, social attention, and friendship | Gives gifts to other students<br>Hugs other students inappropriately<br>Tells elaborate stories to gain the attention of other students<br>Spends excess time socializing during classroom time<br>Engages a peer in a discussion about a prior conflict to preserve or deepen the friendship<br>Holds a birthday party and invites a few new peers to establish new friendships<br>Engages in recreational activities to find ways to socialize more with others and expand the peer group | Some of the inappropriate approach behaviors might be related to a threat or perceived threat of loss of social connections<br>Becomes silent when asked to speak in front of others to save face in case the answer is wrong or to avoid feelings of anxiety, shame, or embarrassment<br>Remains silent or lies about having broken a rule to save face and not lose friendships<br>Avoids discussion of conflicts with a friend, for fear of losing the friendship |
| Self-efficacy and a sense of personal competence | Works hard to gain good grades<br>Seeks out and gains skills in personal or recreational activities such as skating, playing a musical instrument, playing a sport to enhance the sense of personal efficacy | Avoids doing work to maintain positive relationships with academically less able peers who are part of the perceived cool group<br>Looks distracted, busies self with drawing or playing with screen-based toys to avoid the frustration or the embarrassment of not being able to do work<br>Works hard in areas in which he or she is already skilled, while avoiding tasks or activities that are difficult (prevent feelings of loss of efficacy when faced with challenges)<br>Works hard to master academic skills and thereby avoid negative feelings associated with loss of social relations at home or elsewhere |
| Altruistic behaviors and needs | Offers a helping hand to a teacher to gain praise or social approval<br>Offers a helping hand to a peer because she or he is in need, without any desire to gain friendship or social approval from that peer<br>Organizes a conference about bullying to help reduce bullying incidents at school for all students | Acts as teacher's helper instead of doing classroom work to avoid feelings of lack of personal efficacy, because the work is too hard<br>Acts as teacher's helper to avoid feelings of social isolation from peers |

will not suffice to ensure persistence toward that goal, especially if the goal cannot be reached over the short term. Students often start out with the right motivation and the right behaviors, but then quickly lose their motivation to persist until they successfully reach their goal. The capacity to maintain motivation over the longer term is referred to as *motivational vigor* or *goal persistence*. Goal persistence and motivational vigor are possible when the underlying arousal is high enough, when the underlying emotional valence is mostly positive, and when both can be maintained over an extended period of time

Goal persistence and motivational vigor are dependent on personal and environmental resources (Ford, 1992). Personal resources include cognitive skills such as executive skills, general knowledge, and the other skills discussed in this book. Environmental resources are material supports such as computers and textbooks, as well as caring adults who can provide direct instruction, guidance, and mentorship when needed. Even those students who are interested in learning and participating in school activities will not persist if they lack the resources to do so. The intensity of arousal and the positive emotional valence needed for goal persistence can both become depleted when personal and environmental resources are not consistently available.

***Summary of Concepts Related to Motivation*** Understanding student behavior requires adults to theorize about the motivations that underlie human behaviors in general. All observable behaviors can be interpreted as being fueled by underlying motivations, which include getting sensory-motor, social, personal efficacy, and altruistic needs and incentives addressed. When a school team believes that they have provided for these needs for most students, they can then analyze behaviors in those students who are not participating successfully and who do not appear to be motivated for school-related activities. The analysis begins with observable behaviors. Later in this chapter, the IEP Builder will show how a discussion of motivation can be used to help students align their goals and their behaviors with those expected in the school setting.



## BEHAVIORAL SELF-REGULATION

The introduction to this chapter stated that successful self-regulation is a two-step process, first requiring identifying and perhaps changing underlying affect, and next choosing the right goals and the right behaviors for the situation. The person who self-regulates successfully does not just modify behaviors to reach one goal or another but also takes into consideration why humans should choose one goal or another in a given situation. Successful self-regulation means being conscious of the motivational hierarchy presented in this chapter and choosing goals and behaviors that support the individual's overall long-term success and well-being (Blair, 2002; Blair & Diamond, 2008).

Much of the self-regulation literature discusses a top-down model of self-regulation, meaning that higher order cognitive processes have to act on or regulate affect. When the executive system (specifically, impulse control) fails to regulate emotions and affect, the result is self-regulatory failure (Baumeister & Heatherton, 1996; Heatherton & Wagner, 2011). This perspective is certainly fruitful and is especially pertinent for children and youth, whose executive skills are still developing. Many children do not have the inhibition skills needed to regulate their arousal and their emotions. Their difficulties with self-regulation are expected. For example, they are not able to suppress intense affect, and they end up engaging in automatic and reflexive behaviors that are not beneficial to their long-term success.

Affect always controls behavioral outcomes (Pessoa, 2009). Unless people become conscious of affect, and the automaticity with which most of their decision making occurs, they are likely to continue to show behaviorally maladaptive behaviors, especially in changing environments (Luo & Yu, 2015). They are not likely to select the right behaviors to reach their goals or to support their personal standards or beliefs. By being aware of motivations, the different kinds of arousal and emotions that underlie them, and the different behaviors that flow from them, humans can engage in successful self-regulation. Successful self-regulation manifests when stated standards are aligned with actual behaviors and can result in fulfilling important human motivations over the longer term. Affect and thoughts work together to influence a positive outcome. Successful self-regulation is therefore both top down and bottom up. This dual-process model (Nigg, 2017) can be used to understand connections between cognition and emotion and how the two serve each other in successful self-regulation behaviors (Luo & Yu, 2015).

The capacity to compare one's personal beliefs, values, and goal orientations with one's actual behaviors requires substantial cognitive resources. Many children and youth have difficulty with thinking processes as complex as the ones just listed. This type of thinking requires information about human affect and self-regulation behaviors in general (knowledge), as well as a skill set (self-awareness and practicing self-regulation skills). Most children and youth do not have the knowledge or the experience to show successful self-regulation on a consistent basis. Children and adolescents need adult guidance and feedback for many years to develop these skills. They also need to have adults who have the capacity to think in these complex ways and who can model self-regulation skills.

## Developmental Hierarchy for Self-Regulation Skills: Self-Soothing and Impulse Control

Two primary building blocks for successful self-regulation are the capacity for soothing and self-soothing and the capacity for impulse control and inhibition. These two building blocks underlie self-regulatory successes and failures. They are examples of top-down behavioral regulation and are the key skills that children and youth need to build, so that they can properly understand and reflect on their own behavioral options. Self-regulation means much more than these two skills. Nonetheless, they set the stage for successful self-regulation as children age into adulthood.

***Soothing and Self-Soothing*** In infancy and during the toddler years, extremes of affect are regulated by the environment, typically by caring adults. Adults interpret infant and toddler behaviors and determine when the infant or toddler is experiencing extremes of arousal or extreme emotions. Adults intervene by providing food, removing distressing stimuli, or providing tactile/physical support. In typical parent–child interactions, infants and toddlers might go through thousands of episodes of distress (e.g., hunger, physical discomfort from soiling or wetting, frustrations) or excitement (e.g., joyful bursts of activity prior to bedtime), which then need to be regulated by an adult. The adult provides physical comfort and/or helps to address the arousal and emotion states, and the infant or toddler is soothed in the process. Through these parent–child interactions, the child learns that extremes of affect can be regulated. One can move from an extreme expression of affect to a quieter and more contented state.

As infants age into the toddler and preschool years, they can take on some of their own acts of soothing. Thumb-sucking and holding transitional objects, such as a preferred blanket or toy, can be accessed independently and are common examples of the first acts of self-regulation. As infants and toddlers acquire language, physical and tactile means of soothing shift to verbal mediation. With language, the toddler can speak about affect (e.g., "I'm hungry!" or "I'm mad!"), and words can be used to help regulate affect. Being able to describe and discuss frustrations and being able to verbalize wants and needs are important affect-regulation tools (Vallotton & Ayoub, 2011). With appropriate supports in place, children learn how to use language with adults and other social partners. Even though they are still dependent on adults, they are now able to articulate their affect, describe their physiological and emotional needs, and direct adults to assist in their soothing.

General cognitive developments also result in improved affect regulation. Infants and toddlers learn that certain kinds of arousal and emotions occur at predictable times. For example, they learn that hunger occurs at certain times of the day, a few hours after the last meal, and that they might experience frustration when a parent says that it is time to stop playing and get ready for bed. Even though these experiences of affect may not be agreeable, children also learn that hunger is followed by eating and by feeling satisfied, and that when parents say to stop playing, they will be able to play again the next day. The intensity of the affect diminishes as children learn to regulate their affective responses in a predictable manner. Without environmental supports (e.g., a predictable schedule and routines), it is more difficult for infants, toddlers, and preschoolers to identify patterns in affective experiences. Schedules and routines assist in the child's understanding of the passage of time, helping them to learn that affect occurs in response to predictable situations and that it is time limited. Preschoolers also discover that they may experience extremes of affect in novel situations. New situations may be associated with fear, surprise, or frustration. However, they can be managed successfully with the help of knowledgeable adults. As they learn about these different patterns, toddlers and preschoolers learn that affect can be regulated.

***Inhibition*** Inhibition is the second foundation of self-regulation. As discussed in Chapter 7, there are both hot and cool aspects to inhibition (Zelazo & Cunningham, 2007). Here, the hot form of impulse control is used to suppress excess arousal and emotions (Hermana, Critchley, & Dukaa, 2018). Some researchers refer to this ability as the skill of self-control (Hofmann, Friese, & Strack, 2009). The hot form of inhibition may first emerge as the child's capacity to defer gratification. Preschoolers learn to wait their turn. They learn to follow rules and they learn about "first-then." Children learn that they might need to experience frustration first (e.g., experience the frustration of having to put on their shoes) before experiencing pleasure (once their shoes are on, they can play outside). Inhibition (temporarily) suppresses affect to confer a distal reward.

Inhibition is useful because it can give time for reflection. For example, children can learn to use inhibition skills to temporarily suppress the anger they experience about a peer who said an unkind word. If they can suppress their anger, they can take time to consider their current motivation, compare it to stated standards, and keep in mind the desire for positive long-term outcomes. Whereas the short-term motivation might be to assert safety by being aggressive, the desire for long-term social success is perhaps more important. Instead of lashing out, the student might seek help from an adult to mediate the conflict. Inhibition allows for reflection before acting. Inhibition is critical for following rules and allows children to reflect upon rules and ask: "Do I steal a cookie to meet my physical and sensory needs? Or, do I follow the rules and get praise from adults, thereby meeting my need for social approval?" Many children in the preschool and early-childhood years can take time to stop, think, and weigh their options.

As children better understand routines and time intervals, their inhibition skills can also improve. They can defer the desire to get needs met, for longer periods of time, and can use inhibition to enhance their social success. For example, inhibition is required to follow conversational rules or to follow rules in a game. By using inhibition skills in social situations, the child can fulfill the need for social approval and group membership. Similarly, by applying inhibition skills (interference control), a student can finish her or his homework instead of watching YouTube videos and thereby get personal efficacy needs met. These are just a few of the examples of successful self-regulation thorough inhibition. When applied successfully, inhibition is not just about suppression of affect. It allows for more complex behavioral responses and can help the child engage in behaviors that will confer longer term benefits.

***Beyond Soothing and Inhibition*** As children age into adolescence and adulthood, they learn that affect can be used as a guide for action. The arousal, emotions, and motivations that people experience for certain activities or situations do not always need to be regulated or reduced. Rather, they can be used for creative thinking and can help enhance and ensure that important motivations, such as physical safety and security, social group membership and friendships, self-efficacy, and altruism, can all get fulfilled. For example, by spending more time engaged in a new and exciting sports activity, the student builds a stronger sense of personal efficacy and might also develop new social relations with like-minded peers. The initial burst of excitement related to the sports activity opens up many new possibilities for addressing important human motivations. In a similar vein, a student might experience frustration associated with chronic bullying at school and decide to gather like-minded students to lead to a student-run conference on bullying and to generate strategies for how to respond. Here, frustration about bullying ends up providing the force (arousal) and the emotional valence needed to help the student perform altruistic acts and make the world a better place. Affect reminds people about what matters most to them. People can use affective responses to inspire new interests, develop new skills, and generate new solutions to vexing problems. Affect should be celebrated when it is successfully harnessed and channeled to inspire successful action in the world.

## PERFORMANCE DIFFICULTIES IN AFFECT AND SELF-REGULATION

Performance difficulties in affect refer to the challenges that humans often have in identifying their own affect and in regulating their behaviors successfully. For any situation, children and adults may struggle to identify their state of arousal, their emotions, and/or their motivations. They may also struggle with self-regulation and with getting all of their motivations addressed successfully. Performance difficulties in affect and self-regulation refer to underdeveloped skills in areas such as the ability to use metacognition to reflect on one's affect and one's behaviors, to use self-soothing and inhibition for metacognitive reflection, to use metacognition to discover a broader range of goals and motivations, and to use executive skills to regulate behaviors and bring them in line with the chosen goals and motivations.

Performance difficulties in the identification of affect and in self-regulation skills can cause substantial impairment in function. A core feature of many mental health conditions is a failure to reflect on and (when needed) suppress intense arousal and emotions, perhaps because the arousal or emotions are too intense or because the suppression (inhibition and self-soothing) skills are too weak (Heatherton & Wagner, 2011; Hermana et al., 2018). Some individuals may not even recognize their affect or understand how their affect can lead to faulty decision making. Whenever people do not experience affect with awareness, when affect becomes too intense, or when people do not soothe or suppress affect to create a moment for reflection, they would be expected to have more difficulty with self-regulation. People who are still developing these skills show more difficulty aligning their behaviors with personal or community goals. As a result the motivations and needs listed earlier in this chapter end up not being met.

Performance difficulties in affect and self-regulation are not limited to those people who have mental health conditions or those who may have difficulty with self-soothing or inhibition. Successful recognition of affect and successful self-regulation are inconsistent in most people. People are never conscious or aware of their affect at all times and often do not reflect on the discrepancy between their personal goals, beliefs, or standards and the actual state of their behaviors. They do not show successful self-regulation consistently. The experience of being hungry is a good example. Not all adults recognize when they are hungry, and many might not recognize when a child or student is hungry. Hunger results in heightened arousal for getting physiological needs met, and extra attentional resources are dedicated to the hunger. As long as the hunger is not identified or addressed, people can end up making decisions less successfully. Cognitive resources such as soothing and inhibition are not as available, because attentional resources are dedicated elsewhere. This in turn results in a decreased ability to resist desires (Kelley, Wagner, & Heatherton, 2015). When the ability to resist desires is lower, it is more difficult for a student to resist lashing out when angry, for example, just as it becomes more difficult for an adult to adhere to the promise of sticking to a diet.

It is important to identify performance difficulties in affect and self-regulation that lead to poor long-term outcomes and to differentiate these from expected difficulty with self-regulation. Most children experience and express affect in a relatively unfiltered manner, do not reflect on their affect and its sources, do not reflect on their motivations, and act with only short-term goals in mind. All of the behaviors reflect problems with self-regulation. Poor decision making in childhood occurs as a result of not recognizing the connection between affect and behaviors, limited understanding of time, limited general knowledge, and limited executive skills, among other reasons. Performance difficulties in this area are a normal feature of childhood and adolescence.

Adults who work with children and youth need to recognize developmentally expected difficulties in self-regulation in order to make judgments about problems in affect and self-regulation that might require intervention or specialized attention. For some students, performance difficulties may be due to a developmental disability or mental health condition. Others may not have experienced consistent exposure to quality instruction from primary caregivers. Alternatively, performance difficulties in affect and self-regulation may be caused by environmental factors, such as problems with housing, compromised access to food, or difficult social circumstances. Important needs, such as those described in the Motivation section of this chapter, may have been left unaddressed Each of these variables is important to consider as part of identifying performance difficulties in this area.

## Definition of a Performance Difficulty in Affect and Self-Regulation in the Classroom Setting



Difficulties with affect and self-regulation are likely to show up in many of the classroom participation behaviors listed on a report card. Students may have difficulty with classroom expectations such as following rules of classroom conduct and socializing well with peers. They may also produce low-quality work and fail to meet academic expectations, even with intact thinking abilities. When teachers and other adults see that a student is not performing as successfully as peers, it is important to consider the student's affect, whether arousal is dedicated to something other than learning, and whether the student's emotions and motivations (e.g., physical needs, social needs, self-efficacy needs, and/or altruistic needs) are not being addressed.

***Extremes of Affect*** Extremes of affect almost always interfere with classroom participation. While some incidents of extreme behavior are transient and infrequent, others may be deep seated and require intervention. Intervention is justified when extremes of affect occur often (e.g., daily or weekly), when they last a long time, and when they disrupt learning and participation for the student and for the classroom as a whole.

*Arousal* Extremes of arousal, such as excess hunger, fatigue, or overstimulation, may not be easy to recognize. In some cases, it is the student's lack of participation in classroom activities that gets noticed first, and the underlying problems with arousal only come to light afterward. Some students can have difficulty in regulating their arousal levels because basic physiological processes have not been addressed. Other students may have difficulty regulating their arousal for neurological or neurodevelopmental reasons. For example, they might be overly sensitive to noises, touches, smells, and tastes, which affects their ability to choose behaviors to match the situation. Developmentally immature students or students with cognitive impairments are commonly sensitive to environmental stimuli, as are students with autism. These students can have difficulty regulating their level of arousal successfully and may therefore also show more rigid or inflexible behaviors.

Arousal and emotions are closely interrelated and can be confused with each other. For example, a person who has a phobia of dogs is fearful when faced with one. The emotion that they feel is anxiety, which is associated with the perception of danger, which in turn triggers arousal responses. This chain of events occurs even though it might not be appropriate to dedicate attention to basic survival processes in the situation. The rigid and inflexible fight-flight responses of a dog phobia do not typically confer long-term benefits. A similar phenomenon can occur with other emotions. For example, when a person is sad or angry, he or she might feel hunger, even though they have already had plenty to eat. The emotion triggers a rigid and inflexible response by provoking food-seeking behaviors. In both cases, the arousal processes no longer help to ensure survival and paradoxically interfere with well-being.

*Emotions* Extremes of emotion are also likely to interfere with classroom participation. Extremes of anger are typically easy to recognize and are disruptive not only to the student's own self-regulation but also to others. The anger might manifest as property destruction or aggression toward others. Extremes of anxiety or sadness are also disruptive to the student's self-regulation and participation and may manifest as social withdrawal or limited participation. Anxiety and sadness are not always disruptive to others and may only be noticeable because the student has a sad or anxious or expression; because the student makes comments about being sad or anxious; or because of limited participation.

It is important to remember that both negative and positive emotions can interfere with classroom participation. When happiness or pleasure is too intense, students can also end up not performing well. They might be too excited to concentrate on learning, be overactive, or too talkative. In adolescents and adults, intense happiness or pleasure can be associated with excessive risk taking and poor decision making. Drug use, risky sexual behaviors, and gambling are all associated with intense pleasure-seeking and can result in severe consequences to physical or financial health. Intense emotions can drive choice making. The associated rigid and inflexible behaviors can have a detrimental effect on the individual's mental and emotional well-being.

Just as overly intense emotions can interfere with successful self-regulation, insufficiently intense emotions can also interfere with successful self-regulation. For example, insufficient concern about one's financial future or lack of concern about one's productivity at work can result in poor decision making and can also affect survival. In the classroom, insufficient concern about one's performance can lead to not completing classroom tasks. Like arousal, emotions help support successful behaviors. The emotion has to have the right intensity (level of arousal): Not too strong, not too weak.

To promote success in school, emotions in the classroom need to have both the right level of intensity and be generally positive. Most successful learning occurs when emotions are positive. A negative stance toward schools, classrooms, and learning may be related to prior negative experiences of school, even if the student is a capable and independent learner. Students are likely not to participate successfully when the emotions they experience in the classroom are generally negative, regardless of the intensity of those emotions. Unfortunately, negative emotional valence is commonly associated with learning at school for many students who have identified disabilities.

*Motivation* Adults may notice that a student seems unmotivated and is failing to develop a sense of personal efficacy at school. Some of these students may not be getting their physical and social needs met outside of school and are using the school environment to get those needs met. For example, they might seek out social interactions or affection too intensely, or resort to stealing food or gathering items such as classroom supplies. More commonly, educators express concern when they perceive a lack of motivation. This lack of participation and engagement may be attributable to the student's efforts to avoid the embarrassment or frustration of learning failure. The avoidant behaviors might be a way of preserving the student's sense of personal efficacy.

Table 8.2 provides examples of how motivation influences behaviors in the classroom and includes examples of performance problems.

## HOW TO SET UP AN OBSERVATION

When making observations of students, it is as critical to document observable behaviors as it is to obtain a description of the student's internal experience of the underlying affect. Observations of the student's everyday behaviors may need to occur over many days and, in some cases, over the course of weeks. The observations should occur across settings and should preferably be made by more than one observer. The behavioral observations need to be summarized and synthesized, so that members of the school team, in discussion with the student and with caregivers, can identify patterns of behaviors. Once some behavioral patterns have emerged, it becomes possible to identify the underlying affect (e.g., arousal, emotions, and/or motivations) that help to explain the behaviors.

The behavioral observations should be correlated with information obtained from a student interview. Information about the student's personal experience of the affect can be gathered through a one-to-one conversation, through an interaction with the student, or by observing the student's drawings or play behaviors. Not all students can describe their own affect successfully, whether because of language difficulties or their developmental age. In such cases, professionals may need to infer what the student's internal experience might be. The following sections provide more detailed suggestions for conducting good observations for affect and self-regulation skills. School professionals can use Appendix 8.2, the Affect and Self-Regulation Skills Observation Sheet, to guide their observation and record notes.



### Select the Student

The student selected for observation should have presented with extremes of affect that impact classroom activities. These performance difficulties often show up on a report card and indicate that they interfere with the student's success at school.

### Making Behavioral Observations

Behavioral observations should be made across settings. Affect and self-regulation can look different, depending on the task, the peers, the adults, and the setting or location. If possible, observers should note how successfully the student remains attentive and participates successfully during whole-class instruction, peer-mediated instruction, independent work, recreational activities, and other relevant activities and settings. If the student has more than one teacher, it is important that several teachers (or other adults) have an opportunity to comment on the student's consistency of participation or lack of participation. Observation can also occur during less closely supervised activities, such as lunch, recess, playground activities, and field trips. Observers will also need information about the student's internal experience of affect. The sections that follow provide suggestions both for making observations and for talking with the student about their internal experiences. Using phrases like "I noticed that . . ." and "I wonder if . . ." can be helpful to engage students in conversation about their affect.

***Behavioral Observations of Arousal*** When determining whether a student has performance difficulties related to arousal, the observer should consider the student's overall level of alertness and attentiveness, and whether or not the student is able to complete their work, across different activities. For example, some students might be more alert during independent learning, whereas others are more alert during peer-mediated learning and whole-class instruction. Alternatively, some students may appear to be inattentive in classroom activities. The student may be unable to remain seated successfully, unable to complete work successfully, and unable to respond to questions from the teacher or from peers.

The observer should discuss arousal status with the student. During a one-to-one interview, the observer can share behaviors that have been observed and then ask the student to share perspectives or information about their internal states. The teacher might ask about the students' level of alertness, excitability, or energy. The teacher might say, "I noticed that you were moving around a lot, more than your classmates. Tell me about your energy level. I'm wondering if it is too high." The student might be able to respond that he or she is too excited or too sleepy/tired, or even too hungry. Students with development disabilities may have cognitive or language difficulties that prevent them from sharing their internal feelings or thoughts. In observing students, the behaviors and the pattern of behaviors can be used to determine their level of arousal. Teachers and other professionals at school need very good observation skills to identify when the student is sleepy, awake, overexcited, feeling unwell, or something else entirely. When summarizing the behavioral observations, it is important to quantify the behaviors. Box 8.1 provides specific suggestions for how to quantify the behavioral observations and the student's responses. Quantification of behaviors and internal experiences allows the observer to share information objectively and increases the chances that other adults will have a good sense of the student's affect and self-regulation skills.

## BOX 8.1. How to Quantify Observations

This chapter has focused on observable behaviors that adults should look for when assessing a student's skills in affect and self-regulation. In addition to describing behaviors, the observer also needs to quantify the observed behaviors. School teams may seek assistance from a specialist, such as a behavioral analyst, to decide how to best gather behavioral data quantitatively. However, any adult working with a student who needs instruction in the area of affect and self-regulation can provide measureable information. Without some measures of quantity, it is more difficult to know how a student is performing in contrast to their peers or against a normative standard and how to address the student's self-regulation needs. Equally critical is the question of how to allocate resources to provide the instruction that the student needs. Some students may need instruction in affect and self-regulation weekly or daily, whereas others may need instruction hourly or multiple times per hour. The amount of instruction will depend on how often the student experiences extremes of affect or difficulties with self-regulation. Finally, without quantification, it is much more difficult to measure progress. Quantification should naturally flow from the observations.

### Quantifying Frequency and Duration

Frequency and duration are useful descriptors of observed behaviors. These descriptors can be used for both positive (desired) and negative (undesired) behaviors. The observer should decide which behaviors will be subject to quantification. For the purposes of classroom observations, it is best to start with commonly occurring behaviors, or ones that that are especially important to monitor. For a behavior or symptom such as anger, the observer could estimate how many episodes occurred during the past week and how long they lasted. Hyperactivity and off-task behaviors can also be quantified relatively easily. Based on repeated observations, a teacher could indicate the number of minutes per hour that the student is off task or on task. The analysis of on-task behaviors can be further broken down by the type of task (e.g., independent learning, classroom participation, peer-mediated learning).

The analysis does not have to occur through the formal collection of data. To gather preliminary data, the teacher can jot down notes at the end of each day, or at the end of each hour, to record how many minutes each behavior occurred. It makes a big difference

(continued)

**BOX 8.1.** *(continued)*

whether the behavior of concern occurred once, once every month or two, or once or twice an hour. Similarly, affect or behaviors that last a minute or two are different from affect or behaviors that last for 30–60 minutes. When asked to quantify behaviors or emotions, a common response is for teachers and parents to say, "It's never the same." Behaviors appear random when no time has been put aside to observe them. By taking into consideration the quantifiers discussed here, it is likely that the observer will be able to provide an estimate of frequency and duration, even if only after a day or two of observations and reflection.

Basic indicators of quantity are extremely helpful, especially when communicating with colleagues who do not yet know the student. These data help decide which student needs a more detailed observation (e.g., formal data collection), which student will likely need additional resources, and which student is making sufficient progress. Some of the time, a student may show extreme behaviors, such as safety violations or marked aggression toward other people, and it can be easy for the observer to overfocus on those behavioral extremes, forgetting that the student is also successful much of the time. Data collection, however simple, gives everybody a clearer picture of the student's performance as a whole. Quantifying the behaviors, both positive and negative, helps everybody to remember both successes and failures. Behaviors that are less extreme sometimes have a much bigger impact on the student's performance because they occur more often and account for a larger proportion of lost time. As will be discussed in the IEP Builder later in this chapter, the less extreme but more common behaviors are often best to target for intervention. Quantifying frequency and duration of behaviors, both positive and negative, is extremely helpful.



**Quantifying Severity and Functional Impact**

If desired, the observer can also quantify the severity and the functional impact of the behavior. Off-task behaviors that occur frequently are typically associated with a bigger functional impact. However, it is important to be clear about this. When a student is off task for 2–3 hours per day, the functional impact is obvious. However, the functional impact is different for the student who gets all A grades, as opposed to all D grades, while showing off-task behaviors. Similarly, a student who shows a lot of aggression or anxiety would be expected to have difficulty participating successfully. If the student's grades and social interactions remain positive, the functional impact is lower, and an intervention plan will likely require different and usually less substantial supports.

Aggression merits special mention. Aggression can be verbal only, directed toward objects, directed toward people, or can occur in combination. These different manifestations of anger represent different levels of severity and functional impact and are likely to have different interventions associated with them. The severity and the functional impact of anger are different if there are no safety violations, if nobody gets physically hurt, and when there is no property damage.

**Quantifying Intensity and Valence**

As discussed in the text, observers need to gather information about the student's internal experiences and not focus on observable behaviors alone. Information about the student's internal experiences should also be quantified as much as possible. Likert scales can be useful for quantifying intensity of the student's affect. For any given arousal or emotion, the student can assign a numeric rating to the feeling. The observer might ask, "I'm going to ask you to give me a number that rates how strongly you feel. When you are angry, how angry are you? When you are scared, how scared are you? When you are sleepy, how sleepy are you?" The rating could be on a scale of from 1 to 5 or 1 to 10. The scale can be made up of numbers or if appropriate could be made up of simple faces showing a gradation of feelings from least intense to most intense. If a more simple approach is needed, a binary rating can be used, asking the student to select one of two choices (e.g., not a lot or very much).

Adults can also use Likert scales or other strategies that indicate valence. Many activities can have both positive and negative valence. Adults can ask questions like, "How negative does the anger feel? Is there anything positive about the anger? How happy are you when you are socializing? Is there anything about socializing that feels negative? What makes you feel frustrated about cleanup? What makes you feel happy about cleanup? If we say that zero means 'completely negative' and 10 means 'completely positive' how would you rate your anger? Your happiness? Your frustration?" Over time, it is hoped that the student will be able to describe both the current intensity and valence of symptoms and provide data for how these change over time.

Students can also be prompted to evaluate their motivation(s) by assigning positive or negative valence to different activities (e.g., classroom work, playing a game with friends). This can also be carried out for the different types of arousals or emotions. For example, the adult can ask, "Do you feel positive or negative about math? Do you feel positive or negative about talking with your friends when you're supposed to be doing classroom work? Do you like your anger, or is it too strong or too overwhelming?" Next, the student and adult should discuss an estimate of intensity: The adult can say, "On a scale of from 1 to 10, how positive or how negative do you feel about the activity or the emotion?" Consider using the circumplex model of emotions, in which intensity, valence, and type are all identified graphically (see Figure 8.2).



***Behavioral Observations of Emotions*** When determining whether a student has performance difficulties related to emotions, the observer should consider both the intensity of the emotion, as well as its valence. As is the case with arousal, the student should always be encouraged to express a full range of emotions in ways that are balanced and not disruptive to learning. If students feel and express their emotions too intensely, they will not be able to participate in classroom activities successfully. The observer can use the student's activity level and capacity for on-task behaviors as a way to judge emotional status. The student's nonverbal communication behaviors (facial expressions, gestures, prosody) and verbal communication should be taken into consideration as well.

The observer should also obtain information about the student's emotions directly. This can be done by conducting a one-to-one interview or interaction to discuss emotions. The student may spontaneously make statements about internal states such as arousal, emotions, and/or motivation. The observer can also ask questions to elicit this information. For example, the observer might say such things as, "I've noticed that you often stare into space," "I noticed that you look more sad today," " I've noticed that you were totally quiet when I asked you to answer a question," or "I noticed that you had a frown on your face." The observer might then share, "I was wondering if you were really nervous about not giving the right answer," or "I was wondering if you were feeling frustrated," or "If you can, tell me what you were feeling." Some students can readily share information about their emotional status, whereas others have greater difficulty in doing so. An observer might also be more direct, asking questions like: "Do you feel generally positive and happy about your participation at school? What about the activities that we are doing? Do you mostly feel negative? What emotions are you feeling? Are you feeling nervous or frustrated? Sad or scared?"

Students with more advanced language skills might be able to describe more highly differentiated complex emotions, such as emotions consisting of more than one type, with different intensities and both positive and negative valence. Refer back to Table 8.1 for a list of emotion types, and then take into consideration variables such as intensity, valence, and complexity. Students with limited language skills may reveal information about their internal experiences through the use of puppets or through their play behaviors. Over time, the observer should make a note of the play themes or statements that occur during the child's play and infer underlying emotions or feelings.

Any of the suggestions listed here have to be tailored to each situation. Not all teachers are comfortable asking questions such as the ones listed here, and their role may need to be limited to making behavioral observations without verbal questioning or prompts. Similarly, not all students are comfortable responding to these types of questions, and some may only do so at a later time, on a different day, or with another adult.

***Behavioral Observations of Motivation*** Performance difficulties with motivation can be identified by considering where and when the student participates best. Students who do not participate successfully in the learning activities of the classroom may instead be focused on physiological processes such as eating, using the bathroom, or thinking about food or other physiological functions. Often, students may show withdrawal behaviors and engage in screen-based or social activities, or other off-task behaviors at the expense of learning.

In order to understand their behaviors and underlying affect, teachers can ask students about their level of motivation. For example, the observer might say, "I've noticed that you often speak with your friends in class when you should be focusing on work. What motivates you about speaking with your friends?" Or, alternatively, "Most students I know like socializing at school. Sometimes they socialize so much they don't get their work done. I noticed that you did not get too much work done, so I'm wondering if you were feeling more motivated to socialize today." The observer can then also ask, "When have you noticed that you are motivated to do classroom work? What would motivate you to do classroom work?"

It is useful for students to know that a variety of needs, including physical, social, self-efficacy, and altruistic needs, must be met in order to perform successfully. If the student is not able to have these needs met consistently at school, it may be important to find out if those needs are getting met outside of school. The adult could say, "It's really important to feel successful and to enjoy school." The adult could then ask questions like: "What motivates you about school? Is it your classmates and making friends? Or are you motivated to learn? In which subjects? What types of activities make you feel confident and successful? If you don't feel very motivated by school, what could make you feel more motivated? What types of activities outside of school motivate you? How are you getting all of your needs met, inside and outside of school?"

Students with more limited language or cognitive skills may not be able to describe or discuss their motivations. Careful observations about when the student performs best and when the student is not performing well can help in understanding which activities fulfill the student's motivations. As discussed in the IEP Builder later in this chapter, gathering the information described here will influence the strategies used in the intervention plan.

***Behavioral Observations of Self-Regulation*** Successful self-regulation is straightforward to identify and includes observable behaviors such as following classroom rules of conduct, learning successfully, and seeing the student socialize with peers. In fact, the student's successful participation is just as important to document as the student's failure to participate. In addition to observing for successful performance, students should be asked about their internal experience of performing successfully.

Learning about how students self-regulate, so that their behaviors conform to their goals, standards, and beliefs, is an especially important aspect of the observations. During a one-to-one conversation, the observer can ask the student about the internal experience of self-regulation successes. For example, he or she might say, "I noticed that you were looking frustrated for a while, but then midway through the lesson you opened your book and started to get some work done." Or, "I noticed that you were e-chatting with your neighbor, and I was wondering if you'd get any work done. Then, I noticed that you started to work on the lesson." Another conversation might go like this: "I noticed that your anger lasted about 10 minutes, and then just a few minutes after that, you returned to work. Did you notice that? How did you get from being angry to getting back to work?" As shown in the IEP Builder later in this chapter, it is easier to engage students and help them build successful self-regulation when the conversation is based on the student's successes (however small) as opposed to the student's failures. As such, it is useful to look for those successes as a part of making student observations.

## Discuss With Colleagues

When discussing the student's affect and self-regulation skills, observers can use the framework presented in this chapter to share their findings with colleagues. For example, a teacher might say, "I'm going to describe to you some interfering behaviors that I've observed." The teacher could then share preliminary information as follows:

- How often the behaviors occur (frequency)
- How long the behaviors last (duration)
- The student's description of their internal experience (feelings and emotions)
- The teacher's synthesis of what the underlying affect appears to be (anger, anxiety, fatigue)
- The functional impact upon learning (percent of time lost due to non-participation)
- The student's capacity for self-regulation (ability to return to task)

In some cases, starting with a description of the functional impact of the behaviors, the presentation will have greater clarity and impact. As shown, the presentation should include a description of the behaviors, information as shared by the student, interpretation of the behaviors and their underlying affect, and the student's capacity for successful self-regulation. Colleagues should participate in the conversation and share their observations of the student. The Case Example at the end of this chapter provides a sample of what this conversation could look like.

## IEP BUILDER

To function successfully at school and elsewhere, children and adolescents need the knowledge and the skill to recognize and describe their affect and their self-regulation. By learning about arousal, emotions, motivation, and successful self-regulation, students can also learn to choose goals and behaviors that will fulfill the motivations discussed in this chapter. Most of the time, students learn the vocabulary for identifying affect and successful regulation through modeling, but most adults do not provide explicit instruction in successful self-regulation or discuss the terms with students or colleagues. Classrooms that offer predictability through routines and that help students practice developing inhibition skills, soothing, and taking time for self-reflection can enhance learning in the area of affect and self-regulation. This instruction is especially important for students who may have a disability in this area or who may not receive good modeling at home. Students with disabilities can have intrinsic difficulty in recognizing and describing their affect and in building self-regulation skills, and their IEP should include objectives to improve skills in this area.

Not all of the instruction that the student needs can be provided in the classroom. Some of the modeling and instruction in affect and self-regulation may need to be delivered outside school by professionals trained in this area. It is also likely to be most effective when offered in partnership with the student's parents. What a school team can do is provide the student with the knowledge needed to build self-regulation skills and to help the student practice self-regulation skills within the school setting. Some of those skills, it is hoped, will be carried over into settings outside of the school.

## Educational Objectives and Strategies for Arousal

When a student's arousal levels are not optimal for school and for learning, regulation of the level of arousal depends heavily on environmental supports and/or adult interventions. Hunger, fatigue, feeling unwell, and overexcitement all require environmental supports such as food, a place to lie down, medications, or a quiet space that is free from distraction. In the classroom, optimal arousal can be facilitated by addressing these factors and by providing a predictable schedule and routines. In addition, children and youth need explicit instruction in identifying the feelings associated with arousal.

All students need help developing skills and vocabulary in areas related to physiological needs, such as sleep or rest, hunger, bathroom habits, and personal hygiene. Teaching in this area is perhaps especially important for developmentally immature students, such as preschoolers and students with developmental delay. However, even typically developing teenagers can forget or neglect to address their physiological needs, such as hunger and sleep. Furthermore, they may be confused or preoccupied about private needs related to intimacy and sexuality. Some students may need instruction in managing medical conditions that might affect their level of arousal. Specialized teachers, such as a health care teacher or the school nurse, are sometimes best qualified to have this conversation. When students understand how to identify and describe bodily sensations, they can advocate for and ensure that those needs get met. In turn, they can refocus their attention on learning.



Students can also learn about the strategies used by adults to optimize arousal. For example, daily schedules normally impose times for sleeping, eating, physical activity, fun activities, and demanding or boring activities. Students should learn about how a schedule works and should understand how the schedule helps to optimize arousal. The schedule should help determine at what times of day or week arousal needs to be dedicated to physiological needs and when arousal is needed for classroom learning.

Educators can monitor progress in this area by tracking the student's success in describing arousal and its relationship to sleep–wake cycles, to physiological needs, to safety and security needs, and to learning in the classroom. Progress measures can track how successfully the student is able to describe physiological processes (knowledge) and how well the student is able to advocate for her or his own arousal needs (skill). Another way to measure the student's success in self-regulation is to measure how often the student is either on task or off task. Critically, educators should notice and discuss how often and how quickly the student gets back to task after a period of dysregulation, and whether this occurs with adult support or can occur spontaneously.

## Educational Objectives and Strategies for Emotions

Educational objectives for emotions include teaching the student about basic emotions, social emotions, and complex emotions. Consider using the examples in the following sections to teach about emotions.

***Intensity of Emotions*** Students should be able to discuss the strength of a particular emotion at a given time or situation. Some students may need to rely on a Likert scale that indicates the intensity of emotions using different facial expressions, numbers, or an emotion thermometer.

***Valence of Emotions*** Students should learn about the positive and negative valence of emotions and how positive and negative emotions both affect learning and classroom participation.

***Type and Complexity of Emotions*** Students should learn about different emotion labels. The basic or first-order emotions are happy, angry, scared, and sad. Students can learn to identify these emotions in themselves and in others and can learn about how these emotions become differentiated when they are experienced in different contexts and for different reasons. They can learn about the emotions that are provoked as part of social interactions, including jealousy, shame, guilt, and pride. Finally, they can learn about how emotions are sometimes complex and can be made up of more than one type, with more more than one valence, and more than one intensity. Educators can measure student progress by tracking the level of sophistication that the student brings to the conversation about emotions: For example, how many different emotion labels can the student identify? How well can the student describe differentiation of emotions based on the situation? How well can the student describe social emotions? How well can the student describe complex emotions? Finally, the student should be able to consider emotions in the self as well as emotions in others.

***Causes and Consequences of Emotions*** Educators can teach about the causes and consequences of emotions. Here, the student identifies what types of situations generate what types of emotions. For any given emotion-eliciting event, the best description sometimes emerges through some back-and-forth discussion, which helps to clarify the causes. Once the causes are identified, solutions for responding to the emotion can emerge. For some emotions, a soothing strategy is needed because the emotion is too intense. For other emotions, only a conversation is needed. Having decided that a discussion of emotions is often needed, the student may also need to learn about how and where to conduct the conversation. For example, if the student experiences an emotion, should he or she speak about it right away, defer discussion until later, or ignore it altogether? Is the emotion a sign that someone needs to provide some support or soothing? Is the emotion an opportunity to engage in problem solving or creative thinking? Is the emotion not relevant to the situation and should be ignored for later discussion?

***Measuring Progress in Understanding and Responding to Emotions*** Educators can measure progress in both knowledge and skills related to emotions. Students can show improvements in their knowledge of terms such as *intensity* and *valence* and the types of emotions that they experience or that they may see in others. Students may understand concepts such as the differentiation of emotions and the differences between basic and social emotions and between basic and complex emotions. Over the course of the year, students may show progress by providing a more detailed description of emotions, by identifying a larger range of emotions, or supplying a better description of their intensity and valence. Students may become more skilled at identifying the causes of emotions and what to do once they emerge.

Progress in skills also needs to be taken into consideration. The student should become more skilled at applying the knowledge of emotions to real-time situations that involve emotions. The student should become more adept at identifying soothing strategies for overwhelming emotions. Alternatively, the student should become more skilled at discussing emotions with the right person at the right time when problem solving is needed. For some students, progress can be measured by monitoring the intensity (frequency and duration) of emotions. For other students, progress can be measured by the sophistication of the student's description of emotions. For still other students, progress can be measured when the student provides a more detailed description of the emotion, its causes, and what to do with the emotion once identified and described. Some students can learn to use their awareness of emotions to solve social or classroom problems. Other students may simply show better overall participation, with improved frequency and duration of on-task behaviors. The frequency and duration of social interactions may also improve. Progress can be measured by the student's awareness of her or his own emotions, as well as the emotions of others.

## Educational Objectives and Strategies for Motivation

In order to help students align their goals and motivations with the activities offered by the school, adults need to speak to students about motivation. Students need to understand how the activities of school are designed to address important motivations. When the student's behaviors and goals are not aligned with those of the school, the student and adult may need to work together to align the goals and behaviors more successfully.

Students can expand or enhance their motivation for school-related activities when they understand what motivation means. The structure provided in the Motivation section is a good starting point. Students need to learn about physiological needs, social needs, self-efficacy needs, and altruistic needs. They need to see and understand how school-related activities are designed to meet these needs and that these needs also must be met elsewhere before successful learning can occur.

To expand the number of activities that students will recognize as motivating, they may need to think about first-order motivations that have to be addressed before the activities of school become meaningful to them. Physiological processes, safety and security, and social group membership all have to be in place, at least most of the time, so that students can become motivated to learn. At the same time, students need to learn about how school-related activities can help to build friendships, build a sense of personal efficacy, and address altruistic needs as well.

It may take some students time to appreciate what adults say about the value of school. However, as students develop their personal resources and start to see how school fulfills important motivations, they will also start to align their behaviors to the goal(s) of schooling. At times, providing resources such as books, computers, learning supports, and more mentorship opportunities, can all make a big difference.

When learning about motivation is hampered by the student's difficult with self-regulation, he or she may need to learn to analyze behaviors (the student's own and those of others). For example, the student may discover that even though all students want to have a sense of personal efficacy, they do not always behave in their own best interests. They sometimes show off-task behaviors or are disruptive. It is important for students to recognize how their own behaviors can prevent them from reaching their goals.



***Teach About Approach and Withdrawal Behaviors as Motivational in Origin*** Students may need to learn about approach–withdrawal behaviors and how different motivations and different goals can compete for their attention. When a student is not engaged by learning and is engaged in off-task behaviors or appears to be unmotivated for classroom activities, a teacher or therapist should initiate a discussion about motivation and could start out by bringing awareness to off-task behavior. The student may need help understanding the function of off-task behaviors, for example, to avoid (withdraw from) the negative emotions of feeling unsuccessful. If the student persists in being unmotivated, the adult could clarify the point by saying something like, "I think that this activity is not capturing your interest and might be making you feel unsuccessful. However, this activity is important because it's teaching you a really important skill. By mastering this skill, you will feel more successful as a learner." The student might say, "The work is too hard; I don't want to do it" but is not very likely to say, "I feel incompetent when I try to do this work, so I'm just going to avoid it." The student is also unlikely to ask, "What can I do to feel more competent?" However, this is the question that adults need to answer. Adults can help the students frame the question correctly so that they can start to reflect upon their behaviors. As another example, disruptive classroom behaviors can be analyzed through the lens of motivation. Instead of telling the student that he or she is being defiant or disruptive, the teacher might instead take the student aside for a private conversation and say, "I can imagine that it's fun to throw paper balls, especially if you reach your target and everyone laughs!" The teacher highlights the current motivation, which is to get social needs met. The teacher could then add, "But, I'm wondering if part of the reason that you are throwing paper balls is also because the work that I gave you is challenging and is making you feel unsuccessful." By introducing this idea, it becomes possible to discuss ways to develop success and personal efficacy through more appropriate classroom behaviors.

***Teach Students About How Motivation Is Related to Personal Efficacy and Mastery*** The educator or therapist can direct the student's attention toward the motivation for personal efficacy: "I know that you want to feel successful. Let's find a way to make this activity make you feel more successful. Maybe there are a few things that you can do to show yourself that you can be successful. I want to celebrate your successes with you." Judicious use of positive feedback can help the student identify her or his own successes, even when they are small. Fulfilling one's need for personal efficacy is important for all students, for the struggling learner and also for the advanced learner who finds classroom work boring or unfulfilling. Both successful and unsuccessful learners need to know that they are developing mastery in a skill before they will participate consistently in classroom settings.

***Teach About How Motivation Is Related to Personal and Environmental Resources*** Students may need to learn about how the environment can support or facilitate their motivation for learning. For example, the teacher could say, "I'm going to find ways to shape this activity to help you feel successful. Maybe I can break it down into smaller steps or you can work on it more slowly. We might also be able to work together for a while and then you can continue on without me." By providing extra mentorship, by offering more material supports, or by reducing the demands on the student's cognitive resources, the teacher can help the student align school-related goals and behaviors with the motivations discussed in the framework.

***Measuring Progress in Understanding and Expanding Motivation*** Teaching staff can gauge progress by measuring how successfully the student is able to describe motivation concepts (in the self and in others). Progress can also be measured by monitoring the student's capacity to self-advocate and show successful self-regulation behaviors. Adults can monitor how often and how successfully the student identifies the need for self-soothing and makes use of adult supports, or how long it takes for the student to return to and remain on task. Progress can also be measured by documenting improvements in how often and for how long the student is able to participate successfully in classroom activities and in learning or how often and for how long the student is off task and not participating. The student who shows successful self-regulation might also show the ability to assist others and advocate for successful interactions and successful learning for the classroom as a whole.



## Accommodations for Arousal, Emotions, and Motivation

The following sections provide general information and suggestions for students who may have difficulty with their expression of affect and with successful self-regulation. The strategies are designed to optimize arousal and emotions, so that the entire hierarchy of motivations can be fulfilled. The suggestions begin with the need to provide quality instruction in general education, a first priority for all students. Quality instruction is not defined consistently but includes features such as having an organized classroom, clearly defined classroom rules of conduct that the students can all see are being followed consistently, and delivering instruction in the right sequence and with the right scope and pace for the majority of the students in the class. Quality instruction in general education can then be supplemented with specific strategies or interventions to help students develop successful self-regulation skills.

***Accommodations That Help Address Arousal: Physiological, Safety, and Security Needs*** Children and youth need significant support to ensure that needs associated with nutrition, sleep, physical safety and health are secured. Arousal processes are regulated successfully when students do not have concerns about their safety inside and outside of school, and when students have a consistent schedule that allows them to predict how their day will go. Part of that consistency is the presence of familiar adults, with whom interactions have to be generally positive and supportive.

Schools should take into consideration the student's arousal needs beyond the boundaries of the school building and the school day. School, home, and other environments have to work in concert to ensure successful self-regulation behaviors. Educators and therapists can discuss with caregivers the importance and relevance of factors that help with successful self-regulation, such as having consistent times for sleeping, eating, and other activities of the daily routine. These factors have to be paired with a generally positive parent–child relationship. Without these basic supports both at school and elsewhere, it is much more difficult for students to show successful self-regulation and participation at school. Not all parents and other care providers received these basic supports when they were young and may therefore not realize how important they are to integrate them into their own home. Over time and using a supportive approach, educators can help parents and other caregivers to reflect on these variables and understand their importance to the overall well-being of the child. They can also help parents find environmental and personal resources to help them provide for their children's needs. This is especially important for parents who did not receive these supports when they were children.

*Have a Classroom Schedule and Routine and Make Sure That Schedules and Routines Are Clearly Understandable to the Student* Structure and predictability in the environment help students manage their level of arousal. When the student understands and follows the schedule, physiological needs such as food, access to the bathroom, and resting times all can get addressed and do not end up interfering with the alertness for learning. The schedule needs to be set up explicitly and should be designed to help the student make predictions about what will happen next in the schedule. It is also important for the student to understand the concept of sequences: How one activity follows another, and how each activity can be broken down into a sequence. Young students, students with developmental delays, and those with difficulties in their executive skills and self-regulation skills commonly need explicit instruction in scheduling. Some may need a personal schedule that is more detailed than the one normally provided to all of the students, and they may need prompting from adults to use the schedule. The personal schedule can be provided in written or pictorial form.

*Provide the Right Level of Stimulation in the Classroom* Once the student's physiological needs have been met, and once the student has a sense of the predictability of schedules and activities, educators and therapists can consider whether the student needs special attention concerning the level of stimulation and the intensity of sensory inputs. Some students may need a reduction in sensory inputs by reducing the intensity of classroom stimulation, such as noise levels or visual stimulation. Noise levels can be reduced by placing mufflers in the bottoms of chair legs, for example, or by using other techniques to reduce ambient noise and reverberation. See Chapter 2 for additional suggestions and details. Some students may need a reduction in visual stimulation, such as lowering ambient light and reducing visual clutter. See Chapter 1 for additional information. In contrast, students sometimes need to increase their level of arousal with increased stimulation such as by providing exposure to exciting or interesting noises (e.g., music), visual stimuli (e.g., a movie), motor activities, or novel and unexpected activities.

The correct match of appropriate stimulation will vary by student and will depend upon the student's sensitivity to environmental inputs and the student's tolerance for variations in the schedule.

*Consider Using Sensory Integration Therapy Techniques* Sensory integration therapy, a type of therapy used by occupational therapists, is sometimes used to optimize arousal levels. These therapies have a limited evidence base, but they may be useful in some situations (American Academy of Pediatrics, 2012). Sensory integration therapy involves exposing the student to sensory experience such as touch, visual stimuli, kinesthetic (movement) stimuli, and auditory stimuli. One important goal of the therapy is to reduce sensory sensitivities and to optimize the student's arousal levels and readiness for learning. It is not clear how much of the benefit of sensory integration therapies is related to the sensory activities themselves, as opposed to the language and executive skills that are also acquired as part of the therapy (Baranek, 2002). If sensory activities prove to be helpful to the student, they should be used. Usually, as language and executive skills improve, sensory integration therapy is effective as an accommodation or intervention (Rogers & Ozonoff, 2005).

***Accommodations That Help to Foster the Right Mix of Positive and Negative Emotional Valence*** Positive emotional valence is associated with thinking more broadly and making associations with disparate aspects of a learning activity. Negative emotional valence is associated with detail-oriented learning and can enhance memorization. Students need the right balance between positive emotions such as happiness and excitement and negative emotions such as frustration or worry for goal persistence. Positive emotional valence is associated with persistence and "want to" goals, while negative emotional valence is associated with "have to" goals (Inzlicht, Schmeichel, & Macrae, 2014). Stated another way, approach behaviors, designed to get important needs met, are easier to sustain than avoidance behaviors, which are designed to prevent or to avoid consequences (Graham, 2011). Successful learning includes a mixture of both. For example, a student may strongly wish to avoid the frustration and negative valence associated with having to stay after school to complete unfinished work. The prospect of having to stay after school can result in the decision to work harder during class. However, the capacity to sustain the decision to work harder in class has to be associated with some positive emotional valence. The student has to experience success and some positive valence in the work as assigned. One way to develop the right balance between positive and negative emotional valence is to use corrective feedback, rewards, and consequences judiciously. See Box 8.2 for a discussion of these three very important variables.



## BOX 8.2. Corrective Feedback, Rewards, and Consequences

**Use Negative Feedback Judiciously to Confer Negative Emotional Valence**
When children and youth receive negative feedback ("Don't do that!"), they learn what to avoid, such as lying, cheating, or stealing, and risky behaviors, such as crossing the street without looking both ways. A negative emotional valence produces a withdrawal response from these "don't do" behaviors and helps to ensure that important safety and social norms are maintained. They can be associated with consequences and punishments when needed.

**Use Positive Feedback Judiciously to Confer Positive Emotional Valence**
Although corrective feedback and consequences can be useful to teach important safety-related skills or to teach about what *not* to do, they are less useful for building the skills

*(continued)*

**BOX 8.2.** *(continued)*

needed for what students *do* need to do. Positive emotional valence is more likely to be associated with skills building and goal persistence. When adults provide positive feedback to students, even for very small successes, they can build skills and develop a sense of self-efficacy. It is important to remember that the positive feedback must be clearly tied to evidence of skills building. For example, a teacher can say, "You got three out of ten math problems right. Let's look at why you were successful on those. After that, we can figure out how to increase your success on the rest of the math problems." Providing positive feedback judiciously takes some thoughtful reflection. It has to be specific, and it has to be tied clearly to skills building. It has to show the student that he or she is becoming more successful in meeting physical and social needs, building a sense of personal efficacy, and showing greater capacity for altruism.

**Use Rewards, Privileges, and Consequences Judiciously**

Rewards and privileges are often used to enhance motivation for classroom-related activities. They can help ensure compliance to adult-imposed rules, but they do not necessarily enhance motivation for the activity or behavior that is being rewarded. Students need to build an intrinsic desire to participate in classroom activities, not a desire for rewards. Students are less likely to acquire intrinsic motivation for learning when the reward is not related to the activity and when rewards are controlled externally (i.e., by the adult). Excessive environmental control is not always effective in building motivation toward specific goals (Botvinick & Braver, 2015). Rewards given by adults are useful for showing the student when the adult perceives the student as successful. However, students may or may not see themselves as successful just because an adult sees them that way. Many young students and students with disabilities may not have the metacognitive and self-regulation skills needed to know when they have done something successfully and need adults to point out and explain successes when they occur. However, as metacognition and self-regulation skills improve, students need to be able to judge their own performance and experience pride in their own successes. Classroom participation and goal persistence for learning improve once students can judge their own performance and can experience their successes on their own.



***Accommodations That Help Ensure Social Needs Are Met: Social Inclusion, Group Membership, and Friendships*** A teacher or therapist's prior positive relationship with the student is critical to successful teaching in affect and self-regulation. Positive interactions help reduce overarousal whereas negative interactions increase it (El-Sheikh & Erath, 2011). Developing positive emotional valence toward people at school and toward learning in general comes from positive interactions with teaching staff and others. Any teacher or other adult working in the school setting can facilitate positive student–adult interactions by providing positive feedback about the student's successes and by expressing curiosity about the student's interests, aspirations, and personal stories. Most students appreciate positive feedback, especially if it is specific. They also appreciate someone else's genuine interest in their thoughts and experiences. This is true even if the student is reluctant to share personal information. Students with underdeveloped language skills or developmental delays may not be able to engage in a conversation about their inner life with adults. However, they certainly notice it when adults make time to observe and interact with them.

In addition to having a positive relationship with the teacher, the student has to have positive relations with peers. Educators should foster social inclusion because students benefit from being part of a social group, either in the classroom or elsewhere at school. Social group membership allows students to feel secure but also fulfills a psychological need for friendship, sets the stage for participation in in peer-mediated learning, and is helpful in cultivating feelings of altruism toward others. Some students may need explicit instruction in social interactions and social skills, so that they experience a sense of belonging and inclusion. Chapter 6 provides examples for how to develop social skills in students.

***Accommodations That Help to Build the Motivation for Personal Efficacy*** Most of the strategies listed in this chapter can help build personal efficacy. One strategy not yet mentioned is building on what is already motivating for the student. At times, this means using the student's strengths in skills or activities outside the classroom to overcome weaknesses or difficulties that the student might be experiencing in the classroom. Some seemingly unmotivated students may be motivated for social activities or for sensory-motor activities, such as sports or screen time. If screen-based activities provide a sense of efficacy or success, perhaps the student can write an essay or complete a project about screen-based toys. Alternatively, the teacher could use analogies related to screen-based activities to teach concepts in basic academic subjects such as reading, writing, and math or content areas. If social activities are motivating to the student, consider using peer-mediated instruction. If recreational, adaptive, or vocational interests are motivating to the student, find out if this is where the student feels the most successful. Educators can use a student's sense of personal efficacy in activities outside the classroom, and then see whether that personal efficacy could be developed inside the classroom.

#### ***Accommodations That Help Build Goal Persistence***

*Enhance Environmental Resources* School professionals can enhance environmental resources for students who are not motivated for classroom learning. For example, schools can provide computers, textbooks, more varied ways of sharing or accessing information (e.g., universal design for learning) and human resources (e.g., more adults who can be helpful in solving problems or ensuring the student's learning success).

*Modify the Demands on the Student's Personal Resources by Making Changes in the Scope, Sequence, and/or Pace* Educators should ensure that the lesson plan covers enough material to keep the student engaged. At the same time, the scope of the lesson plan should not be so large that it becomes overwhelming. The lesson plan should be well organized and taught in a logical sequence to foster understanding. The pace of the lesson plan should be adjusted to allow the student to feel mastery by using the appropriately sized steps. Students need mentoring and coaching support when learning breakdowns occur by using clarifying examples, by providing explanations in more than one manner, and/or by using real-life experiences to illustrate the learning objectives. At times, the teacher may need to address frustration about learning to make the lesson less overwhelming. At times, the teacher may need to break the task down into smaller components or steps.

*Accommodations for Building Affect and Successful Self-Regulation Skills: Stop and Review* When providing accommodations or strategies to improve students' self-regulation skills, a critical component is to stop and review. Any of the theories or strategies listed in this chapter can work successfully. However, none of them will work all of the time with every student. Teaching successful self-regulation is a skill that is developed through frequent practice. The student may need to become dysregulated and experience some frustration and failure in order to then master self-regulation and move on to the next challenge. Each episode of dysregulation, frustration, or difficulty can potentially become a moment for learning self-regulation. The teacher and student can both review and analyze their own behaviors, the strategies that were used in the past, and the strategy that may prove helpful going forward. When the strategies discussed in this chapter do not seem to be working, educators should take a step back and consider why the student is not performing successfully. See Box 8.3 for possible interventions or modifications that could be offered and that might help a dysregulated student perform more successfully. The questions listed there are useful to review with the student and may be useful to re-review in an iterative manner over the course of days, weeks, or months.

### BOX 8.3. Key Questions to Ask and Answer When a Student Is Not Showing the Self-Regulation Needed to Be Successful in the Classroom

1. What do the student's current behaviors suggest about her or his motivation? Students are always motivated by something. It is often something in which they feel personally successful. Find out what their current motivations and goals are and have a conversation with them about different motivations that are possible and the different goals and behaviors that fulfill those motivations. If the student is not highly verbal, you will have to make your own determinations about what is motivating to the student.
2. What is the intensity of the arousal? How can the level of arousal be optimized? Find out whether the student has any physiological needs, such as fatigue, hunger, or illness. Address those factors. Provide examples to the student of when he or she showed the right level of attention/arousal to learning so that the student knows what you are referring to.
3. What is the valence of the emotion? The student may be experiencing emotions that are interfering with participation. What are those emotions? Are they caused by any factors that can be addressed during the school day? Are they related to factors outside school? When does the student experience positive emotions related to learning?
4. How can you meet all the student's motivations? Learning and participation at school should fulfill as many motivations as possible. Tasks and activities can be rewarding for sensory-motor reasons (e.g., learning by seeing and doing). Tasks and activities can be made more rewarding by including a social aspect. Finally, tasks and activities may need to be modified so that the student experiences mastery and self-efficacy. All three modifications can be made simultaneously. Adaptive or vocational skills training can sometimes fulfill more motivations than can desktop and language-based tasks and activities.
5. What does the student know about her or his own behaviors and underlying motivations? Using reframing, see if you can encourage more participation by analyzing the student's behaviors. Describe and discuss approach behaviors as distinct from avoidance behaviors. Ask the student about her or his behaviors and how to categorize them. What is the student showing approach behaviors toward? Which behaviors are avoidance behaviors? What is the student trying to avoid? Are all four of the student's motivations being met? Is the student showing the right behavior for the right motivation, just not at the right time? Are the student's behaviors going to primarily help ensure physical safety and security, social group membership, self-efficacy, and altruism? Is the student going to lose access to one or more of these motivations? See whether you can encourage more on-task behavior by highlighting the student's desire for personal efficacy or even for altruism. If this is not possible, see whether the student is working on fulfilling more basic motivations.

6. Do motivations need to be shifted? Starting with activities that are motivating to the student, see whether you can piggyback the student's motivation for one activity (e.g., a recreational interest, social interests) to the activities and demands of the classroom.
7. Do the demands on the student's personal resources need to be changed? When a student is unmotivated, it may be because the task is too hard. You may need to consider aspects of the scope, sequencing, and pacing of the lesson or provide accommodations to ensure the student's participation.
8. Are more environmental resources required? Consider providing additional environmental resources, such as material supports or attentive adults who can provide more social approbation or assist with problem solving. This can enhance goal persistence.
9. Do the classroom and learning demands need to be adjusted? Successful learning requires the just right level of challenge. The scope, sequence, and pace of the lesson plan should be stimulating but not overwhelming. Remember that some students have the potential for accelerated learning. Those students sometimes do not perform well because the scope of learning is too narrow and the pace of learning is too slow.
10. What is the student's narrative about her or his participation at school? Some students avoid learning because they have forgotten what it means to feel successful. Students such as this may need a lot more time to rediscover what it means to be a successful learner and a full member of the learning community. How can the student develop a personal narrative that includes a sense of personal efficacy, social inclusion, and altruism? The student may have the skills needed to participate successfully but may need help to think about school differently. Alternatively, the student may need to build missing skills (academic skills, classroom participation skills) in order to feel motivated by classroom participation and academic learning.



## CASE EXAMPLE

Ricky is a third-grade student who has been served through an IEP since kindergarten. His attention span is short, and his frustration tolerance is low. He has learning difficulties in some areas of the curriculum but is able to perform at grade level when supported with accommodations and with some specialized instruction. Ricky's report card indicates difficulty with participation behaviors, especially in the general education classroom. He does not always listen to instructions or follow classroom rules consistently. His inability to participate consistently is related to inattention, a high level of arousal, and difficulty managing intense emotions.

Ricky has a pattern of showing excessive frustration during times of transitions, especially when shifting toward nonpreferred tasks or activities. Use of a schedule and the provision of advance warning helps to reduce many, but not all, of these episodes. His teacher shared that, some of the time, the frustration seems to come out of nowhere. In the past, Ricky had explosive outbursts when asked to transition from preferred to nonpreferred activities. He would scream, fall to the floor, or throw his classroom materials. At times, he would push furniture or kick his chair.

Last year, Ricky had several episodes during which he could not be consoled, and it took him more than an hour before he was ready to return to classroom work. For one of those episodes, he was sent home early. Episodes of aggression toward teaching staff occurred several times during his second-grade year. This was a concern for the team, because he had not shown such behaviors in his earlier years. Thus far in his third-grade year, he has not shown any episodes of aggression toward staff. In fact, he seems to have made gains overall with episodes occurring less often and being shorter in duration. Overall participation in classroom activities has increased. Ricky has always needed shorter work periods because of his limited attention span. However, this year he is commonly able to work for 20 minutes at a time and can participate for longer stretches during group activities. Even when he does have an outburst, he now returns to work much more quickly.

Ricky has consistently shown sensitivities to excessive noises and other types of stimuli and seems distressed when the fire alarm rings. The classroom staff set up an advance warning system for him to let him know before a fire drill occurs, allowing him to leave the building with an adult if the noise and tumult become too stressful. That said, his tolerance for noises has improved. As a kindergarten student, he was much more distressed by different types of noises, not just the fire drill. However, only very loud and unexpected noises now affect him.

Ricky's parents have noticed the same types of behaviors at home and are concerned about the impact that his frustration is having on peer relations and on learning at school. They have used time-outs and rewards to encourage compliance at home, but they are not sure whether this has changed his behaviors very much. They report that it is often difficult to get him to bed on time. He can become very engrossed in screen-based toys and games, and he usually resists bedtime routines. Even though screen time is a factor in falling asleep so late, his parents stated that he has always had difficulty falling asleep at night, even when he was a toddler and preschooler. His day seems to go better on weekends, when they let him sleep later in the morning. Of course, weekend days are not as demanding as school days, which may contribute to his improved performance on weekends. The family is seeking professional counseling services to help improve his compliance.

The team reviewed some behavioral data gathered during his past years and compared it with his current performance. In kindergarten and first grade, Ricky's outbursts occurred several times a day and lasted up to 30 minutes. Anger and frustration now emerge only a few times per week. They consist of him yelling or raising his voice. Episodes now last only 1–3 minutes. Episodes that include aggression toward furniture or classroom materials occur two or three times per month. The team is encouraged by this progress. However, they also note that Ricky's behaviors still look immature when compared with his grade-level peers. They would like to help him continue to make improvements, but it is not clear to them how they should teach him more successful self-regulation. When teaching staff ask him about the internal experience of his frustration and explosive outbursts, he usually just says, "It's because I don't like it." It is not clear what he dislikes. He might tell his teacher that a noise was bothering him, even though he has tolerated louder and more disruptive noises in the past. When asked about classroom activities in general, Ricky is able to explain that he enjoys morning meeting time and some of the academic activities provided by his teacher. He is not always able to identify which activities of the day are frustrating for him.

During a meeting with his parents, the school psychologist reviewed some of the information that the team had gathered. Ricky was present in the psychologist's office, busying himself with some of the psychologist's toys. The psychologist said, "Ricky knows that he gets angry more than he should, but he can't explain why." Almost immediately, Ricky became attentive and alert and exclaimed, "That's what I keep trying to tell my Mom!" His parents were surprised by his statement, as he had never said anything to them about his anger before.

## Case Analysis

Ricky shows several typical features of a student with difficulty in the expression of affect and with self-regulation. The sections that follow analyze his affect and self-regulation skills using the terms presented in this chapter.

### *Analysis of Ricky's Arousal*

Ricky is easily overaroused. He is overly reactive to sudden noises. He reacts in an explosive manner when he could instead show more minor frustration or no frustration at all. Even though Ricky's reactions have become shorter and less frequent with age, the current frequency and duration of episodes are not expected for his age or grade. Ricky's own surprise and confusion about his behaviors merits special mention. Even though he has a desire to perform successfully, his very automatic and sudden outbursts prevent him from doing so consistently. His behaviors suggest a neurologically based difficulty in the expression of his arousal, which is more intense than expected given the environment. Ricky's parents reported difficulty falling asleep at night. A long latency for falling asleep is a feature that commonly co-occurs in children with sensory sensitivities, which Ricky also experiences.

### *Analysis of Ricky's Emotions*

Ricky shows frustration most often when he is interrupted or when bothered by sensory sensitivities, but the pattern is not always consistent. Ricky is able to express basic emotions, such as being happy or angry, but his vocabulary for social emotions is not as well developed. He expresses positive emotions about his social interactions some of the time, but also shows frustration in his social interactions because his peers do not always do as he asks. He can express when he is mad at a peer but is not yet clear about when he feels pride, such as for good work. Teaching staff usually have to point out his successes, in response to which he shows that he is happy with his performance. He shows some guilt about his outbursts, especially when teaching staff (or his parents) express disapproval. When staff work with him to understand his emotions, his responses are usually a bit vague.

### *Analysis of Ricky's Motivation*

Ricky enjoys screen-based activities. This is common for many children. However, he seems to retreat to screen-based activities more often than other children his age. He appears to feel successful when interacting with a screen. The screen-based toy also fulfills the need for excitement and stimulation. Ricky is socially motivated, and he often seeks out the company of peers. He can play successfully in organized social activities, but he struggles with small-group play interactions because he can be very bossy. His peers have found him to be insistent on following his own agenda. He maintains friendships with a few peers and seems to enjoy peer interactions more when he is playing with only one friend at a time. Ricky does experience successes at school and he is developing a sense of personal efficacy. However, success in learning often only comes after a lot of effort. One of the reasons he engages in screen-based activities so often is because he feels successful in these activities. Ricky is not yet thinking altruistically. He knows that he is supposed to be helpful toward other students but would typically not think about lending a helping hand or saying a kind word unless prompted by an adult.

### *Analysis of Ricky's Self-Regulation*

Ricky has limited insight into his own arousal and self-regulation processes. He knows that he has explosive outbursts more often than his peers. In fact, he seems to experience some guilt about this and often refuses to discuss his outbursts with anyone because they are a source of embarrassment for him. The history suggests that his overarousal exceeds his capacity for inhibition, resulting in excessively intense emotions. He relies heavily on adults to help manage his outbursts. His parents and teaching staff believe that he would like to perform better, but they are not clear about what they could do to help his performance improve.

## Educational Objectives and Strategies for Ricky

The objectives and strategies outlined in the following sections would be appropriate for developing Ricky's arousal and self-regulation skills.

### *Educational Objectives and Accommodations for Ricky's Arousal*

Given the intensity of his arousal, the team allows Ricky to wear headphones during portions of the day. Classroom staff put pads under the chair feet to reduce the impact of classroom noise and created a quiet space for him in the corner of the classroom. They provide advance warning about transitions using a timer, which helps Ricky predict when transitions will occur, but also provokes frustration at times. Even with advance warning, he does not like to stop a preferred activity (such as screen time). One of the teaching goals is for Ricky to be able to access his schedule more independently. By teaching him about his schedule and by getting him to think about all the activities that are to come, his team hopes that he will show less frustration. His teacher decided to no longer provide information about upcoming events on the schedule. Instead, she asks him to tell her what is on the schedule. She tries to avoid telling him to use the schedule, but when needed, she prompts him to use it. This strategy has helped him to remember to put things away as needed, to prepare materials for the upcoming lesson as needed, and to tolerate the frustration of upcoming interruptions more successfully.



### *Educational Objectives and Strategies for Ricky's Emotions*

The team dedicated time in his IEP to provide instruction about emotions and how to manage them. Ricky has learned to use a chart with different colors to represent different states of arousal and emotions. Ricky is not usually very motivated to use it when he gets angry, but he is willing to use it when he has his one-to-one instruction with the school counselor. Having heard Ricky show that he is clearly thinking about his emotional outbursts and seems unable to control them, the psychologist recommended a slight change in plan. He suggested that instead of speaking with Ricky about his anger and focusing on the source of his anger (such as overstimulation or the demands of transitioning), adults should instead focus on his self-regulation. What this means is that adults should point out when his frustration comes to an *end* and when successful classroom participation restarts. The psychologist believes that Ricky needs to develop his awareness of what he did to *regain* his calm, not necessarily what made him *lose* his calm. As a first step, the psychologist suggested counting the number of minutes of each episode of anger. The logic for using this strategy is to remind Ricky that whenever anger starts, it also always stops. Ricky knows that the countdown will eventually lead to self-regulation and helps him to focus on a future state of calm (self-regulation) instead of focusing on the current state of anger. The psychologist said to the team, "You can tell Ricky that whenever he has an outburst, you are going to do a countdown together to see how long his frustration lasts. That way, you can celebrate with him whenever the episodes comes to an end." The psychologist also counseled the team not to place any expectations on how fast the anger should dissipate: "Just tell him that you are both going to see how long the anger lasts. You can measure duration by counting or by using the clock. The purpose of monitoring the duration of the episodes is to enhance his self-awareness about how and when the anger ends, not to think about when the anger begins."

The classroom staff responded with enthusiasm to this new idea, but they also thought of something else. They knew that the most common cause of Ricky's dysregulation were moments of transition, especially when having to switch to a nonpreferred activity. Given Ricky's inability to describe the causes of his own frustration, they decided to develop a social story with Ricky to enhance his level of awareness. The social story would contain photos of Ricky in his calm state, and maybe some drawings of him when upset. The social story would develop his awareness of his own anger and would be designed to celebrate his successful self-regulation abilities.

Once the team agreed to this plan, the school psychologist explained the plan to Ricky. The psychologist started out by saying, "I was so interested to hear what you said earlier! You told me how hard it is to figure out why you get angry. I have an idea I want to share with you." The psychologist paused here, to make sure that Ricky was paying attention. Then, the psychologist added, "I'm pretty sure you're going to have an anger episode again this week. Maybe even later today! That's okay. We are going to use it as a chance to do something really important. We're going to figure out how you always get back on track. That's the thing that I want you to remember: You always get back on track, right?" Ricky nodded. The psychologist repeated himself by saying, "Yeah, it's amazing, you always get back on track! The teachers are going to do some observing to help you to figure out how you do it."

The classroom staff provided Ricky with additional information about their strategy, including the creation of a social story and use of the clock to count the number of minutes of his episodes. By monitoring the duration of episodes and by focusing on the end of the episodes, Ricky and the team were able to start to celebrate the success of returning to normal participation, as opposed to being frustrated that Ricky had yet another outburst. By pointing out to him when he is being attentive and productive, Ricky is able to develop an internal sense of what it feels like and looks like when he is successful.

### *Educational Objectives and Strategies for Ricky's Motivation and Goal Persistence*

Ricky's motivation was not felt to be an important area to address, as he always maintained his motivation for learning and for classroom participation. That said, the team working with him knew that they had to be respectful of his personal (cognitive) resources. By considering the scope, sequencing, and pace of the lesson plan, they made modifications to reduce task demands to about 20 minutes. They continue to help to work toward grade-expected reading, writing, and math skills. However, they are proceeding more slowly. They suspect that when he transitions into fourth grade, he will need more small-group instruction and will end up spending less time with his grade-level peers.

### *Educational Objectives and Strategies for Ricky's Self-Regulation*

The team used Ricky's emotion (frustration) as a teachable moment for teaching self-regulation. They extended this strategy by developing more questions about other emotions and by helping him to think about his self-regulation skills also. Whenever they find him not focused on learning, they avoid telling him to focus on his work. Instead, they ask Ricky to share his own perspective first. For example, they ask him questions such as, "Where is your attention now? Are you feeling positive or negative about this task/activity? What is your goal now? What steps do you need to take to reach your goal? Do you need anything from me to get you there?" Questions such as these have become a useful part of their overall teaching strategy. As with most strategies, these metacognitive questions do not always get results right away. Ricky sometimes still reacts with frustration because he assumes that the teacher's question means that he is not behaving or that something is wrong. However, by using questions such as these, Ricky usually does not respond in such a defensive manner. More often, he ends up showing more problem-solving behaviors and more successful self-regulation.

## Working With Culturally and Linguistically Diverse Learners

When helping culturally and linguistically diverse learners develop skills related to self-regulation and affect, consider the following strategies:

### *Teach Language and Gestures That Accurately Express Emotions*

It is important to spend time teaching students the language necessary to accurately identify and describe very intense feelings that they may be experiencing.

With some languages, words used to describe emotions and affect do not necessarily translate easily from one language to another. For example, the word *ambiente* in Spanish expresses social and emotional aspects of an environment, which is not the case for the word *ambience* in English. The English language learner may need to understand these differences in order to communicate successfully in English. Culturally and linguistically diverse learners also need to know what different gestures mean in English since an appropriate gesture in one language maybe considered rude or obscene in another. The "thumbs-up" sign and the "perfect" sign (thumb and index finger create a circle) are gestures that communicate positive affect in English. However, in other cultures they can be perceived as very vulgar.

### *Provide Clear Instruction on Acceptable Behaviors*

Culturally and linguistic diverse learners and their families may be unfamiliar with the types of responses that schools, especially those in the United States, may have when students use especially graphic or violent language to express their feelings. Many schools adopt the practice of "zero tolerance," very strict standards that prohibit emotional language that contains any hint of violence. Both the student and the student's family need to be made aware of this cultural norm and need to know that students are expected to use emotion terms when describing intense feelings. Students who use violent language will need to explain their intentions clearly, so that professionals can respond to the situation successfully. It is important for learners to be aware of appropriate means of expressing their emotions, especially when those emotions are intense.



## CONCLUSION

This chapter covered several critical topics to help the reader understand terms related to affect and self-regulation. The terms used to cover these topics included *arousal, emotions,* and *motivation.* Different authors sometimes use different terms from those presented here or use the same terms differently. To add to the confusion, the terms are highly overlapping, which can create confusion for practitioners. The reader is invited to review this chapter again and to compare the content provided here with terms that may already be in use in the practitioner's current school setting. Prior to any discussion of a student's needs, it is important to have a list of terms and a shared understanding of them.

It can be difficult to know where to start the intervention and teaching process for those students who are clearly not performing well at school, especially when the difficulty appears to be related to difficulty in the recognition and expression of affect and in self-regulation skills. This chapter presented the most important concepts that need to be considered for students who show difficulties in this area. The purpose of sharing the concepts listed in this chapter is to help school professionals describe successful self-regulation and to describe performance difficulties in self-regulation more accurately. The information provided in this chapter should deepen understanding about why and how students show poor self-regulation skills and how school practitioners can come together and develop plans that can enhance successful self-regulation. By using the terms and ideas presented in this chapter, school professionals can use existent strategies in the school setting to develop creative solutions for the many students whose self-regulation difficulties interfere with their performance. Critically, the strategies should be discussed with the student. The student needs to develop competence in affect and self-regulation as a base of knowledge and as a set of skills. This chapter concludes Section II, Developmental Frameworks. Section III, Educational Frameworks, covers reading, writing, and math skills.

## REFERENCES


Abe, J. A., & Izard, C. E. (1999). The developmental functions of emotions: An analysis in terms of differential emotions theory. *Cognition and Emotion, 13*(5), 523–554.

Affect. (n.d.). In *American Psychological Association dictionary*. Retrieved from https://dictionary.apa.org/affect

American Academy of Pediatrics. (2012). Policy statement: Sensory integration therapies for children with developmental and behavioral disorders. *Pediatrics, 129*(6), 1186–1189.

Ball, S. (1982). Motivation. In H. E. Mitzel (Ed.), *Encyclopedia of educational research* (5th ed., pp. 1256–1263). New York, NY: Macmillan.

Baranek, G. (2002). Efficacy of sensory and motor interventions for children with autism. *Journal of Autism and Developmental Disorders, 32*(5), 397–422.

Barrett, L. F. (2006a). Are emotions natural kinds? *Perspectives on Psychological Science, 1*(1), 28–58.

Barrett, L. F. (2006b). Solving the emotion paradox: Categorization and the experience of emotion. *Personality and Social Psychology Review, 10*(1), 20–46.

Barrett, L. F., Gendron, M., & Huang, Y-M. (2009). Do discrete emotions exist? *Philsophical Psychology, 22*(4), 427–437.

Barrett, L. F., Mesquita, B., Ochsner, K. N., & Gross, J. J. (2007). The experience of emotion. *Annual Review of Psychology, 58*(1), 373–403.

Baumeister, R. F., & Heatherton, T. F. (1996). Self-regulation failure: An overview. *Psychological Inquiry, 7*(1), 1–15.

Berridge, K. C. (2004). Motivation concepts in behavioral neuroscience. *Physiology & Behavior, 81*, 179–209.

Blair, C. (2002). Integrating cognition and emotion in a neurobiological conceptualization of children's functioning at school entry. *American Psychologist, 57*(2), 111–127.

Blair, C., & Diamond, A. (2008). Biological processes in prevention and intervention: The promotion of self-regulation as a means of preventing school failure. *Development and Psychopathology, 20*(3), 899–911.

Blair, C., & Raver, C. C. (2015). School readiness and self-regulation: A developmental psychobiological approach. *Annual Review of Psychology, 66*, 711–731.

Botvinick, M., & Braver, T. (2015). Motivation and cognitive control: From behavior to neural mechanism. *Annual Review of Psychology, 66*, 83–113.

Braver, T. S., Krug, M. K., Chiew, K. S., Kool, W., Westbrook, J. A., Clement, N. J., . . . Somerville, L. H. (2014). Mechanisms of motivation–cognition interaction: Challenges and opportunities. *Cognitive Affective Behavioral, 14*(2), 443–472.

Cacioppo J. T., & Gardner W. L. (1999). Emotion. *Annual Review of Psychology, 50*, 191–214.

Carver, C. S., & Harmon-Jones, E. (2009). Anger is an approach-related affect: Evidence and implications. *Psychological Bulletin, 135*(2), 183–204.

de Leceal, L., Carter, M. E., & Adamantidis, A. (2012). Shining light on wakefulness and arousal. *Biological Psychiatry, 71*(12), 1046–1052.

Denham, S. A., Ferrier, D. E., Howarth, G. Z., Herndon, K. J., & Bassett, H. H. (2016). Key considerations in assessing young children's emotional competence. *Cambridge Journal of Education, 46*(3), 299–317.

Dinsmore, D. L., Alexander, P. A., & Loughlin, S. M. (2008). Focusing the conceptual lens on metacognition, self-regulation, and self-regulated learning. *Educational Psychology Review, 20*(4), 391–409.

El-Sheikh, M., & Erath, S. A. (2011) Family conflict, autonomic nervous system functioning, and child adaptation: State of the science and future directions. *Development and Psychopathology 23*(2011), 703–721.

Ford, M. E. (1992). *Motivating humans: Goals, emotions, and personal agency beliefs.* Newbury Park, CA: Sage.

Forness, S. R., Freeman, S. F. N., Paparella, T., Kauffman, J. M., & Walker, H. M. (2012). Special education implications of point and cumulative prevalence for children with emotional or behavioral disorders. *Journal of Emotional and Behavioral Disorders,20*(1), 4–18.

Garner, P. (2010). Emotional competence and its influences in teaching and learning. *Educational Psychology Review, 22*(3), 297–321.

Graham, S., & Weiner, B. (2011). Motivation: Past, present, and future. In K. R. Harris, S. Graham, & T. Urdan (Eds.), *Educational psychology handbook: Vol. 1. Theories, constructs, and critical issues* (pp. 367–397). Washington, DC: American Psychological Association.

Heatherton, T. F., & Wagner, D. D. (2011). Cognitive neuroscience of self-regulation failure. *Trends in Cognitive Sciences, 15*(3), 132–139.

Heckhausen, H., & Kuhl, J. (1985). From wishes to action: The dead ends and short-cuts on the long way to action. In M. Frese & J. Sabini (Eds.), *Goal-directed behavior: The concept of action in psychology* (pp. 134–159). Hillsdale, NJ: Lawrence Erlbaum.

Heckhausen, J. (2000). Evolutionary perspectives on human motivation. *American Behavioral Scientist, 43*(6), 1015–1029.

Hermana, A. M., Critchley, H. D., & Dukaa, T. (2018). The role of emotions and physiological arousal in modulating impulsive behavior. *Biological Psychiatry, 133*, 30–43.

Hofmann, W., Friese, M., & Strack, F. (2009). Impulse and self-control from a dual-systems perspective. *Perspectives on Psychological Science, 4*(2), 1–15.

Hofmann, W., Schmeichel, B. J., & Baddeley, A. D. (2012). Executive functions and self-regulation. *Trends in Cognitive Sciences, 16*(3), 174-180.

Inzlicht, M., Schmeichel, B. J., & Macrae, C. N. (2014). Why self-control seems (but may not be) limited. *Trends in Cognitive Sciences, 18*(3), 127–133.

Izard, C. E. (2010). The many meanings/aspects of emotion: Definitions, functions, activation, and regulation. *Emotion Review, 2*(4), 363–370.

Izard, C. E. (2011). Norms and functions of emotions: Matters of emotion–cognition interactions. *Emotion Review, 3*(4), 371–378.

Izard, C. E., Fine, S., Mostow, A., Trentacosta, C., & Campbell, J. (2002). Emotion processes in normal and abnormal development and preventive intervention. *Development and Psychopathology, 14*(4), 781–797.

Kelley, W. M., Wagner, D. D., & Heatherton, T. F. (2015). In search of a human self-regulation system. *Annual Review of Neuroscience, 38*, 389–411.

Kreibig, S. (2010). Autonomic nervous system activity in emotion: A review. *Biological Psychology, 84*, 394–421.

Lanata, A., Valenza, G., and Scilingo, E. P. The role of nonlinear dynamics in affective valence and arousal recognition. *IEEE Transactions on Affective Computing, 3*(2), pp. 237–249, 2012. doi:10.1109/T-AFFC.2011.30.

Levenson, R. W. (1999). The intrapersonal functions of emotion. *Cognition and Emotion, 13*(5), 481–504.

Levine, L. J., & Edelstein, R. S. (2009). Emotion and memory narrowing: A review and goal-relevance approach. *Cognition and Emotion, 23*(5), 833–875.

Luo, J., & Yu, R. (2015). Follow the heart or the head? The interactive influence model of emotion and cognition. *Frontiers in Psychology, 6*(583), 1–14.

Nigg, J. T. (2017). Annual research review: On the relations among self-regulation, self-control, executive functioning, effortful control, cognitive control, impulsivity, risk-taking, and inhibition for developmental psychopathology. *Journal of Child Psychology and Psychiatry 58*(4), 361–383.

Pessoa, L. (2009). How do emotion and motivation direct executive control? *Trends in Cognitive Sciences, 13*(4), 160–166.

Pfaff, D. W. (2006). *Brain arousal and information theory*. Cambridge, MA: Harvard University Press.

Rogers, S., & Ozonoff, S. (2005). Annotation: What do we know about sensory dysfunction in autism? A critical review of the empirical evidence. *Journal of Child Psychology and Psychiatry, 46*(12), 1255–1268.

Rottenberg, J., & Gross, J. J. (2007). Emotion and emotion regulation: A map for psychotherapy researchers. *Clinical Psychology: Science and Practice, 14*(4), 323–328.

Russell, J. A. (1980). A circumplex model of affect. *Journal of Personality and Social Psychology, 39*(6), 1161–1178.

Ryan, R. (2012). Motivation and the organization of human behavior: Three reasons for the re-emergence of a field. In R. M. Ryan (Ed.), *Oxford handbook of human motivation* (pp. 2–14). New York, NY: Oxford University Press.

Valiente, C., Swanson, J., & Eisenberg, N. (2012). Linking students' emotions and academic achievement: When and why emotions matter. *Child Development Perspectives, 6*(2), 129–135.

Vallotton, C., & Ayoub, C. (2011). Use your words: The role of language in the development of toddlers' self-regulation. *Early Childhood Research Quarterly, 26*(2), 169–181.

Wolters, C. A. (2003). Regulation of motivation: Evaluating an underemphasized aspect of self-regulated learning. *Educational Psychologist, 38*(4), 189–205.

Zelazo, P. D., & Cunningham, W. A. (2007). Executive function: Mechanisms underlying emotion regulation. In J. Gross (Ed.), *Handbook of emotion regulation* (pp. 135–138). New York, NY: Guildford Press.

APPENDIX 8.1 **Affect and Self-Regulation Skills Framework**

The Affect and Self-Regulation Skills Framework is summarized here. School professionals can use this form as a quick reference for the skill sets and skills that need to be taken into consideration when making observations and developing an intervention plan.

| Skill sets | Functions and skills | Examples of functions and skills in action | Sample performance difficulties | Potential strategies, accommodations, or educational objectives |
|---|---|---|---|---|
| Arousal | Maintain an optimal level of alertness and attentiveness to internal stimuli, environmental stimuli, tasks, activities, or goals | The student is able to recognize biological arousal processes that may need to be addressed, including hunger, sleep, fight-flight responses, sexual needs, among others.<br><br>The student is able to label and identify arousal needs and communicate those needs to others as needed.<br><br>The student is able to maintain the right level of arousal or attentiveness to classroom and social activities because biological arousal processes and needs are being met consistently. | The student does not recognize arousal processes and their relationship to biological needs. The student does not advocate for getting biological needs met and relies on adults to ensure that these needs get met successfully (e.g., needs related to eating, voiding, sleeping).<br><br>The student experiences arousal as either too intense or not intense enough and is not able to judge what the "right" level of arousal is for a given situation.<br><br>The student is unable to sustain the right level of arousal or attentiveness to activities that require sustained attention and focus, such as classroom tasks or social activities. | Teach the student the vocabulary needed to identify and describe her or his arousal processes, including hunger, sleepiness or fatigue, pain, fight–flight responses, and even sexual responses.<br><br>Teach the student the vocabulary needed to describe arousal and its relationship to attention and focus to task.<br><br>Teach the student strategies used to regulate arousal so that it is more appropriate to the situation. In school, this typically means regulating arousal so that it is aligned with classroom activities and tasks. You can ask the student how they can harness their attentiveness and alertness in the service of learning.<br><br>Provide strategies for the student to self-soothe when arousal is too intense or becomes overwhelming. |

(continued)

| Skill sets | Functions and skills | Examples of functions and skills in action | Sample performance difficulties | Potential strategies, accommodations, or educational objectives |
|---|---|---|---|---|
| Emotions | The capacity to recognize and understand the emotional responses of self and others to a variety of situations | The student is able to recognize the right type of emotion for a given situation. For example, the student can recognize basic emotions, such as happy, mad, scared, and sad, and the types of situations that provoke those feelings.<br><br>The student is able to recognize social emotions, such as pride, jealousy, shame, and embarrassment, and the types of situations that provoke those emotions.<br><br>The student is able to recognize complex emotions, such as blends of the emotions listed previously.<br><br>The student is able to identify the right intensity of emotions for the situation in self and in others. For example, the student can recognize when anger or anxiety are too intense for the situation and are disruptive to self and others. The student can recognize when the emotion is not intense enough for the situation and interferes with safety or with social success.<br><br>The student is able to recognize that positive and negative emotions both have an important role to play for optimal success and health.<br><br>*Causes and consequences:* The student is able to identify the causes of emotions and the types of actions that may need to be taken in response to those emotions. | The student has difficulty recognizing basic emotions in self and others.<br><br>The student has difficulty recognizing social emotions in self and others.<br><br>The student has difficulty recognizing complex emotions (mixed intensity, valence, and types of emotions) in self and others.<br><br>The student has difficulty recognizing the right intensity of emotions for a given situation, in self and/or in others.<br><br>The student has difficulty recognizing the important role of both positive and negative emotions for survival and successful action in the world.<br><br>The student has difficulty using emotions as a guide for succesful action in the world. The student has difficulty making use of adult support and guidance in choosing the best course of action in response to an emotion. | Teach the vocabulary needed to identify and describe emotions in self and others. This vocabulary includes the following terms:<br>• Basic emotions: Happy, mad, scared, sad<br>• Social emotions: Pride, shame, embarrassment, disgust, jealousy<br>• Intensity of emotions: High or low<br>• Valence of emotions: Positive or negative<br>• Complex emotions: Blends of the preceding emotions and descriptors of emotions<br>• Causes and consequences: How emotions are elicited by a situation and how emotions lead to an action.<br><br>Teach about how emotions guide and drive positive and negative action in the world.<br><br>In many emotional situations, it is appropriate to ask the student what type of emotion they are feeling, whether or not it is the right emotion for the situation, whether or not the intensity matches the situation, what they plan or wish to do with the emotion, and what they could do for the best long-term outcome. |

| Skill sets | Functions and skills | Examples of functions and skills in action | Sample performance difficulties | Potential strategies, accommodations, or educational objectives |
|---|---|---|---|---|
| Motivation | The capacity to understand and meet all of the key needs that motivate humans: Physical safety and sensory-motor needs, social needs, self-efficacy, and altruism | The student can recognize how her or his behaviors are designed to meet or are motivated by the needs listed in the column to the left.<br><br>The student can recognize that all human behaviors can be explained by the needs listed in the left-hand column and can be categorized as "approach" behaviors or "withdrawal" behaviors. The student recognizes that approach behaviors are designed to ensure that the needs listed in the left column are met, while withdrawal or avoidance behaviors are designed to prevent the loss of those same needs.<br><br>Many behaviors consist of a mixture of approach and withdrawal and can serve more than one motivational goal or set of needs. | The student does not recognize the need to ensure physical safety and security and relies on adults to get physical needs met.<br><br>The student does not recognize the need for social group membership and social connectedness and relies on adults to get social needs met.<br><br>The student does not recognize the need for personal efficacy needs to get met and over-focuses on getting the first two needs met (physical, sensory-motor needs, and social needs). Class-clown behaviors and an over-focus on screen-based activities while at school are two examples that illustrate approach behaviors for meeting social and sensory motor needs, respectively, and/or are withdrawal behaviors designed to "save face" and avoid the exerience of shame or embarrassment related to lack of efficacy.<br><br>The student recognizes all of the needs listed in the motivation section but does not know how to get those needs met in the school setting.<br><br>The student lacks personal and/or environmental resources to ensure that all of the motivations are addressed and that all needs get met successfully while at school. | Teach about all of the needs that humans can have, as outlined in the list of motivations.<br><br>Teach how all of the needs get addressed and/or get met.<br><br>Teach how arousal and emotions can drive and guide action so that all needs get met consistently.<br><br>Teach how to analyze human behaviors as either approach, withdrawal, or a mixture of the two. Teach how human behavior is always designed to get important personal needs met.<br><br>When a student is not motivated for classroom activities, you can ask the student where their motivation lies, which needs they are currently fulfilling, what time is best for fulfilling those needs. Teach students how to describe their own behaviors by using terms such as *motivation* ("Right now, I'm motivated to . . ."), *approach* ("My behaviors are designed to access or get more of . . ."), and *withdrawal* ("My behaviors are designed to avoid . . .").<br><br>Discuss with the student how teaching staff couild help to orient their motivation for classroom activities (addressing personal efficacy needs).<br><br>Think with the student about the skills needed so they could be more motivated by classroom activities or tasks. Think with the student about the environmental or human resources needed to enhance motivation for classroom activities. |

*(continued)*

| Skill sets | Functions and skills | Examples of functions and skills in action | Sample performance difficulties | Potential strategies, accommodations, or educational objectives |
|---|---|---|---|---|
| Self-regulation | The capacity to notice one's own behaviors, determine whether those behaviors are aligned to one's personal standards and goals, and change the behaviors so as to be successfully aligned with personal standards and goals<br><br>The capacity to change one's behaviors as needed, to fulfill all of the motivations listed previously, and ensure positive long-term outcomes. | The student recognizes that arousal needs have to be met to ensure physical safety and sensory-motor stimulation. The student changes her or his behaviors so that those needs get met consistently and at the right time(s).<br><br>The student recognizes that emotional needs have to be met to ensure group membership and social connectendess.<br><br>The student changes behaviors so that those social needs can get met.<br><br>The student recognizes the need for a sense of personal efficacy, and can change behaviors to ensure that personal efficacy needs get met.<br><br>The student recognizes personal standards and goals and changes behaviors so that they are so aligned. As a result, the student is able to meet all of the needs in the motivational hierarchy over longer time intervals. | The student often experiences overarousal or underarousal and has difficulty identifying the right level of arousal for a given situation. The student is therefore unable to use arousal to guide action and regulate behaviors successfully.<br><br>The student experiences emotions too intensely or not intensely enough and has difficulty identifying the right intensity level of emotion for a given situation. The student is therefore unable to use emotions to guide action and regulate behaviors successfully.<br><br>The student is not aware of how school activities are designed to enhance a sense of personal efficacy and success and does not participate in school activities for this reason.<br><br>The student is not aware of the list of motivations and needs and does not have a way to express how to get those needs met.<br><br>The student *does* understand the need to fulfill all of the motivations listed in this table but overrelies on avoidance behaviors to make sure that those motivations are not lost or taken away.<br><br>The student does not have the metacognition and self-reflection skills needed to identify arousal, emotions, and/or motivation. The student has only limited self-soothing and inhibition skills and has difficulty reflecting upon her or his affect for this reason.<br><br>The student does not have the metacognition and self-reflection skills or the experience needed to identify personal standards, beliefs, and goals.<br><br>The student does not have the metacognition skills needed to change goals, create subgoals, and change behaviors so that personal standards are met and important personal goals can be reached. | Teach about all of the preceding concepts.<br><br>Teach the student how to observe her or his own behaviors; use adults and peers to describe the student's behaviors to the student.<br><br>Teach the student about the arousal and emotional processes that drive her or his behaviors and how those drives are designed to get personal needs met. Help the student understand how behaviors sometimes are designed to get immediate needs met but are not effective in getting long-term needs met.<br><br>Teach the student how to identify personal goals. Discuss how those goals are or are not successful in getting their personal needs met.<br><br>Teach the student how to identify pesonal standards and goals and help the student compare her or his behaviors against those standards or goals.<br><br>Teach the student about successful self-regulation. Teach about self-soothing and inhibition skills and how to use them. Ask the student how their behaviors support personal standards and goals. Discuss with the student how they are going to make sure that their needs will get met consistently over the longer term.<br><br>Use previewing and provide a prior lesson about self-regulation so that conversations about motivation do not come as a surprise to the student when they are discovered to be lacking in motivation. Use examples from personal experience and practice, if appropriate. Support the student in choosing new goals that may be difficult for the student to achieve because of underdeveloped personal resources.<br><br>Teach the student how to change her or his goals and how to reach those goals. See also Chapter 7. |

APPENDIX 8.2 **Affect and Self-Regulation Skills Observation Sheet**

| Skill sets | Functions and skills | Example skills or deficits in this student | Potential strategies, accommodations, or educational objectives |
|---|---|---|---|
| Arousal | Maintain an optimal level of alertness and attentiveness to internal stimuli, environmental stimuli, tasks, activities, or goals | | |
| Emotions | The capacity to recognize and understand the emotional responses of self and others to a variety of situations | | |
| Motivation | The capacity to understand and meet all of the key needs that motivate humans: Physical safety and sensory-motor needs, social needs, self-efficacy, and altruism | | |
| Self-regulation | The capacity to notice one's own behaviors, determine whether those behaviors are aligned to one's personal standards and goals, and change the behaviors so as to be successfully aligned with personal standards and goals<br>The capacity to change one's behaviors as needed and fulfill all of the motivations listed previously | | |

# Educational Frameworks

# Reading Skills

## INTRODUCTION AND GENERAL DEFINITIONS

This chapter on reading skills serves as the introduction to Section III. As with all skills discussed in this book, success in reading requires intact neurological structures and functions. When the brain is developing normally, the neurological and developmental foundations discussed in the first two sections can be harnessed to develop the skill of reading. However, unlike the other skills discussed thus far, there are no biological structures or functions specifically dedicated to reading. Reading, writing, and math are not biologically programmed to unfold or develop as a part of normal child development. They are acquired only if taught explicitly. This chapter will focus on the acquisition of reading skills.

Reading requires matching visual symbols to spoken words. The act of matching symbols (letters and letter combinations) to their associated sounds (phonemes) is a specific skill called *phonics*. Phonics is the essential skill needed for reading. Acquisition of reading skills depends on intact neurological structures, such as the audiological capacity of hearing and discriminating sounds, as well as the formal (receptive) language functions of phonological awareness. In addition, reading requires the formal (expressive) language skill of speech-sound production and the visual capacity to recognize symbols on a page. All of the skills just listed have to be in place before phonics (matching sounds to their symbols) is possible. A similar process of integration is needed for writing, which also has phonics at its core. Although writing skills won't be discussed until the next chapter, it is important to keep writing in mind throughout the discussion of reading. When someone reads, the skill of phonics is used to decode words, meaning that they sound out the letters on the page. In writing, the skill of phonics is used to encode words, meaning that they print and spell the words from actual or imagined speech.



## HOW THIS FRAMEWORK WAS CONSTRUCTED

Unlike some of the previous chapters, the literature on reading and the terms used to describe reading are relatively consistent across researchers and practitioners. The Reading Skills Framework was developed from several sources, but two commonly recognized sources stand out as especially important: The National Reading Panel (2001) and Common Core State Standards (2010). Other references are listed in the body of the text.

Reading is often separated into two skill sets: Phonics and reading comprehension (Gildroy & Deshler, 2005). Each of these is made up of component skills. Using this categorization, phonics consists of phonological awareness, sound–symbol correspondences, and reading fluency. Reading comprehension consists of reading comprehension for words, reading comprehension for sentences and text, and the interpretation of text. The terms and definitions of this framework are organized into three skills related to phonics and four groups of skills related to reading comprehension. The purpose of separating reading skills in this manner is to be consistent with commonly used interventions for reading and commonly used measures of reading progress.

This framework addresses skills related specifically to reading. However, reading success is not only about mastering phonics and comprehension. It is also dependent on components outside the domain of reading (Joshi, Gooden, & Bentum, 2008), including all of the other skills discussed thus far in this book. For example, language skills are important to reading (Grizzle & Simms, 2005; Hulme & Snowling, 2014; Semrud-Clikeman, 2009; Snowling & Hulme, 2010; van der Lely & Marshall, 2010). See Chapter 4 for a review of terms. Working memory (Berninger & O'Malley, 2011; Gathercole & Pickering, 2000), motivation, and ecological factors also must be considered (Joshi et al., 2008).

## HOW CAN THIS FRAMEWORK HELP ME?

Reading is central to education and to learning. All adults involved in the education of students should be able to assist those students who have reading difficulty. School professionals can do so only when they themselves understand the component skills of reading, can discuss those component skills with the student, and can target relevant components through an intervention plan. Both preservice and in-service teachers often do not have the training and expertise needed to teach literacy skills to students who struggle with reading (Washburn, Joshi, & Binks-Cantrell, 2011; Washburn, Malatesha Joshi, & Cantrell, 2011). This framework introduces and explains all the skills involved in reading to help school professionals make more accurate observations of reading success and difficulty and allow them to discuss observation results with colleagues.

School professionals can use the terms presented in this chapter to discuss a student's reading abilities with team members, the student's family, and the student. As is true for all of the skills discussed in this book, good observations of a student's reading performance in the classroom should be integrated into a comprehensive description of that student's skills across all areas of development. Classroom observations and the student's performance on standardized measures can be interpreted using the terms discussed in this chapter, which are also important for measuring the student's progress. Repeated observations of the student's performance can be analyzed to measure progress in the student's reading skills and assess responsiveness to the teaching and intervention plan.



## READING SKILLS FRAMEWORK: TERMS AND DEFINITIONS

The framework presented here provides specific definitions and examples of terms helpful to discussing a student's reading skills.

The Reading Skills Framework consists of the following skill sets and skills:

1. Phonological awareness (phonemic awareness)
2. Phonics
3. Reading fluency

4. Reading comprehension
    a. Reading vocabulary and linguistic complexity
    b. Reading comprehension for sentences and syntactic complexity
    c. Reading comprehension for paragraphs and text: Elements and structures in text
    d. Understanding and interpreting content of text. Interrelationships within the text, between text and other events, and reader variables

The sections that follow define each of the terms and concepts outlined in the Reading Skills Framework. The framework is also available in summary form in Appendix 9.1.

## Phonological Awareness

Phonological awareness refers to the capacity to segment words into their component syllables and component sounds. The National Reading Panel report (2001) uses the term *phonemic awareness* in reference to this skill. Phonological or phonemic awareness is a receptive language skill. As mentioned in Chapter 4, the English language has 45 phonemes. Each of the vowels and consonants used in spoken English is a phoneme. Sound combinations, such as /ch/ or /th/, are also phonemes. Each alphabet letter and many letter combinations represent one or more phonemes (Crystal, 1997). Students need to be able to identify all the sounds of the English language to develop phonological awareness. They also need to be able to produce those sounds (speech-sound production). Because both of these skills are prerequisites for successful reading, students with hearing impairment are at very high risk of reading difficulty. Reading skills in the student who is deaf or hard of hearing depend on the student's residual hearing functions, capacity for discriminating phonetic contrasts, and phonological awareness for the English language in particular (Zupran & Dempsey, 2013).



## Phonics

Phonics is the capacity to match phonemes to printed symbols. Matching a sound to its symbol is a separate skill from phonological awareness, which involves hearing and discriminating sounds in spoken speech. When faced with letters on the page, the student has to hear the sound in his or her mind and then produce that sound (speech-sound production). Speech-sound production can occur by speaking aloud or by producing the sounds as internalized speech. The ability to identify a sound by looking at its printed symbol is called decoding. The term *phonics* is used in the Writing Skills Framework (Chapter 10) as well. Just as reading requires phonics skills to decode the sounds in printed words, writing requires phonics skills to encode spoken sounds into printed words.

## Reading Fluency

Reading fluency refers to the speed (the number of words read per minute) at which a student can read text. Reading fluency consists of more than one type of skill; it requires not only fluent decoding skills but also automatic word recognition skills. The National Reading Panel discusses how the term *reading fluency* has shifted over time (2001, Chap. 3). Vocabulary knowledge and comprehension greatly enhance reading fluency and automaticity. For the Reading Skills Framework, it is important to recognize that reading fluency is dependent on rapid decoding and automatic word recognition without having to decode. Fluency and automaticity also depend upon rapidly connecting the word with its meaning. The fluent reader is able to decode, automatically recognize, and comprehend words quickly. Problems with fluent decoding and automatic word recognition affect reading comprehension (National Reading Panel, 2001). This is true regardless of the student's understanding of word meanings (vocabulary).

## Reading Comprehension

Phonological awareness, phonics, and reading fluency are three of the essential skills of reading. They serve as prerequisites to successful reading comprehension, which requires connecting printed text with language. Printed text is not only connected with the meaning of individual words (reading vocabulary) but also with larger ideas expressed through sentences and paragraphs. How ideas are expressed in language is discussed in Chapter 4. Reading comprehension includes having an understanding of the different elements and structures used in text (Akhondi, Malayeri, & Samad, 2011). The terms *elements* and *structures* are defined later in this section. The Common Core Standards discuss text-level comprehension as the analysis of key ideas and details, as well as the analysis of craft (interpretation of words and phrases) and structure. The following paragraphs discuss the component skills of reading comprehension.

***Reading Comprehension for Words*** Reading comprehension of individual words is sometimes referred to as reading vocabulary and is related to a student's vocabulary in both oral and printed language. The National Reading Panel references the term *reading vocabulary* in its chapter on comprehension (2001, Chap. 4) as a measure of a person's word bank in spoken language. A student's reading vocabulary is more constrained if their spoken (aural-oral, receptive-expressive) vocabulary is constrained. Students with a limited vocabulary have difficulty comprehending what they read, regardless of their decoding and fluency skills (Nation, Cocksey, & Taylor, 2010). An important goal of reading instruction is to expand the student's vocabulary for both printed and spoken words. Comprehension of vocabulary facilitates decoding and automatic word recognition.



*Reading Vocabulary and Linguistic Complexity* The capacity to understand words depends on a student's exposure to language and successful language development. It also depends on the student's exposure to new or different types of words through formal education and life experiences. Stated another way, reading vocabulary depends upon general knowledge.

*Linguistic complexity* is a term used to understand the depth and breadth of a student's vocabulary in both spoken and printed language and can be measured in different ways. For example, a word has greater linguistic complexity if it is made up of multiple syllables instead of a single syllable. Words are more complex if they are used rarely or when they refer to an abstract idea as opposed to a concrete object or simple fact. Literary devices, such as humor, onomatopoeia (e.g., words that sound like their meaning, such as "sizzle" or "boom"), flashback, or alliteration (e.g., two or more words with a repeating initial consonant sound, such as "Peter Piper picked a peck of pickled peppers"), also reflect greater linguistic complexity. These devices often include words that have a dual meaning or that serve more than one purpose in the sentence or text. The depth and breadth of a student's reading vocabulary therefore depend on the student's vocabulary in spoken language, their understanding of language more generally (e.g., all of the morphemes, word roots, and prefixes and suffixes that exist in a language), their general knowledge of the world, their capacity to engage in abstract thinking, and their capacity to look at the multiple purposes and meanings that words can represent. All of these facets of language are used to define linguistic complexity.

***Reading Comprehension for Sentences and Syntactic Complexity*** Reading comprehension for sentences depends on the student's understanding of the morpho-syntax of English. The student has to understand morphemes and word order, as discussed in Chapter 4, as well as the elements of sentences in print, such as punctuation and grammar. Sentence-level reading comprehension is affected by syntactic complexity. Phrases and short sentences have a lower level of complexity compared to compound sentences that have subordinate clauses. Sentence-level reading requires a student to be able to read, differentiate, and understand phrases, incomplete sentences, compound sentences, and complex sentences, all of which contribute to *syntactic complexity*. The Common Core Standards include syntactic complexity in the sections dedicated to key ideas and details, as well as craft and structure.

***Reading Comprehension for Paragraphs and Text*** Reading comprehension at the paragraph and text level requires yet more skills. The elements and structure of text are important aspects of reading comprehension. *Elements* refer to the components that make up the text. *Structures* refer to the organization of ideas in text.

*Elements of Text* Successful reading requires the student to identify elements of both literary and expository text. Literary text contains elements such as character, plot, setting, major events, problem, and solution. In reading comprehension, the student must be able to identify elements such as these and respond to comprehension questions related to these elements. The teacher might ask the student to provide a list of the characters in a story, describe the setting, identify the main problem that the protagonist has to solve, or to describe the solution to the problem. Another way to assess reading comprehension might be to hypothesize about what a character from the story might do under a different circumstance, how the author might end the story with a different solution, or how different characters within the text might respond to the same situation. Expository or informational text includes elements such as the title, table of contents, charts and graphs, maps, illustrations, index, headings and subheadings, and other such features. When assessing reading comprehension for informational text, the teacher could begin by asking the student to identify different elements. The teacher could also ask more detailed questions and have the student summarize the most important information revealed by different elements of the text. For example, the teacher could ask the student to identify the key ideas of the text and explain how they are communicated by the table of contents, by pictures, or by titles and subtitles. Poetry, prose, fiction, fables, and dramatic literature all have their own elements, which are different from those of business letters, instruction manuals, newspaper articles, science reports, and web pages.



*Structures of Text* Successful reading requires an understanding of text structure, which is how ideas are presented. Explicit instruction about text structure results in improved reading comprehension skills (Hebert, Bohaty, & Nelson, 2016). Using structure as the method of analysis, the teacher could ask the student to first identify the structure of individual paragraphs, such the topic sentence, supporting sentences, and concluding sentence. This structure is especially evident in informational text but can also be present in literary text. By identifying these structures, students can more easily identify main ideas, supporting ideas, and conclusions in the text. Other common text structures such as description, chronological sequence, cause and effect, compare and contrast, and problem and solution (Meyer, 1985) can apply to whole texts and are often used in essay writing. However they can also apply to many different types of text, and they are important to know because they support reading comprehension.

Additional structures exist for other types and purposes of writing. For example, a narrative text can be organized according to goals and can include a goal path. The goal path may or may not be chronological or even sequential. For example, a writer could tell a story about a problem and a goal that involves moving back and forth in time and between different episodes. The story and the goal path could include substructures, such as a problem-and-solution or cause-and-effect substructure (a story within the story). Poetry, prose, fiction, fables, and dramatic literature, business letters, instruction manuals, newspaper articles, science reports, and web pages also have characteristic structures and elements. Reading comprehension requires students to be able to identify these structures and comment on the interrelationship between them and the elements and the ideas presented in the text.

***Reading Comprehension and the Interpretation of Text*** The words, sentences, elements, and structures discussed in the preceding paragraphs influence a student's comprehension of text. The reader must be able to comprehend the linguistic and syntactic complexity, elements, and structures of the text to master the content. Readers vary in their ability to recognize and understand these aspects of text, depending on their vocabulary, their mastery of formal language, and their prior exposure to the elements and structures listed in the previous section. However, even when these aspects of text are properly matched to the student's knowledge, additional reader variables as described below also affect reading comprehension and interpretation of text.

*Understanding the Key Ideas as Presented by the Author* The organizational structure can influence the reader's interpretation of what is or is not important. One aspect of reading comprehension requires the reader to identify how the author decided to present the ideas in the text and how the author underscores which ideas are more important than others. The importance of the ideas as presented by the author might vary depending on the text structure, the number of elements dedicated to an idea, and the linguistic and syntactic complexity used to present those ideas. Ideas that are more important might be presented earlier in the text, repeated more often, explained more fully, and explained using more precise language that includes technical terms. Ideas that are less important might be presented later, emerge less often, explained less fully, and be conveyed with less precision. By identifying key ideas, the student can also understand interrelationships among the main ideas, supporting ideas, elements, and structures.

*Understanding Key Ideas and Their Relationship to Ideas Outside the Text* Key ideas in the text might be associated with historical events or with other works of writing such as newspaper articles, plays, or poems. By making associations with contemporary or past events or texts produced elsewhere, the text influences how the reader understands the key ideas and enables the reader to assess which ideas are most important. When a reader links the ideas inside the text with ideas from other sources, the reader is enhancing their comprehension of the printed text. The Common Core Standards refer to this skill as the integration of knowledge and ideas.



*Understanding Key Ideas and Their Relationship With Ideas Not Explicitly Stated or Referenced by the Author* Using the knowledge discussed above, students can interpret and understand text even when the writing is not explicit. For example, in narrative, one aspect of interpretation is the narrator's evaluation. This might show up in how the narrator makes links between the elements of the story (e.g., persons, places, and event) and the goal path (the structure of the narrative). For example, the student might examine how the setting affects a character's action or the narrative's plot development. The student might examine how the main plot is related to subplots or consider how internal or external conflicts (within the character, between characters, and between the character and society) give rise to subsequent events or how these conflicts support the theme. Understanding text structures such as chronological sequences, cause-and-effect sequences, and compare-and-contrast structures can help the reader make inferences about aspects of the plot not stated explicitly by the author. A narrator or author may also make links to general knowledge or information not contained in the text itself. The same types of interpretation are commonly required for narrative text but are sometimes also required for expository text.

*Reader Variables in the Understanding and Interpretation of Text* The discussion thus far has focused on reading comprehension for those ideas that the author intended to convey, either directly or indirectly. However, there is also a subjective aspect to reading comprehension, referred to as *reader variables*. In reading, a student has to make links with prior personal experiences and with her or his own general knowledge of the world. In so doing, the student makes the text meaningful in a personal way. The Common Core Standards refer to these reader features as *reader and task considerations*. As will be discussed in Chapter 10, the quality of written text depends in part on how successfully the author takes into consideration reader and task considerations. A successful text not only is understood by the reader but also influences the reader in some way. A good text can illuminate important concepts for a reader, teach them something new, make it easier to perform a skill of some sort, or inspire a reader to act differently in the world. The text itself does not have any control over reader variables. The reader alone can make the text personally meaningful depending on personal reader variables. How a given text influences the reader is known only to that reader. It is not a feature that is embedded in the text alone. Box 9.1 summarizes the key ideas related to reading comprehension.

**BOX 9.1. Key Factors to Consider for Reading Comprehension**

Successful reading comprehension depends on how well the reader recognizes and understands the following features of text. In addition, reading comprehension depends on reader variables, that is, how the reader makes the text meaningful to him- or herself.

1. Words: Linguistic complexity of the text
2. Sentences: Syntactic complexity of the text
3. Elements: The number and type of elements in the text
4. Structure: The structure and substructures of the text
5. Interrelationships:
    a. Of ideas within the text
    b. Of ideas in the text with ideas outside of the text
6. Reader variables:
    a. The relationship of ideas in the text with ideas and knowledge already held by the reader
    b. Relevance of the ideas in the text to the tasks that the reader may need to carry out
    c. The likelihood that the text will influence the reader's knowledge base, skill base, or actions in the world

## PERFORMANCE DIFFICULTIES IN READING

Performance difficulties in reading are identifiable through everyday observations of the student's reading skills and also by analyzing a student's report card, which typically has specific items related to decoding words and reading fluency, as well as reading comprehension. In the early grades, report cards often reveal whether the student has difficulty with phonics, reading fluency, and/or reading comprehension. When phonics and reading fluency are not affected, the report card may reveal reading difficulty due to challenges in executive or language skills.

During classroom observations, it is often easy to identify struggling readers. They may have difficulty pronouncing words in spoken language or when reading aloud. Students with dyslexia have a very specific difficulty in matching letters (printed symbols) to their corresponding sounds (Shaywitz et al., 1998) and may find it difficult to remember which sound goes with which letter or letter combination. This difficulty can occur even when the student has normal phonological awareness. The student may be able to discriminate and produce speech sounds in oral-aural language without difficulty but have difficulty doing so when reading printed words. Even when these students succeed in matching sounds to their corresponding letters, the process can be effortful (even exhausting) and often characterized by mispronouncing words or reading that is so slow and laborious that it interferes with comprehension. When a student is not able to decode (sound out) words successfully, encoding (writing and spelling) is also affected.

The reader who is struggling with decoding typically has difficulty with reading comprehension and may not be able to respond to even very basic comprehension questions such as identifying the main ideas of a text. Some readers who decode successfully but read slowly also have difficulty with reading comprehension. The reader who has not yet mastered reading fluency can be identified by their slow pace of reading and because of poor reading comprehension. Slow readers can end up not comprehending text because they are expending too much mental energy on the decoding aspect of reading. Readers may also have difficulty with reading comprehension, in the absence of decoding difficulties, because of gaps in language development and general knowledge. When this occurs, the vocabulary demands of the text might exceed the reader's vocabulary in formal language (word bank) or other receptive language skills.

Executive skills also play a role in reading comprehension difficulties (De Franchis, Usai, Viterbori, & Traverso, 2017; van der Sluis, de Jong, & van der Liej, 2007). For example, working memory and inhibition skills are important in reading decoding, especially when decoding unfamiliar words. The reader has to remember rules of decoding while connecting the printed word with language and connecting the meaning of the word into the text as a whole. This requires working memory and inhibition as the reader moves back and forth between mechanical and semantic aspects of reading. Working memory is also needed to retain important points of each paragraph or section of text and to use this information to understand new content that is yet to come. The reading comprehension skills discussed earlier in this chapter (the words, sentences, elements, and structures that make up the text) pose challenges to the student who does not have the working memory to retain and make use of all of these concepts while reading. Students with under-developed executive skills may not have the inhibition and set-shifting skills needed to move back and forth between concrete and abstract meaning, between supporting and main ideas, and between paragraph-level structure and text structure. They may also not have the planning skills needed to sequence the information gleaned from text, an important aspect to remembering and understanding all of the interrelationships between text elements and text structures. When working memory and inhibition skills are overtaxed, it is harder for the student to register, remember, and comprehend the text. This difficulty is especially apparent as the texts and reading expectations become longer and more complex. The demands on the student's executive skills may account for some or all of the student's reading difficulties, regardless of the student's decoding skills.



## HOW TO SET UP AN OBSERVATION

Observations made of routine classroom reading demands, and analyzed using the Reading Skills Framework, can help identify all of the components of reading. By using the Reading Skills Framework summarized in Appendix 9.1 and the Reading Skills Observation Sheet in Appendix 9.2, practitioners can decide whether a formal or standardized evaluation is needed. A standardized measure makes it possible to analyze the process of reading with greater detail than is possible based on informal classroom observations alone. Decisions related to the student's instruction depend on an accurate understanding of the components of reading that are affected in any given reader, especially in the area of decoding. Regardless of the type of observation (standardized or naturalistic), it is important to observe and assess all components of reading.

The focus here is on naturalistic observations. As discussed in Chapter 4, one of the advantages of classroom or naturalistic observations is seeing how the student performs in context. Reading in context (e.g., reading a text or reading in order to participate in various classroom activities) commonly places demands on skills other than just reading skills, such as executive skills and general knowledge. Standardized measures do not typically reflect how successfully a student applies their skills in reading and related areas (such as working memory and motivation) while in classroom settings. These types of measure also do not necessarily capture text-level comprehension or inference skills. It is therefore important to understand how a student responds to reading demands in these natural contexts, outside of a formal testing session using standardized measures. Each of the many different variables that impact reading should then inform the intervention plan (Fletcher et al., 2002).

## Select the Student

A teacher who has experience working with a student can often make an accurate judgment of her or his reading skills through naturalistic observations. Any student who seems to be below grade level in reading can be selected for a more detailed observation and/or for evaluation by using standardized measures. Students may be selected for a variety of reasons, including difficulties at the level of speech-sound production, phonics (decoding), or reading fluency. Alternatively, the selected student may exhibit more generalized difficulty in classroom participation and in learning.

## Obtain a Reading Performance Sample

Before beginning the observation of the student's reading skills, the observer should select a text for the student to read. When choosing a text for the observation, the observer should consider its linguistic and syntactic complexity. For texts that have an assigned grade level, observers might choose one that is aligned with the student's grade. Alternatively, the observer might choose a text that is one or two grade levels lower and then introduce texts that are at progressively higher grade levels to see at which point the student is most successful.

For students with developmental delays and/or students with limited reading skills, the texts may initially need to include many pictures so the observer can gain a sense of the student's formal language skills. Chapter 4 provides an example of how to do this. The language sample obtained by looking at pictures can provide an indication of the level of text complexity that might be appropriate. The observer can also generate single-syllable words in on a computer and sample reading behaviors using samples of text that vary in font sizes and length of passage. Text complexity is usually considered to be higher as the number of words increases and the number of pictures decreases. As the observer makes more observations, the ratio of words to pictures can be increased. The observer should also take into consideration the complexity of the language (linguistic complexity) and sentences (syntactic complexity). Audio clips, videoclips, or transcripts of the student's reading performance can be extremely helpful, but preference should be given to observing the student in real time.

***Observations for Phonological Awareness*** Good articulation is a prerequisite for successful reading and provides evidence of secure phonological awareness skills. Unclear speech is an indicator that the student's phonological awareness may be affected. Observe and make an assessment of the student's articulation skills and overall intelligibility.

***Observations for Phonics*** The student should be able to identify letters and the sounds associated with each letter. Verify whether the student can identify all the sounds associated with the letters of the alphabet and whether the student can identify the sounds associated with all the phonemes of English. Remember that there are 45 phonemes in English, even though there are only 26 letters. Some students with reading difficulty may be able to decode individual letters or simple consonant–vowel–consonant words but have difficulty with longer words or with multiple-letter phonemes. Some students may be able to sound out individual words but not be able to sound out words in connected text. Some students can decode connected text, but their pace of reading is slow. During the observation, take into consideration the student's decoding skills at these different levels of decoding difficulty.

***Observations for Reading Fluency*** The student needs to be able to decode words fluently and to automatically recognize certain words without the need to decode. Formal measures may be needed to identify a student with reading fluency difficulty, because they capture performance on a standardized scale (e.g., words read per minute). Still, natural observations can help a teacher understand a student's reading fluency, especially as compared with other students in the same class or grade. Remember that reading vocabulary can influence the speed of decoding and automaticity. The purpose of fluency and automaticity in reading is to quickly link the decoded word with its meaning. This link cannot occur as easily if the student does not also have a good vocabulary in spoken language.

***Observations for Reading Comprehension*** The observer can assess reading comprehension by asking the student about the meaning of words and sentences in the text. When language comprehension is not a concern, the observer can assess more advanced aspects of reading comprehension. For example, reading comprehension can be assessed by asking the student to respond to questions related to the content of the text, to paraphrase the text, and/or to identify text elements and text structures. In narrative text, the observer should determine whether the student can respond to questions about the characters or the goal path. For expository text, it would be important to know whether the student can summarize the main idea or present a few of the important ideas from the text. The observer can assess whether the student can identify important text types (fiction and different types of nonfiction), text elements (table of contents, titles and subtitles, and elements used for specialized purposes such as in letters, plays, or poems), and text structures (compare and contrast, free form, and structures used for specialized purposes such as letters, recipes, or plays).



***Observation for Reading Skills as Affected by Developmental Skills and Frameworks Outside of Reading*** Developmental domains and frameworks outside of reading decoding and reading comprehension may be important to consider for some students. For example, when assessing a student's reading comprehension, consider the demands being placed on the student's language skills and working memory skills. A student can appear to have difficulty with reading comprehension when, in fact, they are actually struggling to express what she or he knows (expressive language difficulty) or to remember key information (working memory weaknesses). Some students may not be able to respond to reading comprehension questions because they do not have the expressive language skills to do so. However, they may be able to show their reading skills another way. For example, a student might demonstrate stronger reading comprehension skills if required to respond to multiple-choice questions instead of open-ended questions, if given more time to respond, or if provided texts that contain many pictures. The distinctions among reading decoding, language comprehension, working memory skills or other executive skills, and expressive language skills are useful to make, because each will inform needed interventions in different ways. The IEP Builder in this chapter provides some illustrative examples.

## Analyze and Interpret the Observations

After observing the student, the observer will have to make a determination about whether the student shows reading difficulty. By using the Reading Skills Framework, it is possible to make logical guesses about which aspects of reading appear to be the most affected: Phonological awareness and phonics, reading fluency, reading vocabulary, and/or reading comprehension. It is also possible to identify reading difficulties that may be related to domains outside of the Reading Skills Framework.

## Discussion of Findings With Colleagues

After the observation, the observer should discuss the student's performance with colleagues. The discussion should be used to help identify the source(s) of the student's reading difficulty, determine whether there is a need for a formal evaluation, and generate ideas for interventions.

Reading instruction should address all of the aspects of reading as outlined by the National Reading Panel and discussed in this chapter. A simple way to plan reading instruction, and to develop educational objectives for reading instruction, is to divide instruction into phonics-based instruction and reading comprehension instruction (Duff & Clarke, 2011). Within these two basic subdivisions, instruction should take into consideration the component skills that students need to master.

The purpose of the IEP Builder is not to fully address all of the important aspects of reading instruction. Only key aspects of reading acquisition and reading instruction will be discussed here. Educators and other school professionals can use the information contained in this chapter to ensure that the student's reading curriculum addresses all the skills presented in the framework. Another important aspect to consider is that reading instruction must be integrated with writing instruction (Berninger, Abbott, Nagy, & Carlisle, 2010) and with listening comprehension and spoken language. The acronym POSSuM summarizes all of the components needed for effective reading instruction, which includes instruction in **P**honics, **O**rthography, **S**ematics, **S**yntax, and **M**orphemes (Wolf et al., 2009; Wolf & Stoodley, 2008). For a comprehensive discussion of all the different components of reading instruction, see Horowitz-Kraus and Finucane (2016) and Tunmer (2008, and additional articles in that issue of *Reading and Writing*). See Brooks (2017) for a review of evidence-based literacy instruction. Teachers with limited experience in reading instruction should review the excellent articles listed in the References section and consult with their school's reading specialist.

## Educational Objectives and Strategies for Teaching Reading

The choice of educational objectives for any student will depend on the student's progress in each of the skill sets and skills listed in the following sections. In typically developing learners, language development precedes reading development. Enhancing and expanding a student's language skills always serves the development of reading skills. Students with limited language skills, but who have phonological awareness and can identify symbols, can be taught how to decode words. However, future reading comprehension is dependent on language skills. With this in mind, the discussion that follows focuses on skills specifically related to reading.

***Educational Objectives and Strategies for Pre-reading Skills*** Reading instruction starts with teaching such emergent literacy skills such as looking at pages in a book, scanning pictures, scanning from left to right, gaining meaning from pictures, speaking with adults about the experience of looking at pictures, and looking at the content of printed materials. The student can learn to identify a few symbols such as icons, letters, and single printed words. Progress measures can be used to track how well the student uses books and printed materials to engage in oral discussion or respond to basic questions. For students with developmental limitations, success in pre-reading skills can be assessed through the student's comprehension of pictures, icons, or familiar single printed words in context.

***Educational Objectives and Strategies for Phonological Awareness*** In typically developing students, phonological awareness evolves as part of language development and is securely in place before formal reading instruction starts in kindergarten or first grade. Students are taught phonological skills by using activities such as rhyming, breaking words into their component phonemes, and breaking words into their component syllables. Students are also taught to blend phonemes in speech; to identify beginning, middle, and ending sounds of spoken words; and to blend phonemes in spoken language. Progress in phonological awareness can be measured by considering how many phonemes the student is able to recognize or discriminate and to produce in speech.

***Educational Objectives and Strategies for Phonics*** Formal reading instruction starts with teaching the letters of the alphabet, how to match letters to their sounds, and how to match sounds with their letters. This is the skill of phonics. Instruction in phonics typically starts in kindergarten or first grade. In typical learners, it takes approximately 2.5 years to learn all the sound–symbol relationships required for successful reading in English. Reading curricula provide ways to measure the number of sound–symbol relationships understood by the student and how many of those symbols the student can decode accurately. Progress monitoring usually occurs as part of reading instruction or occurs as part of a standardized measure of reading skills. Progress includes the capacity to decode greater numbers of phonemes, more complex phonemes, and phonemes in connected text. Decoding becomes more automatized as phonics skills improve, resulting in greater reading fluency and greater comprehension. The student should also develop the skill of identifying and repairing decoding errors. For example, a decoding error might be obvious when the word produced does not make sense within the sentence or within the text as a whole.



***Educational Objectives and Strategies for Reading Fluency*** Reading fluency instruction can be delivered separately from decoding (phonics) instruction. Common estimates of oral reading fluency range from averages of 23–53 words per minute in first grade to 127–150 words per minute by middle school (Hasbrouk & Tindal, 2006). To track the student's progress, school professionals can measure how many words a student decodes accurately during a 1-minute time interval. Some judgment is needed to discern whether a student is reading below the level expected for her or his age, as the norms listed above are for average performance. Progress monitoring for reading fluency is usually carried out as a part of reading instruction or as part of standardized evaluation of reading skills. It is useful to depend on a standardized measure of reading fluency, both to identify accurately a student's reading fluency abilities and to measure the student's responsiveness to instruction.

***Educational Objectives and Strategies for Reading Vocabulary*** Students improve their reading vocabulary by learning to read (decoding, fluency, and automatic word retrieval) and by learning new vocabulary words through reading. Students can also acquire new words through oral language. There are different ways in which the student's vocabulary can be expanded, using both reading and formal language as the platform for learning. Students learn to identify the meaning of words by breaking words down into component parts, by learning about the multiple meanings of words (e.g., *light* can mean more than one thing) or similar meanings between words (e.g., *tired* as opposed to *exhausted*), and by using context clues.

Reading vocabulary instruction also involves instruction in linguistic categories of words and semantic categories of words. Students can learn words to represent linguistic categories such as plants, animals, or tools. These words can be mastered as part of content vocabulary for grade-level curriculum. Students can also learn semantic categories of words, such as parts of sentences (e.g., verbs, nouns, adjectives) or types of words (e.g., antonyms, homonyms, synonyms). They can learn that words are used for the purposes of imagery, flashback, foreshadowing, hyperbole, symbolism, humor, suspense, personification, exaggeration, dialogue, description, or alliteration. These words can be mastered when students read connected text. As the student builds vocabulary, they also learn about the difference between concrete and literal meaning versus abstract and conceptual meaning and how words can, at times, be both concrete and abstract. Standardized measures can be used to monitor the progress of the student's reading vocabulary skills.

***Educational Objectives and Strategies for Reading Comprehension*** Just as reading decoding is taught in a systematic manner, so too should instruction for reading comprehension be systematic (Williams, 2005). When reading instruction shifts toward reading comprehension, it is equally accurate to say that the student is participating in literacy and content instruction. In most instances, third grade is when a shift occurs from learning to read to reading to learn. Reading comprehension includes the full range of reading comprehension skills discussed in this chapter. Student progress can be measured by evaluating the student's comprehension of vocabulary, ability to identify and understand different types of sentences, ability to identify different types of text elements and text structures, and capacity to interpret text. Box 9.2 discusses additional aspects of reading comprehension instruction.

**BOX 9.2. Reading Strategy Instruction**

Reading comprehension can be enhanced with reading strategy instruction, using strategies such as identifying the main ideas; summarization; self-questioning, mnemonics, and graphic organizers; and self-monitoring tools such as a checklist or prompt card (Solis et al., 2012). Reading strategies often consist of specific questions that the student needs to ask when engaged in reading. The teacher can ask the student to respond to the questions and instructions listed below. See Roehling, Hebert, Nelson, and Bohaty (2017) and Bakken and Whedon (2002) for additional strategies for reading comprehension for expository text.

1. **Reading at the Word and Sentence Levels**
    a. Underline words that you do not understand. Think of a different word to say the same thing.
    b. Put a circle around symbols that you do not understand.
2. **Reading at the Paragraph Level**
    a. Count the number of sentences in this paragraph.
    b. What is the opening sentence?
    c. What is the closing sentence?
    d. List the sentences that you do not understand.
    e. What is the main idea?

*(continued)*

**BOX 9.2.** *(continued)*

f. How many examples does the author give to support the main idea?

g. List one thing that you learned from reading this paragraph.

h. List any literary elements that you discovered from reading this paragraph, for example, dialogue; examples of description; and imagery, repetition, flashback, foreshadowing, hyperbole, symbolism, humor, suspense, personification, and exaggeration.

**3. Reading at the Text Level**

a. How many paragraphs are there? List the main idea in each paragraph.

b. What is the main idea of the text? What are the supporting ideas?

c. What type of text is this? For example, is it a poem, letter, essay, instruction manual, or newspaper article? Why did the author use the structure that she or he chose?

d. What is the purpose of this text? Is it to persuade, inform, or entertain?

e. How did the author organize his or her ideas? (Examples include sequential, chronological, cause and effect, compare and contrast, description.)

f. List or identify the following elements: Character, setting, plot, problem, solution.

g. What are the main events? How many episodes are there in this story?

h. What type of structure(s) do you see in this text? (Examples include compare and contrast; categorization; point by point; temporal sequence.)

**Use of Graphic or Visual Organizers**
Reading comprehension strategies can include graphics, such as balloons or boxes on a page, which the student fills out when answering questions such as those listed above. Graphic organizers can help the student visually divide a story into its beginning, middle, and end; list episodes or key ideas; and isolate supporting information for each episode or key idea. Drawing connections between the balloons or boxes with lines and arrows can help students demonstrate their understanding of the flow of ideas in the text.



## Accommodations for Reading

When reading is not the primary task of learning, information can be shared in ways other than through print. Students with more limited reading skills can expand their vocabulary and knowledge when information is presented in oral form, for example, through conversations or presentations or through visual media such as films or videos. For students with more limited reading proficiency, consider using texts with more graphics and pictures and fewer words. Readability measures and text complexity measures are ways to identify appropriate reading material for some learners (Kotula, 2003). For example, young readers can read more successfully when the text includes a lot of pictures and when there are only a few words or one or two sentences per page. Struggling readers may also perform better with these types of text and when he or she can simultaneously listen to the text being read aloud by another person or in recorded formats.

Remember that some students have reading difficulty not related to reading decoding. The struggling reader may have difficulty with limited language and associated difficulty with comprehension or have difficulty with reading comprehension because of difficulties in working memory and other executive skills. Still others may have difficulty showing what they know after reading a text because of difficulty in their expressive language. The accommodations used for each of these situations will vary. The reader who has difficulty because of limited language may need more visual information to circumvent comprehension difficulties related to language. That student may also need exposure to more content areas to build language and vocabulary skills. The reader with language and working memory difficulties may need text delivered visually (using pictures) and verbally (using printed text as well as spoken words) and may need the information contained in the text to be sequenced in a logical order so that sequencing/planning demands are reduced. For example, the information contained in the text may need to be organized in graphic format (e.g., using bubbles, boxes, or numerical categories). For narrative text, school professionals can reduce the load on working memory and on planning skills by providing pictures that have a clearly defined sequence or story line, with relatively obvious cause-and-effect relationships and a limited number of events or episodes.

## CASE EXAMPLE

Ellen is a 10-year-old student who is finishing the fifth grade. Ellen participated in a reading evaluation at the end of her fifth-grade year, using text taken from a commonly used reading assessment tool (Wiederholt & Bryant, 2012). The case example here is presented in printed text. It is important for the reader to remember that reading must be analyzed aurally. Observations in a classroom setting must be made while the student is reading or by using an audioclip of the student reading. Keep this in mind when reading the transcript below. The analysis following the transcript of Ellen's reading performance here more fully describes Ellen's reading difficulties to make up for the lack of audio. Bracketed words within the transcript indicate the correct decoding of the word or phrase.

> *Over the world farmer face many difficult problems. Fruits vegetables and other plants are fre freq frequently attacked by insects and diseases that can wipe out in . . . in . . . intire crop . . . crop* [entire crops]. *Farmers attempt to control these pests by using chemicals but these pois poisons can make our food unsafe to eat. They can also harm useful insects and birds at many seasons of the year* [at any season of the year] *weather may also destroy crops. Ex extreme heat or co cold too much rain or too little hail or high wings* [. . . too much rain or too little, hail or high winds . . .] *all can ser ious dis disgrate crop ial* [can seriously decrease crop yields]. *Unlikely pest* [unlike pests, severe] *weather con . . . condi c . . . condictions are usually impossible to protect or control.*

After she finished reading, Ellen responded to the following reading comprehension questions. Her answers are noted in italics.

1. What is the main idea of this story? *Stop animals from eating it.*
2. What is a worker's main goal in this story? *Get rid of animals that do stuff on plants.*
3. What one word was used to describe heat and cold? *Um . . .*
4. How are pests and weather contrasted in this story? *Um . . .*
5. What specific weather conditions are described in this story? Name two. *Rain and sun.*

### Case Analysis

Ellen shows characteristic behaviors of a student with dyslexia, which is a phonics-based reading disability. All too often, school teams are uncomfortable thinking about dyslexia (a medical term) and its educational equivalent, a specific learning disability in reading. As is common in many children with dyslexia, Ellen's disability lies in phonics (reading decoding, and reading fluency). A more detailed analysis of Ellen's reading skills helps identify the components of Ellen's reading disability and helps to inform the content of her intervention plan.

### Analysis of Phonological Awareness

The transcript does not reveal any errors in articulation. Most of the words that Ellen read out loud were also pronounced correctly and clearly, at least when she was able to decode normally. There is no concern about Ellen's phonological awareness.

### Analysis of Phonics

Ellen has marked difficulty in sounding out many of the words presented in the reading passage. The transcript reveals Ellen's decoding difficulty in several places. For example, Ellen had difficulty decoding words such as *frequently, poisons, decrease,* and *yield.* It is important to notice that Ellen identifies more words correctly than incorrectly, which can be a source of confusion to an untrained observer. Given her reading successes, the observer needs to discover whether her reading errors are merely reflective of her lack of familiarity with a few vocabulary words. In this case, Ellen's decoding is too effortful to be attributed solely to lack of familiarity. Remember that Ellen has had many years of reading practice. She has become adept at guessing, relying on visual appearance of unknown words or making approximations based upon memorization of features of familiar or frequently occurring words. This is a good skill to have and helps with reading fluency, when it works! However, memorization of familiar words is not a skill that Ellen can rely upon when reading new or unfamiliar texts. Without secure decoding skills, she will continue to have difficulty comprehending text.

### Analysis of Reading Fluency



An average reader for Ellen's age and grade should be able to read 110–140 words per minute. A low average performance for her age and grade would be 85–99 words per minute. It took Ellen 1 minute and 45 seconds to read the 96 words of this passage. Based on this one reading sample, her oral reading fluency score is below 55 words per minute, far below age expectations. Ellen has normally developed articulation, prosody, and intonation in spoken language (see Chapter 4 for definitions of these terms). However, she was not able to bring her normal speech into her reading, because she was dedicating so much energy to reading decoding. She gave each word equal emphasis. It was difficult to differentiate one sentence from the next, because she did not pause between sentences. She did not use normal intonation or expression in her reading, even though she is capable of doing so in her speech.

### Analysis of Reading Comprehension

Ellen's difficulty in decoding resulted in very substantial difficulty in reading comprehension. Because of the energy she had to expend deciphering the words of the text, she was not able to dedicate cognitive resources to understanding the text. Her literal comprehension of the text was very limited. Therefore, she is not ready to master inferential aspects of text comprehension at her current reading decoding level.

### Educational Strategies for Building Ellen's Phonological Awareness Skills

A teacher who is skilled and qualified to teach reading to a student with a phonics-based reading disability (dyslexia) should assess Ellen's phonological awareness. Even though her phonological awareness appears to be intact in everyday speech, it may be useful to know if she has difficulty discriminating certain phonemes aurally and needs to receive instruction in oral-aural phoneme discrimination skills.

### Educational Strategies for Teaching Phonics

The primary focus for Ellen's reading instruction should be to teach her phonics and decoding skills. At the same time, Ellen needs to be taught spelling/encoding skills. Teaching reading decoding and spelling (encoding) at the same time reinforces the phonics-based instruction that she needs. Phonics instruction proceeds in a logical manner from least complex to more complex phonemes, letters, and letter combinations. A teacher who is qualified to teach reading to students with reading disabilities can determine which phonemes Ellen has mastered and which phonemes she still needs to master.

### Educational Strategies for Improving Ellen's Reading Fluency

In addition to instruction in decoding, Ellen needs instruction in reading fluency. Reading fluency is taught through frequent reading of text that does not place substantial burden on decoding skills and that the student can use to pair meaning with the printed word. Stated another way, the student is asked to read more straightforward text, to read it quickly, and to read it with comprehension. By pairing reading decoding with reading comprehension, fluency can improve.

### Educational Strategies for Building Ellen's Reading Comprehension Skills

In addition to instruction in phonics, Ellen should receive instruction in reading comprehension. She can expand her vocabulary, her ability to understand different types of sentences, and her understanding of text elements and text structures. Ellen may need substantial accommodations for her reading decoding difficulties so that she can access the content of reading and develop her comprehension of text. She can expand her understanding of printed text through oral discussion, text-to-voice software, videos, and classroom discussion. She can continue to expand her reading comprehension skills by reading printed text but will need substantial aural-oral support to circumvent her decoding difficulties. For example, an adult can assist with difficult-to-decode text and prompt Ellen to use clues in the text that help access meaning (e.g., use of elements such as pictures, graphs, titles, and subtitles in text). Given her disability, she will need substantial special education accommodations and supports. Her educational program would need to be delivered in a setting that can provide those supports.

Ellen is already at the end of grade five. She shows a substantial impairment in reading. The degree of her impairment may be related to limited access to quality instruction. Ellen's instruction should be intensive, meaning that it should include small group instruction (less than three students), frequent sessions (three to five sessions weekly), and extra time (30–60 minutes per session). Instruction has to address all components of reading as shown above. For students like Ellen, instruction should be delivered by a teacher qualified to teach students with a reading disability (Shaywitz, Morris, & Shaywitz, 2008).



## Working With Culturally and Linguistically Diverse Learners

School professionals should keep the following concepts in mind when working with culturally and linguistically diverse learners on reading skills:

### *Concepts About Phonics*

Many languages are entirely phonetic where a letter or pair of letters represents a predictable sound with very few exceptions. Spanish is a predictable language and is easy for most individuals to sound

*(continued)*

out letters and words. English is not a predictable language, as there are often many different pronunciations for the same letters or letter combinations. Children who can speak and read Spanish easily may therefore struggle with reading in English because of its variable pronunciation rules.

### *Concepts About Print*

In English, reading occurs from left to right and top to bottom. In other languages, such as Japanese and Arabic, reading occurs from right to left. Children who are accustomed to reading Japanese or Arabic may instinctively open a book in a way that to speakers of English and Spanish would seem backward.

## CONCLUSION

This chapter presented the framework dedicated to reading skills. It reviewed reading skills related to phonics including phonological awareness, phonics, and reading fluency. It also reviewed skills related to reading comprehension such as reading vocabulary, understanding the elements and structures of text, and being able to interpret the text. Both skill sets (phonics and reading comprehension) need to be developed in all learners, but especially in those with reading difficulty. Reading always should be taught in the context of language and literacy. Good reading skills serve as a foundation for good writing. The next chapter is dedicated to writing skills.

## REFERENCES


Akhondi, M., Malayeri, F. A., & Samad, A. A. (2011). How to teach expository text structure to facilitate reading comprehension. *The Reading Teacher, 64*(5), 368–372.

Bakken, J. P., & Whedon, C. K. (2002). Teaching text structure to improve reading comprehension. *Intervention in School and Clinic, 37*(4), 229–233.

Berninger, V., Abbott, R. D., Nagy, W., & Carlisle, J. (2010). Growth in phonological, orthographic, and morphological awareness in grades 1 to 6. *Journal of Psycholinguistic Research, 39*(2), 141–163.

Berninger, V. W., & O'Malley, M. O. (2011). Evidence-based diagnosis and treatment for specific learning disabilities involving impairments in written and/or oral language. *Journal of Learning Disabilities, 44*(2), 167–183.

Brooks, G. (2017). What works for pupils with literacy difficulties? The effectiveness of intervention schemes. Retrieved from http://www.interventionsforliteracy.org.uk/wp-content/uploads/2017/11/What-Works-5th-edition-Rev-Oct-2016.pdf

Common Core State Standards. (2018). Retrieved from www.corestandards.org, September 2018

Crystal, D. (1997). *The Cambridge encyclopedia of language* (2nd ed., p. 162). Cambridge, United Kingdom: Cambridge University Press.

De Franchis, V., Usai, M. C., Viterbori, P., & Traverso, L. (2017). Preschool executive functioning and literacy achievement in grades 1 and 3 of primary school: A longitudinal study. *Learning and Individual Differences, 54*, 184–195.

Duff, F., & Clarke, P. J. (2011). Practitioner review: Reading disorders: What are the effective interventions and how should they be implemented and evaluated? *Journal of Child Psychology and Psychiatry, 52*(1), 3–12.

Fletcher, J. M., Foorman, B. R., Boudousquie, B., Barnes, M. A., Schatschneider, C., & Francis, D. J. (2002). Assessment of reading and learning disabilities: A research-based intervention-oriented approach. *Journal of School Psychology, 40*(1), 27–63.

Gathercole, S. E., & Pickering, S. J. (2000). Working memory deficits in children with low achievements in the national curriculum at 7 years of age. *British Journal of Educational Psychology, 70*(2), 177–194.

Gildroy, P., & Deshler, D. D. (2005). Reading development and suggestions for teaching reading to students with learning disabilities. *Insights on Learning Disabilities, 2*(2), 1–10.

Grizzle, K. L., & Simms, M. D. (2005). Early language development and language learning disabilities. *Pediatrics in Review, 25*(8), 274–283.
Hasbrouk, J., & Tindal, G. A. (2006). Oral reading fluency norms: A valuable assessment tool for reading teachers. *The Reading Teacher, 59*(7), 636–644.
Hebert, M., Bohaty, J. J., & Nelson, J. R. (2016). The effects of text structure instruction on expository reading comprehension: A meta-analysis. *Journal of Educational Psychology, 108*(5), 609–629.
Horowitz-Kraus, T., & Finucane, S. (2016). Separating the different domains of reading intervention programs: A review. *SAGE Open, 6*(2), 1–26.
Hulme, C., & Snowling, M. J. (2014). The interface between spoken and written language: Developmental disorders. *Philosophical Transactions of the Royal Society, 369*(1634), 2–8.
Joshi, R. M., Gooden, R., & Bentum, K. E. (2008). Diagnosis and treatment of reading disabilities based on the component model of reading: Alternative to the discrepancy model of LD. *Journal of Learning Disabilities, 41*(1), 67–84.
Kotula, A. W. (2003). Matching readers to instructional materials: The use of classic readability measures for students with language learning disabilities and dyslexia. *Topics in Language Disorders, 23*(3), 190–203.
Meyer, B. J. F. (1985). Prose analysis: Purposes, procedures, and problems. In B. K. Britton & J. Black (Eds.), *Understanding expository text: A theoretical and practical handbook for analyzing explanatory text* (pp. 269–304). Hillsdale, NJ: Erlbaum.
Nation, K., Cocksey, J., & Taylor, J. S. (2010). A longitudinal investigation of early reading and language skills in children with poor reading comprehension. *Journal of Child Psychology and Psychiatry, 51*(9), 1031–1039.
National Reading Panel. (2001). Retrieved from https://www.nichd.nih.gov/sites/default/files/publications/pubs/nrp/Documents/report.pdf
Roehling, J. V., Hebert, M., Nelson, J. R., & Bohaty, J. J. (2017). Text structure strategies for improving expository reading comprehension. *The Reading Teacher, 71*(1), 71–82.
Semrud-Clikeman, M. (2009). Language-related and learning disorders. In M. Semrud-Clikeman & M. Teeter-Ellison (Eds.), *Child neuropsychology: Assessment and interventions for neurodevelopmental disorders* (2nd ed., pp. 275–327). New York, NY: Springer.
Shaywitz, S. E., Morris, R., & Shaywitz, B. A. (2008). The education of dyslexic children from childhood to young adulthood. *Annual Review of Psychology, 59*, 451–475.
Shaywitz, S. E., Shaywitz, B. A., Pugh, K. R., Fulbright, R. K., Constable, R. T., Mencl, W. E., . . . Gore, J. C. (1998). Functional disruption in the organization of the brain for reading in dyslexia. *Proceedings of the National Academy of Sciences of the United States of America, 95*(5), 2636–2641.
Snowling, M., & Hulme, C. (2010). Evidence-based interventions for reading and language difficulties: Creating a virtuous circle. *British Journal of Educational Psychology, 81*(1), 1–23.
Solis, M., Ciullo, S., Vaughn, S., Pyle, N., Hassaram, B., & Leroux, A. (2012). Reading comprehension interventions for middle school students with learning disabilities: A synthesis of 30 years of research. *Journal of Learning Disabilities, 45*(4), 327–340.
Tunmer, W. (2008). Recent developments in reading intervention research: Introduction to the special issue. *Reading and Writing, 21*(4), 299–316.
van der Lely, H. K. J., & Marshall C. R. (2010). Assessing component language deficits in the early detection of reading difficulty risk. *Journal of Learning Disabilities, 43*(4), 357–368.
van der Sluis, S., de Jong, P. F., & van der Leij, A. (2007). Executive functioning in children, and its relations with reasoning, reading, and arithmetic. *Intelligence, 35*(5), 427–449.
Washburn, E., Joshi, R. M., & Binks-Cantrell, E. S. (2011). Teacher knowledge of basic language concepts and dyslexia. *Dyslexia, 17*(2), 165–183.
Washburn, E., Malatesha Joshi, R., & Cantrell, E. B. (2011). Are preservice teachers prepared to teach struggling readers? *Annals of Dyslexia, 61*(1), 21–43.
Wiederholt, J. L., & Bryant, B. B. (2012). Gray Oral Reading Test, fifth edition. *Journal of Psychoeducational Assessment, 31*(5), 516–520.
Williams, J. P. (2005). Instruction in reading comprehension for primary-grade students: A focus on text structure. *Journal of Special Education, 39*(1), 6–18.
Wolf, M., Barzillai, M., Miller, L., Gottwald, S., Spencer, K., & Norton, E. (2009). The RAVE-O intervention: Connecting neuroscience to classroom practice. *Mind, Brain, and Education, 3*(2), 84–93.
Wolf, M., & Stoodley, C. J. (2008). *Proust and the squid: The story and science of the reading brain*. Cambridge, United Kingdom: Icon Books.
Zupran, B., & Dempsey, L. (2013). Facilitating emergent literacy skills in children with hearing loss. *Deafness and Education International, 15*(3), 130–148.

## APPENDIX 9.1 Reading Skills Framework

The Reading Skills Framework is summarized here. School professionals can use this form as a quick reference for the skill sets and skills that need to be taken into consideration when making observations and developing an intervention plan.

| Skill sets | Functions and skills | Examples of functions and skills in action | Sample performance difficulties | Potential strategies, accommodations, or educational objectives |
|---|---|---|---|---|
| Phonological awareness | The capacity to hear, discriminate, and produce (articulate) the sounds of English | The student is able to discriminate between different words and between similar-sounding words.<br>The student is able to speak clearly and does not make articulation errors. | The student is unable to discriminate words from one another during listening comprehension tasks and makes comprehension errors.<br>The student is unable to discriminate similar-sounding words.<br>The student's articulation is poor, affecting intelligibility for the listener.<br>The student's articulation is not yet mature, but the student remains 100% intelligible. | Develop awareness of the sounds of English through listening comprehension tasks<br>Improve articulation skills |
| Phonics | The capacity to match sounds of English with their printed letters and letter combinations | The student is able to sound out (decode) letters printed on the page.<br>The student is able to sound out (decode) simple words in print.<br>The student is able to sound out (decode) multisyllable words or complex letter combinations in print. | The student does not show an understanding for how the letters of the alphabet match the sounds of spoken English.<br>The student is unable to match all of the sounds of English with their spoken letters or letter combinations.<br>The student is unable to sound out printed words unless she or he is already familiar with the word.<br>The student is unable to sound out multisyllable words or words with complex letter combinations. | Instruction may need to include instruction in phonological awareness and articulation.<br>Phonics instruction: Phonics instruction consists of significant drill-and-practice in the recognition of letters and their associated sounds. Phonics instruction teaches how to decode printed words (into their component sounds) and how to encode sounds into their appropriate letters (spelling). |
| Reading fluency | The capacity to read (decode) words fluently and smoothly | The student is able to sound out words smoothly and fluently.<br>The student is able to sound out words in connected text (e.g., sentence- or paragraph-level text).<br>The student is able to recognize instantly a large number of familiar words.<br>Instant word recognition depends in part on reading vocabulary. See next section. | The student is able to decode words but is unable to do so smoothly or fluently.<br>The student is able to decode single words, but has difficulty reading words in connected text. Reading is effortful or halting.<br>The student is able to recognize and decode familiar words smoothly or fluently but is unable to do so for unfamiliar words.<br>The student has only a limited number of words that are recognized instantly, without the need for decoding. | The student may need instruction in phonological awareness and phonics.<br>The student may need fluency instruction.<br>Fluency instruction involves reading large amounts of text, learning to read more fluently, and learning to connect meaning to decoded text. |

| Skill sets | Functions and skills | Examples of functions and skills in action | Sample performance difficulties | Potential strategies, accommodations, or educational objectives |
|---|---|---|---|---|
| Reading comprehension | Reading vocabulary: The capacity to understand words in printed text | The student is able to recognize and understand familiar printed words instantly.<br><br>The student is able to quickly decode words and recognize the meaning of the word.<br><br>The student is able to decode a word and, using her or his vocabulary, make a good guess at the meaning of the word.<br><br>The student uses knowledge of words (e.g., prefixes, suffixes, common roots) to identify the meaning of unfamiliar words.<br><br>The student understands words with higher linguistic complexity (e.g., multisyllable words, words with unusual spelling, technical words). | The student is unable to decode and comprehend familiar printed words instantly.<br><br>The student is unable to comprehend familiar words quickly even after successful decoding.<br><br>The student can decode words successfully but cannot understand the words because of a low vocabulary (small word bank).<br><br>The student is able to decode words with higher linguistic complexity but is not necessarily able to understand the words because of limited understanding of word structures.<br><br>The student has a limited understanding of higher complexity words (e.g., multisyllable words, words with unusual spelling, technical words). | Provide vocabulary instruction:<br><br>The student may need language therapy or language instruction to build knowledge of words (e.g., parts of words, such as word endings, word roots).<br><br>Vocabulary increases through literacy and general academic instruction.<br><br>Vocabulary increases through reading but can also increase through other classroom activities such as disussion and learning through videotapes or lectures. |
| | Sentences: The ability to read and understand sentences and to read at different levels of syntactic complexity | The student is able to decode printed text at the sentence level.<br><br>The student is able to decode and understand different types of sentences in printed text, including an understanding of punctuation and grammar.<br><br>The student is able to decode and understand sentences of varying length and complexity. | The student is unable to understand sentence-level text because of limited language skills or limited understanding of punctuation and grammar.<br><br>The student can decode and understand simple sentences but not complex sentences or sentences with complex syntax. | The student may need instruction in building decoding skills and vocabulary.<br><br>The student may need language therapy or language instruction to build knowledge about morphemes (parts of words, such as word endings) and syntax (word order) in language.<br><br>The student may need to build knowledge about different types of sentences and punctuation in English. |

*(continued)*

| Skill sets | Functions and skills | Examples of functions and skills in action | Sample performance difficulties | Potential strategies, accommodations, or educational objectives |
|---|---|---|---|---|
| | Paragraphs and text: The ability to read and understand paragraphs and text consisting of multiple paragraphs | The student can read connected text (paragraphs and multiple-paragraph text) and comprehends the content (e.g., as evidenced by answering comprehension questions).<br><br>The student recognizes elements in text, such as indentation for a paragraph, opening and closing sentences, and titles and subtitles. The student uses these elements to comprehend the text.<br><br>The student recognizes and understands structure of text, such as compare-contrast structure, chronological structure, free-form structure, and structures related to different genres of writing.<br><br>The student can identify key ideas in text, using knoweldge of elements and structures. | The student is able to decode text (paragraphs and multiple paragraphs) but may not comprehend what he or she reads.<br><br>The student can answer basic comprehension questions but may be unable to answer more complex comprehension questions that require identifying elements and structures in text.<br><br>The student may not know how to identify all of the elements and structures in different genres of text. | The student may need instruction in the skills listed previously.<br><br>The student may need reading strategy instruction. Reading strategy instruction helps to reinforce comprehension by assisting the student in identifying key words, key ideas, key elements, and structures that are important to comprehending the text. |
| | Interpretation of text:<br><br>Understanding key ideas<br><br>Interrelationships within the text<br><br>Interrelationships outside the text<br><br>Reader variables | The student is able to identify key ideas and supporting ideas in text.<br><br>The student is able to understand interrelationships of key ideas, elements, and/or structures within the text.<br><br>The student is able to understand interrelationships between the text and events or works of writing outside the text.<br><br>The reader is able to use the text to inform her or his thinking or change her or his behaviors. | The student is unable to identify key ideas or supporting ideas in text.<br><br>The student is unable to recognize interrelationships within the text and has difficulty answering comprehension questions for this reason.<br><br>The student has difficulty recognizing interrelationships between the text and events or works outside of the text.<br><br>The text does not respond to the reader's needs and does not influence the reader's thinking or change the reader's behaviors. | The student may need instruction in the skills listed previously.<br><br>Reading strategy instruction can help the student be strategic and systematic in identifying key ideas and supporting ideas and in comprehending text by using knowledge of elements and structures.<br><br>Reading strategy instruction can be used to help the student consider interrelationships between key ideas.<br><br>Literacy instruction and improvements in general knowledge help the reader to understand text at a deeper level and make connections inside and outside the text. |

## APPENDIX 9.2 Reading Skills Observation Sheet

| Skill sets | Functions and skills | Example skills or deficits in this student | Potential strategies, accommodations, or educational objectives |
|---|---|---|---|
| Phonological awareness | The capacity to hear, discriminate, and produce (articulate) the sounds of English | | |
| Phonics | The capacity to match sounds of English with their printed letters and letter combinations | | |
| Reading fluency | The capacity to read (decode) words fluently and smoothly | | |
| Reading comprehension | Reading vocabulary: The capacity to understand words in printed text<br><br>The capacity to read and understand sentences and different levels of syntactic complexity<br><br>Paragraphs and text: The ability to read and understand paragraphs and text consisting of multiple paragraphs<br><br>Interpretation of text:<br>Understanding key ideas<br>Interrelationships within the text<br>Interrelationships outside the text<br>Reader variables | | |

# Writing Skills

## INTRODUCTION AND GENERAL DEFINITIONS

Writing is the second educational framework and the focus of this chapter. Narrowly defined, writing consists of using visual symbols to represent spoken words. In English, the symbols are the letters of the English language, and the letters represent speech sounds. In other languages, such as Mandarin, the visual symbols do correspond to spoken words but do not represent speech sounds. Writing can also refer to broader concepts including sharing ideas and/or having a particular writing style. The digital age has changed the meaning of writing because so much digital media now includes videos and images that are embedded in and inseparable from text. These factors influence the definition of writing and how writing is taught (Rijlaarsdam et al., 2012). Despite these complexities and advances, writing in English still begins with a secure understanding of sound-to-symbol correspondences. Like reading, writing is an acquired skill that must be taught.

The prior chapter discussed how the topic of reading can be divided into two skill sets: phonics and reading comprehension. Writing can also be divided into two main components: transcription skills and text-generation skills (Hayes & Berninger, 2009). Transcription skills involve converting linguistic information (sounds, words) into written symbols, via handwriting (or keyboarding) and spelling. Text generation refers to producing and capturing ideas in sentences, paragraphs, and full-length text (Hayes & Berninger, 2009). The Writing Skills Framework that follows explains these two skill sets in more detail.

Writing cannot be separated easily from the other frameworks in this book. The reading and writing frameworks have many points of overlap. Phonics in particular and language in general are essential components of both reading and writing, which is why difficulties in these areas so commonly co-occur (Costa, Edwards, & Hooper, 2016). Like reading, writing is related to and dependent on language; ideas cannot be expressed in writing before they are expressed in language. Instruction in language enhances writing and reading skills. As such, there is an important role for both the speech-language pathologist and the literacy teacher in writing instruction (Fallon & Katz, 2011). Instruction in language enhances writing and reading skills.

One way to understand the interrelationship between writing and language is to think of the language system as having the following four parts:

1. Language by hand (writing)
2. Language by ear (receptive language skills, listening comprehension)

3. Language by mouth (expressive language skills, speech production)
4. Language by eye (reading)

All four language systems have similarities in their development and follow the same hierarchy discussed in Chapter 4: Sounds, words, phrases, sentences, and paragraphs. Development in any one of these four systems affects the development in the other three systems. However, the development of each system is also somewhat separate. Each requires different types of developmental stimulation and/or instruction and intervention (Berninger, 2000; Berninger & Richards, 2002a). Even when all four language systems are developing normally, writing skills may not develop successfully. Organizing ideas in both spoken and written language requires the use of executive skills, and motor skills are needed for successful handwriting. Motivation and ecological factors also need to be considered (Graham, Harris, & Larsen, 2001; Joshi, Gooden, & Bentum, 2008). Difficulties in any of these areas can affect the successful development of writing.

## HOW THIS FRAMEWORK WAS CONSTRUCTED

Unlike the case for reading, there is not a National Writing Panel Report that details the components of writing or describes different types of writing instruction. The Writing Skills Framework was therefore developed using content and recommendations from the National Reading Panel (2001), the Writing Framework of the National Assessment of Educational Progress (U.S. Department of Education, 2017), and Common Core State Standards (CCSS, 2010). Additional references are listed throughout this chapter. Consistent with the other chapters in this book, the Writing Skills Framework is based on a developmental hierarchy that starts with lower order or first-order skills and proceeds to higher order and more complex skills.

The framework divides writing into three main components: Mechanics (which corresponds to transcription skills), elements and structures (which corresponds to text-generation skills), and quality (which refers to subjective aspects of writing). The mechanics of writing refers to the skills needed to write individual words and some sentence-level skills. The mechanics of writing include handwriting skills, spelling skills, and correct use of English language conventions, such as punctuation and grammar. These skills are mostly rule based and rule bound. Elements and structures are those aspects of writing that define the type of text being produced. They include features such as tables and graphs, address lines and date in a letter, and characters and plot in a story. Structures describes the different ways that ideas are presented. For example, a paragraph has an opening sentence, supporting ideas, and a closing statement. A larger text can present its ideas in descriptive manner, in chronological order, or in a categorical approach. Elements and structures often follow certain conventions but are not necessarily rule bound. The quality of writing refers to those aspects of written expression that are most subjective and provide opportunities for creativity. Quality features of writing will vary according to the intentions of the writer and the receptivity of the audience. See Box 10.1 for an alternative framework, proposed by the Common Core State Standards.



### BOX 10.1. The Writing Skills Framework and the Common Core State Standards

The Common Core State Standards (CCSS, 2010), used in creating the Writing Skills Framework, provides its own framework for writing based on college-entry text-writing goals. In the CCSS, writing is divided into the following three types:

1. Argument
2. Information/explanatory text
3. Narrative

Within each of these text-writing goals, the CCSS provides a way to analyze writing quality using three different methods: Quantitative, qualitative, and other variables related to the reader and to the purpose of the text. Within each of these, the CCSS analyzes the complexity of the ideas in the text, the complexity of the sentences of the text, the choice of words in the text, and the mechanics of the writing (roughly in that order). The Writing Skills Framework in this book takes the reverse approach. It describes the mechanics of writing first. It then proceeds to elements and structures in text, often dictated or influenced by the type of text. Finally, it takes into consideration quality measures such as the choice of words, the complexity of the sentences, and the ideas of the text and their relevance to the reader.

## HOW CAN THIS FRAMEWORK HELP ME?

During the course of their school years, students are expected to become increasingly skilled, efficient and confident writers. It is therefore important that all adults involved in the education of students understand how writing skills are acquired. Nationally, most students perform well below the proficient level in writing (U.S. Department of Education, 2011), an indication that good writing instruction, although essential to learning, is clearly lacking. Adults can assist students who struggle to write only if they understand the components of writing and are able to discuss the components of writing with students. They also need to be able to target all the components that comprise writing instruction. Educators and therapists can use the terms presented in this chapter to discuss a student's writing skills with team members, students, and family members and to help assess and monitor the student's progress.

## WRITING SKILLS FRAMEWORK: TERMS AND DEFINITIONS

The framework presented in this section provides more specific definitions and examples of the terms introduced above. By understanding a student's writing skills at the level of detail presented in the framework, practitioners will be able to more effectively discuss writing skills with the student and with colleagues. Writing is divided into three skill sets: Mechanics, elements and structures, and quality. These terms are defined in the sections that follow.



The Writing Skills Framework includes the following terms:

1. Mechanics of writing
    a. Handwriting
    b. Spelling
    c. Writing fluency (transcription fluency): Words
    d. Writing fluency (transcription fluency): Sentences
2. Elements and structures in writing
    a. Sentences: Syntactic complexity
    b. Paragraphs
        i. Elements: Subtitles and indentation
        ii. Structures: Organizational structure of paragraphs (e.g., topic sentence, supporting ideas, concluding sentence)

(continued)

c. Text
    i. Elements: Titles, subtitles, table of contents, index, and other elements
    ii. Structures: Text genre, form, and organizational schemata
3. Quality of writing
    a. Linguistic and syntactic complexity
    b. Content:
        i. Density of ideas
        ii. Interrelationships between ideas (within the text and with other sources)
        iii. Relevance of the ideas to the audience
        iv. Impact of the ideas on the audience

Each of these terms and concepts is defined and explained in the sections that follow. The Writing Skills Framework is also summarized and available in Appendix 10.1 for quick reference.

## Mechanics of Writing

The mechanics of writing typically refers to handwriting and spelling. In this framework, we have chosen to also include punctuation and grammar as part of the mechanics of writing.

***Handwriting*** Handwriting is a motor skill and refers to the act of printing or writing letters, using a pencil or pen. For students who cannot use a pencil or pen successfully, keyboarding may be an alternative. Good handwriting skills are important because they affect the very purpose for which writing is taking place: To convey knowledge in an intentional way. Deficits or delays in fine motor function affect handwriting and as a result can have an impact on the writing text (Berninger & Rutberg, 1992a; Graham, Harris, & Fink, 2000; Santangelo & Graham, 2016). This statement is true even with the use of keyboarding to generate text (Cahill, 2009). Good handwriting does not imply good spelling, which is a separate skill.



***Spelling (Encoding)*** Spelling requires the translation (encoding) of speech sounds into written symbols (letters). Correct spelling is determined by the sound–symbol correspondences of the English language and requires the same phonics skills discussed in Chapter 9. Encoding in writing is the opposite of decoding in reading, but requires the same skill (phonics). From an early age, both handwriting and spelling skills have an impact on the quality of writing at the text level (Puranik & Alotaiba, 2012). Box 10.2 provides information about the developmental trajectory of spelling skills, which is important to understand when teaching spelling.

**BOX 10.2. The Development of Spelling Skills With Age**

A young learner might understand that the sound /ee/ is spelled with the letter *e* but not that there are other ways to print the same sound (e.g., /ea/ or /ie/). Over time, the student should show a more fully developed phonemic skill set, mastering all the different ways that the sound /ee/ can be spelled.

There is a relatively predictable trajectory for how students learn to map the sounds of English into the letters of English. The Common Core State Standards (2010) provides information about the order in which students encode sounds to graphemes (letters). Partially phonetic spelling is a stage in learning spelling that reflects the student's ability to encode sounds to graphemes or letters but does not include the many spelling exceptions found in English. Fully formed spelling refers to the ability to spell correctly, including those words that are not spelled in predictable ways.

***Mechanics: Writing Fluency or Transcription Fluency*** Handwriting and spelling are two separate skills that, when combined, result in a transcription. The goal is for transcription to be automatized, requiring the student to print or draw letters automatically, without having to think about their shape. The student also needs to learn to spell words automatically, without having to go through the steps of encoding sounds (phonemes) to graphemes. This is referred to as transcription fluency or writing fluency. When writing (transcription) is not fluent, it is more difficult for students to produce quality compositions (Graham, Berninger, Abbott, Abbott, & Whitaker, 1997; Hayes & Berninger, 2009).

***Mechanics: Writing Fluency and Sentence-level Writing*** The skill of writing sentences requires an understanding of both the elements and structures involved. Elements and structures are defined in the next section. The mechanics of writing sentences successfully includes an understanding of punctuation (English language conventions) and grammar (morphosyntax). English language conventions include rules such as capitalization, ending marks, and indentation of paragraphs, among others. Grammatical rules include rules about parts of sentences (e.g., subject, object, verb, and agreement). These mechanics are rule bound. Correct and fluent use of mechanics is a prerequisite for successful writing.

## Elements and Structures in Writing

The following sections provide examples of elements and structures in writing. Elements and structures are primarily relevant to writing at the text level (text-generation skills). The term *elements* refers to rule-based aspects of text. Elements include features such as a title page, an index, or chapter titles. They are essential for different types of text and are similar or the same regardless of text type. Pagination and correct numerical identification of charts or graphs are also the same or similar across most texts. The term *structure* refers to how ideas are organized in text. The organizational structure of a written composition will vary depending on whether, for example, the text is an essay, a poem, or a newspaper article. Much of the time, the structure of writing should be sequential, with a clear beginning, middle, and end. Even though structures follow certain conventions, they are less rule-bound and more flexible than elements. They can vary depending on the purpose and style of the writing.



***Elements and Structures of Sentences*** The elements of sentences are words, punctuation, and grammatical markings and are subsumed under the definition of mechanics. The structure of sentence-level writing refers to those aspects of writing that change according to the purpose of the writing. Sentence structure varies with different types of text and becomes more complex as students advance into higher grades. Sentences can be simple, consisting of a single clause, or complex and contain subordinate clauses or be compound sentences. Sentence-level writing skill also entails being able to write different types of sentences (e.g., statements, questions, dialogue), each of which has a different structure and requires different punctuation. Some judgment is needed to determine which of these structures is the most appropriate for any given text.

***Elements and Structures of Paragraphs*** As with sentences, writers must understand the elements and structures involved in writing successful paragraphs. One important structural element is the convention of indenting to signal the start of a new paragraph. A key structure of paragraphs is that they consist of one or more sentences. They have an opening sentence, supporting information, and a concluding sentence. Although this organizational structure is common for paragraphs and is very important to master, it is not universal.

***Elements and Structures of Full-Length Text*** As with each of the components of writing just discussed, texts have certain kinds of elements and structures, depending on the purpose, genre, or form of the writing. Different genres of text require different elements. For example, informational text requires elements such as titles, subtitles, headings, and subheadings, and/or an index. Some types of text require accompanying illustrations, maps, and/or charts. A recipe has a list of ingredients and a chronological description of the cooking method. A business letter has a date, salutation, and signature line. A play has dialogue and stage directions. Even a narrative has predictable elements, such as a character and a plot. The content served by these elements can vary widely, but the form of these elements is primarily the same across informational text, recipes, letters, plays, and narratives. Elements are used in relatively conventional ways and can be rule bound.

Just as texts have to have certain elements, they also have to have a structure. Text structure varies according to the type of writing required for the situation. For example, an essay can be written using more than one structure, but typically relies on the following types: 1) chronological, 2) compare and contrast, 3) categorical, 4) descriptive, and 5) free form. These organizational structures are common in many different kinds of text. Other types of organizational structures apply to other type of text, such as the structure used for a newspaper article, a recipe, or a play. Elements and structures are dictated by the genre or the form. These elements and structures need to be respected for the writing to succeed. The correct use of elements and structures are critical aspects of text quality. They are prerequisites for meeting the needs and expectations of the audience and the intended purpose of the text.

## Quality of Writing



Even though the term *quality* may seem subjective, many qualitative aspects of writing can be assessed objectively. For example, the mechanics of writing (handwriting, spelling, punctuation, and grammar) leave little room for interpretation. Because they are bound by rules, they can be assessed as being done correctly or incorrectly. Quality writing consists of legible handwriting, accurate spelling, correct use of punctuation, and correct use of grammar. Difficult-to-read handwriting with incorrect spelling and improper use of punctuation and grammar can interfere with the effectiveness of the text for the reader and constitute lower quality writing. In addition to using mechanics correctly, students have to use the right vocabulary to convey their ideas. Errors in word choice, such as mistakenly using the word *intricate* instead of *intrinsic,* or more subtle choices such as *mix* instead of *combine* affect the quality of writing. Rules and vocabulary knowledge help determine the correct word selection and use for the intended meaning.

Elements and structures of text are also somewhat rule bound. It is not difficult to identify the correct or successful use of elements and structures, once the purpose of the text is established. The writing teacher and the student can both assess the mechanics, elements, and structures of writing relatively easily. Yet, the quality of writing depends on more than just the successful application of these features and often includes concepts that are more difficult to assess objectively. The following sections provide parameters for measuring the quality of writing and help to increase objectivity during the writing process.

***Linguistic Complexity*** To produce quality writing, the right word may need to be selected from among a set of words that all have a similar meaning. This concept is referred to as linguistic complexity, which includes factors such as the length of the word (one syllable versus multiple syllables), the specificity of the word (a word with a general meaning versus a technical term that has a very precise meaning), and the concreteness or abstractness of the word (e.g., *elevated* can mean to lift up but can also refer to an idea or a behavior that is more refined or more global). Some of the terms discussed in Chapter 9, such as alliteration, hyperbole, and exaggeration, are linguistically complex because they refer to concepts and are defined through multiple examples. In typically developing students, linguistic complexity advances with age (Beers & Nagy, 2011), meaning that children learn to use progressively longer, more precise, and more abstract words as their writing improves. Linguistic complexity can be measured by a teacher or by a computer (CCSS, 2010). Lower linguistic complexity sometimes signals lower quality writing and is commonly seen in children with language impairment. See sample studies by Fey, Catts, Proctor-Williams, Tomblin, and Zhang, 2004; McNamara, Crossley, and McCarthy, 2010; Ravit, 2006; Scott & Windsor, 2000a; and Sun and Nippold, 2012.

Even though a higher level of linguistic complexity can be evidence of quality writing in children and youth, the relationship between the two is nuanced. Higher linguistic complexity does not always signal quality writing, which is dependent on the purpose and the intended audience of the writing. Concrete, literal, and single-definition words are more appropriate for some kinds of audiences and purposes, whereas less common, abstract, and conceptual words are more appropriate for others. For example, writing intended for young readers, or for conveying a message quickly and clearly to a very broad audience, should normally be linguistically simple and include words with only one meaning. In contrast, writing that includes precise words are more appropriate to use for knowledgeable audiences or for the reader who needs to increase their level of understanding of a specialized field of study or a specific area of interest. Writing intended to introduce important topics related to social policy or legislation will need to include specialized terms and conceptual and abstract language. This is in contrast to writing intended to provide entertainment or display humor, which often includes word choice and language that is ambiguous and reflects multiple meanings.

***Syntactic Complexity*** Sentences have different levels of construction, ranging from simple to compound to complex. As children age, they can write in more complex sentences, and levels of complexity can be measured objectively. For example, a teacher or a computer program can capture the number of single-clause sentences, sentences with subordinate clauses, or the number of compound sentences. A computer can also measure the number of words per sentence or the number of clauses per sentence, both of which can be used to measure the syntactic complexity of the text (DuBay 2004, 2007). While useful, these measures, intended to serve as an index of readability, have important limitations and are not useful in the analysis of all types of text (Bailin & Grafstein, 2001). As is also the case for linguistic complexity, the preferred level of syntactic complexity depends on the purpose of the writing (Beers & Nagy, 2009). For some types of writing, a simpler sentence structure might be the correct one to use.



***Quality of Content of the Text*** The quality of content is the most subjective aspect of writing and depends on the needs of the audience and the purpose of the text. The following ideas can be used or adapted to make judgments about the quality of writing.

*Density of Ideas in the Text* One aspect of quality is related to the density of ideas in the text. The number of ideas presented in the text can be measured quantitatively and qualitatively. For example, an indirect measure of the density of ideas is to measure the number of sentences or the number of clauses in the text. Another way to measure the density of ideas is to assess the number of ideas presented in each paragraph. Like linguistic and syntactic complexity, the best density measurement will depend upon the needs of the audience. For some writing, only a few ideas should be presented in the text. For technical texts and for the more advanced reader, a higher number of ideas may be needed.

*Interrelationship of Ideas Within and Between Texts* One way to measure quality of a text is to measure the extent to which the text creates interrelationships between ideas within the text, as well as relationships with ideas outside the text. A text that makes connections within the text can be easier or more enjoyable to read, like when the writer both introduces a character and elaborates upon their place of birth and the geography of the location. In expository text, a writer might make connections between the text and recent or historical events. Connections such as these make the writing clearer and more interesting, relevant, and understandable to a larger number of readers, all of which contributes to its higher quality.

*Relevance of the Ideas to the Target Audience* Quality writing depends on the relevance of the ideas to the target audience. Readers will respond differently to a text depending on their background knowledge and experiences. These factors also influence the reader's own interpretation of the quality of the text (Bailin & Grafstein, 2001; CCSS, 2010). For informational text, the reader who needs the information to solve a problem or answer a question will find the text useful and may rate it as being of high quality. For narrative text, a reader who has had similar experiences as those described in the novel may find the novel more pleasurable. The quality of the text therefore requires a successful match between text and reader. This concept is as true for linguistic and syntactic complexity as it is for the number and relevance of the ideas presented in the text.

*Impact on the Target Audience* The quality measures discussed above may ultimately be unimportant if the writing does not have an impact on the reader. The impact might be as simple as invoking emotion in the reader or more complex, such as changing the reader's world view or even altering how the reader behaves as a result of reading the text. Quality is thus not necessarily located inside the text. It can also be judged by the interaction of the reader with the text and measured by how the reader is affected by the interaction.



## PERFORMANCE DIFFICULTIES IN WRITING

Performance difficulties in writing are often easily identified in the student's report card in the section that focuses on literacy and language arts. Indicators of performance difficulties will show up in items such as written work or writing fluency. Writing samples, which should be analyzed based on mechanics, elements, structures, and quality as discussed above, can help identify specific performance difficulties. The sections that follow take a closer look at how performance difficulties related to writing skills can present.

### Performance Difficulties in Handwriting

Students may struggle with handwriting because of an underlying motor or organizational difficulty, among other factors. Students with a motor impairment, such as low muscle tone or spasticity may experience handwriting difficulties. Students may also have handwriting difficulty when they are not able to organize information in two-dimensional space, due to poor eye–hand coordination or difficulties with spatial awareness. Performance difficulties in handwriting may be evident by irregular letter formation, inconsistent letter size, or inconsistent spacing.

Some handwriting difficulties are appropriate at younger ages. For example, a preschool-age child might show writing skills that consist of scribbles, wavy lines, or letter-like symbols. This level of performance is acceptable for a preschooler but is no longer acceptable in kindergarten or first grade. When children enter the primary school years, their writing may be irregular and unsteady, but it should become smooth and consistent during the early elementary school grades.

## Performance Difficulties in Spelling

Young students need to master phonics to be able to spell correctly. Spelling errors are expected in young students who have not yet mastered phonics. Students with dyslexia, a phonics-based reading disability, are expected to make spelling errors for the same reason, even when they are older. Notably, not all spelling is mastered through phonics. Some spelling skills are mastered only through formal instruction and memorization, as is the case for irregular words. Students who have not had consistent access to writing and spelling instruction will show more spelling errors and limited ability to evaluate their spelling work and make edits and corrections, even with feedback from adults.

## Performance Difficulties in Writing Fluency or Transcription Fluency

Even as some students master handwriting and spelling, they may struggle to combine handwriting with spelling to transcribe their ideas quickly and efficiently. Underdeveloped writing fluency interferes with all of the higher level aspects of writing presented in the Writing Skills Framework. It is more difficult to produce quality compositions when writing fluency is low (Graham et al., 1997; Hayes & Berninger, 2009). Challenges with writing fluency can be due to handwriting difficulties, difficulties with phonics (encoding and spelling), and/or difficulties with the automatic retrieval and application of these skills. Low writing fluency can be easily identified by counting the number of words or sentences that a student can transcribe within a given time interval. Students who can only produce compositions more successfully when using dictation software may have underlying difficulties in writing fluency. For these students, other aspects related to the mechanics of writing should also be considered.

## Performance Difficulties in Generating Words and Sentences

A student may produce low quality text because of a limited vocabulary or underdeveloped skills in generating longer and more complex sentences. The successful student can write using words and sentences of varying complexity (varied linguistic and syntactic complexity). Students with language impairment or those with global learning delays may experience difficulty in sentence-level writing, whether or not they have difficulty in the mechanics of writing, such as correct punctuation and correct use of grammar.

## Performance Problems in Writing Paragraphs and Full-Length Text

Students with limited handwriting, spelling, writing fluency, and/or language skills are expected to have greater difficulty writing at the text level. Text-level writing difficulties may be characterized by incorrect use of elements and structures such as missing titles and subtitles or other features that identify the genre or purpose. More significantly, paragraphs may lack the structure of an opening sentence, supporting details, and closing sentences. Students with underdeveloped executive skills often have difficulty writing at the text level, even if they do not have any difficulty with handwriting, spelling, or writing at the sentence level. These students may struggle to generate text because of their difficulty gathering and organizing ideas from their reading and then organizing those ideas in their writing. Performance difficulties in written text may show up because ideas are not presented in a logical sequence, are not linked sequentially, do not follow a commonly accepted structure (e.g., compare and contrast, personal narrative), and/or do not fulfill the purpose of the writing. Performance difficulties in writing are expected in many school-age children, as it takes many years of close mentorship and instruction to master writing skills. That said, comparison with grade- and age-level expectations can help define whether performance problems in writing require remediation or intervention. The Common Core State Standards provides examples of writing at different ages and for different grades, with accompanying analysis.

## HOW TO SET UP AN OBSERVATION FOR WRITING

The Writing Skills Framework is useful for planning an observation of a student's writing skills. The observer should have reviewed an outline of the framework, as provided in Appendix 10.1, and be prepared to make observations and analyze those observations going from lower order skills to higher order skills. Observers can also use Appendix 10.2, the Writing Skills Observation Sheet, to inform their observation. The writing sample could be a writing assignment completed by the student as part of a general education curriculum or a sample generated specifically for the observation. The writing sample should be analyzed for mechanics, elements and structures, and quality. When assessing for quality, observers should consider if the writing sample follows necessary rules of mechanics and adheres to important conventions for elements and structures that fulfill the intended purpose of the writing. For writing samples from students who are more advanced, observers should look for quality markers such as the linguistic and syntactic complexity, the density of ideas, and factors related to the intended audience. The observer can select those aspects of the Writing Skills Framework that are the most relevant to the writing demands for the situation and focus only on those. The observer can use the appendices as a prompting tool to help organize the observation. Box 10.3 offers a scheme for organizing the observation.

### BOX 10.3. A Structure for Making Observations of Writing Skills

1. Mechanics
    a. Neatness of letter formation
    b. Correct spelling
    c. Correct use of punctuation and grammar
    d. Writing fluency
        i. Ability to transcribe smoothly and efficiently during copying tasks
        ii. Ability to transcribe smoothly and fluently during composing text
2. Elements and structures
    a. Elements: Successful use of elements in the text, including conventional elements of informational text such as titles, subtitles, indices, and tables; in narrative, successful use of character, location, events, and plot
    b. Structure: Successful use of structure. Paragraphs have a topic sentence and supporting sentences; informational text has a larger structure such as compare and contrast, sequential or chronological, categorical, or descriptive
3. Quality: The ability of the text to meet the needs of the audience. Linguistic and syntactic complexity are key factors; other factors may be identifiable only after getting feedback from the readers

Isaacson (n.d.) provides a summary article that presents many of the same principles discussed in this chapter and offers an alternate structure for the analysis of writing, starting with writing fluency (how many words were written within a specified period of time) and then moving to other aspects of writing, such as content, conventions (correct handwriting, spelling), syntax, vocabulary, and purpose. His scheme also includes looking at the organizational structure of the text and the organizational structure of individual paragraphs.

While standardized assessments can help identify features of a student's writing difficulty, they do not necessarily provide the same level of detail provided by a good observation and subsequent analysis. Naturalistic observations are recommended to compare the student's performance on standardized measures with performance in the classroom, which is typically more challenging because of the other demands that compete for the student's attention. Text-generation skills in particular are not assessed in a consistent manner through standardized measures, especially when writing demands go beyond the paragraph level. Naturalistic observations of a student's composition skills are thus critical to include in the observations.

The CCSS (2010) provides a comprehensive list of writing (composition) samples, organized by age and grade. The reader is invited to use these samples to understand writing skills by grade and to practice analyzing writing by using the Writing Skills Framework.

## Select the Student

A teacher who has experience working with a particular student can likely make a well-informed guess about their writing abilities based on classroom observations and identify them as needing closer attention. Certainly, any student whose report card suggests below grade level performance in writing skills warrants a more careful review. There are many different types of students who are at risk for writing difficulty, including those with a language impairment, reading difficulty, motor and coordination problems, global learning delays, and/or underdeveloped executive skills. At times, a teacher may suspect that the student is likely to have writing difficulties based on these difficulties.

## Obtain a Writing Sample

It may not be necessary to set up a special writing observation. Any written work already produced by the student can be a good starting point, with the exception of writing fluency that needs to be observed in real time. Some students may be reluctant to produce written text upon asking. They may even be reluctant to write down the first word. For these students, who may protest that they don't know how to write or that they cannot write, it is a question of finding the right starting point. For instance, students who won't attempt a full page of written text might be able to produce a paragraph. Others who balk at writing a paragraph might be amenable to generating a single sentence. Still others, with encouragement, may be able to produce single words or even single letters or shapes. And those students who cannot use a pencil or pen may be able to show some writing skills on a keyboard. It is important to be creative and flexible in choosing the right starting point for the observation

To start the writing observation process, the observer may first engage the student in conversation, perhaps about preferred hobbies, pets, or favorite activities outside of school. Then, the observer can ask the student to write about what was just shared. If the student protests and says, "I don't know how to write!" or "I don't like writing!" the observer could offer to start writing as the student dictates or could write down a few key words from their conversation and ask the student to use them in their sentences. A picture or picture series is another way to support writing, especially at the paragraph level. Pictures placed into a sequential storyline reduce the burden on the student's language skills and executive skills and allow the student to focus more exclusively on writing.

***Observations for the Mechanics of Writing: Handwriting, Spelling, and English Language Conventions*** The mechanics of writing include making observations of handwriting, spelling, punctuation, and grammar.

*Handwriting Skills* When observing a student's handwriting, the observer should take notes on the following aspects of handwriting: Letterform readability, slant, spacing, and line straightness. The observations can also take into consideration the biomechanical aspects of handwriting, such as how the pencil is held in the hand and how much downward pressure is used to print or write letters on the page (Rosenblum, Weiss, & Parush, 2003).

*Spelling Skills* Difficulties with spelling often accompany underdeveloped handwriting skills. The effort involved in handwriting can sometimes use up mental resources that would otherwise be dedicated to spelling. Limited spelling skills can also be the result of difficulties with phonics. The observer should consider the student's reading skills, especially phonics, and establish the extent to which the student has mastered decoding, encoding, and accurate spelling.

*Punctuation and Grammar* The writing sample should be reviewed for correct use of English language conventions, such as punctuation, grammar, and fully formed sentences.

***Observations for Elements and Structures in Writing*** This section is focused on making observations and analyzing elements and structures of writing in sentences, paragraphs, and text.

*Elements and Structures of Sentences* The elements of sentences are discussed in the section dedicated to the mechanics of writing. To make observations of structures, the observer can focus on the complexity and variety of sentences produced by the student. Sentences can be simple or compound, can contain subordinate clauses, and can be complex.

*Elements and Structures in Paragraphs* Depending on the type of writing sample, the observer should take notice of the elements that are appropriate or necessary to the text. For example, paragraphs require an indentation and may require a subtitle. Paragraphs should be structured with a topic or opening sentence, supporting details, and concluding sentence or transitional sentence.



*Elements and Structures in Full-Length Text* For full-length narrative text, the observer can review the text to identify literary elements such as characters, events, setting, plot, and goal path. Not all of these elements may be obvious from reviewing a single paragraph. For informational text, elements include indentation of the paragraph, titles and subtitles, graphs and charts, boxes, glossary, and indexes. The observer should also note the structure of the text. Elements and structures vary depending upon the type of writing, such as an essay, a newspaper article, a recipe, or a play. Many full-length texts make use of the structures discussed in this framework, including compare and contrast, categorical, chronological or temporal, and free form. The text should include linking devices that help the reader understand and make connections between different ideas presented in the text.

***Making Observations of the Quality of Writing*** All quality writing requires good mechanics, the right elements and structures for the purpose or genre of the text, and the successful execution of those elements and structures. These aspects of writing leave some room for interpretation but are usually bound by rules and conventions and are not that subjective. In addition, quality of writing needs to take into consideration the needs of the audience, as highlighted by the factors listed below.

*Linguistic Complexity* The observer should take into consideration the level of the student's vocabulary in writing. The choice of words can be simple or complex. For example, the observation should take into consideration if the text includes only general nouns and verbs or more precise and technical nouns and verbs. The observer should take into consideration whether the student uses adjectives, adverbs, and other parts of speech.

*Syntactic Complexity* The student may produce simple sentences, compound sentences, and/or sentences with subordinate clauses. They may also produce declaratives, interrogatives, or exclamations. It is important to note whether the complexity and variety of sentence structure is high or low and the extent to which these factors help the student convey his or her intended messages and meaning in writing.

*Density of Ideas in Text and Interrelationships Between Ideas* One parameter of quality writing is to identify the number of ideas in the text. This can be done using syntactic measures. Each sentence or each clause can be documented as representing one idea and can serve as an objective measure of text density. Another way to measure the density of ideas in text is to count the number of subjects or topics discussed. Those ideas may have links with one another and may be linked by the writer to ideas, events, and works of writing not contained in the text.

*Relevance and Impact on the Audience* The most subjective aspect of writing is the effect that it has on the reader. The reader's responsiveness to the text is not something that the writer can control, but successful writers know their audience and can produce text at the right level of linguistic and syntactic complexity, with the right elements and structures, and the right content to impact the readers. However, only the responses of the audience can help determine whether the writing achieved the intended impact. The relevance and impact of the text on the audience is therefore not measurable by looking at the text alone.

## Analyze and Interpret the Observations

Using the Writing Skills Framework, the observer can make a judgment about the student's areas of writing strengths and difficulty. The previous sections showed how a teacher or other practitioner can make observations of writing and identify key components of writing. Upon completing the observations, the practitioner has to analyze and make an interpretation of the success of the student's performance. For many students who struggle to learn, the writing sample will likely range in length from one or two sentences to a few paragraphs at most. Observations will likely focus on the mechanics of writing (handwriting, spelling, punctuation, and appropriate grammar) and the ability of the student to write different types of sentences and a well-structured paragraph. The writing should include appropriate and clear vocabulary. The analysis and the interpretation of these students' writing samples should be relatively straightforward.

For students writing at a higher level, the observer can take the analysis further. The observer may need to review the students' ability to use commonly occurring elements and commonly needed structures in writing. Analysis of elements and structures requires a longer text, at least several paragraphs. The most common elements of narrative text include problem, characters, events, setting, and solution. The most common elements of informational text include the elements that define a business letter, a newspaper article, a book report, among others. The elements that are the most important to observe and analyze will be defined by the curriculum.

Analysis of written work samples produced by more advanced writers, and typically not students who struggle with learning, may include quality parameters. For example, the text produced is likely to be longer than just a few paragraphs. As is true for the analysis of more basic work products, the observer will have to take into consideration whether the mechanics, elements, and structures are used accurately and successfully, as well as how well matched the subject matter is to the intended audience. The analysis should determine whether the writer chose the right level of linguistic complexity, syntactic complexity, elements, and structures to fulfill the purpose of the writing and whether they met the needs of the audience.

## Discuss Findings With Colleagues

After obtaining and analyzing a writing sample, the observer can discuss the student's performance with colleagues. By sharing writing samples and by using a systematic format of analysis, the group can more successfully identify writing difficulties that the student may need to address. This conversation will help guide the decision for a more detailed evaluation and will also influence decisions about instruction and intervention strategies.

The earlier sections of this chapter lead naturally to selecting the most appropriate writing objectives and strategies for the student. Using the framework, the team can decide which components of writing are most challenging for the student and should be targeted for extra (or intensive) instruction. The following sections explain in greater detail the process of choosing the best objectives, strategies, and accommodations for the student.

## General Information About Writing Instruction

Instruction in writing should be an integral part of a larger literacy instruction program. Writing instruction should be used to support reading (Duff & Clarke, 2011) and must take into consideration all four aspects of language development: Language by ear, by mouth, by eye, and by hand. This means writing instruction requires instruction in reading and language as well as in handwriting, spelling, and composition skills (Berninger et al., 2006a; Berninger, Abbott, Nagy, & Carlisle, 2010).

An intervention plan for the struggling writer requires an observation and analysis of that student's skills, using the Writing Skills Framework. The analysis should identify which writing skills the student has mastered and which next steps the student might be ready to master. Those next steps should inform the instructional plan. Depending on the student's strengths and difficulties, instruction may need to focus on fine motor skills and handwriting, spelling, sentence-level writing, paragraph-level writing, or writing full text. Once these skills have been mastered, writing instruction can then focus on quality parameters, such as linguistic complexity, syntactic complexity, and text structures for different genres. Finally, writing instruction can move toward factors such as the purpose and audience. The intervention plan follows logically from the analysis and should address all areas of difficulty (Berninger & O'Malley, 2011).

For the struggling writer, teaching should include the full spectrum of writing skills. Instruction should include aspects such as grapho-motor training to improve legibility of handwriting, orthographic training to improve spelling, explicit instruction in writing compositions, and transfer of writing skills to reading skills (Berninger et al., 2002b, 2006b). Explicit instruction for writing compositions should include the use of strategy instruction, which involves teaching students strategies for planning, revising, and editing their compositions. Within strategy instruction, students need to be taught strategies for summarizing reading material and how to organize ideas prior to writing a first draft. Teaching should provide good models for different types of writing, so that the students have exposure to a full range of different structures in writing. Finally, students should participate in peer-mediated learning, working with other students to plan, draft, revise, and edit their compositions (Graham, Harris, & Larsen, 2001; Graham & Perin, 2007a).

The reader is referred to a number of excellent works on the topic of writing instruction, which provide a description of the components of writing and how to promote the development of writing. These works include textbooks such as *Instruction and Assessment for Struggling Writers* (Troia, 2009) and *Brain Literacy for Educators and Psychologists* (Berninger & Richards, 2002a); evidence-based resources available online, such as Interventions for Literacy (Brooks, 2016) and "Writing Next" (Graham & Perin, 2007b); and web sites, such as ReadingRockets.org. See Datchuk and Kubina (2012) for a review of sentence-level writing instruction and its components. See also a summary of approaches for teaching writing at both the text and word levels (Graham et al., 2001). The more specific suggestions in the sections below should be considered as a framework for writing instruction and may not cover all the effective strategies that can possibly be used in writing instruction.

## Educational Objectives and Strategies for Writing

This section introduces objectives and strategies that a team might select for a student who has writing performance difficulties. The strategies are organized according to the length of text that the student needs to improve.

### Educational Objectives and Strategies for Pre-writing Skills

*Mechanics of Writing* Pre-writing objectives for handwriting and spelling can include scribbling, drawing shapes, and copying shapes; letter identification; and phonics to understand sound–symbol relationships.

*Text-Level Compositions* Pre-writing instruction for compositions can include organizing pictures into an appropriate sequence. Text-generation or composition skills can be developed even in the absence of handwriting and keyboarding skills. For example, a student could dictate an oral narrative and then use a computer to organize the ideas into a logical sequence. See Chapter 4 for more information on how narrative develops with age. The objectives for improving a student's oral narrative can be used to help the student improve written compositions.

### Educational Objectives and Strategies for the Mechanics of Writing



*Handwriting* Handwriting instruction has a positive impact on legibility and fluency of handwriting and the quality of compositions (Graham et al., 2000; Santangelo & Graham, 2016). In multisensory approaches, the motor system is engaged to produce letters by using finger painting, by using a pencil or pen, or by building letters with blocks or pieces of wood. However, handwriting instruction should not just be a type of motor instruction. Effective handwriting instruction requires explicit practice in letter and word formation (Hoy, Egan, & Feder, 2011), and must be embedded in spelling instruction, as well as in writing instruction as a whole.

*Spelling* Accurate spelling is an important educational objective. There are different ways in which spelling is taught, and the best method for a given student depends on the student's phonics skills and language skills and the student's preference for memorization-based learning versus more conceptual learning. Spelling instruction requires learning the alphabetic principle and phonics. Spelling instruction can be provided by making available lists of spelling words. This type of learning requires rote memorization, which may appeal to some students, but is not sufficient to build the level of skill proficiency for students to become independent readers and spellers. Finally, some spelling can be taught by analyzing different types and parts of words as part of vocabulary instruction in reading. By grouping words into semantic categories, word roots, prefixes and suffixes, or similar orthographic patterns, the student masters new vocabulary while also learning about spelling. Spelling instruction should be integrated into reading and writing as a whole (Scott, 2000b). Explicit and systematic instruction should accompany opportunities for incidental or natural learning (Graham, 1999). The Common Core State Standards outlines an order in which spelling skills can be taught (CCSS, 2010). See Graham and Weintraub (1996) and Datchuk and Kubina (2012) for a review of word-level writing instruction.

*Writing Fluency* Handwriting and spelling instruction improves writing fluency. The more the student practices the skill of integrating handwriting, keyboarding, and spelling (i.e., transcription skills), the more fluently the student can write sentences and full-length text. See Graham and Weintraub (1996) and Datchuk and Kubina (2012) for a review of word-level writing instruction.

*Mechanics of Sentence-Level Writing* Students need to be able to use the correct punctuation for different types of sentences (e.g., periods, commas, capitalization, question marks, exclamation marks, quotation marks) and to write grammatically correct sentences. Educational objectives can be developed for using appropriate grammar (morpho-syntax), such as appropriate subject–verb agreement and correct placement of adjectives and adverbs.

### *Educational Objectives and Strategies for Writing at the Paragraph and Text Levels*

*Paragraph Writing* To build skills in writing at the paragraph level, students need to learn how to organize their thoughts in a paragraph by having a main idea or topic sentence, followed by multiple supporting ideas and a concluding sentence. Strategy instruction is an effective way to teach students about how to organize their ideas in writing for paragraphs and for full-length text. In strategy instruction, the student learns how to identify the main idea and supporting ideas and details and how to write a concluding sentence. For both narrative and informational text, cycles of planning, composing, revising, and editing are required. Self-regulated strategy development is an important component to writing (Graham, Harris, & Mason, 2005).



*Text Writing* Objectives include teaching students to write in different types of genres and to identify the elements and structures that are relevant to each. National and state curriculum standards provide guidance about teaching writing at the text level. As discussed in the section Paragraph Writing, strategy instruction is a primary means by which students learn to write full-length text. Both narrative and informational text require cycles of planning, composing, revising, and editing. Strategy instruction helps students through these cycles and is focused on producing a coherent and logical structure. Within the text structures, the right elements also need to be present. Sometimes, the elements make up part of the structure. For example, in narrative, the elements consist of an opening problem, characters, events, settings, solution, and a goal path. These elements help to make up the structure, such as the chronological structure used so often in narrative. To generate educational objectives, the student can be asked to write a clear and logically consistent storyline that includes the elements of narrative just listed. The narrative may need to include use of descriptive language, sensory language, and/or dialogue.

Similar objectives apply to writing informational text. Informational text has to include elements such as titles, subtitles, graphs, charts, and tables, which can help inform the structure. Educational objectives for informational text can include the selection of pertinent or relevant information to set the context or background. The text may need to include a summary or paraphrasing of key ideas. The text may need to state and maintain a focus or point of view as when responding to a question. The information may need to be presented in a specific kind of structure, such as a compare-and-contrast structure, a categorical structure, or a chronological or temporal structure. Other types of expository text are associated with other types of elements and structures. Recipes, e-mail messages, text messages, letters, and invitations all have their own text structures.

***Educational Objectives and Strategies to Address the Quality of Writing*** Quality writing requires an understanding of the target audience and the ability to write in a way that is appropriate for that audience. Educational objectives to improve the quality of writing may focus on the identification of the target audience and purpose. For example, the student may need to decide which terms should be explained in the text and how to explain them in a manner that suits the intended audience. The student may need to develop strategies to engage an audience that might be unfamiliar with the topic, such as providing a case example or by making a connection to current events. The student should be able to choose the right level of linguistic and syntactic complexity for a particular audience and purpose. Objectives can also be developed for writing for the purpose of persuading, informing, or entertaining the audience. Not all the quality parameters are necessarily measurable and not all readers of a text will necessarily be able to provide feedback or insight into the ability of the text to persuade, inform, or entertain. However, the ability of the text to do so still merits discussion and analysis.

## Accommodations for Writing

To provide accommodations for a student's writing difficulties, educators and practitioners need information about which specific areas of writing are most affected. In general, lower order skills have to be in place before higher order skills can be mastered. When higher order skills, such as writing full-length text, are the focus of educational objectives, lower order skills may need to be accommodated. Assuring quality instruction for lower order skills and to bring lower order skills to mastery is one way to address this issue. Another way to address the issue is to remove the demand on lower order skills, so that the student can focus on higher level skills or higher level thinking.

*Accommodations for Handwriting and Spelling* At times, eliminating the need for accurate handwriting or spelling can free up the mind of the young writer to expand into writing compositions. For example, if a student has difficulty with spelling but can otherwise produce a well-structured essay, an accommodation might be to ignore spelling when grading the student's work, focusing instead on the successful use of text elements and text structures. Similarly, fine motor weaknesses can interfere with all aspects of writing. Circumventing the fine motor demands of writing by using dictation software or scribing can allow the student to demonstrate content knowledge and skills in higher order aspects of writing.



*Accommodations for Writing Compositions* As writing objectives move to the paragraph and text levels, the demands on the student's language and executive skills increase. A student may need to work on a single skill or a few of the higher level skills in writing one at a time, such as focusing only on the organizational structure. The accommodation might be for the student to use simpler sentences and words (i.e., reduced linguistic and syntactic complexity) while honing his or her ability to structure a text.

Writing strategy instruction can lead to reduced demands on the student's executive system. The student with underdeveloped executive skills may need much more one-to-one instruction to be able to use the strategy successfully. At times, the strategy may necessitate close supervision and extended time to develop and use efficiently. For example, the student might need much more supervision for the first step (gathering research) than for the second step (writing down what was learned).

*Accommodations Provided by a Computer* Computerized technology can assist by providing many accommodations, including supporting the student's handwriting skills (keyboarding and speech recognition), spelling skills (word processing and spell check), linguistic complexity (word prediction, thesaurus to improve linguistic complexity or appropriateness), and text-level skills such as planning, writing, and revising (concept mapping and organizing software). The efficacy of these computerized accommodations for students with different learning profiles, however, is not yet clear (Batorowicz, Missiuna, & Pollock, 2012).

## CASE EXAMPLE

Recall the language samples provided by Leonard presented in Chapter 4. Several years later, when Leonard was 8 years 1 month old, his special education team met again at their annual review. Leonard's teacher shared information about his writing skills as he was approaching the end of second grade. Leonard's teacher stated that he needs help writing narratives, and that he does best when an adult lets him talk through events prior to writing down his thoughts. Leonard is able to organize thoughts when given extra time and after he has written them down. Leonard's teacher also provided information about his other literacy skills. She stated that his reading skills are improving but continue to be below grade level. Even though he can decode text at grade level, he has difficulty responding successfully to comprehension questions and performs better when asked to respond to multiple-choice questions. When looking at language skills, Leonard's teacher commented that he continues to need instructions broken down into steps, needs extra reminders to follow through on tasks, and frequently makes off-topic comments. His academic skills were rated as progressing toward the standards. Leonard's teacher shared the writing sample in Figure 10.1. Leonard was asked to produce a new writing sample in response to the six-picture stimulus that he had used 3 years earlier (the story "The Fisherman and the Cat").

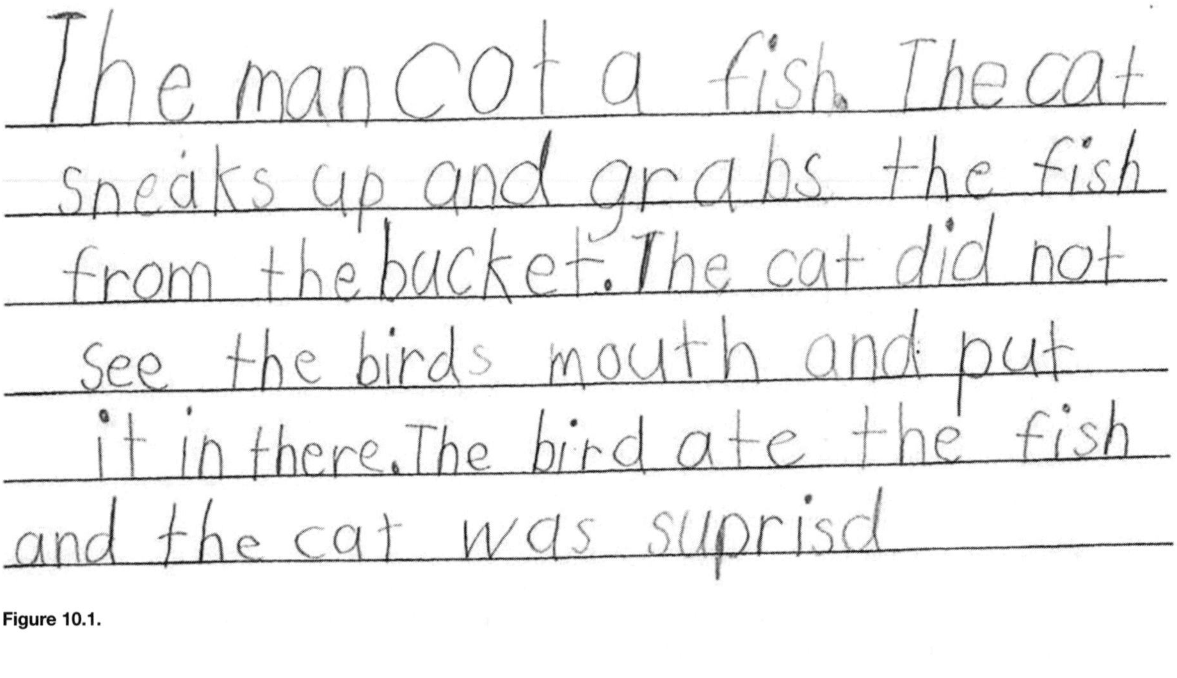

The man Cot a fish. The cat
sneaks up and grabs the fish
from the bucket. The cat did not
see the birds mouth and put
it in there. The bird ate the fish
and the cat was suprisd

**Figure 10.1.**

## Analysis of Leonard's Writing Sample

In reviewing Leonard's writing sample, his team offered the following points of analysis:

### *Handwriting and Spelling*

Leonard showed good handwriting/transcription skills. Spelling errors are consistent with the phonetic spelling errors seen in young writers at his age and grade level.

### *Linguistic Complexity*

Linguistic complexity is low. Leonard used one-syllable words with concrete meaning only.

### *Syntactic Complexity*

Sentence structure is correct but simple, with only one clause per sentence.

### *Paragraph Structure*

The sequence of the sentences is correct, but there are no linking devices and the relationship between each of the sentences is not clearly marked. It is useful to remember that the paragraph writing sample was supported through the use of pictures, something that is not always true in a second-grade classroom. The pictures reduced demands on Leonard's executive skills, notably working memory and planning. Even though the writing skills shown in the sample look largely appropriate for his grade, other students in his class would be able to produce a similar paragraph without the support of pictures. Further analysis of other writing samples is needed to confirm the preliminary impressions of his grade-level performance.

### *Quality of Writing*

At this grade level, quality of writing can be assessed using conventional standards for letter formation, spelling, grammar, and linguistic and syntactic complexity. Quality parameters related to the purpose of the writing and the audience are typically not the focus of instruction at this grade level.



## Educational Objectives for Leonard

Having made observations of Leonard's writing sample and analyzing those observations more closely, Leonard's team can identify targets for improving his writing. Using the framework helps facilitate the choice of objectives that might be the most appropriate for Leonard. The framework also ensures that objectives are chosen in a comprehensive manner. Based on the points of analysis, his team might recommend the following objectives for Leonard:

### *Transcription Objectives for Leonard*

Leonard has secure handwriting skills and spells words correctly. Educational objectives should include spelling objectives. This is consistent with his age and grade.

### *Sentence-Level Writing Objectives for Leonard*

Leonard should expand his repertoire of sentence-writing skills. He should learn how to write longer sentences, such as those with more than one clause, and will continue to need instruction in the use of punctuation.

### Paragraph-Level Writing Objectives

Paragraph-writing is an objective for Leonard's peers and is appropriate for Leonard as well. Instruction should focus on writing a five-sentence paragraph with sentences in proper sequence. Leonard needs to develop a repertoire of linking devices, so that the connections between each of the sentences is clear. Leonard would be expected to have greater difficulty in this area compared to his peers and may continue to need more supports in order to write paragraphs successfully.

### Text Structures

Leonard may be able to experiment in writing different genres and in using different types of text structure. An important focus should still remain on writing a good paragraph, however exposure to different genres of writing could be helpful and enjoyable. In higher grades, Leonard will learn to write different types of text structures.

### Objectives to Improve the Quality of Leonard's Writing

Leonard can expand his repertoire of words by increasing linguistic complexity. He will also learn how to tailor writing to the audience and how to write for the intended purpose. These skills might be more appropriate to teach as his writing skills improve.

## An Additional Writing Sample: Benjamin, 8 Years 9 Months Old

Benjamin, another 8-year-old boy, completed a writing sample using the same stimulus that Leonard used (see Chapter 4). He produced the writing sample in Figure 10.2 at the beginning of third grade. He was older than Leonard at the time of sampling but had received only slightly more instruction. Benjamin's second-grade teacher rated his performance in all areas as meeting standards at the end of the previous year. Benjamin was provided with the same picture supports as those provided to Leonard.

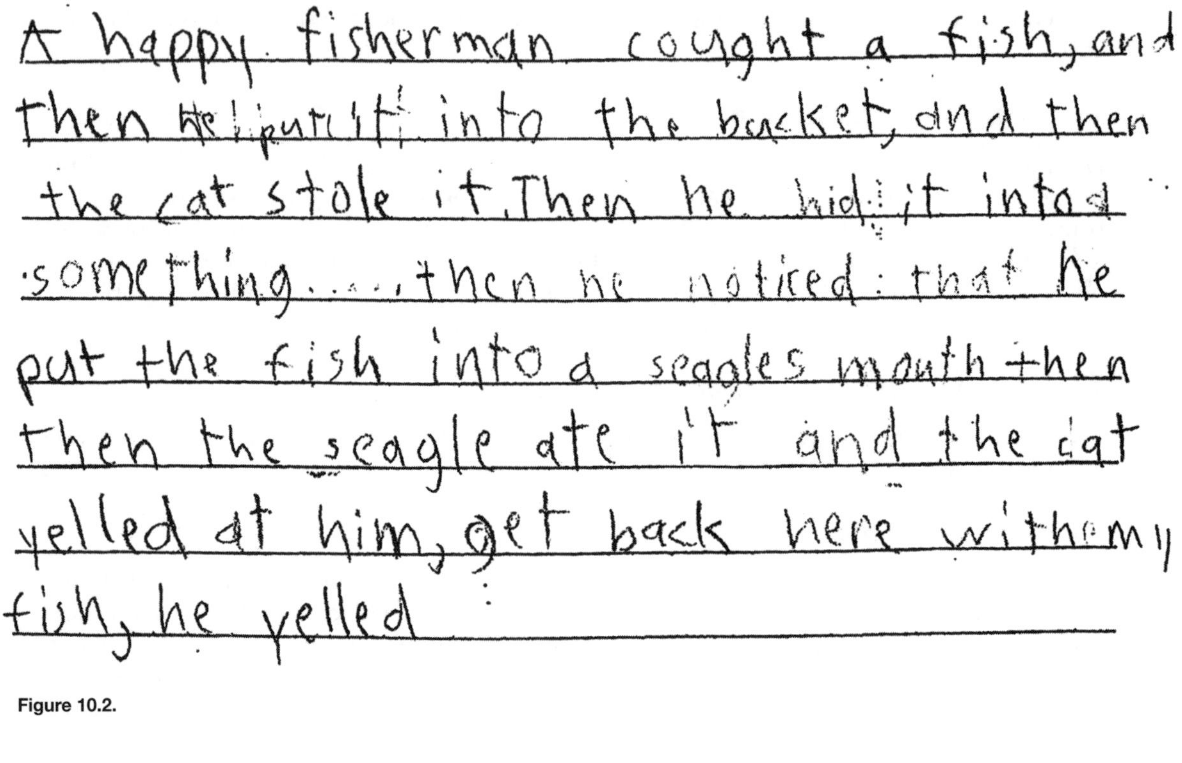

A happy fisherman cought a fish, and
then he put it into the backet, and then
the cat stole it. Then he hid it into a
something....then he noticed that he
put the fish into a seagles mouth then
then the seagle ate it and the cat
yelled at him, get back here with my
fish, he yelled

Figure 10.2.

***Analysis of Benjamin's Transcription Skills***

Benjamin's sample reveals secure handwriting skills. He makes phonetic spelling errors that are still consistent for his age and grade.

***Analysis of Benjamin's Sentence-Writing Skills***

Benjamin produced longer sentences than Leonard was able to produce. Some of the sentences have subordinate clauses. He made punctuation errors in several places and also produced run-on sentences.

***Analysis of Benjamin's Paragraph-Writing Skills***

The sentences are linked with one another by using the word *then*. This is an early emerging way to create links in a narrative. Additional writing samples would help confirm that Benjamin is performing at grade level in his writing skills.

***Analysis of Linguistic Complexity***

Linguistic complexity is higher than was the case for Leonard. Benjamin used descriptors (*happy, surprised*) and expressed himself using written dialogue.

Benjamin's writing skills are more advanced than Leonard's writing skills. The main purpose in presenting both writing samples is to show the reader the similarities and the differences that students can bring to the same writing task. Regardless of the level of the student's performance, the Writing Skills Framework provides a systematic way to analyze writing and to develop educational objectives that can help the student improve his or her writing.

### Working With Culturally and Linguistically Diverse Learners

Expectations and rules for writing differ widely between cultures. School professionals must consider these differences and provide instruction that explains how American English handles these elements. Two examples of such variations are discussed below.

#### *Letter Formation*

Culturally and linguistically diverse learners and their families may be unaware that the way letters are formed or joined in cursive differs from culture to culture. In some languages, the way capital or uppercase letters are formed, such as with the letters *A* and *G*, differ from the way the way they are formed in American and/or British English. This can be especially frustrating because there can be one or more letters that are not exact representatives of the letters used in English. Ideally learners can be taught how to form these letters according to the expectations of the school. However, schools should avoid sending correspondence home to families in cursive, even if the family can read and write English, since this can easily lead to misunderstandings.

#### *Style*

Culturally and linguistically diverse learners may be unaware that there is a great deal of variation in the style that is used to produce pieces of writing for different purposes and audiences. Learners need to be made aware that, in English, simple grammar and short sentences are used to write about simple topics. Likewise, they will need to learn that a more complex writing style is needed for more complicated topics.



## CONCLUSIONS

This chapter closes the second of three chapters dedicated to educational frameworks. Chapter 9 reviewed the Reading Skills Framework and this chapter reviewed the Writing Skills Framework. Although these two chapters may seem basic for teachers who are experienced in literacy instruction, it is important for all team members to understand how literacy skills develop over several years and how reading and writing are interrelated with language skills. When all school professionals understand the development of early literacy skills, they are in a better position to understand reading and writing difficulties in students who may already be in higher grades. Chapters 9 and 10 highlight the important interconnections among language, reading, and writing skills. The next chapter, Chapter 11 on math skills, is the final chapter in Section III, Educational Frameworks. It is also the final framework of the book.

## REFERENCES


Bailin, A., & Grafstein, A. (2001). The linguistic assumptions underlying readability formulae: A critique. *Language and Communication, 21*(3), 285–301.

Batorowicz, B., Missiuna, C. A., & Pollock, N. A. (2012). Technology supporting written productivity in children with learning disabilities: A critical review. *Canadian Journal of Occupational Therapy, 79*(4), 211–224.

Beers, S. F., & Nagy, W. E. (2009). Syntactic complexity as a predictor of adolescent writing quality: Which measures? Which genre? *Reading and Writing 22*(2), 185–200.

Beers, S. F., & Nagy, W. E. (2011). Writing development in four genres from grades three to seven: Syntactic complexity and genre differentiation. *Reading and Writing, 24*(2), 183–202.

Berninger, V., Abbott, R. D., Nagy, W., & Carlisle, J. (2010). Growth in phonological, orthographic, and morphological awareness in grades 1 to 6. *Journal of Psycholinguistics, 38*(2), 141–163.

Berninger, V., & O'Malley, M. (2011). Evidence-based diagnosis and treatment for specific learning disabilities involving impairments in written and/or oral language. *Journal of Learning Disabilities, 44*(2), 167–183.

Berninger, V., & Richards, T. (2002a). Building a writing brain neurologically. In V. W. Berninger & T. L. Richards, *Brain literacy for educators and psychologists* (pp. 168–169). New York, NY: Academic Press.

Berninger, V., & Rutberg, J. (1992a). Relationship of finger function to beginning writing: Application to diagnosis of writing disability. *Developmental Medicine and Child Neurology, 34*(3), 198–215.

Berninger, V., Yates, C., Cartwright, A., Rutberg, J., Remy, E., & Abbott, R. (1992b). Lower-level developmental skills in beginning writing. *Reading and Writing,* 4(3), 257–280.

Berninger, V. W. (2000). Development of language by hand and its connections with language by ear, mouth, and eye. *Topics in Language Disorders, 20*(4), 65–84.

Berninger, V. W., Abbott, R. D., Jones, J., Wolf, B. J., Gould, L, Anderson-Youngstrom, M. A., . . . Apel, K. (2006a). Early development of language by hand: Composing, reading, listening, and speaking connections; three letter-writing modes; and fast mapping in spelling. *Developmental Neuropsychology, 29*(1), 61–92.

Berninger V. W., Rutberg, J. E., Abbott, R. D., Garcia, N., Anderson-Youngstrom, M., Brooks, A., & Fulton, C. (2006b). Tier 1 and Tier 2 early intervention for handwriting and composing. *Journal of School Psychology, 44*(3), 3–30.

Berninger, V. W., Vaughan, K., Abbott, R. D., Begay, K., Coleman, K. B., Curtin, G., . . . Graham, S. (2002b). Teaching spelling and composition alone and together: Implications for the simple view of writing. *Journal of Educational Psychology, 94*(2), 291–304.

Brooks, G. (2016). What works for pupils with literacy difficulties? The effectiveness of intervention schemes. Retrieved from https://www.helenarkell.org.uk/documents/files/What-works-for-children-and-young-people-with-literacy-difficulties-5th-edition.pdf

Cahill, S. M. (2009). Where does handwriting fit in? Strategies to support academic achievement. *Intervention in School and Clinic, 44*(4), 223–228.

Common Core State Standards. (2010). Retrieved from www.corestandards.org

Costa, L.-J., Edwards, C. N., & Hooper, S. R. (2016). Writing disabilities and reading disabilities in elementary school students: Rates of co-occurrence and cognitive burden. *Learning Disability Quarterly, 39*(1), 17–30.

Datchuk, S. M., & Kubina, R. M. (2012). A review of teaching sentence-level writing skills to students with writing difficulties and learning disabilities. *Remedial and Special Education, 34*(3), 180–192.

DuBay, W. (2004). The principles of readability. Retrieved from https://files.eric.ed.gov/fulltext/ED490073.pdf

DuBay, W. (2007). The classic readability studies. Retrieved from https://eric.ed.gov/?id=ED506404

Duff, F. J., & Clarke, P. J. (2011). Practitioner review: Reading disorders: What are the effective interventions and how should they be implemented and evaluated? *Journal of Child Psychology and Psychiatry, 52*(1), 3–12.

Fallon, K., & Katz, L. A. (2011). Providing written language services in the schools: The time is now. *Language, Speech, and Hearing Services in Schools, 42*(1), 3–17.

Fey, M., Catts, H., Proctor-Williams, K., Tomblin, J. B., & Zhang, X. (2004). Oral and written story composition skills of children with language impairment. *Journal of Speech, Language, and Hearing Research, 47*(6), 1301–1318.

Graham, S. (1999). Handwriting and spelling instruction for students with learning disabilities: A review. *Learning Disability Quarterly, 22*(2), 78–98.

Graham, S., Berninger, V., Abbott, R., Abbott, S., & Whitaker, D. (1997). Role of mechanics in composing of elementary school students: A new methodological approach. *Journal of Educational Psychology, 89*(1), 170–182.

Graham, S., Harris, K. R., and Fink, B. (2000). Is handwriting causally related to learning to write? Treatment of handwriting problems in beginning writers. *Journal of Educational Psychology, 4*(4), 620–633.

Graham, S., Harris, K., & Larsen, L. (2001). Prevention and intervention of writing difficulties for students with learning disabilities. *Learning Disabilities Research & Practice, 16*(2), 74–84.

Graham, S., Harris, K. R., & Mason, L. (2005). Improving the writing performance, knowledge, and self-efficacy of struggling young writers: The effects of self-regulated strategy development. *Contemporary Educational Psychology, 30*(2), 207–241.

Graham, S., & Perin, D. (2007a). A meta-analysis of writing instruction for adolescent students. *Journal of Educational Psychology, 99*(3), 445–476.

Graham, S., & Perin, D. (2007b). Writing next: Effective strategies to improve writing of adolescents in middle and high schools. Retrieved from https://www.carnegie.org/

Graham, S., & Weintraub, N. (1996). A review of handwriting research: Progress and prospects from 1980 to 1994. *Educational Psychology Review, 8*(1), 7–87.

Hayes, J. R., & Berninger, V. W. (2009). Relationships between idea generation and transcription: How act of writing shapes what children write. In R. K. Braverman, K. Lunsford, S. McLoed, S. Null, & A. S. P. Rogers (Eds.), *Traditions of writing research* (pp. 166–180). New York, NY: Routledge.

Hoy, M. M. P., Egan, M. Y., & Feder, K. P. (2011). A systematic review of interventions to improve handwriting. *Canadian Journal of Occupational Therapy, 78*(1), 13–25.

Isaacson, S. (n.d.). Simple ways to assess the writing skills of students with learning disabilities. Retrieved from http://www.readingrockets.org/article/simple-ways-assess-writing-skills-students-learning-disabilities

Joshi, R. M., Gooden, R., & Bentum, K. E. (2008). Diagnosis and treatment of reading disabilities based on the component model of reading: Alternative to the discrepancy model of LD. *Journal of Learning Disabilities, 41*(1), 67–84.

McNamara, D. S., Crossley, S. A., & McCarthy, P. M. (2010). Linguistic features of writing quality. *Written Communication, 27*(1), 57–86.

National Reading Panel. (2001). Retrieved from https://www.nichd.nih.gov/sites/default/files/publications/pubs/nrp/Documents/report.pdf

Puranik, C. S., & Alotaiba, S. (2012). Examining the contribution of handwriting and spelling to written expression in kindergarten students. *Reading and Writing, 25*(7), 1523–1546.

Ravit, D. (2006). Semantic development in textual contexts during the school years: Noun scale analyses. *Journal of Child Language, 33*(4), 791–821.

Rijlaarsdam. G., Van den Bergh, H., Couzijn, M., Hanssen, T., Braaksma, M., Tillema, M., . . . Baedts, M. (2012). Writing. In K. R. Harris, S. Graham, & T. Urdan (Eds.), *APA educational psychology handbook: Vol. 3. Application to learning and teaching* (pp. 189–227). Washington, DC: American Psychological Association.

Rosenblum, S., Weiss, P. L., & Parush, S. (2003). Product and process evaluation of handwriting difficulties. *Educational Psychology Review, 15*(1), 41–81.

Santangelo, T., & Graham, S. (2016). A comprehensive meta-analysis of handwriting research. *Educational Psychology Review, 28*(2), 225–265.

Scott, C. M., & Windsor, J. (2000a). General language performance measures in spoken and written narrative and expository discourse of school-age children with language learning disabilities. *Journal of Speech, Language, and Hearing Research, 43*(2), 324–339.

Scott, M. (2000b). Principles and methods of spelling instruction: Applications for poor spellers. *Topics in Language Disorders, 20*(3), 66–82.

Sun, L., & Nippold, M. A. (2012). Narrative writing in children and adolescents: Examining the literate lexicon. *Language, Speech, and Hearing Services in Schools, 43*(1), 2–13.

Troia, G. A. (Ed.). (2009). *Instruction and assessment for struggling writers: Evidence-based practices.* New York, NY: Guilford Press.

U.S. Department of Education. (2017). National Assessment of Educational Progress Writing Framework. Retrieved from www.nagb.org/content

U.S. Department of Education and Institute of Education Sciences. (2011). The Nation's Report Card: Writing. National Assessment of Educational Progress. Retrieved from https://nces.ed.gov/nationsreportcard

## APPENDIX 10.1 Writing Skills Framework

The Writing Skills Framework is summarized here. School professionals can use this form as a quick reference for the skill sets and skills that need to be taken into consideration when making observations and developing an intervention plan.

| Skill sets | Skills | Examples of skills in action | Sample performance difficulties | Potential strategies, accommodations, or educational objectives |
|---|---|---|---|---|
| Mechanics of writing | Handwriting | The student is able to produce letters in print using handwriting. | The student has difficulty with letter formation in handwriting. Writing is illegible or irregular.<br>The student can produce letters and words in handwriting, but handwriting speed is slow and letter formation is uneven. | Teach handwriting skills through handwriting instruction and/or with occupational therapy interventions. |
| | Spelling | The student is able to spell phonetically.<br>The student is able to spell common words accurately.<br>The student is able to spell irregularly spelled words accurately.<br>The student can guess at or know correct spelling of unfamiliar words using knowledge of word structures. | The student is unable to spell words phonetically.<br>The student is unable to spell common words correctly.<br>The student is unable to spell irregularly spelled words.<br>The student is unable to spell unfamiliar words using knowledge of word structures. | Teach phonics.<br>Teach spelling through drill and practice and through general education spelling instruction. |
| | Writing fluency:<br>Smooth transcription of spoken words into correctly spelled handwritten words | The student is able to write by hand and spell accurately in a smooth manner.<br>The student shows automaticity in both handwriting and spelling for grade-level words. | The student is unable to print words in handwriting while also spelling words correctly. Either handwriting or spelling skills are underdeveloped. Transcription is slow and effortful and includes excessive errors.<br>The student is able to print words smoothly and spell them accurately, but transcription speed is slow and interferes with writing compositions. | Teach writing fluency through writing large volume of words, sentences, and/or text.<br>Accommodate for handwriting difficulty by using transcription software when text-level writing (composition) is the goal.<br>Accommodate for spelling difficulty by allowing access to word recognition software, dictionary, spell check functions, and other resources, especially when text-level writing is the goal. |
| | Writing fluency and the mechanics of sentences:<br>Smooth transcription of spoken sentences into correctly spelled sentences with correct punctuation | The student is able to write sentences smoothly, including appropriate punctuation and correct grammar (correct spelling, correct word order). | The student is able to print and form words smoothly and spell accurately but is slow to produce sentence and/or makes excessive errors in punctuation and grammar. | Transcription fluency at the word level is necessary for successful writing at the sentence level. Teach transcription fluency if needed.<br>Allow use of spell check and grammar check functions in computer software if teaching text-level writing skills (compositions) is the goal. |

| Skill sets | Skills | Examples of skills in action | Sample performance difficulties | Potential strategies, accommodations, or educational objectives |
|---|---|---|---|---|
| Elements and structures | Sentence writing | The student is able to write a variety of sentence types, including simple, compound, subordinate clause, and complex. | The student is able to transcribe words and produce sentences smoothly and accurately, but sentence structure is simple and contains only few words and/or one clause. | Transcription difficulties can interfere with writing at the text level. Teach in the preceding areas or provide accommodations as needed.<br>Teach about different types of sentences and sentence structures in spoken language and then in written language. |
| | Paragraph writing | The student is able to write a well-structured paragraph that has appropriate indentation, an introductory sentence, supporting sentences, and a concluding sentence. | The student is able to produce several sentences to produce a paragraph but is unable to produce a paragraph that is organized with an opening sentence, supporting ideas, and closing sentence. The paragraph may consist of unconnected sentences or sentences written in illogical order. | Instruction in the preceding areas may be needed to teach about paragraph writing.<br>Teach about single-paragraph writing. Substantial practice is needed for students to master paragraph-level writing. |
| | Full-length text writing:<br>Elements: Titles, subtitles, table of contents, index, and other elements<br>Structures: Text genre, form, and organizational schemata | The student is able to write a text that includes an opening paragraph, supporting ideas presented in supporting paragraphs, and a concluding paragraph.<br>The student is able to write multiple-paragraph text that includes appropriate key elements such as titles, subtitles, table of contents, and index. | The student is able to produce a well-structured paragraph but is not yet producing a multiple-paragraph text that is structured with an opening paragraph, supporting paragraphs, and a concluding paragraph.<br>The student can write a multiple-paragraph text but is not using text elements to enhance and clarify ideas in text.<br>The student can write a multiple-paragraph text but is unable to produce different types of text structures and writes in only one or two genres. | Use writing strategy instruction to teach about writing multiple-paragraph text.<br>Teach about text structures, such as compare-contrast structure, chronological structures, and free-form structure.<br>Substantial practice is needed for students to master multiple-paragraph-level writing. |
| Quality of writing | Linguistic complexity | The student is able to choose the right level of linguistic complexity for the genre and purpose of writing. | The student uses simple vocabulary and does not modify the choice of words (linguistic complexity) to suit the needs of the audience. | Teach the student how to change vocabulary or sentence structure to suit the needs of the audience. |
| | Syntactic complexity | The student is able to choose the right level of syntactic complexity for the genre and the purpose of writing. | The student uses only simple sentence structures and does not modify sentence structure to make the writing more interesting or more appropriate to the audience. | |

*(continued)*

| Skill sets | Skills | Examples of skills in action | Sample performance difficulties | Potential strategies, accommodations, or educational objectives |
|---|---|---|---|---|
| | Content: Density of ideas, interrelationships between ideas (within the text and with other sources), relevance of the ideas to the audience, impact of the ideas on the audience | The student presents a sufficient number of key ideas in the text.<br><br>The student shows interrelationships between key ideas in the text and between the text and other sources.<br><br>The student makes the key ideas relevant to the chosen audience.<br><br>The student's writing has an impact on the reader by influencing the thoughts or actions of the reader in some way. | The student shares only a limited number of ideas in text.<br><br>The student does not produce a text that shows interrelationships of ideas within the text.<br><br>The student does not produce a text that shows interrelationships of ideas in text with ideas or events outside of the text.<br><br>The student does not choose or explain her or his ideas to suit the needs of the intended audience.<br><br>The student's writing does not have an impact on the audience or does not have the impact that was intended. | Teach the student about the number of ideas shared in the text and how to make interrelationships between ideas more noticeable. This can be done through text elements as well as text structures.<br><br>Teach how to make the ideas presented in the text interesting or relevant to the intended audience. |

APPENDIX 10.2 **Writing Skills Observation Sheet**

| Skill sets | Skills | Example skills and deficits in this student | Potential strategies, accommodations, or educational objectives |
|---|---|---|---|
| Mechanics of writing | Handwriting<br><br>Spelling<br><br>Writing fluency:<br>Smooth transcription of spoken words into correctly spelled handwritten words<br><br>Writing fluency and the mechanics of sentences:<br>Smooth transcription of spoken sentences into correctly spelled sentences with correct punctuation | | |
| Elements and structures | Sentence writing<br><br>Paragraph writing<br><br>Full-length text writing<br><br>Elements: Titles, subtitles, table of contents, index, and other elements<br><br>Structure: Text genre, form, and organizational schemata | | |
| Quality of writing | Linguistic complexity<br><br>Syntactic complexity<br><br>Content: Density of ideas, interrelationships between ideas (within the text and with other sources), relevance of the ideas to the audience, and impact of the ideas on the audience | | |

# Math Skills

## INTRODUCTION AND GENERAL DEFINITIONS

As discussed in the preceding chapters, reading and writing are key foundations for learning; Math skills must be put on equal footing. They are just as critical to academic success. Underdeveloped math skills are correlated with significant academic and adaptive deficits throughout the school years and into adulthood, and failure to develop math skills substantially affects employment opportunities (Geary, 2011).

If math could be reduced to just one foundational skill, it would be the ability to understand and discriminate different quantities and differences in magnitude, referred to as number sense. Number sense is the first math skill to develop and is the most essential. It enables people to identify differences and similarities between sets of quantities (Butterworth, 2010). It emerges as early as infancy (Dehaene, Dehaene-Lambertz, & Cohen, 1998) and sets the stage for all the early numerical abilities that are taught in preschool and kindergarten (see Box 11.1).

In addition to the understanding of quantity, math involves performing *operations* or *calculations,* terms that are interchangeable and refer to the act of manipulating quantities. Math operations and calculations are possible once a student has understood numerals, the symbols used to represent quantities. See Box 11.1 for definitions of *number, numeral,* and *numeron*. In order to perform calculations, young learners must have a representational system of numbers and be able to match numerical symbols (numerals) to different quantities. Number sense and calculations are subsequently integrated with other skills. Reading, writing, executive skills, and spatial skills (understanding the three-dimensionality of quantities) are all included in math skills. This chapter discusses the development of math skills, starting with number sense and calculations and then incorporating other skills necessary in math.



### BOX 11.1. Numbers, Numerals, and Numerons

1. Number: A mathematical value, an amount, or a quantity
2. Numeral: The symbol that is used to represent a specific quantity. In Western cultures, Arabic numerals are used to represent quantities
3. Numeron: Any symbolic representation of value, amount, or quantity (e.g., notches on a piece of wood, beads on an abacus, a printed symbol or word)

## HOW THIS FRAMEWORK WAS CONSTRUCTED

The Math Skills Framework was created using the Common Core State Standards (CCSS, 2010), as well as expertise from research cited in this chapter's references. One challenge in creating this framework was in structuring it into lower order and higher order skills. Math does not lend itself to this structure as successfully as do reading and writing. The development of math skills starts out with the lower order skills of number sense and calculations. However, as math skills develop, number sense continues to develop. As math skills become more complex, students deepen their understanding of number sense and perform increasingly complex calculations. There are many skill sets and skills that are needed for students to build skills in math and solve higher order math problems. In addition to allowing students to understand numbers more deeply and perform more complex math calculations, higher order math skills also are dependent on domain-general skills such as language skills and executive skills (Dowker, 2005; Geary & Moore, 2016; Kucian & von Aster, 2015; Luculano, 2016). The Math Skills Framework was constructed with these concepts in mind.

## HOW CAN THIS FRAMEWORK HELP ME?

Math is a critical educational foundation. Nationally, most students perform below the proficient level in math (National Assessment of Educational Progress, 2017). To teach math effectively and to assist students who struggle with math, adults need to understand the components of math, discuss them with students, and target relevant components for additional instruction and intervention. School professionals can use the terms presented in this chapter to discuss a student's math skills with team members and with the student and the student's family. As is true for all the student observations proposed in this book, comprehensive observations of a student's performance in math can help all team members understand and address the math learning needs of the student. Repeated observations of the student's performance can serve to measure progress in the student's math skills and assess responsiveness to the teaching and intervention plan.

## MATH SKILLS FRAMEWORK: TERMS AND DEFINITIONS

Math skills begin with number sense and calculations. These lower-order math skills are at the core of any math task, regardless of complexity. Demands in math can increase very quickly as number problems related to number sense shift from concrete and tangible entities to ones that are abstract. Math also becomes more complex as quantities are subject to increasingly longer calculations that involve more and more steps. Still, in the end, the focus of any math problem remains one of quantities and how they are manipulated.



The Math Skills Framework includes the following terms and concepts:

1. Number sense
2. Math operations or math calculations
3. Math fluency
4. Math facts
5. Math comprehension and application of math to larger contexts
   a. Language, reading, and writing skills in math
   b. Executive skills in math
   c. Spatial awareness in math

Each component of the framework is defined and explained in the sections that follow. The framework is also summarized and available in Appendix 11.1 to this chapter for quick reference.

## Number Sense

*Number sense* and *numerosity* are the terms used to describe an innate understanding of quantity. Number sense includes the basic understanding of how quantities are different from one another. Quantities can be represented as approximate or very precise, concrete, or abstract. Any of these different quantities can be manipulated in math calculations (Ansari & Karmiloff-Smith, 2002).

In early development, number sense first manifests as a nonsymbolic skill for understanding quantity. Children can recognize small quantities easily and do not necessarily need words or symbols to understand quantities when the number sets are small. This skill is sometimes referred to as the approximate number system (ANS) (Karolis & Butterworth, 2016). For example, without necessarily knowing numerals, infants and young children can recognize differences between sets of four and seven items. Number sense continues to develop as children age and as they apply their understanding of approximate quantities to different situations (Feigensen, Dehaene, & Spelke, 2004; Gilmore, McCarthy, & Spelke, 2010; Mussolin, Nus, Leybaert, & Conent, 2016). However, as number sets become larger (e.g., beyond 7–10 items), the approximate number system is no longer adequate. It becomes important to represent larger sets using a precise number system. Quantities are represented as words (*two, five*) and as symbols (2, 5). Precise identification of quantities using numerals allows children to differentiate more precisely between sets of objects, especially when the sets are similar in size. Simultaneously, it leads to the development of a *number line,* which refers to both the visual representation of numbers along a line and the understanding that numbers are organized in an unchanging sequence. The development of a number line is a symbolic accomplishment because the young math learner has matched numerals (numeric symbols) to quantities. The number line is also an achievement in understanding basic relations between and among numbers (Carr, 2012; Geary, 2011).

In preschool and in the early school years, the development of number sense includes several components. Children first learn about small and approximate quantities, learn to represent those quantities precisely using number words and number symbols, and learn to apply precise terms to larger quantities. Children also learn to understand quantities in different ways. They first understand quantities concretely and visually as objects with three dimensions that can be held and viewed from different angles. They then learn to understand quantities in two dimensions, such as by interpreting a photograph or a drawing of one or more objects. Next, they understand the three-dimensionality of objects in their mind's eye and can visualize three dimensions even if there is no physical object to see. Some of these skills are discussed in Chapter 1. When learning math, the young math student must also understand quantities symbolically, as imaginary entities represented by numerals (Butterworth, 2005). Once children understand quantities using numerals, they can create a number line and develop counting principles (Carr, 2012). The later acquisition of math calculations (discussed in the next section) helps children expand their understanding of numbers and of number sense, deepening their understanding of how quantities are related to one another.



There are different ways in which the skill of number sense can be identified and measured in students (Berch, 2005; Dehaene, 1992). Children who have developed number sense can instantly recognize differences in size between sets of objects and can recognize differences between small sets of numbers, without the need for any counting. They can also identify differences in size by counting, a skill that is especially important for quantities that are close to each other such as 4 and 5. They understand that counting always occurs in the same order, that numbers can be applied to any set of objects, and that numbers can be represented on a number line, where each number has a fixed position. See Box 11.2 for a review of basic components of number sense that are critical in early childhood. Box 11.3 takes the conversation further and discusses developments in number sense as children age.

## BOX 11.2. Early Examples of Number Sense

Subitizing, estimation, encoding, counting, 1:1 correspondence, order irrelevance, stable order of numbers and numeration, and abstraction are all aspects of number sense. They are discussed below in the order that they are most likely to emerge, beginning in infancy.

**Subitizing**
Subitizing refers to the implicit understanding of the exact quantity of a small collection of objects or symbols. Subitizing involves instant recognition of a quantity. It does not include mapping words to quantities, that is, it does not include labeling quantities using a symbol or word. In preferential looking paradigms (a research strategy that helps to identify cognitive skills in infancy) infants can, for example, distinguish a set of three items from a set of five items. Children can intuitively apprehend or understand differences in size, number, and volume.

**Estimation**
Estimation is an extension of subitizing. It is similar to subitizing, because it involves an instant understanding of the difference between quantities. However, the sets are much larger than just three or five and the differences can apply to noncountable entities. For example, in preschool and kindergarten, students can make accurate comparisons between objects that are longer and shorter, lighter and heavier, warmer and colder, and so forth. Without necessarily counting or measuring, they can make meaningful comparisons between different types of quantities.

**Encoding**
As language develops, humans match words and symbols to quantities. In math, the number 1 is used to encode "one-ness," whereas the number 5 is used to encode "five-ness." Similarly, "one-ness" and "five-ness" can be encoded by speaking or writing the words *one* or *five*. Children need to understand and use numerals, and they learn to shift between number symbols (numerals) and number words. They also learn to shift between precise and approximate quantities.

**Counting**
Counting requires visual or spatial discrimination skills. Each object being counted has to be visualized as separate. Counting requires working memory, because the child has to remember which objects have already been counted. Counting also requires serial attention, meaning that all objects need to be counted until the end is reached. Counting is defined in terms of the five principles, described below. The list uses the word *number*, even though it is more accurate to use the word *numeron*. All the skills listed below emerge in the preschool years (Geary, Hamson, & Hoard, 2000; Gelman & Galistell, 1978).

**Five Principles of Counting**

1. *1:1 Correspondence:* There is a 1:1 correspondence between each number and item being counted. Each number can be used only once as it is mapped on to an object (e.g., only one item can occupy a given spot on a number line).
2. *Order Irrelevance:* The order in which the items of a set are mapped on to number words is irrelevant to the counting process. Counting can occur from right to left, left to right, top to bottom, or bottom to top, as long as only one number is assigned to each object. In mature counting, only one pattern (e.g., left to right) is typically used.
3. *Stable Order of Numbers and Numeration:* It does not matter which item in a set is counted first or last. However, the numbers used in the act of counting must have a stable order. Numbers and counting always occur in the same order, even though

objects can be placed into different configurations and can be counted in different ways. Numeration is the skill of remembering numbers in sequence.

4. *Abstraction:* All sorts of physical objects, as well as symbols and even purely mental constructs, can be counted. As students develop their counting skills, they can shift from counting visible items (e.g., tangible blocks) to counting virtual and imagined items (e.g., nonexistent blocks). They can also shift from counting visually imagined items to linguistic or cognitive concepts such as "the number of blocks needed to build a tower that is 1 mile high." Conceptual shifts continue when children learn to apply numbers to money or to measures of weight, distance, or time. Numbers can also be applied to activities, as when a younger learner uses counting principles for concepts such as "the number of jobs that I have to do today."
5. *Cardinality:* The last number used during a count represents a property of the entire set. This is referred to as its cardinality. The last number used for counting is the same as the number of items counted.

## BOX 11.3. Developments in Number Sense

Box 11.2 showed that number sense is an early emerging skill that is a critical precursor for mastery of math calculations. However, just as mastery of math calculations is dependent on number sense, a fuller understanding of number sense is dependent on mastering math calculations. Many of the math skills taught beyond the primary school years continue to deepen and broaden a student's understanding of numbers and number sense.

**Numbers and Measurements**
In primary and elementary school, number sense continues to develop as students apply numbers to entities such as measurements. They learn that numbers apply to real or imaginary weights, distances, and time and that calculations can be applied to those entities. When they learn about surface area (e.g., multiplication of two distances) and speed (e.g., distance divided by time), they are no longer working just with simple numbers. Rather, they are working with numbers that are the product of an equation. As students learn about more ways in which numbers can be represented and manipulated, they deepen their understanding of numbers and number sense.

**Different Types of Numbers**
Elementary school students transition from understanding whole numbers to understanding fractions, decimals, and percentages. They learn about rational numbers (comparisons between negative and positive numbers) and irrational numbers, such as $\pi$ (Pi). As students learn about new types of numbers, they also deepen their understanding of numbers and number sense.

**Equations and Algebra**
In middle school, students are introduced to algebra, demanding a shift of focus from numbers to equations. Equations represent an equality between two or more entities that may or may not include any actual numbers. The focus of study now becomes the relationship between quantities, differences and similarities in the magnitude of the relationship, and the different ways that the relationship can be expressed. The focus is no longer on the quantities themselves (Carr, 2012). All of these developments are examples of developments in number sense as well as in operations.

## Math Operations or Math Calculations

Operations refers to addition, subtraction, multiplication, and division skills that are also referred to as math calculations. Students spend a significant portion of their math instruction learning basic addition, subtraction, multiplication, and division problems from first through fifth grades (CCSS, 2010). They learn about the interrelationships among these operations and calculations and how each provides information about how numbers are related to one another. They therefore expand the student's number sense. For example, the quantity 20 can be identified by multiplying 10 by 2, by subtracting 80 from 100, or by adding the number 5 to itself four times.

During this period of early math learning, children need to learn to carry out procedures with accuracy as well as carry out procedures more quickly, especially as math calculations become more complex. They also start to memorize the results of common math calculations and store them in long-term memory (Geary et al., 2000). The student's underlying number sense plays a role in mastering math operations. Without number sense, math operations are much more difficult to carry out successfully. In dyscalculia (math learning disability), math calculations are not performed successfully because of an underdeveloped number sense (Geary, 2010).

## Math Fluency and Math Facts

Math fluency refers to the speed at which a student performs math calculations. Math calculations are performed more quickly and more fluently as the student becomes more skilled at performing those calculations. This increasing skill is due to greater efficiency in following the steps of math calculations. With greater fluency and deeper understanding, children acquire math facts. Math facts or math fact retrieval refers to the automatic retrieval of answers to routine addition, subtraction, multiplication, and division problems. Automatic retrieval of basic math facts is needed for answering multiple-step calculations. Automatic retrieval allows the student to perform longer and more complex math calculations without having to perform each operation separately.

The distinction between math fluency and math facts is not made clear in the literature. A similar issue was raised in the Reading Skills Framework. When learning to read fluently, the student must decode rapidly. However, reading fluency also depends on instant recognition of words without any decoding and the instant retrieval of word meaning from the student's formal language (vocabulary). A similar phenomenon exists in math fluency, which depends not only on fluency in the operations discussed but also on the instant recognition of answers to math problems, without having to perform the operation at all. The student's underlying number sense (similar to vocabulary and meaning in reading skills) allows for instant recognition and retrieval of math facts. It also allows the student to verify the answers to math facts and judge the reasonableness of those answers.



The instant recognition of answers to basic operations is especially important as the number of units of information needed to solve math problems increases. For example, multiple-step calculations, which often include embedded calculations and calculations that are derived from word problems, usually require several steps. To solve multiple-step problems fluently, the student must be able to shift between two or three calculations that are embedded into one another, remember the answers, and then perform another calculation. Completing all of these steps successfully partially depends on the automatic retrieval of math facts for each portion of the math problem. It is not efficient to perform a separate calculation for each step of a multiple-step math problem.

Math fluency, math facts, and automatic retrieval should be securely in place by the end of fourth or fifth grade. Almost all students with math learning disability demonstrate problems with accurate and automatic retrieval of basic arithmetic combinations well beyond this point in their school career. Difficulties with the automatic retrieval of math facts can be due to underdeveloped number sense, difficulty performing calculations, or other factors such as problems in executive skills or reading skills (Dowker, 2005; Jordan, Hanich, & Kaplan, 2003).

## Math Comprehension and Application of Math to Larger Contexts

***Language, Reading, and Writing in Math*** Language and reading skills have an impact on math performance (Harrison, McLeod, Berthelsen, & Walker, 2009; Korhonen, Linnanmaki, Adademi, & Aiunio, 2012), even if they are not considered core components of math. Reading skills are required for tackling word problems and for reading numerical math equations. Similarly, writing skills such as handwriting are needed to correctly print numbers and symbols and to write out numerical equations.

***Executive Skills in Math*** Executive skills are important for successful performance in math. The triad of basic executive skills—shifting, inhibiting, and working memory, discussed in Chapter 7—(Miyake et al., 2000) are critical in solving math problems. Working memory is especially important (Friso-van den Bos, van der Ven, Kroesbergen, & van Luit, 2013) as students have to manipulate information in working memory while engaged in solving math problems. For example, they have to remember and switch back and forth between spoken and written words, between symbolic and nonsymbolic quantities, and between concrete and abstract quantities (Geary et al., 2000). Switching back and forth between these different representations requires shifting cognitive set. Working memory is needed to retain information for ready access, such as retrieving and remembering math facts or remembering the rules for embedded calculations while performing a multiple-step math problem (Caviola, 2012; Friso-van den Bos et al., 2013).

When first attempting a complex math problem, a student may need to use inhibition to suppress attention to irrelevant information or to suppress distractors coming from elsewhere (Fias, Menon, & Szucs, 2013). The student then needs to plan the steps of the problem correctly (sequencing or planning skills). While performing a multiple-step math problem, the student needs to remember the results of an intermediate step to then carry out operations in later steps, all of which requires working memory. The student needs to remember and make use of number sense to check the reasonableness of answers. Metacognition is important for carrying out error detection and error correction procedures (Polya, 1957). The role of executive skills has been illustrated in observational studies of middle school–age students solving math problems (Kotsopoulos & Lee, 2012).

***Spatial Awareness in Math*** Math requires an understanding of space. Understanding space in two dimensions is needed when, for example, students have to properly align numbers into rows and columns to perform calculations or when they have to identify data points on a graph. Two-dimensional and three-dimensional understanding of space is needed when solving problems related to distance, surface area, and volume. Students cannot rely on concrete representations of space. Space has to be represented in the mind's eye. Not only does space have to be understood in the imagination, it also has to be accurately associated with numbers. The math learner has to correlate volume, surface area, or weight with numerical representations of quantity. Spatial awareness is usually thought of as a purely visual skill, however, it is also developed with other modalities (e.g., hearing and sound localization, touch and kinesthetic awareness) and plays an important role in the development and mastery of skills in math. The reader is invited to review relevant sections in Chapters 1, 2, and 3 to understand more fully all of the skills implicated in spatial awareness.

## PERFORMANCE DIFFICULTIES IN MATH SKILLS

*Math learning disability* and *dyscalculia* are terms commonly used to indicate math learning difficulty. There is a lack of consensus about how to define these overlapping terms (Soares, Evans, & Patel, 2018). Both can be defined as the result of gaps in one or more of the following basic math skills: Number sense, math calculations, math fluency, and automatic retrieval of math facts (Dowker, 2005; Geary, 2010). Some experts emphasize gaps in these first-order math skills as the specific underlying causes of dyscalculia and consider deficits in domain-general skills, such as executive, language, and visual-spatial skills, to account for a broader set of difficulties in math, referred to as math learning disability (Kucian & von Aster, 2015). Students with math difficulties may struggle to develop one or more of the skills discussed in the Math Skills Framework. The following sections provide examples of how math performance difficulties can manifest.

### Performance Difficulties in Number Sense

Young students with underdeveloped number sense may have difficulty mastering the early skills related to number sense. They may struggle to identify numbers either as symbols or as words, to learn to count, to understand counting principles (e.g., order irrelevance and cardinality), or to develop a number line. As math calculations are introduced into the curriculum, they may over rely on concrete representations of numbers in order to solve math problems. For example, they may use their fingers or concrete manipulatives such as objects or rods (commonly used in math instruction with young learners) or pictures during counting. Students with an underdeveloped number sense may make significant errors in their calculations and may struggle to judge the reasonableness or lack of reasonableness of their answers. Deficits in number sense manifest in the early school years and underlie later math learning difficulties (Ansari & Karmiloff-Smith, 2002; von Aster & Shalev, 2007).

### Performance Difficulties in Operations/Calculations

Often, the student who has difficulty with math calculations has an underlying difficulty with number sense. Calculations that are very far from being correct are especially suggestive of underlying problems in number sense. Errors in calculations can also be due to not following the procedures correctly or not remembering all the steps required for solving problems, especially as numbers get larger. Mistakes can occur as a result of the student confusing addition and subtraction, transcribing numbers incorrectly, misaligning numbers on the page, or failing to detect and correct errors. Errors in performing math calculations can reflect underdeveloped number sense but can also reflect domain-general factors such as difficulties with two- and three-dimensional spatial skills or difficulties with executive skills.



### Performance Difficulties in Math Fluency and Math Facts Retrieval

Students with underdeveloped math fluency may be slow to carry out calculations, because they are still learning how to automatize the procedures for arriving at correct responses during math operations. Students may also have difficulty with the automatic retrieval needed for solving math problems. For example, when performing a larger problem that includes several operations or embedded calculations, a student needs to have developed automaticity in retrieving answers to simple calculations such as 5 + 8 or 7 × 7. If the student cannot retrieve math facts automatically, the performance in these multiple-step problems is much slower. As is the case for difficulties in handwriting and writing fluency and their impact on writing compositions, the more energy that gets expended in solving lower order aspects of the math problems (such as basic calculations in math), the more difficulty the student would be expected to have in solving higher order or more complex math problems.

### Performance Difficulties in Reading Decoding and Reading Comprehension Skills

Math performance difficulties can arise when a student needs to read and understand math word problems. Errors can occur if a student does not decode whole words accurately and subsequently writes out numerals incorrectly. Students can also fail to decode math symbols correctly and make errors in math calculations for this reason. Students who have difficulty with reading fluency and comprehension may also misunderstand the words in math, struggle to differentiate what information is most relevant, and have trouble writing out a numeric equation. Both reading comprehension and executive skills are essential components in solving word problems in math.

### Performance Difficulties in Executive Skills

A student may show a variety of difficulties when dysfunctions in executive skills affect math performance. Working memory, shifting cognitive set, inhibition skills, and planning are all important in solving math problems. Working memory difficulties may have an especially big impact. The student might make copying or transcription (oral to print) errors because the student's working memory capacity is insufficient to the task. It may be difficult for the student to remember and retrieve math facts while also remembering the rules for embedded calculations and then perform those calculations. The student might also forget the product of the calculation needed to carry out all the subsequent steps needed to solve the problem. Working memory, inhibition, shifting cognitive set, and planning are important when translating word problems into problems written as numerals. The student needs to remember the most pertinent information from the word problem, while also inhibiting irrelevant information from the word problem. For example, consider the following word problem: "Billy picked seventeen apples on Saturday. It was very hot outside and the temperature was over eighty degrees! He met four people on the way home. All of them said that they were thirsty, and asked where he had picked all of his apples. By the time he got home, only fourteen apples were left in his basket. Write a numeric equation that will help you understand how many apples disappeared between the time he picked the apples (at two o'clock pm) and the time he got home (at five o'clock pm)." In addition to selecting only the most relevant information, the student must rewrite the words into numerals, sequence them properly, line them up in the correct rows and columns, and decide what operations need to be applied, all before starting to solve the problem (Caviola, 2012; Cornoldi & Lucangeli, 2004; Geary et al., 2000).

### Performance Difficulties in Spatial Awareness and Visual Working Memory

Underdeveloped spatial awareness, in both two and three dimensions, affects performance in math. Two-dimensional spatial skills are required to align numbers and calculations on the page, produce and order information correctly in a graph, and understand concepts of surface area. Errors can occur when numbers are not aligned successfully, when data are not graphed properly, or when numerals are not properly assigned to the spatial dimensions of the math problem. Two- and three-dimensional spatial skills are needed to visualize numbers and their calculations. If a math word problem concerns the surface area of a soccer field, the student needs to be able to visualize the field and understand the numerals that represent length and width, before deciding what calculations are needed to determine the surface area. The student with limited visual working memory difficulty may not be able to do so as successfully. Number processing slows down when the student needs concrete visual information (e.g. pictures, manipulatives) to solve math problems or when the student needs to write down every bit of information. The same issues apply to measurements (e.g., distance between home and school, the volume of a beaker), counting data (e.g., how many containers of milk are there in the cafeteria refrigerator and how many middle schoolers are expected to buy one for their lunch), and/or geometric forms (e.g., sphere, parallelogram). All of these math problems require the capacity to visualize quantities and then manipulate the quantities as part of a math calculation.

### Performance Difficulties With Complex Math Problems (Mixed Representations)

For many students, math becomes challenging when transitioning from simple numbers and basic calculations to complex multistep math problems. Similarly, math is more complex when moving from concrete whole numbers (e.g., assigning a number to a series of objects) to more abstract concepts such as measurements. Fractions, decimals, percentages, and negative numbers may also be more difficult because they are not as easily manipulated as equations involving whole numbers. Students have to master a variety of ways of representing and manipulating quantities and must become skilled at assigning numbers to many different types of quantities: Concrete and abstract, visible and invisible, whole numbers and other types of numbers. In addition to this, they have to retain and remember the interrelationships between numbers in an equation. As their skills improve, students must learn to solve more purely theoretical math problems such as those that include negative numbers or that do not include any numbers at all. For example, in algebra, quantities are no longer represented numerically. The focus is not on quantities, but on interrelationships between quantities.

## HOW TO SET UP AN OBSERVATION

To understand a student's math learning difficulties, school professionals should begin by setting up an observation. A student's difficulties may be related to basic math skills of number sense and calculations or to domain-general skills such as language, executive, and spatial skills. It is useful to review a student's performance with all these skills in mind, because it helps to identify strategies that are most appropriate to inform instruction and intervention.

Math learning difficulties are easier to identify in students who are still mastering skills related to number sense and calculations. In older children, math performance difficulty may be related to a variety of lower order math skills, such as number sense, calculations, fluency, and automatic retrieval. However, math performance difficulties may also be due to difficulties in language, reading comprehension, executive skills, and spatial skills. These types of learning difficulties are more likely to manifest when students have to complete multiple-step math problems that are more abstract and require more complex thinking.



### Select the Student

A student's difficulties in math performance should be evident from his or her educational history and from teacher ratings and comments on the report card. Before setting up an observation, school professionals can also review completed work samples to both preview math performance and look for patterns of weakness over time and across different types of assignments. Work samples can reveal errors in such areas as transcribing, following procedures, or not checking work.

### Obtain a Math Work Sample

The most accurate information comes from making observations in real time. To set up a real-time observation, the observer must first decide what types of math problems are most appropriate for starting the observation and analysis. For example, a multiple-step math word problem is a more demanding place to start than a multiple-step math problem that is already transcribed as a numerical equation. A multiple-step math problem may be too challenging for some students, who may need to start with a single-step addition, subtraction, multiplication, or division problem. For other students, the observation may need to start at a more basic level by asking the student to demonstrate an understanding of counting principles and other foundational number sense skills.

School professionals can use Appendix 11.2, the Math Skills Observation Sheet, to record their observations. For any math calculation, the observer should notice how slowly or how quickly the student performs the procedure. This provides information about the student's math fluency and automatic retrieval of math facts. Alternatively, the observer may focus on how accurately the student performs the procedure, assessing the student's ability to perform math calculations with fidelity. If calculations are too advanced for the student, simpler tasks should be offered, for example, asking the student to count objects or show an understanding of differences in magnitude of numbers, such as objects shown in photos or concrete manipulatives, skills that look at number sense specifically. Regardless of the task, the observer should look for behaviors that point to problems in the areas of math facts (automatic retrieval), math fluency, calculations, and number sense. After conducting a real-time observation, the observer may also use a standardized assessment to confirm initial impressions and probe further to reveal whether or not the student's challenges meet criteria for a math learning disability. The following sections provide more detailed suggestions for how to make observations of these skills.

### *Observations of Number Sense*

*Approximate Number System* The student can show an understanding of the approximate number system when asked to recognize differences in quantities or magnitude. This is relatively easy to measure when asking the student to compare very small quantities (1–5 items) or quantities that are very different in size (100 blocks versus 10 blocks). As number sense skills improve, the student is able to recognize differences in size that are smaller. This capacity emerges as students develop their understanding of numerals, and when they can use numerals and counting to understand differences in sizes of quantities. The approximate number system is useful in the interpretation of data. The interpretation of bar graphs, scatter plots, and other graphic representations of data often relies on the approximate number system, as well as on counting principles. These examples of the approximate number system also require an understanding of two-dimensional space. They are more highly abstract representations of quantities and may be out of the reach of students with early-emerging math skills.

*Numbers, Numerals, and the Number Line* If the student already shows an understanding of numbers, the observer can verify that the student has all the basic number sense skills discussed in this chapter. For example, the observer can ask the student to order numbers along a number line or simply to count objects. When a student is able to count, they can also recognize differences in quantities that are smaller than the ones discussed above, especially when they can use real objects or photos of objects for counting. They should be able to recognize differences between 8 and 10, and even between 87 and 95. The observer can ask the student to perform different types of calculations using manipulatives or pictures. Some students who perform calculations using numbers printed on the page may have difficulties in their calculations because of underlying difficulties with number sense. These students are not yet likely to able to use their understanding of approximate number sense to check the reasonableness of their answers.

*Advances in Number Sense* Some students may be able to show their understanding of number sense by showing that they can count and by showing that they understand counting principles such as order irrelevance, cardinality, estimation, and approximation. The observer can then ask the student to respond to number sense questions that relate to measurement concepts such as distance, weight, time, and/or money; to identify measurements related to objects and distances in the classroom or school building; or time concepts that are reflected in a daily schedule. A simple starting point is to ask the student to show what the measurement means and to show an understanding of similarities and differences in magnitude (e.g., which of two objects weighs more, which of two distances or time intervals is longer). These observations can be made using concrete manipulatives and then using numerals. Later developments in number sense include understanding how different types of calculations are related to one another. To sample a student's knowledge and skill, the observer can ask the student to show or explain how multiplication is related to addition.

Some students may show a good understanding of whole numbers but may have difficulty with complex numbers, such as fractions, decimals, percentages, and negative numbers. They may also have difficulty understanding how numbers apply to measures such as surface area, volume, or speed. These are more complex measurements than the examples cited earlier because they represent an equation (multiplication) and therefore cannot be separated from math calculations. As representations of data may become more complex, they can be sampled to show the student's understanding of numbers and how they apply to different problem-solving demands. All of these skills then lead to algebra, where numbers are no longer the primary focus of analysis and interrelationships of quantities become the focus of learning. By analyzing work samples, the observer should be able to identify the student's number sense skills and the degree to which those skills have been developed.

***Observations of Calculations*** The second important area to review is the student's ability to perform math calculations. The student has to be able to show that they can follow procedures for adding, subtracting, multiplying and dividing, and do so with fidelity. The student also has to show an ability to check work for errors and make corrections as needed. Number sense skills must be in place for the student to master math calculations, check the reasonableness of answers, and show an understanding of the interrelationships between calculations. When making observations for math calculations, it is useful to verify the student's performance with whole numbers before asking the student to perform calculations for more complex types of numbers, such as fractions, measurements, irrational numbers, or negative numbers.

***Analysis of Math Fluency and Math Facts Retrieval*** A third important area to review is the speed with which the student can perform math calculations, including the automatic recognition of math facts. Difficulties with math fluency will be obvious when the student's math fluency is substantially lower than expected for age or grade. These difficulties may be easier to identify by using standardized measures (e.g., a series of math operations as part of a timed test and comparing the student's performance in different skill areas against population norms). Math fluency is strongly influenced by the student's ability to memorize and automatically retrieve simple math facts. One way to break down the process to look at the automatic retrieval of math facts is to consider all one-digit addition, subtraction, multiplication, and division problems with any other digit. The observations should first focus on addition and subtraction procedures before sampling performance in multiplication and division. Very slow performance or excess reliance on concrete manipulatives (such as using the fingers for counting) provide evidence of difficulties with math facts retrieval.



***Analysis of Working Memory in Math*** When evaluating working memory, the observer will have to take into consideration all the steps involved in solving a math problem. Difficulties in working memory show up as math problems start to contain more steps and as more intermediate steps need to be held in working memory. Examples include transcribing from the white board to the page, transcribing between math word problems and numerals, understanding all the embedded calculations that may be present in the math problems, and remembering the answers to intermediate calculations while performing calculations in series. The observer should notice whether the student performs multiple-step problems mentally and ask them to speak each step out loud or write out the steps as they prepare to solve a problem. The observer should analyze the number and types of errors. So-called careless errors are those not related to a student's difficulties with the math concepts (number sense and calculation skills), but rather a consequence of not remembering intermediate steps or forgetting to compute intermediate calculations within a larger math problem. Errors of this kind are likely related to working memory.

***Analysis of Word Problems in Math*** The observer can assess the student's ability to read and translate words into numerals in math word problems. Reading decoding and reading comprehension problems can both interfere with correctly writing a math equation using numerals. Working memory, inhibition, and shifting are also implicated in transcribing word problems into numerals. The challenge for some students lies in shifting between words (language) and numerals. In addition, numeric equations have to be sequenced correctly, which requires planning skills.

***Analysis of Spatial Concepts and Complex Numbers*** The observer can assess math skills not related to concrete entities or basic counting principles. Math problems are more complex when numbers are assigned to measurements (e.g., distance, weight, time), and when numbers are assigned to products of measurements (e.g., volume, speed) or to other representations of numbers (e.g., geometric shapes, data). More complex numbers also include fractions, decimals, percentages, negative numbers, and irrational numbers. As numbers become more complex, the student has to identify and separate the components that make up the (more complex) number, sequence the equation successfully, and arrive at the right answer. For example, understanding how much paint is needed to cover the surface area of a wall requires an understanding of surface area (the product of two length measurements), volume (the product of three length measurements), and the interrelationship between the two (volume of paint needed for a standard surface area in square feet). Math problems are more complex when they also include a time component (time needed to paint a surface area) and the costs involved (painter's hourly rate and cost per gallon of paint). Math problems such as these require greater abstraction (assigning numerals to spatial concepts). They also require the student to order and complete the calculations correctly to arrive at the right answer. Problems such as these place substantial burden on working memory, as the student shifts attention between different quantities, the numerals and calculations that represent those quantities, the words in the problem, and the sequence in which calculations have to get solved. Working memory and planning demands increase further as numbers are represented as fractions, decimals, percentages, or irrational numbers. Number sense demands also increase as the student shifts toward using irrational numbers and algebra and has to focus on interrelationships and equivalencies instead of on quantities.



## Analysis and Interpretation

After obtaining a math work sample and making observations, the practitioner can review and analyze the observations. The Math Skills Framework helps to structure the observation and analysis, ensuring that the observer takes each skill and skill set into account. By using the Math Skills Framework, the practitioner should be able to attribute math learning difficulty to missing or underdeveloped math skills, such as number sense, calculations, math fluency, and automatic retrieval, and domain-general skills, such as language skills, executive skills, and spatial awareness.

## Discuss Findings With Colleagues

After analyzing the findings, the observer can then discuss the student's performance with colleagues, including members of the student support team, the special education team, the special education teacher, and others. The discussion should help reach consensus about the specific math skills that are not yet at age or grade level and whether a formal evaluation is needed.

IEP BUILDER

## General Information About Teaching Math Skills

In a review of interventions for students with dyscalculia in primary schools (Monei & Pedro, 2017), it was found that most interventions focused on teaching students math calculations, math fluency, automatic retrieval, and number sense. Examples of instruction included the explicit use and practice in strategy instruction, including identifying the key question, the appropriate operations and numbers to use for obtaining a solution, and the best use of visual strategies. In a comprehensive review of instructional strategies for third-grade students (Kingsdorf & Krawec, 2016), intervention practices used most often included step-by-step teacher models, multiple exemplars, and immediate and explicit positive and corrective feedback. Intervention practices also included the use of visual representations to help the student understand numbers and their interrelationships. Finally, instruction included the use of self-strategies (self-monitoring and self-regulation strategies) for error detection and error correction.

These summaries list a wide range of educational objectives and strategies that can be implemented when teaching students with dyscalculia and/or math learning difficulty. However, as discussed earlier in the chapter, there is a lack of consensus in the field about the definition of *dyscalculia* and *math learning difficulty*. Neither of these terms is precise enough to identify the difficulties that a given student is likely to have or the strategies that the student is likely to need. Interventions most appropriate to individual students can only be identified after careful observation, successful analysis, and collaborative planning about how to address the student's particular areas of difficulty. Suggestions for assisting students with math learning difficulty follow logically from the framework provided in this chapter. Teachers can develop an intervention plan based on whether students need to develop number sense, calculations, math fluency, automatic recall, or decomposing complex math problems into their component parts (working memory and planning skills, including reading skills for math word problems). Strategies, goals, and objectives will also depend upon whether the difficulties lie in the realm of language skills, executive skills, or visual-spatial skills. The suggestions listed in the IEP Builder were derived from references cited in this chapter, as well as those listed here: Butterworth, Varma, and Laurillard (2011); Gersten and colleagues (2009); Kaufman and von Aster (2012); Lembke, Hampton, and Beyers (2012); Mazzocco and Myers (2003); and Montague (2011).



## Educational Objectives for Math

The educational objectives in the following sections are organized by skill set. The practitioner will have to understand the student's development of number sense, math calculations, math fluency, and ability to solve complex math problems to select the most appropriate objectives, based on an analysis of the student's current performance.

**_Educational Objectives and Strategies for Number Sense_** A key educational objective may be to build a student's number sense, which can be accomplished in a number of ways. Instruction can start by focusing on small quantities that are represented concretely and/or visually. Using objects and/or pictures of objects, the student may need to spend extra time making connections among approximate quantities, small quantities, actual objects, pictures of objects, and precise numbers (Fuchs & Powell, 2012). Some students need to master the vocabulary of number sense, by learning words such as *bigger/smaller, tall/short,* and *more/less.* Once the student has developed the prerequisite vocabulary and both an approximate and precise understanding of numbers, they are ready to work on developing a number line, after which they can begin to learn about calculations. Number sense also deepens and expands as the student learns to assign numbers and numerals to different types of quantities, such as measurements (e.g., weight, height, distance, time), data, and geometric shapes (e.g., volumes).

Even though calculations are considered a separate skill in this framework, the practitioner can use calculations and interrelationships between calculations as a means to deepen the student's number sense. For example, the practitioner can teach the student to check the reasonableness of answers when completing math calculations. A student who understands what is reasonable knows that he or she can arrive at the solution to a math problem in more than one way. A reasonable answer might be a number that is close to an estimate of the answer. For example, if a student says that the product of 360 × 4.2 = 151,200, he or she should be able to self-correct their work after realizing that 4 × 400 (two numbers that are close to the numbers in the equation) are only equal to 1,600.

A reasonable answer might also be one that makes sense in real-world terms. For example, when the solution to a word problem about the number of hours needed to complete a paint job is excessively high, the student should be able to check whether the answer is reasonable. A painter will not need several days to paint a room but might several hours. A more complex problem might be to check whether it is reasonable to assume that a barrel filled with 40 apples will produce 40 gallons of apple juice. Without necessarily knowing the precise answer to a math problem, the student is using number sense skills to check the reasonableness of their response.

**_Educational Objectives and Strategies for Calculations/Operations_** Some students may need to relearn and practice the procedures for addition, subtraction, multiplication, and division. This objective is reached through explicitly identifying the procedures involved and providing extra practice. The student may need to master single-digit calculations before proceeding to two-digit calculations or master one- and two-digit calculations more fully before moving to multiple-step calculations and embedded calculations. In order to understand and perform calculations successfully, the student will need to expand his or her number sense skills as a part of the instruction. The student will also need to learn about the interrelations between addition and multiplication or division and subtraction.



**_Educational Objectives and Strategies for Math Fluency and Math Facts Retrieval_** Math fluency and math facts are improved through drill and practice. However, students also need to memorize the answers to different types of problems. Counting strategies and reasoning strategies help improve the memorization of math facts. Drill and practice are also important and are enhanced when the student also has a foundation of conceptual knowledge (number sense) and procedural knowledge (how to set up and calculate answers to problems). By discovering patterns and relations between numbers, math facts are retained with greater ease and success (Baroody, Bajwa, & Eiland, 2009).

**_Educational Objectives and Strategies for Executive Skills in Math_** The student with math learning difficulty might not perform successfully because of difficulties with working memory or planning. Before attributing the math difficulty to underdeveloped executive skills such as these, it is important to be sure that the difficulty is not related to number sense or difficulties with calculation. These two areas can be difficult to disentangle. To identify underdeveloped executive skills as the primary difficulty, see whether the student shows secure number sense skills and calculation skills for one-step or simple math problems and seems to show difficulties only when the math problems are more complex (e.g., multistep math problems, math problems with embedded calculations, math word problems).

Regardless of the cause of the math problem, many students with difficulty with more complex math problems benefit from strategy instruction. Strategy instruction helps to reduce demands on executive skills and is especially useful for solving math problems beyond basic calculations, for example, multiple-step problems and problems that involve different types of quantities (e.g., weight, distance, speed, volume) and different types of numbers (e.g., whole numbers, fractions, decimals, negative numbers). Strategy instruction could include steps such as think-aloud strategies to verbalize the problem, explain the steps, and explain the answer to a peer. The strategy could include a more generalizable sequence such as reading the problem, highlighting key words, solving the problems, and checking the work. Sometimes, the strategy may need to include reciting the rules for calculations and embedded calculations. Strategies such as this support both working memory and planning. Strategy instruction should also support the (metacognitive) skill of detecting and correcting errors.

***Educational Objectives and Strategies for Reading Skills in Math*** Reading strategy instruction may be needed to help students read math word problems accurately. Strategy instruction for math word problems can help the student identify, retain, and synthesize key points for subsequent transcription into a numerical equation. For example, the strategy could specify component steps: "First, write out all of the number words in this word problem. Which numeral goes with which number word? Second, write out all of the words that make you think this is an addition problem / subtraction problem / multiplication problem/division problem. Third, write out all of the equations that you can see in this problem. Fourth, write out all of the words that tell you about the order of the calculations. What should the order be?"

## Educational Accommodations for Math

Accommodations for math should typically be designed for use when number sense and math calculations have been mastered. Both of these skill sets are critical to all math problems. Accommodations should not be designed to circumvent number sense and calculation skills needed to fully understand the math problem, regardless of the complexity of the math problem.



***Accommodations for Number Sense*** Students with math learning difficulties may be able to subitize only small sets (e.g., three items) as opposed to larger sets (e.g., five or six items). To accommodate a student's limited subitizing abilities, teachers can use smaller sets of numbers in instruction and represent quantities in more than one way (e.g., visually, kinesthetically, linguistically; using concrete objects or pictures). This is especially useful for students with limited visual-spatial skills or limited visual-spatial working memory. Both real objects and two-dimensional images can help the student with limited number sense make sense of calculations and more complex equations.

***Accommodations for Calculations and Operations*** To accommodate for difficulty with calculations and operations, students can be provided with a calculator. This helps to overcome challenges posed by limited working memory needed to access math facts or overcome difficulty with multiple-step problems. Calculators themselves do not teach number sense, calculations, math fluency, or math facts retrieval and should not be provided when those skills are the focus of the math lesson. A calculator may be appropriate to use when the student needs to focus on ordering equations in a complex math problem, or when the student is focusing on translating word problems into numerical problems. In these circumstances, the calculator can slightly reduce the work needed to solve multiple-step problems and allow the student to focus on the language and executive skills needed to solve them.

***Accommodations for Math Fluency and Math Facts*** To perform successfully in math, students need robust skills in conducting calculations, in assessing the reasonableness of the answers obtained in those calculations, and in carrying out math operations accurately. Without these skills, it is not possible to learn all the other types of math skills discussed in this chapter, including mastering the concepts related to number sense itself. Accommodations through use of a calculator are appropriate when math fluency and math facts are not the focus of the lesson.

***Accommodations for Reading and Writing Skills in Math*** Students may have difficulty mapping number words to their corresponding numerals because of reading difficulty. Educators and other school professionals can accommodate students by reading problems orally or by allowing students to use voice dictation software. Similar strategies might apply to writing. Voice dictation software or scribing by an adult can help circumvent writing difficulty that might interfere with doing math.

***Accommodations for Executive Skills in Math*** Students with underdeveloped working memory and/or inhibition skills may need more prompting by adults to make use of strategies for solving math problems. For example, providing access to preprinted math facts or a summary list of rules for embedded calculations can help circumvent working memory problems. The student may need a summary of instructions for solving word problems or multistep problems to circumvent difficulties with planning. Strategies such as teacher prompting may also be needed to ensure that the student reviews his or her work for errors.

***Accommodations for Spatial Awareness in Math*** Some students may need access to tangible objects or images of objects in order to understand quantities. Lack of understanding of space and volume can make it very difficult to solve math problems, especially when poor spatial awareness contributes to difficulties with number sense. Some students may need to develop their spatial awareness through manipulatives, using touch and kinesthetic cues. Presenting math problems visually or via touch can help these students understand numerical aspects of problems more successfully. Students who have difficulty writing out math problems in a logical order may benefit from graph paper to help ensure that numbers are aligned into their appropriate columns and rows and that errors do not occur because of misaligned numbers. Graphic organizers can also be effective tools in both instruction and in planning and self-monitoring of performance.



## CASE EXAMPLE

Sebastian, a 9-year-old student in third grade, completed a set of math calculation problems as shown in Figure 11.1. The sample was taken from a standardized tool, commonly used in schools for the assessment of math learning difficulty (Connolly, 2007). Review the sample and focus on his performance in number sense and math calculations.

| (24) | (25) | (26) |
|---|---|---|
| 2 + 6 = 8 | 7<br>+ 2<br>9 | 7<br>− 4<br>3 |

| (27) | (28) | (29) |
|---|---|---|
| 9<br>− 2<br>7 | 9<br>(+)7<br>10 | 37<br>+ 61<br>97 |

| (30) | (31) | (32) |
|---|---|---|
| 48<br>− 25<br>24 | 14<br>− 8<br>14 | 57<br>(+)36<br>813 |

| (33) | (34) | (35) |
|---|---|---|
| 5 × 2 = | 674<br>+ 47 | 7<br>× 3 |

Page 1

**Figure 11.1.** Sebastien's math sample was collected using an adapted version of the KeyMath-3 Diagnostic Assessment (Connolly, 2007).

| 1. | 2. | 3. |
|---|---|---|
| $\begin{array}{r}321\\ \times 3\\ \hline 963\end{array}$ | $\begin{array}{r}74\\ -55\\ \hline 21\end{array}$ | $2\overset{3}{\sqrt{6}}$ |
| **4.** | **5.** | **6.** |
| $\begin{array}{r}533\\ -67\\ \hline 134\end{array}$ | $49 \times 10 =$ | $\begin{array}{r}411\\ -84\\ \hline 473\end{array}$ |

| 7. | 8. | 9. |
|---|---|---|
| $x + 24 = 48$<br>$x =$ | $3\sqrt{48}$ | $\begin{array}{r}78\\ \times 6\\ \hline\end{array}$ |
| **10.** | **11.** | **12.** |
| $\frac{3}{5} - \frac{1}{5} = \frac{2}{5}$ | $(-3) \times (-8) = 16$ | $6\sqrt{102}$ |



MATH SKILLS

### Observations of Sebastian's Math Fluency

Sebastian's math fluency (the number of calculations performed per minute) was not documented in this specific test. The observer noted that his performance was effortful and slower than expected for his age and grade, an important consideration in determining the nature and impact of his learning difficulty.

### Observations of Sebastian's Ability to Perform Calculations

In addition to slow performance, it was found that Sebastian did not use calculation procedures correctly. Although he performed successfully for single-digit addition and subtraction, his performance faltered when solving double-digit problems in both addition and subtraction. He also shows errors for multiplication and division.

### Observations and Interpretation of Sebastian's Number Sense

The magnitude of Sebastian's errors points to difficulties with number sense. Some of his errors might be attributed to carelessness, for example, 37 + 61 does not equal 97, but is close enough to suggest it was a careless counting error. Similarly, the problem 48 – 25 does not equal 24. His answer is only one number off and could also be due to carelessness. In contrast, the equation 14 – 8 cannot possibly equal 14, and the addition problem 57 + 36 cannot possibly equal 813. Errors on page 2 reveal a mixture of incorrect procedures in math, as well as unreasonable answers. In looking at the test as a whole, Sebastian can perform some math calculations successfully, but his success is limited to single-digit calculations and is likely based on memorization of a procedure. The magnitude of his errors suggests that his understanding of math calculations is limited to procedural aspects of math. He does not self-check his work and may not understand the unreasonableness of his answers. Interventions should focus primarily on developing number sense, with ongoing instruction in math calculations to strengthen and deepen his number sense skills.

### Educational Goals, Objectives, and Strategies for Sebastian

Having determined that Sebastian's difficulties lie primarily in the area of number sense, practitioners working with Sebastian should seek additional information about his math skills. This can be done by doing more observations or by conducting more in-depth assessment. It would be important to review Sebastian's basic number sense skills, such as his understanding of a number line and basic principles of counting such as 1:1 correspondence and cardinality. If these skills are not yet fully in place, he may need to work with manipulatives and enhance his early number sense skills. If counting skills and his number line skills appear to be fully developed, he may be ready to learn how calculations enhance understanding of numbers and deepen his number sense skills. Manipulatives and/or greater use of images (photos, drawings of objects) can help him learn about addition and subtraction and how these math calculations help understand numbers more generally. Sebastian does not appear ready to work on developing multiplication or division skills. The objectives listed in the section Educational Objectives and Strategies for Number Sense in the IEP Builder include additional suggestions.



## Working With Culturally and Linguistically Diverse Learners

Preferred math systems and notations vary across cultures and languages. School professionals should consider the following differences when working with culturally and linguistically diverse learners:

### *Math and Measurements*

Culturally and linguistically diverse learners and their families may need to learn that measurements are expressed differently in different countries. Many culturally and linguistically diverse parents have grown up in traditions where they are only using the metric system. As such, they may be used to reporting and processing information in measures like kilograms, centimeters, or Celsius, rather than pounds, inches, or Farenheit. To help families get acquainted with the school's preferred system of measurement, professionals can ensure that information sent to families includes metric equivalents. For example, a school policy document should say "Schools will be closed if the temperature goes below 28 degrees Fahrenheit or minus one degree Celsius."

### *Different Styles of Denoting Math Operations*

Culturally and linguistically diverse learners may have different styles of denoting math operations. For example. when a student has to do a math division problem, he or she may switch the position of the dividend and the divisor and may use different symbols to carry out the division problem. School professionals should provide instruction on how to notate and complete these operations.

## CONCLUSIONS

This chapter closes the section on educational frameworks and is the final framework presented in this book. There are several ways in which the reader may now wish to make use of all the frameworks. Each framework is designed to deepen the practitioner's awareness of the skill sets and skills needed to perform successfully at school, to make more detailed and more accurate observations of student learning, and to identify the educational objectives that the student may need to master so that he or she can learn more successfully. The reader may wish to start by using a framework that is familiar or that lies within her or his area of expertise. The practitioner might then select students and conduct observations that take into consideration the skill sets and skills from other frameworks.

Any student experiencing learning difficulty at school is likely to have difficulties with skills in more than one of the frameworks, not just one. Understanding all of the frameworks will deepen awareness of learning difficulties that are both within and outside of a practitioner's area of expertise. For example, understanding language, executive skills, and affect and self-regulation skills helps in understanding student performance in reading, writing, and math. Be sure to review more than one framework when learning about the skills and needs of an individual student.

Just as a single disability category, such as learning disability or autism, does not provide enough information about a student's performance, so too is it limiting to focus on one framework only. All of the student's performance difficulties need to be identified. For many students, this means that potentially all the frameworks may need to be reviewed. For students with any type of learning difficulty, educational objectives and strategies will often be needed from multiple frameworks. Planning decisions will need to be shaped with input from the parents and student and from one or more practitioners on the student's team.

Our vision is that the frameworks presented in this book can and should be used to structure observations of students, structure conversations held with colleagues, structure the choice of educational objectives and accommodations selected for any given student, and inform progress monitoring. The frameworks can help practitioners identify how one curriculum or educational method addresses (or fails to address) certain skill sets and skills and can help the practitioner make adjustments to ensure that the students' learning needs are addressed in a comprehensive manner. Learning needs are addressed in a comprehensive manner. As practitioners continue to use the frameworks to guide their practice, it is likely that they will be able to choose effective learning objectives and strategies more quickly and with greater precision. Finally, they may find that more time can be allocated to teaching as opposed to assessment.

Our vision for this book is also that it will allow for improvements in the often challenging team decision-making process. We hope that you will use the frameworks to share your expertise with colleagues and help them expand their skills in observation, communication, and intervention. In so doing, practitioners can learn from each other for the benefit of students and everyone in the school community. Appendices A and B provide tools and suggestions to help fulfill this vision. We hope that you will enjoy the process of learning and discovery as much as we have enjoyed sharing our frameworks with you.

## REFERENCES


Ansari, D., & Karmiloff-Smith, A. (2002). Atypical trajectories of number development: A neuroconstructivist perspective. *Trends in Cognitive Sciences, 6*(12), 511–516.

Baroody, A. J., Bajwa, N. P., & Eiland, M. (2009). Why can't Johnny remember the basic facts? *Developmental Disabilities Research Reviews, 15*(1), 69–79.

Berch, D. B. (2005). Making sense of number sense: Implications for children with mathematical disabilities. *Journal of Learning Disabilities, 38*(4), 333–339.

Butterworth, B. (2005). Development of arithmetical abilities. *Journal of Child Psychology and Psychiatry, 45*(1), 3–18.

Butterworth, B. (2010). Foundational numerical capacities and the origins of dyscalculia. *Trends in Cognitive Sciences, 14*(12), 534–541.

Butterworth, B., Varma, S., & Laurillard, D. (2011). Dyscalculia: From brain to education. *Science, 332,* 1049–1053.

Carr, M. (2012). Critical transitions: Arithmetic to algebra. In K. R. Harris, S. Graham, & T. Urda (Eds.), *APA educational psychology handbook, Vol. 3: Application to learning and teaching* (pp. 229–255). Washington, DC: American Psychological Society.

Caviola, S. (2012). The involvement of working memory in children's exact and approximate mental addition. *Journal of Experimental Child Psychology, 112*(2), 141–160.

Common Core State Standards. (2010). Retrieved from www.corestandards.org

Connolly, A. J. (2007). *KeyMath-3 Diagnostic Assessment.* Upper Saddle River, NJ: Pearson.

Cornoldi, C., & Lucangeli, D. (2004). Arithmetic education and learning disabilities in Italy. *Journal of Learning Disabilities, 37*(1), 42–49.

Dehaene, S. (1992). Varieties of numerical abilities. *Cognition, 44,* 1–42.

Dehaene, S., Dehaene-Lambertz, G., & Cohen, L. (1998). Abstract representations of numbers in the animal and human brain. *Trends in Neuroscience, 21,* 355–361.

Dowker, A. (2005). Early identification and intervention for students with mathematics difficulties. *Journal of Learning Disabilities, 38*(4), 324–332.

Feigensen, L., Dehaene, S., & Spelke, E. (2004). Core systems of number. *Trends in Cognitive Sciences, 8*(7), 307–314.

Fias, W., Menon, V., & Szucs, D. (2013). Multiple components of developmental dyscalculia. *Trends in Neuroscience and Education, 2*(2), 43–47.

Friso-van den Bos, I., van der Ven, S. H., Kroesbergen, E. H., & van Luit, J. E. (2013). Working memory and mathematics in primary school children: A meta-analysis. *Educational Research Review, 10,* 29–44.

Fuchs, L. S., & Powell, S. R. (2012). Early numerical competencies and students with mathematics difficulty. *Focus on Exceptional Children, 44*(5), 1–21.

Geary, D. (2010). Mathematical disabilities: Reflections on cognitive, neuropsychological, and genetic components. *Learning and Individual Differences, 20*(2), 130–133.

Geary, D. (2011). Consequences, characteristics, and causes of mathematical learning disabilities and persistent low achievement in mathematics. *Journal of Developmental-Behavioral Pediatrics, 32*(3), 250–263.

Geary, D. C., Hamson, C. O., & Hoard, M. K. (2000). Numerical and arithmetical cognition: A longitudinal study of process and concept deficits in children with learning disability. *Journal of Experimental Child Psychology, 77*(3), 236–263.

Geary, D. C., & Moore, A. M. (2016). Cognitive and brain systems underlying early mathematical development. In M. Cappelletti & W. Fias (Eds.), *Progress in brain research* (Vol. 227, pp. 75–103). Amsterdam, the Netherlands: Elsevier.

Gelman, R., & Gallistel, C. R. (1978). *The child's understanding of number.* Cambridge, MA: Harvard University Press.

Gersten, R., Chard, D. J., Jaynathi, M., Baker, S. K., Morphy, P., & Flojo, J. (2009). Mathematics instruction for students with learning disabilities: A meta-analysis of instructional components. *Review of Educational Research, 79*(3), 1202–1242.

Gilmore, C. K., McCarthy, S. E., & Spelke, E. S. (2010). Non-symbolic arithmetic abilities and mathematics achievement in the first year of formal schooling. *Cognition, 115*(3), 394–406.

Harrison, L. J., McLeod, S., Berthelsen, D., & Walker, S. (2009). Literacy, numeracy, and learning in school-aged children identified as having speech and language impairment in early childhood. *International Journal of Speech-Language Pathology, 11*(5), 392–403.

Jordan, N. C., Hanich, L. B., & Kaplan, D. (2003). Arithmetic fact mastery in young children: A longitudinal investigation. *Journal of Experimental Child Psychology, 85*(2), 103–119.

Karolis, V., & Butterworth, B. (2016). What counts in estimation? The nature of the preverbal system. In M. Cappelletti & W. Fias (Eds.), *Progress in brain research* (Vol. 227, pp. 29–51). Amsterdam, the Netherlands: Elsevier.

Kaufmann, L., & von Aster, M. (2012). The diagnosis and management of dyscalculia. *Deutsches Arzteblatt International, 109*(45), 767–778.

Kingsdorf, S., & Krawec, J. (2016). A broad look at the literature on math word problem solving interventions for third graders. *Cogent Education, 3*(1), 3–13.

Korhonen, J., Linnanmaki, K., Akademi, A., & Aiunio, P. (2012). Language and mathematical performance: A comparison of lower secondary school students with different level of mathematical skills. *Scandinavian Journal of Educational Research, 56*(3), 333–344.

Kotsopoulos, D., & Lee, J. (2012), A naturalistic study of executive function and mathematical problem-solving. *Journal of Mathematical Behavior, 31*(2), 196–208.

Kucian, K., & von Aster, M. (2015). Developmental dyscalculia. *European Journal of Pediatrics, 174*(1), 1–13.

Lembke, E. S., Hampton, D., & Beyers, S. J. (2012). Response to intervention in mathematics: Critical elements. *Psychology in the Schools, 49*(3), 257–272.

Luculano, T. (2016). Neurocognitive accounts of developmental dyscalculia and its remediation. In M. Cappelletti & W. Fias (Eds.), *Progress in brain research* (Vol. 227, pp. 305–333). Amsterdam, the Netherlands: Elsevier.

Mazzoco, M. M., & Myers, G. F. (2003). Complexities in identifying and defining mathematics learning disability in the primary school age years. *Annals of Dyslexia, 53*(1), 218–253.

Miyake, A., Friedman, N. P., Emerson, M. J., Witzki, A. H., Howerter, A., & Wager, T. D. (2000). The unity and diversity of executive functions and their contributions to complex "frontal lobe" tasks: A latent variable analysis. *Cognitive Psychology, 41*(1), 49–100.

Monei, T., & Pedro, A. (2017). A systematic review of interventions for children presenting with dyslcalculia in primary schools. *Educational Psychology in Practice, 33*(3), 277–293.

Montague, M. (2011). Effective instruction in mathematics for students with learning difficulties. In C. Wyatt-Smith, J. Elkins, & S. Gunn (Eds.), *Multiple perspectives on difficulties in learning literacy and numeracy* (pp. 295–313). New York, NY: Springer.

Mussolin, C., Nus, J., Leybaert, J., & Content, A. (2016). How approximate and exact number skills are related to each other across development: A review. *Developmental Review, 39*, 1–15.

National Assessment of Educational Progress. (2017). NAEP Mathematics Report Card. Retrieved from https://www.nationsreportcard.gov/math_2017

Polya, G. (1957). *How to solve it: A new aspect of mathematical method* (2nd ed.). Princeton, NJ: Princeton University Press.

Soares, N., Evans, T., & Patel, D. R. (2018). Specific learning disability in mathematics: A comprehensive review. *Translational Pediatrics, 7*(1), 48–62.

von Aster, M. G., & Shalev, R. S. (2007). Number development and developmental dyscalculia. *Developmental Medicine and Child Neurology, 49*(11), 868–873.

APPENDIX 11.1 **Math Skills Framework**

The Math Skills Framework is summarized here. School professionals can use this form as a quick reference for the skill sets and skills that need to be taken into consideration when making observations and developing an intervention plan.

| Skill sets | Functions and skills | Examples of functions and skills in action | Sample performance difficulties | Potential strategies, accommodations, or educational objectives |
|---|---|---|---|---|
| Number sense | The understanding of quantities and how they are the same or different from one another | The student is able to recognize differences in size for small sets of quantities and/or when there is a substantial difference in size between the two sets.<br>The student is able to recognize differences in size for differently sized sets even if the difference between the two is small.<br>The student is able to count visible objects.<br>The student shows counting skills and an understanding of counting principles (e.g., 1:1 correspondence, order irrelevance, cardinality).<br>The student has developed a number line and is able to use numerals to represent quantities instead of relying on tangible objects to represent quantities. | The student has not developed quantity-related vocabulary, such as smaller/bigger, tall/short, heavy/light.<br>The student is unable to recognize differences in size even when the set of objects is small and/or when the differences in quantity are large.<br>The student is not yet able to count.<br>The student is able to count by rote but has not developed principles of counting (e.g., 1:1 correspondence, order irrelevance, cardinality).<br>The student has not developed a number line. | Teach the words for quantities, such as smaller/bigger, tall/short, heavy/light.<br>Teach the student to make correlations between quantities and the adjectives listed above.<br>Teach the student to estimate quantities and to compare them with each other.<br>Teach the student to count while also teaching counting principles and help the student develop a number line. |
| Advances in number sense | Measurements, estimation, complex numbers, multiple step math problems, and algebra | *Measurements:* The student can apply numbers to different types of measurable entities (e.g., distance, time, temperature, weight, money).<br>The student is able to apply and manipulate numbers to measures that include embedded calculations (e.g., speed, surface area, volume).<br>*Applying numbers to estimates:* The student can use estimation in the interpretation of data and statistics and to check the reasonableness of answers. | The student is unable to apply numbers to different types of measures (abstraction), as listed in the left column.<br>The student is able to apply (abstract) numbers to some measures (e.g. distance, temperature, time, weight, money) and can perform operations on those types of measures but may show confusion when asked to apply and manipulate numbers when they refer to measurements that include embedded calculations (e.g., speed, surface area, volume). | The student may need to focus on building the skills listed previously.<br>The student may need strategies to help solve multiple-step math problems. The strategy may be to include a list of math rules and the order in which math problems need to be solved. Or, the student may need to make use of a list of solutions to common math problems. |

| Skill sets | Functions and skills | Examples of functions and skills in action | Sample performance difficulties | Potential strategies, accommodations, or educational objectives |
|---|---|---|---|---|
| | | *Complex numbers:* The student understands and can perform operations on complex numbers such as fractions, percentages, decimals; negative numbers, irrational numbers; and numbers with embedded calculations such as numbers squared, square roots of numbers.<br><br>*Complex math problems:* The student can perform multiple-step math problems that include one or several of the different types of numbers and/or measurements.<br><br>*Algebra:* The student understands relationships for nonnumerical equations. | The student is unable to perform operations successfully when working with complex numbers that are also an equation (e.g., fractions, percentages, decimals, numbers squared, square roots of number).<br><br>The student is unable to perform multiple step calculations for simple numbers.<br><br>The student is unable to perform multiple-step calculations for any of the measurements or numbers listed previously.<br><br>The student is unable to abstract numbers and number sense to solve (nonnumerical) algebraic problems. | The student may need visual representations of measurements so that he or she can also learn how to abstract numbers and apply them to measurements.<br><br>The student may need explicit instruction in the relationship of math calculations to numbers such as fractions, decimals, square roots, numbers squared. |
| Math operations or math calculations | The four operations of adding, subtracting, multiplying, and dividing | The student shows the capacity to add, subtract, divide, and multiply single-digit numbers, two-digit numbers, multiple-digit numbers.<br><br>The student is able to use number sense to check the reasonableness of answers and can correct errors as needed. | The student is unable to perform calculations in math accurately.<br><br>The student is able to peform adding and subtracting but not multiplication or division in math.<br><br>The student is able to perform single-digit calculations reliably but cannot perform multiple-digit calculations accurately. | Many students with difficulty with math calculations have difficulties in their number sense. Instruction may need to return to the use of concrete quantities so that the student understands quantities and makes a connection between different quantities and the numerals used to represent them.<br><br>Teach the steps needed to perform math calculations accurately and successfully.<br><br>Develop a list of instructions that the student can use when in doubt about how to perform math calculations. |

*(continued)*

| Skill sets | Functions and skills | Examples of functions and skills in action | Sample performance difficulties | Potential strategies, accommodations, or educational objectives |
|---|---|---|---|---|
| Math fluency | The capacity to perform the four operations of math smoothly and fluently | The student is able to complete adding and subtracting smoothly and fluently.<br>The student is able to complete adding, subtracting, multiplying, and dividing smoothly and accurately. | The student is able to perform some or all of the math calculations listed here but performs them slowly or with effort.<br>The student makes excessive errors. | Teach fluency in math by having the student perform many math calculations.<br>In complex math problems, consider use of a calculator to allow the student to peform calculations more quickly. |
| Math facts | Instant recognition (automatic retrieval) of answers to math calculations | The student is able to automatically retrieve answers to a variety of one-digit math calculations.<br>The student is able to automatically retrieve answers to one- and two-digit math calculations, without the need to perform the calculation. For example, the student can automatically retrieve the fact that 7 × 7 = 49 without the need to perform the calculation. | The student is unable to automatically retrieve correct answers to common math calculations.<br>The student is able to automatically retrieve correct answers to single-digit math calculations only, not two-digit or multiple-digit math calculations. | Teach automaticity in math by teaching memorization of math facts.<br>Consider providing a sheet or table of solutions to common math calculations; consider use of a calculator for complex math problems or math problems with higher abstraction. |
| Math comprehension and application of math to larger contexts | Language, reading, and writing skills in math | The student is able to identify key words that are related to numbers and/or calculations.<br>The student is able to write out and solve a numeric equation, as translated from a math word problem. | The student has not developed the vocabulary or language needed to identify numerals and operations in math word problems.<br>The student is unable to write out a numeric equation as described in a math word problem.<br>The student is unable to separate relevant from nonrelevant information in a math word problem and therefore cannot write an equation successfully. | The student may need to build the skills listed previously.<br>Teach students the vocabulary needed to solve math calculations (i.e., teach the language of math). |

| Skill sets | Functions and skills | Examples of functions and skills in action | Sample performance difficulties | Potential strategies, accommodations, or educational objectives |
|---|---|---|---|---|
| | Executive skills in math | The student is able to perform multiple-step math problems and to use working memory to apply rules for calculations and retain solutions to embedded calculations while solving a multiple-step math problem.<br><br>The student is able to write out equations in a logical order so that the calculations are carried out in the right order and the student can arrive at a correct answer (planning skills).<br><br>The student uses metacognition to detect and correct errors, using estimation, using number sense and the reasonableness of the answer, and by reviewing accuracy of the procedure. | The student is unable to remember the math calculation rules or the solution to common math problems while also attempting to solve a multiple-step math problem, resulting in excessive errors (working memory difficulty).<br><br>The student is unable to write out multiple-step calculations so that the steps are completed in the right order (planning difficulty).<br><br>The student does not have the metacognitive skills or the attention span to detect and correct errors by comparing answers to estimates, by using number sense to assess the reasonableness of the answer, and/or by verifying that procedures were carried out accurately. | The student may need instruction in all of the skills listed previously.<br><br>The student may need working memory aids, such as a list of solutions to common math problems or a reminder sheet for the procedures of math, in order to solve multiple-step math problems.<br><br>The student may need graphic organizers to help ensure that calculations are written in the correct order.<br><br>The student may need prompts to detect and correct errors (e.g., by comparing against an estimate, by using number sense to check the reasonableness of the answer, and/or to verify that the procedure was carried out correctly). |
| | Spatial awareness in math | The student is able to align numbers onto the page and ensure that math procedures are carried out correctly by placing numbers into their correct columns and rows (two-dimensional spatial awareness).<br><br>The student understands how numbers apply to volume and space (e.g., geometry and measurements, two- and three-dimensional spatial awareness). | The student is unable to align numbers successfully on the page because of transcription errors.<br><br>The student is unable to align numbers successfully on the page because of difficulties in two-dimensional spatial awareness (not recognizing rows and columns accurately and consequently making errors).<br><br>The student has difficulty solving math problems that include measures of volume or space. | The student may need graph paper to help organize information in the two dimensions of the page.<br><br>The student may need to use concrete objects/manipulatives in order to solve math problems related to space or volume. |

## APPENDIX 11.2 Math Skills Observation Sheet

| Skill sets | Functions and skills | Example skills and deficits in this student | Potential strategies, accommodations, or educational objectives |
|---|---|---|---|
| Number sense | The understanding of quantities and how they are the same or different from one another | | |
| Advances in number sense | Measurements, estimation, complex numbers, complex multiple-step math problems, and algebra | | |
| Math operations or math calculations | The four operations of adding, subtracting, multiplyng, and dividing | | |
| Math fluency | The capacity to perform the four procedures of math calculations smoothly and fluently | | |
| Math facts | Instant recognition (automatic retrieval) of answers to math calculations | | |
| Math comprehension and application of math to larger contexts | Language, reading, and writing skills in math<br><br>Executive skills in math<br><br>Spatial awareness in math | | |

# Implementing the Frameworks

## Suggestions for Professionals

After reviewing each of the frameworks offered in this book, school professionals will need to practice implementing the approach in their classroom. Practice should involve making behavioral observations of real students to evaluate the skill sets and skills discussed in each of the frameworks. Any student behavior can be analyzed using any of the frameworks. At times, the observations will quickly confirm that the student's performance within a given framework is intact and is developing as expected. In other circumstances, the observations will reveal that some of the student's skills are not developing typically.

Still, not all learning difficulties are obvious to the untrained eye. To support practice, school professionals can reference the Skills Frameworks and the Skills Observation Sheets in the appendices that accompany each chapter; these provide a structure to prompt the observer to make observations of a student's skills in greater detail. The full set of Skills Frameworks and Skills Observation Sheets is also available online for download (see the About the Online Materials at the front of the book for more information). To further guide implementation, school professionals can consider the suggestions that follow. These guidelines are designed to help practitioners integrate the frameworks into everyday practice.

1. **Read Chapter 1.** All school professionals should start by reading Chapter 1. Chapter 1 sets the stage for all the remaining chapters and helps to orient the reader to the overarching concepts of the book. The first chapter also helps you to understand the structure of each of the subsequent chapters. After reading the introductory chapter, select one or several of the subsequent chapters. It could be the chapter that is the most familiar or the least familiar to you, the most relevant to your area of training, the most interesting to you personally, and so forth.

2. **Read the frameworks.** You may wish to start out by reading the chapter that corresponds to your area of expertise. Once you have done so, you can start to read other chapters and think about how those chapters deepen your understanding of your area of expertise. If you are not sure where to start, consider the following suggestions:

    a. ***Read about reading, writing, math, and language skills first.*** It may be logical to start with all the skills related to language, literacy, and math, given their importance in most school programs. Start out by identifying the reading, writing, or math skills that your student has already mastered. Then identify the formal language skills that the student has mastered. These four frameworks are a good starting point for most practitioners working in schools. If you are a practitioner working with students with severe disabilities, or if you are primarily working in a vocational setting, you may choose a different order.

    b. ***Read about less familiar and more complex skill sets and skills.*** Depending on your area of expertise, some of the frameworks in this book may seem more difficult to master. Pragmatic language skills, social skills, executive skills, and affect and self-regulation skills are more difficult to observe, analyze, and interpret successfully. One reason why these observations are more difficult to carry out is that they are so interrelated—with each other and with other frameworks. Another reason why these skills are more difficult to observe, analyze, and interpret is because the student's performance can be so much more variable. A student's performance in literacy and math skills tends to be consistent from one day to the next. The same is not true for pragmatic language skills, social skills, executive skills, and affect and self-regulation skills. Some days the student might seem to perform successfully, whereas on other days the student does not perform as successfully. To understand these skills, you will often need to make multiple observations. You may need to make observations over the course of several days and to make those observations in different environments within the school building. Only by making many observations will you be able to detect patterns of performance difficulty and performance successes. To identify these patterns, you may need to consult with your expert colleagues. The descriptors *frequency* and *duration* are very important to keep in mind when making observations. How often and for how long does the student show successes? How often and for how long does the student show difficulties?

c. ***Read about the least commonly affected skills: Neurological frameworks.*** Neurological frameworks are listed last. This is not because they are less important. In fact, they are a foundation for all of the other frameworks presented in this book. That said, the functions and skills described in the neurological frameworks are less commonly affected in students served in special education, especially those who are served in general education settings. Statistically speaking, most students do not have substantial impairments in these skills. Depending on the student population that you serve, you may choose to read about the neurological frameworks last.

3. **Observe your students.** Make a habit of observing students. Observe them in the everyday tasks and activities that are expected in the classroom: Following routines and rules; participating in conversations and discussions with peers; socializing with peers and making friends; completing academic tasks such as reading, writing, and math; participating in activities such as physical education, art, and music. Keep a mental list of the neurological, developmental, and academic skills that underlie all student performance. Make a habit of choosing one or two frameworks. Take a guess about how successfully the student is performing based on a short observation. Consider the following questions as a prompt:

    a. What does the activity tell you about the student's reading, writing, or math skills?

    b. What does the activity tell you about the student's formal language skills?

    c. What does the activity tell you about the student's pragmatic language and social skills?

    d. What does the activity tell you about executive skills and affect and self-regulation skills?

    e. What does the activity tell you about the student's neurological functions and skills?

4. **Analyze and interpret student behaviors.** As you make more and more observations, you will discover yourself making more detailed observations. As you make more and more observations of a specific student, you might discover contradictions. You might find that you have to change your initial impressions. Take your time! You will end up with a more accurate interpretation if you keep observing. Be sure to use the list of skill sets and skills in the worksheets to guide your observations, analysis, and interpretation.

5. **Share your observations, analysis, and interpretations with colleagues.** Speak with your colleagues, especially the experts. Find out how they make their observations. Find out how they relate observations with the skill sets and skills discussed in this book. How often do you and your colleagues end up agreeing about a student's performance successes and difficulties?

6. **Make a decision about whether a standardized assessment is needed.** When speaking with your expert colleagues, make a decision about whether a standardized assessment is needed. The standardized assessment is useful for making a more detailed analysis of the student's behaviors. For example, you may decide that a formal or standardized assessment such as an academic assessment, an occupational therapy assessment, a speech-language assessment, or another assessment is needed. Standardized assessments help to confirm your interpretation that the student is having performance difficulties. Formal assessments can help to break down complex learning activities or learning behaviors into their components and thereby help identify specific areas for remediation.

7. **Ask the experts to explain student behaviors using the frameworks.** After a standardized measure is completed, be sure to ask the experts on your team to share their observations, analysis, and interpretations of the student's performance using the structure of the most pertinent framework(s). The experts should share information about the student's behaviors during the standardized measure. The experts should provide examples of how those student behaviors are likely to manifest in everyday classroom settings and activities. Then, the experts should share information about the skill sets and skills that may be underdeveloped in the student. It is the responsibility of the team to identify targets for remediation or intervention. The team needs the expert to translate standardized assessment findings into the terminology presented in each framework. Be sure to show how all of the observations, standardized or not standardized, relate to the skill sets and skills discussed and described in this book. This is the best way to identify targets for remediation.

8. **Ask the experts to share sample educational objectives.** Student behaviors, work samples, and performance during a standardized measure are the means by which a student's skill sets and skills are assessed. The student's difficulties in skills sets and skills then determine the educational objectives that are the most appropriate for the student. During team meetings, ask your expert colleagues to share useful or important educational objectives that you could develop for the student. Into which domain does the educational objective fall? What are the essential skills that the objective helps to build or develop?

9. **Intervention plan and IEP Builder.** After the above discussion, the team will be ready to develop more specific educational objectives for the student. Measurable objectives may be created as required for a responsiveness to intervention (RTI) plan, an accommodation plan, or an individualized education program (IEP) under special education law. Some interventions can also be provided as part of general education.

# Implementing the Frameworks

## Suggestions for Team Leaders

After teams read this book and begin to consider how to put the frameworks into practice, team leaders should ensure that the educational team (student support team, special education team) discussion is dedicated to a comprehensive description of the student's performance. Before meeting, multiple team members should observe the student, including use of both standardized measures and naturalistic observation.

The team discussion should include an analysis that will tell the team about the student's skills and difficulties. In order to understand the student's performance fully, communication, collaboration, and partnering are essential. The practitioners who work with the student regularly need to share their observations and need to make connections between their observations and the student's skills and difficulties. As appropriate or necessary, team leaders, or experts in certain frameworks, should facilitate making these connections for the team. This logic applies to a student in general education and to a student being served in special education. It applies to the student who has not yet undergone any formal evaluation, as well as to the student who has completed a formal evaluation. The brief guide that follows includes an effective way to structure team meetings to facilitate rich discussion and analysis. To begin the meeting, team leaders should prompt the team to do the following:

1. **Describe the student's performance and identify performance difficulties.** Team members should have work samples and observations to share, especially when the student is not performing successfully. For example, team members should be prepared to discuss how the student performs in the following activities:

   a. Following classroom routines and rules

   b. Participating in conversations with peers during peer-mediated learning

   c. Socializing with peers and making friends

   d. Reading, writing, and math

   e. Working in academic content areas

   f. Engaging in physical education, art, and music

   Work samples can be used to discuss and describe a student's performance in reading, writing, and math. Behavioral observations are typically needed to describe a student's performance in language skills, pragmatic language skills, social skills, executive skills, and affect and self-regulation skills. Each team member should be prepared to share some work samples, and/or provide a description (it could be a video- or audioclip) of the student's everyday behaviors.

2. **Analyze and interpret.** Team members should be prepared to analyze the work and behavioral samples to identify successes and difficulties in the student's functions, skill sets, and skills. For example, team members should know how to analyze work samples using the terms discussed in the reading, writing, and math chapters. Team members should know how to discuss behavioral examples (including video- and audioclips) using the terms presented in the developmental chapters (language skills, pragmatic language skills, social skills, executive skills, and affect and self-regulation skills). Finally, team members should take into consideration neurological functions, skill sets, and skills, as appropriate. Not all team members will be able to analyze student behaviors this way or make accurate interpretations. In the service of professional development, the less experienced member of the team can still be invited to share initial impressions. For example, each team member who presents work or behavioral samples can be asked to identify what he or she believes to be the student's performance difficulties and how those performance difficulties are related to the skill sets and skills as presented in each of the frameworks.

Even just making a guess about which framework is the most pertinent framework for a given behavior or work sample is a good place for the novice to start. After gathering initial impressions, the team can discuss the student's performance as a group and can also turn to the expert. The expert can provide a more detailed analysis and a more accurate interpretation to the whole group.

3. **Confirm the presence of performance problems.** Confirmation of performance difficulties occurs when those difficulties are persistent over time and are present during multiple observations, and when multiple observers agree. After the team has confirmed the presence of performance difficulties, the team can decide whether an intervention should be trialed and/or whether a formal evaluation is needed. For both decisions, the team will need to think about the most relevant frameworks, skill sets, and skills. The more often each team member considers neurological, developmental, and educational frameworks a part of their observations, the more often each team member will be able to participate in decision making. With practice, the decision-making process should take less time.

4. **Identify educational objectives or strategies to be delivered through general education or as a responsiveness to intervention trial.** After the discussion, the team leader can take the team through a step-by-step decision-making process. There may be good agreement about performance difficulties in a given framework. However, the discussion for any student should never be limited to one framework only. Regardless of the number of observations made, the team as a whole should always discuss or take into consideration all of the frameworks. Performance difficulties in one framework are often related to performance difficulties in other frameworks. A framework that is left undiscussed will never be included for analysis or interpretation. The result can be that the team ends up missing important aspects of the student's profile. Given the very close interrelationships between frameworks, it is critical to be systematic and comprehensive and to consider all of the frameworks, even if it's to decide as a team that the framework does not warrant further discussion. The team leader can use a process such as outlined here:

    a. ***Neurological frameworks.*** The team will have to decide whether there are any performance problems in vision, hearing, or motor skills. The majority of students in special education do not have problems with vision or hearing. Most students do not have significant motor impairments, though many students with disabilities have milder motor problems such as low tone, joint laxity, or problems with coordination. The team should take into consideration whether vision, hearing, or motor skills are areas of strength or need. These difficulties are typically easy to recognize. When identified as an area of need, the team should start to identify the specific skill sets and skills that are developing successfully and those that are not developing successfully and need attention. By the end of the meeting, the team should be prepared to request or suggest further evaluation of vision and/or hearing, if appropriate. By the end of the meeting, the team should be prepared to make suggestions for motor supports if needed or to suggest a formal evaluation.

    b. ***Developmental frameworks.*** Developmental frameworks are an important area for the team to review carefully. A majority of special education services and supports are dedicated to improving the student's performance in the developmental frameworks discussed in this book. Developmental frameworks are highly interrelated. All team members will likely need to participate in a discussion about formal and pragmatic language, executive skills, social skills, and affect and self-regulation skills. The team will have to decide which of these are areas of strength and which are areas of need. By the end of the meeting, participants should have information about which developmental frameworks are affected. They should also leave the meeting with some educational objectives or strategies that might help the student improve her or his performance. These objectives or strategies can be used to assess responsiveness to intervention. In addition, the team may elect to conduct formal evaluations to clarify initial impressions.

c. ***Educational frameworks.*** The team will have to decide whether educational frameworks are areas of strength or need. The teachers working with the student should leave the meeting with information about which educational skill sets or skills appear to be the most affected and what types of educational objectives the student might be ready to master. The team should consider whether or not general education supports, such as Title I or response to intervention (RTI) services are justified. The team may also decide to recommend a formal evaluation for special education eligibility.

5. **Identify developmental skill sets and skills that may need to be analyzed further as part of a comprehensive formal evaluation.** Based on the team's observations, formal or standardized evaluations may be needed. For a given student, potentially all of the frameworks, skill sets, and skills discussed in this book may require a standardized evaluation. The one or two frameworks that were initially raised for discussion may not be the only frameworks that need a thorough analysis. Observations of the student's performance in the activities listed in number 1 can also be a way to inform testing/evaluation decisions. By considering all of the activities listed in number 1, the team may discover performance difficulties that were not considered as concerns in the original referral. The examples in number 6 can be used to guide the team's decision making.

6. **Examples of different evaluations and the specialists who can perform them.**

   a. ***Vision.*** An evaluation for vision may be undertaken by the school nurse or by an outside professional such as an ophthalmologist or optometrist. The school nurse can assist in making an appropriate referral. The team may also decide that a functional visual assessment is needed. The functional visual assessment could be carried out by a teacher of the visually impaired or by an optometrist or ophthalmologist who is also specialized to do a functional visual assessment. The referral question might be related to the student's visual acuity only, or the questions might be related to skill sets such as the student's oculomotor skills, ocular skills, or visual processing skills. The team will need to know what types of training or intervention will be needed, such as orientation and mobility training, accommodations for ocular impairments, or strategies for visual processing difficulties.

   b. ***Hearing.*** A hearing evaluation may be undertaken by the school nurse or by an outside professional such as an audiologist. The school nurse can assist in making a referral for outside testing. The team may also decide that an evaluation is needed by a teacher of the hearing impaired or by an audiologist specialized to conduct evaluations and consult with schools. The referral question might be to determine auditory acuity, auditory processing, or the types of amplification devices that the student may need. Alternatively, the consultation with the audiologist may be needed to address questions about classroom acoustics.

   c. ***Motor skills.*** The team may decide that a physical or occupational therapy evaluation is needed. The referral question might be related to problems in motor structure and motor functions, such as cerebral palsy, hypotonia, or other problems affecting muscles, bones, or joints. The referral question might be more limited and designed to address questions about low tone or lack of coordination. For any student with motor performance difficulties, the team will have to know if educational and therapeutic and educational objectives should be targeted toward accommodations for limited rudimentary and fundamental movement patterns, if the student will be working toward differentiation of movement patterns and improving functional movement sequences, and/or if the student will need objectives related to motor control.

d. ***Formal and pragmatic language skills.*** The team may decide that a speech-language evaluation should be conducted by the district speech pathologist. The referral questions might be related to either formal language, pragmatic language, or both. The team should offer specific examples of performance problems in either formal or pragmatic language as justification for the request to evaluate.

e. ***Social skills.*** The team may decide that the student needs an evaluation of her or his social skills. Social skills are highly dependent on formal language skills, pragmatic language skills, executive skills, and affect and self-regulation skills. Social skills are also dependent on social cognition. Several professionals could be involved in analyzing the student's social skills. For example, the behavioral analyst, the speech pathologist, and the school psychologist may all be important to include. Teachers of students with emotional impairments or teachers of students with autism can be helpful in understanding and assessing social skills. The team will need to know if social skills instruction should be geared toward teaching the social cognition skills discussed in Chapter 6 or if the student's socializing difficulties are best addressed by targeting language skills, executive skills, and affect and self-regulation skills.

f. ***Executive skills, affect and self-regulation skills.*** Difficulties in executive skills and affect and self-regulation skills often co-occur. Performance problems will usually or often be related to classroom participation and to social skills. A behavioral analyst, school psychologist, and teacher of students with emotional impairments can all be helpful in understanding strengths and needs in this area. The team will need to understand how well the student is able to describe and use executive skills and affect and self-regulation skills, and how all of the team members can support learning in this area.

g. ***Educational domains:*** Reading, writing, and math. The school psychologist and the special education teacher who completes academic evaluations may need to conduct evaluations of reading, writing, and math. All team members would benefit from knowing which educational goals and objectives are most appropriate to target for the student. It can make a difference to know if the student is working on phonics or reading comprehension; mechanics of writing versus text-generation skills; or number sense, calculations, and/or more complex skills in math.

7. **Share findings with the family and with the student.** The team leader should inform the family and the student of the team's decision to conduct an evaluation. The team should inform the family of the results of the evaluation(s) after they are completed. If sharing results with the student can enhance student participation and performance, results should also be presented to the student. The format for sharing findings with the family and the student can follow the format presented in prior sections. It is also shown here:

    a. **Performance difficulties as evident from work samples and everyday classroom participation behaviors.** The student and the family first need to know what constitutes performance difficulties and what evidence the team has for stating that the student has performance difficulties. The team can certainly share test scores and information related to the student's performance during the testing situation. However, it is much more valuable and instructive to all team members to learn about the student's performance successes and difficulties in everyday activities at school. Team members should be prepared to share information about performance difficulties in everyday classroom activities.

b. **Performance difficulties and their relationship to frameworks, skill sets, and skills.** The team should be prepared to discuss with the family how the performance difficulties are related to the frameworks, skill sets, and skills discussed in this book. For example, if the student has a math or reading difficulty, which skill set or skill seems to be at issue? If the student has performance difficulties in formal language, which skill is missing or underdeveloped? If the student has performance difficulties in following classroom rules or routines, is the problem due to executive skills? Affect and self-regulation skills? Which skill set or skills within these two frameworks seem to be the most affected? As part of this conversation, the team should share the student's underlying strengths. Within a given framework, which skills are already present? Which of these can be used as a foundation upon which the student can continue to build?

c. **Educational objectives and strategies.** The student and the family need to know what types of educational objectives and strategies the team will use to remediate or ameliorate the student's performance. Educational objectives will likely need to be developed based upon the student's strengths and the next steps that the student is ready to take within each framework. Which skill sets and skills will be the focus of the program? How will the expert support the student's growth? How will other team members support the student's growth? How should the family support the student's growth? Finally, how should adults discuss this skill set with the student and help the student improve her or his performance?

d. **Progress monitoring.** The intervention plan and IEP Builder in each chapter of this book provides guidance about the types of educational objectives that are appropriate to each framework. If relevant to a given student, these objectives need to be refined further so that they can meet the criteria for measurable objectives as required in an Individualized Education Program (IEP). Once the objectives have been written to be measurable, the team should measure and share progress with the student and the family. Qualitative measures, such as intermittent frequency and duration counts of on-task and preferred behaviors and intermittent comparative analysis of how skills have progressed over time, should also be shared with the student and the student's family. Progress monitoring of this type can be just as important to share with the student as is any progress monitoring mandated through special education procedures. Progress monitoring can help practitioners not only assess the student's skill development. It also serves the purpose of refining the practitioner's observation skills.

# Index

Tables and figures are indicated by *t* and *f*, respectively.